THOMAS CARLYLE

Reminiscences

Edited by
CHARLES ELIOT NORTON

Introduction by
IAN CAMPBELL
Lecturer in the Department of English
at the University of Edinburgh

J. M. Dent & Sons Ltd, London

No. 875   ISBN (if a hardback): 0 460 00875 7
No. 1875   ISBN (if a paperback): 0 460 01875 2

Published with the support of the Scottish Arts Council

CONTENTS

THOMAS CARLYLE

A BIOGRAPHICAL NOTE

THOMAS CARLYLE was born in 1795, the son of a moderately prosperous stonemason in Ecclefechan. This small Scottish village, a staging post on the mail route from Glasgow to London, afforded him an elementary education and a rigid religious background; after further schooling in nearby Annan he matriculated at the University of Edinburgh in 1809, not yet fourteen years old. Although destined for the ministry of the Church, Carlyle soon found his early faith assailed by sceptical questions and doubts, which alienated him both from his family and from his ambitions to enter the Church. After teaching in schools, which he loathed, and living precariously as a literary freelance in Edinburgh, Carlyle underwent spiritual agonies of doubt and uncertainty which were to become the source for the 'Everlasting NO' of *Sartor Resartus*. Reunited with his family, encouraged and animated by a growing intimacy with Jane Welsh between 1821 and 1826, Carlyle gradually constructed a new life philosophy for himself, using salvaged parts of his childhood Christianity, and half-assimilated fragments from German literature and thought, the understanding of which he pioneered in Britain. In 1826 he married, and in 1828 the Carlyles moved from Edinburgh (where they had led a brilliant but impecunious existence) to their isolated farm of Craigenputtoch, in Dumfries-shire, where they lived (with short holidays) till 1834. Chief among the productions of these early years are *Sartor Resartus*, the important and seminal *Critical and Miscellaneous Essays*, German essays and translated texts, and a magnificent correspondence with family and friends.

In 1834 the Carlyles moved to London, and spent the remainder of their lives based in Chelsea. As 'Sage of Chelsea' Carlyle slowly rose to fame and recognition; Jane was always a formidable conversationalist, wit, letter writer and hostess. First as historian, Carlyle captured the literary imagination of London, of Britain, and eventually of the world. *The French Revolution* made him famous, and the other major contributions to historical studies were his lives of Cromwell and

Frederick the Great of Prussia. To Carlyle history and ethics were inextricable; he grew more and more conspicuous as a writer on morals, on social reform, and (especially in *Past and Present*) tried to marshal the facts of history in a coherent form to illustrate the shortcomings of the present from the study of the past. His bold, energetic, tempestuous style helped make his work widely read and quoted. Increasingly he alienated many liberal thinkers by his uncompromising views on the expediency of slavery (*The Nigger Question*), by his support of Governor Eyre, by his advocacy of relentless physical force in draconian measures to cure the social evils of his time (*Latter-Day Pamphlets*). People quoted him, attacked him, agreed with him, revered him for his untiring call for moral reform, for work, for Christian reconstruction of a faithless age: no one could ignore the urgency or the relevance of his message.

After the death of Jane Welsh in 1866 Carlyle was a spent force in his major published work. His energies were diverted into the writing of these *Reminiscences*, and into the continuing flood of letters he produced. When palsy impaired his ability to write, he talked on (he was one of the formidable conversationalists, if not indeed the most formidable, of his age), and until his severe illnesses late in the eighteen-seventies his home in Chelsea was the centre of attraction and pilgrimage for scores of literary figures. He died in 1881, mourned by the whole nation. He refused a tomb in Westminster Abbey, and chose instead, as his wife had done, to be buried with his family in his native place. The gesture was symbolic; although living in London, he had remained loyal to many features of his Scottish upbringing. As Sage of Chelsea he was a major, if a spent, force when he died. He had, in his published work, spanned almost fifty years of the nineteenth century, an incalculable force in enlarging British sympathy with continental literature, in advocating moral reform and social reconstruction, and in advancing the art of history. His correspondence, now being published, will add to this achievement that of being, with his wife, almost certainly the most brilliant letter writer of his age.

INTRODUCTION

ON 2nd April 1866 Thomas Carlyle rose in the Music Hall, George Street, in Edinburgh, to deliver his inaugural address as Rector of the University of Edinburgh. The hall was full to capacity with students, civic dignitaries and literary figures who had travelled from all over Britain. It was a great occasion for them, and it was a great occasion for Thomas Carlyle; in 1809 he had entered the University of Edinburgh as a very raw undergraduate, poor, without friends, with few advantages in life apart from an excellent upbringing, wide general reading and a notable gift of speech. His gift of speech had not failed him; the Inaugural Address was a triumphant success, and under the title *On the Choice of Books* it is still widely known.

Carlyle spoke in his address of the university as a place where he had learned little but to use books, in his own words to 'go into the books that treated of these things, and try anything I wanted to make myself master of gradually, as I found it suit me'. This had been his practice all through a life full of reading, of self-education. His greatest ally had been his wife, Jane Welsh Carlyle, and in poor health she stayed in London, anxiously awaiting the telegram which carried to her the news of her husband's success.

In a few days she was dead. Worn out by ill health, she succumbed apparently to a heart attack in her carriage. The telegram announcing her death found Thomas Carlyle holidaying in his native Dumfries-shire, and struck him like a thunderbolt. It was the second time in his life he had learned of the death of a dearly loved relation at a distance; the first time, in 1832, had been in London when his father died in far-off Ecclefechan. That event had given rise to agonized reflections and reminiscences of his youth, and the debt he owed to his strong-minded and pious father. The death of Jane was a more catastrophic blow. Carlyle was over seventy years old, his life's work as historian and moral leader almost complete. His reputation, despite his unpopular views of slavery, on the treatment of the Irish and the poor classes generally, stood high. He was seen as an indispensable part of Victorian morality, a man of Christian principles who could be trusted, who called the age to moral reformation. Yet in private life

Jane's death was a terrible blow. It was, as he movingly wrote
on her tombstone, as if the light of his life had gone out.

His reaction in 1866 was as it had been in 1832 on hearing
of his father's death—his mind roamed back over earlier
scenes and events, and as a result of these agonized broodings
and recollections came the following pages of *Reminiscences*.
The *Reminiscences* are based in style on the spoken memories
with which Carlyle loved to entertain his friends. 'Those who
enjoyed the privilege of visiting Carlyle,' wrote one of his early
biographers, 'especially if they were fellow countrymen, can
testify how vivid were his reminiscences of his early days at
Ecclefechan and Annan, and how he liked nothing better than
to hear of the old companions of his boyhood.' [1] From his own
memories, and those of his audience, he would compose a glowing
narrative which combined personal reminiscences with acute
and frequently devastating commentary on the literature,
politics and personalities of the day. The performance was
delivered in a brilliant, energetic style, relieved by moments of
pathos and recollected emotion; many of the hearers have
testified to the extraordinary effect of these monologues, and
many rushed, Boswell-like, to preserve in their notebooks what
they could remember of the night's talk. Carlyle's *bons mots*
found their way into the popular talk of London, but the style
which enlivened these reminiscences was considered even more
remarkable. Certainly it was

. . . never for an instant commonplace. The whole diction was always
original and intensely vivid, and it was more saturated and interlaced with
metaphor than any other conversation I have ever heard. . . . On religious
matters his language had a sublimity and an air of inspiration which always
reminded me (and many others) of what a Hebrew prophet must have been;
and sometimes when very earnest he had a strangely solemn way of turning
and looking full in the hearer's face for a second before speaking, which
added extraordinarily to the impressiveness of what he said.[2]

The pieces which follow, and which together form the *Reminiscences*, are a crystallization of many such nights' talk, trans-
ferred to paper at a time in Carlyle's life when he could not
bear company, when talk and conversation, normally essential
to his character, were more than his hypersensitive nerves
could stand.

They are, in short, produced under stress. This important
fact is often forgotten in discussion of these pieces, which at
their first appearance sent the literary world of the 1880s into
passionate literary argument. They were not, to Carlyle,
serious employment, not a 'task' but a mere 'Quasi-Task'

[1] W. H. Wylie, *Thomas Carlyle, the Man and his Books* (London, 1881), 341.
[2] *A Memoir of the Right Honourable William Edward Hartpole Lecky, by
his Wife* (London, 1909), 93–4.

(page 342) which, he found, 'calms and soothes me as I go on' (page 307). Yet he acutely saw that they might turn out to be 'more about myself than him' when he saw Edward Irving's life in restrospect, closely interwoven with his own at the time of his first meeting with Jane. The *Reminiscences* were painful as well as soothing, personal, acutely and embarrassingly personal; and they were produced at a time when dispassionate self-criticism was not possible. Carlyle clearly saw this.

> Everything admonishes me to *end* here my poor scrawlings and weak reminiscences of days that are no more.
> I still mainly mean to *burn* this Book before my own departure; but feel that I shall always have a kind of grudge to do it, and an indolent excuse, 'Not *yet;* wait, any day that can be done!'—and that it *is* possible the thing *may* be left behind me, legible to interested survivors,—*friends* only, I will hope, and with *worthy* curiosity, not *un*worthy!
> In which event, I solemnly forbid them, each and all, to *publish* this Bit of Writing *as it stands here;* and warn them that *without fit editing* no *part* of it should be printed (nor so far as I can order, *shall* ever be);—and that the '*fit* editing' of perhaps nine-tenths of it will, after I am gone, have become *impossible.*
>
> T. C. (Saturday, 28th July 1866)   [page 169]

The editing, 'fit' or unfit, of the *Reminiscences*, was to be a *cause célèbre* of late nineteenth-century Britain. Carlyle's chosen biographer, James Anthony Froude, was given by Carlyle a very large number of manuscripts from which to compose his study, and these included the *Reminiscences*, which Carlyle had not destroyed. Froude recognized their value both to a biographer and to the student of autobiography in English. Plainly, he thought, they must be made available to the public, and so in addition to employing extracts in his life of Carlyle, Froude published an edition of the *Reminiscences* a few weeks after Carlyle's death. What appeared was essentially what is in this text, without '"Christopher North"' or 'Sir William Hamilton'. Carlyle had just died, his memory was revered not only throughout Britain, but throughout the civilized world, as one of the great moral forces of the nineteenth century. Tributes in the press were long and hyperbolic in their praise. Many felt his day was over, that his opinions had lost their relevance to the world of 1881, yet few would have denied his stature in his century.

The publication of the *Reminiscences* burst on this situation like a thunderstorm. They reveal everything about their writer, his moods, his secret motivations, his regrets. Worse still, they reveal his opinions about his contemporaries, not always respectful or flattering ones. As Carlyle grew older his tolerance lessened, his nerves became more frayed, his memory recaptured less and less the bright spots of his youth and dwelt more on the gloomy. One example is his treatment of the time he spent (between 1826 and 1828) in Edinburgh with Jane, living in suburban Comely Bank. They were the centre of a brilliant circle, whom they entertained at weekly 'at-homes', and they enjoyed enormously the interest and the stimulus which these friends brought to their home. Yet in writing of these years, much later, in the *Reminiscences*, Carlyle said that 'nobody except Jeffrey seemed to either of us a valuable acquisition' (page 55). A typical judgment of the *Reminiscences*, showing their danger to the biographer, for indeed Jeffrey was the only permanently important or famous friend they made at the time, yet this is the over-simplified judgment of retrospect, not a fair or well-balanced reflection of true facts. The brilliant circle fades into obscurity; Jeffrey (because he is most famous) stands out in the memory. He came to Craigenputtoch, he carried a breath of Edinburgh gaiety into their lives after they were forced to retire to country obscurity, but so did many Edinburgh figures; they are forgotten. The judgment is as unfair as it is inaccurate, springing partly from the passage of forty years, partly from a jaundiced view of life at the time of writing.

It was the accumulation of passages like these, some much more personal and unpleasant, which made the *Reminiscences* offensive to many at the time of their first publication. Living figures, or close relatives of those who had known Carlyle, were distressed (and appalled) by contemptuous private judgments and dismissals. Offended too were the friends and relatives of Carlyle himself. These were distressed by revelations of the stress in the marriage between the Carlyles, and by the damage which they forecast (all too accurately) this would do to Carlyle's reputation. To many a new Carlyle emerged from the pages of this autobiography, a domineering, bullying, sarcastic, insensitive Carlyle, embodying his defects in a style so memorable as to ensure the immortality of his insults. It was a picture which some of Froude's descriptions helped to reinforce, and Froude's *Life* seemed to many merely an underlining of the more terrible passages of the *Reminiscences*. The living Carlyle, kind, friendly, discreet, charitable, was gone. In life he was sarcastic and scornful, but he was also immensely kind; on balance, people remembered the kindness, and forgave the scorn. No such balance is possible on reading the *Reminiscences*. The man is gone, the words remain. Offence is inevitable.

Yet Carlyle must be allowed to speak in his own defence. Writing of Lockhart's *Life of Scott*, he had said:

How delicate, decent is English Biography, bless its mealy mouth! A Damocles' sword of *Respectability* hangs forever over the poor English life-writer (as it does over poor English Life in general), and reduces him to the verge of paralysis ... The English biographer has long felt that if in writing his Man's Biography, he wrote down anything that could by possibility offend any man, he had written wrong. The plain consequence was, that, properly speaking, no biography whatever could be produced . . . [Yet] no man lives without jostling and being jostled; in all ways he has to *elbow* himself through the world, giving and receiving offence. His life is a battle, in so far as it is an entity at all.[1]

Ironic words, these, written fifty years before the storm which was to break over his own biographer's head. His point, however, is sound. As a major literary figure for forty years and more, coming into contact with many of his contemporaries at every point, Carlyle could not fail to give offence, and to have a poor opinion of some people. Add to this his admission that he inherited his father's tendency to exaggeration, '. . . in description and for the sake chiefly of *humorous* effect' (page 4), and his famous style, and the *Reminiscences* were bound to give offence.

The storm which followed their publication came close to overwhelming Froude. Clearly many of Carlyle's admirers felt they had been betrayed, and Carlyle too, by Froude's failure to perform the 'fit editing' of the manuscript. Members of the family found a graver reason to distrust the editor. When the papers eventually found their way back to the family's hands, it became obvious that the published text had had only superficial treatment, and that the accuracy of its transcription was very poor indeed. The storm over this point became ludicrously overheated (and its less pleasant details may be followed in W. H. Dunn's *Froude and Carlyle*, London, 1931), for Froude's slips of the pen very rarely amounted to more than mistaken transliterations, not often to omissions and changes which altered the meaning. Froude's edition was unsatisfactory because its text was carelessly transcribed from the original. Hence the edition of Charles Eliot Norton appeared in 1887, produced from the manuscript at the request of Carlyle's niece, Mary Aitken Carlyle. More accurate, though still imperfect, it was clearly the better edition, and has remained the standard one. Its text is largely the basis for the present edition.

The dispassionate modern reader, torn neither by outrage following on Carlyle's attack on nineteeth-century figures, nor by anger at Froude's too intimate revelations, will see Carlyle's *Reminiscences* not as a literary landmine, but as an autobiography, or an essay in autobiography, of unusually high quality. In any systematic sense it was certainly not auto-

[1] T. Carlyle, 'Sir Walter Scott', first published in the *London and Westminster Review* in 1838, and here quoted from the *Critical and Miscellaneous Essays* (London, 1867), IV, 140–1. Everyman's Library No. 703. *Essays: Scottish and Other Critical Miscellanies* (London, 1915), I, 60.

biography, for its coverage of Carlyle's life is capricious in the extreme, event following event as the fancy (or the association of ideas) took Carlyle's mind. For autobiography, the *Reminiscences* have been used, cautiously, in conjunction with Carlyle's diaries, in so far as these are available in passages quoted in Froude's life and in the *Two Note Books* published by Charles Eliot Norton.

Although not strictly speaking autobiography, the *Reminiscences* do tell us a great deal about Carlyle, and also a great deal about his times. Carlyle, as his correspondence shows, had an enormous acquaintance, a vast experience, a tenacious memory. Far from damaging Carlyle's reputation, the *Reminiscences* may in time take their place beside the many volumes of Carlyle's 'collected' works as one of his greatest achievements. As prophet, stylist, letter-writer extraordinary and Sage, Carlyle was a major figure of his century, and here is one clue to a fuller understanding of his life and intellectual history.

The University of Edinburgh,   IAN CAMPBELL.
1972

SELECT BIBLIOGRAPHY

COLLECTED WORKS. 'Centenary' Edition (ed. H. D. Traill), 30 vols., New York, 1896–9; the standard edition. *Collectanea Thomas Carlyle 1821–1855*, 1903; a rare but important compilation.

SEPARATE WORKS. *Wilhelm Meister's Apprenticeship. A Novel from the German of Goethe*, 3 vols., Edinburgh, 1824. *The Life of Schiller*, 1825. *German Romance* (including *Wilheim Meister's Travels*), 4 vols., Edinburgh, 1827. *Sartor Resartus; the Life and Opinions of Herr Teufelsdröckh*, Boston, 1836. *The French Revolution. A History*, 3 vols., 1837. *Lectures on the History of Literature*, 1838. *Critical and Miscellaneous Essays*, 4 vols., Boston, 1838. *Chartism*, 1840. *On Heroes, Hero-Worship, and the Heroic in History*, 1841. *Past and Present*, 1843. *Oliver Cromwell's Letters and Speeches*, 2 vols., 1845. *Latter-Day Pamphlets*, 1850. *Life of John Sterling*, 1851. *The History of Friedrich II of Prussia, called Frederick the Great*, 6 vols., 1858–65. *On the Choice of Books* [inaugural address at Edinburgh, 2nd April 1866], 1866. *The Early Kings of Norway: Also an Essay on the Portraits of John Knox*, 1875. *Reminiscences* (ed. J. A. Froude), 2 vols., 1881; (ed. C. E. Norton), 2 vols., 1887. *Reminiscences of my Irish Journey in 1849*, 1882. *Last Words of Thomas Carlyle*, 1892; reprinted 1972. *Two Notebooks of Thomas Carlyle*, New York, 1898; reprinted part of Carlyle's voluminous diaries, still largely unpublinted. *Journey to Germany, Autumn 1858*, New Haven, 1940. *Carlyle's Unfinished History of German Literature* (ed. H. Shine), Lexington, 1951.

LETTERS (of great importance to students of the Victorian age). *Letters to Mrs B. Montagu and B. W. Procter*, 1881. *Correspondence of Carlyle and Emerson* (ed. C. E. Norton), 2 vols., 1883; ed. J. Slater, New York, 1964. *Early Letters of Carlyle, 1814–1821* (ed. C. E. Norton), 2 vols., 1886. *Correspondence between Goethe and Carlyle* (ed. C. E. Norton), 1887. *Letters of Thomas Carlyle, 1826–1836* (ed. C. E. Norton), 2 vols, 1888. *Letters of Carlyle to his Youngest Sister*, Boston, 1899. *New Letters of Thomas Carlyle* (ed. A. Carlyle), 1904. *Love Letters of Carlyle and Jane Welsh* (ed. A. Carlyle), 2 vols., 1909. *Letters of Thomas Carlyle to John Stuart Mill, John Sterling and Robert Browning* (ed. A. Carlyle), 1923. *New Letters of Carlyle to Eckermann* (ed. W. A. Speck), Yale Review, XV, 1926. *Letters of Carlyle to William Graham* (ed. J. Graham), Princeton, 1950. *Carlyle: Letters to his Wife* (ed. T. Bliss), 1953. *Letters of Thomas Carlyle to his Brother Alexander* (ed. E. W. Marrs, Jr.), Cambridge, Mass., 1968. The Complete Duke-Edinburgh edition of Carlyle's correspondence (general editor C. R. Sanders) is in progress; vols i–iv (1812–28) were published in 1970.

PERIODICALS TO WHICH CARLYLE CONTRIBUTED. Brewster's *Edinburgh Encyclopaedia*, vols. xiv, xv, xvi. *The Dumfries and Galloway Courier*, 1813–1827. *Edinburgh Review*, 1827–32. *New Edinburgh Review*, 1821, 1822. *Fraser's Magazine*, 1830–5, 1837, 1839, 1844, 1847, 1849, 1875. *Westminster Review*, 1831, 1837, 1838, 1842, 1855. *Foreign Review*, 1828, 1829. *Foreign Quarterly Review*, 1831–3, 1843. *New Monthly Magazine*, 1832. *Nation* (Dublin), 1849. *Examiner*, 1839, 1848. *Spectator*, 1848. *Leigh Hunt's Journal*, 1850, 1857. *Keepsake*, 1852. *Proceedings of the Society of Antiquaries of Scotland*, 1855. *Macmillan's Magazine*, 1863, 1867. *The Times*, 19th June 1844; 28th November 1876; 5th May 1877.

BIOGRAPHY AND CRITICISM. M. C. Conway, *Thomas Carlyle*, 1881. H. J. Nicoll, *Thomas Carlyle*, Edinburgh, 1881. R. H. Shepherd and C. N. Williamson, *Memoirs of Carlyle*, 2 vols., 1881; an early attempt to offer

xvi   SELECT BIBLIOGRAPHY

critical guidance. J. A. Froude, *Thomas Carlyle*, 4 vols., 1882–4; often care-
less, but essential. D. Masson, *Edinburgh Sketches and Memories*, 1892. J.
Nichol, *Thomas Carlyle* (English Men of Letters series), 1892. F. Espinasse,
'The Carlyles and a Segment of their Circle', in *Literary Recollections and
Sketches*, 1893. J. M. Sloan, *The Carlyle Country*, 1904. W. Allingham, *A
Diary*, 1907. L. Cazamian, *Carlyle*, Paris, 1913 (Eng. tr. 1932). A. Ralli,
Guide to Carlyle, 2 vols., 1920. D. A. Wilson, Life of Thomas Carlyle, 6 vols.,
1923–34 (vol. vi completed by D. W. MacArthur); the main corrective to
Froude. E. Neff, *Carlyle*, 1932. C. F. Harrold, *Carlyle and German Thought
1819–1834*, 1934; a work not yet superseded. A. L. Drummond, *Edward
Irving and his Circle* [1937]. Basil Willey, *Nineteenth Century Studies*, 1949;
important for Carlyle's thought and style. L. and E. Hanson, *Necessary
Evil: the Life of Jane Welsh Carlyle*, 1952. J. Symons, *Carlyle: the Life and
Ideas of a Prophet*, 1952. J. Holloway, The Victorian Saga, 1953; ranks in
importance with Willey (*vid. supr.*). Thea Holme, *The Carlyles at Home*,
1965; offers amusement and insight into the Chelsea period. G. B. Tenny-
son, *Sartor called Resartus*, Princeton, 1965. A. LaValley, *Carlyle and the
Idea of the Modern: Studies in Carlyle's Prophetic Literature and its Relation
to Blake, Nietzsche, Marx, and Others*, Yale, 1968. J. P. Siegel, *Carlyle*
(Critical Heritage series), 1971.

C. F. Harrold, 'On the Nature of Carlyle's Calvinism', in *Studies in Philology,*
33, 1936; the pioneer inquiry into Carlyle's religious belief. Ian Campbell,
'James Barrett and Carlyle's "Journal"' in *Notes and Queries*, 17, 1, 1970.

BIBLIOGRAPHY. I. W. Dyer, *A Bibliography of Thomas Carlyle's Writings*,
Portland, Maine, 1928; reprinted 1968.

The place of publication is London, unless otherwise stated.

THE TEXT

The text belongs to two periods. The first, of 'James Carlyle', was produced in London, and the manuscript was passed on to Carlyle's literary
executor, James Anthony Froude, along with numerous others, on Carlyle's
death. It has since passed back to members of the Carlyle family, and
remains in their hands. Prior to this, however, it was made available to
Charles Eliot Norton for his edition of 1887; his text (which is followed in
the present reprint) was set up from manuscript, and his standards of
transliteration and editing were competent.

The remainder of the book belongs to the years 1866–7, in the years
following Jane's death. With the exception of '"Christopher North"' and
'Sir William Hamilton', the manuscripts survive in the National Library
of Scotland, Edinburgh, and from these an edition of the whole *Reminiscences*, with full *apparatus criticus*, is currently in preparation by Professor
Edward Sharples of Wayne State University, Detroit.

Walter Murdoch based his 1932 Everyman edition on Norton's text, and in
corporated a fragment Norton had omitted. This was '"Christopher North"',
published by Alexander Carlyle in *The Nineteenth Century and After* (1920).
Murdoch's note on p. 366 sufficiently explains his reasons for including it,
and it does add a valuable dimension to Carlyle's description of his years in
Edinburgh. The same reasons have prompted the inclusion in the present
edition of the fragment 'Sir William Hamilton', written by Carlyle at
John Veitch's request, and published in Veitch's biography, *Sir William
Hamilton*, 1869.

The present volume reproduces, with literal corrections, the text,
footnotes and index of Murdoch's 1932 edition of Norton's edition. New
introductory matter, biographies of the principal characters, and 'Sir
William Hamilton' make it the most complete edition yet produced.

JAMES CARLYLE

On Tuesday, January the 24th, 1832, I received tidings that my dear and worthy Father had departed out of this world. He was called away, by a death apparently of the mildest, on Sunday morning about six. He had taken what was thought a bad cold on the Monday preceding; but rose every day, and was sometimes out of doors. Occasionally he was insensible (as Pain usually soon made him of late years); but when spoken to recollected himself. He was up and at the Kitchen fire (at Scotsbrig) [1] on the Saturday evening about six: "but was evidently growing fast worse in breathing." "About ten o'clock he fell into a sort of stupor," writes my sister Jane, "still breathing higher and with greater difficulty: he spoke little to any of us, seemingly unconscious of what he did; came over the bedside, and offered up a prayer to Heaven in such accents as it is impossible to forget. He departed almost without a struggle," adds she, "this morning at half-past six." My mother adds, in her own hand: "It is God that has done it; be still, my dear children—Your affectionate Mother—God support us all." The funeral is to be on Friday: the present date is *Wednesday night.*

This stroke, altogether unexpected at the time, but which I have been long anticipating in general, falls heavy on me, as such needs must: yet not so as to stun me or unman me. Natural tears have come to my relief: I can look at my dear Father, and that section of the Past which he has made alive for me, in a certain sacred sanctified light; and give way to what

[1] A farmhouse in the parish of Middlebie, about two miles and a half from Ecclefechan. It was anciently called Gotsbrig, and was once a border "keep" or tower. A portion of the old wall still stands incorporated in the walls of the house. The Carlyles removed to it from Mainhill in May 1826, and James Carlyle, the youngest son, continued tenant of the farm until 1880.

funds, sent me to School and College ; and made me whatever I am or may become. Let me not mourn for my Father ; let me do worthily of him : so shall he still live, even Here, in me ; and his worth plant itself honourably forth into new generations.

I purpose now, while the impression is more pure and clear within me, to mark down the main things I can recollect of my Father : to myself, if I live to after years, it may be instructive and interesting, as the Past grows ever holier the farther we leave it. My mind is calm enough to do it deliberately ; and to do it truly the thought of that pale earnest face which even now lies stiffened into Death in that bed at Scotsbrig, with the infinite All of Worlds looking down on it,—will *certainly* impel me. Neither, should these lines survive myself and be seen by others, can the sight of them do harm to anyone. It is good to know how a true spirit will vindicate itself into truth and freedom, through what obstructions soever ; how the ' acorn cast care- lessly into the wilderness ' will make room for itself, and grow to be an oak. This is one of the cases belonging to that class " the Lives of remarkable men ; " in which, it has been said, " paper and ink should least of all be spared." I call a man remarkable, who becomes a true Workman in this vineyard of the Highest : be his work that of Palace-building and Kingdom- founding, or only of delving and ditching, to me it is no matter, or *next to* none : *all* human work is transitory, small, in itself contemptible ; only the worker thereof and the spirit that dwelt in him is significant. I proceed without order, or almost any forethought ; anxious only to save what I have left, and mark it as it lies in me.

In several respects, I consider my Father as one of the most interesting men I have known. He was a man of perhaps *the* very largest natural endowment of any it has been my lot to converse with : none of us will ever forget that bold glowing style of his, flowing free from the untutored Soul ; full of metaphors (though he knew not what a metaphor was), with all manner of potent words (which he appropriated and applied with a *surprising* accuracy, you often could not guess whence) ; brief, energetic ; and which I should say conveyed the most perfect picture, definite, clear not in ambitious *colours* but in full *white* sunlight, of all the dialects I have ever listened to. Nothing did I ever hear him undertake to render visible, which did not become almost ocularly so. Never shall we again hear such speech as that was : the whole district knew of it ; and laughed joyfully over it, not knowing how otherwise to express the feeling it gave them.   Emphatic I have heard him beyond all men.   In anger he had no need of oaths ; his words were like sharp arrows that smote into the very heart.   The fault was that he exaggerated (which tendency I also inherit) ; yet only in description and for the sake chiefly of *humorous* effect : he was a man of rigid, even scrupulous veracity ; I have often heard him turn back, when he thought his strong words were mis- leading, and correct them into mensurative accuracy.   *Ach, und dies alles ist hin !*

I call him a natural man ; singularly free from all manner of affectation : he was among the last of the true men, which Scotland (on the old system) produced, or can produce ; a man healthy in body and in mind ; fearing God, and diligently working in God's Earth with contentment, hope and unwearied resolution.   *He* was never visited with Doubt ; the old Theorem of the Universe was sufficient for him, and he worked well in it, and in all senses *successfully* and wisely as few now can do ; so quick is the motion of Transition becoming : the new genera- tion almost to a man must make " their Belly their God," and alas even find *that* an empty one.   Thus curiously enough, and blessedly, *he* stood a true man on the verge of the Old ; while his son stands here lovingly surveying him on the verge of the New, and sees the possibility of also being true there.   God make the possibility, blessed possibility, into a reality !

A virtue he had which I should learn to imitate.   *He never spoke of what was disagreeable and past.*   I have often wondered and admired at this.   The thing that he had nothing to *do* with, he did nothing with.   This was a *healthy* mind.   In like manner, I have seen him always when we young ones (half roguishly, and provokingly without doubt) were perhaps repeating sayings of his, sit as if he did not hear us at all : never once did I know him utter a word (only once that I remember of give a look) in such a case.

[*Thursday morning.*]   Another virtue, the example of which has passed strongly into me, was his settled placid indifference to the clamours or the murmurs of Public Opinion.   For the judgment of those that had no right or power to judge him, he seemed simply to care nothing at all.   He very rarely *spoke* of despising such things, he contented himself with altogether disregarding them.   Hollow babble it was ; for him a thing as Fichte said " that did not exist," *das gar nicht existirte.*   There was something truly great in this ; the very perfection of it hid from you the extent of the attainment.

Or rather let me call it a new phasis of the *health* which in mind as in body was conspicuous in him. Like a healthy man, he wanted *only* to get along with his Task : whatsoever could not forward him in this (and how could Public Opinion and much else of the like sort do it ?) was of no moment to him, was not there for him.

This great maxim of Philosophy he had gathered by the teaching of nature alone : That man was created to work, not to speculate, or feel, or dream. Accordingly he set his whole heart thitherwards : he did work wisely and unweariedly (*ohne Hast aber ohne Rast*), and perhaps *performed* more (with the tools he had) than any man I now know. It should have made me sadder than it did to hear the young ones sometimes complaining of his slow punctuality and thoroughness : he would leave nothing till it was *done*. Alas ! the age of Substance and Solidity is gone (for the time) ; that of Show and hollow Superficiality (in all senses) is in full course—

And yet he was a man of open sense : wonderfully so. I could have entertained him for days talking of *any* matter interesting to man. He delighted to hear of *all* things that were worth talking of ; the mode of living men had, the mode of working, their opinions, virtues, whole spiritual and temporal environment. It is some two years ago (in summer) since I entertained him highly (he was hoeing turnips and perhaps I helped him) with an account of the character and manner of existence of Francis Jeffrey. Another evening he enjoyed (probably it was on that very visit) with the heartiest relish my description of the people (I think) of Turkey. The Chinese had astonished him much : in some Magazine (from Little's of Cressfield) he had got a sketch of *Macartney's Embassy*, the memory of which never left him. Adam Smith's *Wealth of Nations*, greatly as it lay out of his course, he had also fallen in with ; and admired, and understood and remembered,—so far as he had any business with it.—I once wrote him about my being in Smithfield Market (seven years ago) ; of my seeing St. Paul's : both things interested him heartily, and dwelt with him. I had hoped to tell him much, much of what I saw in this second visit ; and that many a long cheerful talk would have given us both some sunny hours : but *es konnte nimmer seyn !*—Patience ! Hope !

At the same time he had the most entire and open contempt

for all idle tattle, what he called " clatter." *Any* talk that had
meaning in it he could listen to : what had *no* meaning in it,
above all, what seemed false, he absolutely could and would not
hear ; but abruptly turned aside from it, or if that might not
suit, with the besom of destruction swept it far away from him.
Long may we remember his " I don't believe thee ; " his tongue-
paralysing, cold, indifferent " Hah ! "—I should say of him, as
I did of our Sister [1] whom we lost, that he seldom or never spoke
except actually to convey an idea. Measured by quantity of
words, he was a talker of fully average copiousness ; by extent
of meaning communicated, he was the most copious I have
listened to. How, in few sentences, he would sketch you off an
entire Biography, an entire Object or Transaction : keen,
clear, rugged, genuine, completely rounded in ! His words
came direct from the heart, by the inspiration of the moment :
" It is no idle tale," said he to some laughing rustics, while
stating in his strong way some complaint against them ; and
their laughter died into silence. Dear good Father ! There
looked *honesty* through those clear earnest eyes ; a sincerity
that compelled belief and regard. " Moffat ! " said he one day
to an incorrigible reaper, " thou has every feature of a bad
shearer : high, and rough, and little on't. Thou maun *alter*
thy figure or slant the bog "—pointing to the man's road
homewards.—

He was irascible, choleric, and we all dreaded his wrath. Yet
passion never mastered him, or maddened him ; it rather
inspired him with new vehemence of insight, and more piercing
emphasis of wisdom. It must have been a bold man that did
not quail before that face, when glowing with indignation,
grounded (for so it ever was) on the sense of right, and in resistance of wrong. More than once has he lifted up his strong voice
in Tax Courts and the like before " the Gentlemen " (what he
knew of Highest among men), and rending asunder official
sophistries, thundered even into their deaf ears the indignant
sentence of natural justice, to the conviction of all.—Oh why did
we laugh at these things while we loved them ! There is a
tragic greatness and sacredness in them now.

I can call my Father a brave man (*ein Tapferer*). Man's face
he did not fear ; God he always feared : his Reverence, I think,

[1] Margaret, born 20th September 1803, died 22d June 1830.—" There
are yet few days in which I do not meet on the streets some face that recalls
my Sister Margaret's, and reminds me that *she* is not suffering, but silent,
asleep in the Ecclefechan Churchyard ; her *Life*, her Self where God willed !
What a miracle is all Existence ! "—Carlyle's *Journal*, 8th February 1835.

was considerably mixed with Fear. Yet not slavish Fear ; rather Awe, as of unutterable Depths of Silence, through which flickered a trembling Hope. How he used to speak of Death (especially in late years) or rather to be silent, and *look* of it ! There was no feeling in him here that he cared to hide : he trembled at the really terrible ; the mock-terrible he cared nought for.—That last act of his Life ; when in the last agony, with the thick ghastly vapours of Death rising round him to choke him, he burst through and called with a man's voice on the great God to have mercy on him : that was like the epitome and concluding summary of his whole Life. God gave him strength to wrestle with the King of Terrors, and as it were even then to prevail. All his strength came from God, and ever sought new nourishment there. God be thanked for it.

Let me not mourn that my Father's Force is all spent, that his Valour wars no longer. Has it not gained the victory ? Let me imitate him rather ; let his courageous heart beat anew in me, that when oppression and opposition unjustly threaten, I too may rise with his spirit to front them and subdue them.

On the whole, ought I not to rejoice that God was pleased to give me such a Father ; that from earliest years, I had the example of a real Man (of God's own making) continually before me ? Let me learn of *him ;* let me " write my Books as he built his Houses, and walk as blamelessly through this shadow-world "—(if God so will), to rejoin him at last. Amen !—Alas ! such is the *mis*-education of these days, it is only among what are called the *un*educated classes (those educated by experience) that you can look for *a man.* Even among these, such a sight is growing daily rarer. My Father, in several respects, has not, that I can think of, left his fellow. *Ultimus Romanorum !* Perhaps among Scottish Peasants what Samuel Johnson was among English Authors. I have a sacred pride in my Peasant Father, and would not exchange him even now for any King known to me. Gold, and the guinea-stamp ; the Man, and the Clothes of the Man ! Let me thank God for that greatest of blessings, and strive to live worthily of it.—

Though from the heart and practically even more than in words an independent man, he was by no means an insubordinate one. His bearing towards his Superiors I consider noteworthy, of a piece with himself. I think, in early life, when working at Springkell for a Sir W. Maxwell (the grandfather of the present Baronet), he had got an early respect impressed upon him for the character as well as station of a Gentleman. I have heard him often describe the grave wisdom and dignified deportment of that Maxwell, as of a true " ruler of the people ; " it used to remind me of the Gentlemen in Goethe.   Sir William, like those he ruled over and benignantly (at least gracefully and earnestly) governed, has passed away.—But even for the mere Clothes-screens of rank, my Father testified no contempt : he spoke of them in public or private without acerbity ; testified for them the outward deference which Custom and Convenience prescribed, and felt no degradation therein : their inward claim to regard was a thing which concerned them, not him.   I love to figure him addressing these men, with bared head, by the title of " Your Honour ; " with a manner respectful yet unembarrassed ; a certain manful dignity looking through his own fine face ; with his noble gray head bent patiently to the (alas) unworthy.   Such conduct is perhaps no longer possible.

Withal he had in general a grave natural politeness : I have seen him, when the women were perhaps all in anxiety about the disorder of the house, etc., usher men, with true hospitality, into his mean house ; without any grimace of apologies, or the smallest seeming embarrassment : were the house but a cabin, it was his, and they were welcome to him and what it held.   This was again the *man*.   His Life was " no idle tale," not a Lie, but a Truth, which whoso liked was welcome to come and examine. " An earnest toilsome life," which also *had* a serious issue.

The more I reflect on it, the more must I admire how completely Nature had taught him ; how completely he was devoted to his work, to the Task of his Life ; and content to let *all* pass by unheeded that had not relation to this.   It is a singular fact, for example, that though a man of such openness and clearness, he had never, I believe, read three pages of *Burns's Poems*. Not even when all about him became noisy and enthusiastic (I the loudest) on that matter did he feel it worth while to renew his investigation of it, or once turn his face towards it.   The Poetry *he* liked (he did not call it Poetry) was Truth and the Wisdom of Reality.   Burns indeed could have done nothing for him.   As high a Greatness hung over his world, as over that of Burns (the ever-present greatness of the Infinite itself) : neither was he like Burns called to rebel against the world, but to labour patiently at his Task there ; " uniting the Possible with the Necessary " to bring out the *Real* wherein also lay an Ideal). Burns could not have in any way strengthened him in this course ; and therefore was for him a phenomenon merely.   Nay Rumour had been so busy with Burns, and Destiny and his own

Desert had in very deed so marred his name, that the good rather
avoided him. Yet it was not with aversion that my Father
regarded Burns; at worst with indifference and neglect. I have
heard him speak of once seeing him: standing in " Rob Scott's
Smithy " (at Ecclefechan, no doubt superintending some work)
he heard one say, " There is the Poet Burns ; " he went out to
look, and saw a man with boots on, like a well-dressed farmer,
walking down the village on the opposite side of the burn. This
was all the relation these two men ever had: they were very
nearly coevals.[1]—I know Robert Burns, and I knew my Father;
yet were you to ask me which had the greater natural faculty?
I might perhaps actually pause before replying! Burns had an
infinitely wider Education; my Father a far wholesomer:
besides the one was a man of Musical Utterance, the other wholly
a man of Action, even with Speech subservient thereto. Never,
of all the men I have seen, has one come personally in my way
in whom the Endowment from Nature and the Arena from
Fortune were so utterly out of all proportion. I have said this
often; and partly *know* it. As a man of Speculation (had
Culture ever unfolded him) he must have gone wild and desperate
as Burns: but he was a man of Conduct, and Work keeps all
right. What strange shapeable creatures we are.

My Father's Education was altogether of the worst and most
limited. I believe he was never more than three months at any
school: what he learned there showed what he might have
learned. A solid knowledge of Arithmetic, a fine antique Hand-
writing; these, with other limited *practical* etceteras, were *all*
the things he ever heard mentioned as excellent: he had no
room to strive for more. Poetry, Fiction in general, he had
universally seen treated as not only idle, but *false* and criminal.
This was the spiritual element he had lived in, almost to old age.
But greatly his most important culture he had gathered (and
this too by his own endeavour) from the better men of the district;
the Religious men, to whom as to the most excellent, his own
nature gradually attached and attracted him. He was Religious
with the consent of his whole faculties: without Reason he
would have been nothing; indeed his habit of intellect was
thoroughly free and even incredulous, and strongly enough did
the daily example of this work afterwards on me. " Putting
out the natural eye of his mind to see better with a telescope : "
this was no scheme for *him*. But he was in Annandale, and it
was above fifty years ago; and a Gospel was still preached there

[1] Burns was born in 1759, James Carlyle in 1758. Burns died in 1796.

to the heart of a man, in the tones of a man.   Religion was the Pole-star for my Father : rude and uncultivated as he otherwise was, it made him and kept him " in all points a man."

Oh ! when I think that all the area in Boundless Space he had seen was limited to a circle of some forty miles diameter (he never in his life was farther, or elsewhere so far, from home as at Craigenputtock) ; and all his knowledge of the Boundless Time was derived from his Bible, and what the oral memories of old men could give him, and his own could gather ; and yet, that he was *such*,—I could take shame to myself ; I feel to my Father (so great though so neglected, so generous also towards *me*) a strange tenderness, and mingled pity and reverence ; peculiar to the case ; infinitely soft and near my heart.   Was he not a sacrifice to *me?*   Had I stood in his place, could he not have stood in mine, and more ?   Thou good Father ! well may *I* forever honour thy memory : surely that act was not without its reward.—And was not Nature great, out of such materials to make such a man ?—

Though genuine and coherent, " living and life-giving," he was nevertheless but half developed.   We had all to complain that we *durst not* freely love him.   His heart seemed as if walled in ; he had not the free means to unbosom himself.   My Mother has owned to me that she could never understand him ; that her affection, and (with all their little strifes) her admiration of him was obstructed : it seemed as if an atmosphere of Fear repelled us from him.   To me it was especially so.   Till late years, when he began to respect me more ; and, as it were, to look up to me for instruction, for protection (a relation unspeakably beautiful), I was ever more or less awed and chilled before him : my heart and tongue played freely only with my Mother.   He had an air of deepest gravity, even sternness.   Yet he could laugh with his whole throat, and his whole heart.   I have often seen him weep too ; his voice would thicken and his lips curve while reading the Bible : he had a merciful heart to real distress, though he hated idleness, and for imbecility and fatuity had no tolerance.   Once, and I think once only, I saw him in a passion of tears.   It was when the remains of my Mother's fever hung upon her (in 1817), and seemed to threaten the extinction of her reason : we were all of us nigh desperate, and ourselves mad. He burst, at last, into quite a torrent of grief ; cried piteously and threw himself on the floor, and lay moaning.   I wondered, and had no words, no tears.   It was as if a rock of granite had melted, and was thawing into water.   What unknown

seas of feeling lie in man, and will from time to time break
through !—

He was no niggard, but truly a wisely generous Economist.
He paid his men *handsomely* and with overplus.   He had known
Poverty in the shape of actual want (in boyhood), and never
had one penny which he knew not well how he had come by
(" picked," as he said, " out of the hard stone ") : yet he ever
parted with money as a man that knew when he was getting
money's worth ; that could *give* also, and with a frank liberality,
when the fit occasion called.   I remember, with the peculiar
kind of tenderness that attaches to many similar things in his life,
one or I rather think two times, when he sent *me* to buy a
quarter of a pound of Tobacco to give to some old women whom
he had had gathering Potatoes for him : he nipt off for each a
handsome leash, and handed it her by way of over-and-above.
This was a common principle with him.   I must have been
twelve or thirteen when I fetched this Tobacco.   I love to think
of it.   " The little that a just man hath."   The old women are
now perhaps *all* dead ; he too is dead : but the gift still lives.
[*Thursday night.*]

He was a man singularly free from Affectation.   The feeling
that he had not he could in no wise pretend to have : however
ill the want of it might look, he simply would not and did not
put on the show of it.

Singularly free from Envy I may reckon him too ; the rather
if I consider his keen temper, and the value he naturally (as a
man wholly for Action) set upon *success* in life.   Others that (by
better fortune ; none was more industrious or more prudent)
had grown richer than he, did not seem to provoke the smallest
grudging in him.   They were going their path, he going his ;
one did not impede the other.   He rather seemed to look at
such with a kind of respect, a desire to learn from them : at
lowest with indifference.   In like manner, though he above all
things (indeed in strictness, *solely*) admired Talent, he seemed
never to have measured *himself* anxiously against anyone ; was
content to be taught by whosoever could teach him : one or
two men (immeasurably his inferiors in faculty) he, I do believe,
looked up to ; and thought (with perfect composure) abler
minds than himself.   Complete, at the same time, was his
confidence in his own judgment when it spoke to him decisively :
he was one of those few that could *believe* and *know*, as well as
inquire and *be of opinion*.   When I remember how he admired
Intellectual Force, how much he had of it himself, and yet

how unconsciously and contentedly he gave others credit for superiority, I again see the *healthy* spirit, the genuine man. Nothing could please him better than a well-ordered Discourse of Reason ; the clear Solution and Exposition of any object : and he knew well, in such cases, when the nail had been hit ; and contemptuously enough recognised where it had been missed. He has said of a bad Preacher : " He was like a fly wading among Tar." Clearness, emphatic Clearness, was his highest category of man's thinking power : he delighted always to hear good " Argument ; " he would often say, " I would like to hear thee argue with him : " he said this of Jeffrey and me,— with an air of such simple earnestness (not two years ago) ; and it was his true feeling. I have often pleased him much by arguing with men (as many years ago I was prone to do) in his presence : he rejoiced greatly in my success, at all events in my dexterity and manifested force. Others of us he admired for our " activity," our practical valour and skill ; all of us (generally speaking) for our decent demeanour in the world. It is now one of my greatest blessings (for which I would thank Heaven from the heart) that he lived to see me, through various obstructions, attain some look of doing well. He had " educated " me against much advice, I believe, and chiefly, if not solely, from his own noble faith : James Bell (one of our wise men) had told him : " Educate a boy, and he grows up to despise his ignorant parents." My Father once told me this ; and added : " Thou hast not done so. God be thanked for it ! " I have reason to think my Father was proud of me (not vain, for he never, except provoked, openly bragged of us) ; that here too he lived to " see the pleasure of the Lord prosper in his hands." Oh, was it not a happiness for me ! The fame of all this Planet were not henceforth so precious.—

He was thrifty, patient ; careless of outward accommodation ; had a Spartan indifference to all that. When he quarrelled about such things, it was rather because some human *mismanagement* seemed to look through the evil. Food and all else were simply and solely there as the means for *doing work*. We have lived for months, of old (and when he was not any longer poor), because " by ourselves," on porridge and potatoes with no other condiment than what our own cow yielded. Thus are we not now all beggars ; as the most like us have become. Mother and Father were assiduous, abstemious, frugal without stinginess. They shall not want their reward.

Both still knew what they were doing in this world, and why

they were here : " Man's chief end," my Father could have
answered from the depths of his soul, " is to glorify God and *enjoy
Him* for ever." [1] By this light he walked, choosing his path,
fitting prudence to principle with wonderful skill and manliness—
through " the ruins of a falling Era," not once missing his
footing. Go thou, whom by the hard toil of his arms and his mind
he has struggled to enlighten better, go thou and do likewise !

His death was " unexpected " ? Not so ; every morning and
every evening for perhaps sixty years, he had prayed to the great
Father, in words which I shall now no more hear him impressively
pronounce : " Prepare us for these solemn events, Death,
Judgment, and Eternity." He would pray also : " Forsake
us not now when we are old, and our heads grown gray." God
did not forsake him.—

Ever since I can remember, his honoured head was gray :
indeed he must have been about Forty when I was born. It
was a noble head ; very large ; the upper part of it strikingly
like that of the Poet Goethe : the mouth again bearing marks
of unrefinement ; shut, indeed, and significant ; yet loosely
compressed (as I have seen in the firmest men, if used to hard
manual labour) ; betokening depth, passionateness, force, all
in an element not of languor, yet of toil and patient perennial
Endurance. A face full of meaning, and earnestness.[2] A man
of Strength, and a man of Toil. Jane took a profile [3] of him
when she was last in Annandale : it is the only memorial we
have left ; and worth much to us. He was short of stature ;
yet shorter than usual only in the limbs : of great muscular
strength, far more than even his strong-built frame gave promise
of. In all things he was emphatically *temperate :* through life
guilty (more than can be said of almost any man) of *no* excess.—

He was born (I think, but will inquire better) in the year
1757 ; [4] at a place called Brownknowe, a small farm, not far
from Burnswark Hill in Annandale. I have heard him describe
the anguish of mind he felt when leaving this place, and taking
farewell of " a big stone " whereon he had been wont to sit in
early boyhood, tending the cattle. Perhaps there was a thorn-
tree near it : his heart he said was like to burst. They were
removing to Sibbaldbyside, another farm in the valley of Dryfe.
—He was come to full manhood.—

---

[1] Words from the Scottish *Shorter Catechism.*

[2] " About this hour is the funeral : Irving enters—unsatisfactory."—
T. C.

[3] The profile by Mrs. Carlyle (face only) is done mechanically from
the shadow.   [4] August 1758.

The family was exposed to great privations, while at Brown-knowe. The Mother (Mary Gillespie: [1] she had relatives in Dryfesdale) was left with her children, and had not always meal to make them porridge. My Father was the second son, and fourth child. My Grandfather (Thomas Carlyle, after whom I am named) was an honest, vehement, adventurous, but not an industrious man. He used to collect vigorously and rigorously a sum sufficient for his half year's rent (probably some six or five pounds) ; lay this by ; and for the rest, leave the mother with her little ones to manage very much as they could and would ; himself meanwhile amusing himself ; perhaps hunting, most probably with the Laird of Bridekirk (a swashbuckler of those days, composer of " Bridekirk's Hunting ") partly in the character of kinsman, partly of attendant and henchman. I have heard my Father describe the shifts they were reduced to at home. Once, he said, meal which perhaps had been long scarce and certainly for some time wanting, arrived at last late at night, —she proceeded on the spot to make cakes of it, and had no fuel but straw that she tore from the beds (straw lies under the chaff sacks we all slept on) to do it with : the children all rose to eat. Potatoes were little in use then : a " *wecht*-ful " [2] was stored up to be eaten perhaps about Halloween. My Father often told us how he once, with a providence early manifested, got possession of four potatoes ; and thinking that a time of want might come, hid them carefully against the evil day : he found them long after all grown together ; they had not been needed. I think he once told us his first short-clothes were a hull made mostly or wholly of leather (?). We all only laughed ; for it is now long ago. Thou dear Father ! through what stern obstructions was thy way to manhood to be forced, and, for us and our travelling, made smooth.

My Grandfather, whom I can remember as a slightish wiry-looking old man, had not possessed the wisdom of his Son ; yet perhaps he was more to be pitied than blamed. *His* Mother [3] (whose name I have forgotten) was early left a Widow with two of them, in the parish, perhaps in the village, of Middlebie : Thomas the elder became a joiner, and went to work in Lancashire, perhaps in Lancaster, where he staid more than one

---

[1] Died 1797, aged 70.
[2] A *wecht*, large sieve for winnowing grain.
[3] Isabella Bell (born 1687, died 1759), wife of John Carlyle of Burrens (born 1687, died 1727).

season (he once returned home, in winter, partly by *ice*, skating along the Westmoreland and Cumberland Lakes) : he was in Dumfriesshire in 1745 ; saw the Highlanders come through Ecclefechan (over the Cowden-heights) as they went *down ;* was at Dumfries among them, as they returned back in flight : he had gone by the Lady of Bridekirk's request to look after the Laird, whom as a Whig of some note, they had taken prisoner.[1] His whole adventures there he had minutely described to his children (I too have heard him speak, but briefly, indistinctly, of them) : by my Uncle Frank I once got a full account of the matter ; which shall perhaps be inserted elsewhere. He worked as carpenter, I know not how long, about Middlebie (?), then laid aside that craft (except as a side-business ; for he always had tools, which I myself have assisted him in grinding), and went to Brownknowe to farm. In his latter days he was chiefly supported by my Father ; to whom I remember once hearing him say, with a half-choked tremulous palsied voice : " Thou hast been a good son to me." He died in 1804[2] : I well remember the funeral, which I was at, and that I read (being then a good reader) " *MacEwen on the Types* " (which I have not seen since, but then partially understood, and even liked for its glib smoothness) to the people sitting at the wake. The funeral was in the time of snow : all is still very clear to me. The three brothers, my Father, Frank and Tom spoke together in the dusk, on the street of Ecclefechan, I looking up and listening : Tom proposed that he would bear the whole expense as he had been " rather backward during his Life " (the Deceased's : these were his very words) ; which offer was immediately rejected.—

Old Thomas Carlyle had been proud and poor ; no doubt he was discontented enough : industry was perhaps more difficult in Annandale then (this I do not think very likely) ; at all events, the man in honour (the *man*) of those days, in that rude Border Country, was a drinker, and hunter ; above all a *striker*. My Grandfather did not drink ; but his *stroke* was ever as ready as

[1] Adam Carlyle of Bridekirk was seized on the highway near his own house, by the Pretender's army, in 1745, on its retreat from Carlisle. In passing through Dumfries, he made himself conspicuous at the officers' mess by obstinately refusing to give any sign when Prince Charlie's health was drunk. When the enthusiasm had subsided a little, he stood up alone, and drank " Confusion to the Pretender." Carlyle's grandfather being denied access to him at Dumfries, followed the troops, then on their way to Glasgow, across the Nith ; and mounting a gate, shouted his message as the prisoner marched past, and there received his answer for the Lady.—T. C. *loq.* (1874).
[2] 1806. See *infra*, p. 17 *n.*

his word, and both were sharp enough. He was a fiery man; irascible, indomitable : of the toughness and springiness of steel. An old market-brawl, called " the Ecclefechan Dog-fight," in which he was a principal, survives in tradition there to this day. My Father who in youth too had been in quarrels, and formidable enough in them, but from manhood upwards *abhorred* all such things,—never once spoke to us of this. My Grandfather had a certain religiousness ; but it could not be made dominant and paramount : his life lay in two ; I figure him as very miserable, and pardon (as my Father did) all his irregularities and un-reasons. My Father liked in general to speak of him, when it came in course : he told us sometimes of his once riding down to Annan (when a boy) behind him, on a sack of barley to be shipped ; for which there was then no other mode of conveyance but horseback. On arriving at Annan-bridge, the people demanded three-halfpence of toll-money : this the old man would in no wise pay (for tolls then were reckoned pure imposi-tions) ; got soon into argument about it ; and rather than pay it, turned his horse's head aside, and swam the river (at a dangerous place) to the extreme terror of his boy. Perhaps it was on this same occasion, while the two were on the shore about Whinnyrigg, with many others on the same errand (for a " boat had come in "—from Liverpool probably—and the country must hasten to ship) that a lad, of larger size, jeered at the little boy for his ragged coat, etc. : whereupon the Father, doubtless provoked too, gave him *permission* to fight the wrong-doer,— which he did, and with victory. " Man's inhumanity to man ! "—

I must not dwell on these things : yet will mention the other Brother, my Grand-uncle Francis, still remembered by his title " the Captain of Middlebie." He was bred a shoemaker, and like his elder brother went to travel for work and insight. My Father once described to me, with pity and aversion, how Francis had on some occasion taken to drinking, and to gaming, " far up in England " (at Bristol ?), had lost *all* his money, and gone to bed drunk : he awoke next morning in horrors ; started up (stung by the serpent of remorse), and flinging himself out of bed, broke his leg against a table standing near ; and lay there sprawling,—and had to lie for weeks, with nothing to pay the shot. Perhaps this was the crisis of his life ; perhaps it was to pay the bill of this very tavern, that he went and enlisted himself on board some small-craft man-of-war. A mutiny (as I have heard) took place ; wherein Francis Carlyle, with great daring stood by the Captain and quelled the matter ; for which service he was promoted to the command of a Revenue-ship, and sailed therein chiefly about the Solway Seas, and did feats enough—of which perhaps elsewhere. He had retired, with dignity, on half-pay to his native Middlebie before my birth. I never saw him but once, and then rather memorably. My Grandfather and he, owing to some sort of cloud and misunderstanding, had not had any intercourse for long ; in which division the two families had joined : but now when old Thomas was lying on his probable, and as it proved actual Deathbed, the old rugged Sea-Captain relented, and resolved to see his Brother yet once before he died. He came in a cart to Ecclefechan (a great enterprise then, for the road was all water-cut and nigh impassable with roughness) : I chanced to be standing by when he arrived. He was a grim, broad, to me almost terrible man ; unwieldy so that he could not walk. (My Brother John is said to resemble him : he was my prototype of Smollett's Trunnion.) They lifted him up the steep straight stairs in a chair, to the room of the dying man. The two old Brothers saluted each other hovering over the brink of the grave (they were both above eighty) : in some twenty minutes, the arm-chair was seen again descending (my father bore one corner of it, in front) the old man had parted with his Brother for the last time ; he went away, with few words, but with a face that still dimly haunts me ; and I never saw him more. The business at the moment was quite unknown to me ; but I gathered it in a day or two ; and its full meaning long afterwards grew clear to me. Its outward phasis, now after some twenty-eight years, is plain as I have written. Old Francis also died not long afterwards.[1]

One vague tradition I will mention : that our humble forefathers dwelt long as farmers at *Burrens*, the old Roman Station in Middlebie. Once in times of Border robbery, some Cumberland cattle had been stolen and were chased ; the trace of them disappeared at Burrens, and the angry Cumbrians demanded of the poor farmer what had become of them ? It was vain for him to answer and aver (truly) that he knew nothing of them, had no concern with them : he was seized by the people, and despite his own desperate protestations, despite his wife's shriekings and his children's cries, was hanged on the spot !

[1] This paragraph requires to be corrected by the following dates, viz. : —Francis died 19th August 1803 (aged 77) ; Thomas died 10th January 1806 (aged 84).

The case even in those days was thought piteous; and a perpetual gift of the little farm was made to the poor widow as some compensation. Her children and children's children continued to possess it; till their title was questioned by "the Duke" (of Queensberry) and they (perhaps in my great-grandfather's time, about 1727) were ousted. Date and circumstances for the Tale are all wanting. This is my remotest outlook into the Past; and itself but a cloudy half or whole hallucination: further on there is not even a hallucination. I now return: these things are secular and unsatisfactory.

Bred up in such circumstances, the Boys were accustomed to all manner of hardship; and must trust for upbringing to Nature, to the scanty precepts of their poor Mother, and to what seeds or influences of culture were hanging as it were in the *atmosphere* of their environment. Poor boys! They had to scramble ("'scraffle!'") for their very clothes and food. They knit, they thatched, for hire; above all they hunted. My Father had tried all these things, almost in boyhood. Every dell and *burngate* and *cleugh* of that district he had traversed seeking hares and the like: he used to tell of these pilgrimages: once, I remember, his gun-flint was "tied on with a hatband." He was a *real* hunter, like a wild Indian, from Necessity. The hares' flesh was food: hare-skins (at some sixpence each) would accumulate into the purchase-money of a coat. All these things he used to speak of without either boasting or complaining, not as reproaches to *us*, but as historical merely. On the whole, he never *complained;* either of the past, the present, or the future: he observed and accurately noted all, he made the most and the best of all. His hunting years were not useless to him. Misery was early training the rugged boy into a Stoic;— that, one day, there might be assurance of a Scottish Man.—

One Macleod, "Sandy Macleod," a wandering pensioner invalided out of some Highland Regiment (who had served in America,—I must think with General Wolfe) had strayed to Brownknowe with his old wife, and taken a Cottage of my Grandfather. He, with his wild foreign legends, and strange half-idiotic half-genial ways, was a great figure with the young ones; and I think acted not a little on their character, least of any, however, on my Father, whose early turn for the *practical* and real, made him more heedless of Macleod and his vagaries. The old Pensioner had quaint sayings, not without significance: of a lacrymose complaining man, for example, he said (or perhaps to him) "He might be thankful he was not in Purgatory."

The quaint fashion of speaking, assumed for humour, and most noticeable in my uncle Frank, least or hardly at all in my Father, —was no doubt partly derived from this old wanderer, who was much about their house, working for his rent and so forth; and was partly laughed at, partly wondered at by the young ones.— Tinkers also, nestling in outhouses, melting pot-metal, and with rude feuds and warfare, often came upon the scene. These with passing Highland Drovers were perhaps their only visitors.

Had there not been a natural goodness and indestructible force in my Father, I see not how he could have bodied himself forth from these mean impediments. I suppose, good precepts were not wanting; there was the Bible to read. Old John Orr, the Schoolmaster, used from time to time to lodge with them; he was religious and enthusiastic (though in practice irregular— with drink); in my Grandfather also there seems to have been a certain geniality: for instance, he and a neighbour, Thomas Hogg, read "Anson's Voyage;" also the "Arabian Nights," —for which latter my Father (armed with zealous conviction) scrupled not to censure them openly.—By one means or another at an early age, he had acquired *principles;* lights that not only flickered but shone steadily to guide his way.

It must have been in his teens (perhaps rather early) that he and his elder brother John, with William Bell (afterwards of Wylie-hole, and a noted Drover), and *his* Brother, all met in the kiln at *Relief* [1] to play cards. The corn was dried then *at home:* there was a fire therefore, and perhaps it was both heat and light. The boys had played perhaps often enough, for trifling stakes; and always parted in good humour: one night they came to some disagreement. My Father spoke out, what was in him, about the folly, the sinfulness of quarrelling over a perhaps sinful amusement: the earnest mind persuaded other minds; they threw the cards into the fire; and (I think the younger Bell told my Brother James) no one of the four ever touched a card again through life! My Father certainly never hinted at such a game, since I knew him.—I cannot remember that I, at that age, had any such force of belief; which of us can?

[*Friday night.* My Father is now in his grave; sleeping by the side of his loved ones: his face to the East, under the Hope of meeting the Lord when He shall come to Judgment—when the Times shall be fulfilled. Mysterious Life! Yes, there is a God in man. Silence! since thou hast no voice.—To imitate *him*

---

[1] Farm in Middlebie parish.

I will pause here for the night. God comfort my Mother; God guard them all!]

Of old John Orr I must say another word: my Father, who often spoke of him, though not so much latterly, gave me copious description of that and other antiquarian matters, in one of the pleasantest days I remember; the last time but one (or perhaps two) that we talked together. A tradition of poor old Orr, as of a man of boundless love and natural worth, still faintly lives in Annandale. If I mistake not, he worked also as a Shoemaker: he was heartily devout; yet subject to fits of irregularity; he would vanish for weeks into obscure tippling-houses, then reappear ghastly and haggard in body and mind, shattered in health, torn with gnawing remorse. Perhaps it was in some dark interval of this kind (he was already old) that he bethought him of his Father, and how he was still lying without a Stone of memorial. John had already ordered a Tombstone for him, and it was lying worked, and I suppose lettered and ready, at some mason's establishment (up the water of Mein); but never yet carried to the place. Probably Orr had not a shilling of money to hire any carter with; but he hurried off to the spot, and desperately got the Stone on his back. It was a load that had nigh killed him; he had to set it down ever and anon and rest, and get it up again. The night fell: I think some one found him desperately struggling with it near Mein Mill, and assisted him, and got it set in its place.—Should I not go and look whether it is still to be found there: in Pennersaughs Churchyard?[1]

Though far above all quackery, Orr was actually employed to exorcise a House; some house or room at Orchard in the parish of Hoddam. He entered the haunted place, was closeted in it for some time, speaking or praying: the ghost was really and truly laid, for no one heard more of it. Beautiful reverence even of the rude and ignorant for the infinite nature of Wisdom, in the infinite life of Man!—

Orr, as already said, used to come much about Brownknowe; being habitually *itinerant*, and (though Schoolmaster of Hoddam) without settled home. He commonly, my Father said, slept with some of the Boys, in a place where (as usual) there were several beds. He would call out from the bed, to my Grandfather also in his: "Gudeman, I have found it,"—found

[1] A disused churchyard, about half a mile from Ecclefechan, in which many generations of Carlyles lie buried.

the solution of some problem or other, perhaps arithmetical, which they had been struggling with; or: " Gudeman, what d'ye think of this ? "—I represent him to myself as a squat, pursy kind of figure; grim, dusky, the blandest and most bounteous of Cynics. Also a form of the Past! He was my Father's sole Teacher in " schooling."

It might be in the year (I think, but must inquire of my now sole surviving Aunt) [1] 1773, that one William Brown, a Mason from Peebles came down into Annandale to do some work ; perhaps boarded in my Grandfather's house ; at all events married his eldest daughter and child, my now old and vehement, then young and spirited " Aunt Fanny " (" Aunt Fann.") This worthy man, whose nephew is still Minister of Eskdalemuir (and Author of a Book on the *Jews*) proved the greatest blessing to that household ; my Father could in any case have saved himself ; of the other Brothers it may be doubted whether William Brown was not the primary preserver. They all learned to be Masons from him, or from one another ; instead of miscellaneous labourers and hunters, became regular tradesmen ; the best in all their district (the skilfullest and faithfullest) and the best rewarded—every way. Except my Father, none of them attained a decisive religiousness : but they all had prudence and earnestness ; love of truth ; industry and the blessings it brings. My Father, before my time, though not the eldest had become, in all senses, the head of the house. The eldest was called John. He early got asthma, and for long could not work (though he got his share of the wages still) : I can faintly remember him as a pallid sickly figure, and even one or two insignificant words, and the breathless tone he uttered them in. When seized with extreme fits of sickness, he used to gasp out : " Bring Jamie ; O send for Jamie ! " He died I think in 1802.[2] I remember the funeral ; and perhaps a day before it, how an ill-behaving servant-wench to some crony of hers, lifted up the coverlid from off his pale, ghastly-befilleted head to show it her : unheeding of me, who was alone with them there, and to whom the sight gave

---

[1] Carlyle inquired of her on his return from London, but found her " garrulous," and unable to give dates. She died 26th February 1834, aged 82 years. She had married in 1773. Carlyle says of her in his *Journal :* " She was about 82 ; the last of her family ; a woman of singular vehemence, inflexibility and energy,—all uncultivated, ill directed. Her industry and parsimony were transcendent ; not less her self-help, of which these were forms. She even died refusing help ; unseen ; just as if she had been falling asleep. Τέλος."

[2] Died 12th October 1801, aged 47.

a new pang of horror.—He was the Father of two sons and a daughter, beside whom our boyhood was passed, none of whom have come to anything but insignificance. He was a well-doing man, and left them well ; but their Mother was not wise, nor they decidedly so.—The youngest Brother, my " Uncle Tom," died next : a fiery, passionate, self-secluded warm-loving genuine soul, without fear and without guile : of whom it is recorded that he never from the first tones of speech, " told any lie." A true old-Roman soul, yet so marred, so stunted ; who well deserves a chapter to himself, especially from me, who so lovingly admired him. He departed in my Father's house, in my presence, in the year 1815 : [1] the first Death I had ever understood and laid with its whole emphasis to heart.—Frank followed next ; at an interval of some five years : [2] a quaint, social, cheerful man ; of less earnestness, but more openness ; fond of genealogies, old histories, poems, queer sayings and all curious and *humane* things he could come at. This made him the greatest favourite : the rest were rather feared ; my Father (ultimately at least) universally feared and respected. Frank left two sons, as yet young ; one of whom (my namesake), gone to be a Lawyer, is rather clever, *how* clever I have not fully seen. —All these Brothers were men of evidently rather peculiar endowment : they were (censoriously) noted for their brotherly affection, and coherence ; for their hard sayings, and hard *strikings* (which only my Father ever grew to *heartily* detest) ; all of them became prosperous, got a name and possessions in their degree. It was a kindred, warmly liked, I believe, by those *near* it ; by those at a distance, viewed, at worst and lowest, as something dangerous to meddle with, something *not* to be meddled with.—

What are the rich or the poor ; and how do the simple Annals of the Poor differ from the complex Annals of the Rich, were they never so rich ?—What is *thy* attainment compared with an Alexander's, a Mahomet's, a Napoleon's ? And what was theirs ? A temporary fraction of this Planetkin,—the whole round of which is but a sandgrain in the All ; its whole duration but a moment in Eternity ! The poor life or the rich one, are but the larger or smaller (*very* little smaller) *letters* in which we

---

[1] Thomas, born 1776, died 9th June 1816. Carlyle often said it was his reflections on the death of this uncle, that suggested to him the subject of his chapter on " The Everlasting No," in *Sartor Resartus*.

[2] Francis, born 1761, died 1819. His two sons prospered and were good men, much attached to each other, and to their kindred. They both died about 1880.

write the apophthegm and golden-saying of Life : it may be a
False saying or it may be a True one ; *there* lies it all ; this is of
quite *infinite* moment : the rest is verily and indeed of next to
none.—

Perhaps my Father was William Brown's first Apprentice :
somewhere about his sixteenth year.   Early in the course of the
engagement, work grew scarce in Annandale : the two " slung
their tools " (mallets and irons hung in two equipoised masses
over the shoulders), and crossed the Hills into Nithsdale, to
Auldgarth,[1] where a Bridge was building.   This was my Father's
most *foreign* adventure ; he never again or before saw anything
so new, or (except when he came to Craigenputtock [2] on visits)
so *distant*.   He loved to speak of it : that talking day we had
together, I made him tell it me all over again from the beginning
—as a *whole*, for the first time.   He was a " hewer," and had
some few pence a day.   He could describe with the lucidest
distinctness how the whole work went on ; and " headers " and
" closers " solidly massed together made an impregnable pile.
He used to hear sermon in Closeburn church ; sometimes too in
Dunscore : the men had a refreshment of ale, for which he too
used to table his twopence,—but the grown-up men generously
for most part refused them.   A superintendent of the work,
a mason from Edinburgh, who did nothing but look on, and
(rather decidedly) insist on terms of contract,—" took a great
notion " of him ; was for having him to Edinburgh along with
him.   The master-builder, pleased with his ingenious diligence,
once laid a shilling on his " *banker* " (stone-bench for hewing
on) ; which he rather ungraciously refused.   A flood once
carried off all the cinctures and woodwork : he saw the Master
anxiously, tremulously watch through the rain as the waters
rose ; when they prevailed, and all went headlong, the poor man,
wringing his hands together, spread them out with open palm
down the river,—as if to say : There !
    It was a noble moment, which I regret to have missed, when
my Father going to look at Craigenputtock, saw this Work, for
the first time again, after a space of more than fifty years !
How changed was all else, this thing yet the same.   Then he was
a poor boy, now he was a respected old man ; increased in
worldly goods ; honoured in himself, and in his household.   He
grew alert (Jamie said) and eagerly observant : eagerly, yet with

1 Commonly spelt Auldgirth, about eight miles from Dumfries.
2 See *infra*, p. 83 *n*.

thoughts rise in me without feeling that they are weak and useless. The time till the Funeral was past, I instantly determined on passing with my Wife only, and all others were excluded. I have written to my Mother and to John;[1] have walked far and much (chiefly in the Regent's Park), and considered about many things; if so were I might accomplish this problem: To see clearly what my present calamity *means;* what I have lost, and what lesson my loss was to teach me.

As for the Departed, we ought to say that he was taken home "like a shock of corn fully ripe:" he "had finished the work that was given him to do," and finished it (very greatly more than the most) as became a man; he was summoned too before he had ceased to be interesting, to be lovable (he was to the last the pleasantest man I had to speak with in Scotland); for many years too he had the End ever in his eye, and was studying to make all preparation for what in his strong way he called often "that last, that awful change." Ever at every new parting of late years I have noticed him wring my hand with a tenderer pressure; as if he felt that one other of our few meetings Here was over. Mercifully also has he been spared me, till I am abler to bear his loss; till (by manifold struggles) I too, as he did, feel my feet on the Everlasting Rock, and through Time with its Death can in some degree see into Eternity with its Life. So that I have repeated, not with unwet eyes, let me hope likewise, not with unsoftened heart, these old and forever true words: "Blessed are the Dead that die in the Lord. They do rest from their labours, and their works follow them." Yes, their works follow them: the Force that had been lent my Father he honourably expended in manful welldoing: a portion of this Planet bears beneficent traces of his strong Hand and strong Head; nothing that he undertook to do but he did it faithfully and like a true man. I shall look on the Houses he built with a certain proud interest: they stand firm and sound to the heart, all over his little district: no one that comes after him will ever say, Here was the finger of a hollow Eye-servant. They are little texts, for me, of the Gospel of man's Free-will. Nor will his Deeds and Sayings, in any case, be found unworthy, not false and barren, but genuine and fit. Nay, am not I also the humble James Carlyle's work? I owe him much more than existence; I owe him a noble inspiring example (now that I can read it in that rustic character); it was he *exclusively* that determined on *educating* me, that from his small hard-earned

[1] Dr. Carlyle, then absent in Rome.

sadness. The country was all altered ; broomy knowes were become seed-fields ; trees, then not so much as *seeds*, now waved out broad boughs : the houses, the fields, the men, were of another fashion ; there was little that he could recognise. On reaching the Bridge itself, he started up to his knees (in the cart), sat wholly silent, and seemed on the point of weeping.

Well do I remember the first time I saw this Bridge : twelve years ago in the dusk of a May day ; I had walked from Muirkirk sickly, forlorn, of saddest mood (for it was then my days of darkness) : a rustic answered me : " Auldgarth " ! There it lay silent, red in the red dusk. It was as if half a century of past Time had fatefully, for moments, turned back.

The Master-builder of this Bridge was one Stewart of Minnyive ; who afterwards became my Uncle John Aitken's father-in-law : him I once saw. My Craigenputtock mason, James Hainning's Father, was the Smith that " sharpened the tools." A noble craft it is that of a mason : a good Building will last longer than most Books, than one Book of a million. The Auldgarth Bridge still spans the water, silently defies its chafing : there hangs it, and will hang, grim and strong, when of all the cunning hands that piled it together, perhaps the last now lies powerless in the sleep of death. O Time ! O Time ! wondrous and fearful art thou ; yet there is in man what is above thee.

[*Saturday.*] Of my Father's youth and opening manhood, and with what specialties this period was marked, I have but an imperfect notion. I must inquire further what more is yet to be saved. He was now master of his own actions ; possessed of means by his own earning ; and had to try the world on various sides, and ascertain wherein his own " chief end " in it actually lay. The first impulse of man is to seek for Enjoyment : he tries with more or less impetuosity, more or less irregularity, to conquer for himself a home and blessedness of a mere earthly kind ; not till later (in how many cases never !) does he ascertain that on Earth there is no such home ; that his true home lies beyond the world of Sense, is a celestial home.—Of these experimenting and tentative days my Father did not speak with much pleasure, not at all with exultation. He considered them days of folly, perhaps sinful days. Yet I know well that his life even then was marked by Temperance (in *all* senses) ; that he was abstemious, prudent, industrious, as very few.

I have a dim picture of him in his little world. In summer season diligently, cheerfully labouring with trowel and hammer ;

amused by grave talk, and grave humour, with the elders of the craft : building (*walling*) is an operation that beyond most other manual ones requires incessant consideration, ever-new invention ; I have heard good judges say that he excelled in it all persons they had seen. In the depth of winter, I figure him with the others gathered round his father's hearth (now no longer so poor and desolate) ; hunting (but now happily for amusement, not necessity) ; present here and there at such merry meetings and social doings, as poor Annandale, for poor yet God-created men, might then offer.—Contentions occur ; in these he was no man to be played with ; fearless ; formidable (I think to *all*). In after times, he looked back with sorrow on such things ; yet to me they were not and are not other than interesting and innocent ; scarcely ever, perhaps never, to be considered as *aggressions*, but always as *defences*, manful assertions of man's rights against man that would infringe them,—and victorious ones. I can faintly picture out one scene, which I got from him many years ago : perhaps it was at some " Singing School " ; a huge rude peasant was rudely defying and insulting the party my Father belonged to ; the others quailed, and bore it, till he could bear it no longer ; but clutches his rough adversary (who had been standing I think at some distance, on some sort of height) by the two flanks, swings him with ireful force round in the air hitting his feet against some open door), and hurls him to a distance—supine, lamed, vanquished and utterly humbled. The whole business looks to me to have passed physically in a troublous moonlight ; in the same environment and hue does it now stand in my memory, sad and stern. He would say of such things : " I am wae to think on't "—wae from repentance : Happy who has nothing worse to repent of !—

In the vanities and gallantries of Life (though such in their way came across him) he seems to have very sparingly mingled. One Robert Henderson, a dashing projector and devotee, with a dashing daughter, came often up in conversation : this was perhaps, as it were, my Father's introduction to the " pride of life " ; from which, as his wont was, he appears to have derived little but *instruction*, but expansion, and experience. I have good reason to know that he never addressed any woman except with views that were honest, pure and manly.

But happily he had been enabled very soon, in this choice of the False and Present against the True and Future, to " choose the better part." Happily there still existed in Annandale an influence of Goodness, pure emblems of a Religion : there were yet men living from whom a youth of earnestness might learn by example how to become a man. Old Robert Brand, my Father's maternal uncle, was probably of very great influence on him in this respect : old Robert was a rigorous Religionist, thoroughly filled with a celestial Philosophy of this earthly Life, which shone impressively through his stout decisive, and somewhat cross-grained deeds and words. Sharp sayings of his are still recollected there ; not unworthy of preserving. He was a man of iron firmness, a just man and of wise insight. I think, my Father, consciously and unconsciously, may have learned more from this than from any other individual. From the time when he connected himself openly with the Religious,—became a " Burgher " (strict, not strictest species of Presbyterian Dissenter) may be dated his spiritual majority ; his earthly Life was now enlightened and overcanopied by a heavenly : he was henceforth a Man.—

Annandale had long been a lawless " Border " Country : the people had ceased from foray-riding, but not from its effects ; the " gallant man " of those districts was still a wild, natural, almost animal man. A select few had, only of late, united themselves ; they had built a little Meeting-house at Ecclefechan, thatched with heath, and chosen them a Priest by name John Johnston,—the priestliest man I ever under any ecclesiastical guise was privileged to look upon. He, in his last years, helped me well in my Latin (as he had done many) ; and otherwise procured me far higher benefits. This peasant union, this little heath-thatched house, this simple Evangelist,—together constituted properly the " Church " of that district ; they were the blessing and the saving of many : on me too their pious heaven-sent influences still rest, and live ; let me employ them well. There was, in those days, a " Teacher of the People." He sleeps, not far from my Father (who built his monument) in the Ecclefechan Churchyard ; the Teacher and the Taught : " Blessed," I again say, " are the Dead that die in the Lord. They do rest from their labours, and their works follow them."

My Father, I think, was of the *second* race of religious men in Annandale : old Robert Brand, an ancient herdsman, old John Bretton, and some others that I have seen, were perhaps among the first. Alas, there is no third rising : Time sweeps all away with it so fast at this epoch : the Scottish Church has been short-lived, and was late in reaching thither.—

Perhaps it was in 1791 that my Father married : one Janet

Carlyle, a very distant kinswoman of his own (her father yet, I
believe, lives ; a professor of Religion, but long since suspected
to be none of the most perfect, though not without his worth) :
she brought him one Son ; John, at present a well-doing house-
holder at Cockermouth : [1] she left him and this life in little more
than a year. A mass of long fair woman's hair, which had
belonged to her, lay long in a secret drawer at our house (perhaps
still lies) ; the sight of it used to give me a certain faint horror.
It had been cut from her head, near death, when she was in the
height of fever : she was delirious, and would let none but my
Father cut it. He thought himself sure of infection, nevertheless consented readily, and escaped. Many ways, I have understood he had much to suffer then : yet he never spoke of it ; or
only transiently, and with a historical Stoicism.

Let me here mention the reverent custom the old men had in
Annandale, of treating Death even in their loosest thoughts. It
is now fast passing away ; with my Father was quite invariable.
Had he occasion to speak in the future, he would say : I will do
so and so, never failing to add (were it only against the morrow) :
" if I be spared ; " " if I live." The Dead again he spoke of
with perfect freedom, only with serious gravity (perhaps a
lowering of the voice), and always, even in the most trivial
conversation, adding, " that's gane : " " my Brother John that's
gane," did so and so.—*Ernst ist das Leben.*—

He married again, in the beginning of 1795,[2] my Mother,
Margaret Aitken (a woman of to me the fairest descent, that of
the pious, the just and wise) : She was a faithful helpmate to
him, toiling unweariedly at his side ; to us the best of all Mothers,
to whom for body and soul I owe endless gratitude. By God's
great mercy, she is still left, as a head and centre to us all ; and
may yet cheer us with her pious heroism, through many toils—
If God so please ! I am the eldest child ; and trace deeply in
myself the character of both parents ; also the upbringing and
example of both : the inheritance of their natural *health*,—had
not I and the Time together beat on it too hard.—

It must have been about the period of the first marriage that
my Father and his Brothers, already Master-masons, established
themselves in Ecclefechan. They all henceforth began to take

[1] John emigrated to Canada in 1837, and was a moderately successful
farmer ; he died there in 1872. Carlyle knew but little of his half-brother,
though he was on kindly terms with him, and was generous in the way of
helping him in his old age.
[2] 5th of March.

on a civic existence, to " accumulate " in all senses ; to grow.
They were among the best and truest men of their craft (perhaps
the very best) in that whole district ; and recompensed accordingly.   Their gains, the honest wages of Industry, their savings
were slow but constant ; and in my Father's case continued
(from one source or other) to the end.   He was born and brought
up the poorest ; by his own right hand he had become wealthy,
as he accounted wealth, and in all ways plentifully supplied.
His household goods valued in money may perhaps somewhat
exceed £1000 ; in real inward worth, their value was greater
than that of most kingdoms,—than all Napoleon's conquests,
which did not endure.   He saw his children grow up round him
to guard him and do him honour ; he had (ultimately) a hearty
respect from *all ;* could look forward from the verge of this
Earth, rich and increased in goods, into an Everlasting Country
where through the immeasurable Deeps shone a solemn sober
Hope.   I must reckon my Father one of the most *prosperous*
men I have ever in my life known.

Frugality and assiduity, a certain grave composure, an
earnestness (not without its constraint, then felt as oppressive a
little, yet which now yields its fruit) were the order of our household.   We were all practically taught that *work* (temporal or
spiritual) was the only thing we had to do ; and incited always
by precept and example to do it *well*.   An inflexible element of
Authority encircled us all ; we felt from the first (a useful thing)
that our own *wish* had often nothing to say in the matter.   It
was not a joyful life (what life is ?), yet a safe, quiet one ; above
most others (or any other I have witnessed) a wholesome one.
We were taciturn rather than talkative ; but if little were said,
that little had generally a meaning.   I cannot be thankful
enough for my Parents.

My early, yet not my earliest recollections of my Father had
in them a certain *awe ;* which only now or very lately has passed
into free reverence.   I was parted from him in my tenth year ;
and never *habitually* beside him afterwards.—Of the very earliest
I have saved some ; and would not for money's worth lose them.
All that belongs to him has become very precious to me.

I can remember his carrying me across Mein Water, over a pool
some few yards below where the present Meinfoot Bridge stands.
Perhaps I was in my fifth year.   He was going to Luce I think
to ask after some Joiner.   It was the loveliest summer evening
I recollect.   My memory dawns (or grows light) at the first
aspect of the stream, of the pool spanned by a wooden bow,

without railing, and a single plank broad. He lifted me against his thigh with his right hand, and walked careless along till we were over. My face was turned rather downwards, I looked into the deep clear water, and its reflected skies, with terror yet with confidence that he could save me. Directly after, I, light of heart, asked of him what these " little black things " were that I seemed sometimes to *create* by rubbing the palms of my hands together, and can at this moment (the mind having been doubtless excited by the past peril) remember that I described them in these words : " like penny-rows " (rolls) " but far less." He explained it wholly to me : " my hands were not *clean.*" He was very kind, and I loved him. All around this is Dusk, or Night, before and after.—It is not my *earliest* recollection, not even of him. My earliest of all is a mad passion of rage at my elder Brother John (on a visit to us likely from his grandfather's); in which my Father too figures though dimly, as a kind of cheerful comforter and soother. I had broken my little brown stool, by madly throwing it at my brother ; and felt for perhaps the first time, the united pangs of Loss and of Remorse. I was perhaps hardly more than two years old ; but can get no one to fix the date for me, though all is still quite legible for myself, with many of its [features]. I remember the first " new half-pence " (brought from Dumfries by my Father and Mother for Alick and me) ; and words that my Uncle John said about it : this seems later (in 1799 ?), and might be ascertained. Back wards beyond all, are dim *ruddy* images, of deeper and deeper brown shade into the dark beginnings of being.

I remember, perhaps in my fifth year, his teaching me Arithmetical things : especially how to *divide* (of my Letters taught me by my Mother, I have no recollection whatever ; of reading scarcely any) : he said, " This is the *divider* (divisor), this," etc., and gave me a quite clear notion how to do. My Mother said I would forget it all ; to which he answered : Not so much as they that have never learned it.—Five years or so after, he said to me once : " Tom, I do not grudge thy schooling, now when thy Uncle Frank owns thee to be a better Arithmetician than himself."—

He took me down to Annan Academy on the Whitsunday morning,[1] 1806 ; I trotting at his side in the way alluded to in *Teufelsdröckh*. It was a bright morning, and to me full of moment ; of fluttering boundless Hopes, saddened by parting

[1] 26th May. Whitsunday is a Scotch term-day.

with Mother, with Home ; and which afterwards were cruelly disappointed.   He called once or twice in the grand schoolroom, as he chanced to have business at Annan : once sat down by me (as the master was out), and asked whether I was all well.   The boys did not laugh (as I feared), perhaps durst not.

He was *always* GENEROUS to me in my school expenses ; never by grudging look or word did he give me any pain.   With a noble faith he launched me forth into a world which himself had never been permitted to visit : let me study to act worthily of him there.

He wrote to me duly and affectionately while I was at College ; nothing that was good for me did he fail with his best ability to provide : his simple true counsels and fatherly admonitions have now first attained their fit sacredness of meaning : pity for me if they be thrown away.—

His tolerance for me, his trust in me was great.   When I declined going forward into the Church (though his heart was set upon it), he respected my scruples, my volition, and patiently let me have my way.   In after years, when I had peremptorily ceased from being a Schoolmaster, though he inwardly disapproved of the step as imprudent ; and saw me, in successive summers, lingering beside him in sickliness of body and mind, without outlook towards any good, he had the forbearance to say at worst nothing, never once to whisper discontent with me.   If my dear Mother, with the trustfulness of a Mother's heart, ministered to all my woes, outward and inward, and ever against hope kept prophesying good,—he, with whom I communicated far less, who could not approve my schemes, did nothing that was not kind and fatherly : his roof was my shelter, which a word from him (in those sour days of wounded vanity) would have deprived me of ; he patiently let me have my way ; helping where he could, where he could not help never hindering. —When hope again dawned for me, how hearty was his joy, yet how silent !   I have been a happy Son.—

On my first return from College (in the Spring 1810) I met him in the "Langlands Road," walking out to try whether he would not happen to see me coming.   He had a red plaid about him ; was recovering from a fit of sickness (his first severe one), and there welcomed me back.   It was a bright April day : *where* is it *now ?*—

The great world-revolutions send in their disturbing billows to the remotest creek ; and the overthrow of thrones more slowly overturns also the households of the lowly.   Nevertheless in all

cases the wise man adjusts himself : even in these times, the
hand of the diligent maketh rich. My Father had seen the
American War, the French Revolution, the rise and fall of
Napoleon. The last arrested him strongly : in the Russian
Campaign we bought a London Newspaper, which I read aloud
to a little circle thrice weekly. He was struck with Napoleon,
and would say and look pregnant things about him : empires
won, and empires lost (while *his* little household held together) ;
and now it was all vanished like a tavern brawl !—For the rest,
he never meddled with Politics : he was not there to govern, but
to be governed ; could still *live*, and therefore did not *revolt*. I
have heard him say in late years, with an impressiveness which
all his perceptions carried with them : " that the lot of a poor
man was growing worse and worse ; that the world could not
and would not last as it was ; but mighty changes, of which none
saw the end, were on the way." To him, as one about to take
his departure, the whole was but of secondary moment : he was
looking towards " a city that *had* foundations."—

In the " dear years " (1799 and 1800), when the oatmeal was
as high as ten shillings a stone, he had noticed the labourers
(I have heard him tell) retire each separately to a brook, and
there *drink* instead of dining,—without complaint ; anxious
only to hide it.—

At Langholm he once saw a heap of smuggled Tobacco
publicly burnt. Dragoons were ranged round it with drawn
swords ; some old women stretched through their old withered
arms to snatch a little of it, and the dragoons did not hinder
them.[1]—A natural artist !

The largest sum he ever earned in one year, I think, was
£100 ; by the building of Cressfield House.

He wisely quitted the Mason trade, at the time when the
character of it had changed ; when universal Poverty and Vanity
made *show* and *cheapness* (here as everywhere) be preferred to
Substance ; when as he said emphatically honest trade " was
done." He became Farmer (of a wet clayey spot called Mainhill) in 1815 ; that so " he might keep all his family about him ; "
struggled with his old valour, and here too prevailed. Two ears
of corn are now in many places growing where he found only one ;
unworthy or little worthy men for the time reap the benefit :

[1] It was the common practice of the old Annandale peasant-women to
smoke tobacco.

but it was a benefit done to God's Earth, and God's Mankind will year after year get the good of it.

In his contention with an unjust or perhaps only a mistaken Landlord, he behaved with prudent resolution ; not like a vain braggart but like a practically brave man. It was I that innocently (by my settlement at Hoddam Hill) had involved him in it. I must admire now his *silence,* while we were all so loud and vituperative : he spoke *nothing* on that matter, except only what had practical meaning in it, and in a practical tone. His answers to unjust proposals, meanwhile, were resolute and ever-memorable for their emphasis : " I *will* not do it," said he once ; " I will rather go to Jerusalem, seeking farms, and die without finding one."—" We can live without Sharpe," [1] said he once in my hearing (such a thing only *once*) " and the whole Sharpe creation."—On getting to Scotsbrig, the rest of us all triumphed ; not he : he let the matter stand on its own feet ; was *there* also, not to talk but to work. He even addressed a conciliatory letter to General Sharpe (which I saw right to *write* for him, since he judged prudence better than pride) : but it produced no result, —except indeed the ascertainment that none could be produced ; which itself was one.—

When he first entered our house at Craigenputtock he said in his slow emphatic way, with a certain rustic dignity to my Wife (I had entered introducing him) : " I am grown an *old fellow* " (never can we forgot the pathetic slow earnestness of these two words) " I am grown an old fellow ; and wished to see ye all once more while I had yet opportunity." Jane was greatly struck with him ; and still further opened my eyes to the treasure I possessed in a Father.—

The last thing I gave him was a cake of Cavendish Tobacco sent down by Alick about this time twelvemonth. Through life I had given him very little ; having little to give : he needed little, and from me expected nothing. Thou who wouldst give, give quickly : in the grave thy loved one can receive no kindness.—I had once bought him a pair of silver spectacles ; at receipt of which and the letter that accompanied them (John told me) he was very glad, and nigh weeping. " What I gave I have." He read with these spectacles till his last days ; and no doubt sometimes thought of me in using them.—

The last time I saw him was about the first of August last, a few days before departing hither. He was very kind, seemed prouder of me than ever. What he had never done the like of

---

[1] The landlord referred to above.

before, he said, on hearing me express something which he admired : " Man, it's surely a pity that thou should sit yonder, with nothing but the Eye of Omniscience to see thee ; and thou, with such a gift to speak." His eyes were sparkling mildly, with a kind of deliberate joy.— —Strangely too he offered me on one of those mornings (knowing that I was poor) " two sovereigns " which he had of his own ; and pressed them on my acceptance. They were lying in his Desk, none knew of them : he seemed really anxious and desirous that I should take them ; should take his little hoard, his *all* that he had to give. I said jokingly afterwards that surely he was *fey*.[1] So it has proved.

I shall now no more behold my dear Father with these bodily eyes. With him a whole three-score-and-ten years of the Past has doubly died for me ; it is as if a new leaf in the great Book of Time were turned over. Strange Time ! Endless Time, or of which I see neither end nor beginning ! All rushes on ; man follows man ; his life is as a Tale that has been told. Yet under Time does there not lie Eternity ? Perhaps my Father, all that essentially *was* my Father *is* even now near me, with me. Both he and I are with God. Perhaps, if it so please God, we shall in some higher state of being meet one another, recognise one another : as it is written, " we shall be for ever with God ! " The possibility, nay (in some way) the certainty of perennial existence daily grows plainer to me. " The essence of whatever was, is, or shall be, even now *is*." God is great ; God is good : His will be done, for it will be right !—

As it is, I can think peaceably of the Departed Loved. All that was earthly harsh sinful in our relation has fallen away ; all that was holy in it remains. I can see my dear Father's Life in some measure as the sunk pillar on which mine was to rise and be built ; the waters of Time have now swelled up round his (as they will round mine) ; I can *see* it (all transfigured) though I *touch* it no longer. I might almost say his spirit seems to have entered into me (so clearly do I discern and love him) ; I seem to myself only the continuation, and *second volume* of my Father. —These days that I have spent thinking of him, and of his end, are the peaceablest, the only Sabbath I have had in London. One other of the universal destinies of man has overtaken me.

---

[1] *Fey*, fated to die ; said of a person who does some unusually generous act, or who is seen in any mood surprisingly beyond the bounds of his ordinary temperament ; it is feared the Fate presiding over human destiny is near, actively influencing him in prospect of his death.

Thank Heaven, I know and have known what it is to be a *Son* ;
to *love* a Father, as spirit can love spirit.   God give me to live to
my Father's honour, and to His !—And now beloved Father
farewell, for the last time in this world of shadows !   In the
world of Realities may the great Father again bring us together
in perfect holiness, and perfect love !   Amen !

Sunday night, 29th January 1832.

[The MS. of the following letter, carefully folded, was gummed
by Carlyle into his Journal at the end of the Paper " James
Carlyle," which now forms part of the Reminiscences.   Carlyle
has noted on the margin that this was his Father's last letter,
perhaps the last thing he ever wrote ; and that it was written
" at Jane's request, 21st Sept. 1831, at Scotsbrig, and delivered
by her to John and me in London shortly after."   Spelling and
punctuation have been altered in this printed copy.]

MY DEAR SONS,
        I cannot write you a letter, but just tell you that I am a
frail old sinner that is very likely never to see you any more in
this world.   Be that as it may, I could not help telling that I
feel myself gradually drawing toward the house appointed for
all living, and O God ! may that awful change be much at heart
with every one of us, and may we be daily dying to Sin and living
to Righteousness, and may the God of Jacob be with you and
bless you and keep you in His ways and fear.   I had no more but
leave you in His hands and care.

JAS. CARLYLE.

JANE WELSH CARLYLE

" In the ancient County-Town of Haddington, July 14th, 1801, there was born to a lately wedded pair, not natives of the place, but already reckoned among the best class of people there, a little Daughter, whom they named *Jane Baillie Welsh ;* and whose subsequent and final name (her own common signature for many years) was *Jane Welsh Carlyle,*—and now so stands, now that she is mine in death only, on her and her Father's Tombstone in the Abbey Kirk of that Town.   July 14th, 1801 : I was then in my sixth year, far away in every sense, now near, and infinitely concerned ;—trying doubtfully, after some three years' sad cunctation, if there is anything that I can profitably put on record of her altogether bright beneficent and modest little Life, and Her, as my final task in this world."

[The preceding passage Carlyle has labelled " Rudiments of Preface," and he added at its close, as a memorandum, " something more of Preface ; ' Letters mainly,' ' can be left for friends,' not to be published, any way, till long *after* death."

It is plain that these words were intended to form part of the Preface to the Letters of his Wife, which in 1868–9 he was putting in order and annotating.   They do not properly belong to the following " Bit of Writing."   But they are printed here because in the edition of the *Reminiscences* edited by Froude they appear in a corresponding position, prefixed to Miss Jewsbury's anecdotes of Mrs. Carlyle.

Froude states that Carlyle " had requested Miss Geraldine Jewsbury, his wife's most intimate friend, to tell him any biographical anecdotes which she could remember to have heard from Mrs. Carlyle's lips."   That this statement is incorrect appears from a note addressed by Carlyle to Miss Jewsbury on returning to her the little note-book in which she had written her narrative.   His note was written on the next leaf in the volume, and it is now printed in its place at the end of Miss Jewsbury's pages.[1]]

[1] See *infra*, p. 48.

"IN MEMORIAM JANE WELSH CARLYLE

Ob. April 21, 1866

By Geraldine Jewsbury

" She told me that once, when she was a very little girl, there was going to be a dinner-party at home, and she was left alone with some tempting custards, ranged in their glasses upon a stand. She stood looking at them, and the thought came into her mind ' What *would* be the consequence if I should eat one of them ? ' A whimsical sense of the dismay it would cause took hold of her ; she thought of it again, and scarcely knowing what she was about, she put forth her hand, and—took a little from the top of each ! She was discovered ; the sentence upon her was, to eat *all* the remaining custards, and to hear the company told the reason why there were none for them ! The poor child hated custards for a long time afterwards.

The Bubbly Jock

" On her road to school, when a very small child, she had to pass a gate where a horrid turkey-cock was generally standing. He always ran up to her, gobbling and looking very hideous and alarming. It frightened her at first a good deal ; and she dreaded having to pass the place ; but after a little time she hated the thought of living in fear. The next time she passed the gate several labourers and boys were near, who seemed to enjoy the thought of the turkey running at her. She gathered herself together and made up her mind. The turkey ran at her as usual, gobbling and swelling ; she suddenly darted at him and seized him by the throat and swung him round ! The men clapped their hands, and shouted ' Well done, little Jeannie Welsh ! ' and the Bubbly Jock never molested her again.

Learning Latin

" She was very anxious to learn lessons like a Boy ; and, when a very little thing, she asked her father to let her ' learn Latin like a boy.' Her mother did not wish her to learn so much ; her father always tried to push her forwards ; there was a division of opinion on the subject. Jeannie went to one of the town scholars in Haddington and made him teach her a noun of the first declension (' *Penna*, a pen,' I think it was). Armed with this, she watched her opportunity ; instead of going to bed, she crept under the table, and was concealed by the cover. In a pause of conversation, a little voice was heard, ' *Penna*, a pen ; *pennæ*, of a pen ; ' etc., and as there was a pause of surprise, she crept out, and went up to her father saying, ' I want to learn Latin ; please let me be a boy.' Of course she had her own way in the matter.

School at Haddington

" Boys and girls went to the same school ; they were in separate rooms, except for Arithmetic and Algebra. Jeannie was the best of the girls at Algebra. Of course she had many devoted slaves among the boys ; one of them especially taught her, and helped her all he knew ; but he was quite a poor boy, whilst Jeannie was one of the gentry of the place ; but she felt no difficulty, and they were great friends. She was fond of doing everything difficult that boys did. There was one particularly dangerous feat, to which the boys dared each other ; it was to walk on a *very* narrow ledge on the outside of the bridge overhanging the water ; the ledge went in an arch, and the height was considerable. One fine morning Jeannie got up early and went to the Nungate Bridge ; she lay down on her face and crawled from one end of the bridge to the other, to the imminent risk of either breaking her neck or drowning.

" One day in the boys' school-room, one of the boys said something to displease her. She lifted her hand, doubled it, and hit him hard ; his nose began to bleed, and in the midst of the scuffle the master came in. He saw the traces of the fray, and said in an angry voice, ' You boys, you know, I have forbidden you to fight in school, and have promised that I would flog the next. Who has been fighting this time ? ' Nobody spoke ; and the master grew angry, and threatened *tawse* all round unless the culprit were given up. Of course no boy would tell of a girl, so there was a pause ; in the midst of it, Jeannie looked up and said, ' Please, I gave that black eye ' [*sic*]. The master tried to look grave, and pursed up his mouth ; but the boy was big, and Jeannie was little ; so, instead of the *tawse* he burst out laughing and told her she was ' a little deevil,' and had no business there, and to go her ways back to the girls.

" Her friendship with her schoolfellow-teacher came to an untimely end. An aunt who came on a visit saw her standing by a stile with him, and a book between them. She was scolded, and desired not to keep his company. This made her very sorry, for she knew how good he was to her ; but she never had a notion of disobedience in any matter small or great. She did not know how to tell him or to explain ; she thought it shame to tell him he was not thought good enough, so she determined he should imagine it a fit of caprice, and from that day she never spoke a word to him or took the least notice ; she thought a sudden cessation would pain him less than a gradual coldness. Years and years afterwards, going back on a visit to Haddington, when she was a middle-aged woman, and he was a man married and doing well in the world, she saw him again, and then, for the first time, told him the explanation.

" She was always anxious to work hard, and would sit up half the night over her lessons. One day she had been greatly perplexed by a problem in Euclid ; she *could not* solve it. At last she went to bed ; and in a dream got up and did it, and went to bed again. In the morning she had no consciousness of her dream ; but on looking at her slate, there was the problem solved.

" She was afraid of sleeping too much, and used to tie a weight to one of her ankles that she might awake. Her mother discovered it ; and her father forbade her to rise before five o'clock. She was a most healthy little thing then ; only she did her best to ruin her health, not knowing what she did. She always would push everything to its extreme to find out if possible the ultimate consequence. One day her mother was ill, and a bag of ice had to be applied to her head. Jeannie wanted to know the sensation, and took an opportunity when no one saw her to get hold of the bag, and put it on her own head, and kept it on till she was found lying on the ground insensible.

" She made great progress in Latin, and was in Virgil when nine years old. She always loved her doll ; but when she got into Virgil she thought it shame to care for a doll. On her tenth birthday she built a funeral pile of lead pencils and sticks of cinnamon, and poured some sort of perfume over all, to represent a funeral pile. She then recited the speech of Dido, stabbed her doll and let out all the sawdust ; after which she consumed her to ashes, and then burst into a passion of tears.

Her Appearance in Girlhood

" As a child she was remarkable for her large black eyes with their long curved lashes. As a girl she was extremely pretty,— a graceful and beautifully formed figure, upright and supple,—

a delicate complexion of creamy white with a pale rose tint in the cheeks, lovely eyes full of fire and softness, and with great depths of meaning. Her head was finely formed, with a noble arch, and a broad forehead. Her other features were not regular ; but they did not prevent her from conveying all the impression of being beautiful. Her voice was clear, and full of subtle intonations and capable of great variety of expression. She had it under full control. She danced with much grace ; and she was a good musician. She was ingenious in all works that required dexterity of hand ; she could draw and paint, and she was a good carpenter. She could do anything well to which she chose to give herself. She was fond of logic,—too much so ; and she had a keen clear incisive faculty of seeing through things, and hating all that was make-believe or pretentious. She had good sense that amounted to genius. She loved to learn, and she cultivated all her faculties to the utmost of her power. She was always witty, with a gift for narration ;—in a word she was fascinating and everybody fell in love with her. A relative of hers told me that every man who spoke to her for five minutes felt impelled to make her an offer of marriage ! From which it resulted that a great many men were made unhappy. She seemed born ' for the destruction of mankind.' Another person told me that she was ' the most beautiful starry-looking creature that could be imagined,' with a peculiar grace of manner and motion that was more charming than beauty. She had a great quantity of very fine silky black hair, and she always had a natural taste for dress. The first thing I ever heard about her was that she dressed well,—an excellent gift for a woman.

" Her mother was a beautiful woman, and as charming as her daughter, though not so clever. She had the gift of dressing well also. Genius is profitable for all things, and it saves expense. Once her mother was going to some grand fête, and she wanted her dress to be something specially beautiful. She did not want to spend money. Jeannie was entrusted with a secret mission to gather ivy leaves and trails of ivy of different kinds and sizes, also mosses of various kinds, and was enjoined to silence. Mrs. Welsh arranged these round her dress, and the moss formed a beautiful embossed trimming and the ivy made a graceful scrollwork ; the effect was lovely ; nobody could imagine of what the trimming was composed, but it was generally supposed to be a French trimming of the latest fashion and of fabulous expense.

" She always spoke of her mother with deep affection and

great admiration. She said she was so noble and generous that
no one ever came near her without being the better. She used
to make beautiful presents by saving upon herself,—she econo-
mised upon herself to be generous to others ; and no one ever
served her in the least without experiencing her generosity.
She was almost as charming and as much adored as her daughter.

"Of her *Father* she always spoke with reverence ; he was the
only person who had any real influence over her. But, however
wilful or indulged she might be, *obedience* to her parents—
unquestioning and absolute—lay at the foundation of her life.
She was accustomed to say that this habit of obedience to her
parents was her salvation through life,—that she owed all that
was of value in her character to this habit as the foundation.
Her father, from what she told me, was a man of strong and
noble character,—very true and hating all that was false. She
always spoke of any praise he gave her as of a precious possession. She loved him with a deep reverence ; and she never
spoke of him except to friends whom she valued. It was the
highest token of her regard when she told any one about her
father. She told me that once he was summoned to go a sudden
journey to see a patient ; and he took her with him. It was the
greatest favour and pleasure she had ever had. They travelled
at night, and were to start for their return by a very early hour
in the morning. She used to speak of this journey as something
that made her perfectly happy ; and during that journey, her
father told her he was pleased with her, that her conduct and
character satisfied him. It was not often he praised her ; and
this unreserved flow of communication was very precious to her.
Whilst he went to the sick person, she was sent to bed until it
should be time to return. She had his watch that she might
know the time. When the chaise came round, the landlady
brought her some tea ; but she was in such haste not to keep
him waiting that she forgot the *watch ;* and they had to return
several miles to fetch it ! This was the last time she was with
her father ; a few days afterwards he fell ill of typhus fever, and
would not allow her to come into the room She made her way
once to him, and he sent her away. He died of this illness ; and
it was the very greatest sorrow she ever experienced. She
always relapsed into a deep silence for some time after speaking
of her father. [*Not very correct.* T. C.]

"After her father's death they [' *they, 'no !* T. C.] left Haddington, and went to live at *Templand,* near Thornhill, in Dumfries-

shire. It was a country house, standing in its own grounds, prettily laid out. The house has been described to me as furnished with a certain elegant thrift which gave it a great charm. I do not know how old she was when her father died [*eighteen, just gone*, T. C.], but she was one with whom years did not signify, they conveyed no meaning as to what she was. Before she was fourteen she wrote a *tragedy* in five acts, which was greatly admired and wondered at ; but she never wrote another. She used to speak of it ' as just an explosion.' I don't know what the title was ; she never told me.

" She had no end of ardent lovers, and she owned that some of them had reason to complain. I think it highly probable that if *flirting* were a capital crime, she would have been in danger of being hanged many times over. She told me one story that showed a good deal of character :—There was a young man who was very much in love, and I am afraid he had had reason to hope she cared for him : and she only liked him. She refused him decidedly when he proposed ; but he tried to turn her from her decision, which showed how little he understood her ; for her *will* was very steadfast through life. She refused him peremptorily this time. He then fell ill, and took to his bed, and his mother was very miserable about her son. She was a widow, and had but the one. At last he wrote her another letter, in which he declared that unless she would marry him, he would kill himself. He was in such distraction that it was a very likely thing for him to do. Her mother was very angry indeed, and reproached her bitterly. She was very sorry for the mischief she had done, and took to her bed, and made herself ill with crying. The old servant, Betty, kept imploring her to say just one word to save the young man's mother from her misery. But though she felt horribly guilty and miserable, she was not going to be forced or frightened into anything. She took up the letter once more, which she said was very moving, but a slight point struck her ; and she put down the letter, saying to her mother, ' You need not be frightened, he won't kill himself at all ; look here, he has scratched out one word to substitute another. A man intending anything desperate would not have stopped to scratch out a word, he would have put his pen through it, or left it ! ' That was very sagacious, but the poor young man was very ill, and the doctor brought a bad report of him to the house. She suddenly said, ' We must go away, go away for some time ; he will get well when we are gone.' It was as she said it would be ; her going away set his mind at rest, and he began to recover. In the end he married somebody else, and what became of him I forget, though I think she told me more about him.

" There was another man whom she had allowed to fall in love, and never tried to hinder him, though she refused to marry him. After many years she saw him again. He was then an elderly man ; had made a fortune, and stood high as a county gentleman. He was happily married, and the father of a family. But one day he was driving her somewhere, and he slackened the pace to a walk and said : ' I once thought I would have broken my heart about you, but I think my attachment to you was the best thing that ever happened to me : it made me a better man. It is a part of my life that stands out by itself and belongs to nothing else. I have heard of you from time to time, and I know what a brilliant lot yours has been, and I have felt glad that you were in your rightful place, and I felt glad that I had suffered for your sake, and I have sometimes thought that if I had known I would not have tried to turn you into any other path.' This, as well as I can render it, is the sense of what he said gravely and gently, and I admired it very much when she told me : but it seems to me that it was *much* better as she told it to me. Nobody could help loving her, and nobody but was the better for doing so. She had the gift of calling forth the best qualities that were in people.

" I don't know at what period she knew Irving, but he loved her, and wrote letters and poetry (very true and touching) : but there had been some vague understanding with another person, not a definite engagement, and she insisted that he must keep to it and not go back from what had once been spoken. There had been just then some trial, and a great scandal about a Scotch minister who had broken an engagement of marriage : and she could not bear that the shadow of any similar reproach should be cast on him. Whether if she had cared for him very much she could or would have insisted on such punctilious honour, she did not know herself ; but anyhow that is what she did. After Irving's marriage, years afterwards, there was not much intercourse between them ; the whole course of his life had changed.[1]

. . . . . .

" I do not know in what year she married, nor anything connected with her marriage. I believe that she brought no money

[1] Omitted here, by Froude, probably as uninteresting, an account of " Captain Baillie," a cousin of Mrs. Carlyle, died 1873.

or very little at her marriage. Her father had left everything to her, but she made it over to her mother, and only had what her mother gave her. Of course people thought she was making a dreadfully bad match ; they only saw the *outside* of the thing ; but she had faith in her own insight. Long afterwards, when the world began to admire her husband, at the time he delivered the Lectures on ' Hero Worship,' she gave a little half-scornful laugh, and said ' They tell me things as if they were new that I found out years ago.' She knew the power of help and sympathy that lay in her ; and she knew she had strength to stand the struggle and pause before he was recognised. She told me that she resolved that he should never write for money, only when he wished it, when he had a message in his heart to deliver, she determined that she would make whatever money he gave her answer for all needful purposes ; and she was ever faithful to this resolve. She bent her faculties to economical problems, and she managed so well that comfort was never absent from her house, and no one looking on could have guessed whether they were rich or poor. Until she married, she had never minded household things ; but she took them up when neces-sary, and accomplished them as she accomplished everything else she undertook, well and gracefully. Whatever she had to do she did it with a peculiar personal grace that gave a charm to the most prosaic details. No one who in later years saw her lying on the sofa in broken health, and languor, would guess the amount of energetic hard work she had done in her life. She could do everything and anything, from mending the Venetian blinds to making picture-frames or trimming a dress. Her judgment in all literary matters was thoroughly good ; she could get to the very core of a thing, and her insight was like witch-craft.

" Some of her stories about her servants in the early times were very amusing, but she could make a story about a broom-handle and make it entertaining. Here are some things she told me about their residence at Craigenputtock.

" At first on their marriage they lived in a small pretty house in Edinburgh called Cromlech Bank [*sic*]. Whilst there her first experience of the difficulties of housekeeping began. She had never been accustomed to anything of the kind ; but Mr. Carlyle was obliged to be very careful in diet. She learned to make bread partly from recollecting how she had seen an old servant set to work ; and she used to say that the *first* time she attempted brown bread, it was with awe. She mixed the dough and saw it rise ; and then she put it into the oven, and sat down to watch the oven-door with feelings like Benvenuto Cellini's when he watched his Perseus put into the furnace. She did not feel too sure what it would come out ! But it came out a beautiful crusty loaf, very light and sweet ; and proud of it she was. The first time she tried a pudding, she went into the kitchen and locked the door on herself, having got the servant out of the road. It was to be a suet pudding—not just a common suet pudding but something special—and it was good, being made with care by weight and measure with exactness. Whilst they were in Edinburgh they knew everybody worth knowing ; Lord Jeffrey was a great admirer of hers, and an old friend ; Chalmers, Guthrie, and many others. But Mr. Carlyle's health and work needed perfect quietness and absolute solitude. They went to live at the end of two years at Craigenputtock—a lonely farm-house belonging to Mrs. Welsh, her mother. A house was attached to the farm, beside the regular farmhouse. The farm was let ; and Mr. and Mrs. Carlyle lived in the house, which was separated from the farm-yard and buildings by a yard. A garden and outbuildings were attached to it. They had a cow, and a horse, and poultry. They were fourteen miles from Dumfries, which was the nearest town. The country was uninhabited for miles round, being all moorland, with rocks, and a high steep green hill behind the house. She used to say that the stillness was almost awful, and that when she walked out she could hear the sheep nibbling the grass, and they used to look at her with innocent wonder. The letters came in once a week, which was as often as they sent into Dumfries. All she needed had to be sent for there or done without. One day she had desired the farm-servant to bring her a bottle of yeast. The weather was very hot. The man came back looking scared ; and without the yeast. He said doggedly that he would do anything lawful for her ; but he begged she would never ask him to fetch such an uncanny thing again, for it had just worked and worked till it flew away with the bottle ! When asked where it was, he replied, ' it had a' just gane into the ditch, and he had left it there ! '

" Lord Jeffrey and his family came out twice to visit her ; expecting, as he said, to find that she had hanged herself upon a door-nail. But she did no such thing. It was undoubtedly a great strain upon her nerves from which she never entirely recovered ; but she lived in the solitude cheerfully and willingly for six years. It was a much greater trial than it sounds at first ;

for Mr. Carlyle was engrossed in his work, and had to give himself up to it entirely. It was work and thought with which
he had to wrestle with all his might to bring out the truths he
felt, and to give them due utterance. It was his life that his
work required, and it was his life that he gave, and she gave her
life too, which alone made such life possible for him. All those
who have been strengthened by Mr. Carlyle's written words—
and they have been wells of life to more than have been num-
bered—owe to her a debt of gratitude no less than to him. If
she had not devoted her life to him, he could not have worked ;
and if she had let the care for money weigh on him he could not
have given his best strength to teach. Hers was no holiday
task of pleasant companionship ; she had to live beside him in
silence that the people in the world might profit by his full
strength and receive his message. She lived to see his work
completed, and to see him recognised in full for what he is, and
for what he has done.

" Sometimes she could not send to Dumfries for butcher's
meat ; and then she was reduced to her poultry. She had a
peculiar breed of very long-legged hens, and she used to go into
the yard amongst them with a long stick and point out those
that were to be killed, feeling, she said, like Fouquier Tinville
pricking down his victims.

" One hard winter her servant, Grace, asked leave to go home
to see her parents ; there was some sort of a fair held in her
village. She went and was to return at night. The weather
was bad, and she did not return. The next morning there was
nothing for it but for her to get up to light the fires and prepare
breakfast. The house had beautiful and rather elaborate steel
grates ; it seemed a pity to let them rust, so she cleaned them
carefully, and then looked round for wood to kindle the fire.
There was none in the house ; it all lay in a little outhouse across
the yard. On trying to open the door, she found it was frozen
beyond her power to open it, so Mr. Carlyle had to be roused ;
it took all his strength, and when opened a drift of snow six feet
high fell into the hall ! Mr. Carlyle had to make a path to the
wood-house, and bring over a supply of wood and coal ; after
which he left her to her own resources.

" The fire at length made, the breakfast had to be prepared ;
but it had to be raised from the foundation. The bread had to
be made, the butter to be churned, and the coffee ground. All
was at last accomplished, and the breakfast was successful !
After breakfast she went about the work of the house, as there

was no chance of the servant being able to return.   The work
fell into its natural routine.   Mr. Carlyle always kept a supply
of wood ready ; he cut it, and piled it ready for her use inside the
house ; and he fetched the water, and did things she had not
the strength to do.   The poor cow was her greatest perplexity.
She could continue to get hay down to feed it, but she had never
in her life milked a cow.   The first day the servant of the farmer's
wife, who lived at the end of the yard, milked it for her willingly,
but the next day Mrs. Carlyle heard the poor cow making an
uncomfortable noise ; it had not been milked.   She went herself
to the byre, and took the pail and sat down on the milking stool
and began to try to milk the cow.   It was not at first easy ; but
at last she had the delight of hearing the milk trickle into the
can.   She said she felt quite proud of her success ; and talked to
the cow like a human creature.   The snow continued to lie thick
and heavy on the ground, and it was impossible for her maid to
return.   Mrs. Carlyle got on easily with all the housework, and
kept the whole place bright and clean except the large kitchen
or house place, which grew to need scouring very much.   At
length she took courage to attack it.   Filling up two large pans
of hot water, she knelt down and began to scrub ; having made
a clean space round the large arm-chair by the fireside, she called
Mr. Carlyle and installed him with his pipe to watch her progress.
He regarded her beneficently, and gave her from time to time
words of encouragement.   Half the large floor had been successfully cleansed, and she felt anxious of making a good ending,
when she heard a gurgling sound.   For a moment or two she
took no notice, but it increased and there was a sound of something falling upon the fire, and instantly a great black thick
stream came down the chimney, pouring like a flood along the
floor, taking precisely the lately cleaned portion first in its
course, and extinguishing the fire.   It was too much ; she burst
into tears.   The large fire, made up to heat the water, had melted
the snow on the top of the chimney, it came down mingling
with the soot, and worked destruction to the kitchen floor.   All
that could be done was to dry up the flood.   She had no heart
to recommence her task.   She rekindled the fire and got tea
ready.   That same night her maid came back, having done the
impossible to get home.   She clasped Mrs. Carlyle in her arms,
crying and laughing, saying ' Oh, my dear mistress, my dear
mistress, I dreamed ye were deed ! '

    " During their residence at Craigenputtock, she had a good
little horse, called ' Harry,' on which she sometimes rode long

distances. She was an excellent and fearless horsewoman, and went about like the women used to do before carriages were invented. One day she received news that Lord Jeffrey and his family, with some visitors, were coming. The letter only arrived the day they were expected (for letters only came in one day in the week). She mounted ' Harry ' and galloped off to Dumfries to get what was needed and galloped back, and was all ready and dressed to receive her visitors with no trace of her thirty-mile ride except the charming history she made of it. She said that ' Harry ' understood all was needed of him.

" She had a long and somewhat anxious ride at another time. Mr. Carlyle had gone to London, leaving her to finish winding up affairs at Craigenputtock and to follow him. The last day came. She got the money out of the bank at Dumfries, dined with a friend, and mounted her horse to ride to Ecclefechan, where she was to stay for a day or two. Whether she paid no attention to the road or did not know it I don't know ; but she *lost* her way : and at dusk found herself entering Dumfries from the *other side*, having made a circuit. She alighted at the friend's house where she had dined, to give her horse a rest. She had some tea herself, and then mounted again to proceed on her journey, fearing that those to whom she was going would be alarmed if she did not appear. This time she made sure she was on the right tack. It was growing dusk, and at a joining of two roads she came upon a party of men half-tipsy, coming from a fair. They accosted her, and asked where she was going, and would she come along with them ? She was rather frightened, for she had a good deal of money about her, so she imitated a broad country dialect, and said their road was not hers, and that she had ' a gey piece to ride before she got to Annan.' She whipped her horse, and took the other road, thinking she could easily return to the right track ; but she had again lost her way and, seeing a house with a light in the lower storey, she rode up the avenue which led to it. Some women-servants had got up early, or rather late at night, to begin their washing. She knocked at the window. At first they thought it was one of their sweethearts ; but when they saw a lady on a horse they thought it a ghost. After a while she got them to listen to her, and when she told them her tale they were vehement in their sympathy, and would have had her come in to refresh herself. They gave her a cup of their tea, and one of them came with her to the gate, and set her face towards the right road. She had actually come back to within a mile of Dumfries once more !

The church clocks struck twelve as she set out a third time, and it was after two o'clock in the morning before she arrived, dead tired, she and her horse too, at Ecclefechan ; where however she had long since been given up. The inmates had gone to bed, and it was long before she could make them hear. After a day or two of repose, she proceeded to join Mr. Carlyle in London.

" At first they lived in lodgings with some people who were very kind to them and became much attached to her. They looked upon her as a superior being, of another order, to themselves. The children were brought up to think of her as a sort of fairy lady. One day, a great many years afterwards, when I had come to live in London, it was my birthday, and we resolved to celebrate it ' by doing something ; ' and at last we settled that she should take me to see the daughter of the people she used to lodge with, who had been an affectionate attendant upon her, and who was now very well married, and an extremely happy woman. Mrs. Carlyle said it was a good omen to go and see ' a happy woman ' on such a day ! So she and I, and her dog ' Nero,' who accompanied her wherever she went, set off to Dalston where the ' happy woman ' lived. I forget her name, except that she was called ' *Eliza*.' It was washing day, and the husband was absent ; but I remember a pleasant-looking kind woman, who gave us a nice tea, and rejoiced over Mrs. Carlyle, and said she had brought up her children in the hope of seeing her some day. She lived in a house in a row, with little gardens before them. We saw the children, who were like others ; and we went home by omnibus ; and we had enjoyed our little outing ; and Mrs. Carlyle gave me a pretty lace collar, and Bohemian-glass vase, which is still unbroken. . . .

" I end these ' stories told by herself,' not because there are no more. They give some slight indication of the courage and nobleness and fine qualities which lay in her who is gone. Very few women so truly great come into the world at all ; and no two like her at the same time. Those who were her friends will only go on feeling their loss and their sorrow more and more every day of their own lives.

" G. E. J.

"Chelsea, May 20, 1866."

DEAR GERALDINE,—Few or none of these Narratives are correct in all the details ; some of them, in almost all the details, are *in*correct. I have not *read* carefully beyond a certain point which is marked on the margin.[1] Your *recognition* of the *character* is generally true and faithful ; little of *portraiture* in it that satisfies me. On the whole, all tends to the *mythical ;* it is very strange how much of mythical there already here is !—

As Lady Lothian set you on writing, it seems hard that she should not see what you have written : but I wish you to take *her word of honour* that none else shall ; and my earnest request to you is that, directly *from* her Ladyship, you will bring the Book to me, and consign it to my keeping.

No need that an idle-gazing world should know my lost Darling's History, or mine ;—nor *will* they ever, they may depend upon it ! One fit service, and one only, *they* can do to Her or to Me : cease speaking of us, through all Eternity, as soon as they conveniently can.—Affectionately yours,

T. CARLYLE.

Chelsea, May 22, 1866.

25 *May* 1866. Geraldine returns me this little Book of Myths, *un*shown to anybody, and to be my own henceforth. I do not yet burn it ; as I have done her kind and respectful Letter (" Narratives long ago, on our first acquaintance " etc. etc. and fermenting and agglomerating in my mind ever since !)—in fact, there is a certain mythical truth, in all or most parts of the poor scribble, and it may *wait* its doom, or execution. That of young lovers, especially that of *flirting*, is much exaggerated : if " flirt " mean one who tries to inspire love without feeling it, I do not think she ever was a flirt. But she was very charming, full of grace, talent, clear insight, playful humour, and also of honest dignity and pride ; and not a few young fools, of her own or perhaps a slightly better station, made offers to her,—which, sometimes to their high temporary grief and astonishment, were decisively rejected. The most serious-looking of these affairs, was that of George Rennie, the Junior (not Heir but *Cadet*) of *Phantassie*, Nephew of the first Engineer Rennie ; a clever, decisive, very ambitious, but quite *un*melodious young fellow ; whom we knew afterwards here as sculptor, as M.P. (for a while), —finally as retired Governor of the Falkland Islands, in which latter character he died here, seven or eight years ago. She knew him thoroughly ; had never loved him, but respected various qualities in him, and naturally had some peculiar interest in him to the last. In his final time he used to come pretty often

---

[1] The mark on the margin is near the beginning of a passage omitted by Froude. See *supra*, p. 42 *n.*

down to us here, and was well worth talking to on his Falkland or other experiences : a man of sternly sound common-sense (so called), of strict veracity ; who much contemned imbecility, falsity, or nonsense wherever met with ; had swallowed manfully his many bitter disappointments, and silently awaited death itself for the last year or more (as I could notice), with a fine honest stoicism always complete.—My poor Jane hurried to his House ; and was there for three days, zealously assisting the Widow.

The Wooer who would needs *die* for want of success, was one Fyfe M.D., an extremely conceited, limited, strutting little creature, who well deserved all he got or more.   The end of him had something of tragedy in it, but is not worth recording.— *Dods* is the " Peasant schoolfellow's " name ; about seven or eight years *her* senior, son of a Nurseryman ; now rich abundantly, Banker, etc. etc. ; and an honest and kindly, though clumsy prosaic man.   Never uttered, or could have had the remotest hope or possibility to profit by uttering, his heavy thoughts (age 17–20), of the bright young Fairy (age 10–12).

The Story of her being taken as a child of perhaps seven or eight, to drive with her Father has some truth in it ; but consists of two stories rolled into one.   Child of seven or eight, " with watch forgotten," etc., was to the " Press Inn " (then a noted place ; and to her an ever-memorable expedition beside a Father almost her Divinity).   But drive second, almost still more memorable, was for an afternoon or several hours, as a young girl of eighteen,—over some *district* of her Father's duties ; she waiting in the carriage, unnoticed, while he made his visits. The usually tacit man, tacit especially about his bright Daughter's gifts and merits, took to talking with her that day, in a style quite new ; told her she was a good girl, capable of being useful and precious to him and to the circle she would live in ; that she must summon her utmost judgment and seriousness to choose her path, and *be* what he expected of her ; that he did not think she had ever yet seen the Life-Partner that would be worthy of her (Rennie's or anybody's name he did not mention, I think) ;—in short that he expected her to be wise, as well as good-looking and good.   All this in a tone and manner which filled her poor little heart with surprise, and a kind of sacred joy ; coming from the man she of all men revered.   Often she told me about this.   For it was her last talk with him : on the morrow, perhaps that evening, certainly within a day or two, he caught from some poor old woman patient (who, I think, recovered of it) a typhus fever ; which, under injudicious treatment, killed him in three or four days (September 1819) :— and drowned the world for her in the very blackness of darkness. In effect, it was her first sorrow ; and her greatest of all. It broke her health, permanently, within the next two or three years ; and, in a sense, almost broke her heart. A Father so mourned and loved I have never seen : to the end of her life, his title even to me was " He " and " Him ; " not above twice or thrice, quite in late years, did she ever mention (and then in what a sweet slow tone !), " my Father : " nay, I have a kind of notion (beautiful to me and sad exceedingly) she was never as happy again after that sunniest youth of hers, as in the last eighteen months, and especially the last *two weeks* of her life ; *when,* after wild rain-deluges and black tempests many, the *sun* shone out again, for *another's* sake, with full mild brightness, taking ' sweet farewell.' Oh it is beautiful to me ; and oh it is humbling ; and it is sad ! Where was my Jeannie's *peer* in this world ? and she fell to me, and I *could* not screen her from the bitterest distresses ! God pity and forgive me ; my own burden, too, might have broken a stronger back,—had not she been so loyal and loving. [Enough to-day.]

[*May* 26, Saturday. (*Gone* five weeks, ah me !)].—The Geraldine accounts of her Childhood are substantially correct ; but without the light melodious clearness, and charm of a Fairy Tale all true, which my lost One used to give them in talking to me. She was fond of talking about her childhood ; nowhere in the world did I ever hear of one more beautiful,—all sunny to her and to me, to our last years together.

That of running on the parapets of the Nungate Bridge (John Knox's old suburb), I recollect well ; that of the boy with the bloody nose ; many adventures about skating and leaping ; that of " *Penna, pennæ* " from below the table is already in print, through Mrs. Oliphant's *Life of Irving* [1] (a loyal and clear, but feeble kind of Book, popular in late years). In all things she strove to " be a Boy " in education ; and yet by natural guidance never ceased to be the prettiest and gracefullest of little girls. Full of intelligence, of veracity, vivacity, and bright curiosity. She went into all manner of shops and workshops that were accessible ; eager to see and understand what was going on. One morning (perhaps in her third or fourth year) she went into the shop of a barber, on the opposite side of the street,—*back* from which by a narrow entrance, was her own

[1] *The Life of Edward Irving,* by Mrs. Oliphant (London, 1864), p. 22.

nice, elegant, quiet home. Barber's shop was empty; my Jeannie went in, silently sat down on a bench at the wall, old barber giving her a kind glance, but no word. Presently a customer came in; was soaped and lathered, in silence mainly or altogether; was getting diligently scraped and shaved, my Bonny little Bird, as attentive as possible, and all in perfect silence. Customer at length said, in a pause of the razor, " How is John So-and-so now ? " " He's deid " (*dead*), replied Barber in a rough hollow voice, and instantly pushed on with business again. The bright little child burst into tears, and hurried out. This she told me, not half a year ago. I never saw a picture lovelier than had grown in me of her childhood.

Her first school teacher was Edward Irving; who also gave her private lessons in Latin etc., and became an intimate of the family; it was from him (probably in 1818) that I first heard of her Father and her; some casual mention, the loving and reverential tone of which had struck me. Of the Father he spoke always as of one of the wisest, truest, and most dignified of men; of her as a paragon of gifted young girls. Far away from me, both, and objects of distant reverence and unattainable longing, at that time ! The Father, whom I never saw, died next year (Sept. 1819); her I must have seen first, I think in June 1821. Sight for ever memorable to me :—I looked up at the windows of the old room, in the desolate moonlight of my *last* visit to Haddington (*five weeks ago*, come Wednesday next); and the old summer dusk, and that bright pair of eyes, inquiringly fixed on me (as I noticed, for a moment), came up clear as yesterday, all drowned in woes and death.

Her second teacher (Irving's successor) was a Rev. James Brown, who died in India, whom also I slightly knew. The school, I believe, was and is at the hither, western, end of the Nungate Bridge; and grew famed in the neighbourhood by Irving's new methods and managements,—adopted as far as might be by Brown. A short furlong or so along paved streets, from her Father's house. Thither daily at an early hour (perhaps eight A.M. in summer) might be seen my little Jeannie tripping nimbly and daintily along; her little satchel in hand; dressed by her mother (who had a great talent that way) in tasteful simplicity,—neat bit of pelisse (' light blue,' sometimes) fastened with black belt; dainty little cap, perhaps little *beaver*kin (' with flap turned up ') and I think once at least with modest ' little plume in it.' Fill that figure with *electric* intellect,

ditto love, and generous vivacity of all kinds ; where in Nature
will you find a prettier ?

At home was opulence (*without* waste), elegance, good sense,
silent practical affection and manly wisdom ; from threshold
to roof-tree, no paltriness or unveracity admitted into it. I
often told her how very beautiful her childhood was to me,—so
authentic-looking withal, in her charmingly naïve and humorous
way of telling ;—and that she must have been " the prettiest
little Jenny Spinner " (Scotch name for a long-winged, long-
legged, extremely bright and airy insect) that was dancing on the
summer rays in her time. More enviable lot than all this was I
cannot imagine to myself in any house high or low,—in the
higher and highest still less than the other kind.

Once, I cannot say in what year, nor for how many months,—
but perhaps about six or eight, her age perhaps eight or nine,—
her mother thinking it good, she was sent away to another House
of the Town, to *board* with some kind of Ex-Governess Person,
who had married some Ex-Military ditto, and professed to be
able to educate young ladies and form their *manners* (" better,"
thought the mother, " than with nothing but *men* as here at
home ! ")—and in this place, with a Miss Something, a friend
and playmate of like age, she was fixed down, for a good few
months, and suffered, she and the companion manifold disgust,
even hardships, even want of proper food ; wholly without complaining (too proud and loyal for that) ; till it was, by some accident, found out, and instantly put an end to. This was the little
cup of bitter ; which, I suppose, sweetened into new sweetness
all the other happy years of her home.—Two child *anecdotes* I
will mark, as ready at this moment :

Father and Mother returning from some visit (probably to
Nithsdale) along with her (age, say four), at the Black Bull,
Edinburgh, were ordering dinner. Waiter, rather solemn
personage, inquired, " And what will little Missie eat ? " " A
roasted bumm bee " (*humming* or field bee), answered little
Missie.

" Mamma, wine makes cosy ! " said the little Naturalist once
at home (year *before* perhaps), while sipping a drop of wine
Mamma had given her.

[1] [One of the prettiest stories was of the child's first Ball,
' Dancing School Ball ; ' her first public appearance, as it were,

[1] This passage in brackets is from a loose sheet written in 1868, forming
part of a proposed introduction to the *Letters and Memorials of Jane Welsh
Carlyle.*

on the theatre of the world. Of this, in the daintiest style of kind mockery, I often heard, and have the general image still vivid ; but have lost the express details, or rather, in my ignorance of such things, never completely understood the details. How the evening was so great ; all the higher public there, especially the maternal or paternal sections of it, to see their children dance ; and Jeannie Welsh, probably then about six, had been selected to perform some *Pas seul*, beautiful and difficult, the jewel of the evening, and was privately anxious in her little heart to do it well ; how she was dressed to perfection, with elegance, with simplicity, and at the due hour was carried over in a clothes-basket (streets being muddy and no carriage), and landed safe, pretty silks and pumps [1] uninjured. Through the Ball everything went well and smoothly, nothing to be noted till the *Pas seul* came. My little woman (with a look that I can still fancy) appeared upon the scene, stood waiting for the music ; music began, but alas, alas, it was the wrong music, impossible to dance that *Pas seul* to it ! She shook her little head, looked or made some sign of distress. Music ceased, took counsel, scraped, began again ; again wrong, hopelessly ; the *Pas seul* flatly impossible. Beautiful little Jane, alone against the world, forsaken by the music but not by her presence of mind, plucked up her little skirt, flung it over her head, and curtseying in that veiled manner, withdrew from the adventure amidst general applause and admiration, as I could well believe.]

The second (properly the third) of my anecdotes is not easily intelligible except to myself : Old Walter Welsh, her maternal Grandfather, was a most picturesque, peculiar, generous-hearted, hot-tempered, abrupt and impatient old man. I guess she might be about six ; and was with her mother on a visit, I know not whether at Caplegill (Moffat Water), or at Strathmilligan or Durisdeer (Nithsdale, both these ; Templand was long after) : old Walter, who was of few words though of very lively thought and insight, had a *burr* in pronouncing his *r*, and spoke in *old* style generally. He had taken little Jeannie out to ride on a quiet little pony ; very pleasant winding ride ; and at length, when far enough, old Walter said, Now we will go back by So-and-so, " to vary the scene " (to vah-ry, properly ' to vah-*chy* ' the s*ha*ne). Home at dinner, the company asked her, " Where did you ride to, Pen ? " (*Pen* was her little name there, from Paternal Grandfather's house, " Penfillan," to distinguish her from the other *Welshes* of Walter's household.) **We** rode to *so*,

[1] Dancing-shoes.

then to *so*, answered she, punctually ; then from *so*, returned by *so* " to vah-chy the shane ! " At which, I suppose, the old man himself burst into his cheeriest laugh at the mimicry of tiny little Pen.— —" Mamma, oh mamma, don't expos*ie me !* " exclaimed she once, not yet got quite the length of *speaking*, when her mother for some kind purpose was searching under her clothes.—

I will write of all this no further : the beauty of it is so steeped to me in pain. Why do I *write* at all, for that matter ? Can *I* ever forget ? And is not all this appointed by me rigorously to the *fire* ? Somehow it solaces me to *have* written it ;—and to-morrow, probably, I shall fill out these two remaining pages.[1] Ah me.—She had written at one time something of her own early life ; but she gave up, and burnt it. . . . She wrote at various times in Note-books ; refusing all sight of them even to me : but she has destroyed nearly every vestige of them ;—one little Book, consisting of curious excerpts and jottings *not* biographic (in which she would often look practically for *Addresses*, Street and number as one item), is all that remains,—that I do not mean to burn.

Geraldine's account of *Comley Bank*[2] and Life at Edinburgh, is extremely mythic ; we did grow to " know everybody of mark," or might have grown ; but nobody except Jeffrey[3] seemed to either of us a valuable acquisition. Jeffrey much admired her, and was a pleasant phenomenon to both of us. . . . Wilson, a far *bigger* man, I could have loved, or fancied I could ; but he would not let me try,—being already deep in *whisky-punch*, poor fellow, and apprehensive I might think less of him the better I knew him.—We had a little tea-party (never did I see a smaller or a frugaller, with the tenth part of the human grace and brightness in it) once a week ;—the " brown coffee-pot," the feeble talk of dilettante——, pretty silly——etc. ; ah me, how she knit up all that into a shining thing ! . . . Oh she was noble, very noble, in that early as in all other periods ; and made the ugliest and dullest into something beautiful ! I look back on it as if through rainbows, the bit of sunshine hers, the tears my own.

I was latterly beginning also to get into note and employment.

1 Of the Note-book in which Miss Jewsbury had written.
2 21 Comley Bank, a house in the north-western suburbs of Edinburgh in which Carlyle and his wife lived from the time of their marriage, 17th October 1826, till their removal to Craigenputtock in 1828.
3 See the paper on " Jeffrey " in this volume.

" If I could recover health ! " said I always, with which view and for the sake of cheapness we moved (in May 1828) to Craigenputtock ; she cheerily assenting, though our plans were surely somewhat helpless.[1]

    .   .   .   .   .

[*May* 29.] We must have gone to Craigenputtock[2] early in May 1828 : I remember passing our furniture carts (my Father's carts from Scotsbrig, conducted by my two farming Brothers) somewhere about Elvanfoot, as the coach brought *us* two along. I don't remember our going up to Craigen-puttock (a day or two after), but do well remember what a bewildering *heap* it all was for some time after.

Geraldine's *Craigenputtock* stories are more mythical than any of the rest. Each consists of two or three, in confused exaggerated state, rolled with new confusion into one, and given wholly to *her*, when perhaps they were mainly some servant's in whom she was concerned. That of the kitchen door, which could not be closed again on the snowy morning, etc., that is a fact very visible to me yet ; and how I, coming down for a light to my pipe, found Grace Macdonald (our Edinburgh servant, and a most clever and complete one) in tears and despair, with a stupid farm-servant endeavouring vainly by main force to pull the door to, which, as it had a frame round it, sill and all, for keeping out the wind, could not be shut except by somebody from within (me, *e.g.*) who would first clear out the snow at the sill, and then, with his best speed, shut ; which I easily did. The washing of the kitchen floor, etc. (of which I can remember nothing) must have been years distant, under some quite other servant, and was probably as much of a joyous half-frolic as of anything else. I can remember very well her coming in to me, late at night (eleven or so), with her *first loaf*, looking mere triumphant and quizzical gaiety : " See ! " The loaf was excellent, only the crust a little burnt ; and she compared herself to Cellini and his *Perseus*, of whom we had been reading. From

<hr />

[1] An unimportant commentary on the passage in Miss Jewsbury's narrative relating to Mrs. Carlyle's cousin, see *supra*, p. 42 *n.*, is omitted here.

[2] A farm on the moors about sixteen miles north-west of Dumfries. It was purchased from his father by Dr. Welsh, and on his death in 1819 became the property of his daughter, afterwards Mrs. Carlyle. Dr. Welsh having died suddenly without making provision for his widow, Miss Welsh made it over in life-rent to her mother. Carlyle added a second story to the house, and, with his wife, removed thither from Edinburgh in May 1828. He built a smaller house, which, together with the farm, was let for £200 a year to his brother Alexander. Mrs. Welsh died in 1842, and it then again came into Mrs. Carlyle's possession.

that hour we never wanted excellent bread. In fact, the saving
charm of her life at Craigenputtock, which to another young lady
of her years might have been so gloomy and vacant, was that
of conquering the innumerable Practical Problems that had
arisen for her there ;—all of which, I think all, she triumphantly
mastered. Dairy, poultry-yard, piggery ; I remember one
exquisite pig, which we called *Fixie* (*Quintus Fixlein* of Jean
Paul), and such a little ham of it as could not be equalled.
Her cow gave 24 quarts of milk daily in the two or three best
months of summer ; and such cream, and such butter (though oh,
she had such a problem with that ; owing to a bitter herb
among the grass, not known of till long after by my heroic
Darling, and she triumphed over that too !). That of milking
with her own little hand, I think, could never have been *necessary*
even by accident (plenty of milkmaids within call), and I conclude must have had a spice of frolic or *adventure* in it, for which
she had abundant spirit. Perfection of housekeeping was her
clear and speedy attainment in that new scene. Strange how
she made the Desert blossom for herself and me there ; what a
fairy palace she had made of that wild moorland home of the
poor man ! In my life I have seen no human intelligence that
so genuinely pervaded every fibre of the human existence it
belonged to. From the baking of a loaf, or the darning of a
stocking, up to comporting herself in the highest scenes, or most
intricate emergencies, all was insight, veracity, graceful success
(if you could judge it),—*fidelity* to insight of the fact given.

We had trouble with servants, with many paltry elements
and objects ; and were very poor : but I do not think our days
there were sad,—and certainly not *hers* in especial, but mine
rather. We read together at night,—one winter, through *Don
Quixote* in the original ; Tasso in ditto had come before,—but
that did not last very long. I was diligently writing and reading
there ; wrote most of " the *Miscellanies* " there, for Foreign,
Edinburgh, etc. Reviews (obliged to keep *several* strings to my
bow),—and took serious thought about every part of every one
of them : after finishing an Article, we used to get on horseback,
or mount into our soft old Gig, and drive away, either to her
Mother's (Templand,[1] fourteen miles off), or to my Father and
Mother's (Scotsbrig, seven- or six-and-thirty miles) ;—the
pleasantest journeys I ever made, and the pleasantest visits.
Stay perhaps three days ; hardly ever more than four ; then
back to work and silence. My Father she particularly loved,

[1] See *infra*, p. 105.

and recognised all the grand rude worth and immense originality
that lay in him. Her demeanour at Scotsbrig, throughout in
fact, was like herself, unsurpassable ; and took captive all those
true souls, from oldest to youngest, who by habit and type
might have been so utterly foreign to her. At Templand or
there, our presence always made a sunshiny time. To Templand we sometimes rode on an evening, to return next day early
enough for something of work : this was charming generally.
Once I remember we had come by Barjarg,[1] not by Auldgarth
(Bridge) ; and were riding, the Nith then in flood, from Penfillan
or Penpont neighbourhood : she was fearlessly following or
accompanying me ; and there remained only one little arm to
cross, which did look a thought uglier, but gave me no disturb-
ance, when a farmer figure was seen on the farther bank or fields,
earnestly waving and signalling (could not be *heard* for the
floods) ; but for whom we should surely have had some accident,
ho knows how bad ! Never rode that water again, at least
never in flood I am sure.

[*May* 30.] We were not unhappy at Craigenputtock ; perhaps
these were our happiest days. Useful, continual labour, essentially successful ; that makes even the moor green. I found I
could do fully *twice* as much work in a given time there, as with
my best effort was possible in London,—such the interruptions
etc. Once, in the winter time, I remember counting that for
three months, there had not any stranger, not even a beggar,
called at Craigenputtock door. In summer we had sparsely
visitors, now and then her Mother, or my own, once my Father ;
who never before had been *so far* from his birthplace as when
here (and yet " knew the world " as few of his time did, so well
had he looked at what he did see !). At Auldgarth Brig, which
he had assisted to build when a lad of fifteen, and which was the
beginning of all good to him, and to all his Brothers (and to
me), his emotion, after fifty-five years, was described to me as
strong, conspicuous and *silent*. He delighted us, especially her,
at Craigenputtock ; himself evidently thinking of his *latter end*,
in a most intense awe-stricken, but also quiet and altogether
human way. Since my Sister Margaret's death,[2] he had been

1 At Barjarg, some eight miles from Craigenputtock, there was a library
(" a handsome Library for a Country Gentleman," Carlyle calls it) which
the owner, Mr. Hunter Arundell, had placed at Carlyle's service, and which
was a privilege much prized ; but this good fortune did not come until
September 1833, within eight months of his leaving Craigenputtock for
London, May 1834.
2 See *supra*, p. 6 *n*.

steadily sinking in strength, though we did not then notice it.—
—On the 12th of August (for the *grouse's* sake) Robert Welsh,
her uncle, was pretty certain to be there ; with a tag-raggery
of Dumfries Writers,[1] Dogs, etc. etc., whom, though we liked
him very well, even I, and much more *she* who had to provide,
find beds, etc., felt to be a nuisance. I got at last into the way
of riding off, for some visit or the like, on August 12th : and
unless " Uncle Robert " came in person, she also would answer,
" not at home."

An interesting relation to Goethe had likewise begun in
Comley Bank first, and now went on increasing :[2] " Boxes from
Weimar " (and " to," at least once or twice) were from time to
time a most sunny event ;—I remember her making for Ottilie
a beautiful Highland Bonnet (bright blue velvet, with silvered
thistle etc.), which gave plenty of pleasure on both hands. The
Sketch of Craigenputtock[3] was taken by G. Moir, Advocate
(ultimately Sheriff, Professor,[4] etc., " little Geordie Moir " as we
called him), who was once and no more with us. The visit of
Emerson from Concord, and our quiet night of clear fine talk,
was also very pretty to both of us. The Jeffreys came twice,
expressly, and once we went to Dumfries by appointment to
meet them in passing. Their correspondence was there a steadily
enlivening element. One of the visits, I forget whether first
or last, but from Hazlitt,[5] in London, there came to Jeffrey a
death-bed letter one of the days, and instead of " £10," £50 went
by return : Jeffrey, one of the nights, young Laird of Stroquhan
present, was, what with mimicry of speakers, what with other
cleverness and sprightliness, the most brilliantly amusing
creature I have ever chanced to see. One time we went to
Craigcrook,[6] and returned their visit ;—and, as I can *now* see,
staid at least *a week too long*. His health was beginning to break;
he and I had, nightly, long arguments (far *too* frank and equal

[1] Lawyers.
[2] See the *Correspondence between Goethe and Carlyle*, edited by C. E.
Norton (*Macmillan*, 1887). Carlyle's first letter to Goethe, accompanying
a copy of his translation of *Meister's Apprenticeship*, is dated 24th June
1824 ; Goethe's reply, 30th October 1824.
[3] *Two* sketches ;—they were sent to Goethe, at his request, and engraved
for the translation of Carlyle's *Schiller*, prepared under Goethe's direction,
and for which he wrote an Introductory Preface (*Frankfurt am Main*,
1830). See Carlyle's *Life of Schiller* (Library ed., 1869), *Appendix II*.
[4] Professor of Rhetoric in the Edinburgh University ; translator of
Wallenstein, etc. ; died 1870, aged 71.
[5] Hazlitt died 18th September 1830.
[6] Jeffrey's house, on the eastern slope of Corstorphine Hill, about three
miles north-west of Edinburgh, where (from 1815 until his death,
26th January 1850) Jeffrey's summers were spent.

on my side, I can now see with penitence) about moral matters, perhaps till two or three A.M. He was a most gifted, prompt, ingenious little man (essentially a *Dramatic* Genius, say a melodious Goldoni or more, but made into a Scotch Advocate and Whig) ; never a deeply serious man. He discovered here, I think, that I *could* not be " converted," and that I was of thoughtlessly rugged rustic ways, and faultily irreverent of him (which, alas, I was). The Correspondence became mainly *hers* by degrees ; but was, for years after, a cheerful, lively element,—in spite of Reform Bills and Officialities (ruinous to poor Jeffrey's health and comfort) which, before long, supervened. We were at Haddington on that Craigcrook occasion ; staid with the Donaldsons at Sunnybank (*hodie* Tenterfield), who were her oldest and dearest friends (*hereditarily* and otherwise) in that region. I well remember the gloom of our arrival back to Craigenputtock : a miserable wet, windy November evening, with the yellow leaves all flying about ; and the sound of Brother Alick's stithy (who sometimes amused himself with smithwork, to small purpose), clink-clinking solitary through the blustering element. I said nothing, far was she from ever, in the like case, saying anything ! Indeed I think we at once readjusted ourselves ; and went on diligently with the old degree of industry and satisfaction.

" Old Esther," whose death came, one of our early winters, was a bit of memorability, in that altogether vacant scene. I forget the old woman's surname (perhaps M'George ?) ; but well recal her lumpish heavy figure (lame of a foot), and her honest, quiet, not stupid countenance of mixed ugliness and stoicism. She lived about a mile from us in a poor Cottage of the next Farm (Corson's, of *Nether* Craigenputtock . . .) ; Esther had been a Laird's Daughter, riding her palfrey at one time ; but had gone to wreck, Father and self,—a special " misfortune " (so they delicately name it) being of Esther's own producing. " Misfortune," in the shape ultimately of a solid tall Ditcher, very good to his old mother Esther, had, just before our coming, perished miserably one night on the shoulder of Dunscore Hill (found dead there, next morning) ; which had driven his poor old mother up to this *thriftier* hut, and silent mode of living, in our moorland part of the Parish. She did not beg ; nor had my Jeannie much to have given her of help (perhaps on occasion *milk*, old warm *clothes*, etc.), though always very sorry for her last sad bereavement of the stalwart affectionate Son. I remember one frosty kind of forenoon, while walking meditative to the top of our Hill (now a mass of bare or moorclad whinstone *Crag*, once a woody wilderness, with woody mountain in the middle of it, "Craigen*puttock*," or the stone-mountain, "Craig" of the "Puttock,"—puttock being a sort of *Hawk*, both in Galloway Speech, and in Shakspeare's Old English;[1] "Hill-Forest of the Puttocks"), now a very bare place, the universal silence was complete, all but one click-clack, heard regularly like a far-off *spondee* or *iambus* rather, "click-*clack*," at regular intervals, a great way to my right. No other sound in nature. On looking sharply I discovered it to be old Esther on the highway, crippling along,—towards our house most probably. Poor old soul, thought I; what a desolation; but you *will* meet a kind face too, perhaps! Heaven is over all.

Not long afterwards, poor old Esther sank to bed; death-bed, as my Jane (who had a quick and sure eye in these things) well judged it would be. Sickness did not last above a ten days; my poor Wife zealously assiduous, and with a minimum of fuss or noise. I remember those few poor days; as full of human interest to her (and through her to me) and of a human pity, not painful, but sweet and genuine. She went, walking every morning, especially every night, to arrange the poor bed, etc. (nothing but *rudish* hands, rude though kind enough, being about), the poor old woman evidently gratified by it and heart-thankful, and almost to the very *end* giving clear sign of that. Something pathetic in poor old Esther and her exit :—nay, if I rightly bethink me, that "click-clack" pilgrimage had in fact been a last visit to Craigenputtock with some poor bit of crockery (small gray, lettered butter-plate, which I used to see) "as a wee *memorandum* o' me, mem, when I am gane!" 'Memorandum' was her word; and I remember the poor little platter for years after. Poor old Esther had awoke, that frosty morning, with a feeling that she would soon die, that "the bonny Leddy" had been "unco' guid" to her, and that there was still that "wee bit memorandum." Nay, I think she had, or had once had, the remains, or complete *ghost* of a "fine old riding-habit" once her own, which the curious had seen : but this she had judged it more polite to leave to the Parish. Ah me. *Sunt lachrymæ rerum!*

The gallop to Dumfries and back on "Harry," an excellent, well-paced, well-broken loyal little Horse of hers (thirteen hands or so, an exceeding favourite, and her *last*),—thirty good miles

[1] 'I chose an eagle,
And did avoid a puttock.'—*Cymbeline* Act i. Scene 1.

of swift canter, at the least,—is a fact ; which I well remember, though from home at the moment. Word had come (to *her* virtually, or *properly* perhaps) that the Jeffreys, three and a servant, were to be there, day after to-morrow, perhaps morrow itself ; I was at Scotsbrig ; nothing ready at all (and such narrow means to get ready anything, my Darling Heroine !). She directly mounted Harry, " who seemed to know that he must gallop, and faithfully did it ; " laid her plans while galloping ; ordered everything at Dumfries, sent word to me express ; galloped home ; and stood victoriously prepared at all points to receive the Jeffreys,—who, I think, were all there on my arrival. The night of her *express* is to me very memorable for its own sake : I had been to Burnswark (visit to good old Graham, and walk of three miles to and three from) ; it was ten P.M. of a most still and fine night when I arrived at my Father's door ; heard him making worship, and stood meditative, gratefully, lovingly, till he had ended ; thinking to myself, how good and innocently beautiful and manful on the earth, is all this :—and it was the last time I was ever to hear it. I must have been there twice or oftener [afterwards] in my Father's time ; but the sound of his pious *Coleshill* (that was always his tune), pious Psalm and Prayer, I never heard again. With a noble politeness, very noble when I consider, they kept all that in a fine kind of remoteness from us, knowing (and somehow *forgiving* us completely) that we did not think of it quite as they. My Jane's express would come next morning ;—and of course I made Larry [1] ply his hoofs.

The *second* ride, in Geraldine, is nearly altogether mythical ; being in reality a ride from Dumfries to Scotsbrig (two and a half miles *beyond* " Ecclefechan," where none of us ever passed), with *some* loss of road within the last five miles (wrong turn at Hoddam Brig, I guessed), darkness (night-time in May), money, etc. ; and " terror " enough for a commonplace young lady, but little or nothing of real danger,—and terror not an element at all, I fancy, in her courageous mind. Harry I think cannot have been her Horse (half-killed two years before in an *epidemic;* through which *she* nursed him fondly, he once " kissing her cheek " in gratitude, she always thought) or Harry would have known the road, for we had often ridden and driven it. I was at that time gone to London, in quest of houses.

[*May* 31.] My last considerable bit of *Writing* at Craigen-

[1] *Larry* was Carlyle's horse.

puttock was *Sartor Resartus ;* [1] done, I think, between January
and August 1830 (my Sister Margaret [2] had died while it was
going on). I well remember, where and how (at Templand one
morning) the *germ* of it rose above ground. " Nine months,"
I used to say, it had cost me in writing. Had the perpetual
fluctuation, the uncertainty and unintelligible whimsicality of
Review Editors not proved so intolerable, we might have lingered
longer at Craigenputtock,—" perfectly left alone, and able to
do *more* work, beyond doubt, than elsewhere." But a Book did
seem to promise some *respite* from that, and perhaps further
advantages. Teufelsdröckh was ready ; and (first days of
August [1831]) I decided to make for London. Night before
going, how I still remember it ! I was lying on my back on the
sofa in the drawing-room ; she sitting by the table (late at night,
packing all done I suppose) : her words had a guise of sport
but were profoundly plaintive in meaning, " About to part, who
knows for how long ; and what may have come in the interim ! "
this was her thought, and she was evidently much out of spirits.
" Courage, Dearie, only for a month ! " I would say to her in
some form or other. I went, next morning early, Alick driving :
embarked at Glencaple Quay ; [3] voyage, as far as Liverpool
still vivid to me ; the rest, *till* arrival in London, gone mostly
extinct : let it ! The beggarly history of poor *Sartor among
the Blockheadisms* is not worth my recording, or remembering
—least of all here !—In short, finding that whereas I had got
£100 (if memory serve) for *Schiller* six or seven years before, [4]
and for *Sartor* " at least *thrice* as good," I could not only *not* .
" get £200," but even get no " Murray " or the like to publish
it on " half profits " (Murray, a most stupendous object to me ;
tumbling about, eyeless, with the evidently strong wish to say
" Yes *and* No,"—my first signal experience of that sad human
predicament),—I said, " We will make it *No*, then ; wrap up
our MS. ; wait till this ' Reform Bill ' uproar abate ; and see,
and give our brave little Jeannie a sight of this big Babel, which
is so altered since I saw it last (in 1824–25) ! "— —She came
right willingly ; and had, in spite of her ill-health, which did
not abate but the contrary, an interesting, cheery, and, in spite
of our poor arrangements, a really pleasant winter here. We

[1] Finished in August 1831, not 1830 ; appeared in *Fraser's Magazine*
1833–34 ; first in book form, under Emerson's auspices, in America in
1836–37, and was not reprinted in England until 1838.
[2] See *supra*, p. 6 n.   [3] Five miles beyond Dumfries.
[4] It came out first in the *London Magazine*, 1823–24. Published in
book form in 1825.

lodged in Ampton Street, Gray's Inn Lane, clean and decent pair of rooms, and quiet decent people (the *Daughter* is she whom Geraldine speaks of as having, I might say, " fallen in love " with her,—wanted to be our servant at Craigenputtock etc. !), —reduced from wealth to keeping lodgings, and prettily resigned to it ; really good people. Visitors etc. she had in plenty ; John Mill one of the most interesting, so modest, ingenuous ingenious,—and so very fond of *me* at that time. Mrs. Basil Montagu (already a *correspondent* of hers, now accurately *seen*) was another of the distinguished. Jeffrey, Lord Advocate, often came on an afternoon ;—never *could* learn his road to and from the end of Piccadilly, though I showed it him again and again. In the evening, *miscellany* of hers and mine, often dullish, —had it not been for *her*, and the light she shed on everything. I wrote *Johnson* here ; just before going. News of my Father's death came here : oh, how good and tender she was, and consolatory by every kind art, in those black days ! I remember our walk along Holborn forward into the City, and the *bleeding* mood I was in, she wrapping me like the softest of bandages :— in the City somewhere, two Boys fighting, with a ring of grinning Blackguards round them ; I rushed passionately through, tore the fighters asunder, with some passionate rebuke ("in this world full of death "), she on my arm ; and everybody silently complied. Nothing was *wanting* in her sympathy, or in the manner of it, as even from sincere people there often is. How poor we were ; and yet how rich ! I remember once taking her to Drury Lane Theatre (*Ticket*, from Playwright Kenny belike) along sloppy streets, in a November night (this was *before* my Father's sudden death) ; and how paltry the equipment looked to me, how perfectly unobjectionable to her, who was far above equipments and outer garnitures. Of the theatricality itself that night I can remember absolutely nothing.

Badams, my old Birmingham friend and physician (a most inventive, light-hearted, and genially gallant kind of man ; sadly *eclipsed* within the last five years, ill-married, plunged amid grand mining speculations, which were and showed themselves *sound*, but not till they had driven him to drink brandy instead of water, and next year to die miserably overwhelmed),— Badams with his Wife was living out at Enfield, in a big old rambling sherd of a House among waste gardens ; thither I twice or thrice went, much liking the man, but never now getting any good of him ; she once for three or four days, went with me sorry enough days, had not we and especially she, illuminated

them a little. Charles Lamb and his Sister came daily once or
oftener ; a very sorry pair of phenomena. Insuperable pro-
clivity to *gin*, in poor old Lamb. His talk contemptibly small,
indicating wondrous ignorance and shallowness, even when it
was serious and good-mannered, which it seldom was ; usually
ill-mannered (to a degree), screwed into frosty artificialities,
ghastly make-believe of wit ;—in fact more like " diluted
insanity " (as I defined it) than anything of real jocosity,
" humour," or geniality. A most slender fibre of actual worth
there was in that poor Charles, abundantly recognisable to me
as to others, in his better times and moods ; but he was Cockney
to the marrow ; and Cockneydom, shouting, " Glorious, marvellous, unparalleled in Nature ! " all his days, had quite
bewildered his poor head, and churned nearly all the sense out
of the poor man. He was the *leanest* of mankind, tiny black
breeches buttoned to the knee-cap and no farther, surmounting
spindle-legs also in black, face and head fineish, black, bony,
lean, and of a Jew type rather ; in the eyes a kind of *smoky*
brightness or confused sharpness ; spoke with a stutter ; in
walking tottered and shuffled : emblem of imbecility bodily
and spiritual (something of real *insanity* I have understood),
and yet something too of humane, ingenuous, pathetic, sport-
fully much-enduring. Poor Lamb ! He was infinitely astonished at my Wife ; and her quiet encounter of his too
ghastly London wit by cheerful native ditto. Adieu, poor
Lamb ! He soon after died ; as did Badams, much more to
the sorrow of us both. Badams at our last parting (in Ampton
Street, four or more months after this), burst into tears :
" Pressed down like *putty* under feet," we heard him murmuring
" and no strength more in me to rise ! " We invited him to
Craigenputtock, with our best temptations, next Summer ;
but it was too late ; he answered, almost as with tears, " No,
alas,"—and shortly died.[1]

We had come home, last days of previous March : wild
journey by heavy Coach, I outside, to Liverpool : to Birmingham
it was good, and Inn there good ; but next day (a Sunday, I
think) we were quite over-loaded ; and had our adventures,
especially on the street in Liverpool, rescuing our luggage after
dark. But at Uncle John's,[2] again, in Maryland Street, all
became so bright. At mid-day, somewhere, we dined pleasantly
tête-à-tête,—in the belly of the Coach, from my Dear One's

[1] September 1833.
[2] Mr. John Welsh, Mrs. Carlyle's maternal uncle.

stores (to save expense doubtless), but the rest of the day had been unpleasantly chaotic even to me,—though from her, as usual, there was nothing but patient goodness. Our dinners at Maryland Street I still remember, our days generally as pleasant,—our departure in the Annan Steamer; a bright sunshiny forenoon, Uncle etc. zealously helping and escorting; sick, sick my poor woman must have been; but she retired out of sight, and would suffer with her best grace in silence :—ah me, I recollect now a tight, clean, brandy-barrel she had bought : to " hold such quantities of luggage, and be a water-barrel, for the rain at Craigenputtock ! "—how touching to me at this moment !—And an excellent water-barrel it proved; the purest *tea* I ever tasted, made from the rain it stored for us. —At Whinnyrigg, I remember, Brother Alick and others of them were waiting to receive us : there were *tears* among us (my Father gone, while *we* returned); *she* wept bitterly, I recollect,—her sympathetic heart girdled in much sickness and dispiritment of her own withal : but my Mother was very kind and cordially good and respectful to her always. We returned in some days to Craigenputtock, and were again at peace there. Alick, I think, had by this time left; a new tenant there (a peaceable but dull stupid fellow); and our summers and winters for the future (1832–1834) were lonelier than ever. *Good* Servants too were hardly procurable; difficult anywhere, still more so at Craigenputtock where the choice was so limited. However, we pushed along; *writing* still brisk; *Sartor* getting published in *Fraser*, etc. etc. We had not at first any thought of leaving. And indeed would the Review Editors but have stood *steady* (instead of for ever changeful), and domestic service gone on comfortably,—perhaps we might have continued still a good while. We went one winter (1833) to Edinburgh; the Jeffreys absent in official regions. A most dreary contemptible kind of element we found Edinburgh to be (partly by accident, or baddish behaviour of two individuals, Dr. Irving one of them, in reference to his poor kinswoman's *furnished house*) : a locality and life-element never to be spoken of in comparison with London and the frank friends there. To London accordingly, in the course of next winter and its new paltry experiences of house-service etc., we determined to go. Our home-coming I remember; missed the coach in Princes Street; waited perdue till following morning; bright weather,—but my poor Jeannie so ill by the ride, that she could not drive from Thornhill to Templand (half a mile), but had to go or stagger hanging on my arm, and instantly took to bed with one of her terrible headaches. Such headaches I never witnessed in my life ; agony of retching (never anything but phlegm) and of spasmodic writhing, that would last from twenty-four to sixty hours, never the smallest help affordable. Oh, what of pain, *pain*, my poor Jeannie had to bear in this thorny pilgrimage of life ; the unwitnessed Heroine, or witnessed only by me,—who never till now *see* it *wholly !*

She was very hearty for London, when I spoke of it, though *till* then her voice on the subject had never been heard. " Burn our ships ! " she gaily said, one day—i.e. dismantle our House ; carry all our furniture with us. And accordingly here it still is (mostly all of it her Father's furniture ; whose character of solidly noble is visibly written on it : " respect what is *truly* made to its purpose ; detest what is *falsely*, and have no concern with it ! "). My own heart could not have been more emphatic on that subject ; honour to him for its worth to me, not as furniture alone. My Writing-table, solid mahogany, well devised, always *handy*, yet *steady* as the *rocks*, is the best I ever saw : " no Book could be too good for being written here," it has often mutely told me. *His* Watch, commissioned by him in Clerkenwell, has measured my time, for forty years ;—and would still guide you to the *longitude*, could anybody now take the trouble of completely regulating it (but old Whitelaw in Edinburgh, perhaps thirty-five years ago, was the last that did). Repeatedly have upholsterers asked, " Who made these chairs, ma'am ? " In Cockneydom, nobody in our day ; ' unexampled prosperity ' makes another kind. Abhorrence, quite equal to my own, of *cheap and nasty*, I have nowhere seen, certainly nowhere else seen completely accomplished, as poor mine could never manage almost in the least degree to be. My *pride*, fierce and sore as it might be, was never hurt by that furniture of his in the house called mine ; on the contrary my *piety* was touched ; and ever and anon have this *Table* etc. been a silent solemn sermon to me. Oh, shall not victory at last be to the Handful of Brave ; in spite of the rotten multitudinous canaille, who *seem* to inherit all the world and its forces and steel-weapons and culinary and stage properties ? Courage ; and be true to one another !

[*June* 3.] I remember well my departure (middle of May, 1834),[1] she staying to superintend packing and settling ; in gig,

---

1 " LONDON, May 14th, 1834. What a word is there ! I left home on Thursday last (five days ago) ; and see myself, still with astonishment, *here* seeking houses. The parting with my Sister Jean, who had driven

I, for the last time ; with many thoughts (forgotten these) ; Brother Alick *voluntarily* waiting at Shillahill Bridge with a *fresh* horse for me ; night at Scotsbrig ; ride to Annan (through a kind of May series of slight showers) ; pretty breakfast waiting us in poor good Mary's (ah me, how strange is all that now, " Mother, you *shall* see me once yearly, and regularly hear from me, while we live ! " etc. etc.) : embarkation at Annan-water Foot, Ben Nelson and James Stuart ; our lifting hawser, and steaming off,—my two dear Brothers (Alick and Jamie) standing silent, apart, feeling I well knew what ;—self-resolute enough, and striving (not *quite* honestly) to feel more so !   Ride to London, all night and all day (I think),—Trades-Union people out processioning (" Help *us ;* what is your sublime Reform Bill else ? " thought they,—and I, gravely saluting one body of them, I remember, and getting grave response from the leader of them).   At sight of London I remember humming to myself a ballad-stanza of *Johnnie o' Braidislea* which my dear old Mother used to sing.

> " For there's seven Foresters in yon Forest ;
> And them I want to see, see,
> And them I want to *see* " (and shoot down) I

Lodged at Ampton Street again ; immense stretches of walking in search of houses.   Camden Town once ; Primrose Hill and its bright dwarfed population in the distance ; Chelsea ; Leigh Hunt's huggermugger, etc. etc.—What is the use of recollecting all that ?

Her arrival I best of all remember : ah me !   She was clear for *this* poor house (which she gradually, as poverty a little withdrew after long years of pushing, has made so beautiful

down with me to Dumfries, was the first of the partings ; that with my dear Mother next day, with poor Mary at Annan, with my two Brothers Alick and Jamie : all these things *were* to be done.   Shall we meet again ; shall our meeting again be for good ?   God grant it !   We are in His hands : this is all the comfort I have.   As to my beloved and now aged Mother, it is sore upon me, so sore as I have felt nothing of the kind since boyhood.   She paid her last visit to Craigenputtock the week before, and had attached me much (if I could have been more attached) by her quiet way of taking that sore trial : she studied not to sink *my* heart, she shed no tear at parting ;—and so I drove off with poor Alick, in quest of new fortunes.   May the Father of All, to whom she daily prays for me, be ever near her !   May He, if it be His will, grant us a glad re-meeting ;—and oh ! if there were an everlasting re-meeting, the reunion in a higher country— ! —But no more of this : words are worse than vain. . . . At Shillahill Bridge the good Alick was waiting for me with his fresh horse : that is one little thing I shall *never* forget, slight as it looks and was.—They are all good to me ; how good, and over good ! "—Carlyle's *Journal.*

and comfortable) in preference to all my other samples : and *here* we spent our two-and-thirty years of hard battle against Fate ; hard but not quite unvictorious, when she left me, as in her car of heaven's fire. My noble one ! I say deliberately *her* part in the stern battle, and except myself none knows how stern, was brighter, and braver than my own. Thanks, Darling for your shining words and acts, which were continual in my eyes, and in no other mortal's. Worthless I was your divinity ; wrapt in your perpetual love of me and pride in me, in defiance of all men and things. Oh was it not beautiful, all this that I have lost forever ! And I was Thomas the *Doubter*, the Unhoping ; till now the only Half-believing, in myself and my priceless opulences !—At my return from Annandale, after *French Revolution*,[1] she so cheerily recounted to me all the good " items ; " item after item, " Oh, it has had a great success, Dear ! "—to no purpose ; and at length beautifully lost patience with me for my incredulous humour. My life has not wanted at any time what I used to call ' *desperate* hope ' to all lengths ; but of common ' *hoping* hope ' it has had but little ; and has been shrouded since youthhood (almost since boyhood, for my school-years, at Annan, were very miserable, harsh, barren and worse) in continual gloom and grimness, as of a man set too nakedly *versus* the Devil and all men. Could I be easy to live with ? She flickered round me, like perpetual radiance ; and in spite of my glooms and my misdoings, would at no moment cease to love me and help me. What of bounty too is in Heaven!

[*Monday, June* 4, 1866. Yesterday all spent against my will in foreign talk : " National Portrait Exhibition " (Tyndall's kindness), American Pike (Belgian Minister), Mazzini (kind and sad) etc. etc. : At midnight, alone upon the streets, I felt only gloomier and sorer than ever,—as if *she* had been defrauded of my thoughts every instant they had been away from her.]

We proceeded all through Belgrave Square hither, with our Servant, our looser luggage, ourselves and a little canary bird (" Chico " which she had brought with her from Craigenputtock) ; one hackney coach rumbling on with us all. Chico, in Belgrave Square, burst into singing, which we took as a good omen. We were all of us striving to be cheerful (she needed no effort of striving) : but we " had burnt our ships," and at bottom the case was grave. I don't remember our arriving at this door ;

---

[1] The *French Revolution* was published in early summer 1837 ; the *Diamond Necklace, Mirabeau,* and *Parliamentary History of the French Revolution* were also published in that year.

but I do the cheerful Gypsy life we had here among the litter and carpenters, for three incipient days.[1] Leigh Hunt was in the next street, sending kind *un*practical messages ; in the evenings, I think, personally coming in ; we had made acquaintance with him (properly he with us), just before leaving in Spring 1832. Huggermugger was the type of his Economics, in all respects, financial and other ; but he was himself a pretty man, in clean cotton nightgown,[2] and with the airiest kindly style of sparkling talk,—wanting only wisdom of a sound kind, and true insight into fact. A great want !

I remember going with my Dear One (and Eliza Miles, the " Daughter " of Ampton Street, as escort), to some dim ironmonger's shop, to buy kettles and pans, on the thriftiest of fair terms. How noble and more than royal is the look of that to me now, and of my Royal One then ! California is dross and dirt to the experiences I have had.— —A tinderbox with steel and flint was part of our outfit (incredible as it may seem at this date) : I could myself burn rags into tinder ; and I have groped my way to the kitchen, in sleepless nights, to strike a light, for my pipe, in that manner. . . . *Chico* got a Wife by and by (Oh the wit there was about that and its sequels), produced two bright yellow young ones, who, so soon as they were fledged, got out into the trees of the garden, and vanished towards swift destruction ; upon which, villain Chico finding his poor wife fallen so tattery and ugly, took to pecking a hole in her head ; pecked it, and killed her : by and by ending his own disreputable life. I had begun *The French Revolution* (trees at that time before our window—a tale by these too on her part) : infinitesimal little matters of that kind hovered round me like bright fireflies, irradiated by *her* light ! Breakfast, early, was in the back part of this ground-floor room ; details of gradual intentions etc. as to *French Revolution*, advices, approval or criticism, always beautifully wise, and so soft and loving, had they even been foolish !

We were not at all unhappy during those three years of *French Revolution ;* at least she was not ; her health perhaps being better than mine, which latter was in a strangely painful, and as if conflagrated condition towards the end. She had made the house " a little Eden round her " (so neat and graceful in its

---

[1] " 5 *Great Cheyne Row, Chelsea ; Friday,* 21*st June* 1834. Adventures enough, seeking Houses ; ups and downs ; cross-purposes, good-fortunes ; at length a glad meeting with my Wife, a house got, and all well that ends well. We have been here since Tuesday gone a week."—Carlyle's *Journal.*

[2] *Nightgown* in its old sense, equivalent to the modern Dressing-gown.

simplicity and thrifty poverty) ; " little Paradise round you,"
—those were Edward Irving's words to her, on his visit to us ;
short affectionate visit, the first and the last (October [1] 1834) ;
on horseback, just about setting off for Glasgow, where he died,
December following : I watched him till at the corner of Cook's
Grounds,[2] he vanished, and we never saw him more. Much
consulting about him we had already had : a *Letter* to Henry
Drummond (about delivering him from the fools and fanatics
that were agitating him to death, as I clearly saw) lay on the
mantelpiece here for some days, in doubt, and was then burnt.
Brother, Father, rational Friend, I could not think of, except
Henry ; and him I had seen only once, not without clear view
of his unsoundness too. Practically we had long ago had to
take leave of poor Irving : but we both knew him well, and all
his *brotherhoods* to us first and last, and mourned him in our
hearts as a lost Hero. Nobler men I have seen few if any, till
the foul gulfs of London Pulpit-Popularity sucked him in, and
tragically swallowed him.

We were beginning to find a " friend " or two here ; that is,
an eligible acquaintance,—none as yet very dear to us, though
several brought a certain pleasure. Leigh Hunt was here
almost nightly, three or four times a week, I should reckon ;—
he came always neatly dressed, was thoroughly courteous,
friendly of spirit, and talked—like a singing bird. Good
insight, plenty of a kind of humour too ;—I remember little
warbles in the turns of his fine voice which were full of fun and
charm. We gave him Scotch Porridge to supper (" nothing
in nature so interesting and delightful ") ; *she* played him Scotch
tunes ; a man he to understand and feel them well. His talk
was often enough (perhaps at first oftenest) Literary-Bio-
graphical, Autobiographical, wandering into Criticism, *Reform
of Society*, Progress, etc. etc.,—on which latter points he gradually found me very shocking (I believe,—so fatal to his rose-
coloured visions on the subject). An innocent-hearted, but
misguided, in fact rather foolish, *un*practical and often much-
suffering man. John Mill was another steady visitor (had by
this time introduced his Mrs. Taylor too,—a very Will-o'-
wispish " Iridescence " of a creature ; meaning nothing bad
either). She at first considered my Jane to be a rustic spirit

[1] Not in October.—" Irving gone on a journey ; very unhealthy ; was
here one day : but departed, I know not whither, when I called. Another
Opfer der Zeit."—Carlyle's *Journal*, 8th September 1834.
[2] Street at the top of Cheyne Row, Chelsea.

fit for rather tutoring and twirling about when the humour took her ; but got taught better (to her lasting memory) before long. Mill was very useful about *French Revolution ;* [1] lent me all his Books, which were quite a Collection on that subject ; gave me, frankly, clearly and with zeal, all his better knowledge than my own (which was pretty frequently of some use in this or the other detail) : being full of eagerness for such an advocate in that cause as he felt I should be. His evenings here were sensibly agreeable for most part. Talk rather wintry (" *saw-dust* "-ish, as old Sterling once called it) ; but always well-informed and sincere. The Mrs. Taylor business was becoming more and more of questionable benefit to him (we could see), but on that subject we were strictly silent ; and he was very pretty still. For several years he came hither, and walked with me every Sunday,—Dialogues fallen all dim, except that they were never in the least genial to me, and that I took them as one would wine where no nectar is to be had,—or even thin ale where no wine. *Her* view of him was very kindly, though precisely to the same effect. How well do I still remember that night when he came to tell us, pale as Hector's ghost, that my unfortunate First Volume was burnt ! [2] It was like *half*

1 " The First Book of that *French Revolution* is finished some three weeks ago : I, after a pause spent in reading etc., have begun the Second. . . . Soul and body both very *sick ;* yet I have a kind of sacred defiance : *trötzend das Schicksal.* It has become clear to me that I *have* honestly more force and faculty in me than belong to the most I see ; also it was always clear that no honestly exerted force can be utterly lost ; were it long years after I am dead, in regions far distant from this, under names far distant from thine, the seed thou sowest will spring. The great difficulty is to keep one's own *self* in right balance : not despondent, not exasperated, defiant ; free and clear. O for faith ! Food and raiment thou hast never lacked, and shalt not.

" Nevertheless it is now some three and twenty months since I have earned one penny by my craft of Literature : be this recorded as a fact and document of the Literary History of this time. I have been *ready* to work ; I am abler than ever to work ; know no fault I have committed : and yet so it stands. To *ask* able Editors to employ you will not improve but worsen the matter : you are like a Spinster waiting to be married ; one knows how she has to behave ! I have some serious thoughts of quitting this Periodical Craft one good time for all : *it* is not synonymous with a life of wisdom ; when want is approaching one must have done with whims. If Literature will refuse me both bread and a stomach to digest bread with, then surely the case is growing clear."—Carlyle's *Journal,* 7th February 1835.

2 " Last night at tea, Mill's rap was heard at the door : he entered pale unable to speak ; gasped out to my Wife to go down and speak with Mrs. Taylor ; and came forward (led by my hand, and astonished looks) the very picture of desperation. After various inarticulate and articulate utterances to merely the same effect, he informs me that my First Volume (left out by him in too careless a manner, after or while reading it) was

sentence of death to us both; and we had to pretend to take it lightly, so dismal and ghastly was *his* horror at it, and try to talk of other matters. He staid three mortal hours or so; his departure quite a relief to us. Oh the burst of sympathy my poor Darling then gave me; flinging her arms round my neck, and openly lamenting, condoling, and encouraging like a nobler second self! Under Heaven is nothing beautifuller. We sat talking till late; " *shall* be written again," my fixed word and resolution to her. Which proved to be such a task as I never tried before or since. I wrote out *Feast of Pikes* (vol. ii.), and then went at it,—found it fairly *impossible* for about a fortnight; passed three weeks (reading Marryat's novels), tried, cautious-cautiously, as on ice paper-thin, once more; and in short had a job more like breaking my heart than any other in my experience. Jeannie, alone of beings, burnt like a steady lamp beside me. I forget how much of money we still had: I think there was at first something like £300; perhaps £280 to front London with. Nor can I in the least remember where we had gathered such a sum;—except that it was our own, no part of it borrowed or *given* us by anybody. " Fit to last till *French Revolution* is ready ! "—and she had no misgivings at all. Mill was penitently liberal: sent me £200 (in a day or two), of which I kept £100 (actual cost of house while I had written burnt volume); upon which he bought me *Biographie Universelle*, which I got bound, and still have. Wish I could find a way of getting the now much macerated, changed, and fanaticised " John Stuart Mill " to take that £100 back; but I fear there is no way !

How my Incomparable One contrived to beat out these exiguous resources into covering the appointed space I cannot

except four or five bits of leaves *irrevocably* ANNIHILATED ! I remember and can still remember less of it than of anything I ever wrote with such toil : *it* is gone ; the whole world and myself backed by it could not bring that back : nay the old spirit too is fled. I find it took five months of steadfast, occasionally excessive, and always sickly and painful toil.— Mill very injudiciously staid with us till late ; and I had to make an effort and speak, as if indifferent, about other common matters ; he left us however in a *relapsed* state ; one of the pitiablest.—My dear Wife has been very kind and become dearer to me. The night has been full of emotion ; occasionally sharp pain (something cutting or hard-grasping me round the heart), occasionally with sweet consolations. I dreamed of my Father and Sister Margaret ; alive, yet all defaced with the sleepy stagnancy, swollen hebetude of the Grave,—and again dying in some strange rude country : a horrid dream ! The painfullest too is when you first wake. But, on the whole, should I not thank the Unseen ? for I was not driven out of composure, hardly for moments. ' Walk humbly with thy God.' How I longed for some Psalm or Prayer that I could have *uttered ;* that my loved ones would have joined me in ! But there was none : silence had to be my language."—Carlyle's *Journal,* 7th March 1835.

now see, nor did I then know : but in the like of that, as in her other tasks, she was silently successful always, and never, that I saw, had a misgiving about success.   There would be some trifling increments from *Fraser's Magazine*, perhaps (*Diamond Necklace*, etc. were probably of those years) ; but the *guess* stated above is the nearest I can now come to, and I don't think is in defect of the actuality.—I was very diligent, very desperate (" desperate *hope !* "),—wrote my two (folio) pages (perhaps four or five of print) day by day : then about two P.M. walked out ; always heavy-laden, grim of mood ; sometimes with a feeling not rebellious or impious against God Most High, but otherwise too similar to Satan's stepping the burning marle. Some conviction I had that the Book was worth something,— a pretty constant persuasion that it was not I that could make it better.   Once or twice among the flood of equipages at Hyde-Park Corner, I recollect sternly thinking : " Yes ; and perhaps none of *you* could do what I am at ! "   But generally my feeling was, " I will finish this Book, throw it at your feet ; buy a rifle and spade, and withdraw to the Transatlantic Wildernesses,—far from human beggaries and basenesses ! "   This had a kind of comfort to me ; yet I always knew too, in the background, that this would not practically do.   In short, my nervous-system had got dreadfully irritated and inflamed before I quite ended ; and my desire was *intense*, beyond words, to have done with it.   The *last* paragraph I well remember writing : upstairs in the drawing-room that now is, which was then my writing-room ; beside *her* there, in a gray evening (summer I suppose), soon after tea perhaps ;—and thereupon, with her dear blessing on me, going out to walk.   I had said before going out, " What they will do with this Book, none knows, my Jeannie, lass ; but they have not had, for a two hundred years, any Book that came more truly from a man's very heart ; and so let them trample it under foot and hoof as *they* see best ! " " Pooh, pooh ; they cannot trample that ! " she would cheerily answer ; for her own approval (I think she had read always regularly behind me), especially in vol. iii., was strong and decided.[1]

1 Carlyle, after a long interval in which he wrote nothing in his *Journal*, says—" Not a word written here till now.   Jane fell sick (to the degree of terrifying me) in the saddest circumstances every way, directly after " the last entry in the *Journal*, 21st March 1837.   " Ah me, ever since, it has been unpleasant for me to speak.   Lectures on ' German Literature ' (save the mark !) in the first weeks of May : horrid misery of that, in my then state of nerves !   Book *French Revolution* out about the 1st of June.

We knew the Sterlings by this time, John, and all of them.
Old Sterling very often here ; knew Henry Taylor,[1] etc., the
Wilsons of Eccleston Street, Rev. Mr. Dunn, etc. etc. ; and the
waste wilderness of London was becoming a peopled garden to
us, in some measure, especially to *her*, who had a frank welcome
to every sort of worth and even kindly-singularity in her fellow-
creatures, such as I could at no time rival.

Sprinklings of Foreigners, " Political Refugees," had already
begun to come about us ; to me seldom of any interest, except
for the foreign instruction to be gathered from them (if any),
and the curiosity attached to their foreign ways. Only two of
them had the least charm to me as men : Mazzini whom, I
remember, Mr. Taylor, Mrs. Taylor's (ultimately Mrs. Mill's)
then Husband, an innocent dull good man, brought in to me one
evening ; and Godefroi Cavaignac, whom my Jane had met
somewhere, and thought worth inviting. Mazzini I once or
twice talked with ; recognisably a most valiant, faithful,
considerably gifted and noble soul ; but hopelessly given up to
his Republicanisms, his " Progress," and other Rousseau
fanaticism, for which I had at no time the least credence, or
any considerable respect amid my pity.[2] We soon tired of one
another, Mazzini and I ; and he fell mainly to *her* share ; off
and on, for a good many years, yielding her the charm of a
sincere mutual esteem, and withal a good deal of occasional
amusement from his curious bits of Exile London and Foreign-
life, and his singular Italian-English modes of locution now and
then. For example,—Petrucci having quenched his own fiery
chimney one day, and escaped the fine (as he hoped), " there

Jane's mother here : I off to Scotland by Hull, Leeds, etc., on the 20th of
that month ; where I lay like one buried alive till the middle of September,
when I returned hither, in a kind of dead-alive state, for which there was
no *name*,—of which there was no writing. Why chronicle it ? The late
long effort has really almost killed me. Not the writing of the Book ; but
the writing of it amid such sickness, poverty and despair. The ' reception ' of it, every one says, is good and *so* good : it may be so ; but to
me the blessing of blessings is that *I* am free of it."—Carlyle's *Journal*,
15th November 1837.

   [1] Author of *Philip van Artevelde*, etc., afterwards Sir Henry Taylor.
He died March 1886. See Paper on Wordsworth, *infra*, vol. ii., for notice
of him.

   [2] " Yesterday took leave of Mazzini, who is just about returning permanently to Rome, to publish a Newspaper there. I had not seen him
for a long time : we talked for about an hour, in a cordial and sincere way,
with real emotion (I do believe) on both sides ; and parted, hardly expecting, either of us, to meet again in this world. Mournfully tender, mournfully sublime even, I might call the event to me in the days that now are.
Mazzini is the most *pious* living man I now know."—Carlyle's *Journal*,
8th February 1871.

came to pass a Sweep," with finer nose in the solitary street, who
involved him again.   Or, " *Ma, mio caro, non v'è ci un morto !* "
which, I see, she has copied into her poor little book of *notabilia*.[1]
Her reports of these things to me, as we sat at breakfast or
otherwise, had a tinkle of the finest mirth in them, and in short
a beauty and felicity I have never seen surpassed.   Ah me,
ah me, *whither* fled ?

Cavaignac was considerably more interesting to both of us.
A fine Bayard soul (with figure to correspond), a man full of
seriousness and of genial gaiety withal ; of really fine faculties,
and of a politeness (especially towards women) which was
curiously elaborated into punctiliousness, yet sprang everywhere
from frank nature.   A man very pleasant to converse with,
walk with, or see drop in on an evening, and lead you or follow
you far and wide over the world of intellect and humanly recorded
fact.   A Republican to the bone, but a " Bayard " in that
vesture (if only Bayard had wit and fancy at command).   We
had many dialogues while *French Revolution* struggled through
its last two volumes ; Cavaignac freely discussing with me,
accepting kindly my innumerable dissents from him, and on
the whole elucidating many little points to me.   Punctually
on the *jour de l'an*, came some little gift to her, frugal yet
elegant ; and I have heard him say with a mantling joyous
humour overspreading that sternly sad French face, " *Vous
n'êtes pas Écossaise, Madame ; désormais vous serez Française !* "
I think he must have left us in 1843 ; he and I rode, one summer
forenoon, to Richmond and back (some old *Bonapartist* Colonel
married out there, dull ignorant loud fellow to my feeling) ;
country was beautiful, air balmy, ride altogether *ditto ditto* I
don't remember speaking with him again : " going to Paris
this week " or so, he (on unconditional amnesty, not on con-
ditional like all the others).   He returned once, or indeed twice,
during the three years he still lived : but I was from home the
last time, both of us the first (at Newby Cottage, Annan, oh
dear !)—and I saw him no more.   The younger Brother (" *President* " in 1849 etc.) I had often heard of from him, and learned to
esteem on evidence given, but never saw.   I take him to have
been a second *Godefroi* probably, with less gift of social utterance,
but with a soldier's breeding in return.

1 An undertaker applying to the wrong house, explained to Mazzini,
who had opened the door to him, that he had come with " the coffin."
To which Mazzini answered, with animation, " But, my dear, there is
not here a *Dead !* "

One autumn, and perhaps another, I recollect her making a tour with the elder Sterlings (Thunderer and Wife), which, in spite of the hardships to one so delicate, she rather enjoyed. Thunderer she had at her apron-string, and brought many a comical pirouette out of him from time to time. Good Mrs. Sterling really loved her, and *vice versâ ;* a luminous household circle that to us :—as may be seen in *Life of Sterling,* more at large.

Of money from *French Revolution* I had *here* as yet got absolutely nothing ; Emerson in America, by an edition of his *there,* sent me £150 [1] (" pathetic ! " was her fine word about it ; " but never mind, Dear ") ; after some three years grateful England (through poor scrubby but correctly arithmetical Fraser) £100 ; and I don't remember when, some similar munificence : but I now (and indeed not till recent years do I) see it had been, as *she* called it, " a great *success,*" and greatish of its kind. Money I did get somewhere honestly, Articles in *Fraser,* in poor Mill's (considerably hidebound) *London Review ; Edinburgh* I think was *out* for me before this time. *London Review* was at last due to the charitable faith of young Sir William Molesworth, a poorish narrow creature, but an ardent believer in Mill *Père* (James) and Mill *Fils :* " How much will your Review take to launch it then ? " asked he (all other Radical believers being so close of fist)—" Say £4000," answered Mill. " Here, then," writing a cheque for that amount, rejoined the other. My private (altogether private) feeling, I remember, was, that they could, with profit, have employed me much more extensively in it ; perhaps even (though of this I was candid enough to doubt) made me Editor of it, let me *try* it for a couple of years,—worse I could not have succeeded than poor Mill himself did as Editor

---

[1] " Yesterday came a Letter from Emerson at Concord, New England, informing me that the volumes of *Miscellanies* will be ready by and by ; and—enclosing me a draft for £100, the produce of my *French Revolution* there ! Already £50 had come ; this is £150 in all ; not a farthing having yet been realised *here* by our English bibliopoly. It is very strange this American occurrence ; very gratifying : nothing more so has occurred in the history of my economics. Thanks to the kind friends across the salt waters yonder ! ... This American cash is so welcome *because* I am so poor. Had I been rich, I could not have had that pleasure. *Sic de multis ;* I must own it, bitterly as I often grumble over my poverty. On the whole I shall rejoice to *have been* poor, if in my old days I be not still prosecuted and dogged by the spectre of absolute indigence : that, surely, is ill to bear. —I find too, had this £100 been £1000, it would at bottom have made little difference. What if Fate, as thrifty mothers do, were reserving her sweet condiment till towards the *latter part* of the repast, and giving it out always more liberally the nearer we get to the end ! It were the kindest way of all perhaps."—Carlyle's *Journal,* 6th February 1839.

(*sawdust* to the masthead, and a croakery of crawling things, instead of a speaking by men) ; but I whispered to none but *her* the least hint of all this : and oh, how glad am I now, and for long years back, that apparently nothing of it ever came to the thoughts or the dreams of Mill and Co. ! For I should surely have accepted of it, had the terms been at all tolerable. I had plenty of *Radicalism*, and have, and to all appearance shall have ; but the opposite hemisphere (which never was wanting either, nor will be, as it miserably is in Mill and Co.) had not yet found itself summoned by the trumpet of Time and his Events (1848 : study of *Oliver* etc.) into practical emergence, and emphasis and prominence as now. " Ill luck," take it quietly ; you never are sure but it may be *good* and the *best*.[1]

Our main revenue for perhaps three, or four years (?) now was *Lectures ;*[2] in Edward Street, Portman Square, the only free *room* there was ; earnestly forwarded by Miss and Thomas Wilson, of Eccleston Street (who still live and are good), by Miss Martineau, by Henry Taylor, Frederick Elliot, etc. etc. Brought in, on the average, perhaps £200, for a month's labour : first of them must have been in 1838, I think,—Willis's Rooms, this. " Detestable mixture of Prophecy and Play-actorism," as I sorrowfully defined it : nothing could well be hatefuller to me ; but I was obliged. And she, oh she was my Angel, and unwearied helper and comforter in all that ; how we drove together, poor Two, to our place of execution ; she with a little drop of brandy to give me at the very last,—and shone round me like a bright *aureola*, when all else was black and chaos ! God reward thee, Dear One ; now when I cannot even own my debt. Oh why do we *delay* so much, till Death makes it impossible ? And don't I continue it still with others ? Fools, fools ; we forget that it *has* to end ; lo this *has* ended, and it is such an astonishment to me ; so sternly undeniable, yet as it were incredible !—

---

1 " Mill, I discern, has given Fox the Editorship of that Molesworth Periodical ; seems rather ashamed of it. *A la bonne heure :* is it not probably *better* so ? Trust in God and in thyself ! O could I but ; all *else* were so light, so trivial."—Carlyle's *Journal*, 12th August 1834.

2 There were four Courses of Lectures, the dates of which are as follows, viz.—

    I.   In 1837, Six Lectures on German Literature.
    II. In 1838, Twelve Lectures on the History of Literature, or the Successive Periods of European Culture.
    III. In 1839, Six Lectures on the Revolutions of Modern Europe.
    IV. In 1840, Six Lectures on Heroes and Hero-worship.
    Only the Last Course, *Heroes*, was ever published.

It must have been in this 1838 that her Mother first came to
see us here.[1] I remember giving each of them a sovereign, from
a pocketful of *odd* which I had brought home,—greatly to satisfaction especially of Mrs. Welsh, who I doubt not bought something pretty and symbolic with it. She came perhaps three
times : on one of the later times was that of the " One Soirée,"
with the wax-candles on Mother's part,—and subsequent
remorse on Daughter's. " Burn these last two, on the night
when I lie dead ! " [2] Like a stroke of lightning this has gone
through my heart, cutting and yet healing. *Sacred* be the name
of it ; its praise *silent*. Did I elsewhere meet in the world a soul
so direct from the Empyrean ? My dear old Mother was perhaps equally pious, in the Roman sense, in the British she was
much more so : but starry flashes of this kind she had not,—
from her education etc., could not.

[*June* 6. Surely this is very idle work,—the rather if it is all
to be burnt ! But nothing else yields me any solace at all, in
those days. I will continue it to-morrow. Poor Tablet[3] or
memorial due to me from the lapidary, this day fortnight, at
farthest, surely.]

[*June* 7.] By this time we were getting noticed by select
individuals of the Aristocracy ; and were what is called " rather
rising in society." Ambition that way my Jane never had;
but she took it always as a something of honour done to *me*, and
had her various bits of satisfaction in it. The Spring-Rices
(Lords Monteagle afterwards) were probably the first of their
class that ever asked me out as a distinguished thing. I remember their flunkey arriving here with an express while we were at
dinner ; I remember, too, their Soirée itself in Downing Street,
and the καλοὶ and καλαὶ (as I called them) with their state and
their effulgences, as something new and entertaining to me.
The Stanleys (of Alderley), through the Bullers, we had long since
known, and still know ; but that I suppose was still mostly
theoretic,—or perhaps I *had* dined there, and seen the Hollands
(Lord and Lady), the etc. (as I certainly did ultimately), but
not been judged eligible, or both catchable and eligible ? To me
I can recollect (except what of snob ambition there might be in
me, which I hope was not very much, though for certain it was
not quite wanting either !), there was nothing of charm in any of
them : old Lady Holland I viewed even with aversion, as a kind
of hungry " ornamented witch," looking over at me with merely

---

[1] It was in September 1835.   [2] See *infra*, p. 167.
[3] See *infra*, p. 122 *n*.

carnivorous views (and always questioning her Dr. Allen, when I said anything) ; nor was it till years after (Husband, Allen, etc. all dead) that I discovered remains of beauty in her, a pathetic situation, and distinguished qualities. My Jane I think knew still less of her : in her house neither my Jane nor I ever was. At Marshall's (millionaire of Leeds, and an excellent man, who much esteemed me, and once gave me a horse for health's sake) we had ample assemblages, shining enough in their kind ;—but *she*, I somehow think, probably for saving the cost of " fly " (oh my Queen, *mine* and a true one !), was not so often there as I. On the whole, that too was a thing to be gone through in our career ; and it had its bits of benefits, bits of instructions etc. etc. ; but also its temptations, intricacies, tendencies to vanity etc., to waste of time and faculty ; and in a better sphere of arrangement, would have been a 'game not worth the candle.' Certain of the Aristocracy, however, did seem to me still very *noble ;* and, with due elimination of the grossly worthless (none of whom had we to do with), I should vote at present that, of *classes* known to me in England, the Aristocracy (with its perfection of human politeness, its continual grace of bearing and of acting, steadfast " honour," light address and cheery *stoicism*, if you see *well* into it), is actually yet the best of English Classes.[1] Deep in it *we* never were, promenaders on the shore rather ; but I have known it too, and formed deliberate judgment as above. My Dear One, in theory, did not go so far (I think) in that direction,—in fact was not at the pains to form much " theory ; " but no eye in the world was quicker than hers for individual specimens ;—and to the last she had a great pleasure in consorting more or less with the select of these : Lady William Russell, Dowager Lady Sandwich, Lady etc. etc. (and not in over-quantity). I remember, at first sight of the *first* Lady Ashburton [2] (who was far from regularly

---

[1] " At Alverstoke " (Bay House, The Hon. H. B. Baring's), " in January last,—for the third time now,—and very full of *suffering* in all ways there. Have seen a good deal of the higher ranks, plenty of lords, politicians, fine ladies, etc. etc.—certainly a new *top-dressing* for me that ; nor attainable either without peril : let me see if any *growth* will come of it, and what.— The most striking conclusion to me is, How *like* all men of all ranks in England (and doubtless in every land) intrinsically are to one another. Our Aristocracy, I rather take it, are the *best*, or as good as any class we have ; but their position is fatally awry,—their whole breeding and way of life, ' To go gracefully idle ' (most tragically *so*), and which of them can mend it ? "—Carlyle's *Journal*, 8th February 1848.

[2] Properly, the second Lady Ashburton, first Wife of the second Lord Ashburton.—For a good many years the friendship of Lord and Lady Ashburton was Carlyle's best social resource. He held both in highest

beautiful, but was probably the *chief* of all these great ladies), she said of her to me, " Something in her like a Heathen Goddess ! "—which was a true reading, and in a case not plain at all, but oftener mistaken than rightly taken.

Our first visit to Addiscombe together : a bright summer Sunday ; we walked (*thrift*, I daresay, ah me !) from the near Railway Station ; and my poor Jeannie grew very tired and disheartened, though nothing ill came ; I had been there several times, and she had seen the Lady here (and called her " Heathen Goddess " to me) : this time I had at once joined the company under the shady trees, on their beautiful lawn ; and my little woman, in few minutes, her dress all adjusted, came stepping out, round the corner of the house,—with such a look of lovely innocency, modesty, ingenuousness, gracefully suppressed timidity, and radiancy of native cleverness, intelligence, and dignity, towards the great ladies and great gentlemen ; it seems to me at this moment, I have never seen a more beautiful expression of a human face. Oh my Dearest ; my Dearest that cannot now know how dear ! There are glimpses of Heaven too given us on this Earth, though sorely drowned in terrestrial vulgarities, and sorely " flamed-on from the Hell beneath " too. This must have been about 1843 or so ?

A year or two before, going to see her Mother, she had landed in total wreck of sea-sickness (miserable always at sea, but had taken it as cheapest doubtless)—and been brought up almost speechless, and set down at the Queensberry Arms Inn, Annan. Having no maid, no sign but of trouble and (unprofitable) ladyhood, they took her to a remote bedroom, and left her to her solitary shifts there. Very painful to me, yet beautiful and with a noble pathos in it, to look back upon (from her narrative of it) here and now ! How Mary, my poor but ever faithful " Sister Mary," came to her (on notice), *her* resources few, but her heart overflowing ; could hardly get admittance to the Flunkey

regard. At the time of Lady Ashburton's death he made the following entry in his *Journal* :—

" Monday, 4th May, 4½ P.M., at Paris, died Lady Ashburton : a great and irreparable sorrow to me ; yet with some beautiful consolations in it too. A thing that fills all my mind, since yesterday afternoon that Milnes came to me with the sad news,—which I had never once anticipated, though warned sometimes vaguely to do so. God ' sanctify my sorrow,' as the pious old phrase went ! To her I believe it is a great gain, and the exit has in it much of noble beauty as well as pure sadness,—worthy of such a woman. Adieu, adieu ! "—6th May 1857. On the same day, Lord Ashburton wrote to Carlyle : " She has left me an inheritance of great price, the love of those who loved her. I claim that of you, in her name ; and I am sure it will be rendered to me."

House of Entertainment at all ; got it, however, had a " pint of sherry " with her, had this and that, and perhaps on the third day, got her released from the base place ; of which that is my main recollection now, when I chance to pass it, in its now dim enough condition. Perhaps this was about 1840 ; Mary's husband (now Farmer at the Gill, not a clever man, but a diligent and good-natured) was then a " Carter with two Horses " in Annan,—gradually becoming unable to live in that poor capacity there. They had both been Craigenputtock figures. . . . She loved Mary for her kind-heartedness ; admired and respected her skill and industry in Domestic management of all kinds ; and often contrasted to me her perfect talent in that way, compared to Sister Jean's, who intellectually was far the superior (and had once been her own Pupil and Protégée, about the time we left Comley Bank ; always very kind and grateful to her since, too, but never such a favourite as the other). Mary's Cottage was well known to me too, as I came home by the Steamer, on my visits, and was often riding down to bathe etc. These visits, " once a year to my Mother," were pretty faithfully paid ; and did my *heart* always some good ; but for the rest were unpleasantly chaotic (especially when my poor old Mother, worthiest and dearest of simple hearts, became incapable of management by her own strength, and of almost all enjoyment even from me) : I persisted in them to the last, as did my Woman ; but I think they comprised for both of us (such skinless creatures), in respect of outward *physical* hardship, an amount larger than all the other items of our then life put together.

How well I remember the dismal evening, when we had got word of her Mother's dangerous crisis of illness (a *Stroke*, in fact, which ended it) ; and her wildly impressive look, laden as if with resolution, affection and prophetic woe, while she sat in the railway carriage and rolled away from me into the dark. " Poor, poor Jeannie " thought I ; and yet my sympathy how paltry and imperfect was it to what hers would have been for me ! Stony-hearted ; shame on me ! She was stopped at Liverpool, by news of the *worst ;* I found her sharply wretched, on my following,—and had a strange two or three months, slowly settling everything at Templand ; the " last Country Spring," and my *first* for many long years. Bright, sad, solitary (letters from Lockhart etc.), nocturnal mountain heather-burning, by day the courses of the hail-storms from the mountains, how they came pouring down their respective valleys, deluge-like, and blotted out the sunshine etc. Spring of 1842.

[I ought to have copied my Mother-in-law's *epitaph* at least, or to send for it now to the Minister of Crawford in Clydesdale. Stop to-day ; or even altogether ? No ; can't.]

I find it was in 1842 (20th February) that my poor Mother-in-law died.[1] Wild night for me from Liverpool, through Dumfries (Sister Jean out with tea, etc.), arrived at waste Templand (only John Welsh etc. there ; funeral quite over) : all this and the lonesome, sad, but not unblessed three months almost which I spent there, is still vividly in my mind. I was for trying to keep Templand once, as a summer refuge for us,—one of the most picturesque of locations ; but *her* filial heart abhorred the notion ; and I have never seen more than the chimney-tops of Templand since. Her grief, at my return and for months afterwards, was still poignant, constant :—and oh how inferior my sympathy with her, to what hers would have been with me ; woe on my dull hard ways in comparison ! To her Mother she had been the kindest of Daughters ; life-rent of Craigenputtock settled frankly on her (and such effort to make it practically good to the letter when needful) ;—I recollect one gallop of hers, which Geraldine has not mentioned, gallop from Craigenputtock to Dumfries Bank, and thence to Templand at a stretch, with the half-year's rent, which our procrastinating Brother Alick seldom could or would be punctual with :[2] ah me, gallop which pierces my heart at this moment, and clothes my Darling with a sad radiancy to me. But she had many *remorses*, and indeed had been obliged to have manifold little collisions with her fine high-minded, but often fanciful and fitful Mother,—who was always a Beauty, too, and had whims and thin-skinned ways,

[1] " In February last my good Mother-in-law suddenly died. That will be an unforgettable February, March and April. My poor Wife hurrying off by the first mail-train the evening the Letter came ; in an agony of hope and terror towards Templand,—*too late*, as she found at Liverpool : my following in two days, by night outside the Coach (from Lancaster to Carlisle), and like a kind of ghost, through Annan, Dumfries, in that strange mood : my solitary abode in Templand till the spring storms went by, and the pale Sun had grown hot and strong when I returned. All this makes, in several ways, a new chapter in our history here. My poor Wife has been in deep distress, and is yet, though thank Heaven recovering now. I went to Crawford Churchyard, the wild spring tempests, the wild hills, Dalveen Pass and the lone Resting-place of her whose grave I went to see ! How much that is Heaven-high blended with the lowest things of Earth, lay in all that business for me. But there are no words."—Carlyle's *Journal*, 25th October 1842.

[2] " Alick has written that he cannot keep his farm Craigenputtock longer than Whitsunday, finding it a ruinous concern. . . . I often calculate that the land is all let some thirty *per cent* too high ; and that before it can be reduced the whole existing race of farmers must be ruined."—Carlyle to his Brother John, 21st August 1830.

distasteful enough to such a Daughter. All which, in cruel
aggravation (for all were really small, and had been ridiculous
rather than deep or important), now came remorsefully to mind,
and many of them, I doubt not, *staid.*—Craigenputtock lapsed
to *her*, in 1842, therefore ;—to me she had left the fee-simple of
it by will (in 1824, two years before our marriage),—as I remember she once told me *then*abouts, and never but once : Will
found, the other day, after some difficulty, since her own departure, and the death of any Welsh to whom she could have wished
me to bequeath it. To my kindred it has no relation, nor shall
it go to them : it is much a problem with me how I shall leave it
settled (" Bursaries for Edinburgh College ; " or *what* were best ?)
after my poor interest in it is over. Considerably a problem ;—
and what her wish in it would have actually been ? " Bursaries " had come into my own head, when we heard that poor
final young Welsh was in consumption ; but to her I never
mentioned it (" wait till the young man's *decease* do suggest it ! ")
—and now I have only hypothesis and guess.[1] She never liked
to speak of the thing, even on question (which hardly once or
twice ever rose) ;—and except on question, a stone was not more
silent. Beautiful queenlike woman : I did admire her complete
perfection on this head of the actual " dowry " she had now
brought ; £200 yearly or so,—which to us was a highly considerable sum,—and how she absolutely ignored it, and as it
were had not done it at all. Once or so I can dimly remember
telling her as much (thank God I did so), to which she answered
scarcely by a look, and certainly without word, except perhaps
" Tut ! "

Thus, from this date onward, we were a little richer, easier in
circumstances ; and the *pinch* of Poverty, which had been re-
laxing latterly, changed itself into a gentle *pressure*, or into a
limit and little more. We did not change our habits in any point,
but the grim collar round my neck was sensibly slackened.
Slackened, not removed at all,—for almost twenty years yet.
My Books were not, nor ever will be " popular," productive of
money to any but a contemptible degree : I had lost by the
death of Bookseller Fraser and change to Chapman and Hall ;
—in short, to judge by the running after me by *owls* of Minerva
in those times, and then to hear what day's-wages my Books

1 Carlyle bequeathed Craigenputtock to the University of Edinburgh ;
the income derived from it to be expended in Scholarships, called " The
John Welsh Bursaries." The " Deed of Mortification " (such is the Scotch
name for it) is mostly of Carlyle's writing ; it is characteristic and interesting,—the literary and the legal style made one by very slight touches.

brought me, would have astonished the owl mind! I do not think my literary income was above £200 a year in those decades, —in spite of my continual diligence day by day. *Cromwell* I must have *written*, I think, in 1844 ;[1] but for four years prior it had been a continual toil and misery to me. I forget what was the price of *Cromwell*, greater considerably than in any previous case ;—but the *annual* income was still somewhat as above. I had always £200 or £300 in bank, and continually forgot all about money. My Darling rolled it all over upon *me ;* cared not one straw about it ; only asked for assurance or promissory engagement from me, " *How* little, then ? " and never failed to make it liberally and handsomely do. Honour to her (beyond the ownership of California, I say now) ; and thanks to Poverty that showed me how noble, worshipful and dear she was.

In 1850, after an interval of deep gloom and bottomless dubitation, came *Latter-Day Pamphlets*, which unpleasantly astonished everybody ; set the world upon the strangest suppositions (" Carlyle got deep into whisky ! " said some), ruined my " reputation " (according to the friendliest voices), and, in effect, divided me altogether from the mob of " Progress-of-the-Species " and other vulgar,—but were a great relief to my own *conscience* as a faithful citizen, and have been ever since. My Darling gaily approved ; and we left the thing to take its own sweet will, with great indifferency and loyalty on our part. This did not help our incomings ; in fact I suppose it effectually hindered, and has done so *till quite recently*, any " progress " of ours in that desirable direction, though I did not find that the small steady sale of my Books was sensibly altered from year to year, but quietly stood where it used to be. Chapman (hard-fisted cautious Bibliopole) would not, for about ten years farther, go into any edition of my " Collected Works ; " I did once transiently propose it, once only ;—and remember being sometimes privately a good deal sulky towards the poor man for his judgment on that matter, though decided to leave him strictly to his own light in regard to it, and indeed to avoid him altogether when I had not clear business with him. The " recent return of popularity greater than ever," which I hear of, seems due alone to that late Edinburgh affair ; especially to the Edinburgh *Address ;*[2] and affords new proof of the singularly dark and feeble condition of " Public Judgment " at this time. No

---

[1] Published in December 1845.

[2] Inaugural Address, on his being installed as Lord Rector of the University there ; was delivered on the 2d of April 1866.

idea, or shadow of an idea, is in that Address, but what had been set forth by me tens of times before : and the poor gaping sea of Prurient Blockheadism receives it as a kind of inspired revelation; —and runs to buy my Books (it is said) now when I have got quite done with their buying or refusing to buy.   If they would give me £10,000 a year, and bray unanimously their *hosannahs* heaven-high for the rest of my life,—who *now* would there be to get the smallest joy or profit from it ?   To *me* I feel as if it would be a silent sorrow rather, and would bring me painful retrospections, nothing else.——On the whole, I feel often, as if poor England had really done its very kindest to me, after all. Friends not a few I do at last begin to see that I have had all along ; and these have all, or all but two or three, been decorously silent : enemies I cannot strictly find that I have had any (only blind blockheads running athwart me on their own errand); —and as for the speaking and criticising multitude, who regulate the paying ditto, I perceive that their labours on me have had a twofold result : 1°. That, after so much nonsense said, in all dialects, and so very little sense or real understanding of the matter, I have arrived at a point of indifferency towards all that, which is really very desirable to a human soul that will do well ; and 2°. That, in regard to money, and payment etc. in the money kind, it is essentially the same.   To a degree which, under *both* heads (if it were safe for me to estimate it), I should say was really a far nearer than common approach to completeness. And which, under both heads, so far as it *is* complete, means *victory*, and the very highest kind of " success " !   Thanks to poor anarchic crippled and bewildered England, then ; hasn't it done its very *best* for me, under disguised forms ; and seeming occasionally to do its *worst ?*   Enough of all that.   I had to say only that my dear little Helpmate, in regard to these things also, has been throughout as one sent from Heaven to me.   Never for a moment did she take to blaming England or the world on my behalf ; rather to quizzing my *despondencies* (if any) on that head, and the grotesque stupidities of England and the world : she cared little about Criticisms of me, good or bad ; but I have known her read, when such came to hand, the unfriendliest specimens with real amusement, if their stupidity was of the readable or amusing kind to bystanders.   *Her* opinion of me, it was curiously unalterable from the first !   In Edinburgh for example, in 1826 still, Bookseller Tait (a foolish goosey, innocent but very vulgar kind of mortal), " Oh Mrs. Carlyle, fine criticism in *The Scotsman ;* you will find it at, I think

you will find it at ——." "But what good will it do me?"
answered Mrs. Carlyle, with great good humour; to the
miraculous collapse of Tait, who stood (I dare say) with eyes
staring!

In 1844, late Autumn, I was first at the Grange for a few days
(doing d'Ewes's *Election to the Long Parliament*, I recollect);
she with me next year, I think; and there, or at Addiscombe,
Alverstoke, Bath House,[1] saw on frequent enough occasions, for
twelve years coming, or indeed for nineteen (till the second Lord
Ashburton's death), the choicest specimens of English Aristocracy; and had no difficulty in living with them on free and
altogether human terms, and learning from them by degrees
whatever *they* had to teach us. *Something* actually, though
perhaps not very much, and surely *not* the best. To me, I
should say, more than to her, came what lessons there were;
human friendships we also had; and she too was a favourite
with the better kind,—Lord Lansdowne, for example, had at
last discovered what she was; not without some amazement in
his old retrospective mind, I dare say! But to her the charm
of such circles was at all times insignificant; *human* was what
she looked at, and what she was, in all circles. *Ay de mi:* it is
a mingled yarn, all that of our "Aristocratic" History; and I
need not enter on it here. One evening, at Bath House, I saw
her, in a grand soirée, softly step up, and (unnoticed, as she
thought, by anybody) *kiss* the old Duke of Wellington's
shoulder![2] That perhaps was one of the prettiest things I ever

[1] The Grange and Bath House were residences of Lord Ashburton;
Addiscombe Farm and Alverstoke (Bay House), of his son, the Hon.
H. B. Baring, who succeeded to the title in 1848, and died in 1863.

[2] "By far the most interesting figure present was the old Duke of
Wellington, who appeared between twelve and one, and slowly glided
through the rooms. Truly a beautiful old man; I had never seen till
now how beautiful, and what an expression of graceful simplicity, veracity
and nobleness there is about the old hero, when you see him close at hand.
His very size had hitherto deceived me: he is a shortish, slightish figure,
about five feet eight: of good breadth however, and *all* muscle or bone;
—his legs I think must be the short part of him, for certainly on horseback
at least, I have always taken him to be tall. Eyes beautiful light-blue,
full of mild valour, with infinitely more faculty and geniality than I had
fancied before. The face wholly gentle, wise, valiant and venerable; the
voice too, as I again heard, is *aquiline*, a clear, perfectly equable (*uncracked*,
that is), and perhaps almost musical, but essentially *tenor* or even almost
treble voice. Eighty-two, I understand. He glided slowly along, slightly
saluting this and the other; clean, clear, fresh as the June evening itself;
till the silver-buckle of his stock vanished into the door of the next room
(to make, I suppose, *one* round of the place), and I saw him no more.
Except Dr. Chalmers I have not for many years seen so beautiful an old
man."—Carlyle's *Journal*, 25th June 1850.

saw there. Duke was then very old, and hitched languidly
about, speaking only when spoken to, some "Wow-*wow*,"
which perhaps had little real meaning in it : he had on his
Garter-order, his gold-buckle stock, and was very clean and
trim ; but except making appearance in certain evening parties,
half an hour in each, perhaps hardly knew what he was doing.
From Bath House, we saw his Funeral Procession,[1] a while
after ; and, to our disgust, in one of the Mourning Coaches,
some Official or Dignitary reading a Newspaper. The hearse
(seventeen tons of bronze), the arrangements generally, were
vulgar and disgusting : but the *fact* itself impressed everybody ;
the street rows all silently doffed hat as the Body passed ;—and
London, altogether, seemed to be holding its breath. A dim,
almost wet kind of day. Adieu, adieu.—With Wellington I
don't think either of us had ever spoken ; though we both
esteemed him heartily : I had known his face for nearly thirty
years ; he also, I think had grown to know mine, as that of
somebody who wished him well, not otherwise, I dare say, or the
proprietor's name at all ; but I have seen him gaze at me a little
as we passed on the streets. To speak *to* him, with my notions
of his ways of thinking, and of his *articulate* endowments, was
not among my longings. I went once to the House of Lords,
expressly to hear the sound of his voice, and so complete my
little private Physiognomic Portrait of him : a fine *aquiline*
voice, I found it, quite like the face of him ;—and got a great
instruction and lesson, which has staid with me, out of his little
speech itself (Lord Ellenborough's "Gates of Somnauth" the
subject, about which I cared nothing) ; speech of the most
haggly, hawky, pinched and meagre kind, so far as utterance
and "eloquence" went ; but potent for *conviction* beyond any
other, nay, I may say, quite exclusively of all the others that
night, which were mere "melodious wind" to me (Brougham's,
Derby's, etc. etc.), while *this* hitching, stunted, haggling discourse
of ten or fifteen minutes had made the Duke's opinion completely mine too. I thought of O. Cromwell withal. And have
often since, oftener than ever before, said to myself, "Is not
this (to make your opinion mine) the aim of all 'eloquence,'
rhetoric, and Demosthenic artillery practice ?" And what is
it good for ? Fools : get a *true* insight and belief of your own
as to the matter ; that is the way to get your belief into me, and
it is the only way !—

One of the days while I was first at The Grange (in 1844) was

[1] 18th November 1852.

John Sterling's *death*-day :[1] I had well marked it, with a sad almost remorseful contrast ;—we were at St. Cross and Winchester Cathedral that day.—I think my Wife's latest favourites, and in a sense friends and intimates, among the Aristocracy were the old Dowager Lady Sandwich (died about four years ago, or three) ; *young* Lady Lothian (recent acquaintance) ; and the (Dowager) Lady William Russell, whom I think she had something of real love to, and in a growing condition for the last two or three years. This a clever, high-mannered, massive-minded old lady, now seventy-two. . . .

[*Sunday,* 10*th June ;* weather fiercely hot ; health suffering visibly last week ; *must* take new courses ; form new resolutely definite *plans,*—which requires (or *would* require) a great deal more of strength and calmness than I have at present ! Quiet I am, avoiding almost everybody, and far preferring *silence* to most words I can hear : but clear of vision, *calm* of judgment I am far from being !—Ought I to *quit* this " work " here, which I feel to be very idleness ? I sit in great gloom of heart, but it is gloom all drenched in soft pity (as if *she* were to be " pitied ! ") in benign affection : really it is like a kind of religious course of worship to me, this of " Sitting by her Grave," as I daily do. Oh my Loved one, must I quit even that, then ? Dost *thou,* as if it were *thou,* bid me Rise, go hence, and work at something ? Patience ; yet a little, yet a little !—At least I will quit these vague provinces ; and try to write something more specifically *historical,* on this Paper of *her* providing !—Stop to-day.

11*th June ;* Very mournful little hour : " Parting of her raiment " (I somehow call it) sad *sanction* of what Maggie Welsh had done in it ! Have read the (Dumfries) Copy of her Will, too ; a beautiful *Letter* to her Mother, and other *Deed*[2] (" of Life-

---

[1] " My beloved friend John Sterling died at Ventnor, in the Isle of Wight, on Wednesday, 18th September 1844, about eleven at night. . . .

" For a long while I refused to believe in Sterling's danger ; of late weeks it became sternly apparent to me. . . . I had two notes from him, very affecting to me, and sent him two. He refused to see me, though I think there were few living he loved better. Four days before his death he composed some stanzas of verse addressed to me ; not to be delivered till he were gone. I received them the day before yesterday ; keep them among my precious things. I have had a great loss ; which will gradually become more sensible to me in all its details. He was a noble character, full of brilliancy, of rapid light-flashes in every kind ; and loved me heartily well. Ah me ! These verses were written on Friday the 14th September, that day I was at Winchester. He sat writing at Ventnor in those hours ; such words, in such a mood ! . . . I shall never see John Sterling more, then ; my noble Sterling ! "—Carlyle's *Journal,* 1st October 1844.

[2] Conveying Craigenputtock in life-rent to Mrs. Welsh. See *supra,* p. 56 *n.*

rent "),—all gone, *gone* into the vacant Past:—and have reposited both Documents. Intend to put down something about her Parentage etc., *now ;*—and what of reminiscence most lives with me on that head. Little *Tablet* is not due for ten days yet ; feel it too sad to quit my daily companionship, idle though it be, and almost blamable—no, it is not *blamable,* no !]

John Welsh, Farmer of Penfillan, near Thornhill, Nithsdale, for the greater part of his life, was born, I believe at Craigenputtock, 9th December 1757 ; and was sole Heir of that place, and of many ancestors there ; my Wife's paternal Grandfather,— of whom she had many pretty things to report, in her pleasant interesting way ; genuine affection blending so beautifully with perfect candour, and with arch recognition of whatever was, comically or otherwise, singular in the subject matter. Her Father's name was also John ; which from of old had specially been that of the *Laird,* or of his First-born, as her Father was. This is *one* of the probabilities they used to quote in claiming to come from John Knox's youngest daughter and her husband, the once famous John Welsh, minister of Ayr, etc. : a better probability perhaps is the topographical one that Craigenputtock, which, by site and watershed would belong to Galloway, is still part of Dumfriesshire, and did apparently form part of Collieston, fertile little farm still extant, which probably was an important estate when the antique " John Welsh's Father " had it in Knox's day : (see the *Biographies* [1]),—to which Collieston, Craigenputtock, as moorland, extending from the head of the Glenessland Valley, and a two miles farther southward (quite over the slope and down to Orr, the next river), does seem to have been an appendage. My Jeannie cared little or nothing about these genealogies, but seeing them interest *me,* took some interest in them. Within the last three months (*à propos* of a new Life of the famed John Welsh), she mentioned to me some to me new, and still livelier spark of likelihood, which her " Uncle Robert " (an expert Edinburgh lawyer) had derived from reading the old Craigenputtock law-papers : what this new " spark " of light on the matter was (quite forgotten by me at that time, and looking " new ") I in vain strive to recal ; and have *again* forgotten it (swallowed in the sad Edinburgh hurly-burlies of " three months ago," which have now had such an

---

[1] John Welsh married (about 1595) Elizabeth, third and youngest daughter of Knox. He was not, however, heir of Collieston (as appears from his Father's Will) ; the eldest son being David.—*Life of John Welsh,* by the Rev. J. Young. Edinburgh, 1866.

issue !). To my present judgment there is really good likelihood
of the genealogy, and likelihood all going that way ; but no
certainty attained or perhaps ever attainable. That ' famed
John Welsh ' lies buried (since the end of James I.'s reign) in
some churchyard of Eastern London, name of it known, but
nothing more.[1] His Grandson was minister of Erncray (" Irongray " they please to spell it) near by, in Claver'se's bloody
time ; and there all certainty ends.— —By her Mother's
mother, who was a Baillie, of somewhat noted kindred in Biggar
country, my Jeannie was further said to be descended from
" Sir William Wallace " (the great) ; but this seemed to rest on
nothing but air and vague fireside rumour of obsolete date ; and
she herself, I think, except perhaps in quizzical allusion, never
spoke of it to me at all.   Edward Irving once did (1822 or so) in
his half-laughing Grandison way, as we three sat together
talking : " From Wallace and from Knox," said he, with a
wave of the hands : " there's a Scottish Pedigree for you ! "
The good Irving : so guileless, loyal always, and so hoping and so
generous !

My wife's Grandfather, I can still recollect, died 20th September 1823, aged near sixty-six ;—I was at Kinnaird (Buller's in
Perthshire), and had it in a Letter from *her :* Letters from her
were almost the sole light-points in my dreary miseries there
(fruit of *miserable health* mainly, and of a future blank and
barred to me, as I felt).   Trustfully she gave me details : how
he was sixty-three, near sixty-six (in fact) ; hair still raven-
black, only within a year *eyebrows* had grown quite white ; which
had so softened and sweetened the look of his bright glancing
black eyes, etc. etc.   A still grief lay in the dear Letter, too,
and much affection and respect for her old Grandfather just gone.
Sweet and soft to *me* to look back upon ; and very sad now, from
the threshold of our own grave.   My bonnie Darling, *ja ;* I shall
follow thee very soon, and then—!—

Grandfather's youngest years had been passed at Craigenputtock ; mother had been left a widow there, and could not
bear to part with him ; elder sisters there were, he the only boy.
Jane always thought him to have fine faculty, a beautiful clearness, decision, and integrity of character ; but all this had
grown up in solitude and vacancy, under the silent skies on the
wild moors for most part.   She sometimes spoke of his (and her)
ulterior ancestors ; " several blackguards among them," her

[1] Buried at St. Botolph's, Bishopsgate, 4th April 1662.—Young's *Life
of John Welsh*, p. 407.

old Grandfather used to say ; " but not one blockhead that I
heard of ! "   Of one, flourishing in 1745, there is a story still
current among the country people thereabouts : how, though
this Laird of Craigenputtock had not himself gone at all into the
Rebellion, he received with his best welcome certain other Lairds
or gentlemen of his acquaintance who *had*, and who were now
flying for their life ; kept them there, as in a seclusion lonelier
almost than any other in Scotland ;—heard timefully that
Dragoons were coming for them ; shot them thereupon instantly
away by various well-contrived routes and equipments ; and
waited his Dragoon Guests as if nothing were wrong.   " Such
and such men here with you ; aren't they, you ——! " said they.
" Truly they were, till three hours ago ; and they are *rebels*,
say you ?   Fie, the villains, had I but known or dreamt of that !
But come, let us *chase* immediately : once across the Orr yonder
(and the swamps on this side, which look green enough from
here), you find firm road, and will soon catch the dogs ! "
Welsh mounting his galloway, undertook to guide the Dragoons
through that swamp or " bottom " (still a place that needed
guiding in our time, though there did come at last a " solid
road and bridge ") ; Welsh, trotting cheerily along on his light
galloway, guided the Dragoons in such way that their heavy
animals sank mostly or altogether, in the treacherous element,
safe only for a native galloway and man ; and with much pretended lamentation, seeing them provided with work that would
last till darkness had fallen, rode his ways again.   I believe this
was *true* in substance ; but never heard any of the saved rebels
named.   Maxwells etc., who are of Roman-Catholic Jacobite
type, abound in those parts : a Maxwell, I think, is feudal
superior of Craigenputtock.   This Welsh, I gather, must have
been *grandfather* of my Wife's grandfather : she had strange
stories of his wives (three in succession, married perhaps all,
especially the second and third, for money) ; and how he kept
the last of them, a decrepit ill-natured creature, *in*visible in
some corner of his house ; and used gravely to introduce
visitors to her " gown and bonnet " hanging on a stick as " Mrs
Welsh III."   *Him* his Grandson doubtless ranked among the
" blackguard " section of ancestry ; I suppose his immediate
heir may have died shortly after him and been an unexception-
able man.

In or about 1773, friends persuaded the widow of this latter
that she absolutely must send her Boy away for some kind of
schooling, his age now fourteen : to which she sorrowfully con-

senting, he was despatched to Tynron school (notable at that time) about twelve miles over the hills Nithsdale way, and consigned to a farmer named Hunter, whose kin are now well risen in the world thereabouts, and who was thought to be a safe person for boarding and supervising the young moorland Laird. The young Laird must have learned well at school, for he wrote a fine hand (which I have seen) and had acquired the ordinary elements of country education in a respectable way,— in the course of one year as turned out. Within one year, 16th February 1774, these Hunters had married him to their eldest Girl (about sixteen, three months *younger* than himself), and his school-days were suddenly completed ! [1] This young girl was my Jeannie's Grandmother ; had fourteen children, mostly men (of whom, or of whose male posterity, none now survive, except the three Edinburgh Aunts, youngest of them a month *younger* than my Jane was) ; and thus held the poor Laird's face considerably to the grindstone all his days ! I have seen the Grandmother, in her old age and widowhood ; a respectable-looking old person (lived then with her three daughters in a house they had purchased at Dumfries) ; silently my woman never much liked her or hers (a palpably rather tricky, cunning set these, with a turn for ostentation and hypocrisy in them) ;—and was accustomed to divide her uncles (not without some ground, as I could see) into " Welshes," and " Welshes with a cross of Hunter," traceable oftenest (not always though) in their very physiognomy and complexion. They are now all gone ; the kindred as good as *out*, only their works following them, *talia qualia !*—

This imprudent marriage reduced the poor young man to pecuniary straits (had to *sell* first *Nether* Craigenputtock, a minor part, in order to pay his Sister's portions ; then long years afterwards, in the multitude of his children, *Upper* Craigenputtock, or Craigenputtock Proper, to my Wife's Father this *latter* sale); and though, being a thrifty vigorous and solid manager, he prospered handsomely in his farming, first of Milton, then ditto of Penfillan, the best thing he could try in the circumstances, and got completely above all *money*-difficulties; the same "circumstances" kept him all his days a mere "*Terræ Filius*," restricted to Nithsdale and his own eyesight (which

[1] The whole of the above paragraph requires correction. Carlyle would seem to have written without exact knowledge. There is good reason for believing that the marriage was a runaway match, regretted by the lady's family as much as by the Welshes. Mrs. Carlyle was on intimate terms with these relations, whom she visited, and it is certain, from the way in which she writes to them, that she would not willingly have given them pain.

indeed was excellent) for all the knowledge he could get of this Universe ; and on the whole had made him, such the contrast between native vigour of faculty and accidental contraction of arena, a singular and even interesting man, a Scottish Nithsdale Son of Nature. Highly interesting to his bright young Granddaughter, with the clear eyesight and valiant true heart like his own, when she came to look into him in her childhood and girlhood. He was solidly devout, truth's own self in what he said and did ; had dignity of manners too, in fact a really brave sincere and honourable soul (reverent of talent, honesty, and sound sense, beyond all things) ; and was silently a good deal respected and honourably esteemed (though with a grin here and there) in the district where he lived. For chief or almost sole intimate he had the neighbouring (biggish) Laird, " old Hogan of Waterside," almost close by Penfillan, whose peremptory ways and regularities of mind and conduct, are still remembered in that region,—sorrowfully and strangely as his sons, grandsons, and now great-grandson, have distinguished themselves in the other direction there. It was delightful to hear my Bright One talk of this old Grandfather ; so kindly yet so playfully, with a vein of fond affection, yet with the justest insight. In his Last Will (owing to Hunterian artifices and unkind whisperings, as she thought) he had omitted *her*, though her Father had been such a Second Father to all the rest :— £1000 apiece might be the share of each son and each daughter in this Deed of the old man's ; and my Jane's name was not found there, as if she too had been dead like her beneficent Father. Less care for the *money* no creature in the world could have had ; but the neglect had sensibly grieved her ; though she never at all blamed the old man himself, and before long, as was visible, had forgiven the suspected Hunterian parties themselves,—" Poor souls, so earnest about their paltry bits of interests, which are the vitallest and highest *they* have ! or perhaps it was some whim of the old man himself ? Never mind, never mind ! " And so, as I could perceive, it actually *was abolished* in that generous heart, and not there any longer, before much time had passed. Here are two pictures, a wise and an absurd, two of very many she used to give me of the loved old Grandfather ;—with which surely I may *end :*

1°. " Never hire as servant a very poor person's daughter or son : *they* have seen nothing but confusion, waste, and huggermugger, mere *want* of thrift or method." This was a very wise opinion surely. On the other hand,—

He was himself a tall man, perhaps six feet or more, and stood erect as a column. And he had got gradually into his head, supported by such observation as the arena of Keir Parish and neighbouring localities afforded, the astonishing opinion—

2°. That small people, especially short people, were good for nothing ; and in fine that a man's bodily stature was a correctish sign of his spiritual ! Actually so ; and would often make new people, aspiring to be acquaintances, stand up and be measured, that he might have their inches first of all. Nothing could drive this out of him ; nothing till he went down once to sit on a jury at Dumfries ; and for pleader to him had Francis Jeffrey, a man little above five feet, and evidently the cleverest Advocate one had ever heard or dreamed of !—Ah me, these were such histories and portrayings as I shall never hear again, nor I think did ever hear, for some of the qualities they had.

[*June* 13.] John Welsh, my Wife's Father, was born at *Craigenputtock* (I now find, which gives the place a new interest to me), ' 4th April 1776,'—little more than eighteen years younger than his father, or than his mother. His first three years or so (probably till 26th May 1779, when the Parents may have moved to Milton, in Tynron) must have been passed in those solitudes. At Milton he would see his poor young Sister die,—wonted Playmate sadly vanish from the new hearth ;— and would no doubt have his thoughts about it (my own little Sister Jenny in a similar stage, and my dear Mother's tears about her, I can vividly remember ; the strangely silent white-sheeted room ; white-sheeted linen-curtained bed, and small piece of elevation there, which the joiner was about measuring ; and my own outburst into weeping thereupon, I hardly knew why,—my first passing glance at the Spectre Death !)—more we know not of the Boy's biography there ; except that it seems to have lasted about seven years at Milton ; and that, no doubt, he had been for three or four years at school there (Tynron School, we may well guess) when (1785 or 6) the family shifted with him to Penfillan. There probably he spent some four or three years more ; Tynron still his school, to which he could walk ; and where I conclude he must have got what Latin and other education he had. Very imperfect he himself, as I have evidence, considered it ; and in his busiest time he never ceased to struggle for improvement of it, Touching to know,—and how super- latively well, in other far more important respects, Nature and his own reflections and inspirations had " educated " him. Better than one of many thousands, as I do perceive ! *Close-*

burn (a school still of fame) lay on the other side of Nith River, and would be inaccessible to him, though daily visible.

What year he first went to Edinburgh, or entered the University, I do not know ;—I think he was first a kind of apprentice to a famous Joseph or Charles Bell . . . and with this famed Bell he was a favourite ;—probably I think attending the classes etc., while still learning from Bell.   I rather believe he never took an M.D. degree ; but was, and had to be, content with his Diploma as Surgeon : very necessary to get out of his Father's way, and shift for himself in some honest form !   Went, I should dimly guess, as Assistant to some old Doctor at Haddington on Bell's recommendation,—I know not in what year (say about 1796, his twentieth year, my first in this world).   [Went first, I clearly find, as Regimental Surgeon, 10th August 1796, into the " Perthshire Fencible Cavalry," and served there some three years.   Carefully tied up and reposited by pious hands (seemingly in 1819), I find three old " Commissions " on parchment, with their stamps, seals, signatures, etc. (Surgeon, 10th August 1796 ; Cornet, 15th September 1796 ; and Lieutenant, 5th April 1799) which testify to this ;—after which there could have been no " assistantship " with Somers, but *purchase* and full *practice* at once ;—marriage itself having followed in 1800, the next year after that " Lieutenancy " promotion.] [1]   The old Doctor's name, if I mistake not, was Somers.   Somers finding his Assistant able for everything, a man fast gaining knowledge, and acceptable to all the better Public, or to the Public altogether, agreed in a year or two, to demit, withdraw to country retirement, and declare his assistant successor, on condition, which soon proved easy and easier, of being paid (I know not for how long, possibly for life of self and wife, but it did not last long) an annuity of £200.   Of which I find trace in that poor Account Book of his ; piously preserved by his Daughter ever since his death.

Dr. Welsh's success appears to have been, henceforth and formerly, swift and constant ; till, before long, the whole sphere, or section of life he was placed in had in all senses, pecuniary and other, become his own, and there remained nothing more to conquer in it, only very much to retain by the methods that had acquired it, and to be extremely thankful for as an allotment in this world.   A truly superior man, according to all the evidence I from all quarters have.   A " very valiant man," Edward

1 This passage in brackets is pasted on to the leaf of the Note Book, Carlyle marking in the text that the paragraph was to be corrected by it.

Irving once called him in my hearing. His medical sagacity was reckoned at a higher and higher rate, medical and other *honesty* as well ; for it was by no means as a wise Physician only, but as an honourable exact and quietly dignified man, punctual, faithful in all points, that he was esteemed over the County. It was three years after his death when I first came into the circle which had been his ; and nowhere have I met with a posthumous reputation that seemed to be higher or more unanimous, among all ranks of men. The brave man himself I never saw : but my poor Jeannie, in her best moments, often said to me, about this or that, " Yes, *he* would have done it so ! " " Ah, *he* would have liked you ! " as her highest praise. " Punctuality " Irving described as a thing he much insisted on. Many miles daily of riding (" three strong horses in saddle " always, with inventions against frost etc.) : he had appointed the minute everywhere ; and insisted calmly on having it kept by all interested parties, high or low. Gravely inflexible, wherever right was concerned ; and " very independent " where mere rank etc. attempted to avail upon him. Story of some old valetudinarian Nabal of eminence (Nisbet of Dirleton, immensely rich, continually cockering himself, and suffering) ; grudging audibly once at the many fees he had to pay (from his annual £30,000) :—" Daresay I have to pay you [£160] a year, Dr. Welsh ! "—" Nearly or fully that, I should say ; all of it accurately for work done."— " It's a great deal of money, though ! "—" Work not demanded, drain of payment will cease ; of course, *not* otherwise," answered the Doctor ; and came home with the full understanding that his Dirleton practice and connection had ended. My Jeannie recollected his quiet report of it to Mamma and her, with that corollary :—however, after some short experience (or re-experience of London Doctors) Nabal Nisbet (who had " butter churned *daily* for breakfast," as one item of expenditure) came back, with the necessary *Peccavi* expressed or understood.

One anecdote I always remember, of the *per contra* kind. Riding along one day, on his multifarious business, he noticed a poor wounded partridge, fluttering and struggling about, wing or leg, or both, broken by some sportsman's lead. He alighted, in his haste, or made the groom alight if he had one ; gathered up the poor partridge, looped it gently in his handkerchief ; brought it home ; and, by careful splint and salve and other treatment, had it soon on wing again, and sent it forth healed. This, in so grave and practical a man, had always in it a fine

expressiveness to me :—*she* never told it me but once, long ago ;
and perhaps we never spoke of it again.— —

Some time in Autumn 1800 (I think) the young Haddington
Doctor married : my Wife, his first and only child, was born
14th July (" Bastille-day," as we often called it) *1801* ; —sixty-
four and a half years old when she died.   The Bride was Grace
Welsh of Caplegill (head of Moffat Water in Annandale) ; her
Father an opulent store-farmer up there, native of Nithsdale ;
her Mother, a Baillie from Biggar region, already deceased.
Grace was beautiful,—must have been ; she continued what
might be called beautiful till the very end, in or beyond her
sixtieth year.   *Her* Welshes were Nithsdale people of good
condition, though beyond her grandfather and uncles, big
farmers in Thornhill Parish (the " Welshes of Morton-Mains "
for I know not what length of time before, nor exactly what
after, only that it ceased some thirty or perhaps almost fifty
years ago, in a tragic kind of way) ; I can learn nothing certain
of them from Rev. Walter of Auchtertool, nor from his sister
Maggie here, who are of that genealogy, children of my Mother-
in-law's brother John ; concerning whom perhaps a word afterwards.—When the young Haddington Doctor and his beautiful
Grace had first made acquaintance I know not ; probably on
visits of hers to Morton-Mains, which is but a short step from
Penfillan : acquainted they evidently were, to the degree of
mutually saying, " Be it for life then ; " and, I believe, were and
continued deeply attached to one another.   Sadder widow than
my Mother-in-law, modestly, delicately, yet discernibly was, I
have seldom or never seen ; and my poor Jeannie has told me,
he had great love of her, though obliged to keep it rather secret
or undemonstrative, being well aware of her too sensitive, fanciful, and capricious ways.

[*June* 15.] Mrs. Welsh when I first saw her (1821) must
have been in the [second] year of her widowhood.   I think, when
Irving and I entered, she was sitting in the room with Benjamin [1]
and my Jane, but soon went away.   An air of deep sadness lay
on her, and on everybody, except on poor dying Benjamin, who
affected to be very sprightly, though overwhelmed as he must
have felt himself.   His spirit, as I afterwards learned from his
Niece, who did not love him, or feel grateful to him, was extraordinary, in the worldly-wise kind.   Mrs. Welsh, though
beautiful, a tall *aquiline* figure, of elegant carriage and air, was
not of intellectual or specially distinguished physiognomy; and,

[1] Dr. Welsh's youngest Brother ; he died at Leghorn, in 1822 ; aged 26.

in her severe costume and air, rather repelled me than otherwise at that time. A day or so after, next evening perhaps, both Irving and I were in her Drawing-room, with her Daughter and her, both very humane to me, especially the former, which I noticed with true joy for the moment. I was miserably ill in health ; miserable every way more than enough, in my lonely imprisonment, *such* it was, which lasted many years. The Drawing-room seemed to me the finest apartment I had ever sat or stood in :—in fact it was a room of large and fine proportions, looking out on a garden, on mere gardens or garden walls and sprinkling of trees, across the valley or plain of the Tyne (which lay hidden),—house quite at the back of the Town, facing towards Lethington etc. the best rooms of it ; and everywhere bearing stamp of the late owner's solid temper. Clean, all of it, as spring water ; solid and correct as well as pertinently ornamented : in the Drawing-room, on the tables there, perhaps rather a superfluity of elegant whimwhams. The summer twilight, I remember, was pouring in rich and soft ; I felt as one walking transiently in upper spheres, where I had little right even to make transit. Ah me ! They did not *know* of its *former* tenants when I went to the house again in April last. I remember our all sitting, another evening, in a little parlour off the dining-room (downstairs), and talking a long time ; Irving mainly, and bringing out *me*, the two ladies benevolently listening with not much of speech, but the younger with lively apprehension of all meanings and shades of meaning. Above this parlour I used to sleep, in my visits in after years, while the house was still unsold. Mrs. W. left it at once, autumn 1826, the instant her Jeannie had gone with me ;[1] went to Templand, Nithsdale, to her Father ;—and turned out to have decided never to behold Haddington more.

She was of a most generous, honourable, affectionate turn of mind ; had consummate skill in administering a household ; a goodish well-tending intellect,—something of real drollery in it ; from which my Jeannie, I thought, might have inherited that beautiful lambency and brilliancy of soft genial *humour*, which illuminated her perceptions and discoursings so often to a singular degree, like pure soft morning radiance falling upon a perfect picture, *true* to the facts. Indeed, I once said, " Your mother,

---

[1] It was at the beginning of August that Mrs. and Miss Welsh left Haddington. They staid at Comley Bank for a few weeks, furnishing the house there, and by September were settled at Templand. The marriage was on the 17th October 1826.

my Dear, has narrowly missed being a woman of genius."
Which doubtless was reported by and by in a quizzical manner,
and received with pleasure. For the rest, Mrs. Welsh, as above
said, was far too sensitive ; her beauty, too, had brought
flatteries, conceits perhaps ; she was very variable of humour,
flew off or on upon slight reasons, and, as already said, was not
easy to live with for one wiser than herself, though very easy
for one more foolish, if especially a touch of hypocrisy and perfect assentation were superadded. The married life at Haddington, I always understood, was loyal and happy, sunnier than
most ; but it was so by the Husband's softly and steadily *taking*
the command, I fancy, and knowing how to keep it in a silent
and noble manner. Old Penfillan (I have heard the three
Aunts say) reported once, on returning from a visit at Haddington, " He had seen her one evening in fifteen different humours "
as the night wore on. This, probably, was in his own youngish
years (as well as hers and his son's), and might have a good deal
of satirical exaggeration in it. She was the most exemplary
nurse to her Husband's Brother William, and to other of the Penfillan sons who were brought there for help or furtherance.
William's stay lasted five years, three of them involving two
hours daily upon the " spring-deal " (a stout elastic plank of
twenty or thirty feet long, on which the weak patient gets
himself shaken and secures exercise), she herself, day after day,
doing the part of tramper ;—which perhaps was judged useful,
or as good as necessary, for her own health. William was not in
all points a patient one *could* not have quarrelled with ; and my
Mother-in-law's quiet obedience I cannot reckon other than
exemplary,—even supposing it was partly for her own health
too. This I suppose was actually the case. She had much weak
health, more and more towards the end of life. Her husband
had often signally helped her by his skill and zeal ; once, for six
months long, he, and visibly he alone, had been the means of
keeping her alive. It was a bad inflammation or other disorder
of the liver ; liver disorder was cured, but power of digestion
had ceased ; Doctors from Edinburgh etc. unanimously gave
her up, food of no kind would stay a moment on the stomach,
" What can any mortal of us do ? " Husband persisted ;
found food that would stay (arrowroot perfectly pure ; if by
chance, your pure stock being out, you tried *shop* arrowroot, the
least of starch in it declared it futile) ; for six months kept her
alive and gathering strength on those terms, till she rose again
to her feet. " He much loved her," said my Jeannie ; " but

none could less love what of *follies* she had,"—not a few, though none of them deep at all, the good and even noble soul ! How sadly I remember now, and often before now, the time when she vanished from her kind Jane's sight and mine, never more to meet us in this world. It must have been in autumn 1841 ; she had attended Jane down from Templand, [to Dumfries] probably I was up from Scotsbrig (but don't remember) ; I was, at any rate, to *conduct* to Scotsbrig that night, and on the morrow or so, thence for London. Mrs. Welsh was unusually beautiful, but strangely sad too,—eyes bright, and as if with many tears behind them. Her Daughter too was sad ; so was I, at the sadness of both, and at the evidently boundless feeling of affection which knew not how to be kind enough. Into shops etc. for last gifts, and later than last : at length we had got all done ; and withdrew to Sister Jean's, to order the gig and go. She went with us still ; but feeling what would now be the kindest, heroically rose (still not weeping), and said Adieu there. We watched her, sorrowful both of us, from the end window ; stepping, tall and graceful, feather in bonnet, etc., down Lochmaben Gate, casting no glance *back ;* then vanishing to rightward, into High Street (bonnet feather perhaps, the last thing), and she was gone for ever. *Ay de mi, Ay de mi.* What a thing is Life ; bounded thus by Death ! I do not think we ever spoke of this ; but how could either of us ever forget it at all ?—

Old Walter Welsh, my wife's maternal Grandfather, I had seen twice or thrice, at Templand, before our marriage ; and for the next six or seven years, especially after our removal to Craigenputtock, he was naturally a principal figure in our small circle. He liked his Granddaughter cordially well ; she had been much about him on visits and so forth, from her early childhood ; a bright merry little grig, always pleasant, in the troubled atmosphere of the old Grandfather. " Pen " (*Penfillan* Jeannie, for there was another) he used to call her to the last ; Mother's name in the family was " Grizzie " (Grace). A perfect true affection ran through all branches, my poor little " Pen " well included and returning it well. She was very fond of old Walter (as he privately was of her) ; and got a great deal of affectionate amusement out of him. Me too he found much to like in, though practically we discorded commonly on two points : 1°, that I did and would smoke tobacco ; 2°, that I could not and would not drink, with any freedom, whisky punch, or other liquid stimulants ; a thing breathing the utmost poltroonery in some section of one's mind, thought Walter always.

He for himself cared nothing about drink ; but had the rooted idea (common in his *old* circles) that it belonged in some indissoluble way to good fellowship. We used to presently knit up the peace again ; but tiffs of reproach from him on this score would always arise from time to time ; and had always to be laughed away by me, which was very easy, for I really liked old Walter heartily ; and he was a continual genial study to me over and above : *microcosm* of old Scottish Life as it *had* been ; and man of much singularity, originality and real worth of character, and even of intellect too if you saw well. He abounded in contrasts ; glaring oppositions, contradictions, you would have said in every element of him,—yet all springing from a single centre (you might observe) and honestly uniting themselves there. No better-*natured* man (sympathy, sociality, honest loving-kindness towards all innocent people) ; and yet of men I have hardly seen one of hotter, more impatient *temper*. Sudden, vehement ; breaking out into fierce flashes as of lightning when you touched him the wrong way. Yet they were flashes only, never bolts, and were gone again in a moment ; and the fine old face beaming quietly on you as before. Face uncommonly fine : serious, yet laughing eyes, as if inviting you *in ;* bushy eyebrows, face which you might have called picturesquely shaggy, under its plenty of gray hair, beard itself imperfectly shaved here and there ; features massive yet soft (almost with a tendency to pendulous or flabby in parts) : and nothing but honesty, quick ingenuity, kindliness, and frank manhood as the general expression. He was a most simple man, of stunted utterance, *burred* with his *r* and had a *chewing* kind of way with his words, which, rapid and few, seemed to be forcing their way through laziness or phlegm, and were not extremely distinct till you attended a little (and then, aided by the face etc., they *were* extremely and memorably,—brave old Walter's words, so true too ; as honest almost as my own Father's, though in a strain so different !). Clever things Walter never said or attempted to say ; nor wise things either in any sphere beyond that of sincerely accepted commonplace ; but he very well knew when such were said by others and glanced with a bright look on them, a bright dimpling chuckle sometimes (*smudge* of laughter, the Scotch call it, one of the prettiest words and ditto things) ; and on the whole, hated no kind of talk but the unwise kind. He was serious, pensive, not morose or sad, in these old times. He had the prettiest laugh (once or at most twice, in my presence) that I can remember to have heard,—not the loudest my own Father's still rarer laugh was louder far, though perhaps not more complete ; but his was all of artillery-thunder, *feu de joie* from all guns as the main element ; while in Walter's there was audible something as of infinite flutes and harps, as if the vanquished themselves were invited (or compelled) to partake in the triumph. I remember one such laugh (quite forgot about what), and how the old face looked suddenly so beautiful and young again. " Radiant ever-young Apollo " etc. of Teufelsdröckh's laugh [1] is a reminiscence of that. Now when I think of it, Walter must have had an immense fund of inarticulate gaiety in his composition, a truly fine sense of the ridiculous (excellent *sense* in a man, especially if he never cultivate it, or be conscious of it, as was Walter's case) : and it must have been from him, then, that my Jane derived that beautiful light of humour (*never* going into folly, yet full of tacit fun) which spontaneously illuminated all her best hours. Thanks to Walter ; *she* was of him in this respect : my Father's laugh, too, is mainly mine (a grimmer and inferior kind) ; of my Mother's beautifully sportive vein (which was a *third* kind,—also hereditary I am told) I seem to have inherited less, though not nothing either, nay, perhaps at bottom not even less, had my life chanced to be easier or joyfuller. " Sense of the ridiculous " (worth calling such ; i.e. " brotherly sympathy with the *downward* side ") is withal very indispensable to a man :—Hebrews have it not ; hardly any Jew creature (not even blackguard Heine, to any real length),—hence various *mis*qualities of theirs, perhaps most of their qualities too which have become *Historical*. This is an old remark of mine, though not yet written anywhere.

Walter had been a Buck in his youth, a high-prancing horseman etc. : I forget what image there was of him, in buckskins, pipe hair-dressings, grand equipments ; riding somewhither (with John Welsh of Penfillan I almost think ?)—bright airimage, from some transient discourse I need not say of *whom*. He had married a good and beautiful Miss Baillie (of whom already) ; and settled with her at Caplegill, in the Moffat region ; where all his children were born,—and left with him young ; the mother having died, still in the flower of her age ; ever tenderly remembered by Walter to his last day (as was well understood, though mention was avoided). From her my Jeannie was called " Jane Baillie Welsh " at the time of our marriage ; but after a good few years, when she took to signing " Jane *Welsh* Carlyle," in which I never hindered her, dropped the " Baillie,"

---

[1] *Sartor Resartus* (Everyman edition), p. 24.

I suppose as too long. I have heard her quiz about the " unfortunate Miss Baillie " of the song at a still earlier time. Whether Grace Welsh was married from Caplegill I do not know. Walter had been altogether prosperous in Caplegill ; and all of the Family that I knew (John a merchant in Liverpool, the one remaining of the sons, and Jeannie the one other daughter, a beautiful " Aunt Jeannie " of whom a word by and by) continued warmly attached to it as their real home in this earth : but at the renewal of leases (1801 or so) had lost it in a quite provoking way. By the treachery of a so-called Friend, namely : Friend a neighbouring farmer perhaps, but with an inferior farm, came to *advise* with Walter about rents, probably his own rent first, in this general time of leasing : " I am thinking to offer so-and-so, what say you ? what are *you* going to offer by the bye ? " Walter, the very soul of fidelity himself, made no scruple to answer ;—found by and by that this precious individual had thereupon himself gone and offered for Caplegill the requisite few pounds *more*, and that, according to fixed customs of the Estate, he and not Walter, was declared tenant of Caplegill henceforth. Disdain of such scandalous conduct, astonishment and *quasi* horror at it, could have been stronger in few men than in Walter ; a feeling shared in heartily and irrevocably by all the Family ; who, for the rest, seldom spoke of it, or hardly ever, in my time ; and did not seem to hate the man at all, but to have cut him off as non-extant and left him unmentioned thenceforth.   Perhaps some Welsh he too, of a different stock ? There were Moffat country Welshes, I observed, with whom they rather eagerly (John of Liverpool eagerly) disclaimed all kinship, but it might be on other grounds : this individual's name I never once heard. Nor was the story touched upon except by rare chance and in the lightest way.

After Caplegill, Walter had no more farming prosperity : I believe he was unskilful in the *arable* kind of business, certainly he was unlucky ; shifted about to various places (all in Nithsdale, and I think on a smaller and smaller scale, Castlehill in Durisdeer, Strathmilligan in Tynron, ultimately Templand), and had gradually lost nearly all his capital, which at one time was of an opulent extent (actual number of thousands quite unknown to me) and felt himself becoming old and frail, and as it were thrown out of the game. His Family meanwhile had been scattered abroad, seeking their various fortune : son John to Liverpool (where he had one or perhaps more uncles of mercantile distinction), son William to the West Indies (?) and to early death, whom I often heard lamented by my Mother-in-law ; these and possibly others who were not known to me. John, by this time, had, recovering out of one bit of very bad luck, got into a solid way of business ; and was, he alone of the Brothers, capable of helping his Father a little on the pecuniary side. Right willing to do it, to the utmost of his power or further ! A most munificent, affectionate, and nobly honourable kind of man ; much esteemed by both my Jane and me, foreign as his way of life was to us.

Besides these there was the youngest Daughter, now a woman of thirty or so, the excellent " Aunt Jeannie," so lovable to both of us ; who was said to resemble her Mother (" nearly *as* beautiful, all but the golden hair,"—Jeannie's was fine flaxen, complexion of the fairest) ; who had watched over and waited on her Father, through all his vicissitudes, and everywhere kept a comfortable, frugally effective and even elegant house round him, —and in fact let no wind visit him too roughly. She was a beautifully patient, ingenious and practically thoughtful creature ; always cheerful of face, *suppressing* herself and her sorrows, of which I understood there had been enough,—in order to screen her Father, and make life still soft to him. By aid of John, perhaps slightly of my Mother-in-law, the little Farm of Templand (Queensberry farm, with a strong but gaunt and inconvenient old stone house on it) was leased and equipped for the old man : house thoroughly repaired, garden etc. ; that he might still feel himself an active citizen, and have a civilised habitation, in his weak years. Nothing could be neater, trimmer, in all essential particulars more complete than house and environment, under Aunt Jeannie's fine managing, had in a year or two grown to be. Fine sheltered beautiful and useful garden in front, with trellises, flower-work, and strip of the cleanest river shingle between porch and it : House all clean and complete like a new coin ; steadily kept dry (by industry), bedroom, and every part ; old furniture (of Caplegill) really interesting to the eye, as well as perfect for its duties. Dairy, kitchen etc. : nothing that was fairly needful or useful could you find to be wanting :—the whole matter had the air, to a visitor like myself, as of a rustic Idyl (the seamy side of it all strictly hidden by clever Aunt Jeannie) ;—I think she must have been, what I often heard, one of the best Housekeepers in the world. Dear good little Beauty : it appears too she had met with her tragedies in life,—one tragedy hardest of all upon a woman, betrothed Lover flying off into infamous treason, not against her specially, but

against her Brother and his own honour and conscience (Brother's
Partner he was, if I recollect rightly, and fled with all the funds,
leaving £12,000 of *minus*) ; which annihilated *him* for her, and
closed her poor heart against hopes of that kind, at an early
period of her life.   Much lying on her mind, I always understood,
while she was so cheery, diligent and helpful to everybody round
her !—I forget, or never knew what time they had come to Templand ; but guess it may have been in 1822 or shortly after :
dates of Castlehill and Strathmilligan I never knew, even *order*
of dates :—last summer, I could so easily have known (Deaf-
and-dumb " Mr. Turner," an old Strathmilligan acquaintance,
recognised by *her* in the Dumfries Railway Station, and made to
speak by paper and pencil, I writing for *her* because she could not,
—oh me, oh me, *where is* now that summer Evening, so beautiful, so infinitely sad and strange !   The train rolled off with her
to Thornhill, Holm Hill, and that too, with its setting sun, is
gone).—I almost think Durisdeer (Castlehill) must have been
last before Templand ;   I remember passing that quaint old Kirk
(with village hidden) on my left, one April Evening, on the top of
a Dumfries Coach from Edinburgh, with reveries and pensive
reflections, which must have belonged to 1822 or 1823.   Once,
long after, on one of our London visits, I drove thither sitting by
her, in an afternoon ;   and *saw* the Gypsy Village for the first
time ;   and looked in with her, at the fine Italian Sculptures on
the Queensberry Tomb through a gap in the old kirk wall.
Again a pensive Evening, now so beautiful and sad.

From Childhood upwards she seemed to have been much
about these Homes of old Walter ;   summer visits almost yearly ;
and, after her Father's death, likely to be of longer continuance.
They must have been a quiet, welcome, and right wholesome
element for her young heart and vividly growing mind :   beautiful simplicity and rural Scottish Nature in its very finest form :
frugal, elegant, true and kindly ;   *simplex munditiis* nowhere
more descriptive both for men and things.   To myself, summing
up what I experienced of them, there was a real gain from them
as well as pleasure.   Rough nature I knew well already, or
perhaps too well ;   but here it was reduced to cosmic, and had a
victorious character which was new, and grateful to me, well
nigh poetical.   The old Norse Kings, the Homeric *grazier*
sovereigns of men :   I have felt in reading of them, as if their
ways had a kinship with these (*un*sung) Nithsdale ones.   Poor
" Aunt Jeannie" sickened visibly the Summer after our Marriage ;
Summer 1827, while we were there on visit.   My own little

Jeannie, whom nothing could escape that she had the interest
to fix her lynx-eyed scrutiny upon, discovered just before
our leaving, that her dear Aunt was dangerously ill, and indeed
had long been,—a tumour, now evidently cancerous, growing
on her breast for twelve years past ; which, after effort, she at
last made the poor Aunt confess to ! We were all (I myself by
sympathy, had there been nothing more) thrown into conster-
nation ; made the matter known, at Liverpool etc., to everybody
but old Walter ; and had no need to insist on immediate steps
being taken. My Mother-in-law was an inmate there, and
probably in chief command (had moved thither, quitting
Haddington for good, directly on our marriage) : [1] she at once
took measures ; having indeed a turn herself for *medicining,* and
some skill withal. That autumn Aunt Jeannie and she came to
Edinburgh, had a furnished house close by us, in Comley Bank ;
and then the dismal operation ; successfully, the Doctors all
said,—but alas ! Dim sorrow rests on those weeks to me.
Aunt Jeannie showed her old Heroism ; and my Wife herself
strove to hope : but it was painful, oppressive, sad ;—twice or
so I recollect being in the sick-room ; and the pale yet smiling
face, more excitation in the eyes than usual : one of the times
she was giving us the earnest counsel (my Jane having been
consulting), "To *go* to London, clearly, if I could,—if they
would give me the Professorship there !" (Some Professorship
in Gower Street, perhaps of " Literature," which I had hoped
vaguely [for], not strongly at all, nor ever formally declaring
myself, through Jeffrey from his friend Brougham and consorts,
—which they were kind enough to dispose of *otherwise*). My
own poor little Jeannie ; my poor *pair* of kind little Jeannies !
Poor Templand Jeannie went home again, striving to hope ;
but sickened in winter ; worsened when the spring came ; and
summer 1828 was still some weeks off when she had departed.
Or *were* we at Craigenputtock by that time ? I cannot think
so. No, it must have been in April or March of 1828. The
Funeral, at Crawfurd, I remember sadly well ; old Walter, John
and two Sons (Walter of Auchtertool,[2] and Alick now successor
in Liverpool), with various old Moffat people etc. etc. at the Inn
of Crawfurd ; Pass of Dalveen with Dr. Russell in the dark
(holding candles, both of us, inside the chaise) ; and old Walter's
silent sorrow and my own as we sat together in the vacant
parlour after getting home. " Hah, we'll no see *her* nae mair ! "

[1] See *supra,* p. 99 *n.*
[2] Rev. Walter Welsh of Auchtertool, Fife, who died about 1880.

murmured the old man ; and that was all I heard from him, I
think.

Old Walter now fell entirely to the care of Daughter
"Grizzie," who was unweariedly attentive to him, a most
affectionate Daughter, an excellent housewife too, and had
money enough to support herself and him in their quiet, neat
and frugal way. Templand continued, in all points, as trim and
beautiful as ever ; the old man made no kind of complaint, and
in economics there was even an improvement : but the old
cheery patience of Daughter "Jeannie," magnanimously
effacing herself, and returning all his little spurts of smoke in the
form of lambent kindly flame and radiant light upon him, was no
longer there ; and we did not doubt but he sometimes felt the
change. Templand has a very fine situation ; old Walter's
walk, at the south end of the house, was one of the most picturesque and pretty to be found in the world. Nith valley (river
half a mile off, winding through green holms, now in its borders
of clean shingle, now lost in pleasant woods and bushes) lay
patent to the south, the country sinking perhaps a hundred feet,
rather suddenly, just beyond Templand ; Keir, Penpont,
Tynron lying spread, across the river, all as in a map, full of
cheerful habitations, gentlemen's mansions, well-cultivated
Farms and their cottages and appendages ; spreading up in
irregular slopes and gorges against the finest range of hills,
Barjarg with its trees and mansion atop, to your left hand ;
Tynron Doon, a grand massive lowland mountain (you might call
it) with its white village at the base (behind which, in summer
time was the setting of the sun for you) ; one big pass (Glen-
shinnel, with the clearest river-water I ever saw out of Cumberland) bisecting this expanse of heights, and leading you by the
Clone ("cloven ? ") of Maxwellton, into Glencairn valley, and
over the Black Craig of Dunscore (*Dun-scoir* = Black hill) and to
Craigenputtock if you chose. Westward of Tynron, rose Drumlanrig Castle and woods ; and the view, if you quite turned
your *back* to Dumfries, ended in the Lowthers, Leadhills, and
other lofty mountains, watershed and boundary of Lanarkshire
and Dumfriesshire : rugged, beautifully piled *sierra*, winding
round into the eastern heights (very pretty too) which part
Annandale from Nithsdale. [Alas, what is the use of all this,
here and now ?] Closeburn, mansion, woods and greeneries,
backed by brown steep masses, was on the south-eastern side,
house etc. hiding it from Walter's walk. Walk where you liked,
the view you could reckon unsurpassable,—not the least needing

to be " surpassed." Walter's walk *special* (it never had any
name of that kind ; but from the garden he glided mostly into
it, in fine days, a small green seat at each end of it, and a small
ditto gate, easy to open and shut) was not above 150 yards long :
but he sauntered and walked [in] it as fancy bade him (not with
an *eye* to " regimen," except so far as " fancy " herself might
unconsciously point that way) ; took his newspapers (*Liverpool*,
sent by John) to read there in the sunny seasons, or sat, silent,
but with a quietly alert look, contemplating the glorious
panorama of " sky-covered earth " in that part, and mildly
reaping his poor bit of harvest from it without needing to pay
rent !

We went over often ; were always a most welcome arrival,
surprise oftenest ; and our bits of visits, which could never be
prolonged, were uniformly pleasant on both sides. One of *our*
chief pleasures, I think almost our chief, during those moorland
years. Oh those pleasant gig-drives, in fine leafy twilight, or
deep in the night sometimes, ourselves two alone in the world,
the good " Harry " *faring* us (rather too light for the job, but
always soft and willing), how they rise on me now, benignantly
luminous from the bosom of the grim dead night ! What
would I give for *one*, the very worst of them, at this moment !
Once we had gone to Dumfries, in a soft misty December day
(for a Portrait which my darling wanted, not of *herself !*)—a
bridge was found broken as we went down ; brook unsafe by
night ; we had to try " Cluden (*Lower Cairn*)-Water " road, as
all was mist and pitch-darkness, on our return, road unknown
to me except in general,—and drive like no other in my memory.
Cairn hoarsely roaring on the left (my Darling's side) ; Harry,
with but one lamp-candle (for we had put out the other, lest
both might fall done), bending always to be straight in the light
of that ; I really anxious, though speaking only hopefully ; my
Darling so full of trust in me, really *happy* and opulently interested in these equipments, in these poor and dangerous circumstances,—how opulent is a nobly royal heart. She had the
worthless " Portrait " (pencil-sketch by a wandering German,
announced to us by poor and hospitable Mrs. Richardson, once
a " Novelist " of mark, much a gentlewoman and well loved by
us both) safe in her reticule ; " better far than none," she
cheerfully said of it, and the price, I think, had been 5s., fruit of
her thrift too :—well, could California have made me and her so
rich, had *I* known it (sorry gloomy mortal) just as she did ? To
noble hearts such wealth is there in Poverty itself, and impos-

sible without Poverty! I saw ahead, high in the mist, the minarets of Dunscore Kirk, at last, glad sight; at Mrs. Broatch's cosy rough inn, we got Harry fed, ourselves dried and refreshed (still seven miles to do, but road all plain), and got home safe, after a pleasant day, in spite of all.—Then the drive to Boreland once (George Welsh's, "Uncle George," youngest of the Penfillans), heart of winter, intense calm frost, and through Dumfries, at least thirty-five miles for poor Harry and us; very beautiful, that too, and very strange; past the base of towering New Abbey,[1] huge ruins, piercing grandly into the silent frosty sunset, on this hand, despicable cowhouse of Presbyterian Kirk on that hand (sad new contrast to Devorgilla's *old* bounty) etc. etc. :— of our drive home again I recollect only *her* invincible contentment, and the poor old Cowar-woman[2] offering to warm us with a flame of dry broom, "A'll licht a bruim couw, if ye'll please to come in!" Another time we had gone to "Dumfries Cattle Show" (*first* of its race, which are many since): a kind of *lark*, on our part; and really entertaining, though the day proved shockingly wet and muddy; saw various notabilities there, Sir James Grahame (baddish, proud man, we both thought by physiognomy, and did not afterwards *alter* our opinion much), Ramsay Macculloch (in sky-blue coat, shiningly on visit from London) etc. etc., with none of whom, or few, had we right (or wish) to speak, abundantly occupied with seeing so many fine specimens, biped and quadruped: in afternoon we suddenly determined to take Templand for the night (nearer by some miles, and weather still so wet and muddy); and did so, with the best success, a right glad surprise there. Poor Huskisson had perished near Liverpool, in first trial of the railway, I think, the very day before; at any rate we heard the news, or at least the full particulars there,—the tragedy (spectacular mostly, but not quite, or inhumanly in any sense) of our bright glad evening there. But I must quit these things.

[*June* 18; day wet and muddy. . . . Sad; quiet and sad; "*drowned* in soft regrets and loving sorrow," so I define my common mood at present,—and sometimes estimate it as a kind

[1] Sweetheart Abbey (*Cor Dulce*) is a magnificent ruin seven miles from Dumfries; it was built in the thirteenth century by Devorgilla, widow of John Baliol, whose heart, enclosed in an ivory casket, was buried in the High Altar. It is generally called New Abbey to distinguish it from the older abbey in the neighbourhood (Dundrennan), which this beneficent lady had also founded.

[2] *Cowar-woman*, a maker of broom "couws" or besoms. A wisp of broom, also called a *Cow* or *Couw*, is sometimes used for a temporary blaze on poor hearths in Scotland.

of *religious* worship (course of devotional exercises) I have got
into,—driven by Fate, at the long last !]

The Liverpool children first, then " Uncle John " himself for
a fortnight or so, used to come every summer ; and stir up
Templand's quietude,—to us bystanders, in a purely agreeable
way. Of the children I recollect nothing almost ; nothing that
was not cheerful and auroral or matutinal. The two Boys,
Walter and Alick, came once on visit to us, perhaps oftener, but
once I recollect their lying quiet in their big bed till eleven A.M.,
with exemplary politeness,—for fear of awakening me, who had
been up for two hours, though everybody had forgotten to
announce it to them.   We ran across to Templand rather
oftener than usual on these occasions, and I suppose staid a
shorter time.

My Jeannie had a great love and regard for her " Uncle
John," whose faults she knew well enough, but knew to be of the
surface all, while his worth of many fine kinds ran in the blood,
and never once failed to show in the conduct when called for.
He had all his Father's *veracity*, integrity, abhorrence of dis-
honourable behaviour ; was kind, munificent, frank ; and had
more than his Father's impetuosity, vehemence, and violence,
or perhaps was only more provoked (in his way of life) to exhibit
these qualities now and then.   He was cheerful, musical, politely
conversible ; truly a genial harmonious, loving nature ; but
there was a roar in him too like a lion's.   He had had great mis-
fortunes and provocations ; his way of life, in dusty, sooty, ever
noisy Liverpool, with its dinnerings, wine-drinkings, dull evening
parties issuing in whist, was not *his* element, few men's less,
though he made not the least complaint of it (even to himself, I
think) : but his heart, and all his pleasant memories and
thoughts, were in the breezy Hills of Moffatdale, with the rustic
natives there, and their shepherdings, huntings (brock and fox),
and solitary fishings in the clear streams.   It was beautiful to
see how he made some pilgriming into those or the kindred
localities ; never failed to search out all his Father's old herds-
men (with a sovereign or two for each, punctual as fate) ; and
had a few days' fishing as one item.   He had got his schooling
at Closeburn ; was, if not very learned, a very intelligent inquiring
kind of man ; could talk to you instructively about all manner
of practical things ; and loved to talk with the intelligent,
though nearly all his life was doomed to pass itself with the stupid
or commonplace sort, who were intent upon nothing but " get-
ting-on," and giving dinners or getting them.   Rarely did he

burst out into brief fiery recognition of all this ; yet once at least, before my time, I heard of his doing so in his own drawing-room, with brevity, but with memorable emphasis and fury. He was studiously polite in general, *always* so to those who deserved it, not quite always to those who didn't.

His demeanour in his bankruptcy, his and his Wife's . . . when the villain of a partner eloped, and left him possessor of a *minus* £12,000, with other still painfuller items (Sister Jeannie's incurable heart, for example), was admitted to be beautiful. Creditors had been handsome and gentle, aware how the case stood ; household with all its properties and ornaments left intact, etc. : Wife rigorously locked all her plate away ; Husband laboriously looked out for a new course of business ; ingeniously found or created one, prospered in it, saving every penny possible ;—then, after perhaps seven or eight years, had a great dinner : all the plate out again ; all the creditors there —and under every man's cover punctual sum due, payment complete to every creditor, " Pocket your cheques, Gentlemen, with our poor warmest thanks ;—and let us drink Better Luck for time coming ! " He prospered always afterwards ; but never saved much money ; too hospitable, far too open-handed, for that ; all his dinners, ever since I knew him, were *given* (never dined out, he) ; and in more than one instance, to our knowledge, ruined people were lifted up by him (one widow *Cousin*, one orphan, young daughter of an acquaintance e.g.) as if they had been his own ; sank possibly enough mainly or alto-gether into his hands, and were triumphantly (with patience and in silence) brought through. No wonder my Darling liked this Uncle ; nor had I the least difficulty in liking him !—

Once I remember mounting early, almost with the sun (a kind hand expediting, perhaps sending me), to breakfast at Templand, and spend the day with him there. I rode by the shoulder of the Black Craig (Dunscore Hill), might see Dumfries with its cap of early kitchen-smoke, all shrunk to the size of one's hat, though there were 11,000 souls in it, far away to the right ; descended then by Cairn, by the Clone of Maxwellton (where at length came roads), through fragrant grassy or bushy solitudes ; at the Bridge of Shinnel, looked down into the pellucid glassy pool rushing through its rock chasms, and at a young peasant woman, peeling potatoes by the brink, chubby infant at her knee,—one of the finest mornings, one of the pleasantest rides ; and arrived at Templand in good time and trim for my hosts. The day I forget ; would be spent whole-

somely wandering about, in rational talk on indifferent matters.
—Another time, long after, new from London then, I had
wandered out with him, his two pretty Daughters, and a poor
good Cousin called Robert Macqueen attending ; we gradually
strolled into Crichop Linn (a strange high-lying chasmy place,
near Closeburn) ; there pausing, well aloft, and shaded from the
noon sun, the two Girls, with their Father for *octave* accompaniment, sang us " The Birks of Aberfeldy " so as I have seldom
heard a song ; voices excellent and true, especially his voice
and native expression given ; which stirred my poor London-
fevered heart almost to tears.—One earlier visit from London,
I had driven up, latish, from Dumfries, to see my own little
Woman who was there among them all. No wink could I sleep ;
at length about three A.M., reflecting how miserable I should be
all day, and cause only misery to the others—I (with leave had)
rose, yoked my gig, and drove away the road I had come.
Morning cold and surly, all mortals still quiet, except unhappy
self ; I remember seeing towards Auldgarth, within few yards
of my road, a vigilant industrious heron, mid-leg deep in the
Nith-stream, diligently fishing, dabbing its long bill and hungry
eyes down into the rushing water (tail up stream), and paying
no regard to my wheels or me. The only time I ever saw a
hernshaw (" herrin-shouw " the Annandalers call it) actually
fishing. *Cætera desunt ;* of Dumfries, of the day there, and its
sequences, all trace is gone. It must have been soon after
French Revolution Book ; nerves all inflamed and torn up, body
and mind in a hag-ridden condition (too much their normal one
those many London years).

Of visits *from* Templand there were not so many ; but my
Darling (hampered and gyved as we were by the *genius loci*
and its difficulties) always triumphantly made them do. She
had the genius of a Field-marshal, not to be taken by surprise,
or weight of odds, in these cases ! Oh my beautiful little
Guardian Spirit ! Twice at least there was visit from Uncle
John in person and the Liverpool strangers, escorted by Mother ;
—*my* Mother, too, was there one of the times. Warning I
suppose had been given ; night-quarters etc. all arranged.
Uncle John and boys went down to Orr Water, I attending
without rod, to fish. Tramping about on the mossy brink,
Uncle and I awoke an adder ; we had just passed its under-
ground hole ; alarm rose,—looking round, we saw the vile
sooty-looking fatal abominable wretch, towering up above a
yard high (the only time I ever saw an adder) : one of the boys

snatched a stray branch, hurried up from behind, and with a good hearty switch or two, broke the creature's back.

Another of these dinner days, I was in the throes of a Review Article (*Characteristics*, was it ?), and could not attend the sports; but sauntered about, much on the strain, to small purpose ; *dinner* all the time that I could afford. Smoking outside at the dining-room window,—" Is not every *Day* the conflux of Two Eternities," thought I, " for every man ? " Lines of influence from all the Past, and stretching onwards into all the Future, do intersect there. That little thoughtkin stands in some of my Books : I recollect being thankful (scraggily thankful) for the day of small things.

[Oh my Darling, how dark and sad am I, and seem to have been defrauding *Thee* all this while, and speaking only about others ! I will stop ; and go out.]

[*22d June* . . .] The London bits of *memorabilia* do not disengage themselves from the general mass, as the earlier Craigenputtock ones did ; the years here, *I* still struggling *in* them, lie as a confused heap, *un*beautiful in comparison. Let me pick out (and be speedier) what comes to hand.

She liked London constantly ; and stood in defence of it against me and my atrabilious censures of it ; never had for herself the least wish to quit it again, though I was often talking of that, and her *practice* would have been loyal compliance for my behoof. I well remember my first walking her up to Hyde Park Corner in the summer evening, and her fine interest in everything. At the corner of the Green Park, I found something for her to sit on ; " Hah, there is John Mill coming ! " I said ; and her joyful ingenuous blush is still very beautiful to me. The good Child ! It did not prove to be John Mill (whom she knew since 1831, and liked for my sake): but probably I showed her the Duke of Wellington, whom one often used to see there, striding deliberately along, as if home from his work, about that hour : him (I almost rather think, that same evening), and at any rate, other figures of distinction or notoriety. And we said to one another, " How strange to be in big London here ; isn't it ? "—Our purchase of household kettles and saucepans etc. in the mean Ironmongery, so noble in its poverty and loyalty on her part, is sad and infinitely lovely to me at this moment.

We had plenty of " company " from the very first : John Mill, down from Kensington once a week or oftener ; the " Mrs. Austin " of those days, so popular and almost famous, on such exiguous basis (Translations from the German, rather poorly done, and of original nothing that rose far above the rank of twaddle) : "*femme alors célèbre*," as we used to term the pheno-menon, parodying some phrase I had found in Thiers : Mrs. Austin affected much sisterhood with us (*affected* mainly, though in *kind* wise) ; and was a cheery, sanguine, and generally accept-able member of society,—already *up* to the Marquis of Lans-downe [1] (in a slight sense), much more to all the Radical Officials and notables : Charles Buller, Sir W. Molesworth, etc. etc. of "*alors*." She still lives, this Mrs. Austin, in quiet though eclipsed condition : spring last she was in Town for a couple of weeks ; and my Dear One went twice to see her, though I couldn't manage quite.—Erasmus Darwin,[2] a most diverse kind of mortal, came to seek us out very soon (" had heard of Carlyle in Germany " etc.) ; and continues ever since to be a quiet house-friend, honestly attached ; though his visits latterly have been rarer and rarer, health so poor, I so occupied, etc. etc. He has something of original and sarcastically ingenious in him ; one of the sincerest, naturally truest, and most modest of men. Elder brother of Charles Darwin (the famed *Darwin on Species* of these days), to whom I rather prefer him for intellect, had not his health quite doomed him to silence and patient idleness ;— Grandsons, both, of the first *famed* Erasmus (" Botanic Garden" etc.), who also seems to have gone upon " species " questions ; "*Omnia ex Conchis* " (all from Oysters) being a *dictum* of his (even a *stamp* he sealed with, still extant), as the *present* Erasmus once told me, many long years before this of " Darwin on Species " came up among us ! Wonderful to me, as indicating the *capricious* stupidity of mankind ; never could *read* a page of it, or waste the least thought upon it. Erasmus Darwin it was who named the late Whewell, seeing him sit, all ear (not all *assent*) at some of my Lectures, " The Harmonious Black-smith ; " a really descriptive title. My Dear One had a great favour for this honest Darwin always ; many a road, to shops and the like, he drove her in his Cab ("*Darwingium Cabbum*," comparable to *Georgium Sidus*), in those early days, when even the charge of Omnibuses was a consideration ; and his sparse utterances, *sardonic* often, were a great amusement to her.

[1] " Yesterday Marquis of Lansdowne at Mrs. Austin's. Gray-haired, fine-headed, very polite, intelligent-whiggish looking man. Did not know or catch his name, as I was named to him : thought it ' Lord *Anser* ' (and inwardly grinned over the English of *Anser*) : ' entertained angels un-awares.' "—Carlyle's *Journal*, 27th November 1834.
[2] Erasmus Darwin died in 1881.

" A perfect *gentleman*," she at once discerned him to be ; and of sound worth, and kindliness, in the most unaffected form. " Take me now to *Oxygen* Street ; a dyer's shop there ! " Darwin, without a wrinkle or remark, made for Oxenden Street and drew up at the required door. Amusingly admirable to us both, when she came home.

Our commonest evening sitter, for a good while, was Leigh Hunt, who lived close by, and delighted to sit talking with us (free, cheery, *idly* melodious as bird on bough), or listening, with real feeling, to her old Scotch tunes on the Piano, and winding up with a frugal morsel of Scotch Porridge (endlessly admirable to Hunt) [1]—I think I spoke of this above ? Hunt was always accurately dressed, these evenings, and had a fine chivalrous gentlemanly carriage, polite, affectionate, respectful (especially to her) and yet so free and natural. Her brilliancy and faculty he at once recognised, none better ; but there rose gradually in it, to his astonished eye, something of positive, of practically steadfast, which scared him off, a good deal ; the like in my own case too, still more ;—which he would call " Scotch," " Presbyterian," who knows what ; and which gradually repelled him, in sorrow, not in anger, quite away from us, with rare exceptions, which, in his last years, were almost pathetic to us both. Long before this, he had gone to live in Kensington ;—and we scarcely saw him except by accident. His Household, while in " 4 *Upper* Cheyne Row," within few steps of us here, almost at once disclosed itself to be huggermugger, *un*thrift, and sordid collapse, once for all ; and had to be associated with on cautious terms ; —while he himself emerged out of it in the chivalrous figure I describe. Dark complexion (a trace of the African, I believe), copious clean strong black hair, beautifully-shaped head, fine beaming serious hazel eyes ; *seriousness* and intellect the main expression of the face (to our surprise at first),—he would lean on his elbow against the mantelpiece (fine clean, elastic figure too he had, five feet ten or more), and look round him nearly in silence, before taking leave for the night : " as if I were a *Lar*," said he once, " or permanent Household God here ! " (such his polite *Ariel*-like way). Another time, rising from this *Lar* attitude, he repeated (voice very fine) as if in sport of parody, yet with something of very sad perceptible : " While I to sul-

[1] " Hunt himself seems almost scared off by my Puritanic Stoicism ; talks in a quite tremulous way when he does come. A mind *shattered* by long misery into a kind of unnatural quivering eagerness, which before and instead of all things covets *agreement* with it ? A *good* man."— Carlyle's *Journal*, 8th September 1834.

phurous and penal fire "—as the last thing before vanishing. Poor Hunt ! no more of him. She, I remember, was almost in *tears*, during some last visit of his, and kind and pitying as a Daughter to the now weak and time-worn old man.

[*23d June* 1866, Saturday ; *hot*, and weary of heart.] Allan Cunningham, living in Pimlico, was well within walking distance ; and failed not to come down, now and then ; always friendly, smooth and fond of pleasing : " a solid Dumfries Stone-mason at any rate ! " *she* would define him. He had very smooth manners, much practical shrewdness, some real tone of *melody* lodged in him, *item* a twinkle of bright mockery where he judged it safe : culture only superficial (of the *surface*, truly), reading, information, ways of thinking, all mainly ditto ditto. Had a good will to us evidently ; not an unwelcome face, when he entered, at rare intervals,—always rather *rarer*, as they proved to be :—he got at once into *Nithsdale*, recalled old rustic comicalities (seemed habitually to *dwell* there) ; and had not much of instruction either to give or receive. His resort seemed to be much among Scotch City people ; who presented him with punchbowls, etc. ; and in his own house that was chiefly the (unprofitable) people to be met. We admired always his shrewd sense for managing himself in strange London ; his stalwart healthy figure and ways (bright hazel eyes, bald open brow, sonorous hearty tone of voice ; a tall, perpendicular, quietly manful-looking figure) ; and were sorry sincerely to lose him, as we suddenly did. His widow too is now gone ; some of the sons (especially Colonel Frank, the youngest, and a daughter, who lives with Frank), have still a friendly though far-off relation to this house.[1]

Harriet Martineau had for some years a much more lively intercourse here ;—introduced by Darwin possibly, I forget by whom ; on her return from America, her *Book* upon which was now in progress. Harriet had started into lionhood since our first visit to London ; and was still much run after, by a rather feeble set of persons chiefly. She was not unpleasant to talk with for a little, though through an ear-trumpet, without which she was totally deaf. To admire her literary genius, or even her solidity of common sense, was never possible for either of us : but she had a sharp eye, an imperturbable self-possession, and in all things a swiftness of positive decision, which, joined to her evident loyalty of *intention*, and her frank, guileless, easy

[1] Allan Cunningham died 29th October 1842. Colonel Francis Cunningham and his sister are now also long dead.

ways, we both liked. Her adorers, principally, not exclusively, " poor *whinnering* [1] old moneyed women in their well-hung broughams, otherwise idle," did her a great deal of mischief, and indeed as it proved were gradually turning her fine clear head (so to speak), and leading to sad issues for her. Her talent, which in that sense was very considerable, I used to think, would have made her a quite shining Matron of some big Female Establishment, mistress of some immense Dress-Shop, for instance (if she *had* a dressing-faculty, which perhaps she hadn't); but was totally inadequate to grapple with deep spiritual and social questions,—into which she launched at all turns, nothing doubting. However, she was very fond of us, *me* chiefly, at first, though gradually of both, and I was considerably the *first* that *tired* of her : she was much in the world, we little or hardly at all ; and her frank friendly countenance, eager for practical help had it been possible, was obliging and agreeable in the circumstances, and gratefully acknowledged by us. For the rest, she was full of Nigger fanaticisms ; admirations (e.g.) for her Brother James (a Socinian preacher of due quality). The " exchange of ideas " with her was seldom of behoof in our poor sphere. But she was practically very good. I remember her coming down, on the sudden when it struck her, to demand dinner from us ; and dining pleasantly, with praise of the frugal terms. Her Soirées were frequent and crowded (small house in Fludyer Street [2] full to the door) ; and we, for sake of the notabilities or notorieties wandering about there, were willing to attend. Gradually learning how *in*significant such notabilities nearly all were. Ah me, the thing which it is now touching to reflect on, was the thrift we had to exercise, my little Heroine and I ! My Darling was always dressed to modest perfection (talent conspicuous in that way, I have always understood and heard confirmed) ; but the expense of 10s. 6d. for a " neat fly " was never to be thought of : omnibus, with clogs [3] and the best of care ; that was always our resource. Painful at this moment is the recollection I have of one time : muddy night, between Regent Street and our goal in Fludyer Street, one of her clogs came loose ; I had to clasp it,—with what impatience compared to her fine tolerance, stings me with remorse just now. Surely, even I might have taken a Cab *from Regent Street ;* 1s., 1s. 6d.

1 *Whinnering,* having a falsetto tone of voice suggesting hypocrisy.
2 Fludyer Street is no longer in the London Directory. It was in Westminster, the third turning on the right hand from Charing-cross towards the Abbey and led to St. James's Park
3 Overshoes.

and there could have been no " *quarrel* about fare " (which was always my horror in such cases) : she, beautiful high soul, never whispered or dreamt of such a thing, possibly may have expressly forbidden it, though I cannot recollect that it was proposed in this case. Shame on me ! However, I cleaned perfectly my dirty fingers again (probably in some handy little rainpool in the Park, with diligent wiping) ; *she* entered faultless into the illumination (I need not doubt) : and all still went well enough.

[*24th June* . . .] In a couple of years or so, our poor Harriet, nerves all torn by this racket, of " fame " so-called, fell seriously ill ; threatening of tumour, or I know not what ; removed from London (never has resided there since, except for temporary periods) ; took shelter at Tynemouth, " to be near her brother-in-law, an expert surgeon in Newcastle, and have solitude, and the pure sea air." Solitude she only sometimes had ; and, in perfection, never : for it soon became evident she was constantly in spectacle there, to herself and to the sympathetic adorers (who refreshed themselves with frequent personal visits and continual correspondings), and had, in sad effect, so far as could be managed, the whole world, along with self and company, for a theatre to gaze upon her. *Life in the Sickroom,* with " Christus Consolator " (a paltry print then much canted of), etc. etc. : this, and other sad Books, and actions full of ostentation, done there, gave painful evidence ; followed always by painfuller, till the *Atheism* etc. etc., which I heard described (by the first Lady Ashburton once) as " a stripping of yourself naked, not to the skin only, but to the bone, and walking about in that guise ! " (*clever*, of its kind).

Once in the earliest stage of all this,[1] we made her a visit, my Jane and I ; returning out of Scotland by that route. We were very sorry for her ; not *censorious* in any measure, though the aspects were already questionable, to both of us (as I surmise). We had our lodging in the principal street (rather noisy by night) ; and staid about a week,—not with much profit I think, either to her or ourselves ; I at least with none.

[*25th June.*] There had been, before this, some small note or two of correspondence ; with little hope on my part ; and now I saw it to be hopeless. My hopefuller and kindlier little Darling continued it yet awhile ; and I remember scrubbyish (lively enough, but " sawdustish ") Socinian *didactic* little notes from Tynemouth for a year or two hence ; but the vapidly didactic etc.

---

[1] October 1841 ; Carlyle and his Wife then returning from sea-bathing quarters near Annan.

vein continuing more and more, even she, I could perceive, was getting tired of it : and at length, our poor good Harriet, taking the sublime terror " that her letters might be laid hold of by improper parties in future generations," and demanding them all back that she herself might burn them, produced, after perhaps some retiring pass or two, a complete cessation. We never quarrelled in the least ; we saw the honest ever self-sufficient Harriet, in the company of common friends, still once or twice ; with pleasure rather than otherwise ; but never had more to do with her or say to her. A soul clean as river sand ; but which would evidently grow no *flowers* of *our* planting !— I remember our return home from that week at Tynemouth ; the yelling flight through some detestable smoky chaos, and midnight witch-dance of base-looking nameless dirty towns (or was this some other time, and Lancashire the scene ?). I remember *she* was with me : and her bright laugh (long after, perhaps towards Rugby now) in the face of some innocent young gentleman opposite, who had ingeniously made a *nightcap* for himself of his pocket-handkerchief, and looked really strange (an improvised ' Camus crowned with sedge '),—but was very good-humoured too. *During* the week, I also recollect reading one Play (never any since or before) of Knight's *Edition of Shakespeare ;* and making my reflections on that fatal brood of people, and the nature of " fame " etc. : Sweet friends, for Jesus' sake forbear !

[*26th June* . . .] In those first years, probably from about 1839, we had got acquainted with the Leeds Marshall family ; especially with old Mr. (John) Marshall, the head and founder of it, and the most or really almost only interesting item of it. He had made immense moneys (" wealth now no object to him," Darwin told us in the name of everybody), by skilful, faithful and altogether human conduct in his flax or linen manufactory at Leeds ; and was now settled in opulently shining circumstances in London ; endeavouring to *enjoy* the victory gained. Certain of his sons were carrying on the Leeds " business," in high, quasi-" patriotic " and " morally exemplary," though still prudent and successful style ; the eldest was in Parliament, " a landed gentleman " etc. etc. : wife and daughters were the old man's London household, with sons often incidentally present there. None of them was entertaining to speak with, though all were honest wholesome people. The old man himself, a pale, sorrow-stricken, modest, yet dignified-looking person, full of respect for intellect, wisdom and worth (as he understood the terms) ; low voiced, almost timidly inarticulate (you would have said),—yet with a definite and mildly precise imperativeness to his subalterns, as I have noticed once or twice,—was an amiable, humane and thoroughly respectable phenomenon to me. The house (Grosvenor Street, western division) was resplendent, not gaudy or offensive, with wealth and its fruits and furnishings ; the dinners large, and splendidly served ; guests of distinction (especially on the Whig or Radical side) were to be met with there, and a good sprinkling of promising younger people of the same, or a superior type. Soirées extensive, and sumptuously *illuminated* in all senses ; but generally *not* entertaining. My astonishment at the " Reform " M.P.'s whom I met there, and the notions they seemed to have of " reforming " (and *radical*ling, and quarrelling with their superiors) upon ! We went pretty often (I think I myself far the oftener, as in such cases ; my loyal little Darling taking no manner of offence *not* to participate in my *lionings ;* but behaving like the royal soul she was,—I, dullard egoist, taking no special recognition of such nobleness, till the bar was quite passed, or even not fully then ! Alas, I see it *now*, perhaps better than I ever did !), but we seldom had much real profit, or even real enjoyment for the hour. We never made out together that often-urged " visit to Hallsteads " (grand Mansion and Establishment, near Greystoke, head of Ullswater in Cumberland) ; I myself, partly by accident, and under convoy of James Spedding, was there once, long after, for one night ; [1] and felt very dull and wretched, though the old man and his good old wife etc. were so good. Old Mr. Marshall was a man worth having known ; evidently a great deal of human worth and wisdom lying funded in him. And the world's resources even when he had victory over it to the full, were so exiguous, and perhaps to himself almost contemptible ! I remember well always, he gave me the first *Horse* I ever had in London, and with what noble simplicity of unaffected politeness he did it. " Son William " (the gentleman son, out near Watford) " will be *glad* to take it off your hands through winter ; and in summer it will help your health, you *know !* " And in this way it continued two summers (most part of two), till in the second winter William brought it down ; and it had to be sold, for a trifle— £17, if I recollect, which William would not give to the Anti-Corn-Law Fund (then struggling in the shallows) as I urged, but insisted on handing over to me. And so it ended. I was at

---

[1] On the occasion of their visit to Tynemouth, October 1841.

Headingley (by Leeds) with James Marshall, just wedded to
Spring-Rice's daughter, a languishing patroness of mine ; staid
till third day ; and never happened to return.   And this was
about the sum of my share in the Marshall adventure.   It is
well known the Marshall daughters were all married off (each
of them had £50,000) and what intricate intermarrying with the
Spring-Rices there was. . . . My Jeannie quarrelled with nothing
in Marshalldom ; quite the contrary ; formed a kind of friendship (conquest I believe it was on her side, generously converted
into something of friendship) with Cordelia Marshall, . . . who
became, shortly after, wife, first wife of the late big Whewell, and
aided his position and advancement towards Mastership of
Trinity, etc.   I recollect seeing them both here, and Cordelia's
adoration of her ' Harmonious Blacksmith,' with friendly enough
assent, and some amusement, from us two ; and I don't think
I ever saw Cordelia again.   She soon ceased to write hither ; we
transiently heard . . . that she was very unhappy (Poor innocent
Cordelia !) and transiently, after certain years, that she was
dead, and Whewell had married again.

   I am weary, writing down all this ; so little has my Lost
One to do with it, which alone could be its interest for me !   I
believe I should stop short.   The London years are not definite,
or fertile in disengaged remembrances, like the Scotch ones :
dusty, dim, unbeautiful they still seem to me in comparison ;
and my poor Jeannie's " Problem " (which I believe was sorer,
perhaps far sorer, than ever of old, but in which she again proved
not to be vanquishable, and at length to be triumphant !) is so
mixed with confusing intricacies to me that I cannot sort it out
into clear articulation at all, or give the features of it, as before.
The general type of it is shiningly clear to me : A noble fight
at my side ; a valiant strangling of serpents day after day—
done gaily by her (for most part), as I had to do it angrily and
gloomily ; thus we went on together : *Ay de mi, Ay de mi !*—

   [*June* 27.   Note from Dods yesterday that the *Tablet* [1] was

----

   [1] The Tablet is imbedded in the Tombstone, at Haddington, already
there to mark her Father's resting place, which had now become hers
also.   It bears the following inscription :—

                    " Here likewise now rests

                    " JANE WELSH CARLYLE,

            " Spouse of Thomas Carlyle, Chelsea, London.

   " She was born at Haddington, 14th July 1801 : only child of the above
John Welsh, and of Grace Welsh, Caplegill, Dumfriesshire, his Wife.   In
her bright existence she had more sorrows than are common ; but also a

not come, nor indeed had been expected ; note to-day that it did come yesterday : at this hour probably the mason is hewing out a bed for it ; in the silence of the Abbey Kirk yonder, as completion of her Father's Tomb. The Eternities looking down on him, and on us poor Sons of Time ! Peace, Peace !]

[*June* 28.] By much the tenderest and beautifullest reminiscence to me out of those years is that of the Lecture times. The vilest welter of odious confusions, horrors and repugnancies ; to which, meanwhile, there was conpulsion absolute ;—and to which she was the one irradiation ; noble loving soul, not to be quenched in any chaos that might come. Oh, her love to me ; her cheering, unaffected, useful practicality of help : was not I *rich*, after all ? She had a steady hope in me, too, while I myself had habitually none (except of the " desperate " kind) ; nay a steady contentment with me, and with our lot together, let hope be as it might. " Never mind him, my Dear," whispered Miss Wilson to her, one day, as I stood wriggling in my agony of incipiency, " people like it ; the more of that, the better does the Lecture prove ! " Which was a truth ; though the poor *Sympathiser* might, at the moment, feel it harsh. This Miss Wilson and her brother still live ; opulent, fine, Church of England people (scrupulously orthodox to the secularities not less than the spiritualities of that creed), and Miss Wilson very clever too (i.e. full of strong just insight in her way) ;—who had from the first taken to us, and had us much about them (Spedding, Maurice, etc. attending) then and for some years afterwards ; very desirous to help us, if that could have much done it (for indeed, to me, it was always mainly an indigestion purchased by a loyal kind of weariness. I have seen Sir James Stephen there, but did not then understand him, or that *he* could be a " clever man," as reported by Henry Taylor and other good judges. " He shuts his eyes on you," said the elder Spring-Rice (Lord Monteagle), " and talks as if he were dictating a Colonial Despatch " (most true ;—" teaching you How *Not* to do it," as Dickens defined afterwards) : one of the pattest things I ever heard from Spring-Rice, who had rather a turn for such. Stephen, ultimately, when on half-pay and a Cambridge Professor, used to come down hither pretty often on an evening ;

soft invincibility, a clearness of discernment, and a noble loyalty of heart, which are rare. For forty years she was the true and ever-loving Helpmate of her Husband ; and, by act and word, unweariedly forwarded him, as none else could, in all of worthy that he did or attempted.

" She died at London, 21st April 1866 ; suddenly snatched away from him, and the light of his life as if gone out."

and we heard a great deal of talk from him, recognisably serious and able, though always in that Colonial-Office style, more or less. Colonial-Office *being* an Impotency (as Stephen inarticulately, though he never said or whispered it, well knew), what *could* an earnest and honest kind of man do, but try and teach you How *not* to do it? Stephen seemed to me a master in that art.—

The *Lecture* time fell in the earlier part of the Sterling Period,[1] —which latter must have lasted in all, counting till John's death, about ten years (Autumn 1844 when John died). To my Jeannie, I think, this was clearly the sunniest and wholesomest element in her then outer life. All the Household loved her; and she had virtually, by her sense, by her felt *loyalty*, expressed oftenest in a gay mildly quizzing manner, a real influence, a kind of light *command* one might almost call it, willingly yielded her among them. Details of this are in print (as I said above).—In the same years, Mrs. Buller (Charles's mother) was a very cheerful item to her. Mrs. Buller (a whilom Indian Beauty, Wit and finest Fine Lady), who had, at all times a very recognising eye for talent, and a real reverence for it, very soon made out something of my little woman; and took more and more to her, all the time she lived after. Mrs. Buller's circle was gay and populous at this time (Radical, chiefly Radical, lions of every complexion), and we had as much of it as we would consent to. I remember being at Leatherhead too;—and, after that, a pleasant rustic week at Troston Parsonage (in Suffolk, where Mrs. Buller's youngest son " served," and serves); which Mrs. Buller contrived very well to make the best of, sending me to ride for three days in Oliver Cromwell's country, that she might have the Wife more to herself. My Jane must have been there altogether, I dare say, near a month (had gone before me, returned after me); and I regretted never to have seen the place again. This must have been in September or October 1842; Mrs. Welsh's death in early Spring past. I remember well my feelings in Ely Cathedral, in the close of sunset or dusk; the place was open, free to me without witnesses; people seemed to be tuning the organ, which went in solemn gusts far aloft; the thought of Oliver, and his " Leave off your fooling, and come down, Sir!"[2] was almost as if audible to me. Sleepless night, owing to Cathedral bells; and strange ride next day to St. Ives, to Hinchinbrook, etc., and thence to Cambridge, with

[1] See *supra*, p. 78 *n*.
[2] *Cromwell's Letters and Speeches* (Everyman edition), i. 146.

thundercloud and lightning dogging me to rear, and bursting into torrents few minutes after I got into The Hoop Inn.—

My poor Darling had, for constant accompaniment to all her bits of satisfaction, an altogether weak state of health, continually breaking down, into violent fits of headache in her best times, and in winter-season into cough, etc., in lingering forms of a quite sad and exhausting sort. Wonderful to me how she, so sensitive a creature, maintained her hoping cheerful humour to such a degree, amidst all that ; and, except the pain of inevitable sympathy, and vague flitting fears, gave me no pain. Careful always to screen me from pain, as I by no means always reciprocally was ; alas, no ; miserable egoist in comparison ! At this time, I must have been in the thick of *Cromwell* ; " four years " of abstruse toil, obscure tentations, futile wrestling, and misery, I used to count it had cost me, before I took to editing the *Letters and Speeches* (" to have *them* out of my way ") ; which rapidly drained off the sour swamp water bodily, and left me, beyond all first expectations, quite free of the matter. Often I have thought how miserable my Books must have been to *her ;* and how, though they were none of her choosing, and had come upon her like ill weather or ill health, she at no instant (never once, I do believe) made the least complaint of me or my behaviour (often bad, or at least thoughtless and weak) under them ! Always some quizzing little lesson, the purport and effect of which was to encourage me ; never once anything *worse.* Oh it was noble ;—and I see it so well now, when it is gone from me, and no return possible !

Cromwell was by much the worst Book-time ; till this of *Friedrich ;* which indeed was infinitely worse ; in the dregs of our strength too ;—and lasted for about thirteen years. She was generally in quite weak health, too ; and was often for long weeks or months, miserably ill.

[*28th June.* Interruption here yesterday ; to-day likewise, the whole morning gone, in extraneous fiddle-faddle, and not so much as one word here ! Shame on *me ;* for (though " the world " is a most intrusive, useless, nay plunderous and obstructive affair to me at present), the blame is not chiefly " the world's " but my own ! Froude is now coming ; and with remorse, I must put this away. News of Craik's death, at Belfast, 27th ult., came last night.]

[*29th June.*] It was strange how she contrived to sift out of such a troublous forlorn day as hers, in such case, was, all the available little items ; as she was sure to do,—and to have them ready for me in the evening when my work was done ; in the prettiest little narrative anybody could have given of such things. Never again shall I have such melodious, humanly beautiful Half-hours ; they were the *rainbow* of my poor dripping *day*,—and reminded me that there otherwise *was* a Sun. At this time, and all along, she " did all the society ; " was all brightness to the one or two (oftenest rather dull and prosaic fellows, for all the *better* sort respected my seclusion, especially during that last *Friedrich* time), whom I *needed* to see on my affairs in hand, or who, with more of *brass* than others, managed to intrude upon me : for these she did, in their several kinds, her very best ; all of her own people, whom I might be apt to feel wearisome (dislike any of them I never did, or his or her *discharge from service* would have swiftly followed), she kept beautifully out of my way, saving my " politeness " withal : a very perfect skill she had in all this. And *took* my dark toiling periods, however long sullen and severe they might be, with a loyalty and heart-acquiescence that never failed. The heroic little soul !

Latter-Day Pamphlet time, and especially the time that preceded it (1848 etc.) must have been very sore and heavy : my heart was long overloaded with the meanings at length uttered there, and no way of getting them set forth would answer. I forget what ways I tried, or thought of ; *Times* Newspaper was one (alert, airy, rather vacant editorial gentleman I remember going to once, in Printing House Square) ; but this way, of course, proved *hypothetical* merely,—as all others did, till we, as last shift, gave the rough MSS. to Chapman (in Forster's company one winter Sunday). About *half* of the ultimately *printed* might be in Chapman's hands ; but there was much manipulation as well as addition needed. Forster [1] soon fell away, I could perceive, into terror and surprise ;—as indeed everybody did : " A lost man ! " thought everybody. Not she at any moment ; much amused by the outside pother, she ; and glad to see me getting delivered of my black electricities and consuming fires, in that way. Strange letters came to us, during those nine months of pamphleteering ; strange visitors (of moonstruck unprofitable type for most part), who had, for one reason or another, been each of them wearing himself

[1] John Forster was for forty years a devoted friend of Carlyle's. His kindness and helpfulness to him, especially after Mrs. Carlyle's death, is sufficiently evident from the pages which follow. He was appointed one of the Executors of Carlyle's Will ; but he predeceased Carlyle, having died in 1876.

half-mad on some *one* of the public scandals I was recognising and denouncing. I still remember some of their faces, and the look their paper bundles had. She got a considerable entertainment out of all that ; went along with me in everything (probably *counselling* a little here and there ; a censorship well worth my regarding, and generally *adoptable*, here as everywhere) ; and minded no whit any results that might follow this evident *speaking of the truth.* Somebody, writing from India I think, and clearly meaning kindness, " did hope " (some time afterwards) " the tide would turn, and this lamentable Hostility of the Press die away into friendship again : " at which I remember our innocent laughter,—ignorant till then what " The Press's " feelings were, and leaving " The Press " very welcome to them then. Neuberg [1] helped me zealously, as volunteer amanuensis etc., through all this business ; but I know not that even he approved it all, or any of it *to the bottom.* In the whole world I had one complete Approver ; in that, as in other cases, *one ;* and it was worth all.

On the back of *Latter-Day Pamphlets* followed *Life of Sterling;* [2] a very quiet thing ; but considerably disapproved of too, as I learned ; and utterly revolting to the *Religious people* in particular (to my surprise rather than otherwise) : " Doesn't believe in *us,* then, either ? " Not he, for certain ; *can't,* if you *will* know ! Others urged disdainfully, " What has Sterling

[1] Joseph Neuberg (born near Würzburg 1806 ; died at Hampstead 1867) was, when Carlyle became acquainted with him in 1840, a merchant in Nottingham ; some eight or nine years afterwards, having quitted his business, he generously offered his services as Amanuensis to Carlyle. He was a man " of perfect integrity, of serious reflective temper, of fine and strong faculties (able to *understand* anything presented to him, and of many high aspirations. For the last twenty or twenty-five years, he had been my most attached adherent, ever-loyal, ever-patient, ardent, ever-willing to do me service in every kind :—we were twice in Germany together, where I defined him to be worth ' ten Couriers ' ; in regard to the Book *Friedrich* (especially till he took to translating it, and *I* had not the face to apply so often) his help was truly valuable (or *in*valuable ; sat three months in the State-Paper Office, for example, *excerpting* there, with a skill and rapid felicity not to be rivalled) ; he did all kinds of *excerpting* and *abstracting* etc. etc. as if I myself had done it ;—and, in brief, was an *alter ego* in all the deeper parts of that horrible immensity of drudgery, which I believe would have been impossible to *me* without him. Got no shadow of *reward,* nor sought any ; stood all my spurts of ill-temper, etc., without once wincing ; worked like a patient hero for me, as if *he* had been nothing, I something, and as if it ennobled *his* poor existence so to do ! Perhaps no man of my day had such a *servant* and *subject* (in the noblest sense of these words),—acquired to me without the least effort too ; rather permitted to *give* himself, than in any way asked for."—Carlyle's *Journal,* 3d April 1867. Carlyle had collected materials for a Memoir of Neuberg ; but was unable to carry out his intention of writing it.

[2] *Latter-Day Pamphlets,* published 1850 ; *Life of Sterling,* 1851.

done that he should have a *Life* ? " " *Induced* Carlyle *somehow*
to write him one ! " answered she once (to the Ferguses, I
think) in an arch airy way, which I can well fancy ; and which
shut up the question there.   The book was afterwards greatly
praised,—again, on rather weak terms, I doubt.   What now
will please me best in it, and alone *will*, was then an accidental
quality,—the authentic light, under the due conditions, that is
thrown by it on *her*.   Oh my Dear One ; sad is my soul for the
loss of Thee, and will to the end be, as I compute !   *Lonelier*
creature there is not henceforth in this world ; neither person,
work, or thing going on in it that is of any value, in comparison,
or even at all.   Death I feel almost daily in express fact,
Death is the one haven; and have occasionally a kind of *kingship*,
sorrowful, but sublime, almost godlike, in the feeling that that
is nigh.   Sometimes the image of Her, gone in her car of victory
(in that beautiful death), and as if nodding to me with a smile,
" I am gone, loved one ; work a little longer, if thou still canst ;
if not, follow !   There is no baseness, and no misery *here*.
Courage, courage to the last ! "—that, sometimes, as in this
moment, is inexpressibly beautiful to me, and comes nearer to
bringing *tears* than it once did.   [Stop for to-day.]

[*June* 30.]   In 1852 had come the new-modelling of our
House ;—attended with infinite dusty confusion (head-carpenter
stupid, though honest, fell ill, etc. etc.) ; confusion falling upon
her more than me, and at length upon her altogether.   *She* was
the architect, guiding and directing and contriving genius, in
all that enterprise, seemingly so foreign to her.   But indeed she
was ardent in it ; and she had a talent that way which was
altogether unique in my experience.   An " eye " first of all,
equal in correctness to a joiner's square,—this, up almost from
her childhood, as I understood.   Then a sense of order, sense of
beauty, of wise and thrifty convenience ;—sense of *wisdom*
altogether in fact ; for that was it !   A human intellect shining
luminous in every direction, the highest and the lowest (as I
remarked above) ; in childhood she used to be sent to seek when
things fell lost ; " the best seeker of us all," her Father would
say, or look (as she thought) : for me also she *sought* everything,
with such success as I never saw elsewhere.   It was she who
widened our poor drawing-room (as if by a stroke of genius) and
made it (zealously, at the partial expense of three feet from
her own bedroom) into what it now is, one of the prettiest little
drawing-rooms I ever saw, and made the whole house into what
it now is.   How frugal, too, and how modest about it !   House

was hardly finished, when there arose that of the " Demon-Fowls,"—as she appropriately named them : macaws, Cochin-chinas, endless concert of crowing, cackling, shrieking roosters (from a bad or misled neighbour, next door) which cut us off from sleep or peace, at times altogether, and were like to drive me mad, and her through me, through sympathy with me. From which also she was my deliverer,—had delivered and continued to deliver me from hundreds of such things (Oh my beautiful little *Alcides*, in these new days of Anarchy and the Mud-gods, threatening to crush down a poor man, and kill him with his work still on hand !) I remember well her setting off, one winter morning, from the Grange on this enterprise ;— probably having thought of it most of the night (sleep denied), she said to me next morning the first thing : " Dear, we *must* extinguish those Demon-Fowls, or they will extinguish us ! Rent the house (No. 6, proprietor mad etc. etc.) ourselves ; it is but some £40 a year,—pack away those vile people, and let it stand empty. I will go this very day upon it, if you assent ! " And she went accordingly ; and slew altogether this *Lerna Hydra ;* at far less expense than taking the house, nay almost at no expense at all, except by her fine intellect, tact, just discernment, swiftness of decision, and general nobleness of mind (in short). Oh, my bonny little woman ; mine only in memory now !—

I left the Grange two days after her, on this occasion ; hastening through London, gloomy of mind ; to see my dear old Mother yet once (if I might) before she died. She had, for many months before, been evidently and painfully sinking away,—under no disease, but the ever-increasing infirmities of eighty-three years of time. She had expressed no desire to see me ; but her love from my birth upwards, under all scenes and circumstances, I knew to be emphatically a Mother's. I walked from the Kirtlebridge (" Galls ") Station that dim winter morning ; my one thought, " Shall I see her yet alive ? " She was still there ; weary, very weary, and wishing to be at rest. I think she only at times knew me ; so bewildering were her continual distresses ; once she entirely forgot me ; then, in a minute or two, asked my pardon—ah me, ah me ! It was my Mother, and not my Mother ; the last pale *rim* or sickle of the moon, which had once been *full*, now sinking in the dark seas. This lasted only three days. Saturday night she had her full faculties, but was in nearly unendurable misery ; not breath sufficient etc. etc. : John tried various reliefs, had at last to give a few drops of

laudanum, which eased the misery, and in an hour or two
brought sleep. All next day she lay asleep, breathing equably
but heavily,—her face grand and solemn, almost severe, like a
marble statue ; about four P.M. the breathing suddenly halted ;
recommenced for half an instant, then fluttered,—ceased.[1]
" All the days of my appointed time," she had often said, " will
I wait, *till my change come*." The most beautifully *religious* soul
I ever knew. Proud enough she was, too, though piously
humble ; and full of native intellect, humour, etc., though all
undeveloped. On the *religious* side, looking into the very heart
of the matter, I always reckon her rather *superior* to my Jane,
who in other shapes and with far different exemplars and conditions, had a great deal of noble religion too. Her death filled
me with a kind of *dim amazement*, and crush of *confused* sorrows,
which were very painful, but not so sharply pathetic as I might
have expected. It was the earliest terror of my childhood that
I " might lose my Mother ; " and it had gone with me all my
days :—But, and that is probably the whole account of it, I was
then sunk in the miseries of *Friedrich* etc. etc., in many miseries ;
and was then fifty-eight years of age.—It is strange to me, in
these very days, how *peaceable*, though still sacred and tender,
the memory of my Mother now lies in me. (This very morning,
I got into dreaming confused *nightmare* stuff about some *funeral*
and her ; not hers, nor obviously my Jane's, seemingly my
Father's rather, and she *sending* me on it,—the saddest bewildered stuff. What a dismal debasing and confusing element is
that of a *sick body* on the human soul or *thinking* part !)—

It was in 1852 (September-October, for about a month) that
I had first seen Germany,—gone on my first errand as to *Friedrich :* there was a second, five years afterwards ; this time it
was to *inquire* (of Preuss and Co.) ; to look about me, search for
books, portraits, etc. etc. I went from Scotsbrig (my dear old
Mother painfully weak, though I had no thought it would be the
last time I should see her *afoot*) ;—from Scotsbrig by Leith for
Rotterdam, Köln, Bonn (Neuberg's) ;—and on the whole never
had nearly so (outwardly) unpleasant a journey in my life ; till
the second and last I made thither. But the Chelsea establishment was under carpenters, painters ; till those disappeared,
no *work* possible, scarcely any *living* possible (though my brave
woman did make it possible without complaint) : " Stay so
many weeks, all painting at least shall then be off ! " I returned,
near broken-down utterly, at the set time ; and, alas, was met

[1] Carlyle's Mother died at Scotsbrig, Ecclefechan, 25th December 1853.

by a foul dabblement of paint oozing downstairs : the painters had proved treacherous to her ; time could not be kept ! It was the one instance of such a thing here ; and except the first sick surprise, I now recollect no more of it.

[*Sunday, 1st July.*] " Mamma, *wine* makes cosy ! " said the bright little one, perhaps between two and three years old, her Mother, after some walk with sprinkling of wet or the like, having given her a dram-glass of wine on their getting home : " Mamma, wine makes *cosy !* " said the small silver voice, gaily sipping, getting its new bits of insight into natural philosophy ! What " pictures " has my Beautiful One left me ;—what joys can surround every well-ordered human hearth. I said long since, I never knew so beautiful a childhood. Her little bit of a first chair, its wee wee arms etc., visible to me in the closet at this moment, is still here, and always was ; I have looked at it hundreds of times ; from of *old*, with many thoughts. No daughter or son of *hers* was to sit there ; so it had been appointed us, my Darling. I have no *Book* thousandth-part so beautiful as Thou ; but these were *our* only " Children,"—and, in a true sense, these *were* verily OURS ; and will perhaps live some time in the world, after we are both gone ;—and be of no damage to the poor brute chaos of a world, let us hope ! The Will of the Supreme shall be accomplished : *Amen.* But to proceed.

Shortly after my return from Germany (next summer, I think, while the *Cochin-chinas* were at work, and we could not quit the house, having spent so much on it, and got a long lease), there began a new still worse hurlyburly of the building kind ; that of the new top-story,—whole area of the house to be thrown into one sublime garret-roof, lighted from above, thirty feet by thirty say, and at least eleven feet high ; double-doored, double-windowed ; impervious to sound, to—in short, to every-thing but self and work ! I had my grave doubts about all this ; but John Chorley,[1] in his friendly zeal, warmly urged it on ;

[1] John R. Chorley, Author of *Catálogo de Comedias y Autos de Frey Lope Félix de Vega Carpio* (1860), " which in Spain itself, I understand," writes Carlyle, " has been considered supreme in that kind. For these thirty years past a warm and faithful friend of mine. . . . A man of clear sharp intellect, and fine practical faculties and habits ; of extensive accurate scholarship, and ditto inquiry ; one of the best-informed men to be met with,—decidedly the best-*read* man I knew in London, or indeed elsewhere in these last years. He has left no ' fame ' or general recognition in any kind, behind him,—while so many thousands of far less worth are sounding on the ' popular gale ' (if that could at all help them !) Poor Chorley read constantly for reading's sake, and had not the least regard to ' sounding ' on anybody's tongue or mind. He knew *Classic* Languages like a Scholar, with great accuracy : modern too and their Literatures, German, especially

pushed, superintended ;—and was a good deal disgusted with my
dismal experience of the *result*. Something really good might
have come of it in a scene where good and faithful work was to
be had on the part of all, from *architect* downwards ; but here,
from all (except one good young man of the carpenter trade,
whom I at length noticed thankfully in small matters), the
" work," of planning to begin with, and then of executing, in all
its details, was mere work of Belial, i.e. of the Father of LIES ;
such "work" as I had not conceived the possibility of among the
sons of Adam till *then*. By degrees, I perceived it to be the
ordinary English " work " of this epoch ;—and, with manifold
reflections, deep as Tophet, on the outlooks *this* offered for us all,
endeavoured to be silent as to my own little failure. My new
illustrious " Study " was definable as the *least* inhabitable, and
most entirely detestable and despicable bit of human workman-
ship in that kind. Sad and odious to me *very*. But by many
and long-continued efforts, with endless botherations which
lasted for two or three years after (one winter starved by
" Arnott's improved *grate*," I recollect), I did get it patched
together into something of supportability ; and continued,
though under protest, to inhabit it during all working hours,
as I had indeed from the first done. The whole of the now
printed *Friedrich* was written there (or in summer in the back
court and garden, when driven down by baking heat) ; much
rawer matter, I think, was tentatively on paper, *before* this sublime new " Study." *Friedrich* once done, I quitted the place
for ever ; and it is now a bedroom for the servants. The
" architect " for this beautiful bit of masonry and carpentry
was one " Parsons," really a clever creature, I could see, but
swimming as for dear life in a mere " Mother of Dead Dogs "
(ultimately did become bankrupt) ; his *men* of all types, Irish
hodmen and upwards, for real *mendacity* of hand, for drunken-
ness, greediness, mutinous nomadism, and anarchic malfeasance
throughout, excelled all experience or conception. Shut the *lid*
on their " unexampled prosperity " and them, for evermore.

The sufferings of my poor little woman, throughout all this,
must have been great, though she whispered nothing of them,—

French, and Spanish most of all, with an accuracy and completeness quite
peculiar to him here. . . . *Ay de mi*, no more will he rise up, pen joyfully
flung down, sharp wiry face relapsing into a sunny smile, and kind right-
hand held out, on my entrance at any time ! Friends are falling fast
about me ; sign after sign, ' Thy own turn must be soon ! '—To-morrow is
his Funeral ; half-past eight A.M. ; at which, in spite of the bad hour, I
of course resolve to be."—Carlyle's *Journal*, 3d July 1867.

the rather, as this was my enterprise (both the *Friedrich* and it) ; —indeed it was by her address and invention that I got my sooterkin [1] of a ' study ' improved out of its worst blotches ; it was she, for example, that went silently to Bramah's smith people, and got me a fireplace, of merely human sort, which actually warmed the room, and sent Arnott's miracle about its business. But undoubtedly that *Friedrich* affair, with its many bad adjuncts, was much the *worst* we ever had ; and sorely tried us both. It lasted thirteen years or more.[2] To me a desperate dead-lift pull at that time ; my whole strength devoted to it ; alone, withdrawn from all the world (except some bores who would take no hint, almost nobody came to see me, nor did I wish almost anybody then left living for me), all the world withdrawing from me ; I desperate of ever *getting through* (not to speak of " succeeding ") ; left solitary " with the nightmares " (as I sometimes expressed it), " hugging unclean creatures " (Prussian Blockheadisms) " to my bosom, trying to caress and flatter their secret out of them ! " Why do I speak of all this ? It is now become *coprolite* to me, insignificant as the dung of a thousand centuries ago : I did get through, thank God ; let it now wander into the belly of oblivion for ever. But what I do still, and shall more and more, remember with loving admiration is her behaviour in it. She was habitually in the feeblest health ; often, for long whiles, grievously ill. Yet by an alchemy all her own, she had extracted grains as of gold out of every day, and seldom or never failed to have something bright and pleasant to tell me, when I reached home after my evening ride, the most foredone of men. In all, I rode, during that book, some 30,000 miles, much of it (all the winter part of it) under cloud of night, sun just setting when I mounted. All the rest of the day, I sat silent aloft ; insisting upon work, and *such* work, *invitissimâ Minervâ* for that matter. Home between five and six, with mud mackintoshes off, and, the nightmares locked up for a while, I tried for an hour's sleep before my (solitary, *dietetic*, altogether simple, simple) bit of dinner ; but first *always*, came up for half an hour to the drawing-room and Her ; where a bright kindly fire was sure to be burning (candles hardly lit, all in trustful *chiaroscuro*), and a spoonful of brandy in water, with a pipe of tobacco (which I had learned to take sitting on the rug, with my back to the jamb, and door never so little *open*, so that all

---

[1] Sooterkin : *Hudibras,* part iii. canto ii.
[2] The following are the dates of publication of the *Friedrich* Volumes : I. and II., 1858 ; III., 1862 ; IV., 1864 ; V. and VI., 1865.

the smoke, if I was careful, went up the chimney) : this was the one bright portion of my black day. Oh those evening half-hours, how beautiful and blessed they were,—*not* awaiting me now on my home-coming, for the last ten weeks! She was oftenest reclining on the sofa ; wearied enough, she too, with her day's doings and endurings. But her history, even of what was bad, had such grace and truth, and spontaneous tinkling melody of a naturally cheerful and loving heart, I never any-where enjoyed the like. Her courage, patience, silent heroism, meanwhile, must often have been immense. Within the last two years or so she has told me about my talk to her of the Battle of Mollwitz on these occasions, while that was on the anvil. She was lying on the sofa ; weak, but I knew little how weak, and patient, kind, quiet and good as ever. After tugging and wriggling through what inextricable labyrinth and Sloughs-of-despond, I still well remember, it appears I had at last *conquered* Mollwitz, saw it all clear ahead and round me, and took to telling her about it, in my poor bit of joy, night after night. I recollect she answered little, though kindly always. Privately, she at that time felt convinced she was dying :—dark winter, and such the weight of misery, and utter decay of strength ;—and, night after night, my theme to her, *Mollwitz !* This she owned to me, within the last year or two ;—which how could I listen to without shame and abasement ? Never in my pretended-superior kind of life, have I done, for love of any creature, so supreme a kind of thing. It touches me at this moment with penitence and humiliation, yet with a kind of soft *religious* blessedness too.—She *read* the first two volumes of *Friedrich*, much of it in printer's sheets (while on visit to the aged Misses Donaldson at Haddington) ; her applause (should not I collect her fine Notekins and reposit them here ?) was beautiful and as sunlight to me,—for I knew it was sincere withal, and unerringly straight upon the blot, however exaggerated by her great love of me. The other volumes (hardly even the third, I think) she never read,—I knew too well why ; and submitted without murmur, save once or twice perhaps a little quiz on the subject, which did not afflict her, either. Too weak, too weak by far, for a dismal enterprise of that kind, as I knew too well ! But those Haddington visits were very beautiful to her (and to me through her letters and her) ; and by that time, we were over the hill and " the worst of our days were *past* " (as poor Irving used to give for *toast*, long ago),—worst of them past, though we did not yet quite know it.

[*July* 3.] Volumes One, Two of *Friedrich* were published, I find, in 1858. Probably about two years before that was the *nadir* of my poor Wife's sufferings ;—internal sufferings and dispiritments ; for outward *fortunes* etc. had now, for about ten years, been on a quite tolerable footing, and indeed evidently fast on the improving hand : nor had *they*, at any worst time, ever disheartened her, or darkened her feelings. But in 1856, owing to many circumstances,—my *engrossment* otherwise (sunk in *Friedrich*, in etc. etc. ; far *less* exclusively, very far *less*, than she supposed, poor soul !) ;—and owing *chiefly*, one may fancy, to the deeper downbreak of her own poor health, which from this time, as I now see better, continued its advance upon the *citadel*, or nervous system, and intrinsically grew worse and worse :—in 1856, too evidently, to whatever owing, my poor little Darling was extremely miserable ! Of that year there is a bit of private diary, by chance, left unburnt ; found by me since her death, and not to be destroyed, however tragical and sternly sad are parts of it. She had written, I sometimes knew (though she would never show to me or to mortal any word of them), at different times, various bits of diary ; and was even, at one time, upon a kind of autobiography (had not —— stept into it with swine's foot, most intrusively, though without ill intention—finding it unlocked one day ;—and produced thereby an instantaneous burning of it ; and of all like it which existed at that time). Certain enough, she wrote various bits of diary and private record, unknown to me : but never anything so sore, downhearted, harshly distressed and sad as this (right sure am I !)—which alone remains as specimen ! The rest are all burnt ; no trace of them, seek where I may.

[Here followed Mrs. Carlyle's private diary above referred to ; at the end of which Carlyle has written : " A very sad record ! We went to Scotland soon after ; " (*i.e.* after the date of the last entry in it, 5th July 1856) " she to Auchtertool (cousin Walter's), I to the Gill (sister Mary's)."]

In July 1856, as marked in her sad record, may have been about middle of month, we went to Edinburgh ; a blazing day full of dust and tumult,—which I still very well remember ! Lady Ashburton had got for herself a grand " Queen's saloon " or *ne-plus-ultra* of railway carriages (made for the Queen some time before) costing no end of money ; Lady sat, or lay, in the "saloon; " a common six-seat carriage, immediately contiguous, was accessible from it ; in this the Lady had insisted *we* should ride, with her doctor and her maid ; a mere partition, with a door, dividing us from her. The Lady was very good, cheerful though much unwell ; bore all her difficulties and disappointments with an admirable equanimity and magnanimity : but it was physically almost the uncomfortablest journey I ever made. At Peterborough, the *Ne-plus-ultra* was found to have its axletree *on fire ;* at every station afterwards *buckets* were copiously dashed and poured (the magnanimous Lady saying never a syllable to it) ; and at Newcastle-on-Tyne, they flung the humbug *Ne-plus* away altogether, and our whole party into common carriages. Apart from the burning axle, we had suffered much from dust and even from foul air,—so that, at last, I got the door opened, and sat with my head and shoulders stretched out backward, into the wind. This had alarmed my poor Woman, lest I should tumble out altogether ; and she angrily forbade it, dear loving Woman ; and I complied, not at first knowing why she was angry. This and Lady Ashburton's opening her door to tell us, " Here is Hinchinbrook ! " (a long time before, and with something of pathos traceable in her cheery voice) are nearly all that I now remember of the base and dirty hurlyburly. Lord Ashburton had preceded by some days ; and was waiting for our train, at Edinburgh, 9.30 P.M.—hurlyburly greater and dirtier than ever. They went for Barry's Hotel at once, servants and all,—no time to *inform* us (officially), that *we* too were their guests. But that, too, passed well. We ordered apartments, refreshments of our own there (first of all *baths,* inside of my shirt-collar was as black as ink !)—and before the refreshments were ready, we had a gay and cordial invitation etc. etc. ; found the " Old Bear " (Ellice) [1] in their rooms, I remember, and Lord Ashburton and he with a great deal to say about Edinburgh and its people and phenomena. Next morning, the Ashburtons went for Kinloch-Luichart (fine hunting-seat in Ross-shire) ; and my dear little Woman to her Cousins at Auchtertool ; where, I remember, she was much soothed by their kindness, and improved considerably in health, for the time. The day after seeing her settled there, I made for Annandale, and my Sister Mary's at the Gill. (Maggie Welsh, now here with me, has *helped* in adjusting into clearness the recollection of all this.)—I remember working on final corrections of Books ii. and iii. of *Friedrich,* and reading in *Plato* (Trans-

---

[1] Edward Ellice (M.P. for Coventry) died in 1863, aged 74 :—" called ' *Bear* Ellice ' in society here ; but rather for his oiliness than for any trace of ferocity ever seen in him."—Carlyle, in a Letter of 1852.

lation, and not my first trial of him) while there. My Darling's Letters I remember too (am on search for them just now) ; also visits from Sister Jean and *to* Dumfries and her,—silent nocturnal rides from that town etc., and generally much riding on the (Priestside) Solway Sands, and plenty of sombre occupation to my thoughts.

Late on in Autumn, I met my Jeannie at Kirkcaldy again ; uncomfortably lodged, both of us, and did not loiter (though the people very *kind* . . .) ; I was bound for Rosshire and the Ashburtons (miserable journey thither, sombre, miserable stay there, wet weather, sickly, solitary mostly, etc. etc.) ;—my Wife had gone to her Aunts in Edinburgh, for a night or two, to the Haddington Miss Donaldsons, and in both places, the *latter* especially, had much to please her, and came away with the resolution to go again.

Next year, 1857, she went accordingly ; staid with the Donaldsons (eldest of these old ladies, now well above eighty, and gone stone-blind, was her " godmother," had been at Craigenputtock to see us, the dearest of old friends my wife now had). She was at Auchtertool too, at Edinburgh with her Aunts, once and again ; but the chief element was " Sunny Bank, Haddington," which she began with and ended with ; a stay of some length, each time. Happy to her, and heart-interesting to a high degree, though sorrowfully involved in almost constant bodily pain. It was a Tour for *Health ;* urged on her by me for that end ;—and the poor little Darling seemed inwardly to grudge all along the expense on herself (generous soul !) as if *she* were not worth money spent,—though money was in no scarcity with us now ! I was printing *Friedrich,* volumes i. and ii. here ; totally solitary ; and recollect her Letters of that Tour as altogether genial and delightful,—sad and miserable as the view is which they *now* give me of her endless bodily distresses and even torments, now when I read them again, after nine years, and what has befallen me eleven weeks ago !

[*Sunday, July* 8. Began writing again at the second line of this page ; the intermediate time has been spent in a strenuous search for, and collection of all her letters now discoverable (by Maggie Welsh and me),—which is now completed, or nearly so, —1842–3 the earliest found (though surely there ought to be others, of 1837 etc. ?), and some of almost every year onward to the last. They are exceedingly difficult to arrange ; not having in general any *date ;* so that place often enough, and day and even year throughout, are mainly to be got by the *Post Office*

Stamp, supported by inference and inquiry such as is still possible, at least to me.]

The whole of yesterday I spent in reading and arranging the *letters* of 1857 ; such a day's *reading* as I perhaps never had in my life before. What a piercing radiancy of meaning to me in those dear records, hastily thrown off, full of misery, yet of bright eternal love ; all as if on wings of lightning, tingling through one's very heart of hearts ! Oh, I was blind not to see how *brittle* was that thread of noble celestial (almost more than terrestrial) life ; how much it was all in all to me, and how impossible it should long be left with me. Her sufferings seem little short of those in an hospital fever-ward, as she painfully drags herself about ; and yet constantly there is such an electric shower of all-illuminating brilliancy, penetration, recognition, wise discernment, just enthusiasm, humour, grace, patience, courage, love,—and in fine of spontaneous nobleness of mind and intellect,—as I know not where to parallel ! I have asked myself. Ought all this to be lost, or kept for myself, and the brief time that now belongs to *me ?* Can *nothing* of it be saved, then, for the worthy that still remain among these roaring myriads of profane unworthy ? I really must consider it further ; and already I feel it to have become uncertain to me whether at least this poor Notebook ought to be burnt ere my decease or left to its chances among my survivors ? As to " talent," epistolary and other, these *Letters*, I perceive, equal and surpass whatever of best I know to exist in that kind ; for " talent," " genius," or whatever we may call it, what an evidence, if my little woman needed that to me ! Not all the *Sands* and *Eliots* and babbling *cohue* of " celebrated scribbling women" that have strutted over the world, in my time, could, it seems to me, if all boiled down and distilled to essence, make one such woman. But it is difficult to make these Letters fairly legible ; except myself there is nobody at all that can completely *read* them, as they now are. They abound in allusions, very full of meaning in this circle, but perfectly dark and void in all others : " *Coterie-sprache,*" as the Germans call it, " family-circle dialect," occurs every line or two ; nobody ever so *rich* in that kind as she ; ready to pick up every diamond-spark, out of the common floor-dust, and keep it brightly available ; so that hardly, I think in any house, was there *more* of " Coterie-speech," shining innocently, with a perpetual expressiveness and twinkle generally of quiz and real humour about it, than in ours. She mainly was the creatress of all this ;

unmatchable for quickness (and trueness) in regard to it ;—and in her letters it is continually recurring ; shedding such a lambency of " own fireside " over everything, if you are in the secret. Ah me, ah me !—At least, I have tied up that bundle (the *two* letters touching on *Friedrich* have a paper round them ; the first written in Edinburgh, it appears *how I*) [*Enter* Froude ; almost the only man I care to speak with, in these weeks. Out with him to Battersea Park ; day gray, temperate and windy.]

[*July* 9. Day again all spent in searching and sorting : a box of *hers*, full of strange and sad memorials of her Mother, with a few of Father and infant Self (put up in 1842)—full of poignant meanings to her then and to me now. Her own *christening cap* is there (e.g.), the *lancet* they took her Father's blood with (and so *killed* him, as she always thought) ; Father's door-plate ; " commission in Perth Fencibles," etc. : two or three Christmas notes of mine ; which I could not read without almost sheer weeping. . . .]

[*July* 13. . . . On the whole two days of absence from my little " Shrine of pious Memory " here, where alone it is best for me to be, at present !—I will write down my reminiscence of the " Accident in Cheapside " (1863) ; the opening of what has proved to be the last act of all. Hand sadly shaky, weather extremely hot.]

It must have been near the end of October 1863, when I returned home from my ride, weather soft and muddy, humour dreary and oppressed as usual (nightmare *Friedrich* still pressing heavily as ever), but as usual also, a bright little hope in me that now I was *across* the muddy element, and the lucid twenty minutes of my day were again at hand. To my disappointment, my Jeannie was *not* here ; " had gone to see her Cousin in the City,"—a Mrs. Godby, widow of an important Post-Official, once in Edinburgh, where he had wedded this cousin, and died leaving children ; and in virtue of whom she and they had been brought to London a year to two ago, to a fine situation as " Matron of the Post-office Establishment " (" forty maids under her etc. etc., and well managed by her ") in St. Martin's-le-Grand. She was a good enough creature, this Mrs. Godby (Binnie had been her Scotch name ; she is now Mrs. Something-else, and very prosperous) :—my Jeannie, in those early times, was anxious to be kind to her in the new scene, and had her often here (as often as, for my convenience, seemed to the loyal heart permissible) ; and was herself, on calls and little tea-visits, perhaps still oftener there. A perfectly harmless Scotch cousin, polite and prudent ; almost prettyish . . . ; with good wise instincts ; but no developed intelligence in the articulate kind. Her mother, I think, was my mother-in-law's cousin or connection ; and the young widow and her London friend were always well together. This was, I believe, the last visit my poor wife ever made her, and the last but two she ever received from her, so miserably unexpected were the issues on this side of the matter !

We had been at the Grange for perhaps four or five weeks that autumn ; utterly quiet, nobody there besides ourselves ; Lord Ashburton being in the weakest state, health and life visibly decaying ;—I was permitted to keep *perdu* till three o'clock daily ; and sat writing about Poland I remember. Mournful, but composed and dignifiedly placid the time was to us all. My Jeannie did not complain of health beyond wont, except on one point : that her right arm was strangely lame, getting lamer and lamer, so that at last she could not " *do her hair herself*," but had to call in a maid to fasten the hind part for her. I remember her sadly dispirited looks, when I came in to her in the mornings with my inquiries ; " No sleep," too often the response ; and this lameness, though little was said of it, a most discouraging thing. Oh, what discouragements, continual distresses, pains and miseries my poor little Darling had to bear, remedy for them nowhere, speech about them useless, best to be avoided,—as, except on pressure from myself, it always nobly was ! This part of her life-history was always sad to me ; but it is tenfold more now, as I read in her old *Letters*, and gradually realise, as never before, the continual grinding wretchedness of it, and how, like a winged Psyche, she so soared above it, and refused to be chained or degraded by it.—" Neuralgic rheumatism," the Doctors called this thing ; " neuralgia " by itself, as if confessing that they knew not what to do with it. Some kind of hot half-corrosive ointment was the thing prescribed ;—which did, for a little while each time, remove the pain mostly, the lameness not ;—and I remember to have once seen her beautiful arm (still so beautiful) all stained with spots of *burning*, so zealous had she been in trying, though with small faith in the prescription. This lasted all the time we were at The Grange ; it had begun before, and things rather seemed to be worsening after we returned. Alas, I suppose it was the Siege of the *Citadel* that was now going on ; disease and pain had for thirty or more years been tramping down the *outworks ;* were now got to the *nerves*, to the citadel, and were bent on storming that.

[*14th July, twelfth Saturday since.*] I was disappointed, but

not sorry at the miss of my " twenty minutes ; " that my little
Woman, in her weak languid state, had gone out for exercise,
was glad news ; and I considered that the " twenty minutes "
was only postponed, not lost, but would be repaid me presently
with interest. After sleep and dinner (all forgotten now), I
remember still to have been patient, cheerfully hopeful, " she
is coming, for certain ; and will have something nice to tell me
of news etc., as she always has ! " In that mood I lay on the
sofa, not sleeping, quietly waiting, perhaps for an hour-and-half
more. She had gone in an omnibus, and was to return in one ;
at this time, she had no carriage : with great difficulty I had got
her induced, persuaded and commanded, to take two drives
weekly in a hired brougham (" more difficulty in persuading
you to go into expense, than other men have to persuade their
wives to keep out of it ! ") : on these terms she had agreed to
the two drives weekly, and found a great benefit in them ;—
but, on no terms, could I get her consent to go, *herself*, into the
adventure of purchasing a brougham etc., though she knew it to
be a fixed purpose, and only delayed by absolute want of time
on my part. She could have done it, too, employed the right
people to do it, right well ; and knew how beneficial to her health
it would, likely, be : but no, there was a refined delicacy which
would have perpetually prevented *her ;*—and my " time,"
literally, was *zero ;* I believe, for the last seven years of that
nightmare *Friedrich*, I did not write the smallest message to
friends, or undertake the least business, except upon plain
compulsion of necessity. How lucky that, next autumn, I did
actually, in spite of *Friedrich*, undertake this of the brougham :
it is a mercy of Heaven to me for the rest of my life ! And oh
why was it not undertaken, in spite of all *Friedrichs* and nightmares, years before ! That had been still luckier ; perhaps endlessly so ? But this was not to be.

The visit to Mrs. Godby had been pleasant, and gone all well ;
but now, dusk falling, it had to end,—again by omnibus, as ill-
luck would have it. Mrs. Godby sent one of her maids as escort ;
at the corner of Cheapside, the omnibus was waited for (some
excavations going on near by, as for many years past they seldom cease to do) ; Chelsea omnibus came ; my Darling was in
the act of stepping in (maid stupid, and of no assistance),—when
a cab came rapidly from behind, and, forced by the near exca-
vation, seemed as if it would drive over her, such her frailty, and
want of *speed*. She desperately determined to get on the flag
pavement again ; desperately leaped, and did get upon the

curbstone; but found she was falling over upon the flags, and that she would alight on her right or neuralgic arm, which would be ruin ; spasmodically struggled against this for an instant or two (maid nor nobody assisting), and *had* to fall on the neuralgic arm,—ruined *otherwise* far worse.   For, as afterwards appeared, the muscles of the thigh-bone or sinews attaching them had been torn in that spasmodic instant or two ; and, for three days coming, the torment was excessive, while in the right arm there was no neuralgia perceptible during that time, nor any very manifest new injury afterwards either.   The calamity had happened, however ; and in that condition, my poor Darling, " put into a cab " by the humane people, as her one request to them, arrived at this door,—" later " than I expected ; and after such a " drive from Cheapside " as may be imagined !

I remember well my joy at the sound of her wheels ending in a knock ; then my surprise at the *delay* in her coming up ; at the singular silence of the maids when questioned as to that : thereupon my rushing down ; finding her in the hands of Larkin and them ; in the greatest agony of pain and helplessness I had ever seen her in.   The noble little soul, she had determined I was not to be shocked by it ; Larkin then lived next door ; assiduous to serve us in all things (did *maps, indexes,* even *joinerings* etc. etc.) : him she had resolved to charge with it,— alas, alas, as if you *could* have saved me, noble heroine and martyr !   Poor Larkin was standing helpless ; he and I carried her upstairs in an arm-chair to the side of her bed ; into which she crept by aid of her hands : in few minutes, Barnes (her wise old doctor) was here,—assured me there were no bones broken, no joint out ; applied his bandagings and remedies ; and seemed to think the matter was slighter than it proved to be,—the spasmodic *tearing of sinews* being still a secret to him.

For fifty hours the pain was excruciating ; after that it rapidly abated ; and soon altogether ceased, except when the wounded limb was meddled with never so little.   The poor Patient was heroic, and had throughout been.   Within a week, she had begun contriving rope-machineries, leverages ; and could not only pull her bell, but lift and shift herself about, by means of her arms, into any coveted posture ; and was, as it were, *mistress* of the mischance.   She had her poor little room arranged, under her eye, to a perfection of beauty and convenience ; nothing that was possible to her had been omitted (I remember one little thing the apothecary had furnished : an artificial *champagne-cork* ; turn a screw, and your champagne spurted up, and when

JANE WELSH CARLYLE

you had a spoonful, could be instantly closed down : with what
a bright face she would show me this in action !)—in fact her
sick-room *looked* pleasanter than many a drawing-room (all the
weakness and suffering of it nobly veiled away) ; the select of
her lady-friends were admitted for short whiles, and liked it
well : to me, whenever I entered, all spoke of cheerfully patient
hope ;—the bright side of the cloud always assiduously turned
out for *me*, in my dreary labours ! I might have known, too,
better than I did, that it had a dark side withal, sleeplessness,
sickliness, utter weakness ;—and that " the silver lining " was
due to my Darling's self mainly, and to the inextinguishable
loyalty and hope that dwelt in her. But I merely thought,
" How lucky beyond all my calculations ! "

I still right well remember the night when her bedroom door
(double-door) suddenly opened upon me into the drawing-room,
and she came limping and stooping on her staff, so gracefully,
and with such a childlike joy and triumph, to irradiate my
solitude. Never again will any such bright vision of gladdening
surprise illuminate the darkness for me in that room or any other!
She was in her Indian dressing-gown ; absolutely beautiful,
leaning on her *nibby* staff (a fine hazel, cut and polished from the
Drumlanrig woods, by some friend for *my* service) ; and with
such a kindly brilliancy and loving innocence of expression, like
that of a little child, unconquerable by weakness and years !
A hot-tempered creature, too ; few hotter, on momentary
provocation : but what a fund of soft affection, hope, and melodious innocence and goodness, to temper all that lightning :—
I doubt, candidly, if I ever saw a nobler human soul than this
which (alas, alas, never *rightly* valued till now !) accompanied all
my steps for forty years. Blind and deaf that we are : oh think,
if thou yet love anybody living, wait not till *Death* sweep down
the paltry little dust-clouds and idle dissonances of the moment ;
and all be at last so mournfully clear and beautiful, when it is
too late !

We thought all was now come or fast coming right again ;
and that, in spite of that fearful mischance, we should have a
good winter, and get our dismal " misery of a book " *done*, or
almost done. My own hope and prayer was and had long been
continually that ; *hers* too, I could not doubt, though hint never
came from *her* to that effect ; no hint or look, much less the
smallest word, at any time, by any accident. But I felt well
enough how it was crushing down her existence, as it was crushing down my own,—and the thought that *she* had *not* been at

the choosing of it, and yet must suffer so for it, was occasionally bitter to me. But the practical conclusion always was, "Get done with it, get done with it! For the saving of us both, that is the one outlook." And, sure enough, I did stand by the dismal task with all my time and all my means; day and night, wrestling with it, as with the ugliest dragon, which blotted out the daylight and the rest of the world to me, till I should get it slain. There was perhaps some merit in this; but also, I fear, a *de*merit. Well, well; I could do no better. Sitting smoking upstairs, on nights when sleep was impossible, I had thoughts enough; not permitted to rustle amid my rugs and wrappages lest I awoke *her*, and startled all *chance* of sleep away from her. Weak little Darling, thy sleep is now unbroken; still and serene in the Eternities (as the Most High God has ordered for us); and nobody more in this world will wake for my wakefulness, but for some other reason!—

My poor Woman was what we called "getting well" for several weeks still; she could walk very little, indeed she never more walked much in this world:—but it seems she was out driving, and again out, hopefully for some time (I cannot now remember at all how long); considered to be steadily mending of her accident. [Interruption from Ruskin, *July* 16, must stop again for this day.]

Towards the end of November (perhaps it was in December), she caught some whiff of cold; which, for a day or two, we hoped would pass, as many such had done: but on the contrary, it began to get worse, soon rapidly worse, and developed itself into that frightful universal "neuralgia," under which, it seemed as if no force of human vitality would be able long to stand. "Disease of the nerves" (poisoning of the very *channels* of sensation): such was the *name* the doctors gave it; and for the rest, could *do* nothing further with it; well had they only attempted nothing! I used to compute that *they*, poor souls, had at least *reinforced* the disease to *twice* its natural amount; such the pernicious effect of all their "remedies" and appliances, opiates, etc. etc.; which every new one of them (and there came many) applied anew,—and always with the like *inverse* result. Oh, what a sea of agony my Darling was immersed in; and had to plunge and toss and desperately struggle in, month after month! Sleep had fled. A hideous pain of which she used to say that "common honest pain, were it cutting of one's flesh or sawing of one's bones would be a luxury in comparison,"—seemed to have begirdled her, at all moments and on every side. Her intellect

was clear as starlight, and continued so ; the clearest *intellect*
among us all ; but she dreaded that this too must give way.
" Dear," said she to me, on two occasions, with such a look and
tone as I shall never forget, "*promise* me that you will not put me
into a mad-house, however this go. Do you *promise* me, now ? "
I solemnly did. " Not if I do quite lose my wits ? " " Never,
my Darling ; oh compose thy poor terrified heart ! " Another
time, she punctually directed me about her *burial ;* how her poor
bits of possessions were to be distributed, this to one friend, that
to another (in help of their necessities, for it was the *poor* sort
she had chosen, old indigent Haddington figures),—what employment in the solitary night watches, on her bed of pain : ah
me, ah me !

The house, by day especially, was full of confusion ; Maggie
Welsh had come at my solicitation ; and took a great deal of
patient trouble (herself of an almost obstinate placidity) ; doing
her best among the crowd of doctors, sick-nurses, visitors :—I
mostly sat aloft, sunk, or endeavouring to be sunk, in *work ;*
and till evening, only visited the sick-room at intervals,—first
thing in the morning, perhaps about noon again, and always
(if permissible) at three P.M., when riding time came, etc. etc. ;
—*if* permissible, for sometimes she was reported as " asleep "
when I passed, though it oftenest proved to have been quiescence
of exhaustion, not real sleep. To this hour it is inconceivable
to me how I could continue " working ; " as I nevertheless certainly for much the most part did ! About three times or so, on
a morning it struck me, with a cold shudder as of conviction,
that here did lie death ; that my world must go to shivers, down
to the abyss ; and that " victory " never so complete, up in my
garret, would not save *her,* nor indeed be possible without her.
I remember my morning walks, three of them or so, crushed
under that ghastly spell. But again I said to myself, " No man,
doctor or other, *knows* anything about it. There is still what
appetite there was ; that I can myself understand : "—and
generally, before the day was done, I had decided to *hope* again,
to keep hoping and working. The *after*-cast of the Doctors'
futile opiates were generally the worst phenomena : I remember
her once coming out to the drawing-room sofa, perhaps about
midnight ; decided for trying that—ah me, in vain, palpably in
vain ; and what a look in those bonny eyes, vividly present to
me yet ; unaidable, and like to break one's heart !

One scene with a Catholic sick-nurse I also remember well.
A year or two before this time, she had gone with some acquaint-

ance who was in quest of sick-nurses to an establishment under
Catholic auspices, in Brompton somewhere (the acquaintance,
a Protestant herself, expressing her " certain knowledge " that
this Catholic was the one good kind) ;—where accordingly the
aspect of matters, and especially the manner of the old French
lady who was matron and manager, produced such a favourable
impression, that I recollect my little Woman saying, " If I need
a sick-nurse, that is the place I will apply at."   Appliance now
was made ; a nun duly sent, in consequence :—this was in the
early weeks of the illness ; *household* sick-nursing (Maggie's and
that of the maids alternately) having sufficed till now.   The
nurse was a good-natured young Irish nun ; with a good deal of
brogue, a tolerable share of blarney too, all varnished to the due
extent ; and, for three nights or so, she answered very well.   On
the fourth night, to our surprise, though we found afterwards it
was the common usage, there appeared a new Nun ; new and
very different,—an *elderly* French *young lady* with broken
English enough for her occasions, and a look of rigid earnestness,
in fact, with the air of a life broken down into settled despond-
ency, and abandonment of all hope that was not *ultra*-secular.
An unfavourable change ;—though the poor lady seemed intelligent, well-intentioned ; and her heart-broken aspect inspired
pity and good-wishes, if no attraction.   She commenced by
rather ostentatious performance of her nocturnal Prayers,
" *Beata Maria*," or I know not what other Latin stuff ; which
her poor Patient regarded with great vigilance, though still with
what charity and tolerance were possible.   " You won't understand what I am saying or doing," said the Nun ; " don't mind
me."   " Perhaps I understand it better than yourself," said the
other (who had *Latin* from of old), and did " mind " more than
was expected.   The dreary hours, no sleep, as usual, went on ;
and we heard nothing,—till about three A.M. I was awakened (I,
what never happened before or after, though my door was always
left slightly ajar, and I was right above, usually a deep sleeper),
—awakened by a vehement continuous ringing of my poor
Darling's bell.   I flung on my dressing-gown, awoke Maggie by
a word, and hurried down.   " Put away that woman ! " cried
my poor Jeannie vehemently ; " away, not to come back ! "
I opened the door into the drawing-room ; pointed to the sofa
there, which had wraps and pillows plenty ; and the poor Nun
at once withdrew, looking and murmuring her regrets and
apologies.   " What was she doing to thee, my own poor little
Woman ? "   No very distinct answer was to be had then (and

afterwards there was always a dislike to speak of that hideous
bit of time at all, except on necessity) ; but I learned in general
that during the heavy hours loaded, every moment of them, with
its misery, the Nun had gradually come forward with ghostly
consolations, ill received, no doubt ; and at length, with something more express, about " Blessed Virgin," " *Agnus Dei*," or
whatever it might be ; to which the answer had been : " Hold
your tongue, I tell you ; or I will ring the bell ! " Upon which
the Nun had rushed forward with her dreadfullest supernal
admonitions, " *im*penitent sinner," etc., and a practical attempt
to *prevent* the ringing. Which only made it more immediate
and more decisive. The poor woman expressed to Miss Welsh
much regret, disappointment, real vexation and self-blame ;
lay silent, after that, amid her rugs ; and disappeared, next
morning, in a polite and soft manner : never to reappear, she
or any consort of hers. I was really sorry for this heavy-laden,
pious or quasi-pious and almost broken-hearted Frenchwoman,
—though we could perceive she was under the foul tutelage and
guidance, probably of some dirty muddy-minded semi-*felonious*
Proselytising Irish Priest :—but there was no help for her, in this
instance ; probably, in all England, she could not have found
an agonised human soul more nobly and hopelessly superior
to her and her *poisoned-gingerbread* " consolations."—This
incident threw suddenly a glare of strange and far from
pleasant light over the sublime Popish " Sisters of Charity "
movement ;—and none of us had the least notion to apply
there henceforth.

The doctors were many ; Dr. Quain (who would take no fees)
the most assiduous ; Dr. Blakiston (ditto), from St. Leonard's,
express, one time ;—speaking hope, always, both of these, and
most industrious to help ;—with many more, whom I did not
even see. When any *new* miraculous kind of Doctor was
recommended as such, my poor struggling martyr, conscious too
of grasping at mere straws, could not but wish to see him ; and
he came, did his mischief, and went away. We had even (by
sanction of Barnes, and indeed of sound sense never so sceptical)
a trial of " Animal Magnetism ; " two magnetisers, first a man,
then a *quack* woman (evidently a conscious quack I perceived her
to be),—who at least did no ill, *except* entirely disappoint (if that
were much an exception). By everybody it had been agreed
that a " change of scene " (as usual, when all else has failed) was
the thing to be looked to : " St. Leonard's so soon as the weather
will permit ! " said Dr. Quain and everybody,—especially Dr.

Blakiston, who generously offered his house withal, " Infinitely more room than we need ! " said the sanguine Blakiston always ; and we dimly understood too, from his wife (" Bessie Barnet," an old inmate here, and of distinguished qualities and fortunes), that the doctor would accept " remuneration ; " though this proved quite a mistake. . . . Money for the use of two rooms in his house, we might have anticipated, but did not altogether, he would regard with sovereign superiority.

It was early in March, perhaps 2d March 1864, a cold blowing damp and occasionally raining day, when the flitting thither took effect.   Never shall I see again so sad and dispiriting a scene ; hardly was the day of her last departure for Haddington, departure of what had once been She (the *instant* of *which*, they contrived to hide from me here) so miserable ; for *she* at least was now suffering nothing, but safe in victorious rest for evermore— though then beyond expression suffering.   There was a railway " invalid carriage," so expressly adapted, so etc.,—and evidently costing some ten or twelve times the common expense :—this drove up to the door ; Maggie and she to go in this.   Well do I recollect her look as they bore her downstairs : full of nameless sorrow, yet of clearness, practical management, steady resolution ; in a low small voice she gave her direction, once or twice, as the process went on, and practically it was under her wise management.   The " invalid carriage " was hideous to look upon ; black, low, base-looking,—and you entered it by window, as if it *were* a hearse : I knew well what she was thinking ; but her eye never quailed, she gave her directions as heretofore ; and, in a minute or two, we were all away.   Twice or oftener in the journey, I visited Maggie and her in their prison : no complaint ; but the " invalid carriage," in which I doubt if you could actually sit upright (if you were of *man's* stature or of tall woman's), was evidently a catch-penny humbug ; and she freely admitted afterwards that she would never enter it again, and that in a " coupé to ourselves " she would have been far better.   At St. Leonard's, I remember, there was considerable waiting for " the horses " that should have been ready ; a thrice bleak and dreary scene to all of us (*She* silent as a child) ; the arrival, the dismounting, the ascent of her quasi-bier up Blakiston's long stairs, etc., etc. : ah me !   Dr. Blakiston was really kind.   The sea was hoarsely moaning at our hand, the bleared skies sinking into darkness overhead.   Within doors, however, all was really nice and well-provided (thanks to the skilful Mrs. Blakiston) ; excellent drawing-room, and sitting-room, with bed for *her* ;

bedroom upstairs for Maggie, ditto for servant, within call, etc. etc. ; all clean and quiet : a kind of hope did rise, perhaps even in her, at sight of all this. My mood, when I bethink me, was that of deep misery frozen *torpid ;* singularly dark and stony,— strange to me now ; due in part to the *Friedrich* incubus then. I had to be home again that night, by the last train ;—miscalculated the distance, found no vehicle ; and never in my life saved a train by so infinitesimally small a miss. I had taken mournfully tender leave of my poor much-suffering Heroine (speaking hope to her, when I could more readily have " lifted up my voice and wept "). I was to return in so many days, if nothing went wrong ; *at once,* if anything did ;—I lost nothing by that hurried ride, except at London Station, or in the final cab, a velvet Cap, of her old making ; which I much regretted, and still regret. " I will make you another cap, if I get better," said she lovingly, at our next meeting ; but she never did, or perhaps well could. What matter ? That would have made me still sorrier, had I had it by me now. *Wae's me, wae's me !* [*Wae* is the Scotch *adjective,* too : " *wae, wae,*"—there is no word in English that will express what is my habitual mood in these months.]

I was twice, or perhaps thrice at St. Leonard's (Warrior Square, Blakiston's house, *right* end of it to the sea). Once I recollect being taken by Forster, who was going on a kind of birthday Holiday with his Wife. Blakiston spoke always in a swaggering tone of hope, and there really was some improvement ; but, alas, it was small and slow ; deep misery and pain still too visible : and all we could say was, " We must try St. Leonard's further ; I shall be able to shift down to you in May ! " My little Darling looked sweet gratitude upon me (so thankful always for " the day of small things ! ")—but heaviness, sorrow, and *want* of hope was written on her face ; the sight filling me with sadness, though I always strove to be of Blakiston's opinion. One of my volumes (fourth, I conclude) was coming out at that time ;—during the Forster visit, I remember there was some *review* of this volume, seemingly of a shallow impudent description, concerning which I privately applauded Forster's silent demeanour, and not Blakiston's vocal, one evening at Forster's inn. The dates, or even the number, of these sad preliminary visits, I do not now recollect : they were all of a sad and ambiguous complexion : at home, too, there daily came a letter from Maggie ; but this in general, though it strove to look hopeful, was *ambiguity's* own self ! Much driving in the open air, appe-

tite where it was, sleep at least ditto : all this, I kept saying to
myself, must lead to something good.

Dr. Blakiston, it turned out, would accept no payment for his
rooms ; " a small furnished house of our own " became the only
outlook, therefore ;—and was got, and entered into, some time in
April, some weeks before my arrival in May. Brother John,
before this, had come to visit me here ; ran down to St. Leonard's
one day, and, I could perceive, was silently intending to pass
the summer with us at St. Leonard's. He did so, in an innocent,
self-soothing, kindly and harmless way (the good soul, if good
wishes would always suffice !)—and occasionally was of some
benefit to us, though occasionally also not. It was a quiet
sunny day of May when we went down together ;—I read most
of " Sterne's Life " (just out, by some Irishman, named Fitz-
something) ; looked out on the old *Wilhelmus Conquestor*
localities ; on Lewes, for one thing (de " *Le Ouse*,"—Ouse the
dirty river there is *still* named) ; on Pevensey, Bexhill etc., with
no unmixed feeling, yet not with absolute misery, as we rolled
along. I forget if Maggie Welsh was still there at St. Leonard's.
My Darling, certain enough, came down to meet us, attempting
to sit at dinner (by my request, or wish already signified) ; but
too evidently it would not do. Mary Craik was sent for (from
Belfast) instead of Maggie Welsh who " was wanted " at Liverpool, and did then or a few days afterwards return thither,—
Mary Craik succeeding, who was very gentle, quiet, prudent,
and did well in her post. . . . Miss Jewsbury had *offered* " for
a fortnight,"—" say No, and write to Mary Craik," was my poor
Jane's direction to me (more practical sense in her sick head,
than in all the sound ones together !—So it was with her *throughout*) . . .

I had settled all my Book affairs the best I could : I got at
once installed into a poor closet on the ground-floor, with
window to the north (keep that open and the door ajar, there
will be fresh air !)—Book box was at once converted into Book
press (of rough deal, but covered with newspaper *veneering*
where necessary), and fairly held and kept at hand the main
books I wanted ; camp-desk, table or two, drawer or two, were
put in immediate seasonablest use ; in this closet there was
hardly room to turn ; and I felt as if crushed, all my apparatus
and I, into a stocking, and *there* bidden *work*. But I really did
it withal, to a respectable degree, Printer never pausing for me,
work daily going on ; and this doubtless was my real anchorage
in that sea of trouble, sadness and confusion, for the two months

it endured. I have spoken elsewhere of my poor Darling's hopeless wretchedness, which daily cut my heart, and might have cut a very stranger's : those drives with her (" daily, one of your drives, is with *me*,"—and I saw her gratitude, poor soul, looking out through her despair ; and sometimes she would *try* to talk to me, about street sights, persons etc. ; and it was like a bright lamp flickering out into extinction again), drives mainly on the streets to escape the dust, or still dismaller if we did venture into the haggard, parched lanes, and their vile whirlwinds : Oh my Darling, I would have cut the Universe in two for thee,—and *this* was all I had to share with thee, as we were !—

St. Leonard's, now that I look back upon it, is very odious to my fancy, yet not without points of interest. I rode a great deal too,—two hours and a half daily my lowest stint ; bathed also, and remember the bright morning air, bright Beachy Head and everlasting Sea, as things of blessing to me ; the *old* lanes of Sussex too, old cottages, peasants, old vanishing ways of life, were abundantly touching : but the *new* part, and it was all getting " new," was uniformly detestable and even horrible to me. Nothing but dust, noise, squalor, and the universal tearing and digging as if of gigantic human *swine, not* finding any worms or roots that would be useful to them ! The very " houses " they were building, each " a congeries of rotten bandboxes " (as our own poor " furnished house " had taught me, if I still needed teaching), were " built " as if for nomad apes, not for men. The " moneys " to be realised, the etc. etc. : does or can God's *blessing* rest on all that ? My dialogues with the dusty sceneries there (Fairlight, Crowhurst, Battle, Rye even, and Winchelsea), with the novelties and the antiquities, were very sad for most part, and very grim,—here and there with a kind of wild interest too. Battle I did arrive at, one evening, through the chaotic roads ; Battle, in the rustle or silence of incipient dusk, was really affecting to me ;—and I saw it to be a good post of fence for King Harold, and wondered if the Bastard did " land at Pevensey," or not near Hastings somewhere (Bexhill or so ?) and what the marchings and preliminaries had really been. (Faithful study, continued for long years or decades, upon the old Norman romances etc., and upon the ground, would still tell some fit person, I believe.) But there shrieks the railway, " shares " at such and such a premium ; let us make for home ! My Brother, for a few times at first, used to accompany me on those rides ; but soon gave in (not being bound to it like me) ; and Noggs [1] and I had nothing for it but solitary contemplation and what mute " dialogues " with Nature and Art we could each get up for himself.   I usually got home towards nine P.M. (half-past eight the rigorous rule) ; and in a gray dusty evening, from some windy hill-top, or in the intricate old narrow lanes of a thousand years ago, one's reflections were apt to be of a sombre sort.—My poor little Jeannie (thanks to her, the loving one) would not fail to be waiting for me, and sit trying to talk or listen, while I had tea ; trying her best, sick and weary as she was ; but always very soon withdrew after that ; quite worn down, and longing for solitary *silence*, and even a *sleepless* bed, as was her likeliest prospect for most part. How utterly sad is all that ! yes ; and there is a kind of devout blessing in it too (so nobly was it borne, and conquered in a sort) ; and I would not have it altered now, after what has come, if I even could.

[*Sunday, 22d July.*]   We lived in the place called " Marina " (what a name !) almost quite at the west end of St. Leonard's ; a new house (bearing marks of thrifty, wise, and modestly-elegant habits in the old-lady owners just gone from it) ; and for the rest, decidedly the *worst*-built house I have ever been within.   A scandal to human nature, it and its fellows ; which are everywhere, and are not objected to by an enlightened public, as appears !   No more of *it*,—except our farewell malison ; and pity for the poor Old Ladies who perhaps are still there !

My poor suffering woman had at first, for some weeks, a vestige of improvement, or at least of new hope and alleviation thereby : she " slept " (or tried for sleep) in the one tolerable bedroom ; second floor, fronting the sea ; darkened and ventilated, made the tidiest we could ; Miss Craik slept close by. I remember our settlings for the night ; my last journey up, to sit a few minutes, and see that the adjustments *were* complete,— a " Nun's lamp " was left glimmering within reach ; my poor little woman *strove* to look as contented as she could, and to exchange a few friendly words with me as our last for the night. Then in the morning, there sometimes *had* been an hour or two of sleep ; what news for us all !   And even brother John, for a while, was admitted to step up and congratulate, after breakfast.   But this didn't last ; hardly into June, even in that slight degree.   And the days were always heavy ; so sad to her, so painful, dreary, without hope : what a time, even in my *reflex* of it !   Dante's *Purgatory* I could now liken it to ; both

1 Carlyle's horse (named after Newman Noggs, in *Nicholas Nickleby*).

of us, especially my Loved One by me, " bent like corbels," under our unbearable loads as we wended on,—yet in me always with a kind of steadily glimmering hope ! Dante's *Purgatory ;* not his *Hell*, for there was a sacred blessedness in it withal ; not wholly the society of devils, but among *their* hootings and tormentings something still pointing afar off towards Heaven withal. Thank God !

At the *beginning* of June, she still had the feeling we were better here than elsewhere ; by her direction, I warned the people we would not quit at " the end of June," as had been bargained, but " of July," as was also within our option, on due notice given. End of *June* proved to be the time, all the same ; the Old Ladies (justly) refusing to *revoke*, and taking their full claim of money, poor old souls, very polite otherwise. Middle of June had not come when that bedroom became impossible : " roaring of the sea," once a lullaby, now a little too loud, on some high-tide or west wind, kept her entirely awake : I exchanged bedrooms with her ; " sea always a lullaby to *me*,"— but, that night, even I did not sleep one wink ; upon which John exchanged with me, who lay to rearward, as I till then had done. Rearward we looked over a Mews (from this room) ; from her now room, into the paltry little " garden ; " overhead of both were clay cliffs, multifarious dog and cock establishments (unquenchable by bribes paid), now and then stray troops of asses, etc. etc. : what a lodging for my poor sufferer ! Sleep became worse and worse ; we spoke of shifting to Bexhill ; " fine airy house to be let there " (fable when we went to look) ; then some quiet old country Inn ? She drove one day (John etc. escorting) to Battle, to examine ; nothing there, or less than nothing. Chelsea home was at least quiet, wholesomely aired and clean : but she had an absolute horror of her old *home* bedroom and drawing-room, where she had endured such torments latterly. " We will new-*paper* them, rearrange them," said Miss Bromley ; and this was actually done in August following (not by Miss Bromley). That " new-*papering* " was somehow to me the saddest of speculations : " Alas, Darling, is that all we can do for thee ? " The weak *weakest* of resources ; and yet what other had we ! As June went on, things became worse and worse. The sequel is mentioned elsewhere : I will here put down only the successive steps and approximate dates of it.

June 29, after nine nights totally without sleep, she announced to us, with a fixity and with a clearness all her own, That she would leave this place to-morrow for London ; try there, not in her own house, but in Mrs. Forster's (Palace-Gate House, Kensington), which was not yet horrible to her.   June 30 (John escorting), she set off by the noon train ; Miss Bromley had come down to see her,—*could* only be allowed to see her in stepping into the train, so desperate was the situation, the mood so *adequate* to it : a moment never to be forgotten by me !   How I " worked " afterwards that day is not on record.   I dimly remember walking back with Miss Bromley and her lady-friend to their hotel ; talking to them (as out of the heart of ice-bergs) ; and painfully somehow sinking into icy or stony rest, worthy of oblivion.

At Forster's there could hardly be a more dubious problem. My poor wandering martyr did get snatches of sleep there ; but found the room so noisy, the scene so foreign etc., she took a further resolution in the course of the night and its watchings ; sent for John, the first thing in the morning ; bade him get places in the night-train for Annandale (my Sister Mary's, all kindness poor Mary, whom she always liked) : " The Gill ; we are not yet at the *end : there ;*—and Nithsdale too is that way ! " John failed not, I dare say, in representations, counter-considerations ; but she was coldly positive ;—and go they did, express of about 330 miles.   Poor Mary was loyal kindness itself ; poor means made noble and more than opulent by the wealth of love and ready will and invention :—I was seldom so agreeably surprised as by a letter in my Darling's own hand, narrating the heads of the adventure, briefly, with a kind of defiant satisfaction, and informing me that she *had* slept, that first Gill night, for almost nine hours !   Whose joy like ours, durst we have hoped it would last, or even though we durst *not !*   She staid about a week still there ;   Mary and kindred eager to get her carriages (rather helplessly in that particular), to do and attempt for her whatever was possible ;   but the success, in sleep especially, grew less and less : in about a week, she went on to Nithsdale, to Dr. and Mrs. Russell, and there slowly improving continued.   Improvement pretty constant ;   fresh air, driving, silence, kindness ;   by the time Mary Craik had got me fitted home to Chelsea, and herself went for Belfast, all this had steadily begun ;   and there were regular *letters* from her, etc. ;   and I could work here with such an alleviation of spirits as had long been a stranger to me.   In August (rooms all " new-*papered*," poor little Jeannie) she came back to me ;   actually there in the cab (John settling) when I ran downstairs ;   looking out on me with the old kind face, a little graver, I might have thought, but as quiet, as composed and wise and good as ever. This was the *end*, I might say, of by far the most *tragic* part of our Tragedy. Act Fifth, though there lay Death in it, was nothing like so unhappy.

[*July* 23.] The last epoch of my Darling's life is to be defined as almost *happy*, in comparison ! It was still loaded with infirmities ; bodily weakness, sleeplessness, continual or almost continual pain, and weary misery, so far as *body* was concerned ; but her noble spirit seemed as if it now had its wings *free ;* and rose above all that to a really singular degree. The Battle was over, and *we* were sore wounded ; but the Battle was over, and *well.* It was remarked by everybody that she had never been observed so cheerful and bright of mind as in this last period. The poor *bodily* department, I constantly hoped this too was slowly recovering ; and that there would remain to us a " sweet farewell " of sunshine after such a day of rains and storms, that would still last a blessed while, all *my* time at least, before the end came. And, alas, it lasted only about twenty months ; and ended as I have seen. It is beautiful still, all that period, the *death* very beautiful to me, and will continue so : let me not repine, but patiently bear what I have got !—While the autumn weather continued good, she kept improving ; I remember mornings when I found her quite wonderfully cheerful, as I looked in upon her bedroom in passing down ; a bright ray of *mirth* in what she would say to me ; inexpressibly pathetic, shining through the wreck of such storms as there had been. How could I but hope ?—It was an inestimable mercy to me (as I often remark) that I did at last throw aside everything for a few days, and actually get her that poor Brougham. Never was soul more grateful for so small a kindness ; which seemed to illuminate, in some sort, all her remaining days for her. It was indeed useful, and necessary, as a means of health ; but still more precious, I doubt not, as a mark of *my* regard for her, —ah me, she never knew fully, nor could I show her in my heavy-laden miserable life, how *much* I had, at all times, regarded, loved and admired her. No telling of her now ;—" five minutes *more* of your dear company in this world ; oh that I had you yet for but five minutes, to tell you *all !* " this is often my thought since April 21.

Friedrich ended in January 1865, as above written ; and we went to Devonshire together ; still prospering and happy, she chiefly, though she was so weak. And her talk with me, and with others there ; nobody had such a charming tongue, for truth, discernment, graceful humour and ingenuity; ever patient too, and smiling over her many pains and sorrows. In May, while I had gone to Scotland, she took to refitting my room here (in the ground floor, and shifting me down from the garret); which she has done, how admirably, and with what labour, the noble loving unwearied little soul! Bad days, especially bad nights overtook her; and she fled, out of the *paint* etc. (I could guess, though all remonstrances of mine were useless, about paint or whatever difficulty); and for a month I had her within reach of me, she in Nithsdale, I at The Gill in Annandale (my Sister Mary's poor little rustic farm-place); within an hour or so of her, by train; and we met (in spite of some disappointments) about weekly; I some three visits which I recollect; met *twice* at Dumfries at least,—and the last time I rode with her in the railway carriage to Annan; express for London she, with a new Maid she had acquired; I not to follow till the " room " were ready. She was the charm of everybody, my poor weak Darling; especially good to *me* unworthy. Oh my own, my own, now lost for ever! The stir and eager curiosities of the poor ignorant people about " T. Carlyle," in our old native land, I could see, were interesting and amusing to her, though she knew their folly and inanity as well as I. Thanks to fate for that too. There has been a great deal more of that since, and far too much of it on any ground it had; but except as pleasure to her, which it really was, as nothing else could have been (my own little Jeannie, loyal to me when there was none else loyal), it had as good as no value to me;—and has now absolutely none, or almost the reverse of one.

She was surely very feeble in the Devonshire time (March, etc., 1865); but I remember her as wonderfully happy; she had long dialogues with Lady Ashburton; used to talk so prettily with me, when I called, in passing up to bed and down from it; she made no complaint; when driving daily through the lanes—sometimes regretted her own poor Brougham and " Bellona " (as " still more one's own "), and contrasted her situation as to *carriage* convenience, with that of far richer ladies. " They have £30,000 a year; cannot command a decent or comfortable vehicle here (*their* vehicles all locked up, 400 miles off, in these wanderings); while *we*— *I* " The Lady Ashburton was kindness itself to her; and we all came up to Town together, rather in improved health she, I not visibly so, being now *vacant* and on the *collapse*,—which is yet hardly over, or fairly on the turn. Will it ever be? I have sometimes thought this dreadful unexpected stroke might perhaps be *providential* withal upon me; and that there lay some other little *work* to do, under changed conditions, before I died. God enable me, if so: God knows.

In Nithsdale, last year, it is yet only fourteen months ago (ah me) how beautiful she was; our three or four half or *quarter* days together, how unique in their sad charm as I now recal them from beyond the grave! That day at Russell's, in the garden etc. at Holmhill; so poorly she, forlorn of outlook (one would have said; one outlook ahead, that of *getting me this room trimmed up,*—the darling ever-loving soul!)—and yet so lively, sprightly even, for my poor sake; "Sir William Gomm" (old Peninsular and Indian General, who had been reading *Friedrich* when she left), what a sparkle that was, her little slap on the table, and arch look, when telling us of him and it! And her own *right* hand was lame; she had only her left to slap with: I cut the meat for her, on her plate, that day at dinner. And our drive to the station at seven P.M.; so sweet, so pure and sad: "We must retrench, Dear!" (in my telling her of some foolish *Bank*-adventure with the *draft* I had left her; "retrench!" oh dear, oh dear!)—Among the last things, she told me that evening was, with deep sympathy, "Mr. Thomson" (a Virginian who sometimes came) "called, one night; he says there is little doubt they will *hang* President Davis!" Upon which I almost resolved to write a Pamphlet upon it,—had not I myself been so ignorant about the matter, so foreign to the whole abominable fratricidal "War" (as they called it; "self-murder of a million brother Englishmen, for the sake of sheer *phantasms,* and totally *false* theories upon the Nigger," as I had reckoned it). In a day or two I found I could not enter upon that thrice-abject Nigger-delirium (viler to me than old witchcraft, or the ravings of John of Münster; considerably viler); and that probably I should do poor Davis nothing but harm.

The second day, at good old Mrs. Ewart's, of Nithbank, is still finer to me. Waiting for me with the carriage; "Better, Dear, fairly better since I shifted to Nithbank!"—the "dinner" ahead there (to my horror), her cautious charming preparation of me for it; our calls at Thornhill (new servant "Jessie," admiring old tailor women,—no, *they* were not of the Shankland kind,[1]—wearisome old women, whom *she* had such an interest

[1] "A Tailor at Thornhill" (Shankland) "who had vehemently laid to heart the *Characteristics* was also a glad phenomenon to me. Let a million voices cry out, How clever! it is still nothing: let one voice cry out, How true! it lends us quite a new force and encouragement."—Carlyle's *Journal,* 6th June 1832.

in, almost wholly for *my* sake) ; then our long drive through the Drumlanrig woods, with such talk from her (careless of the shower that fell, battering on our hood and apron) ; in spite of my habitual dispiritment, and helpless gloom all that summer, I too was cheered for the time. And then the dinner itself, and the bustling rustic company, all this, too, was saved by her, with a quiet little touch here and there, she actually turned it into something of *artistic*, and it was pleasant to everybody.— I was at two or perhaps three dinners, after this, along with her, in London : I partly remarked, what is now clearer to me, with what easy perfection she had taken her position in these things ; that of a person *recognised* for quietly *superior* if she cared to be so ; and also of a suffering aged woman, accepting her age, and feebleness, with such a grace, polite composure and simplicity as—as all of you might imitate, impartial bystanders would have said ! The Minister's Assistant, poor young fellow, was gently ordered out by her, to sing *me*, " Hame cam our gudeman at e'en,"—which made him completely happy, and set the dull drawing-room all into illumination till tea entered. He, the assistant, took me to the station (too late for *her* that evening).

The third day was at Dumfries ; Sister Jean's and the Railway Station : more hampered and obstructed, but still good,— beautiful as ever on her part. *Dumb* Turner, at the Station, etc. ; evening falling, ruddy opulence of sky,—how beautiful, how brief and *wae !*—The fourth time was only a ride from Dumfries to Annan, as she went home : sad and afflictive to me, seeing such a journey ahead for her (and nothing but the new " Jessie," as attendant, some carriages off) ; I little thought it was to be the *last* bit of railwaying we did together. These, I believe, were all our meetings in the Scotland of last year. One day I stood watching " her train " at The Gill, as appointed ; Brother Jamie too had been summoned over by her desire : but at Dumfries she felt so weak, in the hot day, she could only lie down on the sofa, and sadly send John in her stead. Brother Jamie, whose rustic equipoise, fidelity and sharp vernacular sense, she specially loved, was not to behold her at this time or evermore.

[*25th July*. . . . Have to go into my writing-case, and sort and reposit her *last* Letters, and the rings and a *buckle ;—could* not yesterday.]

She was waiting for me the night I returned hither ; she had hurried back from her little visit to Miss Bromley [1] (after the

---

[1] Visit to Miss Davenport Bromley at Folkestone.

" room " operation) ; must and would be here to receive *me*.
She stood there, bright of face and of soul, her drawing-room all
bright ; and everything to the last film of it in order ; had
arrived only two or three hours before ; and here again *we* were.
Such welcome, after my vile day of railwaying, like Jonah in
the whale's belly ! That was always her way ; bright home,
with its bright face, full of love, and victorious over all disorder,
always shone on me like a star as I journeyed and jumbled along
amid the shriekeries and miseries. Such welcomes could not
await me for ever ; I little knew this was the last of them on
Earth. My *next*,—for a thousand years, I should never forget
the next (of April 23, 1866) ! which now was lying only some
six months away. I might have seen she was very feeble, that ;
but I noticed only [how] refinedly beautiful she was, and thought
of no sorrow ahead ;—did not even think, as I now do, how it
was that she was beautifuller than ever ; as if years and sorrows
had only " worn " the noble texture of her being into greater
fineness, the colour and tissue still all complete !—That night
she said nothing of the room here (down below) ; but next
morning, after breakfast, led me down, with a quiet smile,
expecting her little triumph,—and contentedly had it ; though
I knew not at first the tenth part of her merits in regard to that
poor enterprise, or how consummately it had been *done* to the
bottom, in spite of her weakness (the noble heart !) ; and I
think (remorsefully) I *never* praised her *enough* for her efforts
and successes in regard to it. Too late now !

My return was about the middle of September ; *she* never
travelled more, except daily up and down among her widish
circle of friends, of whom she seemed to grow fonder and fonder,
though generally their qualities were of the *affectionate* and faithfully *honest* kind, and not of the *distinguished*, as a requisite.
She was always very cheerful, and had businesses enough,—though
I recollect some mornings, one in particular, when the sight of
her dear face (haggard from the miseries of the past night) was
a kind of shock to me. Thoughtless mortal : —she rallied always
so soon, and veiled her miseries away :—I was myself the most
collapsed of men ; and had no sunshine in my life but what came
from *her*. Our old laundress, Mrs. Cook, a very meritorious and
very poor and courageous woman, age eighty or more, had
fairly fallen useless that Autumn, and gone into the Workhouse.
I remember a great deal of trouble taken about her, and the
search for her, and settlement of her,—such driving and abstruse
inquiry in the slums of Westminster, and to the Workhouses

indicated ; discovery of her at length, in the *chaos* of some
Kensington Union (a truly *cosmic* body, herself, this poor old
Cook) ; with instantaneous stir in all directions (consulting
with Rector Blunt, interviews with Poor-Law Guardians etc.,
etc.),—and no rest till the poor old Mrs. Cook was got promoted
into some quiet *cosmic* arrangement ; small cell or " cottage "
of your own somewhere, with liberty to read, to be clean, and
to accept a packet of tea, if any friend gave you one, etc., etc. :
a *good* little " triumph " to my Darling ;—I think perhaps the
best she had that spring or winter, and the last *till* my business
and the final one. Of our Rectorship, and what came of *it*,
there is already some record given (*Own* Notebook, marked
" Notebook III.," last pages there).[1]

We were peaceable and happy (comparatively) through
autumn and winter—especially she was ; wonderfully bearing
her sleepless nights and thousandfold infirmities, and gently
picking out of them (my beautiful little heroine !) more bright
fragments for herself and me than many a one in perfect health
and overflowing prosperity could have done. She had one or
two select quality friends among her many others ;—Dowager
Lady William Russell is the only one I will name, who loved her
like a daughter, and was charmed with her talents and graces ;
often astonishing certain quality *snobs* by the way she treated
her, the *un*titled queen. " Mr. Carlyle a great man, yes ; but
Mrs. Carlyle, let me inform you, is no less great as a woman."
Which used to amuse my little Darling ;—not that she needed
protection in such circles ; from the first, her self-possession
there, as everywhere, was complete ; though her modesty and
graceful bashfulness were also great. For timid modesty, with
perfect simplicity, composure, veracity and grace of demeanour,
in entering such scenes, I have never seen her equal. One or
two such *entrances* of hers I remember yet (with my very heart)
as surpassingly beautiful ! Lady William's pretty little " dinners
of three " were every week or two an agreeable and beneficial
event,—to me also, who heard the *report* of them given with such
lucidity and charm.

End of October came somebody about the Edinburgh Rectorship (to which she gently advised me) ; beginning of November
I was elected ; and an inane though rather amusing hurlyburly
of empty congratulations, imaginary businesses, etc. etc., began,
—the *end* of which has been so fatally tragical ! Many were our

1 What follows, on to p. 167 (see footnote there), is taken from the
Notebook here referred to, and runs consecutively.

plans and speculations about her going with *me*; to lodge at
Newbattle, at etc.; the heaps of frivolous letters lying every
morning at breakfast, and which did not entirely cease all
winter, were a kind of entertainment to her; and then, onwards
into March, when the *Address* and Journey had to be thought of
as practical and close at hand. She decided, *un*willingly, and
with various hesitations, *not* to go with me to Edinburgh, in
the inclement weather; not to go even to Fryston (Lord
Houghton's, Richard Milnes's); as to Edinburgh, she said one
day, " You are to speak extempore " (this she more than once
clearly advised, and with sound insight); " now if anything
should happen you, I find on any sudden alarm there is a sharp
twinge comes into my back, which is like to cut my breath, and
seems to stop the heart almost; I should take some fit in the
crowded House;—it will never do, really ! " Alas, the doctors
now tell me, this meant an affection in some ganglion near the
spine; and was a most serious thing, though I did not attach
importance to it; but only assented to her practical conclusion
as perfectly just. She lovingly bantered and beautifully
encouraged me about my Speech, and its hateful ceremonials
and empty botherations; which for a couple of weeks were
giving me, and her through me, considerable trouble, interruption of sleep, etc.: so beautifully borne by her (for my sake),
—so much less so by me for hers. In fact I was very miserable
(angry with myself for getting into such a coil of vanity, sadly
ill in health), and her noble example did not teach me as it should.
Sorrow to me now, when too late !

Thursday—[But I will give over; no end to paltry interruptions; and poor trivialities bursting in upon my most sacred
thoughts (*Monday, 7th May*, 2½ P.M.)]—Thursday 29th March,
about nine A.M., all was ready here (she softly regulating and
forwarding, as her wont was); and Professor Tyndall, full of
good spirits, appeared with a cab for King's Cross Station,—
Fryston Hall to be our lodging till Saturday and Edinburgh. I
was in the saddest sickly mood, full of gloom and misery, but
striving to hide it; she too looked very pale and ill, but seemed
intent only on forgetting nothing that could further me. A little
flask, holding perhaps two glasses, of fine brandy, she brought
me as a thought of her own :—I did keep a little drop of that
brandy (*hers*, such was a superstition I had), and mixed it in
a tumbler of water in that wild scene of the Address,—and afterwards told her I had done so; thank Heaven that I remembered that in one of my hurried Notes. The last I saw of her

was as she stood with her back to the Parlour-door to bid me her good-bye. She kissed me twice (she me once, I her a second time) ; and—oh blind mortals, my one wish and hope was to get back to her again, and be in peace under her bright welcome,— for the rest of my days, as it were !

Tyndall was kind, cheery, inventive, helpful ; the loyalest *Son* could not have more faithfully striven to support his father, under every difficulty that rose. And they were many. At Fryston, no sleep was to be had for *railways* etc. ; I had two nights, the *first* and the *last*, that were totally hideous ;—and the terror lay in them that speaking would be impossible ; that I should utterly break down,—to which, indeed, I had in my mind said, " Well then," and was preparing to treat it with the best *contempt* I could. Tyndall wrote daily to her, and kept up better hopes ; by a long gallop with me the second day, he did get me one good six hours of sleep, and to her made doubtless the most of it : I knew dismally what her anxieties would be, but trust well he reduced them to their *minimum*. Lord Houghton's and Lady's, kindness to me was unbounded ; *she* also was to have been there, but I was thankful not.—Saturday (to *York* etc. with Houghton ; thence, after long wet loiterings to Edinburgh with Tyndall and Huxley) was the *acme* of the three road-days,—my own comfort was that there could be no post to her ;—and I arrived at Edinburgh, the forlornest of all physical wretches ; and had it not been for the kindness of the good Erskines and of their people too, I should have had no sleep there either, and have gone probably from bad to worse. But Tyndall's letter of Sunday would be comforting ; and my poor little Darling would still be in hope, that Monday morning ; though of course in the painfullest anxiety (Tyndall's *telegram* to come to her in the afternoon),—and I know she had quite " gone off her sleep," in those five days since I had left.

Monday at Edinburgh was to me the gloomiest chaotic day, nearly intolerable for confusion, crowding, noisy inanity and misery,—till once I got done. My Speech was delivered as if in a mood of defiant despair, and under the pressure of night-mares. Some feeling that I was *not* speaking lies, alone sustained me. The applause etc., I took for empty noise, which it really was not altogether : the instant I found myself loose, I hurried joyfully out of it, over to my Brother's Lodging (73 George Street, near by) ; to the Students all crowding and shouting round me, I waved my hand prohibitively at the door, perhaps lifted my hat ; and they gave but one cheer more,—something in the tone of *it*, which did for the first time go into my heart : " Poor young men ; so well affected to the poor old brother or grandfather here ; and in such a black whirlpool of a world here, all of us ! "—Brother Jamie, and Son, etc., were sitting within ; Erskine and I went silently walking through the streets, and at night was a kind but wearing and wearying congratulatory dinner. Followed by others such ; unwholesome to me, not joyful to me ; and endured as duties, little more.—But that same afternoon, Tyndall's telegram, emphatic to the uttermost (" A perfect triumph," the three words of it) arrived here ; a joy of joys to my own little Heroine (so beautiful her description of it to me),—which was its one value to me ; nearly *naught* otherwise (in very truth) ; and the *last* of such that could henceforth have any such addition made to it. Alas all " additions " are now ended ; and the thing added to has become only a pain. But I do thank Heaven for this last favour to her that so loved me ; and it will remain a joy to me, if my last in this world. She had to dine with Forster and Dickens that evening, and their way of receiving her good news seemed to have charmed her as much almost as the news itself. From that day forward her little heart appears to have been fuller and fuller of joy, newspapers, etc. etc. making such a jubilation (foolish people, as if " the Address " were anything, or had contained the least thing in it which had not been told you already !) She went out for a two days to Mrs. Oliphant at Windsor ; recovered her sleep, to the old poor average, or nearly so ; and by every testimony, and all the evidence I myself have, was not for many years, if ever, seen in such fine spirits and so hopeful and joyfully serene and victorious frame of mind,—till the last moment. Noble little Heart ; her painful, much enduring, much endeavouring little History now at last crowned with plain victory, in sight of her own people, and of all the world ; everybody now obliged to say my Jeannie was not wrong, she was right, and has made it good ! Surely for this I should be grateful to Heaven ; for this, amid the immeasurable wreck that was preparing for us. She had from an early period formed her own little opinion about *me* (what an Eldorado to me, ungrateful being, blind, ungrateful, condemnable, and heavy-laden, and crushed down into blindness by great misery, as I oftenest was !)—and she never flinched from it an instant, I think, or cared or counted what the world said *to the contrary* (very brave, magnanimous, and noble, truly, she was in all this) ; but to have the world confirm her in it was always a sensible pleasure, which she took no pains to hide.

especially from me. She lived nineteen days after that Edinburgh Monday ; on the nineteenth (April 21, 1866, between
three and four P.M., as near as I can gather and sift), suddenly
as by a thunderbolt from skies all blue, she was snatched from
me : a " death from the gods," the old Romans would have
called it ; the kind of death she many a time expressed her wish
for : and in all my life (as I feel ever since) there fell on me no
misfortune like it ;—which has smitten my whole world into
universal wreck (unless I can repair it in some small measure),
and extinguished whatever light of cheerfulness, and loving
hopefulness life still had in it to me.

The paragraph in *The Times* (Monday, 23d April), which I
believe is by Dr. Quain (a most kind Physician of hers), contains
in briefest compass the true Narrative of her Death,—which I
have searched into all the items of, but have no wish or need to
record here *on paper*, as if *they* were liable to be forgotten, or
erased from the poor heart of me while I live here. She had
" lunched " (dined, for *her*) with the Forsters that day, who
noticed her especial cheerfulness and well-being, " Carlyle coming
home the day after to-morrow ! " She drove away, perhaps
towards three P.M. ; walked (about a hundred and fifty yards)
in Kensington Gardens ; got in again south end of Serpentine
Bridge ; set out that wretched little dog to run by her near
" Victoria Gate " (north-east corner of the Park) ; swift
brougham hurting its foot, instant spring out to help *it* (though
she little loved it, and had taken it only by charity ; woe to
it !), return of the swift-brougham Lady to apologise (*in* the
footpath out [of the brougham], this, opposite Stanhope Place),
re-ascent into her carriage, and Sylvester driving on : this was
the last act of her to me inestimable life ! She had laid off her
bonnet, taken out two combs (that sharp prick in the back
stopping heart and lungs), laid her hands on her lap, right-
hand back uppermost, left-hand palm uppermost ; and leaning
in the left-hand corner of her carriage, she lay dead ! Death,
they tell me, must have followed almost instantly ;—her last
brief thought, if she had any, must have been a pang of sorrow
about *me*. God be gracious to her through Eternity—and oh
to be joined with her again, if that is not too fond a thought ;
free both of us from sin, for evermore ; that were indeed a
Heaven !— —Silvester seems to have spent still about
three-quarters of an hour, suspecting nothing wrong ; drove
down by the Big Drive, then up by the Serpentine, and down
by the Victoria Gate and Big Drive once more ; at the bottom

of that, he half paused for orders ; getting none, looked back over the blinds, saw the two hands ; turned up by the Serpentine again, but after a few yards, looking back, saw the dear little hands again,—drove towards an elderly Lady near by, in the path *beyond* Rotten Row ; begged her to look in ; she half did, elderly Gentleman near her wholly did ; pronounced it death to all appearance, and recommended him to hasten over to St. George's Hospital, which he in a moment did. All in vain, in vain ! Her look of peace, of beautiful absolute repose had struck them much ; very kind, very helpful to *me*, if to no other, —everybody was. For, as I learned ultimately, had it not been for their and John Forster's, and Dr. Quain's and everybody's mercy on me, there must have been, by rule, a Coroner's Inquest held,—which would have been a blotch upon my memory intolerable then, and discordantly ugly for all time coming. It is to Forster's unwearied and invincible efforts, that I am indebted for escape from this sad defilement of my feelings. Indeed *his* kindness then, and all through, in every particular and detail was *un*exampled, of a cordiality and assiduity almost painful to me : thanks to him and perpetual recollection.

Saturday night about half-past nine, I was sitting in Sister Jean's at Dumfries ; thinking of my Railway to Chelsea on Monday, and perhaps of a sprained ankle I had got at Scotsbrig two weeks or so before,—when the fatal telegram (two of them in succession) came ; it had a kind of *stunning* effect upon me ; not for above two days could I estimate the immeasurable depth of it, or the infinite sorrow which had peeled my life all bare, and, in one moment, shattered my poor world to universal ruin. They took me out next day, to wander (as was medically needful) in the green sunny Sabbath fields ; and ever and anon there rose from my sick heart the ejaculation " My poor little Woman ! "—but no full gush of tears came to my relief, nor has yet come ; will it ever ? A stony " Woe's me, woe's me ! " sometimes with infinite tenderness, and pity not for myself, is my habitual mood hitherto. I had been hitching lamely about in the Terregles quarter, my company the green solitudes and fresh Spring breezes,—quietly but far from happily,—about the hour she died. Sixteen hours *after* the telegram,—(Sunday about two P.M.) there came to me a *Letter* from her, written on Saturday before going out ; the cheeriest and merriest of all her several prior ones ;—a Note for *her* written at Scotsbrig, Friday morning, and which *should* have been a pleasure to her at break- fast that morning was not put in till *after* six at Ecclefechan (negligence of ——, excusable, but unforgettable) ; had not left Ecclefechan till ten P.M., nor arrived till two P.M. next day, and lay *un*opened here.

Monday morning, John set off with me for London ;—never, for a thousand years, should I forget that arrival here of ours,— my first *un*welcomed by her ; *she* lay in her coffin, lovely in death ; I kissed her cold brow . . . pale Death and things not mine or *ours* had possession of our poor dwelling. Next day wander over the fatal localities in Hyde Park ; Forster and Brother John settling, apart from me, everything for the morrow. Morrow, Wednesday morning we were under way with our sacred burden ; John and Forster kindly did not speak to me (good Twisleton [1] too was in the train without consulting me) : I looked out upon the Spring fields, the everlasting Skies, in silence; and had for most part a more endurable day,—till Haddington where Dods etc. were waiting with hospitalities, with etc. etc. which almost drove me openly wild. I went out to walk in the moonlit silent streets ; *not* suffered to go alone : I looked up at the windows of the old Room where I had first seen her,—1821 on a Summer evening after Sunset,—five and forty years ago. Edward Irving had brought me out, walking, to Haddington ; *she* the first thing I had to see there. The beautifullest young creature I had ever beheld ; sparkling with grace and talent, though sunk in sorrow (for loss of her Father),[2] and speaking little. I noticed her once looking at me,—Oh Heaven, to think of that now !—

The Dodses (excellent people in their honest homely way) had great pity for me, patience with me ; I retired to my room, slept none all night,—little sleep to me since that telegram night ;—but lay silent in the great Silence. Thursday (26th April 1866), wandered out into the Churchyard etc. : at one P.M. came the Funeral ; silent, small (only twelve old friends, and two *volunteer*, besides us three), very beautiful and noble to me : and I laid her head in the grave of her Father (according to covenant of forty years back) ; and all was ended. In the nave of the old Abbey Kirk, long a ruin, now being saved from further decay, with the skies looking down on her, there sleeps my little Jeannie, and the light of her face will never shine on me more. One other time,—after the *Inscription* is put on,— I have promised myself to be in Haddington. We withdrew, that afternoon ; posted up (by Edinburgh with its many

1 The Hon. Edward Twisleton ; died 1874; aged 63.
2 Dr. Welsh died September 1819.

confusions) towards London all night, and about ten or eleven
A.M. were shovelled out here ; where I am hitching and wandering about, best off in strict solitude (were it only possible) ;
my one solace and employment that of doing all which I can
imagine *she* would have liked me to do. Maggie Welsh and my
Brother are still with me.—I suppose it to be useless to continue
these jottings (Book probably to be *burnt* from all other eyes,
and to myself painful !)—but perhaps will add something to-
morrow still. [8*th May* 1866 ; 9*th* I find !]

Thursday, May 10. (Days all dim to me ; yesterday I was
wrong in date). . . . My one solace and employment hitherto
is that of sorting up, and settling as I judge *she* would have
wished, all that pertained to her beautiful existence and her :
her advice on it all, how *that* wish starts out on me strangely
at many a turn ; and the sharp twinge that reminds me, " No ! "
One's first *awakening* in the morning, the reality all stript so
bare before one, and the puddle of confused dreams at once
gone, is the ghastliest half-hour of the day ;—as I have heard
others remark. On the whole there is no use in writing here.
There is even a lack of *sincerity* in what I write (strange
but true). The thing I *would* say, I cannot. All words are
idle.[1] . . .

MISS JEWSBURY'S ACCOUNT OF THE BURNING OF THE CANDLES.

" On that miserable night, when we were preparing to receive
her, Mrs. Warren[2] came to me and said, that one time when
she was very ill, she said to her, that when the last had come,
she was to go upstairs into the closet of the spare room
and there she would find two wax candles wrapt in paper, and
that those were to be lighted, and burned. She said that after
she came to live in London, she wanted to give a party. Her
mother was staying with her. Her mother wished everything
to be very nice, and went out and bought candles and confec-
tionery : and set out a table, and lighted up the room quite
splendidly, and called her to come and see it, when all was
prepared. *She* was angry ; she said people would say she was
extravagant, and would ruin her husband. She took away two of
the candles and some of the cakes. Her mother was hurt, and
began to weep [I remember the " soirée " well ; heard nothing
of *this !*—T. C.)] *She* was pained at once at what she had done;
she tried to comfort her, and was dreadfully sorry. She took

---

[1] The extract from Notebook III. ends here. See *supra*, p. 160.
[2] The Carlyles' housekeeper at Chelsea.

the candles and wrapped them up, and put them where they could be easily found. We found them and lighted them, and did as she had desired.   G. E. J."

What a strange, beautiful, sublime and almost terrible little action ; silently resolved on, and kept silent from all the Earth, for perhaps twenty-four years ! I never heard a whisper of it, and yet see it to be *true*. The visit must have been about 1837 ; I remember the 'soirée' right well ; the resolution, bright as with heavenly tears and lightning, was probably formed on her mother's death, February 1842. My radiant One ! Must question Warren the first time I have heart (*29th May* 1866).

I have had from Mrs. Warren a clear narrative (shortly after the above date). Geraldine's report is perfectly true ; fact with Mrs. Warren occurred in February or March 1866, " perhaps a month before you went to Edinburgh, sir." I was in the house, it seems, probably asleep upstairs, or gone out for my walk, evening about eight o'clock. My poor Darling was taken with some bad fit ("nausea," and stomach misery perhaps), and had rung for Mrs. Warren, by whom, with some sip of warm liquid, and gentle words, she was soon gradually relieved. Being very grateful and still very miserable and low, she addressed Mrs. Warren as above, " When the last has come, Mrs. Warren ; " and gave her, with brevity a statement of the case, and exacted her promise ; which the other, with cheering counter-words (" Oh, madam, what is all this ! you will see me die first ! ") hypothetically gave. All this was wiped clean away before I got in ; I seem to myself to half recollect one evening, when she did complain of 'nausea so habitual now,' and looked extremely miserable, while I sat at tea (pour it out she always would, herself drinking only hot water, oh heavens !) The candles burnt for two whole nights, says Mrs. Warren (*24th July* 1866).

[*From this point every vacant space of the Notebook being used, Carlyle continues, on a separate paper, wafered on to the last page of it.*]

The paper of this poor Notebook of hers is done ; all I had to say, too (though there lie such volumes yet unsaid), seems to be almost done : and I must sorrowfully end it, and seek for something else. Very sorrowfully still ; for it has been my sacred shrine, and *religious* city of refuge from the *bitterness* of these sorrows, during all the doleful weeks that are past since I took it up : a kind of *devotional* thing (as I once already said), which *softens* all grief into tenderness and infinite pity and repentant love ; one's whole sad *life* drowned as if in *tears* for one, and all the wrath and scorn and other grim elements silently melted away. And now, am I to *leave* it ; to take farewell of *Her* a second time ? Right silent and serene is *She*, my lost Darling yonder, as I often think in my gloom ; no sorrow more for *Her*, —nor will there long be for me. . . .

Everything admonishes me to *end* here my poor scrawlings and weak reminiscences of days that are no more.

I still mainly mean to *burn* this Book before my own departure ; but feel that I shall always have a kind of grudge to do it, and an indolent excuse, " Not *yet ;* wait, any day that can be done ! "— and that it *is* possible the thing *may* be left behind me, legible to interested survivors,—*friends* only, I will hope, and with *worthy* curiosity, not *un*worthy !

In which event, I solemnly forbid them, each and all, to *publish* this Bit of Writing *as it stands here ;* and warn them that *without fit editing* no *part* of it should be printed (nor so far as I can order, *shall* ever be) ;—and that the ' *fit* editing ' of perhaps nine-tenths of it will, after I am gone, have become *impossible*.

T. C. (Saturday, 28th July 1866).

EDWARD IRVING

[Cheyne Row, Autumn 1866.]

EDWARD IRVING died thirty-two years ago (December 1834), in the first months of our adventurous settlement here ; the memory of him is still clear and vivid with me, in all points,— that of his first and only visit to us in this House, in this room, just before leaving for Glasgow (October [1] 1834), which was the last we saw of him, is still as fresh as if it had been yesterday ; —and he has a solemn, massive, sad and even pitiable, though not much blamable, or in heart *ever* blamable, and to me always dear and most friendly aspect, in those vacant Kingdoms of the Past. He was scornfully forgotten at the time of his death ; having indeed sunk a good while before out of the notice of the more intelligent classes. There has since been and now is, in the new theological generation, a kind of revival of him, on rather weak and questionable terms, sentimental mainly, and grounded on no really correct knowledge or insight ; which, however, seems to bespeak some continuance of vague remembrance, for a good while yet, by that class of people, and the many that hang by them.—Being very solitary, and except for converse with the Spirits of my Vanished Ones, very idle in these hours and days, I have bethought me of throwing down (the more rapidly the *better*) something of my recollections of this to me very memorable man ; in hopes they may by possibility be worth something by-and-by to some,—not worth *less* than nothing to anybody (viz. not true and candid according to my best thoughts), if I can help it. *Pergamus*, therefore ;— and be a great deal *swifter*, if you please !——

The Irvings, Edward's father and uncles, lived all within a few miles of my native place, and were of my Father's acquaintance. Two of the uncles, whose little Farm-establishments lay close upon Ecclefechan, were of his familiars, and became mine more or less, especially one of them (" George of Bogside ") who

---

[1] It must have been before October, for Irving had already set out on his journey to Glasgow early in September.

was further a co-religionist of ours (a "*Burgher* Seceder," not
a "Kirkman," as the other was). They were all cheerfully
quiet, rational and honest people, of a good-natured and prudent turn,—something of what might be called a kindly vanity,
a very harmless self-esteem, doing pleasure to the proprietor
and hurt to nobody else, was traceable in all of them. They
were not distinguished by intellect, any of them ; except it
might be intellect in the *unconscious* or instinctive condition
(coming out as prudence of conduct, etc.), of which there were
good indications ;—and of Uncle George, who was prudent
enough and successfully diligent in his affairs (no bad proof of
"intellect" in some shape), though otherwise a most taciturn,
dull, and almost stupid-looking man, I remember this other fact,
that he had one of the *largest heads* in the district, and that my
Father, he, and a clever and original Dr. Little, their neighbour,
never could be fitted in a Hat-shop of the village, but had always
to send their measure to Dumfries to a Hat-maker there.
Whether George had a round head or a long I do not recollect.
There was a fine little spice of innocent, faint, but genuine and
kindly banter in him, now and then. Otherwise I recollect him
only as heavy, hebetated, elderly or old, and more inclined to
quiescence and silence than to talk of or care about anything
exterior to his own interests temporal or spiritual.

Gavin, Edward's Father (name pronounced Ga-yin = Guyon,
as Edward once remarked to me), a tallish man, of rugged
countenance, which broke out oftenest into some innocent fleer
of merriment, or readiness to be merry, when you addressed
him, was a prudent, honest-hearted, rational person, but made
no pretension to superior gifts of mind ; though he too perhaps
may have had such in the undeveloped form,—thus, on ending
his apprenticeship, or by some other lucky opportunity, he had
formed a determination of seeing a little of England in the first
place ; and actually got mounted on a stout pony, accoutre-
ments succinctly complete (road-money "in a belt round his
own body ") ; and rode, and wandered at his will, deliberate
southward, I think for about six weeks ; as far as Wiltshire at
least, for I have heard him speak of Devizes, "*The* Devizes " he
called it, as one of his halting-places. What his precise amount
of profit from this was, I know not at all ; but it bespeaks
something ingenuous and adventurous in the young man. He
was by craft a Tanner ; had settled in Annan, soon began to be
prosperous, wedded well, and continued all his life there. He
was among the younger of those brothers ; but was clearly the

head of them, and indeed had been the making of the principal two, George and John, whom we knew. Gavin was Bailie in Annan, when the furious *Election* sung by Burns (' There were five carlins in the South,'—five burghs, namely) took place ; Gavin voted the right way (Duke of Queensberry's way) ; and got for his two brothers, each the lease of a snug Queensberry Farm, which grew ever the snugger, as dissolute " Old Q." developed himself more and more into a cynical egoist, sensualist and hater of his next heir (the Buccleuch, not a Douglas but a Scott, who now holds both Dukedoms) : a story well known over Scotland, and of altogether lively interest in Annandale (where it meant " entail-leases " and large sums of money) during several years of my youth.

These people, " the Queensberry Farmers," seem to me to have been the happiest set of Yeomen I ever came to see ; not only because they sat easy as to rent, but because they *knew* fully *how* to sit so, and were pious, modest, thrifty men, who neither fell into laggard relaxation of diligence, nor were stung by any madness of ambition ; but faithfully continued to turn all their bits of worldly success into *real* profit for soul and body. They disappeared (in Chancery Lawsuit) fifty years ago. I have seen various kinds of Farmers, cultivated, monied, scientific etc. etc. ; but as desirable a set, not since.

Gavin had married well, perhaps rather above his rank ; a tall, black-eyed handsome woman, Sister of certain Lowthers in that neighbourhood, who did most of the inconsiderable Corn-trade of those parts, and were considered a stiff-necked faithful kind of people, apter to do than to speak,—originally from Cumberland, I believe. For her own share, the Mother of Edward Irving had much of fluent speech in her, and of manage-ment ; thrifty, assiduous, wise, if somewhat fussy ; for the rest, an excellent house-mother, I believe, full of affection and tender anxiety for her children and husband. By degrees she had developed the modest prosperity of her household into something of decidedly " genteel " (Annan " gentility ") ; and, having left the rest of the Irving kindred to their rustic solidities, had probably but little practical familiarity with most of them, though never any quarrel or estrangement that I heard of : her Gavin was never careful of gentility, a roomy simplicity and freedom (as of a man in dressing-gown) his chief aim ; in my time, he seemed mostly to lounge about ; superintended his tanning only from afar, and at length gave it up altogether. There were four other Brothers, three of them small farmers (the two eldest near Ecclefechan, and known to me), and a fourth who followed some cattle-traffic in Annan, and was well esteemed there for his honest simple ways. No Sister of theirs did I ever hear of ; nor what their father had been,—some honest little farmer, he too, I conclude.

Their mother, Edward Irving's aged grandmother, I well remember to have seen, once, perhaps twice, at her son George's fireside ; a good old woman, half in dotage, and the only creature I ever saw spinning with a *distaff* and no other apparatus but tow or wool.—All these Irvings were of blond or even of red complexion ; red hair a prevailing or sole colour in several of their families. Gavin was himself reddish, or at least sandy-blond ; but all his children had beautifully coal-black hair,—except one girl, the youngest of the set but two, who was carroty like her cousins. The brunette Mother, with her swift black eyes, had prevailed so far. Enough now for the genealogy, superabundantly enough. [Stop for the day, 14*th September.*]

One of the circumstances of Irving's boyhood ought not to be neglected by his Biographers : the remarkable schoolmaster he had. " Old Adam Hope," perhaps not yet fifty in Irving's time, was all along a notability in Annan. What had been his specific history or employment before this of schoolmastering, I do not know ; nor was he ever my schoolmaster, except incidentally for a few weeks, once or twice, as substitute for some absentee who had the office ; but I can remember reading in *Sallust* with him, on one such occasion, and how he read it, and drilled us in it ; and I have often enough seen him teach ; and knew him well enough. A bony, strong-built, but lean kind of man ; of brown complexion, and a pair of the sharpest not the sweetest black eyes. Walked in a lounging stooping figure ; in the street, broad-brimmed, and in clean frugal rustic clothes ; in his schoolroom, bare-headed, hands usually crossed over back, and with his effective leather strap (" *Cat*," as he called it, not *tawse*, for it was not *slit* at all) hanging ready over his thumb, if requisite anywhere. In my time, he had a couple of his front teeth quite black ; which were very visible, as his mouth usually wore a settled humanely-contemptuous grin, " Nothing *good* to be expected from *you*, or from those you come of, ye little whelps ; but we must get from you the *best* you have, and not complain of anything : " this was what the grin seemed to say ; but the black teeth (*jet-black*, for he chewed tobacco also, to a slight extent, never spitting) were always mysterious to me,—

till at length I found they were of cork, the product of Adam's frugal penknife, and could be removed at pleasure. He was a man humanely contemptuous of the world ; and valued " suffrages " at a most low figure, in comparison ;—I should judge, an extremely proud man. For the rest, an inexorable logician ; a Calvinist at all points, and Burgher Scotch Seceder to the backbone. He had written a tiny *English Grammar* latterly (after Irving's time, and before mine), which was a very compact, lucid and complete little Piece ; and was regarded by the natives, especially the young natives who had to learn from it, with a certain awe, the feat of Authorship in print being then somewhat stupendous, and beyond example in those parts. He did not know very much, though still a good something, Geometry (of Euclid), Latin, Arithmetic, English Syntax ; but what he did profess or imagine himself to know, he knew in every fibre and to the very bottom. More rigorously solid teacher of the young idea, so far as he could carry it, you might have searched for through the world in vain. Self-delusion, half-knowledge, sham instead of reality, could not get existed in his presence. He had a Socratic way with him ; would accept the poor hapless pupil's half-knowledge, or plausible sham of knowledge, with a kind of welcome, " *Hm, hm, yes ;* " then gently enough begin a chain of inquiries more and more surprising to the poor pupil, till he had reduced him to zero, to mere *non plus ultra,* and the dismal perception that his sham of knowledge had been flat misknowledge with a spice of dis-honesty added. This was what he called " making a boy fast." For the poor boy had to sit in his place, under arrest all day, or day after day, meditating those dismal new-revealed facts, and beating ineffectually his poor brains for some solution of the mystery, and feasible road out. He might apply again at pleasure ; " I have made it out, Sir : " but if again found self-deluded, wanting, it was only a new padlock to those *fastenings* of his. They were very miserable to the poor penitent, or impenitent, wretch.

I remember my Father's once describing to us, a call he had made on Hope, during the mid-day hour of interval ; whom he found reading or writing something not having cared to lock the door and go home ; " with three or four bits of boys sitting prisoners," made fast " in different parts of the room ; all perfectly miserable, each with a rim of black worked out round his eye-sockets " (the effect of salt tears, wiped by knuckles rather dirty) ! Adam, though not cat-like of temper or intention, had a kind of cat-pleasure in surveying and playing with these captive mice,—which was to turn out so beneficial withal. He did not much use the leather strap, I believe, though it always dangled ready ; but contented himself with these spiritual agonies of " making fast," instead. He was a praise and glory to well-doing boys ; a beneficent terror to the ill-doing or dishonest-blockhead sort ;—and did what was in his power to *educe* (or educate) and make available the net amount of faculty discoverable in each, and separate firmly the known from the unknown or misknown in those young heads. On Irving, who always spoke of him with mirthful affection, he had produced quietly not a little effect ; prepared him well for his triumphs in Geometry and Latin, at College ;—and, through life, you could always notice, overhung by such strange draperies, and huge superstructures so foreign to it, something of that old primeval basis of rigorous logic and clear articulation laid for him in boy-hood by old Adam Hope. Old Adam indeed, if you know the Annanites and him, will be curiously found visible there to this day, an argumentative, clear-headed, sound-hearted, if rather conceited and contentious set of people, more given to intellectual pursuits than some of their neighbours. I consider Adam an original, meritorious kind of man ; and regret to think that his sphere was so limited. In my youngest years his brown, quietly-severe face was familiar to me in Ecclefechan Meeting-house (my venerable Mr. Johnston's hearer on Sundays, as will be afterwards noted) ; younger *kindred*, cousins of his, excellent honest people, I have since met (David Hope, Merchant in Glasgow, William Hope, Scholar in Edinburgh, etc.) ; and one tall straight old Uncle of his, very clean always, brown as mahogany and with a head white as snow, I remember very clearly as the picture of gravity and pious seriousness in that poor Ecclefechan Place of Worship,—concerning whom I will report one anecdote, and so end. Old David Hope, that was his name, lived on a little farm close by Solway Shore, a mile or two east of Annan. A wet country, with late harvests ; which (as in this year 1866) are sometimes incredibly difficult to save. Ten days continuously pouring ; then a day, perhaps two days, of drought, part of them it may be of roaring wind,—during which the moments are golden for you (and perhaps you had better work all night), as presently there will be deluges again. David's stuff, one such morning, was all standing dry again, ready to be saved still, if he stood to it, which was much his intention. Breakfast (wholesome hasty porridge) was soon over ; and next in course came family worship, what they call " Taking the Book " (or Books, i.e. taking your *Bibles*, Psalm and Chapter always part of the service) : David was putting on his spectacles, when somebody rushed in, " Such a raging wind risen ; will drive the *stooks* (shocks) into the sea if let alone ! " " Wind ? " answered David ; " Wind canna get ae straw that has been appointed mine ; sit down, and let us worship God " (that rides in the whirlwind) !—There is a kind of citizen which Britain used to have ; very different from the millionaire Hebrews, Rothschild money-changers, Demosthenic Disraelis, and inspired young Göschens, and their " unexampled prosperity." Weep, Britain, if these latter are among the honourable you now have !—

One other circumstance that peculiarly deserves note in Irving's young life, and perhaps the only other one, is also connected with Adam Hope : Irving's young religion. Annandale was not an irreligious country,—though Annan itself (owing to a drunken Clergyman, and the logical habits they cultivated) was more given to sceptical free-thinking than other places ;— the greatly prevailing fashion was, a decent form of devoutness, and pious theoretically anxious regard for things Sacred ; in all which the Irving Household stood fairly on a level with its neighbours, or perhaps above most of them. They went duly to Kirk ; strove still to tolerate and almost to respect their unfortunate Minister (who had succeeded a father greatly esteemed in that office, and was a man of gifts himself, and of much goodnature, though so far gone astray) ; nothing of profane, I believe, or of the least tendency that way, was usually seen, or would have been suffered without protest and grave rebuke in Irving's environment near or remote. At the same time this other fact was visible enough, if you examined : " A man who awoke to the belief that he actually had a soul to be saved or lost was apt to be found among the Dissenting people, and to have given up attendance on the Kirk." It was ungenteel for him to attend the Meeting-house ; but he found it to be altogether salutary. This was the case, throughout, in Irving's district and mine,— as I had remarked for myself, nobody teaching me, at an early period of my investigations into men and things. I concluded it would be generally so over Scotland ; but found when I went north, to Edinburgh, Glasgow, Fife, etc., that it was not, or by no means so perceptibly was. For the rest, all Dissent in Scotland is merely a stricter adherence to the National Kirk in all points ; and the then Dissenterage is definable to moderns simply as a "*Free Kirk*" making no noise." It had quietly (about 1740), after much haggle and remonstrance, " seceded" or walked out of its stipends, officialities, and dignities, greatly to the mute sorrow of religious Scotland ; and was still, in a strict manner, on the united voluntary principle, preaching to the people what of best and sacredest it could. Not that there was not something of rigour, of severity ; a lean-minded con- troversial spirit among certain brethren, (mostly of the laity, I think) ; " narrow-nebs " (narrow of *neb*, i.e. of nose or bill) as the outsiders called them ; of flowerage, or free harmonious beauty, there could not well be much in this system : but really, except on stated occasions (annual fast-day, for instance, when you were reminded that " a testimony had been lifted up," which *you* were now the bearers of), there was little, almost no talk, especially no preaching at all about " patronage," or secular controversy ; but all turned on the weightier and universal matters of the Law, and was considerably entitled to say for itself, " Hear, all men." Very venerable are those old Seceder Clergy to me, now when I look back on them. Most of the chief figures among them, in Irving's time and mine, were hoary old men. Men so like what one might call antique " Evangelists in modern vesture, and Poor Scholars and Gentle- men of Christ," I have nowhere met with in Monasteries or Churches, among Protestant or Papal Clergy, in any country of the world.—All this is altered utterly at present, I grieve to say ; and gone to as good as nothing or worse. It began to alter just about that period, on the death of those old hoary Heads ; and has gone on with increasing velocity ever since. Irving and I were probably among the last products it delivered before gliding off, and then rushing off, into self-consciousness, arrogancy, insincerity, jangle and vulgarity, which I fear are now very much the definition of it. Irving's concern with the matter had been as follows ; brief, but I believe ineffaceable through life.

Adam Hope was a rigid Seceder, as all his kin and connections were ; and in and about Annan, equally rigid some of them, less rigid others, were a considerable number of such,—who indeed, some few years hence, combined themselves into an " Annan Burgher Congregation," and set up a Meeting-house and Minister of their own. For the present they had none, nor had thought of such a thing ; venerable " Mr. Johnston " of Ecclefechan, six miles off, was their only Minister ; and to him, duly on Sunday, Adam and a select group were in the habit of pilgrimage for Sermon. Less zealous brethren would perhaps pretermit in bad weather ; but I suppose it had to be very bad when Adam and most of his group failed to appear. The distance, a six miles twice, was nothing singular in their case ; one family, whose streaming plaids, hung up to drip, I remember to have noticed one wet Sunday, pious Scotch weavers, settled near Carlisle, I was told,—were in the habit of walking fifteen miles twice for their Sermon, since it was not to be had nearer. A curious phasis of things ;—quite vanished now, with whatever of divine and good was in it, and whatever of merely human and not so good. From reflection of his own, aided no doubt, or perhaps awakened by study of Adam Hope and his example (for I think there would not be direct speech or persuasion from Adam in such a matter), the boy Edward joined himself to Adam's pilgriming group, and regularly trotted by their side to Ecclefechan for Sermon, listening, and occasionally joining in their pious discourse thither and back. He might be then in his tenth year ; distinguished hitherto, both his elder brother John and he, by their wild love of sport, as well as readiness in school lessons. John had quite refused this Ecclefechan adventure, and no doubt done what he could to prevent it ; for father and mother looked on it, likewise, with dubious or disapproving eye, " Why run into these ultra courses, sirrah ? " —and Edward had no furtherance in it except from within. How long he persisted I do not know. Possibly a year or two,— or occasionally, almost till he went to College. I have heard him speak of the thing long afterwards,—in a genially mirthful way ; well recognising what a fantastic, pitifully pedantic, and serio-ridiculous set these road-companions of his mostly were. I myself remember two of them, who were by no means heroic to me : " Wullie Drummond," a little man with mournful goggle-eyes, a tailor I almost think ; and " Joe Blacklock " (*Blai-lock*), a rickety stocking-weaver, with protruding chin and one leg *too* short for the other short one, who seemed to me an abundantly solemn, and much too infallible and captious little fellow. Edward threw me off, with gusto, outline likenesses of these among the others ; and we laughed heartily without malice. Edward's religion in after years, though it ran always in the blood and life of him, was never shrieky or narrow ; but even in his last times with their miserable troubles and confusions spoke always with a sonorous deep tone, like the voice of a man, frank and sincere, addressing men. To the last, or almost to the last, I could occasionally raise a genial old Annandale laugh out of him ; which is now pathetic to me to remember.

I will say no more of Irving's boyhood. He must have sat, often enough, in Ecclefechan Meeting-house along with me, but I never noticed or knew ; and had not indeed heard of him till I went to Annan School (1806 ; a new " Academy " forsooth, with Adam Hope for " English Master "), and Irving, perhaps two years before, had left for College. I must bid adieu, also, to that poor Temple of my Childhood ; to me more sacred at this moment than perhaps the biggest Cathedral then extant could have been. Rude, rustic, bare, no Temple in the world was more so ;—but there were sacred lambencies, tongues of authentic flame from Heaven, which kindled what was best in one, what has not yet gone out. Strangely vivid to me some twelve or twenty of those old faces whom I used to see every Sunday ; whose names, employments, precise dwelling-places, I never knew ; but whose portraits are yet clear to me as in a mirror,—their heavy-laden, patient, ever-attentive faces ; fallen solitary, most of them, children all away, wife away for ever (or it might be wife still there ; one such case I well remember, wife constant like a shadow and grown very like her old man) ; the thrifty, cleanly poverty of these good people ; their well-saved old coarse clothes (*tailed* waistcoats down to mid-thigh, a fashion quite dead twenty years before) : all this I occasionally see as with eyes,—sixty or sixty-five years off,—and hear the very voice of my Mother upon it, whom sometimes I would be questioning about these persons of the drama, and endeavouring to describe and identify them to her, for that purpose. Oh, ever-miraculous Time, O Death, O Life !

Probably it was in 1808, April or May, after College time, that I first saw Irving : I had got over my worst miseries in that doleful and hateful " Academy " life of mine (which lasted three years in all) ; had begun, in *spite* of precept, to strike about me, to defend myself by hand and voice ; [1] had made some comrade-ship with one or two of my age, and was reasonably becoming alive in the place and its interests :—I remember to have felt some human curiosity and satisfaction, when the noted Edward Irving, English-master Hope escorting, introduced himself in

[1] Carlyle writes in 1866 : " Mythically *true* is what *Sartor* says of his Schoolfellows, and not half of the truth. Unspeakable is the damage and defilement I got out of those coarse unguided tyrannous cubs,—especially till I revolted against them, and gave stroke for stroke ; as my pious Mother, in her great love of peace and of my best interests, spiritual chiefly, had imprudently forbidden me to do."

our Latin Class-room, one bright forenoon. Hope was essentially
the introducer : this was our " Rector's " Class-room ; Irving's
visit to the school had been specially to Adam Hope, his own old
teacher,—who now brought him down, nothing loth.   Perhaps
our Mathematics gentleman, one Morley (an excellent Cumberland man, whom I loved much, and who taught me well), had
also stept in, in honour of such a stranger ; the road from Adam's
room to ours lay through Mr. Morley's.   Ours was a big airy
room, lighted from both sides ; desks and benches occupying
scarcely the smaller half of the floor ; better half belonged to
the Rector, and to the Classes he " called up " from time to
time.   It was altogether vacant at that moment ; and the
interview, perhaps of ten or fifteen minutes, transacted itself
in a standing posture there.   We were all of us attentive with
eye and ear,—or as attentive as we durst be, while, by theory,
" preparing our lessons."   Irving was scrupulously dressed,
black coat, ditto tight pantaloons in the fashion of the day ;
clerical black his prevailing hue ; and looked very neat, self-
possessed, and enviable : a flourishing slip of a youth ; with
coal-black hair, swarthy clear complexion ; very straight on his
feet ; and, except for the glaring squint alone, decidedly handsome.   We didn't hear everything ; indeed we heard nothing
that was of the least moment or worth remembering ; gathered
in general that the talk was all about Edinburgh, of this Professor
and of that, and their merits and methods (" Wonderful world
up yonder ;—and this fellow has been in it, and can talk of it in
that easy cool way ! ")—the last Professor touched upon, I
think, must have been mathematical Leslie (at that time
totally non-extant to me) ; for the one particular I clearly
recollect was something from Irving about new doctrines, by
somebody (doubtless Leslie), " concerning the circle ; " which
last word he pronounced " cir*cul*," with a certain *preciosity*,
which was noticeable slightly in other parts of his behaviour.
Shortly after this of " circul," he courteously (had been very
courteous all the time, and unassuming in the main), made his
bow ; and the interview melted instantly away.   For seven
years I don't remember to have seen Irving's face again.

Seven years come and gone,—it was now the winter of 1815,—
I had myself been in Edinburgh College ; and above a year ago
had duly quitted it ; had got (by competition at Dumfries,
summer 1814) to be "Mathematical Master" in Annan Academy,
with some potential outlook on Divinity as ultimatum (a *rural*

" Divinity Student," visiting Edinburgh for a few days each year, and " delivering " certain " Discourses ; " six years of that would bring you to the Church-*gate*, as four years of *continuous* " Divinity Hall " would ;—unlucky only that, in my case, I had never had the least enthusiasm for the business, and there were even grave prohibitive doubts more and more rising ahead) : both branches of my situation flatly contradictory to all ideals or wishes of mine ; especially the Annan one, as the closely actual and the daily and hourly pressing on me, while the other lay theoretic, still well ahead, and perhaps avoidable. One attraction, one only, there was in my Annan business : I was supporting myself (even saving some few pounds of my poor £60 or £70 annually, against a rainy day), and not a burden to my ever-generous Father any more ; but in all other points of view, I was abundantly lonesome, uncomfortable and out of place there. Didn't go and visit the people there (" ought to have pushed myself in a little, and sought or silently *invited* invitations," such *their* form of social politeness,—which I was far too shy and proud to be able for) ; had the character of morose, dissocial, etc. etc. ;—in short, thoroughly detested my function and position, though understood to be honestly doing the duties of it ; and held for solacement and company to the few Books I could command, and an accidental friend or two I had in the neighbourhood (Mr. Church of Hitchill, and his wife, Rev. Henry Duncan of Ruthwell, and ditto, these were the two bright and brightest houses for me ; my thanks to them, now and always !).—As to my Schoolmaster function it was never said I *misdid* it much (" a clear and correct " expositor and enforcer) : but from the first, especially with such adjuncts, I disliked it, and by swift degrees grew to hate it more and more. Some four years, in all, I had of it, two in Annan, two in Kirkcaldy (under much improved *social* accompaniments) ;—and at the end, my solitary desperate conclusion was fixed, That I, for my own part, would prefer to perish in the ditch, if necessary, rather than continue living by such a trade :—and peremptorily gave *it* up accordingly. This long preface will serve to explain the small passage of collision that occurred between Irving and me on our first meeting in this world.

I had heard much of Irving all along, how distinguished in studies, how splendidly successful as Teacher, how two Professors had sent him out to Haddington, and how his new Academy and new methods were illuminating and astonishing everything there (alas ! there was one little Pupil he had there,

with her prettiest little " *penna, pennæ* " from under the table,
and " let *me* be a boy, too, Papa ! " [1]—who was to be of endless
moment, and alone was of any moment to me in all that) !—I
don't remember any malicious envy whatever towards this great
Irving of the distance : for his greatness in study and learning
I certainly might have had a tendency, hadn't I struggled against
it, and tried to make it emulation, " Do the like, do thou the
like under difficulties ! "   As to his Schoolmaster success, I
cared little about that, and easily flung that out [when] it came
across me.   But naturally all this betrumpeting of Irving to me
(in which I could sometimes trace some touch of malice to myself) had not awakened in me any love towards this victorious
man : " *ich gönnte ihm*," as the Germans phrase it ; but in all
strictness nothing *more*.

About Christmas time, 1815, I had gone with great pleasure
to see Edinburgh again, and read in Divinity Hall a Latin
Discourse (" *Exegesis* they call it there) on the question, " *Num
detur Religio naturalis ?* "   It was the second, and proved to be
the last, of my performances on that theatre ; my first, an
English Sermon on the words, " Before I was afflicted I went
astray, but now," etc., a very weak and flowery sentimental
Piece, had been achieved in 1814, prior to or few months after
my leaving for Annan.   Piece second too, I suppose, was weak
enough ; but I still remember the kind of innocent satisfaction
I had in turning it into Latin in my solitude ; and my slight and
momentary (by no means deep or sincere) sense of pleasure in
the bits of " compliments " and flimsy " approbations," from
comrades and Professors on both these occasions.   Before
Christmas Day, I had got rid of my " Exegesis," and had still
a week of holiday ahead for old acquaintances and Edinburgh
things, which was the real charm of my official errand thither.

One night, I had gone over to Rose Street to a certain Mr.
(afterwards Dr.) Waugh's there,—who was a kind of maternal
cousin or half-cousin of my own ; had been my school-comrade
(several years older), *item* my predecessor in the Annan " Mathematical Mastership " (*immediate* successor, he, of Morley), and
a great favourite in Annan Society in comparison with some,—
and who, though not without gifts, proved gradually to be
intrinsically a good deal of a fool, and by his insolvencies and
confused futilities, as "Doctor" there in his native place, has
left a kind of remembrance, ludicrous, partly contemptuous,
though not without kindliness too, and even something of

[1] See *supra*, p. 51 *n.*

respect. His Father, with whom I had been boarded while a scholar at Annan, was one of the most respectable and yet laughable of mankind ; a ludicrous caricature of originality, honesty, and faithful discernment and practice, all in the awkward form ;—took much care of his money, however ; which this his only son had now inherited, and did not keep very long. Of Waugh senior, and even of Waugh junior, there might be considerable gossiping and quizzical detailing ; they failed not to rise now and then, especially Waugh senior did not, between Irving and me, always with hearty ha-ha's, and the finest recognition on Irving's part when we came to be companions afterwards :—but whither am I running with so interminable a preface to one of the smallest incidents conceivable !

I was sitting in Waugh junior's that evening, not too vigorously conversing, when Waugh's door went open ; and there stept-in Irving and one Nichol, a Mathematical Teacher in Edinburgh, an intimate of his, a shrewd, merry, and very social kind of person (whom I did not then know, except by name). Irving was over, doubtless, from Kirkcaldy on his holidays ; and had probably been dining with Nichol. The party was duly welcomed ; to myself not unwelcome, though somewhat alarming. Nichol, I perceived, might be by some three or four years the eldest of us, a sharp man, with lips rather quizzically close ; I was by some three or four years the youngest ; and here was Trismegistus Irving, a victorious bashaw, while poor I was so much the reverse. The conversation, in a minute or two, became quite special and my unwilling self the centre of it ; Irving directing upon me a whole series of questions about Annan matters, social or domestic mostly ; of which I knew little, and had less than no wish to speak ; though I strove politely to answer succinctly what I could. In the good Irving all this was very natural ; nor was there in him, I am well sure, the slightest notion to hurt me or be tyrannous to me (far the reverse his mood, at all times, towards all men !)—but there was, I conjecture, something of conscious unquestionable superiority, of careless natural *de haut en bas*, which fretted on me, and which might be rendering my answers more and more succinct. Nay, my small knowledge itself was failing ; and I had, more than once, on certain points (as " Has Mrs. —— got a baby ? Is it son or daughter ? " and the like) to answer candidly, " I don't know." I think three or two such answers to such questions had followed in succession, when Irving, feeling uneasy, and in a dim manner that the game was going wrong, answered in gruffish

yet not ill-natured tone : " You seem to know nothing ! " To
which I, with prompt emphasis, somewhat provoked, replied,
" Sir, by what right do you try my knowledge in this way ?
Are you grand inquisitor, or have you authority to question
people, and cross-question, at discretion ? I have had no
interest to inform myself about the births in Annan ; and care
not if the process of birth and generation there should cease and
determine altogether ! "—" A bad example that," cried Nichol,
breaking into laughter : " that would never do for me " (a fellow
that needs pupils) ! And laughed heartily, joined by Waugh,
by perhaps Irving himself in a sort ;—so that the thing passed
off more smoothly than might have been expected ; though
Irving of course felt a little hurt ; and I think did not altogether
hide it from me, while the interview still lasted, which was only
a short while. This was my first meeting with the man whom I
had afterwards, and very soon, such cause to love. We never
spoke of this small unpleasant passage of fence, I believe ; and
there never was another like it between us in the world. Irving
did not want some due heat of temper, and there was a kind of
joyous swagger traceable in his manners, in this prosperous
young time ; but the basis of him at all times was fine manly
sociality, and the richest truest good-nature. Very different
from the new friend he was about picking up. No swagger in
this latter ; but a want of it which was almost still worse. Not
sanguine and diffusive, he ; but biliary and intense ;—" far too
sarcastic for a young man," said several in the years now
coming.

Within six or eight months of this, probably about the end
of July 1816, happened a new meeting with Irving. Adam
Hope's poor old Wife had died on a sudden ; I went up, the
second or third evening, to testify my silent condolence with the
poor old man (can still remember his gloomy look, speechless,
and the thankful pressure of his hand) : a number of people
were there ; among the rest, to my surprise, Irving (home on
his Kirkcaldy holidays, no doubt), who seemed to be kindly
taking a sort of lead in the little managements. He conducted
worship, I remember ; " taking of the Book," which was the
only fit thing we could settle to ; and he did it in a free-flowing,
modest and altogether appropriate manner,—" *precenting* "
(or leading off the Psalm) too himself, his voice melodiously
strong, his tune *St. Paul's*, truly sung,—which was a new merit
in him to me, quite beyond my own capacities at that time.
If I had been in doubts about his reception of me, after that of

Rose Street, Edinburgh, he quickly and for ever ended them, by a friendliness which, on wider scenes, might have been called chivalrous. At first sight he heartily shook my hand ; welcomed me as if I had been a valued old acquaintance, almost a brother ; and before my leaving, after worship was done, came up to me again, and with the frankest tone said, " You are coming to Kirkcaldy to look about you in a month or two : you know I am there ; my house and all that I can do for you is yours ;— two Annandale people must not be strangers in Fife ! "—The ' doubting Thomas ' durst not quite believe all this, so chivalrous was it ; but felt pleased and relieved by the fine and sincere tone of it ; and thought to himself, " Well, it would be pretty ! " —But to understand the full chivalry of Irving, know first what my errand to Kirkcaldy now was.

Several months before this, rumours had come of some break-up in Irving's triumphant Kirkcaldy kingdom : " A terribly severe master, isn't he ? Brings his pupils on amazingly ; yes truly, but at such an expense of cruelty to them ; very proud, too ; no standing of him ! "—*him*, the least cruel of men, but *expected* and *obliged* to go at high-pressure speed, and no resource left but that of spurring on the laggard :—in short, a portion, perhaps between a third and fourth part, of Irving's Kirkcaldy patrons, feeling these griefs, and finding small comfort or result in complaining to Irving, had gradually determined to be off from him ; and had hit upon a resource which they thought would serve. " Buy off the old Parish Head-Schoolmaster," they said ; " let Hume have his £25 of salary, and go, the lazy, effete old creature ; we will apply again to Professors Christison and Leslie, the same who sent us Irving, to send us *another* ' Classical and Mathematical,' who can start fair."—And accordingly, by a letter from Christison (who had never noticed me while in his class, nor could distinguish me from another " Mr. *Irving* Carlyle," an older, considerably bigger boy, with flaming red hair, wild buck-teeth, and scorched complexion, and the *worst* Latinist of all my acquaintance ;—so ' *dark* ' was the good Professor's ' class-room,' physically and otherwise),—I learnt, much to my surprise and gratification, " That Professor Leslie had been with him ; that etc. etc. (as above) ; and, in brief, that I was the nominee if I would accept." Several letters passed on the subject ; and it had been settled, shortly before this meeting with Irving, that I was, in my near Vacation time (end of August) to visit Kirkcaldy, take a personal view of everything, and then say Yes, if I could, as seemed likely.

Thus stood matters when Irving received me in the way described. Noble, I must say, when you put it altogether! Room for plenty of the vulgarest peddling feelings there was, and there must still have been between us; had either of us, especially had Irving, been of Pedlar nature. And I can say there could no two Kaisers, not Charlemagne and Barbarossa, had they neighboured one another in the Empire of Europe, been more completely rid of all that *sordes*, than were we two Schoolmasters in the Burgh of Kirkcaldy. I made my visit (August coming), which was full of interest to me, saw St. Andrews etc.; saw a fine, frank, wholesome-looking people of the burgher grandees, liked Irving more and more;—and settled to return in a couple of months " for *good*; " which I may well say it *was*, thanks to Irving principally!

George Irving, Edward's youngest brother (who died in London as M.D. beginning practice, about 1833), had met me, as he returned from his lessons, while I *first* came along the street of Kirkcaldy on the sunny afternoon (August 1816), and with blithe looks and words had pointed out where his Brother lived (a biggish simple house on the sands). The *when* of my first call there I do not now remember; but have still brightly in mind how exuberantly good Irving was; how he took me into his Library; a rough, littery, but considerable collection; and said, cheerily flinging out his arms, " Upon all these, you have *will and waygate*," an expressive Annandale phrase of the completest welcome; which I failed not of using by and by. I also recollect lodging for a night or two nights with him about that time,—bright moonshine, waves all dancing and glancing out of window, and beautifully humming and lullabying on that fine long sandy beach, where he and I so often walked and communed afterwards. From the first we honestly liked one another, and grew intimate; nor was there ever, while we both lived, any cloud or grudge between us, or an interruption of our feelings for a day or hour. Blessed conquest, of a Friend in this world! That was mainly all the wealth I had for five or six years coming; and it made my life in Kirkcaldy (i.e. till near 1819, I think) a happy season in comparison, and a genially useful. Youth itself, healthy well-intending youth, is so full of opulences! I always rather like Kirkcaldy to this day; *Annan* the reverse rather, still, when its *gueuseries* come into my head, and my own solitary *quasi-enchanted* position among them,—unpermitted to kick them into the sea!

Irving's Library was of great use to me : Gibbon, Hume, etc.

etc., I think I must have read it almost through ;—inconceivable to me now, with what ardour, with what greedy *velocity*, literally above *ten times* the speed I can now make with any Book. Gibbon, in particular, I recollect to have read at the rate of a volume a day (twelve volumes in all) ; and I have still a fair recollection of it, though seldom looking into it since. It was of all the books perhaps the most impressive on me in my then stage of investigation and state of mind. I by no means completely admired Gibbon, perhaps not more than I now do ; but his winged sarcasms, so quiet, and yet so conclusively transpiercing, and killing dead, were often admirable potent and illuminative to me ; nor did I fail to recognise his grand power of investigating, ascertaining, of grouping and narrating,— though the latter had always, then as now, something of a Drury-Lane character ; the colours strong but coarse, and set off by lights from the side-scenes.—We had books from Edinburgh College-Library too (I remember Bailly's *Histoire de l'Astronomie*, ancient and also modern, which considerably disappointed me) ; on Irving's shelves were the small Didot French Classics in quantity, with my appetite sharp : I must have read (of French and English, for I don't recollect much Classicality, only something of mathematics in intermittent spasms) a great deal during those years.

Irving himself, I found, was not, nor had been, much of a reader ; but he had, with solid ingenuity and judgment, by some briefer process of his own, fished out correctly from many books the substance of what they handled, and of what conclusions they came to ; this he possessed, and could produce, in an *honest* manner always, when occasion came :—he delighted to hear me give accounts of my reading, which were often enough a theme between us, and to me as well a pleasant and profitable one ;—he had gathered, by natural sagacity and insight, from conversation and inquiry, a great deal of practical knowledge, or information on things extant round him, which was quite defective in me the recluse : we never wanted for instructive and pleasant talk while together. He had a most hearty, if not very refined, sense of the ludicrous ; a broad genial laugh in him always ready. His wide just sympathies, his native sagacities, honest-heartedness and good-humour, made him the most delightful of companions. Such colloquies and rich rovings about, in bright scenes, in talk or in silence, I have never had since.

The beach of Kirkcaldy, in summer twilights, a mile of the

smoothest sand, with one long wave coming on, gently, steadily, and breaking in gradual *explosion*, accurately gradual, into harmless melodious *white*, at your hand all the way (the *break* of it, rushing along like a mane of foam, beautifully sounding and advancing, ran from south to north, from West-burn to Kirkcaldy Harbour, through the whole mile's distance) : this was a favourite scene ; beautiful to me still, in the far-away. We roved in the woods, too, sometimes till all was dark. I remember very pleasant strolls to Dysart ; and once or twice to the Caves and queer old Saltworks of Wemyss. Once, on a memorable Saturday, we made pilgrimage, to hear Dr. Chalmers at Dunfermline on the morrow. It was on the inducting a young *Mr.* Chalmers as Minister there (Chalmers *minimus*, as he soon got named) ; the great Chalmers was still in the first flush of his long and always high popularity : " Let us go and hear him, once more ! " said Irving. The summer afternoon was beautiful ; beautiful exceedingly our solitary walk by Burntis-land and the sands and rocks to Inverkeithing,—where we lodged, still in a touchingly beautiful manner (host the Schoolmaster, one Douglas from Haddington, a clever old acquaintance of Irving's, in after years a Radical Editor of mark ; whose wife, for thrifty order, admiration of her husband, etc. etc., was a model and exemplar) : four miles next morning to Dunfermline and its crowded day ; Chalmers Maximus *not* disappointing, —and the fourteen miles, home to Kirkcaldy, ending in late darkness, in rain, and thirsty fatigue, which were cheerfully borne.

Another time, military tents were noticed on the Lomond Hills (on the eastern of the two) : " Trigonometrical Survey ! " said we : " Ramsden's Theodolite, and what not : Let us go ! " and on Saturday we went. Beautiful the airy prospect from that eastern Lomond, far and wide : five or six tents stood on the top, one a black-stained cooking one, with a heap of coals close by ; the rest all closed, and occupants gone,—except one other, partly open at the eaves, through which you could look in, and see a big circular mahogany box (which we took to be the Theodolite), and a saucy-looking cold official gentleman dili-gently walking for exercise, no observation being possible, though the day was so bright. No admittance, however : plenty of fine " County people " had come up ; to whom the Official had been coldly monosyllabic,—as to us also he was ; polite, with a shade of contempt ; and unwilling to let himself into speech. Irving had great skill in these cases ; he remarked, and led us into remarking, courteously this and that about the famous Ramsden and his Instrument, about the famous Trigono-metrical Survey and so forth, till the Official, in a few minutes, had to melt ; invited us exceptionally in for an actual inspection of his Theodolite, which we reverently enjoyed ; and saw through it the Signal Column, a great broad plank he told us, on the top of Ben Lomond, sixty miles off, wavering and shiver-ing like a bit of loose tape, so that no observation could be had. We descended the hill, *re factâ ;* were to lodge in Leslie, other or north side, with the Minister there, where, possibly enough, Irving had engaged to preach for him next day. I do remember a sight of Falkland ruined Palace, black, sternly impressive on me, as we came down ; like a black old bit of coffin or " pro-trusive shin bone," sticking through from the soil of the dead Past. The Kirk, too, of next day I remember ; and a certain tragical Countess of Rothes,—she had been a girl at school in London, fatherless ; in morning walks in the Regent's Park she had noticed a young gardener, had transiently glanced into him, he into her, and had ended by marrying him ; to the horror of Society, and ultimately of herself, I suppose, for he seemed to be a poor little commonplace creature, as he stood there beside her. She was now elderly ; a stately woman, of resolute look though slightly sad, and didn't seem to be soliciting pity. Her I clearly remember ; but not who preached, or what :—and, indeed, both ends of this journey are abolished to me, as if they had never been.

Our voyage to Inchkeith, one afternoon, was again a wholly pleasant adventure, though one of the rashest. There were three of us, Irving's Assistant the third (a hardy, clever kind of man named Donaldson, of Aberdeen origin, Professor Christi-son's Nephew, whom I always rather liked, but who before long, as he could never burst the shell of expert schoolmastering and gerund-grinding, got parted from me nearly altogether) ; our vessel was a row-boat belonging to some neighbour ; in fact, a mere yawl with two oars in it and a bit of helm, reputed to be somewhat crazy and cranky, hadn't the weather been so fine :— nor was Inchkeith our original aim ; original aim had been as follows :—A certain Mr. Glen, Burgher Minister at Annan, with whom I had latterly boarded there, and been (domestically) very happy in comparison, had since, after painful and most unde-served treatment from his contentious congregation, seen him-self obliged to quit the barren wasp's nest of a thing altogether, and with his wife and young family embark on a *Missionary* career, which had been his earliest thought,—as Conscience now reproachfully reminded him, among other considerations. He was a most pure and excellent man ; of correct superior intellect, and of much modest piety and amiability. Things were at last all ready ; and he and his were come to Edinburgh, to embark for Astrachan,—where or whereabouts, accordingly, he continued diligent, zealous, for many years, and was widely esteemed, not by the missionary classes alone. Irving as well as I had an affectionate regard for Glen ; and on a Saturday, eve of Glen's last Sunday in Edinburgh, had come across with me to bid his brave wife and him farewell :—Edinburgh, from Saturday afternoon till the last boat on Sunday evening, this was every now and then a cheery little adventure of ours, always possible again, after the due pause. We found the Glens in an Inn in the Grass Market, much hurried about, and only the Mistress, who was a handsome, brave, and cheery-hearted woman, altogether keeping up her spirits. I heard Glen preach, for the last time, in " Peddie's Meeting-house " (large fine place behind Bristo Street) ; night just sinking as he ended, and the tone of his voice betokening how full the heart was : at the door of Peddie's manse, I stopped to take leave, Mrs. Glen alone was there for me (Glen not to be seen farther) ; she wore her old bright, saucily affectionate smile, fearless, superior to trouble ; but, in a moment, as I took her hand for the last time and said, " Farewell, then ; good be ever with you," she shot all pale as paper ; and we parted mournfully without a word more. This sudden paleness of the spirited woman stuck in my heart like an arrow. All that night, and for some three days more, I had such a bitterness of sorrow as I hardly recollect otherwise : " Parting *sadder* than by death," thought I (in my foolish inexperience !)—" these good people are to live, and we are never to behold each other more ! " Strangely, too, after about four days it went quite off, and I felt it no more.—This was perhaps still the third day ; at all events it was the day of Glen's sailing for St. Petersburg, while Irving and I went watching from Kirkcaldy sands the Leith ships outward bound, afternoon sunny, tide ebbing ; and settled with ourselves which of the big ships was Glen's. " That one, surely," we said at last ;—" and it bends so much this way, one might, by smart rowing, cut into it, and have still a word with the poor Glens ! " Of nautical conclusions none could be falser, more ignorant : but we instantly set about executing it ; hailed Donaldson, who was somewhere within reach ; shoved " Robie Greg's " poor green-painted, rickety yawl into the waves (Robie a good creature who would rejoice to have obliged us); and pushed out with our best speed, to intercept that outward-bound big ship. Irving, I think, though the strongest of us, rather preferred the *helm* post, then and afterwards, and did not much take the oar when he could honourably help it. His steering, I doubt not, was perfect; but in the course of half an hour it became ludicrously apparent that we were the tortoise chasing the hare, and that we should or could, in no wise, ever intercept that big ship. Short counsel, thereupon; and determination, probably on my hint, to make for Inchkeith at least, and treat ourselves to a visit there.

We prosperously reached Inchkeith; ran ourselves into a wild stony little bay (west end of the Island); and stept ashore towards the Lighthouse which was near. Bay, in miniature, was prettily savage, every stone in it, big or little, lying just as the deluges had left them in ages long gone. Whole island was prettily savage. Grass on it mostly wild and scraggy, but equal to the keep of seven cows; some patches, little *bed-quilts* as it were, of weak dishevelled barley trying to grow under difficulties; these, except perhaps a square yard or two of potatoes equally ill off, were the only attempt at crop: inhabitants none except these seven cows and the lighthouse-keeper and his family. Conies probably abounded, but these were *feræ naturæ*, and didn't show face. In a slight hollow about the centre of the Island (whole island, I think, is traversed by a kind of hollow, of which our little bay was the western end), were still traceable some ghastly remnants of the " Russian Graves,"—graves from a Russian Squadron which had wintered thereabouts in 1799 (?) and had there buried its dead; Squadron we had often heard talked of still, what foul creatures these Russian sailors were; how (for one thing) in returning from their sprees in Edinburgh at late hours, they used to climb the lamp-posts in Leith Walk, and drink out the train oil, irresistible by vigilance of the police, so that Leith Walk fell ever and anon into a more or less eclipsed condition, during their stay ! Some wreck of white wooden crosses, rank wild grass, and poor sad, grave-hillocks almost abolished, were all of memorial they had left. The Lighthouse was curious to us; the only one I ever saw before or since. The " revolving light," not produced by a single lamp on its axis, but by ten or a dozen of them, all set in a wide glass cylinder, each with its hollow mirror behind it, *cylinder* alone slowly turning,—was quite a discovery to us.

Lighthouse-keeper, too, in another sphere of inquiry was to me quite new. By far the most life-weary looking mortal I ever saw ;—surely no lover of the picturesque, for in Nature there was nowhere a more glorious view ! He had seven cows, too ; was well fed, I saw, well clad ; had wife and children, fairly eligible-looking ; a shrewd healthy Aberdeen native ; his light-house, especially his cylinder and lamps, all kept shining like a new shilling : a kindly man withal : yet in every feature of face and voice telling you : " Behold the victim of unspeakable ennui ! " We got from him, down below, refection of the best biscuits and new-milk ; I think almost the best in both kinds I have tasted since. A man not greedy of money either :—we left him almost sorrowfully, and never heard of him more.

The scene in our little bay, as we were about proceeding to launch our little boat, seemed to me the beautifullest I had ever beheld : Sun just about setting straight in face of us, behind Ben Lomond far away, Edinburgh with its towers, the great silver mirror of the Frith, girt by such a framework of mountains, cities, rocks and fields and wavy landscape, on all hands of us ; and reaching right under foot (as I remember), came a broad pillar as of gold from the just sinking Sun ; burning axle, as it were, going down to the centre of the world ! But we had to bear a hand, and get our boat launched ; daylight evidently going to end by and by. Kirkcaldy was some five miles off, and probably the tide not in our favour. Gradually the stars came out, and Kirkcaldy crept under its coverlid, showing not itself but its lights. We could still see one another in the fine clear gray ; and pulled along what we could. We had no accident ; not the least ill-luck. Donaldson, and perhaps Irving too, I now think, wore some air of anxiety,—I myself, by my folly, felt nothing ; though I now almost shudder on looking back. We leapt out on Kirkcaldy beach about eleven P.M. ; and then heard sufficiently what a misery and tremor for us various friends had been in.

This was the small adventure to Inchkeith. Glen and family returned to Scotland some fifteen years ago ; he had great approval from his public ; but died in a year or two, and I had never seen him again. His Widow, backed by various Edin-burgh testimonies, applied to Lord Aberdeen, Prime Minister, for a small pension on the " *Literary list* " (Husband " had translated the Bible, or New Testament ? into Persic," among other public merits non-literary) ; and, through her son, earn

estly solicited and urged me to help ; which I did zealously ;
and, by continual dunning of the Duke of Argyll (whom I did
not then personally know, and who was very good and patient
with me), an annual £50 was at last got ; upon which, Mrs. Glen,
adding it to some other small resources, could frugally but
comfortably live. This must have been in 1853. I remember
the young Glen's continual importunity, in the midst of my
Friedrich incipiencies, was not always pleasant ; and my chief
comfort in it was the pleasure which success would give my
Mother. Alas, my good Mother did hear of it ; but pleasure
even in this was beyond her, in the dark valley she was now
travelling ! When she died (Christmas day, 1853), one of my
reflections was, " Too late for *her*, that little bit of kindness ;
my last poor effort, and it came too late ! " That is always a
date for it to me. Young Glen, with his too profuse thanks
etc., was again rather importunate ; poor young soul, he is since
dead. His Mother appeared in person, one morning at my door
in Edinburgh (last spring, in those *Rector* hurries and hurly-
burlies, now so sad to me), T. Erskine just leading me off somewhither : an aged decent widow ; looking kindly on me and
modestly thankful ; so changed I could not have recognised a
feature of her. How *tragic* to one is the sight of " old friends,"
—a thing I always really shrink from, such has my lot been !—
    Irving's visits and mine to Edinburgh were mostly together,
and had always their attraction for us, in the meeting with old
acquaintances and objects of interest ; but except from the
Books procured, could not be accounted of importance. Our
friends were mere Ex-students, cleverish people mostly, but of no
culture or information ; no aspiration beyond (on the best
possible terms) bread and cheese ; their talk in good part was
little other than gossip and more or less ingenious giggle. We
lived habitually, by their means, in a kind of Edinburgh element,
not in the still barer Kirkcaldy one ; and that was all. Irving
now and then perhaps called on some City Clergyman ; but
seemed to have little esteem of them, by his reports to me afterwards. I myself, by this time, was indifferent on that head.
On one of those visits my last feeble tatter of connection with
Divinity Hall affairs or Clerical outlooks was allowed to snap
itself, and fall definitely to the ground (Old " Dr. Ritchie not at
home," when I called to enter myself [1] ;—" Good," answered I ;
" let the omen be fulfilled ! ") Irving on the contrary was
being licensed—probably through *Annan* Presbytery, but I

[1] This was in March 1817.

forget the when and where ; and indeed conjecture it may have
been before my coming to Kirkcaldy.[1]   What alone I well
remember is his often, and notable preaching, in those Kirkcaldy
years of mine.   This gave him an interest in conspicuous clergy-
men (even if stupid), which I had not.   Stupid those Edinburgh
Clergy were not all by any means ; but narrow, ignorant, and
barren to us two, they without exception were.

In Kirkcaldy circles (for poor Kirkcaldy had its circles, and
even its West-End, much more genial to me than Annan used
to be) Irving and I seldom or never met ; he little frequented
them, I hardly at all.   The one house, where I often met him,
besides his own, was the Manse, Rev. Mr. Martin's, which was a
haunt of his, and where, for his sake partly, I was always welcome.   There was a feeble intellectuality current here, the
Minister a precise, innocent, didactic kind of man ; and I now
and then was willing enough to step in,—though various boys
and girls went cackling about ; and Martin himself was pretty
much the only item I really liked.   The girls were some of them
grown up, . . . yet even these, strange to say, in the great
rarity of the article and my ardent devotion to it, were without
charm to me.   Martin himself had a kind of cheery grace and
sociality of way (though much afflicted by *dyspepsia*) ; a clear-
minded, brotherly, well-intentioned man, and, bating a certain
glimmer of vanity which always looked through, altogether
honest, wholesome as Scotch oatmeal.[2]

Irving's preachings as a Licentiate (or ' Probationer ' waiting
for fixed appointment) were always interesting to whoever had
acquaintance with him, especially to me, who was his intimate.
Mixed with but little of self-comparison or other dangerous
ingredient, indeed with loyal recognition on the part of most of
us, and without any grudging or hidden envy, we enjoyed the
broad potency of his delineations, exhortations and free flowing
eloquencies, which had all a manly and original turn ; and then
afterwards there was sure to be, on the part of the public, a great
deal of criticising pro and contra, which also had its entertain-

1 Irving was licensed to preach, at Kirkcaldy, in June 1815.

2 In the passage omitted here, Carlyle goes on to say that Irving became
engaged to Miss Martin, whom he afterwards (in 1823) married, and that
Carlyle did not approve of her influence over Irving.   It would be unpar-
donable to reprint the passage,—all the more as Carlyle had, in Letters
written while he was a guest in Irving's house in London, spoken ap-
provingly of Mrs. Irving as a prudent, judicious housewife, and gratefully
of her kindness to him,—facts, which in those dark days of sad reminiscences, he appears to have forgotten.

ment for us. From the first, Irving read his discourses, but not in a servile manner ; and of attitude, gesture, elocution, there was no neglect :—his voice was very fine ; melodious depth, strength, clearness its chief characteristics ; I have heard more pathetic voices, going more direct to the heart, both in the way of indignation and of pity, but recollect none that better filled the ear. He affected the Miltonic or Old-English Puritan style, and strove visibly to imitate it more and more, till almost the end of his career, when indeed it had become his own, and was the language he used in utmost heat of business, for expressing his meaning. At this time, and for years afterwards, there was something of preconceived intention visible in it, in fact of real " affectation," as there could not well help being :—to his example also, I suppose, I owe something of my own poor affectations in that matter, which are now more or less visible to me, much repented of or not. We were all taught at that time, by Coleridge etc., that the old English Dramatists, Divines, Philosophers, judicious Hooker, Milton, Sir Thomas Browne, were the genuine exemplars ; which I also tried to believe, but never rightly could *as a whole*. The young must learn to speak by imitation of the Older who already do it or have done it : the ultimate rule is, Learn so far as possible to be intelligible and transparent, no notice *taken* of your " style," but solely of what you express by it ; this is your clear rule, and if you *have* anything that is not quite trivial to express to your contemporaries, you will find such rule a great deal more difficult to follow than many people think !

On the whole, poor Irving's style was sufficiently surprising to his hide-bound Presbyterian public ; and this was but a slight circumstance to the novelty of the matter he set forth upon them. Actual practice : " If this thing is true, why not do it ? You had better do it ; there will be nothing but misery and ruin in not doing it ! "—that was the gist and continual purport of all his discoursing ;—to the astonishment and deep offence of hide-bound mankind. There was doubtless something of rashness in the young Irving's way of preaching ; nor perhaps quite enough of pure, complete and serious conviction (which ought to have lain *silent* a good while before it took to speaking) : in general I own to have felt that there was present a certain inflation or spiritual bombast in much of this, a trifle of unconscious playactorism (highly unconscious, but not quite absent) which had been unavoidable to the brave young prophet and reformer. But brave he was ; and bearing full upon the truth, if not yet quite attaining it; and as to the offence he gave, our withers were unwrung; I for one was perhaps rather entertained by it, and grinned in secret to think of the hides it was piercing!—Both in Fife and over in Edinburgh, I have known the offence very rampant. Once, in Kirkcaldy Kirk, which was well filled, and all dead-silent under Irving's grand voice, the door of a pew a good way in front of me (ground floor, right-hand as you fronted the Preacher) banged suddenly open, and there bolted out of it a middle-aged or elderly little man (an insignificant Baker, by position), who, with long swift strides, and face and big eyes all in wrath, came tramping and sounding along the flags, close past my right hand, and vanished out of doors with a slam; Irving quite victoriously disregarding. I remember the violently angry face well enough, but not the least what offence there could have been. A kind of, "Who are you, Sir, that dare to tutor *us* in that manner, and harrow up our ortho-dox quiet skin with your novelties?"—probably that was all.—In Irving's Preaching there was present or prefigured, generous opulence of ability in all kinds (except perhaps the very highest kind, not even prefigured?); but much of it was still crude: and this was the reception it had, for a good few years to come; indeed, to the very end, he never carried all the world along with him, as some have done with far fewer qualities.

In vacation time, twice over, I made a walking Tour with him: First time, I think (but I cannot fix the chronology exactly, though it must lie in *Letters* still hidden here) was to the Trosachs, and home by Loch Lomond, Greenock, Glasgow etc.; many parts of which are still vivid to me. This was probably in 1817.[1] The Tour generally was to be of four; one Pears, who was Irving's housemate or even landlord, School-master of Abbotshall, i.e., of 'The Links,' or *southern extra-burghal* part of Kirkcaldy, a cheerful scatter-brained creature, who went ultimately as Preacher or Professor of something to the Cape of Good Hope; and one Brown (James Brown), who had succeeded Irving in Haddington, and was now Tutor some-where: Tour finally of four, but the full rally was not to be till Stirling; even Pears was gone ahead;—and Irving and I (after an official dinner with the burghal dignitaries of Kirkcaldy, who strove to be pleasant), set out together, on a gray August evening, by Forth sands towards Torryburn. Pears was to have beds ready for us there; and we cheerily walked along, our mostly dark and intricate twenty-two miles: but Pears had nothing,

1 Carlyle's conjecture is correct. It was in 1817.

serviceably ready,—we could not even discover Pears at that dead hour (two A.M.); and had a good deal of groping and adventuring before a poor Inn opened to us, with two coarse clean beds, in which we instantly fell asleep. Pears did in person rouse us next morning about six; but we concordantly met him with mere "ah-ah's," and inarticulate hootings of satirical rebuke, to such extent that Pears, conscious of nothing but heroic punctuality, flung himself out into the rain again, in momentary indignant puff; and strode away for Stirling, where we next saw him after four or five hours. I remember the squalor of our bedroom, in the dim rainy light; and how little we cared for it, in our opulence of youth: the sight of giant Irving, in a shortish shirt, on the sanded floor, drinking patiently a large tankard of "penny-wheep" (the smallest beer in Creation), before beginning to dress, is still present to me as comic; of sublime or tragic the night before, a mysterious great red glow is much more memorable, which had long hung before us in the murky sky; growing gradually brighter and bigger, till at last we found it must be *Carron Ironworks*, on the other side of Forth River; one of the most impressive sights. Our march to Stirling was under pouring rain for most part; but I recollect enjoying the romance of it. "Kincardine, Culross (*Cu'ras*), Clackmannan, here they are, then, what a wonder to be here!" The Links of Forth, the Ochills, Grampians, Forth itself, Stirling, lion-shaped, ahead, like a lion couchant with the castle for his crown,—all this was beautiful in spite of rains, welcome too was the inside of Stirling, with its fine warm inn, and the excellent refection and thorough drying and refitting we got there; Pears and Brown looking pleasantly on; who made a pleasant day of strolling and sight-seeing with us (day now very fine, Stirling all washed), till we marched for Doune in the evening (Brig of Teith, "*voice* of waters," "blue and arrowy Teith,"—Irving and I took that byway, in the dusk); to breakfast in Callander next morning, and get to Loch Katrine in an hour or two more. I have not been in that region again till August last year (four days of magnificently perfect hospitality with Stirling of Keir);—almost surprising to me how mournful it was to 'look on this picture and on that' at an interval of fifty years!—

Irving was in a sort the Captain of our expedition; had been there before; could recommend everything,—was made (unjustly by us) quasi-responsible for everything. The Trosachs I found really grand and impressive, Loch Katrine exquisitely so (my first taste of the beautiful in scenery); not so, any of us, the dirty smoky farm-hut at the entrance, with no provision in it, but bad oatcakes and unacceptable whisky, or the " Mr. Stewart " who somewhat royally presided over it, and dispensed these dainties, expecting to be flattered like an independency, as well as paid like an innkeeper. Poor Irving could not help it :—but in fine the rains, the hardships, the ill diet were beginning to act on us all ; and I could perceive we were in danger (what I have since found usual) of splitting into two parties ; Brown (eight or ten years my senior) leader of the Opposition, myself considerably flattered by him ; though *not* seduced by him into factious courses, only led to see how strong poor Pears was for the Government interest ! This went to no length, never bigger than a summer cloud, or the incipiency of one ; but Brown, in secret, would never quite let it die out (a jealous kind of man, I gradually found ; had been much commended to us, by Irving, as of superior intellect and honesty, —which qualities I likewise found in him, though with the above abatement) ; and there were, or were like to be, divisions of vote in the walking Parliament, two against two ; and had there not been at this point, by a kind of outward and legitimate reason, what proved very sanatory in the case, an actual division of routes, the folly might have lasted longer and become audible and visible, which it never did. Sailing up Loch Katrine, in the top or unpicturesque part, Irving and Pears settled with us (house fully heard) that only we two should go across Loch Lomond, round by Tarbet, Roseneath, Greenock ; they meanwhile making direct for Paisley country (where they had business) ; and so on stepping out, and paying our boatman, they said adieu, and at once struck leftward, we going straight ahead ; rendezvous to be at Glasgow again, on such and such a day. [What feeble trash is all this ; ah me, no better than Irving's " penny-wheep " with the gas *gone out* of it ! Stop to-day, *4th October* 1866.]

The heath was bare, trackless, sun going almost down ; Brown and I (our friends soon disappearing) had an interesting march, good part of it dark, and flavoured just to the right pitch with something of anxiety and sense of danger. The sinking sun threw his reflexes on a tame-looking House with many windows, some way to our right,—the " *Kharrison of Infersnaidt* " [1] (an ancient Anti-*Rob Roy* establishment), as two rough Highland wayfarers had lately informed us ; other house or

---

[1] " The Garrison of Inversnaid," in the county of Stirling, about three miles north of Ben Lomond.

person we did not see; but made for the shoulder of Ben
Lomond and the Boatman's Hut, partly, I think, by the Stars.
Boatman and Huthold were in bed; but he, with a ragged little
Sister or Wife cheerfully roused themselves; cheerfully, and for
most part in silence, rowed us across (under the spangled vault
of midnight, which with the Lake waters silent as if in deep
dream, and several miles broad here, had their due impression
on us) correctly to Tarbet, a most hospitable, clean, and welcome
little country inn (now a huge " Hotel " I hear,—worse luck to
it, with its nasty " Hotel Company, Limited ! ").—On awakening next morning, I heard from below the sound of a churn;
prophecy of new genuine butter, or even of ditto rustic butter-
milk.

Brown and I did very well on our separate branch of pilgrimage; pleasant walk and talk down to the west margin of the
Loch (incomparable among Lochs or Lakes yet known to me),
past Smollett's Pillar; [1] emerge pleasantly on Helensburgh, on
the view of Greenock, and across to Roseneath Manse, where
with a Rev. Mr. Story, not yet quite inducted,—whose *Life*
has since been published,[2]—who was an acquaintance of Brown's,
we were warmly welcomed and well entertained for a couple of
days. Story I never saw again;—but he, acquainted in Haddington neighbourhood, saw some time after, incidentally, a
certain Bright Figure, to whom I am obliged to him at this
moment for speaking favourably of me! " Talent plenty;
fine vein of satire in him ! " something like that;—I suppose
they had been talking of Irving, whom both of them knew and
liked well; *Her*, probably, at that time I had still never seen;
but she told me long afterwards. We have had Story's Son,
Biographer and Successor, here once; who considerably re-
sembles him, but is not so smart and clever.

At Greenock I first saw *Steamers* on the water; queer little
dumpy things, with a red sail to each (and legible name,
" *Defiance* " and such like), bobbing about there, and making
continual passages to Glasgow as their business. Not till about
two years later (1819, if I mistake not), did Forth see a Steamer;
Forth's first was far bigger than the Greenock ones, and called
itself " *The Tug;* " being intended for towing ships in those
narrow waters, as I have often seen it doing; *it* still, and no
rival or congener,—till (in 1825) Leith, spurred on by one Bain,

[1] A pillar, erected to the memory of Smollett, in 1774, which stands near
his birthplace, some three miles north-west of Dumbarton. It bears a
long Latin inscription part of which was written by Dr. Johnson.
[2] *Memoir of the Rev. Robert Story of Roseneath* (1 vol. crown 8vo, 1864).

a kind of scientific Half-pay *Master* R.N., got up a large finely appointed Steamer, or pair of Steamers, for London ; which so successful were they, all Ports then set to imitating.   London alone still held back for a good few years ; it was not till about 1840 that Steamers appeared in the river here.   London was notably shy of the Steamship, great as are its doings now in that line.   An old friend of mine, the late Mr. Strachey,[1] has told me that in his school days, he at one time (early in the Nineties I should guess, say 1795) used to see, in crossing Westminster Bridge, a little *model* Steamship paddling to and fro between him and Blackfriars Bridge, with steam-funnel, paddle-wheels, and the other outfit, exhibiting and recommending itself to London and whatever scientific or other spirit of marine adventure London might have ;—London entirely dead to the phenomenon ; which had to duck under and dive across the Atlantic, before London saw it again when a new generation had risen !   The real inventor of steamships, I have learned credibly elsewhere, the maker and proprietor of that fruitless model on the Thames, was Mr. Millar, Laird of Dalswinton in Dumfriesshire (Poet Burns's Landlord), who spent his life and his estate in that adventure, and is not now to be heard of in those parts,—having had to sell Dalswinton and die quasi-bankrupt (and I should think broken-hearted) after that completing of his painful invention, and finding of London and mankind dead to it. Millar's assistant and work-hand for many years was John Bell, a joiner in the neighbouring village of Thornhill.   Millar being ruined, Bell was out of work and of connection : Bell emigrated to New York ; and there, speaking much of his old Master, and glorious unheeded invention, well known to Bell in its outlines or details,—at length, found one Fulton to listen to him ; and by " Fulton and Bell " (about 1809), an actual Packet Steamer was got launched ; and lucratively plying on the Hudson River, became the miracle of Yankee-land, and gradually of all lands. These I believe are essentially the facts (old Robert M'Queen of Thornhill, Strachey of the India-House, and many other bits of good testimony and of indication, once far apart, curiously coalescing and corresponding for me) ;—and as, possibly enough, the story is not now known in whole to anybody but myself, it may go in here as a digression, *à propos* of those brisk little Greenock steamers, which I first saw, and still so vividly remem-

1 Late Charles Buller's Uncle.   Somersetshire gentleman, ex-Indian, died in 1831, an examiner in the India House.   Colleague of John S. Mill and his Father there.—T. C.

ber, (little " Defiance " etc., saucily bounding about with their red sails in the sun !) on this my tour with Irving.

Those old three days at Roseneath are all very vivid to me, and marked in white : the great blue mountain masses, giant " Cobler " overhanging, bright seas, bright skies ; Roseneath new Mansion (still unfinished, and standing as it did, the present Duke of Argyll has told me), the grand old oaks,—and a certain handfast, middle-aged, practical and most polite " Mr. Campbell " (the Argyll Factor there), with his two Sisters, excellent lean old ladies, with their wild Highland accent, wiredrawn but genuine good-manners and good principles,—and not least their astonishment, and shrill interjections, at once of love and fear, over the talk they contrived to get out of me one evening and perhaps another, when we went across to tea :—all this is still pretty to me to remember. They are all dead, these good souls (Campbell himself, the Duke told me, died only lately, very odd) ; but they were, to my rustic eyes, of a superior, richly furnished stratum of society ; and the new thought that I too might perhaps be ' one-and-somewhat ' (*Ein und Etwas*) among my fellow-creatures by and by, was secretly very welcome at their hands. We rejoined Irving and Pears at Glasgow (transit, place of meeting utterly forgotten) ; I remember our glad embarkation in a track-boat towards Paisley by canal ; visit preappointed for us at Paisley by Irving, in a good old lady's house, whose son was Irving's boarder ; the dusty, sunny Glasgow evening ; and my friend's joy to see Brown and me (or *me* and Brown, I might perhaps put it, as *his* thought). Irving was very good and jocund-hearted : most blithe his good old lady, whom I had seen at Kirkcaldy before ; and we had a pleasant day or two in those neighbourhoods ; the picturesque, the comic, and the genially common all prettily combining, particulars now much forgotten. Pears went to eastward, Dunse, his native country ; " born i' Dunse," equal in sound to *born a dunce*, as Irving's laugh would sometimes remind him ; ' opposition party ' (except it were in the secret of Brown's jealous heart) there was now none. Irving, in truth, was the natural King among us ; and his qualities of captaincy in such a matter were indisputable.

Brown, he, and I went by the Falls of Clyde ; I do not recollect the rest of our route,—except that at " New Lanark," a green silent valley, with fine Cotton-works " of David Dale," *turned* by Clyde Water, we called to see Robert Owen, the then incipient Arch-*Gomeril's* " model school," and thought it (and him,

whom we did not see, and knew only by his pamphlets and it)
a thing of wind, not worth considering farther ;—and that, after
sight of the Falls (which probably was next day), Irving came
out as Captain in a fine new phase. The Falls were very grand
and stormful, nothing to say against the Falls ; but at the last
of them, or possibly it might be about Bothwell Banks farther
on, a woman who officiated as guide and cicerone, most superfluous, unwilling too, but firmly persistent in her purpose,
happened to be in the worst humour ; did nothing but snap and
snarl, and being answered by bits of quiz, towered at length
into foam, and intimated she would now bring somebody who
would ask us, How we could so treat an unprotected female ?—
and vanished to seek the champion or champions. As our
business was done, and the woman paid too, I own (with shame
if needed) my thought would have been to march with decent
celerity on our way, not looking back unless summoned to do it,
and prudently avoiding discrepant circles of that sort. Not so
Irving ; who drew himself up to his full height and breadth,
cudgel in hand, and stood there, flanked by Brown and me,
silently waiting the issue. Issue was, a thickish kind of man,
seemingly the woman's husband, a little older than any of us,
stept out with her ; calmly enough surveying ; and, at respectful
distance,—asked "If we would buy any apples ?"—Upon
which, with negatory grin, we did march. I recollect nothing
more of this route, except that we visited Lead-hills too, joyfully
descended into the mines etc. ; and that Irving, prior to Annan,
must have struck away from us at some point. Brown and I,
on arriving at Mainhill, found my dear good Mother in the saddest
state ; dregs of a bad fever hanging on her,—my profound
sorrow at which seemed to be a surprise to Brown, according to
his Letters afterwards. With Brown, for a year or two ensuing,
I continued to have some not unpleasant correspondence ; a
conscientious, accurate, clear-sighted, but rather narrow and
unfruitful man ;—at present Tutor to some Lockhart of Lee, and
wintering in Edinburgh ; went afterwards to India, as Presbyterian Clergyman somewhere ; and shrank gradually, we heard,
into complete aridity, ' phrenology ' etc., and before long died
there. He had, after Irving, been my dear little Jeannie's
Teacher and Tutor (she never had but these two) ; and the name
of her, like a bright object far above *me* like a star, occasionally
came up between them, on that Journey, I dare say, as at other
times. She retained a child's regard for James Brown ; and,
in this house, he was always a memorable object.

My second Tour with Irving had nothing of *circuit* in it ; a mere walk homeward through the Peebles-Moffat moor country, and is not worth going into in any detail. The region was without roads, often without foot-tracks, had no vestige of inn ; so that there was a kind of knight-errantry in threading your way through it, not to mention the romance that naturally lay in its Ettricks and Yarrows, and old melodious songs and traditions. We walked up Meggat Water to beyond the sources, emerged into Yarrow, not far above St. Mary's Loch ; a charming secluded shepherd country, with excellent shepherd population ;—nowhere setting up to be picturesque, but everywhere honest, comely, well done-to, peaceable and useful, nor anywhere without its solidly characteristic features, hills, mountains, clear rushing streams, cosy nooks and homesteads, all of fine rustic type ; and presented to you *in naturâ*, not as in a Drury Lane with Stage-lights and for a purpose. The vast and yet not savage solitude as an impressive item,—long miles from farm to farm, or even from one shepherd's cottage to another ; no company to you but the rustle of the grass underfoot, the tinkling of the brook, or the voices of innocent primeval things. I repeatedly walked through that country, up to Edinburgh and down, by myself, in subsequent years :—and nowhere remember such affectionately sad, and thoughtful, and in fact interesting and salutary journeys. I have had days clear as Italy (as in this Irving case) ; days moist and dripping, overhung with the infinite of silent gray ;—and perhaps the latter kind were the preferable, in certain moods. You had the world and its waste imbroglios of joy and woe, of light and darkness, to yourself alone. You could strip barefoot, if it suited better ; carry shoes and socks over shoulder hung on your stick : clean shirt and comb were in your pocket ; *omnia mea mecum porto*. You lodged with shepherds who had clean solid cottages, wholesome eggs, milk, oatbread, porridge, clean blankets to their beds, and a great deal of human sense and unadulterated natural politeness; *canty*, shrewd and witty fellows, when you set them talking ; knew, from their hill-tops, every bit of country between Forth and Solway, and all the shepherd inhabitants within fifty miles, —being a kind of confraternity of shepherds from father to son. No sort of peasant labourers I have ever come across seemed to me so happily situated, morally and physically, well-developed, and deserving to be happy, as these shepherds of the Cheviots. *O fortunati nimium !*—But perhaps it is all altered, not a little, now ; as I, sure enough, am, who speak of it !—

Irving's course and mine, from bonny Yarrow onwards by Loch Skene and the *Gray Mare's Tail* (finest of all cataracts, lonesome, simple, grand, that are now in my memory) down into Moffatdale where we lodged in a Shepherd's Cottage, must have been near " Caplegill," old Walter Welsh's farm, though I knew not of it then ! From the shepherd people came good talk, Irving skilful to elicit it :—topography ; Poet Hogg (who was then a celebrity), " *Shirra* Scott " (famed Sir Walter, " Sheriff of Selkirkshire," whose borders we had just emerged from), then gradually stores of local anecdote, personal history, etc. : these good people never once asked *us*, Whence, Whither, or What are you ; but waited till perhaps it voluntarily came, as generally chanced.   Moffatdale, with its green holms and hill-ranges (" Carriferan saddleyoke," actual quasi-*saddle ; * " you can sit astride anywhere, and a stone dropped from either hand will roll and bound a mile : " one of the prettiest hills), with its pleasant groves and farmsteads, voiceful limpid waters rushing fast *for Annan :* all was very beautiful to us ; but what I most remember is Irving's arrival at Mainhill with me to tea,—and how between my Father and him there was such a mutual recognition.   My Father had seen Loch Skene, the Gray Mare's Tail etc. in his youth, and now gave, in few words, such a picture of it all, forty years after sight, as charmed and astonished Irving ; who, on his side, was equally unlike a common man : definite, true, intelligent, frankly courteous, faithful in whatever he spoke about.   My Father and he saw one another (on similar occasions) twice or thrice again, always with increasing esteem ; —and I rather think it was from Irving on this particular occasion that I was first led to compare my Father with other men, and see how immensely superior he, altogether unconsciously, was.   No intellect equal to his, in certain important respects, have I ever met with in the world.   Of my Mother, Irving never made any reading for himself, or could well have made, but only through me, and that too he believed in and loved well.   Generous, all-recognising Irving !—

The Kirkcaldy population were a pleasant honest kind of fellow mortals ; something of quietly fruitful, of good *Old-Scotch* in their works and ways ; more *vernacular*, peaceably fixed, and almost genial, in their mode of life, than I had been used to in the Border home-land.   Fife generally we liked. Those ancient little burghs and sea-villages, with their poor little havens, ' salt-pans,' and weatherbeaten bits of Cyclopean breakwaters and rude innocent machineries, are still kindly to me to think of ;—Kirkcaldy itself had many looms, had Baltic trade, Whale-fishery etc., and was a solidly diligent, yet by no means a panting, puffing, or in any way gambling " Lang Toun," —its flaxmill-machinery, I remember, was turned mainly by *wind*, and curious blue-painted wheels, with oblique vans (how working I never saw), rose from many roofs for that end. We, I in particular, always rather liked the people,—though from the distance chiefly ; chagrined and discouraged by the sad *trade* one had ! Some hospitable human firesides I found, and these were at intervals a fine little element ; but in general we were but onlookers (the one real " Society," our books and our few selves) ;—not even with the bright " young ladies " (what was a sad feature) were we generally on speaking terms. By far the cleverest and brightest, however, an Ex-pupil of Irving's, and genealogically and otherwise (being poorish, proud, and well-bred) rather a kind of alien in the place, I did at last make acquaintance with (at Irving's first, I think, though she rarely came thither) ; some acquaintance ;—and it might easily have been more, had she, and her Aunt, and our economic and other circumstances liked ! She was of the fair-complexioned, softly elegant, softly grave, witty and comely type, and had a good deal of gracefulness, intelligence and other talent. Irving too, it was sometimes thought, found her very interesting, could the Miss-Martin bonds have allowed, which they never would. To me, who had only known her for a few months, and who within a twelve or fifteen months saw the last of her, she continued for perhaps some three years a figure hanging more or less in my fancy, on the usual romantic, or latterly quite elegiac and silent terms, and to this day there is in me a goodwill to her, a candid and gentle pity for her, if needed at all. She was of the Aberdeenshire Gordons, a far-off Huntly, doubt it not ; " Margaret Gordon," born I think in New Brunswick, where her Father, probably in some official post, had died young and poor,—her *accent* was prettily English, and her voice very fine :—an aunt (widow in Fife, childless, with limited resources, but of frugal cultivated turn ; a lean, proud elderly dame, once a " Miss Gordon " herself, sang Scotch songs beautifully, and talked shrewd *Aberdeenish* in accent and otherwise) had adopted her, and brought her hither over seas : and here, as Irving's Ex-pupil, she now cheery though with dim outlooks, was. Irving saw her again in Glasgow, one summer, touring etc., he himself accompanying joyfully,—*not* joining (so I understood it) the retinue of *suitors* or potential ditto ; rather perhaps indicating

gently, " No, I must not ! " for the last time. A year or so
after, we heard the fair Margaret had married some rich insignificant Aberdeen Mr. Something ; who afterwards got into
Parliament, thence out " to Nova Scotia " (or *so*) " as Governor ;"
and I heard of her no more,—except that lately she was still
living about Aberdeen, childless, as the " Dowager Lady "——,
her Mr. Something having got knighted before dying. Poor
Margaret ! Speak to her, since the " good-bye, then " at Kirkcaldy in 1819, I never did or could. I saw her, recognisably to
me, here in her London time (1840 or so), *twice*, once with her
maid in Piccadilly, promenading, little altered ; a second time,
that same year or next, on horseback both of us, and *meeting*
in the gate of Hyde Park, when her *eyes* (but that was all) said
to me almost touchingly, " Yes, yes ; that is you ! "——Enough
of that old matter ; which but half concerns Irving and is now
quite extinct.

In the space of two years, or rather more, we had all got tired
of schoolmastering, and its mean contradictions and poor
results ; Irving and I quite resolute to give *it* up for good ; the
headlong Pears disinclined for it on the there terms longer ; and
in the end of 1819 (or '18 ? at this hour I know not which, and
the old *Letters* that would show are too deep-hidden),[1] we all
three went away ; Irving and I to Edinburgh, Pears to his own
" East Country,"—whom I never saw again with eyes, poor
good rattling soul. Irving's outlooks in Edinburgh were not of
the best, considerably checkered with dubiety, opposition, or
even flat disfavour in some quarters ; but at least they were far
superior to mine :—and indeed I was beginning my four or five
most miserable, dark, sick and heavy-laden years ; Irving,
after some staggerings aback, his seven or eight healthiest and
brightest. He had, I should guess, as one item, several good
hundreds of money to wait upon. My *peculium* I don't recollect,
but it could not have exceeded £100 ; I was without friends,
experience, or connection in the sphere of human business,
was of shy humour, proud enough and to spare,—and had
begun my long curriculum of *dyspepsia*, which has never ended
since !

Irving lived in Bristo Street, more expensive rooms than
mine ; and used to give breakfasts to Intellectualities he fell
in with,—I often a guest with them. They were but stupid
Intellectualities ; and the talk I got into there did not please me
even then, though it was well enough received. A visible gloom

1 Carlyle left Kirkcaldy in November 1818.

occasionally hung over Irving, his old strong sunshine only getting out from time to time. He gave lessons in mathematics, once for a while, to Captain Basil Hall,[1] who had a kind of thin celebrity then; and did not seem to love too well that small lion or his ways with him. Small lion came to propose for me, at one stage; wished me to go out with him " to Dunglas," and there do " *lunars* " in his name, he looking on, and learning of me what would come of its own will : " Lunars " meanwhile were to go as his to the Admiralty, testifying there what a careful studious Captain he was, and help to get him promotion, —so the little wretch smilingly told me. I remember the figure of him in my dim lodging, as a gray, crackling, sniggering spectre, one dusk ; endeavouring to seduce me by affability, in lieu of liberal wages, into this adventure. Wages, I think, were to be smallish (" so poor are we "), but then " the great Playfair is coming on visit,—you will see Professor Playfair ! " I had not the least notion of such an enterprise, on these shining terms ; and Captain Basil with his great Playfair *in posse*, vanished for me into the shades of dusk for good. I don't think Irving ever had any other pupil but this Basil, for perhaps a three months. I had not even Basil ; though private-teaching, to me the poorer, was much more desirable, if it would please to come ; which it generally would not in the least. I was timorously aiming towards " Literature " too ; thought in audacious moments I might perhaps earn some trifle that way, by honest labour somehow, to help my finance : but in that too I was painfully sceptical (talent and opportunity alike doubtful, alike incredible to me, poor down-pressed soul) ; and in fact there came little enough of produce or finance to me from that source, and for the first years absolutely none, in spite of my diligent and desperate efforts which are sad to me to think of even now. " *Acti labores*," yes ; but of such a futile, dismal, lonely, dim and chaotic kind, in a scene all ghastly-*chaos* to one ; sad, dim and ugly as the shores of Styx and Phlegethon, as a nightmare-dream become real ! No more of that ; it did not conquer me, or quite kill me, thank God.— Irving thought of nothing as ultimate but a Clerical career, obstacles once over-come ; in the meanwhile, we heard of robust temporary projects, —" Tour to Switzerland," glaciers, Geneva, " Lake of Thun," very grand to think of, was one of them,—none of which took effect.

I forget how long it was till the then famed Trismegistus Dr.

[1] Died in 1844, aged 56.

Chalmers, fallen in want of an Assistant, cast his eye on Irving :
I think it was in the summer following our advent to Edinburgh ;
I heard duly about it : How Rev. Andrew Thomson, famous
malleus of Theology in that time, had mentioned Irving's name,
had privately engaged to get Chalmers a hearing of him in his,
Andrew's, Church ;[1] how Chalmers heard *incognito*, and there
ensued negotiation ;—once I recollect transiently seeing the
famed Andrew on occasion of it (something Irving had forgotten
with him, and wished me to call for), and what a lean-minded,
iracund, ignorant kind of man Andrew seemed to me ; also,
much more vividly, in Autumn following, one fine airy October
day, in Annandale, Irving, on foot, on his way to Glasgow for
a month of actual trial, had come by Mainhill, and picked me
up ; to walk with him seven or eight miles farther into " Dryfe
Water " (i.e. valley watered by clear swift *Dryfe*, quasi-" Drive,"
—so impetuous and swift is it), where [was] a certain witty
comrade of ours, one Frank Dixon, Preacher at once and Farmer
(only son and heir of his Father who had died in that latter
capacity). We found Frank, I conclude ; though the whole is
now dim to me till we arrived all three, Frank and I to set
Irving on his road to Moffat and bid him good speed, on the top
of a hill, commanding all Upper-Annandale and the grand mass
of Moffat hills, where we paused thoughtful a few moments.
The blue sky was beautifully spotted with white clouds, which,
and their shadows on the wide landscape, the wind was beautifully chasing : " Like *Life* ! " I said, with a kind of emotion, on
which Irving silently pressed my arm, with the hand near it
or perhaps on it, and, a moment after, with no word but his
farewell and ours, strode swiftly away. A mail-coach would
find him at Moffat that same evening (after his walk of about
thirty miles), and carry him to Glasgow to sleep. And the
curtains sink again on Frank and me at this time.

Frank was a notable kind of man ; and one of the memora-
bilities doubtless to Irving as well as me. A most quizzing,
merry, entertaining, guileless and unmalicious man ; with very
considerable logic, reading, contemptuous observation and
intelligence ; much real tenderness too, when not obstructed,
and a mournful true affection, especially for the friends he had
lost by death ! No mean impediment *there* any more (that was
it),—for Frank was very sensitive, easily moved to something
of envy, and as if surprised where contempt was not possible :—

[1] This was in St. George's Church, Edinburgh, in July 1819 ; Irving
began his work as Assistant to Dr. Chalmers in October of the same year.

easy banter was what he habitually dwelt in ; for the rest, an honourable, bright amiable man : alas, and his end was very tragic ! I have hardly seen a man with more opulence of conversation,—wit, fantastic bantering ingenuity, and genial human sense of the ridiculous in men and things. Charles Buller, perhaps ;—but he was of far more refined, delicately managed, and less copious tone (finer by nature, I should say, as well as by culture, though perhaps still more genial of sense, when I now reflect) ; and had nothing of the wild " *Annandale-Rabelais* " turn which had grown up, partly of will, and at length by industry as well, in poor Frank Dixon in the valley of Dryfe, amid his little stock of Books and rustic Phenomena. A slightly built man, nimble-looking and yet lazy-looking, our Annandale Rabelais ; thin, neatly expressive aquiline face, gray genially laughing eyes, something sternly serious and resolute in the squarish fine brow ; nose specially aquiline, thin and rather small,—I well remember the play of point and nostrils there, while his wild home-grown *Gargantuisms* went on. He rocked rather, and negligently wriggled, in walking or standing ; something slightly twisted in the spine, I think ; but he made so much small involuntary tossing and gesticulation while he spoke or listened, you never noticed the twist. What a childlike and yet half imp-like volume of true laughter lay in Frank ; how he would fling back his fine head, left cheek up, not himself laughing much or loud *ever*, but showing you such continents of inward gleesome mirth and victorious mockery of the dear stupid ones who had crossed his sphere of observation ! A wild roll of sombre eloquence lay in him, too ; and I have seen in his sermons sometimes, that brow and aquiline face grow dark, sad, and thunderous like the Eagle of Jove. I always liked poor Frank ; and he me heartily,—after having tried to banter me down, and recognised the mistake, which he loyally did for himself, and never repeated. We had much innocently pleasant talk together first and last.

His end was very tragic,—like that of a sensitive gifted man too much based on laughter ! Having no good prospect of Kirk promotion in Scotland (I think his Edinburgh resource had been mainly that of teaching under Mathematical Nichol for certain hours daily), he, perhaps about a year after Irving went to Glasgow, had accepted some offer to be Presbyterian Chaplain and Preacher to the Scotch in *Bermuda ;* and lifted anchor thither, with many regrets and good wishes from us all. I did not correspond with him there, my own mood and posture being still so dreary and empty. But, before Irving left Glasgow, news came to me (from Irving, I believe) that Frank, struck quite miserable, and lame of heart and nerves, by dyspepsia and dispiritment, was home again, or on his way home, to Dryfesdale, there to lie useless,—Irving recommending me to do for him what kindness I could, and not remember that he used to disbelieve, and be ignorantly cruel, in my own dyspeptic tribulations. This I did not fail of; nor was it burdensome, but otherwise, while near him in Annandale.

Frank was far more wretched than I had been; sunk in spiritual dubieties too, which I, by that time, was getting rid of. He had brought three young Bermuda gentlemen home with him as pupils (had been much a favourite in Society there); with these, in his rough Farmhouse,—" Belkathill " (Bell*top* Hill? near Hook, head part of the pleasant vale of Dryfe),—he settled himself to live. Farm was *his*, but in the hands of a rough-spun Sister and her ploughing Husband; who perhaps were not overglad to see Frank return, with new potentiality of ownership, if he liked,—which truly, I suppose, he never did. They had done some joinering, plank-flooring, in the Farmhouse, which was weather-tight, newish though strait and dim; and there, on rough rustic terms, perhaps with a little disappointment to the young gentlemen, Frank and his Bermudians lived, for some years. He had a nimble quiet pony; rode latterly (for the Bermudians did not stay above a year or two), much about among his cousinry or friends; always halting and baiting with me, when it could be managed. I had at once gone to visit him; found Belkathill on the new terms as interesting as ever. A comfort to me to administer some comfort; interesting even to compare dyspeptic *notes:* besides, Frank, by degrees, would kindle into the old coruscations, and talk as well as ever. I remember some of those visits to him, still more the lonely silent rides thither, as humanly impressive, wholesome, not unpleasant. Especially after my return from Buller Tutorship, and my first London visit; when I was at Hoddam Hill, idly high and dry like Frank (or only translating *German Romance,* etc.), and had a horse of my own. Frank took considerably to my Mother; talked a great deal of his bitter Byronic Scepticism to her,—and seemed to feel, like oil poured into his wounds, her beautifully pious contradictions of him and it. " Really likes to be contradicted, poor Frank! " she would tell me afterwards. He might be called a genuine bit of rustic Dignity; modestly, frugally, in its simplest expression, gliding about among us there.

This lasted till perhaps the beginning of 1826 ;—I don't remember him at Scotsbrig ever ; I suppose the *Lease* of his Farm may have run out that year, not renewed, and that he was now farther away. After my Marriage, perhaps two years after, from Craigenputtock I wrote to him, but never got the least answer, never saw him or *distinctly* heard of him more. Indistinctly I did, with a shock, hear of him once, and then a second final time,— thus : My brother Jamie (youngest brother of us, ten years my junior), riding to Moffat, in 1828 or so, saw near some poor cottage (not a farm at all, ' bare place for a couple of cows,' perhaps it was a Turnpike-keeper's Cottage ?) not far from Moffat, a forlornly miserable-looking figure, walking languidly to and fro, parted from him by the hedge ; whom, in spite of this sunk condition, he recognised clearly for Frank Dixon, who however took no notice of him,—" Perhaps *refuses* to know me," thought Jamie : " They have lost their farm ; Sister and Husband seem to have taken shelter here, and there is the poor gentleman and scholar Frank, sauntering miserably, with an old plaid over his head, and slipshod [1] in a pair of old *clogs !* " That was Jamie's guess ; which he reported to me ; and few months after, grim whisper came, low but certain (no inquest or coroner there), that Frank was dead, and had gone in the *Roman* fashion.[2] What other could he now do ?—The silent, valiant, though vanquished man. He was hardly yet thirty-five ; a man richer in gifts than nine-tenths of the vocal and notable are. I remember him with sorrow and affection. Native-countryman Frank, and his little Life ; what a strange little Island, fifty years off, sunny, homelike, pretty in the memory, yet with tragic thunders waiting it !

Irving's Glasgow news, from the first, were good. Approved of, accepted by the great Doctor and his Congregation ; preaching heartily ; labouring with the ' Visiting Deacons ' (Chalmers's grand " *Parochial* " *Anti-Pauperism Apparatus*, much an object of the Doctor's at this time) ;—seeing and experiencing new things, on all hands of him, in his new wide element. He came occasionally to Edinburgh on visit : I remember him as of prosperous aspect ; a little more carefully, more clerically, dressed than formerly (ample black frock, a little ' *sider*,' longer skirted, than the secular sort, hat of gravish breadth of brim,

---

[1] Slipshod means, in its Scotch sense here, not loose or untidy, but stockingless.

[2] He died in 1832.

all very simple and correct) ; he would talk about the Glasgow
Radical Weavers, and their notable receptions of him, and utterances to him, while visiting their lanes ;—was not copious upon
his great Chalmers, though friendly in what he did say. All
this, of his first year, must have been in 1820 ;—late autumn
1819, the date of his instalment ? I wish I exactly knew !
Year 1819 comes back into my mind as the year of the Radical
" rising " in Glasgow ; and the kind of (altogether imaginary)
" Fight " they attempted on Bonnymuir against the Yeomanry
which had assembled from far and wide. A time of great rages
and absurd terrors and expectations ; a very fierce Radical and
Anti-Radical time. Edinburgh endlessly agitated all round me
by it (not to mention Glasgow in the distance); gentry people full
of zeal and foolish terror and fury, and looking disgustingly
busy and important : courier hussars would come in from the
Glasgow region, covered with mud, breathless for head-quarters
as you took your walk in Princes Street ; and you would hear
old powdered gentlemen in silver spectacles talking with low-
toned but exultant voice about " cordon of troops, Sir " as
you went along. The mass of the people, not the populace
alone, had a quite different feeling, as if the danger from those
West-country Radicals was small or imaginary and their griev-
ances dreadfully real ;—which was with emphasis my own poor
private notion of it. One bleared Sunday morning, I had gone
out for my walk (perhaps seven to eight A.M.) ; at the Riding-
House in Nicolson Street was a kind of straggly group, or small
crowd, with red-coats interspersed : coming up I perceived it
was the " Lothian Yeomanry " (*Mid* or *East*, I know not) just
getting under way for Glasgow to be part of " the cordon " ;
I halted a moment : they took the road, very ill ranked, not
numerous or very dangerous-looking men of war ; but there rose,
from the little crowd, by way of farewell cheer to them, the
strangest shout I have heard human throats utter; not very loud,
or loud even for the small numbers ; but it said as plain as words,
and with infinitely more emphasis of sincerity, " May the Devil
go with *you*, ye peculiarly contemptible, and dead to the distresses of your fellow-creatures ! "—Another morning, months
after, spring and sun now come, and the " cordon " etc. all over,
—I met a gentleman, an Advocate, slightly of my acquaintance,
hurrying along, musket in hand, towards The Links, there to be
drilled as an item of the " Gentlemen Volunteers " now afoot.
" You should have the like of this ! " said he, cheerily patting his
musket. " Hm, yes ; but I haven't yet quite settled on which

side !"—which probably he hoped was quiz, though it really expressed my feeling. Irving too, and all of us juniors, had the same feeling in different intensities, and spoken of only to one another : a sense that revolt against such a load of unveracities, impostures, and quietly inane formalities would one day become indispensable ;—sense which had a kind of rash, false, and quasi-insolent joy in it ; mutiny, revolt, being a light matter to the young.

Irving appeared to take great interest in his Glasgow visitings about among these poor Weavers, and free communings with them as man with men. He was altogether human we heard, and could well believe ; he broke at once into sociality and frank-ness, " would pick a potato from their pot," and in eating it, get at once into free and kindly terms. " Peace be with you here !" was his entering salutation one time, in some weaving shop, which had politely paused and silenced itself on sight of him ; " Peace be with you." " Ay, Sir, if there's *plenty* wi't !" said an angry little weaver, who happened to be on the floor ; and who began indignant response and remonstrance to the Minister and his fine words. " Quite angry and fiery," as Irving described him to us, " a fine thoughtful brow, with the veins on it swollen black, and the eyes under it sparkling and glistening,"—whom, however, he succeeded in pacifying ; and parting with on soft terms. This was one of his anecdotes to us ; I remember that fiery little weaver and his broad brow and swollen veins, a vanished figure of those days, as if I had myself seen him.

By and by, after repeated invitations, which to me were permissions rather, the time came for my paying a return visit. I well remember the first visit, and pieces of the others ; prob-ably there were three or even four in all ; each of them a real holiday to me ! By steamer to Bo'ness, and then by canal skipper of canal-boat and two Glasgow scamps of the period, these are figures of the first voyage, very vivid these, the rest utterly out : I think I always went by Bo'ness, and steam *so far* ; coach the remainder of the road, in all subsequent journeys. Irving lived in Kent Street, eastern end of Glasgow ; ground-floor, tolerably spacious room,—I think he sometimes gave me up his bedroom (me the bad sleeper), and went out himself to some friend's house. David Hope (cousin of old Adam's, but much younger, an excellent guileless man and merchant) was warmly intimate and attached ; the like William Graham, of Burnswark, Annandale, a still more interesting character, with both of whom I made or renewed acquaintance which turned out to be agreeable and lasting : these two were perhaps his most *domestic* and practically trusted friends ; but he had already many, in the better Glasgow circles, and, in generous liking and appreciation, tended to *excess*, never to defect, with one and all of them. " Philosophers " called at Kent Street, whom one did not find so extremely philosophical, though all were amiable and of polite and partly religious turn ; and, in fact, these reviews of Glasgow, on its streets, in its jolly (sometimes *Christmas*) dining-rooms and drawing-rooms, were cordial and instructive to me. The solid style of comfort, freedom and plenty, was new to me in that degree. The *Tontine* (my first evening in Glasgow) was quite a treat to my rustic eyes : several hundreds of such fine, clean, opulent, and enviable or amiable-looking good Scotch gentlemen, sauntering about in trustful gossip, or solidly reading their newspapers,—I remember the shining bald crowns and serene white heads of several ; and the feeling " *O fortunatos nimium*," which they generally gave me. Irving was not with me on this occasion ; had probably left me there for some half-hour, and would come to pick me up again when ready. We made morning calls together too, not very many ; and found once, I recollect, an exuberant bevy of young ladies, which I (silently) took as sample of a great and singular privilege in my friend's way of life. Oftenest it was crotchety, speculative, semi-theological elderly gentlemen whom we met, with curiosity and as yet without weariness on my part ; though of course their laughing chatting daughters would have been better. The Glasgow women of the young-*lady* stamp, seemed to me well-looking, clever enough, good-humoured ; but I noticed (for my own behoof, and without prompting of any kind) that they were not so *well dressed* as their Edinburgh Sisters ; something flary, glary, colours too flagrant and ill-assorted ; want of the harmonious transitions, neatness, and soft Attic art, which I now recognised or remembered for the first time.

Of Dr. Chalmers I heard a great deal ; naturally the continual topic, or one of them ; admiration universal, and as it seemed to me, slightly wearisome, and a good deal indiscriminate and over-done,—which probably (though we were dead-silent on that head) was on occasion Irving's feeling too. But the great man was himself truly lovable, truly loved ; and nothing personally could be more modest, intent on his good industries not on himself or his " fame." Twice that I recollect, I specially saw him ; once at his own house, to breakfast ; company Irving, one Crosby, a young Licentiate, with glaring eyes and no speculation in them, who went afterwards to Birmingham, and thirdly myself. It was a cold vile smoky morning ; house and break-fast-room looked their worst in the dismal light. Doctor himself was hospitably kind ; but spoke little, and engaged none of us in talk. Oftenest, I could see, he was absent ; wandering in distant fields, of abstruse character, to judge by the sorrow-ful glaze which came over his honest eyes and face. I was not ill-pleased to get away ; *ignotus* from one of whom I had gained no new knowledge. The second time was in a rather fine drawing-room (a Mr. Parker's), in a rather solemn evening party ; where the Doctor, perhaps bored by the secularities and trivi-alities elsewhere, put his chair beside mine in some clear space of floor ; and talked earnestly, for a good while, on some scheme he had for proving Christianity by its visible fitness for human nature : " all written in us already," he said, " as in *sympathetic ink ;* Bible awakens it, and you can read ! " I listened respect-fully, not with any real conviction, only with a clear sense of the geniality and goodness of the man. I never saw him again till within a few [weeks] of his death, when he called here, and sat with us an hour,—very agreeable to *Her* and to me, after the long abeyance. She had been with him once on a short Tour in the Highlands ; me too he had got an esteem of,—liked the *Cromwell* especially, and Cromwell's self ditto, which I heartily reckoned creditable of him. He did not speak of that, nor of the Free-Kirk War (though I gave him a chance of that, which he soon softly let drop) : the now memorablest point to me, was of Painter Wilkie, who had been his familiar in youth, and whom he seemed to me to understand well. " Painter's *language*," he said, " was stinted and difficult." Wilkie had told him how, in painting his *Rent-Day*, he thought long and to no purpose, by what means he should signify that the sorrowful Woman, with the children there, had left no Husband at home, but was a Widow under tragical *self*-management,—till one morning, pushing along the Strand, he met a small artisan family going evidently on excursion, and in one of their hands or pockets somewhere was visible the *House-key*. " That will do ! " thought Wilkie ; and prettily introduced the House-key as *coral* in the poor Baby's mouth, just drawn from poor Mammy's pocket, to keep her unconscious little orphan peaceable. He warmly agreed with me in thinking Wilkie a man of real genius, real veracity and simplicity. Chalmers was himself very beautiful to us during that hour ; grave, not too grave, earnest, cordial ; face and figure very little altered, only the head had grown white, and in the eyes and features you could read something of a serene sadness, as if evening and silent star-crowned night were coming on, and the hot noises of the day growing unexpectedly insignificant to one.   We had little thought this would be the last of Chalmers ; but in a few weeks after, he suddenly died [May 1847].

He was a man of much natural dignity, ingenuity, honesty, and kind affection, as well as sound intellect and imagination. A very eminent vivacity lay in him, which could rise to complete impetuosity (glowing conviction, passionate eloquence, fiery play of heart and head),—all in a kind of *rustic* type, one might say, though wonderfully true and tender.   He had a burst of genuine fun too, I have heard ; of the same honest, but most plebeian, broadly natural character : his laugh was a hearty low guffaw ; and his tones, in preaching, would rise to the piercingly pathetic : no preacher ever went so into one's heart.   He was a man essentially of little culture, of narrow sphere, all his life ; such an intellect, professing to be educated, and yet so ill-*read*, so ignorant in all that lay beyond the horizon in place or in time, I have almost nowhere met with.   A man capable of much soaking indolence, lazy brooding, and do-nothingism, as the first stage of his life well indicated ; a man thought to be timid, almost to the verge of cowardice : yet capable of impetuous activity and blazing audacity, as his latter years showed.   I suppose there will never again be such a Preacher in any Christian Church.[1]

Irving's Discourses were far more opulent in ingenious thought than Chalmers's, which indeed were usually the triumphant on-rush of *one* idea with its satellites and supporters ; but Irving's wanted in definite *head*, that is, steady invariably

[1] A slip from a newspaper containing the following extract from Chalmers is here wafered on to the manuscript :

" It is a favourite speculation of mine that if spared to sixty, we then enter on the seventh decade of human life, and that this, if possible, should be turned into the Sabbath of our earthly pilgrimage and spent Sabbatically, as if on the shore of an eternal world, or in the outer courts, as it were, of the temple that is above—the tabernacle in Heaven.   What enamours me all the more of this idea is the retrospect of my mother's widowhood.   I long, if God should spare me, for such an old age as she enjoyed, spent as if at the gate of heaven, and with such a fund of inward peace and hope as made her nine years' widowhood a perfect peace and foretaste of the blessedness that awaits the righteous."

Carlyle writes on the newspaper slip : Had heard it before from Thomas Erskine, with pathetic comment as to what Chalmer's own " Sabbath-decade " had been !

evident *aim*, what one might call definite *head* and *backbone ;*
so that, on arriving, you might see clearly where and how.
That was mostly a defect one felt, in traversing those grand
forest-avenues of his, with their multifarious outlooks to right
and left. He had many thoughts, pregnantly expressed, but
they did not tend all one way. The reason was, there were in
him infinitely more thoughts than in Chalmers ; and he took
far less pains in setting them forth. The uniform custom was,
he shut himself up all Saturday ; became invisible all that day ;
and had his sermon ready before going to bed. Sermon an
hour long or more ; it could not be done in one day, except as a
kind of *extempore* thing. It flowed along, not as a swift rolling
river, but as a broad, deep and bending or meandering one ;
sometimes it left on you the impression almost of a fine noteworthy *lake*. Noteworthy always ; nobody could mistake it
for the Discourse of other than an uncommon man. Originality
and truth of purpose were undeniable in it ; but there was
withal, both in the matter and the manner, a something which
might be suspected of affectation : a noticeable preference and
search for striking quaint and ancient locutions ; a style modelled
on the Miltonic Old-Puritan ; something too in the delivery
which seemed elaborate and of forethought, or might be suspected of being so. He always read, but not in the least slavishly ;
and made abundant rather strong gesticulation in the right
places ; voice one of the finest and powerfullest,—but not a
power quite on the heart, as Chalmers's was, which you felt to be
coming direct *from* the heart.

Irving's preaching was accordingly, a thing not above criticism to the Glasgowites ; and it got a good deal on friendly
terms, as well as " admiration " plenty, in that tempered form ;
—not often admiration pure and simple, as was now always
Chalmers's lot there. Irving no doubt secretly felt the difference, and could have wished it otherwise : but the generous
heart of him was incapable of envying any human excellence,
and instinctively would either bow to it, and to the rewards of
it withal, or rise to loyal emulation of it and them. He seemed
to be much liked by many good people ; a fine friendly and
wholesome element, I thought it for him ; and the criticisms
going, in connection with the genuine admiration going, might be
taken as handsomely *near* the mark.

To me, for his sake, his Glasgow friends were very good ; and
I liked their ways (as I might easily do) much better than some
I had been used to. A romance of novelty lay in them, too ;

it was the *first* time I had looked into opulent burgher life in any
such completeness and composed solidity as here.   We went to
Paisley, several times ; to certain " Carl*i*les " (so they spelt their
name ; " Annan people " of a century back) ; rich enough old
men of religious moral turn, who received me as " a Cousin,"—
their daughters good if not pretty, and one of the sons (Warrand
Carlile, who afterwards became a Clergyman) not quite uninteresting to me for some years coming.   He married the youngest
Sister of Edward Irving ; and, I think, is still preaching somewhere in the West Indies ; wife long since dead ; but one of
their Sons still lives, " *Gavin* Carlile " (or now Carl*y*le), a Free
Kirk Minister here in London (editing his Uncle's Select Works
just now).[1]   David Hope, of Glasgow, always a little stuck
to me afterwards ; an innocent cheerful Nathaniel, ever ready
to oblige : the like much more emphatically did William Graham
of Burnswark, whom I first met in the above City under Irving's
auspices ; and who might, in his way, be called a friend both to
Irving and me, so long as his life lasted, which was thirty odd
years longer.   Other conquests of mine in Glasgow I don't
recollect.   Graham of Burnswark perhaps deserves a paragraph,
—if it could do the good soul any service at all !

Graham was turned of fifty when I first saw him ; a lumpish
heavy but stirring figure ; had got something lamish about one
of the knees or ankles, which gave a certain rocking motion to his
gait ; firm jocund affectionate face, rather reddish with good
cheer, eyes big, blue and laughing, nose defaced with snuff,
fine bald broad-browed head, ditto almost always with an ugly
brown scratch wig.   He was free of hand and of heart ; laughed
with sincerity at not very much of fun ;—liked widely, yet with
some selection, and was widely liked.   The history of him was
curious.   His father, first some small Farmer in " Corrie Water,"
perhaps, was latterly for many years (I forget whether as Farmer
or as Shepherd, but guess the former) stationary at Burnswark, a
notable tabular Hill, of no great height, but *detached* a good way
on every side ; far-seen, almost to the shores of Liverpool,—
indeed commanding, all round, the whole of that huge *saucer*,
fifty to thirty miles in radius, the bottom point of which is now
called Gretna (" Gretan-How," Big Hollow, at the head of
Solway Frith) ; a *Burnswark* beautiful to look on and much
noted from of old.   Has a glorious Roman Camp on the south
flank of it, ' the best preserved in Britain except one ' (says

[1] *The Collected Writings of Edward Irving*, edited by his nephew, the
Rev. G. Carlyle, M.A. (5 volumes, imper. 8vo, London, 1864–65).

General Roy) ; velvet sward covering the whole, but trenches, *prætorium* (three conic mounds) etc. etc., not altered otherwise ; one of the finest limpid *wells* within it ; and a view to Liverpool (as was said), and into Tynedale, and the Cumberland or even Yorkshire mountains, on the one side, and on the other into the Moffat ditto and the Selkirkshire and Eskdale. The name " *Burns*wark " is properly *Birrens*wark (or *fortification* work) : three Roman Stations, with Carlisle (' *Caer-Lewel,* as old as King Solomon ') for mother ; Netherbie, Middlebie, and Ower-bie (or *Upperby* in Eskdale) ;—the specific Roman *Town* of Middlebie is about half a mile below the Kirk (i.e. eastward of it), and is called by the country people " *The Birrens* " (i.e. The *Scrags* or *Haggles,* I should think) ; a place lying all in dimples and wrinkles, with ruined houses if you dig at all ; grassy, but *in*arable ; part of which is still kept sacred *in lea* by " the Duke " (of Queensberry, now of Buccleuch and Queens-berry), while the rest has been all dug to powder in the last sixty or seventy years by the adjoining little Lairds. Many altars, stone figures, tools, axes, etc. were got out of the dug part ;— and it used to be one of the tasks of my boyhood to try what I could do at reading the *Inscriptions* found there ; which was not much, nor almost ever *wholly* enough, though the country folk were thankful for my little Latin faithfully applied, like the light of a damp windlestraw to them in the darkness which was total ! The fable went that from *Birrens* to *Birrenswark* (two and a half miles, for Burnswark lies two good miles on the west or opposite side of the Kirk) there ran a " subterranean passage," complete *tunnel,* equal to *carts* perhaps ; but nobody pretended ever to have seen a trace of it, or indeed did believe it. In my boyhood, passing *Birrens* for the first time, I noticed a small conduit (*cloaca,* I suppose) abruptly ending or issuing in the then recent precipice which had been left by those diggers, and recollect nothing more, except my own poor awe and wonder at the strange scene, strange face-to-face vestige of the vanished Æons. The Caledonian Railway now screams and shudders over this dug part of Birrens. William Graham, whom I am (too idly) writing of, was born at the north-east end of Burnswark ; and passed, in labour, but in health, frugality and joy, the first twenty-five years of his life.

Graham's Father and Mother seem to have been of the best kind of Scottish Peasant ; he had Brothers, two or perhaps three (William was the youngest), who were all respected in their station,—and who all successively emigrated to America, on the following slight first-cause. John Graham, namely, the eldest of the Brothers, had been balloted for the Militia (Dumfriesshire Militia); and, on private consideration with himself, preferred expatriation to soldiering, and quietly took ship to push his fortune in the New World instead. John's adventures there, which probably were rugged enough, are not on record for me; only that, in no great length of time, he found something of success, a solid merchant's-clerkship or the like, with outlooks towards merchant business of his own one day; and invited thither, one by one, all his Brothers to share with him, or push like him there. Philadelphia was the place, at least the ultimate place; and the Firm of " Graham Brothers " gradually rose to be a considerable and well-respected House in that City. William, probably some fifteen years junior of John, was the last Brother that went; after him their only Sister, Parents having now died at Burnswark, was sent-for also; and kept house, for William or for another of the bachelor Brothers,— one at least of them had wedded and has left Pennsylvanian Grahams; William continued bachelor for life; and this only Sister returned ultimately to Annandale, and was William's House-manager there. I remember her well, one of the amiablest of old maids; kind, true, modestly polite to the very heart,— and in such a curious style of polite culture; Pennsylvanian-Yankee grafted on Annandale-Scotch; used to " expect " instead of " *suppose;* " would " guess," too, now and then; and commonly said " Pastor " (which she pronounced " Pawstor ") to signify Clergyman or Minister.

The Graham Brothers' House growing more and more prosperous and opulent in Philadelphia, resolved at last to have a branch in Glasgow (year, say 1814 or so); and despatched William thither,—whose coming, I dimly remember, was heard of in Annandale by his triumphant purchase for himself, in fee-simple, of the Farm and Hill of Burnswark, which happened to come into the market then. His tradings and operations in Glasgow were extensive, not unskilful that I heard of, and were well looked-on, as he himself still more warmly was: but at length (perhaps a year or more before my first sight of him), some grand cargo from or to Philadelphia, some whole fleet of cargoes, all mostly of the same commodity, had, by sudden change of price during the voyage, ruinously misgone; and the fine House of Graham Brothers came to the ground. William was still in the throes of settlement; just about quitting his fine well-appointed mansion in Vincent Street, in a cheerfully stoical humour; and only clinging with invincible tenacity to native Burnswark, which of course was now no longer his, except on Bond with securities,—with interest etc.,—all of excessive extent, his friends said, but could not persuade him, so dear to his heart was that native bit of earth, with the fond 'improvements,' planting and the like, which he had begun upon it.

Poor Graham kept iron hold of Burnswark, ultimately as plain tenant ; good sheep-*farm* at a fair rent ; all attempts otherwise, and they were many and strenuous, having issued in non-success, and the hope of ever recovering himself or it being plainly futile. Graham never merchanted more ; was once in America, on exploratory visit, where his Brothers were in some degree set up again, but had no " £8000 " to spare for his Burns-wark ; he still hung a little to Glasgow, tried various things, rather of a projector sort, all of which miscarried ; till happily he at length ceased visiting Glasgow, and grew altogether rustic, a successful sheep-farmer at any rate ; fat, cheery, happy ; and so, for his last twenty years, rode visiting about among the little Lairds of an intelligent turn, who liked him well, but not with entire acquiescence in all the copious quasi-intelligent talk he had. Irving had a real love for him, with silent deductions in the unimportant respects ; he an entire loyalty and heart-devotedness to Irving. Me also he took up in a very warm manner ; and, for the first few years, was really pleasant and of use to me, especially in my then Annandale summers. Through him I made acquaintance with a really intellectual modest circle, or rather pair of people, a Mr. and Mrs. Johnston, at their place called " Grange," on the edge of the Hill country, seven or eight miles from my Father's : Mrs. Johnston was a Glasgow lady, of really fine culture, manners, and intellect ; one of the smallest voices, and most delicate, gently-smiling figures ; had been in London, etc. ; her Husband was by birth Laird of this pretty Grange ; and had modestly withdrawn to it, finding merchanthood in Glasgow ruinous to weak health. The elegance, the perfect courtesy, the simple purity and beauty I found in both these good people, was an authentic attraction and profit to me in those years : and I still remember them, and that bright little environment of theirs, with a kind of pathetic affection. I as good as lost them on my leaving Annandale ; Mr. Johnston soon after died ; and with Mrs. Johnston there could only be at rare intervals a flying call, sometimes only the attempt at such, which amounted to little.

Graham also I practically more and more lost, from that

epoch (1826, ever memorable to me otherwise !).[1] He hung
about me studiously, and with unabating good-will, on my
Annandale visits to my Mother, to whom he was ever attentive
and respectful for my sake and her own (dear good Mother, best
of Mothers ! He pointed out the light of her ' end-window,'
gable-window, one dark night to me, as I conveyed him from
Scotsbrig, " Will there ever be in the world for you a prettier
light than that ? ").   He was once or more with us at Craigenputtock, ditto at London, and wrote long *Letters*, not unpleasant
to ' read and *burn* : ' but his sphere was shrinking more and more
into dull safety and monotonous rusticity, mine the *reverse*, in
respect of ' safety ' and otherwise ; nay, at length, his faculties
were getting hebetated, wrapt in lazy eupeptic fat :—the last
time I ever, strictly speaking, saw *him* (for he was grown more
completely stupid and oblivious every subsequent time), was
at the ending of my Mother's Funeral (December 1853), day
bitterly cold, heart bitterly sad, at the Gate of Ecclefechan
Kirkyard ; he was sitting in his Gig, just about to go, I ready to
mount for Scotsbrig, and in a day more for London ; he gazed
on me with his big innocent face, big heavy eyes, as if half-
conscious, half-frozen in the cold ; and we shook hands nearly in
silence.

   In the Irving-Glasgow time, and for a while afterwards, there
went on, at Edinburgh too, a kind of cheery visiting and mes-
saging from these good Graham-Hope people ; I do not recollect
the visits as peculiarly successful,—none of them except *one*,
which was on occasion of George IV.'s famed " Visit to Edinburgh," [2] when Graham and Hope (I think, both of them
together) occupied my rooms with grateful satisfaction, I myself
not there.   I had grown disgusted with the fulsome " loyalty "
of all classes in Edinburgh towards this approaching " George-
Fourth Visit ; " whom though called and reckoned a " King,"
I, in my private radicalism of mind, could consider only as a—
what shall I call him ?—and loyalty was not the feeling I had
towards any part of the phenomenon.   At length, reading, one
day, in a public Placard from the Magistrates (of which there
had been several), That on His Majesty's Advent it was expected
that everybody would be carefully well-dressed, ' black coat and
white duck trousers,' if at all convenient,—I grumbled to myself,
"Scandalous flunkeys, I, if I were changing my dress at all,
should incline rather to be in white coat and black trousers!"—
but resolved rather to quit the City altogether, and be absent

---

[1] 1826, the year of Carlyle's marriage.   [2] August 1822.

and silent in such efflorescence of the flunkeyisms. Which I was, for a week or more (in Annandale and at Kirkchrist with the Churches [1] in Galloway,—ride to Lochinbrack Well, by Kenmure Lake, etc., how vivid still !)—and found all comfortably rolled away at my return to Edinburgh.

It was in one of those visits by Irving himself, without any company, that he took me out to Haddington [2] (as recorded elsewhere), to what has since been so momentous through all my subsequent life ! We walked and talked,—a good sixteen miles, in the sunny summer afternoon. He took me round by Athelstaneford (" Elshinford ") Parish, where John Home wrote his " *Douglas*,"—in case of any enthusiasm for Home or it, which I scantly had : we leapt the solitary Kirkyard wall, and found close by us the tombstone of " old Skirving," a more remarkable person, Author of the strangely vigorous Doggrel Ballad on " *Preston-Pans Battle* " (and of the ditto *Answer* to a military *Challenge* which ensued thereupon),[3] " one of the most athletic and best-natured of men," said his epitaph. This is nearly all I recollect of the journey : the end of it, and what I saw *there*, will be memorable to me while life or thought endures. Ah me, ah me !—I think there had been, before this, on Irving's own part some movements of negotiation over to Kirkcaldy for *release* there, and of hinted hope towards Haddington, which was so infinitely preferable ! And something (as I used to gather long afterwards) might have come of it, had not Kirkcaldy been so peremptory, and stood by its bond (as spoken or as written), " Bond or utter Ruin, Sir ! "—upon which Irving had honourably submitted and resigned himself. He seemed to be quite composed upon the matter by this time : I remember in our inn at Haddington that first night, a little passage : we had just seen, in the Minister's house (whom Irving was to *preach* for), a certain shining Miss Augusta,—tall, shapely, airy, giggly, but a consummate fool, whom I have heard called " Miss *Dis*gusta "

---

[1] The Churches late of Hitchill, who had removed to Galloway.

[2] End of May 1821 (Carlyle's first Letter to Miss Welsh, written on his return to Edinburgh, is dated 4th June of that year).

[3] Skirving had in his ballad accused a certain Irish " Lieutenant Smith " of cowardice, and of *running away* at the Battle of Prestonpans. Smith, on his return to his quarters at Haddington, was enraged to find himself an object of ridicule, and sent a challenge to Skirving. Skirving, hard at work amongst his servants, paused, leaning on his spade, considered the challenge, and answered the Military Gentleman who had brought it : " I never saw Lieutenant Smith, and I dinna ken whether I can fecht him or no ; but if he'll come up here, I'll tak' a look o' him ; and if I think I can fecht him, I wull. But if not, I'll do as he did, I'll rin awa'."

by the satirical ;—we were now in our double-bedded room, George Inn, Haddington, stripping, or perhaps each already in his bed, when Irving jocosely said to me, " What would you take to marry Miss Augusta, now? "   " Not for an entire and perfect chrysolite the size of this terraqueous Globe ! " answered I at once, with hearty laughter from Irving.—" And what would you take to marry Miss Jeannie, think you ? "   " Hah, I should not be so hard to deal with there I should imagine ! " upon which another bit of laugh from Irving ; and we composedly went to sleep.   I was supremely dyspeptic and out of health, during those three or four days ; but they were the beginning of a new life to me.

The notablest passage in my Glasgow visits was probably of the year before this Edinburgh-Haddington one on Irving's part.   I was about quitting Edinburgh for Annandale ;[1] and had come round by Glasgow on the road home.   I was utterly out of health as usual ; but had otherwise had my enjoyments. We had come to Paisley as finale, and were lodging pleasantly with the Carliles.   Warrand Carlile hearing I had to go by Muirkirk in Ayrshire, and Irving to return to Glasgow, suggested a convoy of me by Irving and himself, furthered by a fine riding-horse of Warrand's, on the ride-and-tie principle : Irving had cheerfully consented, " You and your horse, as far as you can ; *I* will go on to Drumclog Moss with Carlyle ; then turn home for Glasgow in good time, he on to Muirkirk, which will be about a like distance for him ? "   " Done, done ! "   To me, of course, nothing could be welcomer than this improvised convoy ;—upon which we entered accordingly ; early A.M., a dry brisk April day (far on in April), and one still full of strange dim interest to me.   I never rode-and-tied (especially with three !) before or since, but recollect we had no difficulty with it ; I never was that way again, and there are pieces in [it] still, strangely vivid to me.   Warrand had settled that we should breakfast with a Rev. Mr. French, perhaps some fifteen miles off, after which he and horse would return :   I recollect the Mr. French, a fat apoplectic-looking old gentleman ; in a room of very low ceiling, but plentifully furnished with breakfast materials ; who was very kind to us, and seemed glad and ready to be invaded in this sudden manner by articulate-speaking young men.   Good old soul, I never saw him or heard mention of him again.

Drumclog Moss (after several hours, fallen vacant, wholly

[1] This was towards the end of April 1820.

dim) is the next object that survives, and Irving and I sitting
by ourselves, under the silent bright skies, among the " Peat-
hags " of Drumclog, with a world all silent round us.   These
" Peat-hags " are still pictured in me : brown bog, all *pitted*,
and broken into heathy remnants and bare abrupt wide holes,
four or six feet deep, mostly dry at present ; a flat wilderness of
broken bog, of quagmire not to be trusted (probably *wetter* in
old days than [now], and wet still at rainy seasons),—clearly a
good place for Cameronian Preaching, and dangerously difficult
for Claver'se and horse-soldiery, if " the suffering remnant " had
a few old muskets among them !   Scott's Novels had given the
Claver'se Skirmish here, which all Scotland knew of already, a
double interest in those days.   I know not that we talked much
of this ; but we did of many things, perhaps more confidentially
than ever before.   A colloquy the sum of which is still mournfully beautiful to me, though the details are gone.   I remember
us sitting on the brow of a Peat-hag, the sun shining, our own
voices the one sound ; far, far away to westward over our brown
horizon, towered up, white and visible at the many miles of
distance, a high irregular pyramid,—" Ailsa Craig ! " we at once
guessed, and thought of the seas and oceans over yonder ; but
we did not long dwell on that.   We seem to have seen no human
creature after French (though of course our very road would
have to be inquired of, etc.), to have had no bother, and no need,
of human assistance or society,—not even of dinner or refection,
French's *breakfast* perfectly sufficing us.   The talk had grown
ever friendlier, more interesting : at length the declining sun
said plainly, You must part.   We sauntered slowly into the
Glasgow-Muirkirk highway (know not *how* we knew to find it
without difficulty) ; masons were building at a wayside Cottage
near by, or were packing up on ceasing for the day : we leant
our backs to a dry stone fence (" stone-*dike*," dry-stone wall, very
common in that country), and looking into the western radiance,
continued in talk yet a while, loth both of us to go.   It was here,
just as the sun was sinking, [Irving] actually drew from me by
degrees, in the softest manner, the confession that I did *not*
think as he of Christian Religion, and that it was vain for me to
expect I ever could or should.   This, if this were so, he had pre-
engaged to take *well* of me,—like an elder brother, if I would be
frank with him ;—and right loyally he did so, and to the end of
his life we needed no concealments on that head ; which was
really a step gained.   The sun was about setting, when we turned
away, each on his own path.   Irving would have a good space

farther to go than I (as now occurs to me),—perhaps fifteen or seventeen miles,—and would not be in Kent Street till towards midnight. But he feared no amount of walking ; enjoyed it rather,—as did I in those young years. I felt sad, but affectionate and good, in my clean, utterly quiet little Inn at Muirkirk ; which, and my feelings in it, I still well remember. An innocent little Glasgow Youth (young bagman on his *first* journey, I supposed !) had talked awhile with me in the otherwise solitary little sitting-room : at parting, he shook hands, and with something of sorrow in his tone, said, " Good night, I shall not see *you* again,"—a unique experience of mine in inns.

I was off next morning by four o'clock ; Muirkirk, except possibly its pillar of furnace-smoke, all sleeping round me : concerning which, I remembered, in the silence, something I had heard from my Father, in regard to this famed Iron village (famed long before, but still rural, natural, not all in a roaring whirl, as I imagine it now) ; this is my Father's picture of an incident he had got to know, and never could forget : On the platform of one of the furnaces, a solitary man (' stoker,' if they call him so) was industriously minding his business, now throwing-in new fuel and ore, now poking the white-hot molten mass that was already in ; a poor old maniac woman silently joined him and looked, whom also he was used to, and did not mind ; but, after a little, his back being towards the furnace-mouth, he heard a strange thump or cracking puff ; and turning suddenly the poor old maniac woman was not there ; and, on advancing to the furnace-edge, he saw the figure of her, red-hot, semi-transparent, floating as ashes on the fearful element for some moments ! This had printed itself on my Father's brain ; (*twice* perhaps I heard it from him, which was rare) ; nor will it ever leave my brain either. That day was full of mournful interest to me, in the waste moors, then in bonny Nithsdale (my first sight of it) in the bright but palish almost pathetic sunshine and utter loneliness : about eight P.M., I got well to Dumfries, fifty-four miles, the longest walk I ever made in one day.

Irving's visits to Annandale, one or two every summer, while I spent summer (for cheapness' sake, and health's sake) in solitude at my Father's there, were the sabbath-times of the season to me ; by far the beautifullest days, or rather the only beautiful I had ! Unwearied kindness, all that tenderest anxious affection could do, was always mine from my incomparable Mother, from my dear brothers, little clever active sisters, and from every one, brave Father, in his tacit grim way, not at all *excepted*. There was good talk also; with Mother at evening tea, often on Theology (where I did learn at length, by judicious endeavour, to speak piously and *agreeably* to one so pious, *without* unveracity on my part, nay it was a kind of interesting exercise to wind softly out of those anxious affectionate cavils of her dear heart on such occasions, and *get* real sympathy, real assent, under borrowed forms). Oh her patience with me, Oh her never-tiring love! Blessed be "poverty," which was never indigence in any form, and which has made all that tenfold more dear and sacred to me! With my two eldest brothers also, Alick and John, who were full of ingenuous curiosity, and had (especially John) abundant intellect, there was nice talking, as we roamed about the fields in *gloaming*-time after their work was done,—once I recollect noticing (though probably it happened various times), that little Jean ("*Craw*," as we called her, she alone of us not being blond but black-haired,—one of the cleverest children I ever saw, then possibly about six or seven) had joined us for *her* private behoof, and was assiduously trotting at my knee; cheek, eyes and ear eagerly turned up to me! Good little soul, I thought it, and think it, very pretty of her. She alone of them had nothing to do with *milking* I suppose (her charge would probably be ducks or poultry, all safe to bed now); and was turning her bit of leisure to *this* account instead of another. She was hardly longer than my leg by the whole head and neck. There was a younger and youngest Sister (Jenny) who is now in Canada; of far inferior 'speculative intellect' to Jean; but who has proved to have (we used to think) superior *housekeeping* faculties to hers. The same may be said of Mary the next elder to Jean. Both these, especially Jenny, got stupid or stupidish husbands; but have dextrously and loyally made the most of them and of their families and households,—Hanning, of Hamilton, Canada West; Austin, of The Gill, Annan, are now the names of these two. Jean is Mrs. Aitken, of Dumfries; still a clever, speculative, ardent, affectionate and discerning woman, but much *zersplittert* by the cares of life;—"*zersplittert*," tragically denied *acumination*, or definite consistency and direction to a point; a "tragedy" often repeated in this poor world, the more is the pity for the world too!

All this was something; but in all this I gave more than I got; and it left a sense of isolation, of sadness; as the rest of my imprisoned life all, with emphasis, did. I kept daily studious;

reading diligently (what few books I could get), learning what was possible, German etc. ; sometimes Dr. Brewster turned me to account (on most frugal terms always !) in wretched little translations, compilations, which were very welcome, too, though never other than dreary. Life was all dreary, ' *oury*,' (*Scotticè*), tinted with the hues of imprisonment and impossibility,—hope practically not there, only obstinacy, and a grim steadfastness to strive without hope or with. To all which Irving's advent was the pleasant (temporary) contradiction and *reversal*,—like Sunrising to Night, or impenetrable Fog, and its spectralities ! The time of his coming, the how and when of his movements and possibilities, were always known to me beforehand : on the set day, I started forth, better dressed than usual ; strode along for Annan, which lay pleasantly in sight all the way (seven miles or more from Mainhill) ; in the woods of Mount-Annan I would probably meet Irving strolling towards me ;—and then, what a talk for the three miles down that bonny river's bank, no sound but our own [voices] amid the lullaby of waters and the twittering of birds ! We were sure to have several such walks, whether the first day or not ; and I remember none so well as some (chiefly *one*, which is *not* otherwise of moment !) in that fine locality.

I generally staid at least one night ; on several occasions, two or even more ; and remember no visits with as pure and calm a pleasure. Annan was then at its culminating point ; a fine, bright, self-confident little Town (gone now to dimness, to decay, and almost grass on its streets, by *Railway*-transit) ; bits of travelling notabilities were sometimes to be found alighted there, Edinburgh people, Liverpool people,—with whom it was interesting (to the recluse party) to ' measure minds ' for a little, and be on your best behaviour both as to matter and manner. Musical Thomson (memorable, *more* so than venerable, as the Publisher of Burns's Songs) : him I saw one evening, sitting in the Reading-room ; a clean-brushed commonplace old gentleman in Scratch-wig ; whom we spoke a few words to, and took a good look of. Two young Liverpool Brothers, Nelson their name, Scholars just out of Oxford, were on visit, one time, in the Irving circle, specially at " Provost Dickson's," Irving's Brother-in-law's ;—these were very interesting to me, night after night ; handsome, intelligent, polite, young men, and the first of their species I had seen. Dickson's, on other occasions, was usually my lodging, and Irving's along with me ; but would not be on this,—had I the least remembrance on that head, except that I seem to have been always beautifully well lodged, and that Mrs. Dickson, Irving's eldest Sister, and very like him *minus* the bad eye, and *plus* a fine *dimple* on the bright cheek, was always beneficent and fine to me. Those Nelsons I never saw again ; but have heard once, in late years, that they never *did* anything, but continued ornamentally lounging, with Liverpool as headquarters,—which seemed to be something like the prophecy one might have gathered from those young aspects in the Annan visit, had one been intent to scan them.—A faded Irish Dandy, once picked up by us, is also present : one fine clear morning, Irving and I found this figure lounging about languidly on the streets ; Irving made up to him, invited him home to breakfast ; and home he politely and languidly went with us : " bound for some Cattle-fair," he told us (Norwich perhaps), and waiting for some coach : a par-boiled, insipid " *Agricultural* Dandy," or Old Fogie, of Hibernian type ; wore a superfine light-green frock, snow-white Corduroys ; age above fifty ; face colourless, crow-footed, feebly conceited ;—proved to have nothing in him, but especially nothing *bad*, and we had been human to him ! Breakfast, this morning, I remember, was at " Mrs. Fergusson's " (Irving's third Sister, there were four in all, and there had been three brothers, but were now only two, the youngest and the eldest of the set) : Mrs. Fergusson's breakfast-tea was praised by the Hibernian pilgrim and well deserved it.

Irving was genially happy in those little Annandale " sunny islets " of his year ; happier perhaps than ever elsewhere. All was quietly flourishing in this, his natal element ; Father's house neat and contented ; ditto ditto or (perhaps blooming out a little farther), those of his Daughters, all nestled close to it in place withal : a very prettily thriving group of things and objects, in their limits, in their safe seclusion : and Irving was, silently, but visibly in the hearts of all, the flower and crowning jewel of it. He was quiet, cheerful, genial ; soul unruffled, clear as a mirror ; honestly loving and loved, all round. His time, too, was so *short*, every moment valuable ; —alas, and in so few years after, Ruin's ploughshare had run through it all ; and it was prophesying to you, " Behold, in a little while, the last trace of me will not be here ; and I shall have vanished tragically, and fled into oblivion and darkness, like a bright dream ! " As is, long since, mournfully the fact,—when one passes, pilgrim-like, those old Houses still standing there, which I have once or twice done.

Our dialogues did not turn very much or long on personal topics ; but wandered wide over the world and its ways,—new men of the travelling conspicuous sort, whom he had seen in Glasgow ; new books sometimes, my scope being shut in that respect ; all manner of interesting objects and discoursings : but, to me, the personal, when they did come in course, as they were sure to do now and then, in fit proportion, were naturally the gratefullest of all. Irving's voice to me was one of blessedness and new hope. He would not hear of my gloomy prognostications ; all nonsense that I never should get out of these obstructions and " impossibilities ; " the real impossibility was that such a talent etc. should *not* cut itself clear, one day. He was very generous to everybody's " talent ; " especially to mine, —which to myself was balefully dubious (nothing but bare scaffold-poles, weatherbeaten corner-pieces, of perhaps a " *potential* talent," ever visible to me) :—his predictions about what I *was* to be flew into the completely incredible ; and however welcome, I could only rank them as devout imaginations and quiz them away. " You will see now," he would say ; " one day we two will shake hands across the brook, you as first in Literature, I as first in Divinity ;—and people will say, " Both these fellows are from Annandale : where is Annandale ? " This I have heard him say, more than once, always in a laughing way, and with self-mockery enough to save it from being barrenly vain. He was very sanguine ; I much the reverse ;— and had his consciousness of powers, and his generous ambitions and fore-castings ; never ungenerous, never ignoble : only an enemy could have called him " vain ; " but perhaps an enemy could, or at least would, and occasionally did. His pleasure in being *loved* by others was very great ; and this, if you looked well, was manifest in him when the case offered ; never more, or *worse* than this, in any case ; and this too he had well in check at all times : if this was vanity, then he might by some be called a little vain ; if not, not. To trample on the smallest mortal or be tyrannous even towards the basest of caitiffs, was never at any moment Irving's turn ; no man that I have known had a sunnier type of character, or *so* little of hatred towards any man or thing. On the whole, *less* of rage in him than I ever saw combined with such a fund of courage and conviction. Noble Irving, he was the faithful elder brother of my life in those years ; generous, wise, beneficent, all his dealings and discoursings with me were. Well may I recollect, as blessed things in my existence, those Annan and other visits ; and feel that, beyond all other men, he was helpful to me when I most needed help.

Irving's position at Glasgow, I could dimly perceive, was not without its embarrassments, its discouragements; and evidently enough it was nothing like the ultimatum he was aiming at,—in the road to which, I suppose, he saw the obstructions rather multiplying than decreasing or diminishing. Theological Scotland, above all things, is dubious and jealous of *originality*; and Irving's tendency to take roads of his own was becoming daily more indisputable. He must have been severely *tried in the Sieve*, had he continued in Scotland! Whether that might not have brought him out clearer, more pure and victorious in the end, must remain for ever a question. Much suffering and contradiction it would have cost him, mean enough for most part, and *possibly* with loss of patience, with *mutiny* etc. etc., for ultimate result: but one may now regret that the experiment was never to be made.

Of course, the invitation to London was infinitely welcome to him; summing up, as it were, all of good that had been in Glasgow (for it was the rumours and reports from Glasgow people that had awakened Hatton Garden to his worth); and promising to shoot him aloft over all that had been obstructive there, into wider new elements. The negotiations and correspondings had all passed at a distance from me: but I recollect well our final practical parting, on that occasion. A dim November or December night,[1] between nine and ten, in the Coffee-room of the Black Bull Hotel. He was to start by early coach to-morrow. Glad I was bound to be, and in a sense was; but very sad I could not help being. He himself looked hopeful, but was agitated with anxieties too, doubtless with regrets as well,—more clouded with agitation than I had ever seen the fine habitual solar-light of him before. I was the last friend he had to take farewell of. He showed me old Sir Harry Moncreiff's Testimonial; a Reverend old Presbyterian Scotch Baronet, of venerable quality (the last of his kind) whom I knew well by sight, and by his universal character for integrity, honest orthodoxy, shrewdness and veracity; Sir Harry testified with brevity, in stiff firm, ancient hand, several important things on Irving's behalf; and ended by saying, " All this is my true opinion, and meant to be understood as it is written." At which we had our bit of approving laugh, and thanks to Sir Harry. Irving did

---

[1] It was in December, just before Christmas 1821.

not laugh that night ; laughter was not the mood of either of us.
I gave him as road-companion a bundle of the best cigars (gift
of Graham to me) I almost ever had : he had no practice of smoking ; but could a little, by a time, and agreed that on the
Coach-roof, where he was to ride night and day, a cigar now and
then might be tried with advantage. Months afterwards, I
learnt he had begun by losing every cigar of them,—left the
whole bundle lying on our seat in the Stall of the Coffee-room ;
—this cigar-gift being probably our last transaction there. We
said farewell : and I had in some sense, according to my worst
anticipation, *lost* my friend's society (not my friend himself ever),
from that time.

For a long while I saw nothing of Irving, after this ; heard in
the way of public rumour, or more specific report, chiefly from
Graham and Hope of Glasgow, how grandly acceptable he had
been at Hatton Garden, and what negotiating, deliberating and
contriving had ensued in respect of the impediments there
(" Preacher ignorant of *Gaelic* ? Our fundamental law requires
him to preach *half the Sunday* in that language ! " etc. etc.),—
and how, at length, all these were got over, or tumbled aside,
and the matter settled into adjustment, " Irving our Preacher
talis qualis," to the huge contentment of his Congregation and
all onlookers. Of which latter there were already in London a
select class ; the chief religious people getting to be aware, that
an altogether uncommon man had arrived here to speak to them.
On all these points, and generally on all his experiences in
London, glad enough should I have been to hear from him
abundantly ; but he wrote nothing on such points, nor in fact had
I expected anything : and the truth was, which did a little disappoint me in time, our regular correspondence had here suddenly
come to *finis !* I was not angry : how could I be ? I made no
solicitation or remonstrance ; nor was any poor *pride* kindled (I
think) except strictly, and this in silence, so far as was proper
for self-defence : but I was always sorry more or less, and
regretted it as a great loss I had, by ill-luck, undergone. Taken
from me by ill-luck ;—but then also hadn't it been given me
by good ditto ? Peace, and be silent ! In the first months,
Irving, I doubt not, had intended much correspondence with me,
were the hurlyburly once done ; but no sooner was it so in some
measure, than his flaming popularity had begun, spreading,
mounting without limit, and instead of business hurlyburly
there was whirlwind of conflagration !

Noble good soul, in his last weeks of life, looking back from

that grim shore upon the safe sunny isles and smiling possibilities now forever far behind, he said to Henry Drummond,
" I should have kept Thomas Carlyle closer to me : his counsel,
blame or praise, was always faithful ; and few have such eyes ! "
These words (the first part of them *ipsissima verba*) I know to
have been verily his : must not the most blazing indignation
(had the least vestige of such ever been in me, for one moment)
have died almost into tears at sound of them ?   Perfect abso-
lution there had long been, without inquiry after penitence.   My
ever-generous, loving, and noble Irving !

If in a gloomy moment I had ever fancied that my friend was
lost to me, because no Letters came from him, I had shining
proof to the contrary very soon.   It was in these first months
of Hatton Garden and its imbroglio of affairs, that he did a most
signal benefit to me ; got me appointed Tutor and intellectual
guide and guardian to the young Charles Buller, and his Boy
Brother, now Sir Arthur and an elderly Ex-Indian of mark.
The case had its comic points, too ; seriously important as it
was, to me for one !   Its pleasant real history is briefly this.
Irving's preaching had attracted Mrs. Strachey, Wife of a well-
known Indian Official (of Somersetshire kindred), then an
" Examiner " in the India House, and a man of real worth ; far
diverse as his worth and ways were from those of his beautiful,
enthusiastic, and still youngish Wife :—a bright creature, she,
given wholly (though there lay silent in her a great deal of fine
childlike *mirth* withal, and of innocent *secular* grace and gift) to
things sacred and serious ; emphatically what the Germans call
a *Schöne Seele*.   She had brought Irving into her circle ; found
him good and glorious there almost more than in the pulpit
itself ; had been speaking of him to her elder Sister, Mrs. Buller
(a Calcutta fine-lady, and bright princess of the kind worshipped
there, a once very beautiful, still very witty graceful airy and
ingenuously intelligent woman, of the *gossamer* kind) ; and had
naturally winded up with, " Come and dine with us, come and
see this uncommon man ! "   Mrs. Buller came, saw (I dare say,
with much suppressed quizzery and wonder) the uncommon
man ;   took to him, she also, in her way ;—recognised, as did
her Husband too, the robust practical common-sense that was
in him ; and, after a few meetings, began speaking of a domestic
intricacy there was with a clever, but too mercurial unmanageable
eldest lad of hers, whom they knew not what to do with.   Irving
took sight and survey of this dangerous eldest lad ; Charles
Buller junior, namely ;   age then about fifteen ;   honourably

done with Harrow some weeks or months ago ; still too young for College on his own footing ; and very difficult to dispose of. Irving perceived that though perfectly accomplished in what Harrow could give him, this hungry and highly ingenious youth had fed hitherto on Latin-and-Greek *husks;* totally unsatisfying to his huge appetite : that being a young fellow of the keenest sense for everything from the sublime to the ridiculous, and full of airy ingenuity and fun, he was in the habit, in quiet evenings at home, of starting *theses* with his Mother in favour of Pierce Egan and *Boxiana* (as if the annals of English *boxing* were more nutritive to an existing Englishman than those of the *Peloponnesian War*, etc. etc.) ; against all which, as his Mother vehemently argued, Charles would stand on the defensive, with such swiftness and ingenuity of fence, that frequently the matter kindled between them ; and, both being of hot though most placable temper, one or both grew loud ; and the old gentleman Charles Buller senior, who was very deaf, striking blindly in at this point, would embroil the whole matter into a very bad condition! Irving's recipe, after some consideration, was : " Send this gifted unguided Youth to Edinburgh College ; I know a young man there who could lead him into richer spiritual pastures, and take effective charge of him." Buller thereupon was sent, and his Brother Arthur with him ; boarded with a good old Dr. Fleming (in George's Square), then a Clergyman of mark ; and I (on a salary of £200 a-year) duly took charge. This was a most important thing to me, in the economics and practical departments of my life ;—and I owe it wholly to Irving. On this point, I always should remember, he did " write " copiously enough, to Dr. Fleming and other parties,— and stood up in a gallant and grandiloquent way for every claim and right of his " young Literary Friend ; " who had nothing to do but wait silent, while everything was being adjusted completely to his wish, or beyond it.

From the first, I found my Charles a most manageable, intelligent, cheery and altogether welcome and agreeable phenomenon ; quite a bit of sunshine in my dreary Edinburgh element. I was in waiting for his Brother and him when they landed at Fleming's : we set instantly out on a walk, round by the foot of Salisbury Crags, up from Holyrood, by the Castle and Law-Courts, home again to George's Square ; and really I recollect few more pleasant walks in my life! So all-intelligent, seizing everything you said to him with such a recognition, so loyal-hearted chivalrous, guileless ; so delighted (evidently) with me, as I was with him. Arthur, a two years younger, kept mainly silent, being slightly deaf too ; but I could perceive that he also was a fine little fellow, honest, intelligent, and kind ; and that apparently I had been altogether much in luck in this didactic adventure. Which proved abundantly the fact : the two Youths both took to me with unhesitating liking, and I to them ; and we never had anything of quarrel, or even of weariness and dreariness, between us : such " teaching " as I never did, in any sphere before or since ! Charles, by his qualities, his ingenuous curiosities, his brilliancy of faculty and character, was actually an entertainment to me, rather than a labour ; if we walked together (which I remember sometimes happening), he was the best company I could find in Edinburgh. I had entered him of Dunbar's Third Greek Class in College. In Greek and Latin, in the former in every respect, he was far my superior, and I had to *prepare* my lessons by way of keeping *him* to his work at Dunbar's. Keeping him " to work " was my one difficulty, if there was one, and my essential function. I tried to guide him into reading, into solid inquiry and reflection ; he got some mathematics from me, and might have had more. He got, in brief, what expansion into wider fields of intellect, and more manful modes of thinking and working my poor possibilities could yield him ; and was always generously grateful to me afterwards ; friends of mine, in a fine frank way, beyond what I could be thought to merit, he, Arthur, and all the Family, till death parted us.

This of the Bullers was the product for me of Irving's first months in London ; began, and got under way, in the Spring and Summer of 1822, which followed our winter parting in the Black Bull Inn. I was already getting my head a little up ; translating *Legendre's Geometry* for Brewster, my outlooks somewhat cheerfuller,—I still remember a happy forenoon (Sunday, I fear !) in which I did a *Fifth Book* (or complete " Doctrine of Proportion ") for that work ; complete really, and lucid, and yet one of the *briefest* ever known ; it was begun and done that forenoon, and I have (except correcting the press next week) never seen it since, but still feel as if it were right enough and felicitous in its kind ! I got only £50 for my entire trouble in that *Legendre,* and had already ceased to be in the least proud of *Mathematical* prowess ; but it was an honest job of work honestly done, though perhaps for bread-and-water wages,—and that was such an improvement upon wages producing (in Jean Paul's phrase) only water without the bread !—

Towards Autumn the Buller Family followed to Edinburgh, Mr. and Mrs. Buller with a third very small son, Reginald, who was a curious gesticulating, pen-drawing, etc. little creature, *not* to be under my charge, but who generally *dined* with me at luncheon time, and who afterwards turned out a lazy, hebetated fellow, and is now Parson of Troston, a fat living in Suffolk : these English or Anglo-Indian gentlefolks were all a new species to me, sufficiently exotic in aspect ; but we recognised each other's quality more and more, and did very well together. They had a house in India Street ; saw a great deal of Company (of the Ex-Indian accidental English-gentleman, and native or touring *Lion* genus, for which Mrs. Buller had a lively appetite) ; I still lodged in my old half-rural rooms, " Moray Place, Pilrig Street ; " attended my two Pupils during the day hours (*lunching* with " Regie " by way of dinner) ; and rather seldom, yet to my own taste amply often enough, was of the state " dinners," but walked home to my Books, and to my Brother John, who was now lodging with me and attending College.—Except for *Dyspepsia*, I could have been extremely content ; but that did dismally forbid me, now and afterwards ! Irving and other friends always treated the " ill-health " item as a light matter, which would soon vanish from the account ; but I had a presentiment that it would stay there, and be the Old Man of the Sea to me through life ;—as it has too tragically done, and will do to the end. Woe on it, and not for my own sake alone ;—and yet perhaps a benefit withal has been in it, priceless though hideously painful !—

Of Irving in these two years I recollect almost nothing personal, though all round I heard a great deal of him : and he must have been in my company at least once,—prior to the advent of the elder Bullers, and been giving me counsel and light on the matter ; for I recollect his telling me of *Mrs.* Buller (having, no doubt, portrayed *Mr.* Buller to me in acceptable and clearly intelligible lineaments) That she, she too was a worthy, honourable and quick-sighted lady ; but not without fine-ladyisms, crotchets, caprices,—" somewhat like Mrs. Welsh, you can fancy ; but good too, like her." Ah me, this I perfectly remember, this and nothing more of those Irving interviews and intercourses ; and it is a memento to me of a most important province in my poor world at that time ! I was in constant correspondence (weekly or oftener, sending *Books* etc. etc.) with *Haddington ;* and heard often about Irving, and of things far *more* interesting to me, from that quarter. Gone silent now, closed for ever ; so sad, so strange it all is now !—Irving, I think, had paid a visit there, and certainly sent letters ;—by the above token, I too must have seen him at least once. All this was in his first London Year, or Half-year ; some months before his " popularity " had yet taken *fire*, and made him for a time the property of all the world rather than of his friends.

The news of this latter event, which came in vague, vast, fitful, and decidedly *fuliginous* forms, was not quite welcome to any of us,—perhaps, in secret, not welcome at all. People have their envies, their pitiful self-comparisons ; and feel obliged sometimes to profess, from the teeth outwards, more " joy " than they really have : not an agreeable duty, or quasi-duty, laid on one ! For myself I can say that there was first, something of real joy (" success to the worthy of success ! ") ; second, something (probably not yet much) of honest question for *his* sake, " Can *he* guide it, in that huge element, as *e.g.* Chalmers has done in this smaller one ? " and third, a noticeable quantity of " *Quid tui interest ?* " What business hast thou with it, poor, suffering, hand-cuffed wretch ? To me, these great doings in Hatton Garden came only on the wings of Rumour, the exact nature of them uncertain. To me, for many months back, Irving had fallen totally silent, and this seemed a seal to its being a permanent silence : I had been growing steadily worse in health too, and was silently in habitual wretchedness, ready to say, " Well, whoever is happy and gaining victory, thou art, and art like to be, very miserable, and to gain none at all ! " These were, so far as I can now read, honestly my feelings on the matter. My love to Irving, now that I look at it across those temporary vapours, had *not* abated, never did abate ; but he seemed for the present flown (or *mounted*, if that was it) far away from me ; and I could only say to myself, " Well, well, then ; so it must be."—One heard too, often enough, that in Irving there was visible a certain joyancy and frankness of triumph ; that he took things on the high key, nothing doubting ; and foolish stories circulated about his lofty sayings, sublimities of manner and the like ; something of which I could believe (and yet kindly interpret too) : all which might have been, though it scarcely was, some consolation for our present silence towards one another,—for what could I have *said*, in the circumstances, that would have been, on both sides, agreeable and profitable ?—

It was not till late in Autumn 1823, nearly two years after our parting in the Black Bull Inn, that I fairly, and to a still

memorable measure, saw Irving again.   He was on his Marriage
Jaunt, Miss Martin of Kirkcaldy now become his Life-Partner,
off on a Tour to the Highlands ; and the generous soul had
determined to pass near Kinnaird (right bank of Tay, a mile
below the junction of Tummel and Tay), where I then was with
the Bullers, and pick me up to accompany as far as I would.
I forget where or how our meeting was (at Dunkeld probably) ;
I seem to have lodged with them two nights in successive Inns ;
and certainly parted from them at Loch Tay Village, Sunday
afternoon, where my horse, by some means, must have been
waiting for me : I remember baiting him (excellent cob or
pony " Dolph," i.e. *Bardolph*, bought for me at Lilliesleaf Fair
by my dear Brother Alick, and which I had ridden into the
Highlands for health) at Aberfeldy ; and to have sat, in a kindly
and polite yet very huggermugger cottage, among good peasant
Kirk-people, refreshing themselves on returning home from
Sermon ; sat for perhaps some two hours, till poor Dolph got
rested and refected like his fellow-creatures there.   I even
remember something like a fraction of scrag of mutton and
potatoes eaten by myself,—in strange contrast, had I thought
of that, to Irving's nearly simultaneous dinner, which would
be with My Lord, at Taymouth Castle !   After Aberfeldy
Cottage, the curtain falls.

Irving, on this his Wedding-Jaunt, seemed superlatively
happy ; as was natural to the occasion, or more than natural ;
as if at the top of Fortune's wheel, and in a sense (a generous
sense, it must be owned, and not a *tyrannous* in any measure),
striking the stars with his sublime head.   Mrs. Irving was
demure and quiet, though doubtless not *less* happy at heart ;
really comely in her behaviour . . . Irving had loyally taken
her as the consummate flower of all his victory in the world,—
poor good *tragic* woman ; better probably than the fortune she
had, after all !—

My friend was kind to me as possible ; and bore with my
gloomy humours (for I was ill and miserable to a degree), nay
perhaps as foil to the radiancy of his own sunshine he almost
enjoyed them.   I remember jovial bursts of laughter from him
at my surly sarcastic and dyspeptic utterances.   " Doesn't this
subdue you, Carlyle ? " said he somewhat solemnly : we were
all three standing at the Falls of Aberfeldy (amid " the *Birks* "
of ditto, and memories of song), silent in the October dusk,
perhaps with moon rising,—our ten miles to Taymouth still
ahead,—" Doesn't this subdue you ? "   " Subdue me ?   I

should hope not! I have quite other things to front with defiance, in this world, than a gush of bog-water tumbling over crags as here!" Which produced a joyous and really kind laugh from him as sole answer. He had much to tell me of London, of its fine literary possibilities for a man, of its literary stars, whom he had seen, or knew of: Coleridge in particular who was in the former category, a marvellous sage and man; Hazlitt, who was in the latter, a fine talent too, but tending towards scamphood. "Was at the *Fonthill-Abbey Sale*, the other week, hired to attend as a '*White-bonnet*' there," said he with a laugh. *White-bonnet* intensely vernacular, is the Annandale name for a false bidder merely appointed to raise prices; works so, for his five shillings, at some poor little Annandale Roup (*Ruf*, or vocal Sale) of Standing crop or hypothecated cottage furniture; and the contrast and yet kinship between these little things and the Fonthill great ones, was ludicrous enough. He would not hear of ill-health being any hindrance to me; he had himself no experience in that sad province. All seemed possible to him; all was joyful and running upon wheels. He had suffered much angry criticism in his late triumphs (on his "*Orations*" quite lately), but seemed to accept it all with jocund mockery, as something harmless and beneath him.

Wilson in *Blackwood* had been very scornful, and done his bitterly enough disobliging best: nevertheless Irving, now advising with me, about some detail of our motions or of my own, and finding I still demurred to it, said with true radiancy of look, "Come now, you know I am the *judicious Hooker!*" which was considered one of Wilson's cruellest hits, in that Blackwood *Article*. To myself I remember his answering,— in return evidently for some criticism of my own, on the *Orations*,[1] which was not so laudatory as required, but of which I recollect nothing further :—" Well, Carlyle, I am glad to hear you say all that; it gives me the opinion of another mind on the thing,"—which at least, beyond any doubt, it did! He was in high sunny humour, good Irving. There was no trace of anger left in him; he was jovial, riant, jocose,—jocose rather than serious throughout, which was a new phasis to me. And furthermore, in the serious vein itself there was oftenest something of *falsetto* noticeable (as in that of the waterfall " sub-

[1] *The Oracles of God in Four Orations. For Judgment to Come, an Argument in Nine Parts* (1 vol. London, 1823). Miss Welsh's copy is inscribed " To Jane Welsh my beloved Pupil and most dear friend—and to her Mother whom I love no less—to whose smiles upon his labours the author is indebted for much, very much of his present ardour."

duing" one);—generally speaking, a new height of self-consciousness not yet sure of the manner and carriage that was suitablest for it. He affected to feel his popularity too great, and burdensome; spoke much about a Mrs. Basil Montagu, elderly, sage, lofty, yet humane, whom we got to know afterwards, and to call by his name for her, "the Noble Lady," who had saved him greatly from the dashing floods of that tumultuous and unstable element; hidden him away from it once and again, done kind ministrations, spread sofas for him, and taught him "to rest." The last thing I recollect of him was, on our coming out from Taymouth Kirk (Kirk, Congregation, Minister and Sermon utterly erased from me), how in coming down the broadish little street, he pulled off his big broad hat, and walked, looking mostly to the sky, with his fleece of copious coal-black hair flowing in the wind, and in some spittings of rain that were beginning; how thereupon, in a minute or two, a Livery Servant ran up, "Please, Sir, aren't you the Rev. Edward Irving?" "Yes." "Then my Lord Breadalbane begs you to stop for him one moment." Whereupon *exit Flunkey;* Irving turning to us, with what look of sorrow he could, and "Again found out!" upon which the old Lord came up (Father of the last, or late "Free-Kirk" one, whom I have sometimes seen), and civilly invited him to dinner. Him and Party, I suppose; but to me there was no temptation, or on those terms less than none: so I had Bardolph saddled; and rode for Aberfeldy, as above said. Home, sunk in manifold murky reflections, now lost to me,—and of which only the fewest (and friendliest) were comfortably fit for uttering to the Bullers next day. I saw no more of Irving for this time. But he had been at Haddington too, was perhaps again corresponding a little there; and I heard occasionally of him, in the beautiful, bright, and kindly quizzing style that was natural there.

I was myself writing *Schiller* in those months, a task Irving had encouraged me in, and prepared the way for in the *London Magazine;*—three successive Parts there were; I know not how far advanced at this period; know only that I was nightly working at the thing in a serious, sad, and totally solitary way. My two rooms were in the *Old* "Mansion" of Kinnaird, some three or four hundred yards from the New, and on a lower level, over-shadowed with wood; thither I always retired directly after tea, and for most part had the edifice all to myself; good candles, good wood fire, place dry enough, tolerably clean, and such *silence* and total absence of company good or bad, as I never experienced before or since. I remember still the grand *sough* of those woods, or perhaps in the stillest times, the distant ripple of Tay ; nothing else to converse with but this and my own thoughts, which never for a moment pretended to be joyful, and were sometimes pathetically sad. I was in the miserablest dyspeptic health, uncertain whether I ought not even to *quit* on that account, and at times almost resolving to do it ; dumb, far away from all my Loved ones ;—my poor *Schiller*, nothing considerable of a *work* even to my own judgment, had to be steadily persisted in, as the only protection and resource in this inarticulate huge *wilderness*, actual and symbolical. My Editor I think was complimentary ; but I knew better. The *Times* Newspaper once brought me, without commentary at all, an " eloquent " passage reprinted (about the *Tragedy* of " noble Literary Life ") ; which I remember to have read with more pleasure, in this utter isolation, and as the *first* public nod of approval I had ever had, than any criticism or laudation that has ever come to me since. For about two hours it had lighted in the desolations of my inner man a strange little glow of illumination : but here too, on a little reflection, I 'knew better;' and the winter afternoon was not over when I saw clearly how very small this conquest was, and things were in their *statu quo* again.

Schiller done, I began *Wilhelm Meister ;* a task I liked perhaps rather better, too scanty as my knowledge of the element, and even of the language still was. Two years before, I had at length, after some repulsions, got into the heart of *Wilhelm Meister*, and eagerly read it through ;—my sally out, after finishing, along the vacant streets of Edinburgh (a windless, Scotch-misty Sunday night) is still vivid to me : " Grand, surely, harmoniously built together, far-seeing, wise and true : when, for many years, or almost in my life before, have I read such a Book ? " Which I was now, really in part as a kind of duty, conscientiously translating for my countrymen, if they would read it,—as a select few of them have ever since kept doing. I finished it the next Spring, not at Kinnaird, but at Mainhill (a month or two there, with my best of nurses and of hostesses, my Mother ; blessed voiceless or low-voiced time, still sweet to me !), with *London* now silently ahead and the Bullers there, or to *be* there : of Kinnaird life they had now had enough ; and I (and my miserable health) far more than enough some time before ! But that is not my subject here. I had ridden to Edinburgh, there to consult a Doctor ; having at last reduced my complexities

to a single question, " Is this disease curable by medicine ; or
is it chronic, incurable except by regimen, if even so ? " This
question I earnestly put ; got response, " It is all *tobacco*, Sir ;
give up tobacco ; " gave it instantly and strictly up ;—found,
after long months, that I might as well have ridden sixty miles
in the opposite direction, and " poured my sorrows into the long
hairy ear of the first jackass I came upon," as into this select
medical man's, whose name I will not mention.

After these still months at Mainhill, my printing at Edinburgh
was all finished, and I went thither with my *Preface* in my
pocket ; finished that and the rest of the *Meister* business
(£180 of *payment* the choicest part of it !) rapidly off ; made a
visit to Haddington,—what a retrospect to me now, encircled
by the Silences and the Eternities ; most beautiful, most sad
(I remember the *gimp bonnet* she wore, and her anxious silent
thoughts, and my own, mutually legible both of them, in part,
—my own little Darling, now at rest, and far away !)—which
was the last thing in Scotland. Of the Leith Smack, every
figure and event in which is curiously present, though so unimportant, I will say nothing : only that we entered London
River on a beautiful May [1] morning ; scene very impressive
to me, and still very vivid in me ; and that soon after mid-day,
I landed safe in Irving's, as appointed.

Irving lived in Myddelton Terrace (*hodie* Myddelton *Square*),
Islington, No. 4 ;—it was a new place, houses bright and smart,
but inwardly bad as usual. Only one side of the now Square
was built, the western side, which has its back towards Battle-
Bridge region ; Irving's house was fourth from the northern
end of that, which of course had its *left-hand* on the New Road.
The place was airy, not uncheerful ; our chief prospect from the
front was a good space of green ground, and in it, on the hither
edge of it, the big open *reservoir* of Myddelton's " New River "
(now above two centuries *old*, for that matter, but recently made
new again and all cased in tight masonry), on the spacious
expanses of smooth flags surrounding which, it was pleasant on
fine mornings to take our early promenade, with the free sky
overhead, and the New Road with its lively traffic and vehicula-
tion seven or eight good yards below our level. I remember
several pretty strolls here, ourselves two, while breakfast was
getting ready close by, and the esplanade, a high little island
lifted free out of the noises and jostlings, was all our own.

[1] It was in the beginning of June.

Irving had received me with the old true friendliness, wife and household eager to imitate him therein. I seem to have staid a good two or three weeks with them at that time (Buller arrangements not yet ready, nay sometimes threatening to become uncertain altogether !)—and, off and on, during the next ten months, I saw a great deal of my old Friend and his new affairs and posture. That first afternoon, with its curious phenomena, is still very lively in me. Basil Montagu's eldest son (" Noble Lady's " *step*-son ; she was Basil's *third* Wife, and had four kinds of children at home, a most sad miscellany, as I afterwards found), ' Mr. Montagu junior,' accidental guest at our neat little early dinner ; my first specimen of the London Dandy,—*broken* Dandy, very mild of manner, who went all to shivers, and died miserable, soon after : this was novelty first. Then, during or before his stay with us, dash of a brave carriage driving up, and entry of a strangely-complexioned young lady, with soft brown eyes and floods of *bronze*-red hair, really a pretty-looking, smiling and amiable, though most foreign bit of magnificence and kindly splendour ; whom they welcomed by the name of " dear Kitty,"—Kitty Kirkpatrick, Charles Buller's cousin or half-cousin, Mrs. Strachey's full cousin, with whom she lived ; her birth, as I afterwards found, an Indian *Romance*, mother a sublime *Begum*, father a ditto English Official, mutually adoring, wedding, living withdrawn in their own private paradise, Romance famous in the East. A very singular " dear Kitty ; " who seemed bashful withal, and soon went away,—twitching off, in the lobby (as I could notice, not without wonder), the loose label which was sticking to my trunk or bag, still there as she tripped past, and carrying it off in her pretty hand : with what imaginable object then, in Heaven's name ? To show it to Mrs. Strachey I afterwards guessed ; to whom, privately, poor I had been prophesied of, in the usual grandiloquent terms. This might be called novelty second, if not first and far greatest ! Then after dinner, in the drawing-room, which was prettily furnished, the *Romance* of said furnishing,—which had all been done, as if by beneficent fairies, in some temporary absence of the owners ; " We had decided on not furnishing it," Irving told me ; " not till we had more money ready ; and, on our return, this was how we found it. The people here are of a nobleness you have never before seen ! "—" And don't you yet guess at all who can have done it ? " " H'm, perhaps we guess vaguely ; but it is their Secret, and we should not break it against their will." It turned out to have been Mrs. Strachey and dear Kitty, both of whom were rich and openhanded, that had done this fine stroke of art-magic ; one of the many munificences achieved by them in this new province. Perhaps the " Noble Lady " had, at first, been suspected ; but how innocently she,—not flush in that way at all, though notably so in others ! The talk about these and other noble souls, and new phenomena, strange to me, and half-incredible in such interpretation, left me wondering and con-fusedly guessing over the much that I had heard and seen, this day.

Irving's London element and mode of existence had its questionable aspects, from the first ; and one could easily per-ceive, here as elsewhere, that the ideal of fancy and the actual of fact, were two very different things. It was as the former that my Friend, according to old habit, strove to represent it to himself, and to *make it be ;* and it was as the latter that it obstinately continued being ! There were beautiful items in his present scene of life, but a great majority which, under specious figure, were intrinsically poor, vulgar and importunate ; and introduced largely into one's existence the character of *huggermugger,* not of greatness or success in any real sense. He was, inwardly, I could observe, nothing like so happy as in old days ; inwardly confused, anxious, dissatisfied ; though, as it were, denying it to himself, and striving, if not to " talk big," which he hardly ever did, to *think* big upon all this. We had many strolls together, no doubt much dialogue, but it has nearly all gone from me,—probably not so worthy of remembrance as our old communings were. Crowds of visitors came about him, and ten times or a hundred times as many would have come if allowed ; well-dressed, decorous people ; but for most part, tiresome, ignorant, weak, or even silly and absurd. He per-suaded himself that at least he " loved their love ; "—and of this latter, in the kind they had to offer him, there did seem to be no lack. He and I were walking, one bright Summer evening, somewhere in the outskirts of Islington, in what was or had once been *fields,* and was again coarsely green in general, but with symptoms of past devastation by bricklayers (who have now doubtless covered it all with their dirty " human dog-hutches of the period ! ")—when in some smoothish hollower spot, there suddenly disclosed itself a considerable company of altogether fine-looking young girls, who had set themselves to dance ; all in airy bonnets, silks and flounces ; merrily alert, nimble as young fawns ; tripping it, to their own rhythm, on the light fantastic toe : with the bright beams of the setting sun gilding them, and the hum and smoke of huge London shoved aside as foil or background, nothing could be prettier. At sight of us they suddenly stopped, all looking round ; and one of the prettiest, a dainty little thing, stept radiantly out to Irving, " Oh, oh, Mr. Irving ! " and, blushing and smiling, offered her pretty lips to be kissed, which Irving gallantly stooped down to accept, as well worth while. Whereupon, after some benedictory or Pastoral words, we went on our way. Probably I rallied him on such opulence of luck provided for a man ; to which he could answer properly, as a *spiritual* Shepherd, not a secular.

There were several Scotch Merchant-people, among those that came about him, substantial City men, of shrewd insight and good honest sense, several of whom seemed truly attached and reverent,—one William Hamilton, a very honest, shrewd and pious Nithsdale man, who wedded a Sister of Mrs. Irving's by and by, and whom I knew till his death, was probably the chief of these ; as an old good Mr. Dinwiddie, very zealous, very simple and far from shrewd, might perhaps be reckoned at or near the other end of the series :—a Sir Peter Laurie, afterwards of Aldermanic and even Mayoral celebrity, came also pretty often ; but seemed privately to look quite from the aldermanic point of view, on Irving and the new " Caledonian Chapel " they were struggling to get built (old Mr. Dinwiddie especially struggling) ;—and indeed once, to me at Paris a while after this, likened Irving and Dinwiddie to " Harlequin and Blast " whom he had seen in some Farce then current ; Harlequin conjuring up the most glorious possibilities (like this of their " Caledonian Chapel "), and Blast loyally following him with swift destruction on attempting to help. Sir Peter rather took to me, but not I much to him ; a long-sighted satirical *Ex-Saddler* I found him to be, and nothing better,—nay something of an *Ex*-Scotchman too, which I could still less forgive. I went with the Irvings once to his house (Crescent, head of Portland Place) to a Christmas dinner this same year; very sumptuous, very cockneyish, strange and unadmirable to me ;—and don't remember to have met him again. On our coming to live in London, he had rather grown in civic fame and importance ; and possibly (for I am not quite sure) on the feeble chance of his being of some help, I sent him some indication or other (a project beliks, and my card with it ; one of several *air-castles* I was anxiously building at that time before taking to *French Revolution !*) ;—but if so, he took no notice, gave no sign. Some years afterwards I met him in my rides in the Park ; evidently recognisant, and willing or wishful to speak ; but it never came to effect, there being now no charm in it.   Then again, years afterwards, when *Latter-day Pamphlets* were coming out, he wrote me, on that of *Model Prisons* a knowing, approving, kindly and civil Letter ; to which I willingly responded by a kindly and civil.   Not very long after that I think, he died,[1]—riding diligently almost to the end.   Poor Sir Peter, he was nothing of a bad man, very far other indeed ; but had lived in a loud-roaring, big, pretentious and intrinsically barren sphere ;   unconscious wholly that he might have risen to the top in a considerably nobler and fruitfuller one.   What a tragic, treacherous stepdame is vulgar Fortune to her children ! Sir Peter's wealth has gone now in good part to somebody concerned in " discovering," not for the final time, " *the* source of the Nile" (blessings on it !)—a Captain Grant, I think, companion to a ditto Speke ;   having married Sir Peter's Scotch Niece and Lady Heiress, a good clever girl, once of *Haddington* ... who made her way to my Loved One on the ground of common country, in late years, and used to be rather liked here, in the few visits she made.   Grant and she, who are now gone to India, called after marriage, but found nobody,—nor now ever will.

By far the most distinguished Two, and to me the alone important, of Irving's London Circle, were Mrs. Strachey (Mrs. Buller's younger sister), and the " Noble Lady," Mrs. Basil Montagu ;   with both of whom, and their households, I became acquainted by his means.   One of my first visits was, along with him, to Goodenough-House, Shooter's Hill, where they [the Stracheys] oftenest were in Summer.   I remember our entering the little winding avenue, and seeing in a kind of open conservatory or verandah, on our approach to the House, the effulgent vision of " dear Kitty," busied among the roses, and almost buried under them, who, on sight of us, glided hastily in.   The before and after, and all other incidents of that first visit, are quite lost to me ;   but I made a good many visits there and in Town, and grew familiar with my ground.

Of Mrs. Strachey I have spoken already ;   to this day, long years after her death, I regard her as a singular pearl of a woman; pure as dew, yet full of love ;   incapable of unveracity to herself or others.   *Examiner* Strachey had long been an Official (judge etc.) in Bengal, where Brothers of his were, and Sons still are : eldest Son is now master, by inheritance, of the Family Estate in Somersetshire ;—one of the Brothers had translated a curious old Hindoo Treatise on *Algebra*, which had made his name

1 Sir Peter Laurie died 1861 ; aged 83.

familiar to me. Edward (that, I think, was the Examiner's name) might be a few years turned of fifty, at this time; his Wife twenty years younger, with a number of pretty children,—the eldest hardly fourteen, and only one of them a girl. They lived in Fitzroy Square, a fine-enough house; and had a very pleasant country establishment at Shooter's Hill, where in Summer time they were all commonly to be found. I have seldom seen a pleasanter place: a panorama of green, flowery, clean and decorated country all round; an umbrageous little Park, with roses, gardens; a modestly-excellent House,—from the drawing-room window a continual view of ships, multiform and multitudinous, sailing up or down the River (about a mile off), smoky London as background, the clear sky overhead; and, within doors, honesty, good sense and smiling seriousness the rule and not the exception. Edward Strachey was a genially-abrupt man; 'Utilitarian' and Democrat by creed, yet beyond all things he loved *Chaucer* and kept reading him. A man rather tacit than discursive; but willing to speak, and doing it well, in a fine tinkling, mellow-toned voice, in an ingenious aphoristic way;—had withal a pretty vein of quiz, which he seldom indulged in: a man sharply impatient of pretence, of sham and untruth in all forms,—especially contemptuous of "quality" pretensions and affectations, which he scattered grinningly to the winds. Dressed in the simplest form; walked daily to the India House and back, though there were fine carriages in store for the women part;—scorned cheerfully "the general humbug of the world," and honestly strove to do his own bit of duty, spiced by Chaucer and what else of inward harmony or condiment he had. Of religion in articulate shape, he had none; but much respected his Wife's, whom, and whose truthfulness in that as in all things, he tenderly esteemed and loved. A man of many qualities: comfortable to be near. At his house, both in Town and here, I have seen pleasant graceful people; whose style of manners, if nothing else, struck me as new and superior.

Mrs. Strachey took to me from the first, nor ever swerved: it strikes me now, more than it then did, she silently could have liked to see "dear Kitty" and myself come together, and so continue near her, both of us, through life: the good kind soul,—and Kitty, too, was charming in her beautiful *Begum* sort, had wealth abundant, and might perhaps have been charmed? None knows. She had one of the prettiest smiles, a visible sense of humour (the slight merry curl of her upper lip, *right side* of it only, the carriage of her head and eyes, on such occasions, the quiet little things she said in that kind, and her low-toned hearty laugh, were noticeable) ; this was perhaps her most spiritual quality ; of developed intellect she had not much, though not wanting in discernment. Amiable, affectionate, graceful ; might be called attractive (not *slim* enough for the title " pretty," not *tall* enough for " beautiful ") ; had something low-voiced, languidly harmonious, placid, sensuous, loved perfumes etc. : a Half-*Begum* in short ; interesting specimen of the Semi-oriental Englishwoman.   Still lives, near Exeter (the prize of some idle Ex-Captain of Sepoys), with many children, whom she watches over with a passionate instinct ; and has not quite forgotten me, as I had evidence once in late years, thanks to her kind little heart.

The Montagu establishment (25 Bedford Square) was still more notable, and as unlike this as possible. Might be defined, not quite satirically, as a most singular social and spiritual *ménagerie ;* which, indeed, was well known and much noted and criticised in certain Literary and other circles. Basil Montagu, a Chancery Barrister in excellent practice, hugely a *sage* too, busy all his days upon "Bacon's Works," and continually preaching a superfinest morality, about benevolence, munificence, health, peace, unfailing happiness,—much a bore to you by degrees, and considerably a humbug if you probed too strictly. Age at this time might be about sixty ; good middle stature ; face rather fine under its grizzled hair (brow very prominent) ; wore oftenest a kind of smile, not false or consciously so, but insignificant, and as if feebly defensive against the intrusions of a rude world. On going to Hinchinbrook long after, I found he was strikingly like the dissolute, questionable Earl of Sandwich (Foote's " Jemmy Diddler " [1]) ; who indeed had been father of him, in a highly tragic way ! [His mother,] pretty Miss Ray, carefully educated for that function ; Rev. ex-dragoon Hackman taking this so dreadfully to heart that (being if not an ex-lover, a lover, Bless the mark !) he shot her as she came out of Drury Lane Theatre one night, and got well hanged for

---

1 Carlyle's memory was at fault here. " Jemmy *Twitcher* " is the name of a character in Gay's *Beggar's Opera*, and was a nickname applied to John, Earl of Sandwich, who died in 1792. Gray's satirical poem on Lord Sandwich, *The Candidate*, begins—

" When sly Jemmy Twitcher had smugged up his face,
    With a lick of court whitewash, and pious grimace."

" Jeremy Diddler " is the name of a character in Kenny's farce of *Raising the Wind.*

it.[1] The story is musty rather, and there is a loose foolish old book upon it called *Love and Madness* which is not worth reading. Poor Basil ! no wonder he had his peculiarities, coming by such a genesis, and with a life of his own which had been brimful of difficulties and confusions ! It cannot be said he managed *it* ill, but far the contrary, all things considered. Nobody can deny that he wished all the world rather well, could wishing have done it ; express malice against anybody or anything he seldom or never showed. I myself experienced much kind flattery (if that were a benefit), much soothing treatment in his house ; and learned several things there which were of use afterwards, and not alloyed by the least harm done me. But it was his wife, the " Noble Lady," who in all senses presided there, to whom I stand debtor, and should be thankful for all this.

Basil had been thrice married ; children of all his marriages, and one child of the now Mrs. Montagu's own by a previous marriage, were present in the house ; a most difficult miscellany. . . . Only the eldest child, Emily, the one daughter Basil had, succeeded in the world ; made a good match (in Turin country somewhere), and is still doing well. Emily was Basil's only daughter, but she was not his wife's only one : Mrs. Montagu had by her former marriage, which had been brief, one daughter, six or eight years older than Emily Montagu ; Anne Skepper the name of this one, and York or Yorkshire her birthplace : a brisk, witty, prettyish, sufficiently clear-eyed and sharp-tongued young lady,—bride, or affianced, at this time, of the Poet " Barry Cornwall," i.e. Bryan W. Procter, whose wife, both of them still prosperously living, she now is. Anne rather liked me, I her ; an evidently true, sensible and practical young lady, in a house considerably in want of such an article. She was the *fourth* genealogic species among those children ; visibly the eldest, all but Basil's first son (now gone) ; and did, and might well, pass for the flower of the collection.

Ruling such a miscellany of a household, with Basil Montagu at the head of it, and an almost still stranger miscellaneous society that fluctuated through it, Mrs. Montagu had a problem like few others. But she, if anyone, was equal to it. A more constant and consummate *Artist* in that kind you could nowhere meet with ; truly a remarkable and partly a high and tragical woman ; now about fifty, with the remains of a certain queenly beauty, which she still took strict care of. A tall, rather thin

figure ; face pale, intelligent and penetrating, nose fine, rather
large, and decisively Roman ; pair of bright, not soft, but sharp
and small black eyes, with a cold smile as of inquiry in them ;
fine brow, fine chin, both rather prominent : thin lips always
gently shut, as if till the inquiry were completed, and the time
came for something of royal speech upon it.   She had a slight
Yorkshire accent ; but spoke—Dr. Hugh Blair could not have
picked a hole in it, and you might have printed every word,—
as queenlike, gentle, soothing, measured, prettily royal,—towards
subjects whom she wished to love her.   The voice was modu-
lated, low, not inharmonious, yet there was something of
metallic in it, akin to that smile in the eyes.   One durst not quite
love this high personage as she wished to be loved !   Her very
dress was notable, always the same, and in a fashion of its own :
kind of widow's-cap fastened below the chin ; darkish puce-
coloured silk all the rest,—and (I used to hear from one who
knew !) was admirable, and must have required daily the
fastening of sixty or eighty pins.

There were many criticisms of Mrs. Montagu, often angry
ones ; but the truth is, she did love, and aspire to, human
excellence ;—and her road to it was no better than a steep hill
of jingling boulders and sliding sand.   There remained, therefore, nothing, if you still aspired, but to succeed ill, and put the
best face on it.   Which she amply did.   I have heard her speak
of the Spartan Boy who let the fox, hidden under his robe, eat
him rather than rob him of his honour from the theft.

In early life she had made some visit to Nithsdale (to the
" Craiks of Arbigland "), and had seen Burns ; of whom her
worship continued fervent, her few recollections always a jewel
she was ready to produce : she must have been strikingly
beautiful at that time, and Burns's recognition and adoration
would not be wanting ;—the most royally courteous of mankind,
she always defined him, as the first mark of his genius.   I think
I have heard that, at a Ball in Dumfries, she had frugally constructed some dress by sewing real flowers upon it ; and shone,
by that bit of art, and by her fine bearing, as the cynosure of all
eyes.   Her Father, I gradually understood (not from herself),
had been a man of inconsiderable wealth or position, a Wine-
merchant in York, his name Benson ; her first Husband, Mr.
Skepper, some young Lawyer there, of German extraction ;—
and that the " Romance " of her wedding Montagu, which she
sometimes touched on, had been, prosaically, nothing but this :
Seeing herself, on Skepper's death, left destitute with a young

girl, she consented to take charge of Montagu's motherless confused family, under the name of " Governess," bringing her own little Anne as appendage ; had succeeded well, and better and better, for some time, perhaps some years, in that ticklish capacity ; whereupon, at length, offer of marriage, which she accepted. Her sovereignty in the house had to be soft, judicious, politic ; but it was constant and valid,—felt to be beneficial withal. " She is like one in command of a mutinous ship, which is ready to take fire ! " Irving once said to me. By this time he had begun to discover that this " Noble Lady " was in essentiality an Artist ; and hadn't perhaps loved him so much as tried to buy love from him, by soft ministrations, by the skilfullest flattery liberally laid on. He continued always to look kindly towards her ; but had now, or did by and by, let drop the old epithet. Whether she had done him good or ill, would be hard to say,—ill perhaps ? In this liberal London, pitch your sphere one step lower than *yourself*, and you can get what amount of flattery you will consent to ; everybody has it like paper-money for the printing, and will buy a small amount of ware by any quantity of it. The generous Irving did not find out this so soon as some surlier fellows of us !—

On one of the first fine mornings, Mrs. Montagu, along with Irving, took me out to see Coleridge at Highgate. My impressions of the man and of the place are conveyed, faithfully enough, in the *Life of Sterling ;* that first interview in particular, of which I had expected very little, was idle and unsatisfactory, and yielded me nothing,—Coleridge, a puffy, anxious, obstructed-looking, fattish old man, hobbled about with us, talking with a kind of solemn emphasis on matters which were of no interest (and even *reading* pieces in *proof* of his opinions thereon) ; I had him to myself once or twice, in *narrow* parts of the garden-walks ; and tried hard to get something about *Kant* and Co. from him, about " reason " *versus* " understanding," and the like ; but in vain : nothing came from him that was of use to me, that day, or in fact any day. The sight and sound of a sage who was so venerated by those about me, and whom I too would willingly have venerated, but could not,—this was all. Several times afterward, Montagu, on Coleridge's " Thursday Evening," carried Irving and me out, and returned blessing Heaven (I not) for what we had received ; Irving and I walked out more than once on mornings, too ; and found the Dodona Oracle humanely ready to act,—but never (to me, nor to Irving either I suspect) explanatory of the question put. Good Irving strove always to think that he was getting priceless wisdom out of this great man ; but must have had his misgivings. Except by the Montagu-Irving channel, I at no time communicated with Coleridge : I had never, on my own strength, had much esteem for him ; and found slowly, in spite of myself, that I was getting to have less and less. Early in 1825 was my last sight of him ; a Print of Porson brought some trifling utterance, " Sensuality, such a *dissolutor* even of the features of a man's face ! "—and I remember nothing more. On my second visit to London (autumn 1831), Irving and I had appointed a day for pilgrimage to Highgate ; but the day was one rain-deluge, and we couldn't even try. Soon after our settling here (late in 1834) Coleridge was reported to be dying ; and died : [1] I had seen the last of him almost a decade ago.

A great " worship of genius " habitually went on at Montagu's, from self and wife especially ; Coleridge the Head of the *Lares* there, though he never appeared in person, but only wrote a word or two of Note on occasion. A confused dim miscellany of " geniuses " (mostly nondescript and harmlessly useless) hovered fitfully about the establishment ;—I think those of any reality had tired, and gone away. There was much talk and laud of Charles Lamb and his *Pepe* etc. ; but he never appeared : at his own house I saw him once ; once I gradually felt to have been enough for me. Poor Lamb, such a " divine genius " you could find in the then London only ! Hazlitt, whom I had a kind of curiosity about, was not now " of the admitted " (such the hint) ; at any rate, kept strictly away. There was a " Crabbe Robinson " (who had been in Weimar, etc. ; who was *first* of the " Own Correspondents " now so numerous, this is now his real distinction) ; there was a Mr. Fearn " profound in Metaphysics " (dull utterly, and dry) ; there was a *Dr.* Sir Anthony Carlile, of name in Medicine ; native of Durham, and a hard-headed fellow, but Utilitarian to the bone,—who had defined Poetry (to Irving once) as " the pro-d*ooction* of a rude *Aage* !" We were clansmen, he and I ; but had nothing of mutual attraction,—nor of repulsion either, for the man didn't want for shrewd sense in his way. I heard continual talk and admiration of " the grand old English Writers " (Fuller, Sir Thomas Browne, and various others, *Milton* more rarely),—this was the orthodox strain ; but there was little considerable of actual knowledge, and of critical appreciation

[1] The Carlyles settled in Chelsea 10th of June. Coleridge died 25th July 1834.

almost nothing, at the back of it anywhere ; and in the end it did one next to no good, yet perhaps not quite none,— deducting, in accurate balance, all the ill that might be in it.

Nobody pleased me so much in this miscellany as Procter (Barry Cornwall), who, for the fair Anne Skepper's sake, was very constantly there. Anne and he were to have been, and were still to be, married ; but some disaster or entanglement in Procter's Attorney Business had occurred (some Partner defalcating or the like), and Procter, in evident distress and dispiritment, was waiting the slow conclusion of this ; which, and the wedding thereupon, happily took place in winter following. A decidedly rather pretty little fellow, Procter, bodily and spiritually ; manners prepossessing, slightly London-elegant, not unpleasant ; clear judgment in him, though of narrow field ; a sound honourable morality ; and airy friendly ways. Of slight neat figure, vigorous for his size ; fine genially rugged little face, fine head,—something curiously dreamy in the eyes of him, lids *drooping* at the *outer* ends, into a cordially meditative and beautiful expression. Would break out suddenly, now and then, into opera attitude and " *Là ci darem la mano* " for a moment ;—had something of real fun, though in London style. Me he had invited to " his garret," as he called it ; and was always good and kind, and so continues, though I hardly see him once in the quarter of a century.—The next to Procter in my esteem, and the considerably more important to me just then, was a young Mr. Badams, in great and romantic estimation here, and present every now and then, though his place and business lay in Birmingham ; a most cheery, gifted, really amiable man,—with whom not long afterwards, I, more or less *romantically*, went to Birmingham ; and, though *not* " cured of dyspepsia " there (alas, not the least) had two or three singular and interesting months, as will be seen, if we have room. But indeed it is shameful to speak so much of myself in what was meant for another mainly. Badams, Procter etc. were of Irving's London Circle ; and came to me through Irving : that is my one excuse, so far as it will go.

Irving's Preaching at Hatton Garden, which I regularly attended while in his House, and occasionally afterwards, did not strike me as superior to his Scotch performances of past time, or, in private fact, inspire me with any complete or pleasant feeling. Assent to them I could not, except under very wide reservations ; nor, granting all his postulates, did either matter or manner carry me captive, or at any time perfect my admira-

tion. The force and weight of what he urged was undeniable,
the potent faculty at work, like that of Samson heavily striding
along with the Gates of Gaza on his shoulders ; but there was a
want of spontaneity and simplicity, a something of strained and
aggravated, of elaborately intentional, which kept jarring on
the mind : one felt the bad element to be, and to have been,
unwholesome to the honourable soul. The doors were crowded
long before opening, and you got in by ticket : but the first
sublime rush of what once seemed more than popularity, and
had been nothing more,—Lady Jersey " sitting on the Pulpit
steps," Canning, Brougham, Mackintosh, etc. rushing, day after
day,—was now quite over ; and there remained only a popularity of " the people " (not of the *plebs* at all, but never higher
than of the well-dressed *populus* henceforth) ; which was a sad
change to the sanguine man. One noticed that at heart he
was not happy, but anxious, struggling, questioning the future ;
—happiness, alas, he was no more to have, even in the old
measure, in this world ! At sight of Canning, Brougham,
Lady Jersey and Co. crowding round him, and listening week
after week, as if to the message of Salvation, the noblest and
joyfullest thought (I know this on perfect authority) had taken
possession of his noble, too sanguine, and too trustful mind :
" That Christian Religion was to be a truth again, not a paltry
form, and to rule the world,—he, unworthy, even he the chosen
instrument ! " Mrs. Strachey, who had seen him, in her own
house, in these moods, spoke to me once of this, and once only ;
reporting some of his expressions, with an affectionate sorrow.
Cruelly blasted all these hopes soon were ;—but Irving never,
to the end of his life, could consent to give them up. That was
the key to all his subsequent procedures, extravagances, aberrations, so far as I could understand them. Whatever of blame
(and there was on the very surface a fond *credulity* etc., with
perhaps, farther down, and as root to such credulity, some excess
of *Self-love*, which I define always as ' love that others should
love him,' *not* as any worse kind), with that degree of blame
Irving must stand charged ; with that, and with no more, so
far as I could testify or understand. Good Mrs. Oliphant, and
probably her public, have much mistaken me on this point :
that Irving to the very last had abundant " popularity," and
confluence of auditors sufficient for the largest pulpit " vanity,"
I knew and know ;—but also that his once immeasurable quasi-
celestial hope remained cruelly blasted, refusing the least *bud*
farther ; and that without this, all else availed him nothing.

Fallacious semblances of bud it did shoot out, again and again, under his continual fostering and forcing ; but real bud never more :—and the case, in itself, is easy to understand.

He had much quiet seriousness, beautiful piety and charity, in this bad time of agitation and disquietude ; and I was often honestly sorry for him :—Here was still the old true man, and his new element seemed so false and abominable. Honestly ; though not so purely sorry as now, now when element and man are alike gone, and all that was or partook of paltry in one's own view of them is also mournfully gone ! He had endless patience with the mean people crowding about him, and jostling his life to pieces ; hoped always they were not so mean ; never complained of the uncomfortable huggermugger his life was now grown to be ; took everything, wife, servant, guests, world, by the favourablest handle. He had infinite delight in a little baby boy there now was, went dandling about with it in his giant arms, tick-ticking to it, laughing and playing to it,—would turn seriously round to me, with a face sorrowful rather than otherwise, and say, " Ah, Carlyle, this little creature has been sent me to soften my hard heart, which did need it ! "

Towards all distressed people, not absolutely criminal, his kindness, frank helpfulness, long-suffering and assiduity, were in truth wonderful to me. Especially in one case, that of a " Reverend Mr. Macbeth ; " which I thought ill of from the first, and which did turn out hopeless. Macbeth was a Scotch Preacher, or Licentiate, who had failed of a Kirk,—as he deserved to do, though his talents were good ;—and was now hanging very miscellaneously on London, with no outlooks that were not bog meteors, and a steadily increasing tendency to strong drink. He knew Town well, and its babble, and bits of temporary cynosures and frequented haunts, good and perhaps bad ;—took me one evening to the Poet Campbell's, whom I had already seen, but *not* successfully. Macbeth had a sharp, sarcastic, clever kind of tongue ; not much real knowledge ; but was amusing to talk with on a chance walk through the streets ;—older than myself by a dozen years or more. Like him I did not ; there was nothing of wisdom, generosity or worth in him ; but in secret, evidently discernible a great deal of bankrupt vanity, which had taken quite the malignant shape. Undeniable envy, spite and bitterness, looked through every part of him. A tallish slouching lean figure ; face sorrowful, malignant, black ; not unlike the picture of a devil. To me he had privately much the reverse of liking ; I have seen him, in

Irving's and elsewhere (perhaps with a little drink on his stomach, poor soul), break out into oblique little spurts of positive spite,—which I understood to mean merely, " Young Jacka-napes, getting yourself noticed and honoured, while a mature man of real genius is " etc. ! and took no notice of, to the silent comfort of self and neighbours.

This broken Macbeth had been hanging a good while about Irving, who had taken much earnest pains to rescue and arrest him on the edge of the precipices ; but latterly had begun to see that it was hopeless, and had rather left him to his own bad courses. One evening, it was in dirty Winter weather, and I was present, there came to Irving or to Mrs. Irving, dated from some dark Tavern in the Holborn precincts, a piteous little Note from Macbeth : " Ruined again (tempted, O how cunningly, to my old sin) ; been drinking these three weeks, and now have a chalk-score and no money, and can't get out. Oh help a perishing sinner ! " The majority were of opinion, " Pshaw, it is totally hopeless ! " but Irving, after some minutes of serious consideration, decided, " No, not *totally*,"—and directly got into a Hackney-coach, wife and he, proper moneys in pocket ; paid the poor devil's tavern-score (some £2 : 10s. or so, if I remember), and brought him groaning home out of his purgatory again,— for he was in much bodily suffering too. I remember to have been taken up to see him, one evening, in his bedroom (comfort-able airy place), a week or two after : he was in clean dressing-gown and night-cap, walking about the floor ; affected to turn away his face, and to be quite " ashamed," etc. etc., when Irving introduced me ; which, as I could discern it to be painful hypocrisy merely, forbade my visit to be other than quite brief. Comment I made none, here or downstairs ; was actually a little sorry, but without hope ; and rather think this was my last sight of Macbeth. Another time, which could *not* now be distant, when he lay again under chalk-score and bodily sickness in his drinking-shop, there would be no deliverance but to the hospital ; and there I suppose the poor creature tragically ended. He was not without talent ; had written a " Book *on the Sabbath*," better or worse ; and, I almost think, was under-stood, with all his impenitences and malignities, to have real love for his poor old Scotch Mother. After that night in the clean airy bedroom, I have no recollection or tradition of him ;—a vanished quantity, hardly once in my thoughts, for above forty years past.—There were other disastrous or unpleasant figures whom I met at Irving's ; a Danish fanatic of Calvinistic species (repeatedly, and had to beat him off) ; a good many fanatics of different kinds ; one insolent " Bishop of Toronto," triumphant Canadian, but *Aberdeen* by dialect (once only, from whom Irving defended me) ; etc. etc. ;—but of these I say nothing. Irving, though they made his House-element and Life-element continually muddy for him, was endlessly patient with them all.

This my first visit to London, lasted, with interruptions, from early June 1824 till [end of February] 1825 ; during which I repeatedly lodged for a little while at Irving's, his house ever open to me like a brother's ; but cannot now recollect the times or their circumstances. The above recollections extend vaguely over the whole period,—during the last four or five months of which I had my own rooms in a Southampton Street near by, and was still in almost constant familiarity. My own situation was very wretched,—primarily from a state of health, which nobody could be expected to understand, or sympathise with, and about which I had as much as possible to be silent. The accursed hag, *Dyspepsia*, had got me bitted and bridled ; and was ever striving to make my waking living Day a thing of ghastly Nightmares ! I resisted what I could ; never did yield or surrender to her ; but she kept my heart right heavy, my battle very sore and hopeless ;—one could not call it hope, but only desperate obstinacy, refusing to flinch, that animated me. " Obstinacy *as of ten mules*," I have sometimes called it since ;— but in candid truth there was something *worthily human* in it too ; and I have had through life, among my manifold unspeakable blessings, no other real bower-anchor to ride by in the rough seas. Human " obstinacy," grounded on real human faith and insight, is good and the *best*.

All was change, too, at this time, with me ; all uncertainty. Mrs. Buller, the bright, the ardent, airy, was a changeful lady ! The original program had been, We were all to shift to Cornwall ; live in some beautiful Buller cottage there was, about East Looe or West (on her eldest Brother-in-law's property) ; with this as a fixed thing, I had arrived in London, asking myself " What kind of thing will it be ? " It proved to have become already a thing all of the winds ;—gone like a dream of the night (by some " accident " or other) ! For four or five weeks coming, there was new scheme, followed always by newer and newest ; all of which (by some " accident " or other) proved successively inexecutable. Greatly to my annoyance and regret, as may be imagined. The only thing that did ever take effect was a shifting of Charles and me out to solitary lodgings at Kew

Green ;[1] an isolating of us two (*pro tempore*) over our lessons there.   One of the dreariest and uncomfortablest things to both of us ; lasted for about a fortnight,—till Charles (I suppose privately pleading) put an end to it, as intolerable, and useless both (for one *could* not " study," but only pretend to do it, in such an element !)   Other wild projects rose rapidly, rapidly vanished futile ; the end was, in a week or two after, I deliberately counselled that Charles should go direct for Cambridge next term, in the meantime making ready under some fit College " grinder ; " I myself, not without regret, taking leave of the enterprise.   Which proposal, after some affectionate resistance on the part of Charles, was at length (rather suddenly, I recollect) acceded to by the elder people ;—and, one bright summer morning (still vivid to me), I stept out of a house in Foley Place, with polite *farewell* sounding through me ; and the thought as I walked along Regent Street, That here I was without employment henceforth.   Money was no longer quite wanting ; enough of money for some years to come : but the question, What to do next ? was not a little embarrassing, and indeed was intrinsically abstruse enough.

I must have been lodging again with Irving when this finale came : I recollect, Charles Buller and I, a day or some days after quitting Kew, had rendezvoused by appointment in Regent *Square* (St. Pancras), where Irving and a great company were laying the foundation of the " Caledonian Chapel " (which still stands there), and Irving of course had to deliver an Address. Of the Address, which was going on when we arrived, I could hear nothing, such the confusing crowd and the unfavourable locality (a muddy chaos of rubbish and excavations, Irving and the actors shut off from us by a circle of rude bricklayers' planks); but I well remember Irving's glowing face, streaming hair, and deeply-moved tones, as he spoke ;—and withal that Charles Buller brought me some new futility of a Proposal, and how sad he looked, good youth, when I had directly to reply with " No, alas I cannot, Charles ! "—This was but a few days before the Buller finale.—

Twenty years after, riding discursively towards Tottenham, one summer evening, with the breath of the wind from Northward, and London hanging to my right hand, like a grim and vast sierra, I saw among the peaks, easily ascertainable, the high minarets of that Chapel ; and thought with myself, " Ah, you fatal *tombstone* of my lost Friend ; and did a soul so strong and

[1] In June 1824.

high avail only to build you ! "—and felt sad enough and rather angry in looking at the thing.

It was not many days after this of the Regent-Square Address, which was quickly followed by termination with the Bullers, that I found myself one bright Sunday morning [1] on the top of a swift Coach for Birmingham, with intent towards the " Mr. Badams " above mentioned, and a considerable visit there,— for health's sake mainly ! Badams and the Montagus had eagerly proposed and counselled this step ; Badams himself was so eager about it, and seemed so frank, cheery, ingenious and friendly a man, that I had listened to his pleadings with far more regard than usual in such a case, and without assenting had been seriously considering the proposal for some weeks before (during the Kew-Green seclusion and perhaps earlier) ; he was in London twice or thrice, while things hung in deliberation, and was each time, more eager and persuasive on me. In fine I had assented ; and was rolling along, through sunny England (the first considerable space I had yet seen of it), with really pleasant recognition of its fertile beauties, and air of long-continued cleanliness, contentment and well-being. Stony Stratford, Fenny Stratford, and the good people coming out of Church ; Coventry, etc. etc.: all this is still a picture. Our coach was of the swiftest in the world ; appointments perfect to a hair,—one and a half minutes the time allowed for changing horses ;—our coachman, in dress etc., resembled a " sporting *gentleman ;* " and scornfully called any groundling whom he disliked, " You Radical ! " for one symptom. I don't remember a finer ride,—as if on the Arrow of Abaris,[2] with lips shut and nothing to do but look. My reception at Ashsted (western end of Birmingham, not far from the great *Watt's* house of that name) and instalment in the Badams's domesticities must have well corresponded to my expectations, as I have now no memory of it : my visit in whole, which lasted for above three months, may be pronounced interesting, idle, pleasant, and successful, though singular.

Apart from the nimbus of Montagu romance in the first accounts I had got of Badams, he was a gifted, amiable and remarkable man,—who proved altogether friendly, beneficent, so far as he went with me ; and whose final history, had I time for it, would be tragical in its kind ! He was eldest boy of a

---

[1] July 1824.
[2] The flying arrow received from Apollo, on which Abaris, at his own will, sped through space.

well-doing but not opulent master-workman (Plumber, I think) in Warwick Town ; got marked for the ready talents he showed, especially for some Picture he had, on his own resources and unaided inventions, copied, in the Warwick-Castle Gallery, with " wonderful success " ;—and in fine, was taken hold of by the famous Dr. Parr and others of that vicinity, and lived some time as one of Parr's Scholars in Parr's House,—learning I know not what ; not taking very kindly to the *Æolic Digamma* department, I should apprehend ! He retained a kindly and respectful remembrance about this Trismegistus of the then Pedants ; but always in brief quizzical form. Having declared for Medicine, he was sent to Edinburgh College ; studied there, for one session or more ; but,—" being desirous to marry some beautiful lady-love " (said the Montagus), or otherwise determined on a shorter road to fortune,—he now cut loose from his patrons, and modestly planted himself in Birmingham, with purpose of turning to account some chemical ideas he had gathered in the Classes here ; rivalling of *French* green vitriol by purely *English* methods (" no *husks of grapes*, for you and your vitriol, ye English ; your vitriol only *half* the selling-price of ours ! "),— that I believe was it : and Badams had fairly succeeded in it, and in other branches of the colour business ; and had a modest manufactory, of twenty or fewer hands, and full of thrifty and curious ingenuity ; at the outer corner of which, fronting on two streets, was his modest but comfortable dwelling-house, where I now lived with him as guest. Simplicity, and a pure and direct aim at the essential (aim good, and generally success-ful),—that was our rule in this establishment ; which was, and continued, always innocently comfortable and home-like to me. The lowest floor, opening rearward on the manufactory, was exclusively given up to an excellent " Mrs. Barnet " (with husband and family of two) who, in perfection and in silence, kept house to us, her husband (whom Badams only tolerated for her sake) working out of doors among the twenty ; we lived in the two upper floors, entering from our street door, and wearing a modestly civilised air. Everything has still a living look to me in that place ; not even the bad —— (who never showed his badness) but has claims on me ; still more the vener-able lean and brown old " *Grandfather* Barnet," who used to go " for our Letters," and hardly ever *spoke* except by his fine and mournful old *eyes :* these Barnets, with the workmen generally, and their quiet steady ways, were pleasant to observe ;—but especially our excellent, sad, pure and silent Mrs. Barnet, correct

as an eight-day clock, and making hardly as much noise!
Always dressed in modest black ; tall, clean, well-looking, light
of foot and hand ; she was much loved by Badams as a friend of
his Mother's, and a woman of real worth, bearing well a heavy
enough load of sorrows (chronic " disease of the heart," to crown
them, he would add). I remember the sight of her, on after-
noons, in some lighted closet there was, cutting out the bit of
bread for her children's luncheon, two clean pretty little girls,
who stood looking up with hope ; her silence, and theirs, and the
fine human relation between them,—as one of my pleasant
glimpses into English humble life. The younger of these pretty
children died within few years ; the elder, " *Bessy* Barnet," a
creature of distinguished qualities who has had intricate vicissitudes, and fortunate escapes, staid with us here, as our first
servant (servant and friend both in one) for about a year ; then
went home ; and, after long and complete disappearance from
our thoughts and affairs, re-emerged, most modestly triumphant,
not very long ago, as Wife of the accomplished Dr. ―― of St.
Leonards,—in which capacity she showed a generous exaggerated " gratitude " to her old Mistress and me, and set herself
and her Husband unweariedly to help, in that our sad St.
Leonards' season of woe and toil, which has now ended in eternal
peace to One of us, and cannot, nor can Dr. ――'s and his
" Bessy's " kindness in it, ever be forgotten while the Other of
us still lingers here !—Ah me, ah me !—

My Birmingham visit, except as it continually kept me riding
about in the open air, did nothing for me in the anti-dyspeptic
way ; but in the social and spiritually consolatory way, it was
really of benefit. Badams was a horse-fancier, skilful on horseback ; kept a choice two-or-three of horses here ; and, in theory,
professed the obligation to " ride for health," but very seldom
by himself did it,—it was always along with me, and not tenth-
part so often as I, during this sojourn. With me red " Taffy,"
the briskest of Welsh Ponies, went galloping daily far and wide,
unless I were still better mounted (for exercise to the other high-
going sort) ; and many were the pleasant rides I had in these
Warwickshire lanes and heaths, and real good they did me,—
if Badams's medicinal and dietetic formalities (to which I strictly
conformed) did me little or none. His unaffected kindness, and
cheerful human sociality and friendliness, manifest at all times,
could not but be of use to me, too. Seldom have I seen a franker,
trustier, cheerier form of human kindliness than Badams's ;—
how I remember the laughing eyes and sunny figure of him,

breaking into my room on mornings, himself half-dressed (*waist-band in hand*, was a common aspect, and hair all flying):
" What ? Not up yet,—monster ! " The smile of his eyes,
the sound of his voice, were so bright and practically *true*, on
these occasions.   A tight middle-sized handsome kind of man ;
eyes blue, sparkling, soft, nose and other features inclining to
the pointed,—complexion, which was the weak part, tending
rather to bluish, face always shaven bare, and no whiskers
left : a man full of hope, full of natural intellect, ingenuity,
invention ; essentially a gentleman ; and really looked well,
and jauntily aristocratic, when dressed for riding, or the like,
which was always a careful preliminary.   Slight rusticity of
accent rather did him good ; so prompt, mildly emphatic and
expressive were the words that came from him.   His faults were
a too sanguine temper, and a defective inner *sternness* of *veracity* :
—true he was, but not sternly enough, and would listen to
Imagination and delusive Hope, when Fact said No :—for which
two faults, partly recognisable to me even then, I little expected
he would by and by pay so dear !

We had a pleasant time together ; many pleasant summer
rides and out-door talks and in ;—to Guy's Cliff, Warwick Castle,
Sutton Coldfield, Kenilworth, etc., on holidays ; or miscellaneously over the furzy heaths, and leafy ruralities in common
evenings : I remember well a ride we made to Kenilworth, one
Saturday afternoon, by the " Wood of Arden " and its monstrous
old Oaks, on to the famous Ruin itself (*fresh* in the Scott Novels
then), and a big jolly Farmer friend of Badams's, who lodged us,
nice polite Wife and he, in a finely human way, till Monday
morning,—with much talk about " Old Parr," [1] in whose Parish,
Hatton, we then were : Old Parr would have been desirabler
to me than the great old Ruin (now mainly a skeleton, part of
it a coarse farmhouse, which was the most interesting part) ;
but Badams didn't propose a call on his old Pedant Friend, and
I could not be said to regret the omission (a saving of so much
trouble withal) : there was a sort of pride felt in their Dr. Parr
over all this region ; yet everybody seemed to consider him a
ridiculous old fellow, whose strength of intellect was mainly
gone to self-will and fantasticality ; they all mimicked his *lisp*,
and talked of his wig and tobacco-pipe (" No pipe, no Parr ! "
his avowed principle when asked to dinner among fine people).
The old man came to Edinburgh on a visit to Dr. Gregory,

1 Samuel Parr, born 1747, died 1825 ; nicknamed " Old Parr " after
Thomas Parr who died in 1635 and was reported to be 152 years old.

perhaps the very next year ; and there too, for a year following, there lingered tradition of good-natured grins and gossip, which one heard of : but the man himself I never saw, nor, though rather liking him, sensibly cared to see.

Another memorable gallop (we always went at galloping or cantering pace, and Badams was proud of his cattle and their really great prowess) was one morning out to Hagley ; to the "top of the Clent Hill," for a view, after breakfasting at Hagley Tap, and then return. Distance from Birmingham is about seventeen miles ; " The Leasowes " (Poet Shenstone's Place) is about midway (visible enough, to left, in the level sun-rays, as you gallop *out*) ; after which comes a singular *Terra di Lavoro*, or wholly Metallic Country, Hales Owen the heart of it,—thick along the wayside, little forges built of single-brick, hardly bigger than sentry-boxes, and in each of them, with bellows, stake and hammer, a woman busy making nails ; fine tall young women, several of them, old others, but all in clean aprons, clean white calico-jackets (must have been *Monday* morning) their look industrious and patient ;—seems as if all the nails of the world were getting made here, on very unexpected terms ! Hales Owen itself had much sunk under the improved highway, but was cheerfully jingling, as we cantered through. Hagley Tap, and its quiet Green, was all our own ; not to be matched *out* of England. Lord Lyttelton's mansion I have ever since in my eye as a noble-looking place, when his now Lordship comes athwart me ; a rational, ruggedly considerate kind of man, whom I could have liked to see there (as he was good enough to wish), had there been a *Fortunatus' travelling-carpet* at my disposal. Smoke-pillars many, in a definite, straight or spiral shape,—the Dudley " Black Country," under favourable omens,—visible from " the top of ' the Clent Hill ' " ; after which, and the aristocratic roof-works, attics, and grand chimney-tops of Hagley mansion, the curtain quite drops.

Of persons also I met some notable, or quasi-notable. " Joe Parkes," then a small Birmingham Attorney, afterwards the famous Reform-Club ditto, was a visitor at Badams's in rare evenings ; a rather pleasant talking, shrewd enough little fellow, with bad teeth, and a knowing lightly satirical way ;—whom Badams thought little of, but tolerated for his (Joe's) Mother's sake, as he did Parkes Senior, who was her second husband. The famous Joe I never saw again, though hearing often of his preferments, performances and him,—till he died, not long since ; " writing a new *Discovery of Junius*," it was rumoured ;

fit enough task for such a man. Bessy Parkes (of " the Rights
of Women ") is a daughter of his.   There were Phipsons, too,
" Unitarian people," very good to me : a young fellow of them,
still young though become a Pin Manufacturer, had been at
Erlangen University, and could float along in light airy anecdotic
fashion, by a time ;—he re-emerged on me four or five years ago,
living at Putney, head grown white from red, but heart still
light ; introducing a Chemical Son of his, whom I thought not
unlikely to push himself in the world by that course.   Kennedy
(of Cambridge) afterwards great as " Master of Shrewsbury
School," was polite to me, but unproductive.   Others—But
why should I speak of them at all ?   Accidentally one Sunday
evening I heard the famous " Dr. Hall " (of Leicester) preach :
a flabby puffy, but massy, earnest forcible-looking man (' *homme
alors célèbre* ' !) ; Sermon extempore, text, " God who cannot
lie : "—he proved beyond shadow of doubt, in a really forcible
but most superfluous way, that God never lied (' had no need to
do it,' etc., etc.) : " As good prove that God never fought a
duel ! " sniffed Badams, on my reporting at home.

" Jemmy Belcher " was a smirking little dumpy Unitarian
Bookseller, in the Bull-ring ; regarded as a kind of curiosity
and favourite among these people, and had seen me : one
showery day I took shelter in his shop ; picked up a new
Magazine,—found in it a cleverish and completely hostile
criticism of my *Wilhelm Meister*, of my Goethe and Self, etc. ;
read it faithfully to the end, and have never set eye on it since.
On stepping out, my bad spirits did not feel much elevated by
the dose just swallowed : but I thought with myself, " This
man is perhaps right on some points ; if so, let him be
admonitory ! "   And he was so (on a *Scotticism* or perhaps
two) ;—and I did reasonably soon (in not above a couple of
hours) dismiss him to the Devil, or to Jericho, as an ill-given
*un*serviceable kind of Entity in my course through this world.
It was De Quincey, as I often enough heard afterwards from
foolish talking persons :—" what matter who, ye foolish *talking*
persons ? " would have been my *silent* answer, as it generally
pretty much was :—I recollect too, how, in Edinburgh, a year or
two after, poor De Quincey, whom I wished to know, was reported
to tremble at the thought of such a thing ; and did fly pale as
ashes, poor little soul, the first time we actually met.   He was
a pretty little creature, full of wire-drawn ingenuities ; bankrupt enthusiasms, bankrupt pride ; with the finest silver-toned
low voice, and most elaborate gently-winding courtesies and

ingenuities in conversation : " What wouldn't one give to have him in a Box, and take him out to talk ! " (That was *Her* criticism of him ; and it was right good.) A bright, ready and melodious talker ; but in the end an inconclusive and long-winded. One of the smallest man-figures I ever saw ; shaped like a pair of tongs ; and hardly above five feet in all : when he sat, you would have taken him, by candlelight, for the beauti-fullest little Child ; blue-eyed, blonde-haired, sparkling face,—had there not been a something too, which said, " *Eccovi*, this Child has been in Hell ! " After leaving Edinburgh, I never saw him, hardly ever heard of him. His fate,—owing to opium etc.,—was hard and sore ; poor fine-strung, weak creature, launched *so* into the " Literary " career of ambition, and mother of dead-dogs.—That peculiar kind of " meeting " with him was among the phenomena of my then Birmingham (" Brom-wich-ham," *Brumagem*, as you were forced to call it).

Irving himself once, perhaps twice, came to us ; in respect of a " Scotch Chapel " newly set on foot there, and rather in tottering condition ; Preacher in it one Crosbie, whom I had seen once at Glasgow in Dr. Chalmers's, a silent guest along with me ; whose chief characteristic here was helpless dispiritment, under *dyspepsia* which had come upon him, hapless innocent lazy soul. The people were very kind to him ; but he was help-less,—and I think, soon after me, went away. What became of the Chapel since, I didn't hear. The Rev. Mr. Martin of Kirk-caldy, with his Reverend Father, and perhaps a Sister, passed through Birmingham ; bound for London, to christen some new child of Irving's ; and, being received in a kind of gala by those Scotch-Chapel people, caused me a noisy not pleasant day. Another day, positively painful, though otherwise instructive, I had, in the Dudley " Black Country " (which I had once seen from the distance), roving about among the coal-and-metal mines there,—in company or neighbourhood of Mr. Airy, now " Astronomer Royal," whom I have never seen since. Our party was but of four : some opulent retired Dissenting Minister had decided on a holiday ovation to Airy, who had just issued from Cambridge, as a Trismegistus, chief of Wranglers, and mathematical wonder ; and had come to Birmingham, on visit to some footlicker whose people lived there : " I will show Trismegistus Airy our Mine-Country," said the Reverend old Friend of Enlightenment ; " and Mr. G——, Airy footlicker, shall accompany ! " That was his happy thought ;—and Badams, hearing of it from him, had suggested me (not quite unknown to him) as a fourth figure. I was ill in health; but thought it right to go. We inspected blast furnaces, descended into coal-mines; poked about industriously into Nature's and Art's sooty arcana, all day (with a short recess for luncheon), and returned at night, in the Reverend's postchaise,—thoroughly wearied and disgusted, one of us at least. Nature's sooty arcana were welcome and even pleasant to me, Art's also more or less: —thus, in the belly of the deepest mine, climbing over a huge jingle of new-loosened coal, there met me on the very summit a pair of small cheerful human *eyes* (face there was none discernible at first, so totally black was *it*, and so dim were our candles); then a ditto ditto of *lips* internally red; which I perceived, with a comic interest, were begging beer from me! Nor was Airy himself in the least an offence, or indeed sensibly a concern. A hardy little figure, of edacious energetic physiognomy, eyes hard, if strong, not fine; seemed three or four years younger than I; and to be, in secret, serenely, not insolently, enjoying his glory, which I made him right welcome to do, on those terms. In fact, he and I hardly spoke together twice or thrice; and had as good as no relation to each other. The old Reverend had taken possession of Airy, and was all day at his elbow. And to me, fatal allotment, had fallen the "Footlicker," one of the foolishest, conceited ever-babbling blockheads I can remember to have met. What a day of *boring* (not of the mine strata only)! I felt as if driven half-crazy; and mark it to this hour with *coal*!

But enough, and far more, of *my* Birmingham reminiscences! Irving himself had been with us; Badams was every few weeks up in London for a day or two; Mrs. Strachey too, sometimes wrote to me: London was still in a sense my head-quarters. Early in September (it must have been), I took kind leave of Badams and his daily kind influences,—hoping, both of us, it might be only temporary leave;—and revisited London; at least, passed through it, to Dover and the Sea-Coast; where Mrs. Strachey had contrived a fine Sea-party, to consist of herself with appendages, of the Irvings and of me, for a few bright weeks! I remember a tiny bit of my journey, solitary on the coach-roof, between Canterbury and Bridge: nothing else whatever of person or of place from Birmingham to that, nor anything immediately onwards from that!—The Irvings had a dim but snuggish house rented, in some street near the shore, and I was to lodge with them; Mrs. Strachey was in a brighter place near by; detached new *row*, called *Liverpool Terrace* at that time (now buried among streets, and hardly discoverable by me last Autumn, when I pilgrimed thither again after forty-two years!). Mrs. Strachey had Kitty with her ; and was soon expecting her Husband. Both households were in full action, or daily getting into it, when I arrived.[1]

We walked together, all of us together sometimes, at other times in threes or twos ; we dined after at Mrs. Strachey's ; read commonly in the evenings at Irving's, Irving *reader*,—in Phineas Fletcher's *Purple Island* for one thing ; over which Irving strove to be solemn, and Kitty and I rather *not*, throwing in now and then a little spice of laughter and quiz. I never saw the book again ; nor, in spite of some real worth it had, and of much half-real laudation, cared greatly to see it. Mrs. Strachey, I suspect, didn't find the Sea-party so idyllic as her forecast of it ; in a fortnight or so, Strachey came, and then there was a new and far livelier element of Anti-humbug, Anti-*ennui*, which could not improve matters. She determined on sending Strachey, Kitty and me off on a visit to Paris for ten days, and having the Irvings all to herself. We went accordingly ; saw Paris, saw a bit of France, nothing like so common a feat as now ; and the memory of that is still almost complete, if that were a legitimate part of my subject.

The journey out,—weather fine, and novelty awaiting young curiosity at every step,—was very pleasant. Montreuil, Noailles, Abbeville, Beauvais : interesting names start into facts ; Sterne's *Sentimental Journey* (especially) is alive in one from the first stage onwards,—at Nampont, on the dirty little street, you almost expect to see the Dead Ass lying! Our second night was at Beauvais : glimpse of the old Cathedral next morning went for nothing (*was* in fact nothing to me) ; but the glimpse I had had, the night before, as we drove in this way, of the *Coffee-house* near by, and in it no company but one tall, sashy, epauletted, well-dressed Officer striding dismally to and fro, was, and still is, impressive on me, as an almost unrivalled image of human *ennui*. I rode usually outside ; fair Kitty sometimes, and Strachey oftener, sitting by me,—on the hindward seat : carriage, I think, was Kitty's own, and except her maid we had no servants. Postilion could not tell me where " *Crécy* " was, when we were in the neighbourhood. Country in itself, till near Paris, ugly ; but all gilded with the light of young lively wonder. Little scrubby Boys, playing at ball, on their scrubby patch of Parish-green, how strange! " *Charité,*

[1] This is a mistake. Miss Kirkpatrick, the Irvings and **Carlyle** were all at Dover for some time before the Stracheys arrived.

Madame, pour une pauvre misérable ; qu'elle en a bien besoin ! "
sang the poor lame beggar girl, at the carriage door. None of
us spoke French well ; Strachey's grew ever worse as we proceeded ; and at length was quite an amusement to hear. At
Paris he gave it up altogether ; and would speak nothing but
English ; which, aided by his vivid looks and gestures, he found,
in shops and the like, to answer much better. " *Quelque chose à
boire, Monsieur !* " said a respectful exceptional Postilion at
the Coach-window, before quitting, " *Nong, vous avez drivé
devilish slow !* " answered Strachey readily, in a positive half-
quizzing tone. This was on the way home :—followed by a
storm of laughter on our part, and an angry blush on the
Postilion's.

From about Montmorency (with the Shadow of Rousseau !)
—especially from St. Denis, to Paris, the drive was quite beautiful, and full of interesting expectation. Magnificent broad
highway, great old trees and then potherb gardens on each hand ;
all silent too, in the brilliant October afternoon, hardly one
vehicle or person met,—till, on mounting the shoulder of Mont-
martre, an iron-gate, and *douanier* with his brief question before
opening, and Paris wholly and at once lay at our feet. A huge
bowl, or deepish *saucer* of seven miles in diameter, not a breath
of smoke or dimness anywhere, every roof and dome and spire
and chimney-top clearly visible, and the skylights sparkling
like diamonds : I have never, since or before, seen so fine a
view of a Town. I think the fair Miss Kitty was sitting by me ;
but the curious *speckled straw-hats* and costumes and physiogno-
mies of the Faubourg St. (*Fashionable*—I forget it at this
moment !) are the memorablest circumstance to me. We
alighted in the Rue de la Paix (clean and good Hôtel, not now
a Hôtel) ; admired our rooms all covered with mirror, our
grates, or grate-*backs*, each with a *Cupidon* cast on it ;—and
roved about the Boulevards, in a happy humour, till sunset or
later. Decidedly later, in the still dusk, I remember sitting
down, in the Place Vendôme, on the steps of the Column there,
to smoke a cigar ; hardly had I arranged myself, when a bustle
of military was heard round me : clean, trim, handsome soldiers,
blue-and-white, ranked themselves in some quotity, drummers
and drums especially faultless ; and after a *Shoulder Arms* or
so, marched off in parties, drums fiercely and finely clangouring
their *ran-tan-plan ;*—setting the watch or watches of this human
city, as I understood it. " Ha, my tight little fellows in blue,
you also have got drums, then ; none better ;—and all the world

is of kin, whether it all agree or not ! " was my childlike reflection, as I silently looked on.

Paris proved vastly entertaining to me ; ' walking about the streets would, of itself ' (as Gray the poet says), ' have amused me for weeks.' I met two young Irishmen, who had seen me once at Irving's ; who were excellent *ciceroni*. They were on their way to " the Liberation of Greece ; " a totally wild-goose errand, as then seemed to me,—and as perhaps they themselves secretly guessed,—but which entitled them to call on everybody for an " autograph to our album," their main employment just now. They were clever enough young fellows ; and soon came home again out of Greece : the considerably taller and cleverer, black-haired and with a strong Irish accent, was called Tennent, whom I never saw again ; the milky, smaller blondine figure, cousin to him, was Emerson,—whom I met twenty-five years afterwards, at Allan Cunningham's, as *Sir* Emerson *Tennent*,[1] late Governor of Ceylon ; and complimented, simpleton that I was, on the now finely *brown* colour of his *hair !* We have not met since. There was also, of their acquaintance, a pleasant Mr. Malcolm, " Ex-Lieutenant of the *Forty-second ;* " native of the Orkney Islands, only son of a Clergyman there ; who, as a young ardent lad, had joined Wellington's Army at the *Siege of St. Sebastian,* and got badly wounded, lame for life, at the *Battle of Thoulouse* that same season. Peace coming, he was invalided on half-pay ; and now lived with his widowed mother, in some clean upper-floor in Edinburgh, on frugal, kind and pretty terms, hanging loosely by Literature, for which he had some talent. We used to see him in Edinburgh, with pleasure and favour, on setting up our own poor Household there. He was an amiable, intelligent little fellow ; of lively talk and speculation, always cheerful, and with a traceable vein of humour, and of pathos withal (there being much of sadness and affection hidden in him),—all kept, as his natural voice was, in a fine *low* melodious tone. He wrote, in Periodicals, ' Annuals ' and the like vehicles, really pretty verses ; and was by degrees establishing something like a real reputation, which might have risen higher and higher, in that kind : but his wound still hung about him ; and he soon died,—a year or two after our quitting Edinburgh, which was the last we saw of him : his mother we had never seen.

---

[1] There is a trifling error here. Allan Cunningham was not alive " twenty-five years afterwards " (died 1842).—Emerson Tennent died in 1869, aged 65.

Poor little Malcolm, he quietly loved his mother very much, his vanished father too ; and had pieties and purities, very alien to the wild reckless ways, of practice and of theory, which the Army had led him into ! Most of his army habitudes (with one private exception, I think, nearly *all*) he had successfully washed off from him ; to the reprobate ' theories ' he had never been but heartily abhorrent. "No God, I tell you ;—and will prove it to you on the spot ! " said some elder blackguard Lieutenant, among a group of them, in their tent one evening (a Hanoverian, if I recollect) : "On the spot ; none ! "—"How then ? " exclaimed Ensign Malcolm much shocked. The Hanoverian lifted his canteen, turned the bottom of it up, "Empty, you see ; we have no more rum : " then holding it aloft into the air, said, in a tone of request, "Fill us that ; " paused an instant, turned it bottom up, empty still ; and with a victorious glance at his companions, set it down again, as a thing that spoke for itself. This was one of Malcolm's war-experiences ; of which he could pleasantly report a great many. These, and the physical agonies and horrors witnessed and felt, had given him a complete disgust for War. He could not walk far, always had a marked halt in walking ; but was otherwise my pleasantest companion in Paris.

Poor *Louis Dix-huit* had been "lying in state," as we passed through St. Denis ; Paris was all plastered with placards, ' *Le Roi est mort, vive le Roi !* '—announcing, from Châteaubriand, a Pamphlet of that title. I made no effort to see Châteaubriand; did not see his Pamphlet either : in the Streets, Galleries, *Cafés* I had enough and to spare. Washington Irving was said to be in Paris ; a kind of lion at that time, whose Books I somewhat esteemed : one day the Emerson Tennent people bragged that they had engaged him to breakfast with us at a certain *Café*, next morning ; we all attended duly, Strachey among the rest ; but no Washington came,—"Couldn't rightly come," said Malcolm to me in a judicious *aside*, as we cheerfully break-fasted without him. I never saw Washington at all, but still have a mild esteem of the good man. To the Louvre Gallery alone or accompanied, I went often ; got rather faintish good of the Pictures there, but at least no *harm*,—being mute and deaf on the subject. Sir Peter Laurie came on me there one day ; took me to dinner, and plenty of hard-headed London talk. Another day, nobody with me and very few in the Gallery at all, there suddenly came storming past, with dishevelled hair, and large besoms in their hand, which they shoved out on any bit of paper or the like, a row of wild Savoyards, distractedly proclaiming, " Le Roi ! " " Le Roi ! " and almost oversetting people, in their fierce speed to clear the way. Le Roi, *Charles Dix* in person, soon appeared accordingly with three or four attendants ; very ugly people, especially one of them (who had blear-eyes and small bottle-nose, never identifiable to my inquiries since),—Charles himself was a swart, slightish insipid-looking man, but with much the air of a gentleman ; insipidly endeavouring to smile, and be popular, as he walked past ; sparse public indifferent to him, and silent nearly all. I had a real sympathy with the poor gentleman, but could not bring up the least *Vive le Roi*, in the circumstances ! We understood he was going to look at a certain Picture, or Painting now on the easel, in a room at the very end (*entrance*-end) of the Gallery, which one had often enough seen, generally with profane mockery if with any feeling ; Picture of or belonging to the Birth or Baptism of what they called " the Child of Miracle " (the assassinated Duc de Berri's posthumous child, *hodie* " Henri V. *in partibus* "),—Picture as yet distressingly ugly ; mostly in a smear of dead-colours, brown and even green, and with a kind of horror in the subject of it as well. How tragical are men, once more ;—how merciless withal to one another ! I had not the least real *pity* for *Charles Dix's* pious pilgriming to such an object ;—the poor *Mother* of it, and her immense hopes and pains, I did not even think of then. This was all I ever saw of the Legitimate Bourbon Line ; with which, and its tragedies, I was to have more concern within the next ten years.

My reminiscences of Paris, and its old aspects and localities, were of visible use to me in writing of the *Revolution* by and by ; the rest could only be reckoned under the head of amusement, but had its vague profits withal, and still has. Old Legendre,[1] the Mathematician (whose *Geometry* I had translated in Edinburgh) was the only man of real note with whom I exchanged a few words. A tall, bony, gray, old man ; who received me with dignity and kindness ; introduced me to his Niece, a brisk little brown gentlewoman who kept house for him ; asked about my stay here, and finding I was just about to go, answered " *Diantre !* " with an obliging air of regret : his rugged, sagacious, sad and stoical old face is still dimly present with me. At a meeting of the *Institut* I saw, and well remember, the figure of Trismegistus Laplace ; the skirt of his long blue-silk *dressing-*

[1] Adrien Marie Legendre, born 1752, died 1833.

gown (such his costume, unique in the place, his age and his fame being also unique) even touched me as he passed, on the session's rising.   He was tall, thin, clean, serene ; his face, perfectly smooth as a healthy man of fifty's, bespoke intelligence keen and ardent, rather than deep or great ; in the eyes was a dreamy smile, with something of pathos in it and perhaps something of contempt.   The session itself was profoundly stupid ; some lout of a Provincial reading about *Vers à Soie,*—and big Vauquelin the chemist (noticed by me) fallen sound asleep.   Strachey and I went one evening to call upon a M. de Chézy,[1] Professor of *Persic,* with whom he, or his brother and he, had communicated while in India.   We found him high aloft ; but in a clean snug apartment ; burly, hearty, glad enough to see us ;—only that Strachey would speak no French ; and introduced himself with some shrill-sounding sentence, the first word of which was clearly " *Salaam !* "   Chézy tried lamely, for a pass or two, what Persian he could muster ; but hastened to get out of it,—and to talk even to me who owned to a little French, since Strachey would own to none.   We had rather an amusing twenty minutes; Chézy a glowing and very emphatic man :—" *ce hideux reptile de Langlès,*" was a phrase he had once used to Strachey's Brother, of his chief French rival in the Persic field !—I heard Cuvier lecture, one day : fine strong German kind of face ; ditto intelligence, as manifested in the Lecture ; which reminded me of one of old Dr. Gregory's in Edinburgh.   I was at a sermon in Ste. Géneviève's, main audience 500 or so of serving-maids, preacher a dizened fool, in *hourglass* hat, who ran to and fro in his balcony or pulpit, and seemed much contented with himself ; heard another foolish preacher, Protestant, at the *Oratoire* (" *Console-toi, O France !* " on the death of *Louis Dix-huit*) ;— looked silently into The *Morgue* one morning (infinitely better *Sermon,* that stern old grayhaired Corpse lying there !) ;[2] looked into the Hôtel-Dieu, and its poor sick-beds, once ; was much in the Pont-Neuf region (*on tond les chiens et coupe les chats, et va en ville,* etc. etc.), much in the Palais Royal and adjacencies ;— and, the night before leaving, found I ought to visit one Theatre ; and, by happy accident, came upon Talma playing there.   A heavy shortish numb-footed man ; face like a warming-pan for size, and with a strange most ponderous yet delicate expression in the big dull-glowing black eyes and it : incomparably the best

---

[1] Antoine Léonard de Chézy, Professor of *Sanskrit,* Collège de France, born 1773, died 1832.   Langlès was Professor of *Persic.*
[2] See *Early Letters of Thomas Carlyle* (Macmillan and Co., 1886), ii, 282.

actor I ever saw. Play was *Œdipe* (Voltaire's very *first*) ; place the *Théâtre Français :* Talma died within about a year after.[1]

Of the journey home I can remember nothing but the French part,—if any part of it were worth remembering :—at Dover I must still have found the Irvings ;[2] and poor outskirts, and insignificant fractions, of solitary Dialogues on the Kent shore (far inferior to our old *Fife* ones!) have not yet entirely vanished: *e.g.* strolling together on the beach, one evening, we had repeatedly passed at some distance certain building operations ; upon which, by and by, the bricklayers seemed to be getting into much vivacity,—crowding round the last gable-top, in fact, just about finishing their House there. Irving grasped my arm, said in a low tone of serious emotion : " See, they are going to bring out their topstone with shouting ! " I inquired of a poor man, what it was ; " You see, Sir, they gets allowance of beer," answered he ; that was all, a silent deglutition of some beer ! Irving sank from his Scriptural altitudes ; I, no doubt, profanely laughing rather. There are other lingering films of this sort, but I can give them no date, of before or after : and find nothing quite distinct till that of our posting up to London ; I should say, of the Stracheys posting, who took me as guest,—the Irvings *being* now clearly gone. Canterbury and the Shrine of St. Thomas I did see ; but it must have been before. We had a pleasant drive throughout, weather still sunny though cool ; and about nine or ten P.M., of the second day, I was set down at a little Tavern on Shooter's Hill ; where some London Mail or Diligence soon picked me up (fare one shilling, transaction then very common), and speedily landed me within reach of hospitable Pentonville (4 Myddelton Terrace there), which gave me a welcome like itself. There I must have staid a few days, and not above a few.

I was now again in London (probably about the middle of November) ;[3] hither after much sad musing and moping I had decided on returning for another while. My wretched *Schiller* (of which I felt then the intrinsic wretchedness, or utter *leanness* and commonplace) was to be stitched together from the *London Magazine,* and put forth with some trimmings and additions as a Book :—" £100 for it, on publication in that shape " (*zero* till then) ; that was the bargain made ; and I had come to fulfil

[1] 19th October 1826.

[2] The trip lasted only twelve days. They returned to Dover 6th November 1824 ; the Irvings were not there ; had left for London " only a few hours before."

[3] Arrived in London on the 9th November.

that,—almost more uncertain than ever about all beyond that.
I soon got lodgings in Southampton Street, Islington, in Irving's
vicinity ; and did henceforth, with my best diligence, endeavour
to fulfil that,—at a far slower rate than I had expected.   I
frequently called on Irving (he never or not often on me, which
I did not take amiss), and frequently saw him otherwise : but
have already written down miscellaneously most of the remembrances that belong to this specific date of months.   On the
whole, I think now, he felt a good deal unhappy ; probably
getting deeper and deeper sunk, in manifold cares of his own ;
and that our communication had not the old copiousness and
flowing freedom, nay that even since I left for Birmingham
there was perhaps a diminution.   London " Pulpit Popularity "
the smoke of that foul witch's cauldron ;—there never was anything else to blame !   I stuck rigorously to my work, to my
Badams regimen : though it did little for me : I was sick of
body and of mind, in endless dubiety, very desolate and miserable ; and the case itself, since nobody could help, admonished
me to silence.   One day, on the road down to Battle-Bridge, I
remember recognising Irving's broad hat, atop, amid the tide
of passengers, and his little child sitting on his arm : Wife
probably near by,—" Why should *I* hurry up ; they are parted
from me, the old days are no more ! " was my sad reflection
in my sad humour.

Another morning, what was wholesomer and better, happening
to notice, as I stood looking out on the bit of green under my
bedroom window, a trim and rather pretty Hen actively paddling
about and picking up what food might be discoverable : " See,"
I said to myself ; " look, thou fool ! Here is a two-legged
creature with scarcely half a thimbleful of poor brains ; thou
call'st thyself a man, with nobody knows how much brain, and
reason etc. dwelling in it ; and behold, how the one *life* is
regulated, and how the other ! In God's name, concentrate,
collect, whatever of ' reason ' thou hast, and direct it on the one
thing needful ! "—Irving, when we did get into intimate dialogue, was affectionate to me as ever ; and had, as always to
the end, a great deal of practical sense, and insight into things
about him : but he could not much help me ; how could anybody but myself ? By degrees I was doing so ; taking counsel
of that *Symbolic* HEN !—and settling a good few things : first
and most of all, That I would, renouncing ambitions, " fine
openings," and the advice of all bystanders, and friends *who
didn't know, go home* to Annandale, were this work done ; pro-

vide myself a place where I could ride, follow regimen, and be free of *noises* (which were unendurable), till if possible I could recover a little health. Much followed out of that ; all manner of adjustments gathering round it. As head of these latter, I had offered to let my Dearest be free of me, and of any virtual engagement she might think there was ; but she would not hear of it, not of that, the Noble Soul ; but stood resolved to share my dark lot along with me, be [it] what it might. Alas, her love was never known completely to me, and how celestial it was, till I had lost her ! " Oh for one five-minutes more of her," I have often said, since April last, " to tell her with what perfect love, and admiration as of the beautifullest of known human souls, I did intrinsically always regard her ! " But all minutes of the time are irrevocably past :—be wise, all ye living, and remember that time *passes* and does not return !—

I had, apart from regular work upon *Schiller*, a good deal of talking with people, and social moving about, which was not disagreeable. With Allan Cunningham I had made ready acquaintance ; a cheerful social man,—" solid Dumfries Mason, with a surface polish given him," was one good judge's definition, years afterwards ! He got at once *into Nithsdale* when you talked with him ; which, though clever and satirical, I didn't very much enjoy : Allan had sense and shrewdness on all points, especially the practical ; but, *out* of Nithsdale, except for his perennial good-humour, and quiet cautions (which might have been exemplary to me), was not instructive. I was at the christening of one of Allan's children, over in Irving's, where there was a cheery evening, and the Cunninghams to sleep there, one other of the Guests, a pleasant enough Yorkshire youth, going with me to a spare-room I could command. My commonest walk was fieldwards, or down into the City (by many different old lanes and routes) ; more rarely, by Portland Place (*Fitzroy Square* and Mrs. Strachey's, probably *first*), to Piccadilly and the West End. One muddy evening there came to me, what enlightened all the mirk and mud, ' by the Herren Grafen von Bentinck's ' (Servant), a short Letter from Goethe in Weimar ! [1] It was in answer to the copy of *Wilhelm Meister* which (doubt-less with some profoundly reverent bit of Note) I had despatched to him six months ago, without answer till now. He was kind, though distant, brief ; apologised, by his ' great age (*hohen Jahren*),' for the delay ; till at length the Herren Grafen von Bentinck's passage homewards had operated on him as a hint

[1] Middle of December 1824.

to do the needful,—' and likewise to procure for both parties,'
(Herren Grafen and Self !) ' an agreeable acquaintance ; ' of
which latter, naturally, neither I nor the Herren Grafen ever
heard more. Some twenty years afterwards a certain Lord
George Bentinck, whom newspapers called the " *stable* minded,"
from his previous *turf* propensities, suddenly quitting all these,
and taking to Statistics and Tory Politics, became famous or
noisy for a good few months, chiefly by intricate *Statistics* and
dull vehemence, so far as I could see ; a stupid enough phenomenon for me, till he suddenly died,[1] poor gentleman ;—I then
remembered that this was probably one of the Herren Grafen
von Bentinck, whose acquaintance I had missed, as above.

One day Irving took me with him on a curious little errand
he had. It was a bright Summer morning ; must therefore have
preceded the Birmingham and Dover period : his errand was
this. A certain loquacious extensive Glasgow *Publisher* (Dr.
Chalmers's, especially ; had been a schoolmaster, " Collins "
perhaps his name) was in London for several weeks on business ;
and often came to Irving,—wasting (as I rather used to think)
a good deal of his time, in zealous discourse about many vague
things ; in particular, about the villany of common Publishers ;
how, for example, on their " *Half-profits* System," they would
show the poor Author a Printer's Account pretending to be paid
in full, Printer's signature visibly appended,—Printer having
really touched a sum *less* by 25 per cent. ;—and *sic de cæteris ;*
all an arranged juggle, to cheat the poor Author, and sadly
convince him that his moiety of profit was nearly or altogether
zero divided by *two !* Irving could not believe it ; denied stoutly
on behalf of his own Printer, one Bensley, a noted man in his
craft ;—and getting nothing but negatory smiles, and kindly
but inexorable contradiction, said he would go next morning and
see. We walked along, somewhere Holborn-wards ; found
Bensley and Wife in a bright, quiet, comfortable room ; just
finishing breakfast ; a fattish, solid, rational and really amiable-
looking pair of people, especially the Wife, who had a fine,
plump, cheerfully experienced matronly air ;—by both of whom
we (i.e. Irving, for I had nothing to do but be silent) were warmly
and honourably welcomed, and constrained at least to sit since
we would do nothing better. Irving with grave courtesy laid
the case before Bensley (perhaps showed him his old signature
and account), and asked, If that was or was not really the sum
he had received ? Bensley, with body and face, writhed uneasily ;

1 1848.

evidently loth to lie, but evidently obliged by the laws of trade to do it. " Yes, on the whole, that was the sum ! " Upon which we directly went our ways,—both of us convinced, I believe, though only one of us said so. Irving had a high opinion of men ; and was always mortified when, in any instance, he found it no longer tenable.

Another time (this also was of the Ante-Birmingham time) we made an excursion with certain ornate City gentlemen called Jupp, father and three sons ; and had a day's boating, from London Bridge to Twickenham, perhaps to Teddington, and back ! The three young Jupps were fine handsome gentle- manly fellows, of City type ; so was Jupp senior, a veteran boater of renown, full of Thames " wit " and the like ; his house, in some cleanest, stillest brick-paved Court near Guildhall, where he held some lucrative office, was a picture of opulent comfort ; so was, or so had been, the good little plumpish elderly Mrs. Jupp, still rosy, though now wrinkly as well, and manifesting sickly maternal anxieties (of *anti*-boating kind), which Jupp senior promptly discomfited with gay City repartee as fast as they rose. One of the Sons had perhaps been at Cambridge ; at anyrate, the youngest of them, who much fell to my share, had a beautiful passion to go to some such place, as to the *summum bonum* of man ;—and there was with us, of their acquaintance, an actual Cantab, a pleasant polite little fellow, who talked intelligently with me upon College matters, and didn't row. My Scotch ' *Mea mater est mala sus* ' (which needs only two *commas* to make it perfectly respectful : ' Go, mother, the swine is eating the apples ') he could not interpret ; but said, Had it been pronounced in [the] English way, the last vowel of ' *meā* ' would have helped him. Legendre's *Geometry*, etc. he pretended to know, and didn't (being in fact weak on the mathe- matical side).—" Oh no, *not* translated, I assure you ! "—Upon which, " Bless you, Sir, I translated it myself ! " somewhat took him aback, and the tone on that string grew low enough. But the grand novelty was Jupp senior's wit, " *Mens tuus ego*," [1] when he took snuff ; and so on : he was very good-humoured and absurd ;—escorting me, out of the wherry, towards some Tavern (on an Island about Twickenham,—*leanish* kind of Tavern, nothing but tea in it), Jupp senior was spoken to, from a first- floor window, by one of his Sons : " Good Heavens ! " cried he, starting violently : " Speak ? I thought you were the Sign of the Saracen's Head ! "—it was 10 P.M. or so before we victoriously

---

[1] i.e. " Mind your eye ! "

" shot London Bridge," the perils of which feat had been an interjectional topic with our junior Jupps, but were to me, at that time, profoundly unknown and indifferent. Irving, during this whole day, had been passive, taciturn, kindly taking in the summer glories of land and river, and the human kindness of the Jupps ; but looking serious, pensive, almost sad, and preferring silence. The worship of these Jupps was hearty, but too evidently worth almost nothing. Worship as to a mere Katerfelto or thing wondered at : " See, how the people turn round on him ! " said the youngest Jupp to me, as we walked the streets. I never went boating more, nor probably did Irving : one time quite enough.[1]

Irving was sorrowfully occupied at this period, as I now perceive, in scanning and surveying the *wrong-side* of that immense Popularity, the outer or right side of which had been so splendid and had given rise to such sacred and glorious hopes. The crowd of people flocking round him continued, in abated, but still superabundant quantity and vivacity ; but it was not of the old high quality any more, the thought that Christian religion was again to dominate all minds, and the world to become an Eden by his humble thrice-blessed means, was fatally declaring itself to have been a dream. And he could not consent to believe it such ; never he ! That was the secret of his inward quasi-desperate resolutions, breaking out into the wild struggles, and clutchings, towards the unattainable, the unregainable, which were more and more conspicuous in the sequel. He was now, I gradually found, listening to certain Interpreters of Prophecy ; thinking to cast his own great faculty into that hopeless quagmire along with them. These and the like resolutions, and the dark humour which was the mother of them, had been on the growing hand, during all this first London visit of mine ; and were fast coming to outward development by the time I left for Scotland again.

About the beginning of March 1825, I had at length, after fierce struggling and various disappointments from the delay of others, got my poor business winded up ; *Schiller* published, paid for,—left to the natural neglect of mankind (which was perfect, so far as I ever heard, or much cared) ;—and, in humble, but condensed, resolute and quiet humour, was making my bits of packages, bidding my poor adieus, just in act to go. Everybody thought me headstrong and foolish ; Irving less so than

---

1 This unimportant paragraph, written on a *rider* (or attached slip) which had got displaced in the MS., was omitted in the first edition.

others, though he too could have no understanding of my dyspeptic miseries, my intolerable sufferings from *noises* etc. etc. He was always kind, and spoke hope, if personal topics turned up. Perhaps it was the very day before my departure, at least it is the last I recollect of him, we were walking in the streets, multifariously discoursing : a dim gray day, but dry and airy ; —at the corner of Cockspur Street, we paused for a moment, meeting " Sir John Sinclair " (*Statistical Account of Scotland*, etc. etc.), whom I had never seen before, and never saw again. A lean old man, tall but stooping, in tartan cloak ; face very wrinkly, nose blue ; physiognomy vague and with [*sic*] distinction (as one might have expected it to be) ; he spoke to Irving with benignant respect ; whether to me at all I don't recollect. A little farther on in Parliament Street, somewhere near the *Admiralty* (that now is, and perhaps then was), we ascended certain stairs, narrow, newish, wooden staircase the last of them, and came into a bare clean comfortless official little room (fire gone out), where an elderly official little gentleman was seated, within rails, busy in the red-tape line. This was the Honourable Something or other, great in Scripture Prophecy, in which he had started some sublime new idea, well worth prosecuting, as Irving had assured me. Their mutual greetings were cordial and respectful ; and a lively dialogue [ensued] on Prophetic matters, especially on the sublime new idea,—I strictly unparticipant, sitting silently apart till it were done. The Honourable Something had a look of perfect politeness, perfect silliness ; his face, heavily wrinkled, went smiling and shuttling about, at a wonderful rate, and in the smile there seemed to me to be lodged a frozen sorrow, as if bordering on craze. On coming out, I asked Irving, perhaps too markedly, " Do you really think that gentleman can throw any light to you on anything whatever ? " To which he answered, good-naturedly, but in a grave tone, " Yes, I do." Of which the fruits were seen before long. This is the last thing I can recollect of Irving in my London visit,—except perhaps some gray shadow of him giving me Farewell, with express " Blessing."

I paused some days at Birmingham ; got rich Gifts sent after me by Mrs. Strachey (beautiful desk, gold pencil, etc., which were soon *Another's*, ah me, and are still here !).[1]—I saw Manchester too, for the first time (strange *Bagman* ways, in the Palace Inn there),—walked to Oldham, savage-looking scene

---

[1] On one handle of the desk is engraved : THOMAS CARLYLE ; and on the other : LIBERTAS, VERITAS, PAUPERTAS.

of Sunday morning ; old schoolfellow of mine, very stupid but
very kind, being *Curate* there ; shot off, too, over the Yorkshire
Moors to Marsden, where another boy-and-College-friend of
mine was (George Johnston, since Surgeon in Gloucester) ; and
spent three dingy but impressive days in poking into those
mute wildernesses and their rough habitudes and populations.
At four o'clock, in my Palace Inn (Boots having forgotten me),
awoke by good luck of myself, and saved my place on the coach
roof.   Remember the Blackburns, Boltons and their smoke-
clouds, to right and to left, grimly black amid the gray March
winds.   Lancashire was not all smoky then, but only smoky
in parts.   Remember the Bush Inn at Carlisle, and quiet
luxurious shelter it yielded for the night ; much different from
now (" Betty, a pan o' *cooals !* " shouted the waiter, an Eskdale
man by dialect, and in five minutes the trim Betty had done her
feat, and your clean sleek bed was comfortably warm).   At
Ecclefechan, next day, within two miles or so of my Father's,
while the coach was changing horses, I noticed through the
window my little Sister Jean earnestly looking up for me ; she,
with Jenny the youngest of us all, was at School in the village ;
and had come out daily of late to inspect the coach in hope of
me ;—always in vain till this day : her bonny little blush, and
radiancy of look, when I let down the window and suddenly
disclosed myself, are still present to me.—In four days' time, I
now (2d December 1866) hope to see this brave *Jean* again (now
" Mrs. Aitken," from Dumfries, and a hardy, hearty Wife and
Mother) ; Jenny, poor little thing, has had her crosses and
difficulties, but has managed them well ; and now lives, contented
enough and industrious as ever, with Husband and three or
two daughters, in Hamilton, Canada West,—not far from which
are my Brother Alick too, and others dear to me.   Double,
double, toil and trouble,—such, with result or without it, are
our wanderings in this world !—

My poor little establishment at Hoddam Hill (close by the
" Tower of *Repentance*," [1] as if symbolically !) I do not mean to
speak of here.   A neat compact little Farm, rent £100, which my
Father had leased for me ; on which was a prettyish-looking
Cottage for dwelling-house (had been the Factor's place, who

[1] A square Tower, near Hoddam Castle which was once the property
of the Lords Herries ; above the door of it are carved a Serpent and a
Dove (emblems of remorse and grace), and between them the word
Repentance.   Scott gives a note respecting the vague traditions connected
with this Tower.   See " The Complaint of the Lord Herries," *Minstrelsy
of the Scottish Border* (four vol. edition, Edinburgh, 1869), iv. 307.

was retiring),—and from the windows, such a " view " (fifty miles in radius, from beyond Tyndale to beyond St. Bees, Solway Frith and all the Fells to Ingleborough inclusive) as Britain or the world could hardly have matched ! Here the ploughing etc. was already in progress (which I often rode across to see) ; and, here at term-day (26th May 1825) I established myself ; set up my Books and bits of implements and *Lares ;* and took to doing *German Romance* as my daily work ; " ten pages daily " my stint, which, barring some rare accident, I faithfully accomplished. Brother Alick was my practical *farmer ;* ever-kind and beloved Mother, with one of the little girls, was generally there,—Brother John, too, oftenest, who had just taken his degree ;—these, with a little man and ditto maid, were our establishment. It lasted only one year ; owing, I believe, to indistinctness of bargain, first of all, and then to arbitrary high-handed temper of our Landlord (used to a rather prostrate style of obedience, and not finding it here, but a polite appeal to fair-play instead), our whole summer and autumn were defaced by a great deal of paltry bother on that head, superadded to the others ; and at last, Lease of Mainhill, too, being nearly out, it was decided to quit said Landlord's territories altogether, and so end his controversies with us. Next 26th of May, we went, all of us, to Scotsbrig (a much better farm, which was now bidden for, and got) ; and where, as turned out, I continued only a few months :—wedded, and to Edinburgh in October following. Ah me, what a *retrospect* now !

With all its manifold petty troubles, this year at Hoddam Hill has a rustic beauty and dignity to me ; and lies now like a not ignoble russet-coated Idyll in my memory ; one of the quietest on the whole, and perhaps the most triumphantly important of my life. I lived very silent, diligent, had long solitary rides (on my wild Irish horse " Larry," good for the *dietetic* part) ;—my meditatings, musings and reflections were continual ; thoughts went wandering (or travelling) through Eternity, through Time, and through Space, so far as poor I had scanned or known ;—and were now, to my endless solacement, coming back with *tidings* to me ! This year I found that I had conquered all my scepticisms, agonising doubtings, fearful wrestlings with the foul and vile and soul-murdering Mud-gods of my Epoch ; had escaped, as from a worse than Tartarus, with all its Phlegethons and Stygian quagmires ; and was emerging, free in spirit, into the eternal blue of ether,—where, blessed be

Heaven, I have, for the spiritual part, ever since lived ; looking down upon the welterings of my poor fellow-creatures, in such multitudes and millions, still stuck in that fatal element ; and have had no concern whatever in their Puseyisms, Ritualisms, Metaphysical controversies and cobwebberies ; and no feeling of my own, except honest silent pity for the serious or religious part of them, and occasional indignation, for the poor world's sake, at the frivolous, *secular* and impious part, with their Universal Suffrages, their Nigger Emancipations, Sluggard-and-Scoundrel Protection Societies, and " Unexampled Pros-perities," for the time being !—What my pious joy and gratitude then was, let the pious soul figure.   In a fine and veritable sense, I, poor, obscure, without outlook, almost without worldly hope, had become independent of the world ;—what was death itself, from the world, to what I had come through ?   I understood well what the old Christian people meant by their " Conversion," by God's Infinite Mercy to them :—I had, in effect, gained an immense victory ; and, for a number of years, had, in spite of nerves and chagrins, a constant inward happiness that was quite royal and supreme ; in which all temporal evil was transient and insignificant ; and which essentially remains with me still, though far oftener *eclipsed*, and lying deeper *down*, than then. Once more, thank Heaven for its highest gift.   I then felt, and still feel, endlessly indebted to *Goethe* in the business ; he, in his fashion, I perceived, had travelled the steep rocky road before me,—the first of the moderns.   Bodily health itself seemed improving ; bodily health was all I had really lost, in this grand spiritual battle now gained ; and that too, I may have hoped, would gradually return altogether,—which it never did, and was far enough from doing ! Meanwhile my thoughts were very peace-able, full of pity and humanity as they had never been before. Nowhere can I recollect of myself such pious musings ; commun-ings, silent and spontaneous, with Fact and Nature, as in these poor Annandale localities.   The sound of the Kirk-bell, once or twice on Sunday mornings (from Hoddam Kirk, about a mile off on the plain below me), was strangely touching,—like the departing voice of eighteen hundred years.   Frank Dixon, at rare intervals, called in passing.   Nay once, for about ten days, my Dearest and Beautifullest herself came across, out of Nithsdale, to " pay my Mother a visit,"—where she gained all hearts ; and we mounted our swift little horses and careered about !   No wonder I call that year *idyllic*, in spite of its russet coat.   My Darling and I were at The Grange (Mrs. Johnston's), at Annan (Mrs. Dickson's) ; and we rode together to Dumfries, where her Aunts and Grandmother were, whom she was to pause with, on this her road home to Templand. How beautiful, how sad and strange all that now looks ! Her beautiful little heart was evidently much cast-down ; right sorry to part, though we hoped it was but for some short while. I remember the Heights of Mouswald, with Dumfries, and the granite Mountains lying in panorama seven or eight miles off to our left ; and what she artlessly yet finely said to me there. Oh, my Darling, not Andromache dressed in all the art of a Racine looks more high and queenly to me, or is more of a *tragic poem*, than thou and thy noble Pilgrimage beside me, in this poor thorny muddy world !—

I had next to no direct correspondence with Irving ; a little Note or so on business, nothing more. Nor was Mrs. Montagu much more instructive on that head, who wrote me high-sounding amiable things, which I could not but respond to, more or less, though dimly aware of their quality : nor did the sincere and ardent Mrs. Strachey, who wrote seldomer, almost ever touch upon Irving. But by some occasional unmelodious *clang* in all the Newspapers (twice over I think in this year), we could sufficiently, and with little satisfaction, construe his way of life. Twice over he had leaped the barriers ; and given rise to criticism,—of the customary idle sort, loudish universally, and nowhere accurately just. Case first was of Preaching to the London Missionary Society (" Missionary " I will call it, though it might be " Bible " or another) : on their grand Anniversary these people had appointed him the honour of addressing them, and were numerously assembled,—expecting some flourishes of eloquence, and flatteries to their illustrious divinely-blessed Society ; ingeniously done, and especially with fit *brevity ;* dinner itself waiting, I suppose, close in the rear. Irving emerged into his Speaking Place at the due moment : but, instead of treating men and office-bearers to a short comfortable dose of honey and butter, opened into strict sharp inquiries, Rhada-manthine expositions of duty and ideal ; issuing perhaps in actual criticism and admonition, gall and vinegar instead of honey ;—at any rate, keeping the poor people locked up there for " above two hours," instead of one hour, or less, with dinner *hot* at the end of it ! This was much criticised ; " plainly wrong, and produced by love of singularity and too much pride in one-self ! " voted everybody. For in fact a man suddenly holding up the naked inexorable Ideal in face of the clothed (and in

England generally plump, comfortable and pot-bellied) Reality, is doing an unexpected and a questionable thing !

The next escapade was still worse. At some public meeting of probably the same " Missionary Society," Irving again held up his Ideal,—I think, not without murmurs from former sufferers by it ;—and ended by solemnly putting down, not his name to the Subscription-List, but an actual Gold Watch, which he said had just arrived to him from his beloved Brother lately dead in India. (This Brother was John, the eldest of the three, an Indian Army-Surgeon ; whom I remember once meeting on a " common stair " in Edinburgh, on return I suppose from some call on a comrade higher up ; a taller man than even Edward, and with a blooming, placid, not very intelligent face, and no squint ; whom I easily recognised by family-likeness, but never saw again or before.) That of the Gold Watch tabled had in reality a touch of rash ostentation ; and was bitterly crowed over by the able editors for a time. On the whole, one could gather too clearly that Irving's course was beset with pitfalls, barking dogs, and dangers and difficulties unwarned-of ; and that, for one who took so little counsel with prudence, he perhaps carried his head too high. I had a certain harsh kind of sorrow about poor Irving, and my loss of him (and his loss of *me*, on such poor terms as these seemed to be !)—but I carelessly trusted in his strength against whatever mistakes and impediments ; and felt that for the present it was better to be absolved from corresponding with him.

That same year, late in Autumn, he was at Annan, only for a night and a day,—returning from some farther journey, perhaps to Glasgow or Edinburgh, and had to go on again for London next day. I rode down from Hoddam Hill before nightfall ; found him sitting in the snug little Parlour beside his Father and Mother ; beautifully domestic ;—I think it was the last time I ever saw those good old people : we sat only a few minutes ; my thoughts sadly contrasting the beautiful affectionate safety here, and the wild tempestuous hostilities and perils yonder. He left his blessing to each, by name, in a low soft voice : there was something almost tragical to me, as he turned round (hitting his hat on the little door-lintel) and, next moment, was on the dark street, followed only by me. We stept over to Robert Dickson's, his Brother-in-law's, and sat there, still talking, for perhaps an hour. Probably, his plan of journey was, to catch the Glasgow-London Mail at Gretna ; and to *walk* thither, the night being dry, and time at discretion. Walk, I remember, he did ; and talk in the interim, three or at most four of us now. He looked sad and serious ; not in the least downhearted ;—told us (probably in answer to some question of mine) that the Projected " London University " (now of Gower Street) seemed to be progressing towards fulfilment ; and how, at some meeting, Poet Campbell arguing loudly for a purely *Secular* System, had, on sight of Irving entering, at once stopt short, and, in the politest way he could, sat down without another word on the subject. " It will be *un*religious, secretly anti-religious, all the same," said Irving to us. Whether he reported of the Projected *Athenæum Club* (dear to Basil Montagu, among others), I don't recollect ; probably not, as he or I had little interest in that. When the time had come for setting out, and we were all on foot, he called for his three little Nieces, having their Mother by him ; had them each successively set standing on a chair ; laid his hand on the head first of one, with a " Mary Dickson, the Lord bless you ! " then of the next by name, and of the next ; " The Lord bless you ! "—in a sad and solemn tone (with something of elaboration noticeable in it, too), which was painful and dreary to me. A dreary visit altogether, though an unabatedly affectionate on both sides : in what a contrast, thought I, to the old sunshiny visits, when Glasgow was headquarters, and everybody was obscure, frank to his feelings, and safe ! Mrs. Dickson, I think, had tears in her eyes : her, too, he doubtless blessed, but without hand on head. Dickson and the rest of us escorted him a little way ; would then take leave in the common form ;—but even that latter circumstance I do not perfectly recal, only the fact of our escorting ; and, before the visit and after it, all is now fallen dark.

Irving did not re-emerge for many months ; and found me then in very greatly changed circumstances : his next visit was to *us*, at Comley Bank, Edinburgh, not to *me* any longer ! It was probably in Spring, 1827 ; a visit of only half an hour ; more resembling a " call " from neighbour on neighbour. I think it was connected with Scripture-Prophecy work, in which he was now deep : at any rate, he was now preaching and communing on something or other, to numbers of people in Edinburgh ; and we had heard of him for perhaps a week before as shiningly busy in that way, when, in some interval, he made this little run over to Comley Bank and us. He was very friendly ; but had a look of trouble, of haste, and confused controversy and anxiety ; sadly unlike his old good self. In dialect too and manner, things had not bettered themselves, but the contrary : he talked with an undeniable self-consciousness, and something which you could not but admit to be religious mannerism ;— never quite recovered out of that, in spite of our, especially of *her* efforts, while he staid. At parting he proposed " to pray " with us ;—and did, in standing posture ; ignoring, or conscientiously defying, our pretty evident reluctance. " Farewell," he said soon after ; " I must go, then,—and suffer persecution, as my fathers have done ! "   Much painful contradiction he evidently had, from the world about him ; but also much zealous favour ;—and was going, that same evening, to a Public Dinner given in honour of him, as we and everybody knew.   This was, I think, the *nadir* of my poor Irving ; veiled and hooded in these miserable manifold *crapes* and formulas, so that his brave old self never *once* looked fairly through,—which had not been, nor was again, quite the case, in any other visit or interview.   It made one drearily sad ; " dreary," that was the word ; and we had to consider ourselves as not a little *divorced* from him, and bidden " Shift for yourselves ! "

We saw him once again in Scotland ; at Craigenputtock, and had him for a night, or I almost think for two,—on greatly improved terms.   He was again on some kind of Church business, but it seemed to be of cheerfuller and wider scope than that of Scriptural-Prophecy, last time ; Glasgow was now his goal, with frequent preaching as he went along, the regular clergy actively countenancing.   I remember dining with him at our Parish Minister's, good Mr. Bryden's, with certain Reverends of the neighbourhood (the Dow of Irongray one of them, who afterwards went crazy on the " Gift of Tongues " affair [1]) ; I think it must have been from Bryden's that I brought him up to Craigenputtock ; where he was quite alone with us, and franker and happier than I had seen him for a long time.   It was beautiful summer weather ; pleasant to saunter in, with old friends, in the safe green solitudes, no sound audible but that of our own voices and of the birds and woods.   He talked to me of Henry Drummond, as of a fine, a great, evangelical, yet courtly and indeed universal gentleman, whom Prophetic Studies had brought to him ;—whom I was to *know* on my next coming to London, more joy to me !   We had been discoursing of Religion, with mildly-worded but entire frankness on my part as usual ; and something I said had struck Irving as unexpectedly ortho-

---

[1] The Rev. David Dow was ejected from the Scotch Kirk for " heresy."

dox ; who thereupon ejaculated, " Well, I am right glad to hear that ;—and will not forget it, where it may do you good with one whom I know of,"—with Henry Drummond namely !—which had led him into that topic, perhaps not quite for the first time. There had been big " Prophetic Conferences " etc. held at Drummond's House (Albury, Surrey) ; who continued ever after an ardent Irvingite ; and rose by degrees, in the " Tongues " business, to be Hierophant and Chief over Irving himself. He was far the richest of the Sect, and alone belonged to the Aristocratic Circles ; abundant in speculation as well as in money ; a sharp, elastic, haughty kind of man, had considerable ardour, disorderly force of intellect and character, and especially an insatiable love of shining and figuring. In a different element I had afterwards plentiful knowledge of Henry ; and, if I got no good of him, got also no mischief, which might have been extremely possible !——

We strolled pleasantly, in loose group, Irving the centre of it, over the fields. I remember an excellent little Portraiture of *Methodism* from him, on a green knoll where we had loosely sat down: " Not a good religion, Sir," said he, confidentially, shaking his head, in answer to my question : " far too little of spiritual conscience, far too much of temporal appetite. Goes hunting and watching after its own emotions, that is, mainly, its own *nervous-system ;* an essentially sensuous religion, depending on the body, not on the soul ! " " Fit only for a gross and vulgar-minded people," I perhaps added : " a religion so-called, and the essence of it principally *cowardice* and *hunger ;* terror of pain, and appetite for pleasure, both carried to the infinite ? " To which he would sorrowfully assent, in a considerable degree. My brother John, lately come home from Germany, said to me next day, " That was a pretty little *Schilderung* (Portraiture) he threw off for us, that of the Methodists ; wasn't it ? "

At Dunscore in the evening, there was Sermon, and abundant rustic concourse ; not in the Kirk, but round it in the Kirkyard, for convenience of room. I attended, with most of our people (*one* of us not ; busy she, at home, ' field-marshalling,' the noble little soul !)—I remember nothing of sermon or subject except that it went along flowingly, like true discourse direct from the inner reservoirs, and that everybody seemed to listen with respectful satisfaction. We rode pleasantly home in the dusk ; and soon afterwards would retire, Irving having to " catch the Glasgow Coach " early next day. Next day, correct to time, he and I were on horseback, soon after breakfast ; and rode leisurely along towards Auldgarth Bridge, some ten miles from us, where the Coach was to pass. Irving's talk, or what of it I remember, turned chiefly, and in a cheerful tone, upon Touring to the Continent ; a beautiful six weeks of *rest*, which he was to have in that form (and I to be taken with him, as *dragoman*, were it nothing more !)—which I did not at the time believe in ; and which was far enough from ever coming. On nearing the goal, he became a little anxious about his Coach : but we were there in perfect time, " still fifteen minutes to spare,"—and stept into the Inn to wait, over a real or (on my part) theoretic glass of ale. Irving was still but midway in his glass, when the Coach, sooner than expected, was announced : " Does not *change* here ; changes at Thornhill ! "—so that there was not a moment to be lost. Irving sprang hastily to the Coach-roof (no other seat left) ; and was at once bowled away, waving me his kind farewell, and vanishing among the woods. This was probably the last time I ever had Irving as my guest,—nay as guest for nights, or even a night, it was probably the first time. In Scotland I never saw him again. Our next meeting was in London, autumn of the year 1831.

By that time, there had been changes both with him and me ; with him a sad-enough change,—namely, *deposition* from the Scottish Established Kirk ; which he felt to be a sore blow, though to me it seemed but the whiff of a *telum imbelle* for such a man. What the particulars of his heresy were, I never knew or have totally forgotten : some doctrine he held about the Human Nature of the Divine Man, that Christ's human nature was liable to sin like our own, and continually tempted thereto, while, by his divine nobleness he kept it continually perfect, and pure from sin,—this doctrine, which as an impartial bystander, I, from Irving's point of view and from my own, entirely assented to, Irving had, by voice and pen, been publishing ; and I remember hearing vaguely of its being much canvassed, up and down,— always with impatience and a boundless contempt when I did hear of it—(" The *Gig* of Respectability again ! " I would say or think to myself : " They consider it more honourable to their Supreme of the World to have had his work done for him than to have done it himself : *Flunkeys* irredeemable ; carrying their *plush* into Highest Heaven ! ")—this I do remember ; but whether this was the damning heresy of Irving, this or some other, I do not now know. Indeed my own grief on the matter, and it had become a chronic, dull and perennial grief, was, That such a soul had anything to do with " heresies," and mean puddles of that helpless sort ; and was not rather working in his proper sphere, infinite spaces above all that ! Deposed he certainly was ; the fact is still recorded in my memory : and by a kind of accident I have the approximate *date* of it too ;—Allan Cunningham having had a Public Dinner given him in Dumfries, at which I, with great effort, attended ; and Allan's first talk to me, on meeting, having been about Irving's late troubles, and about my own soon coming to London with a MS. Book in my pocket, with *Sartor Resartus,* namely ! The whole of which circumstances have, naturally, imprinted themselves on me, while so much else has faded out.

The first genesis of *Sartor* I remember well enough, and the very spot (at Templand) where the notion of astonishment at *Clothes* first struck me : the Book had taken me, in all, some nine months, which are not present now, except confusedly and in mass ; but that of being wearied with the fluctuations of *Review* work, and of having decided on London again, with *Sartor* as a *Book* to be offered there, is still vivid to me ;—vivid above all, that *Dinner to Allan,* whither I had gone, not against my deliberate will, yet with a very great repugnance ; knowing and hating the multiplex bother of it, and that I should have some kind of Speech to make ! " Speech " done, however (*taliter qualiter,* some short rough words upon " *Burns,*" which did well enough), the thing became not unpleasant ;—and I still well remember it all. Especially how, at length, probably near midnight, I rose to go ; decisively resisting all invitations to " sleep in Dumfries ; " must and would drive home (knowing well *who* was waiting for me there !)—and drove accordingly, with only one circumstance now worth mention.

Dumfries streets, all silent, empty, were lying clear as day, in the purest moonlight ; a very beautiful and shiny midnight,— when I stept down, with some one or two for escort of honour ; got into my poor old Gig (Brother Alick's gift or procurement to me !)—and with brief farewell, rattled briskly away. I had sixteen good miles ahead, fourteen of them *Parish* road, narrower than Highway, but otherwise not to be complained of ; and the Night and the sleeping world seemed all my own for the little enterprise. A small black mare, nimble, loyal, wise (whom I well remember : " as useful a beast," said my dear Mother once of her, in fine expressive Scotch, while we drove together, " as ever *as* little skin covered ") :—this was all my team. Soon after leaving the Highway,—or perhaps it was almost before, for I was well wrapt up, warm enough, contented to be out of

my affair, wearied too with so much noise and sipping of wine,—
I too, like the world, had fallen sound asleep. Must have sat,
in deep perfect sleep (probably with the reins hung over the whip
and its case), for about ten miles ! There were ascents, descents
steep enough ; dangerous fenceless parts ; narrow bridges with
little parapet (especially one, called " Rowting," i.e. bellowing
or roaring " Brig," spanning a grand loud cataract, in quite an
intricate way, for there was abrupt turn, just at the end of it,
with rapid descent, and *wrong* road to be avoided) ; " Rowting
Brig," " Milltown Brig " (also with intricacy of wrong roads) :—
not very long after which latter, in the bottom of Glenessland,
roads a little rumbly there, owing to recent inundation, I awoke ;
safe as if Jehu had been driving me, and within four miles of
home. Considerably astonished ; but nothing like so grateful
as I now am, on looking back on the affair, and my brave little
mare's performance in it. Ah me, in this Creation, rough and
honest, though not made for our sake only, how many things,
lifeless and living,—living *persons*, some of them, and *their* life
beautiful as azure and heaven,—beneficently help us forward,
while we journey together, and have not yet bidden sorrowful
farewell ! My little Darling sat waiting for me, in the depths of
the desert ; and, better or worse, the Dumfries Dinner was over.
This must have been in July [1] 1831.

Thirteen months before there had fallen on me, and on us all,
a very great, most tender, painful and solemn grief : the death
of my eldest Sister, Margaret ; who, after sore struggles, had
quitted us, in the flower of her youth, age about twenty-seven. She
was the charm of her old Father's life ; deeply respected as well
as loved by her Mother and all of us, by none more than me ;
and was, in fact, in the simple, modest, comely and rustic form,
as intelligent, quietly valiant, quietly wise and heroic a young
woman as I have almost ever seen : very dear and estimable to
my Jeannie, too, who had zealously striven to help her, and now
mourned for her along with me. " The shortest night of 1830 ; "
that was her last in this world. The year before, for many
months, she had suffered nameless miseries, with a stoicism all
her own ; Doctors, unable to help, saw her with astonishment
rally and apparently recover,—" by her own force of character
alone ! " said one of them. Never shall I forget that bright
Summer Evening (late Summer, 1829), when, contemplatively
lounging with my pipe outside the window, I heard unexpectedly the sound of horses' feet ; and, up our little " Avenue,"

[1] It was on the 22d July.

pacing under the trees, overhung by the yellow sunlight, appeared my Brother John and she, unexpectedly from Scotsbrig ; bright to look upon, cheery of face, and the welcomest interruption to our solitude : " dear Mag, dear Mag, once more ! " Nay John had brought me, from Dumfries Post-Office, a long Letter from Goethe ;[1] one of the finest I ever had from him ; (Son's death perhaps mentioned in it ?)—Letter all so white, so *pure* externally and internally, so high and heroic,—this, too, seemed bright to me, as the summer sunset, in which I stood reading it. Seldom was a cheerfuller evening at Craigenputtock. Margaret staid perhaps a fortnight ; quietly cheerful all the time : but was judged (by a very quick *Eye* in such things) to be still far from well. She sickened again in March or April next, on some cold or accident ; grew worse than ever, herself now falling nearly hopeless (" Cannot stand a second bout like last year's ! " she once whispered to one of her sisters) : we had brought her to Dumfries, in the hope of better medical help, which was utterly vain ; Mother and Sister Mary waited on her, with trembling anxiety, I often there ; few days before the end, my Jeannie (in the dusk of such a day of gloomy hurlyburly to us all !) carried her on her knees, in a *sedan*, to some new or suburban *garden*-lodging we had got (but did not *then* tell me what the dying one had said to her). In fine, towards midnight, June 21–22, I alone still up, an express from Dumfries rapped on my window : " Grown worse ; you and your Brother wanted yonder ! " Alick and I were soon on horseback ; rode diligently through the slumbering woods (ever memorable to me, that night, and its phenomena of woods and sky) ;—found all finished, hours ago ; only a weeping Mother and Sister left, with whom neither of us could help weeping. Poor Alick's face, when I met him at the door with such news (for he had staid behind me, getting rid of the horses) ; the mute struggle, mute and vain, as of the rugged rock *not* to dissolve itself,—is still visible to me. Why do I evoke these bitter sorrows and miseries, which have mercifully long lain as if asleep ? I will not farther : that day, 22d June 1830, full of sacred sorrow and of paltry botheration of business (for we had, after some hours and a little consultation, sent Mary and my Mother home), is to be counted among the painfullest of my life ;—and in the evening, having at last reached the silence of the woods, I remember fairly lifting up my voice and weeping aloud, a long time.—

[1] For this letter, see *Correspondence between Goethe and Carlyle* (Macmillan and Co., 1887), p. 127.

[Half of another *written sheet* goes with me to Mentone, to try whether it (it, and something better, might I hope ?) cannot be finished there.—Chelsea, Wednesday, 19 *Dec.* 1866.]

All this has nothing to do with Irving ; little even with the journey I was now making towards him,—except that in the tumultuous agitations of the latter, it came all, in poignant clearness and completeness, into my mind again ; and continued with me, in the background or the foreground, during most of the time I was in London. From Whitehaven onwards to Liverpool, amid the noise and jostle of a crowd of high-dressed vulgar-looking people who joined us there, and with their " hot brandies," dice-boxes, etc., down below, and the blaring of brass bands, and idle babblers and worshippers of the nocturnal picturesque, made deck and cabin almost equally a delirium,— this, all this of fourteen months ago, in my poor head and heart, was the one thing awake, and the saturnalia round it a kind of mad nightmare *dream.* At London, too, perhaps a week or so after my arrival, somebody had given me a ticket to see Macready ; and, stepping out of the evening sun, I found myself in Drury Lane Theatre,—which was all darkened, carefully lamplit ; play just beginning or going to begin : out of my gratis box (front box on the lower tier), I sat gazing into that painted scene and its mimings ; but heard nothing, saw nothing ;—*her* green grave, and Ecclefechan silent little Kirkyard far away, and how the evening sun at this same moment would be shining *there ;* generally that was the main thing I saw or thought of ; and tragical enough that was, without any Macready ! Of Macready, that time, I remember nothing ; and suppose I must have come soon away.

Irving was now living in Judd-Street, New Road ; a bigger, much better old House than the former new one ; and much handier for the new " Caledonian Chapel," which stood, spacious and grand, in Regent *Square*, and was quite dissevered from Hatton-Garden and its concerns. I stept over to him, on the evening of my arrival ; found him sitting quiet and alone, brotherly as ever in his reception of me.

[*27th December* 1866. *Ceased* at London, perhaps three weeks ago, mere hubbub and uncertainty intervening ; *begins* again at Mentone on the *Riviera Occidentale*, whither I have been pushed and pulled in the most unheard-of way, Professor Tyndall, Lady Ashburton, friends, foes all conspiring ; a journey like " *chaos* come again," and an arrival and continuance hitherto still *liker* ditto (wakeful nights each, especially the one just gone) :—in which strange circumstances, bright sun shining, blue sea faintly murmuring, orange groves glowing out of window, Mentone hidden, and Ventimiglia Cape in view ; all earth a kind of Paradise, inhabitant a kind of quasi-Satan,—I endeavour to proceed the best I can.]

Our talk was good and edifying : he was by this time deep in Prophecy and other aberrations ; surrounded by weak people, mostly echoes of himself and his incredible notions : but he was willing to hear me, too, on secularities ; candid like a second-self in judging of what one said in the way of opinion ; and wise and even shrewd in regard to anything of business if you consulted him on that side. He objected clearly to my Reform-Bill notions ; found *Democracy* a thing forbidden, leading down to outer darkness ; I, a thing inevitable, and *obliged* to lead whithersoever it could. We had several colloquies on that subject ; on which, though my own poor convictions are widened, not altered, I should now have more sympathy with his than was then the case. We also talked on Religion and Christianity " Evidences,"—our notions, of course, more divergent than ever. " It is sacred, my friend ; we can call it sacred : such a *Civitas Dei* as was never built before ; wholly the grandest series of work ever hitherto done by the Human Soul,—the Highest God (doubt it not) assenting and inspiring all along ! " This I remember once saying plainly ; which was not an encouragement to prosecute the topic. We were in fact, hopelessly divided, to what tragical extent both of us might well feel ! But something still remained ; and this we (*he* at least, for I think in friendship he was the nobler of the two) were the only more anxious to retain and make good. I recollect breakfasting with him and the like, a strange set of ignorant conceited fanatics forming the body of the party, and greatly spoiling it for me. Irving's own kindness was evidently in essence unabated ; how sorrowful, at once provoking and pathetic, that I or he could henceforth get so little good of it !—

We were to have gone and seen Coleridge together ; had fixed a day for that object ; but the day proved one long deluge, no stirring out possible ; and we did not appoint another. I never saw Coleridge more ; he died the year after our final removal to London : [1] a man much pitied and recognised by me ; never excessively esteemed in any respect, and latterly, on the

[1] This is a mistake ; Coleridge died 25th July 1834.

intellectual or spiritual side, less and less. The Father of
Puseyism and of much vain Phantasmal Moonshine, which still
vexes this poor earth,—as I have elsewhere described him.
Irving and I did not, on the whole, see much of one another
during this *Sartor Resartus* visit ; our circles, our courses and
employments were so altogether diverse. Early in the visit, he
walked me to Belgrave Square to dine with Henry Drummond ;
beautiful promenade through the crowd and stir of Piccadilly
which was then somewhat of a novelty to me : Irving, I heard
afterwards, was judged, from the broad hat, brown skin and
flowing black hair to be in all probability the One-string Fiddler
Paganini, a tall, lean taciturn abstruse-looking figure, who was
then, after his sort, astonishing the idle of mankind. Henry
Drummond, house all in summer *déshabille*, carpets up, etc.,
received us with abundance of respect, and of aristocratic pococurantism withal (the latter perhaps rather in a *conscious* condition) ; gave us plenty of talk, and received well what was
given (chiefly on the rotten social state of England ; on the
" Swing " outrages, " half the year in raising wheat, t'other half
in burning it," which were then alarming everybody), all rather
in epigrammatic exaggerative style, and with wisdom sometimes
sacrificed to " wit " ;—gave us, in short, a pleasant enough
dinner and evening : but left me, as Mazzini used to describe it,
" cold." A man of elastic pungent decisive nature ; full of
fine qualities and capabilities,—but well nigh cracked by an
enormous conceit of himself, which, both as pride and vanity
(in strange partnership, mutually agreeable), seemed to pervade
every fibre of him, and render his life a restless inconsistency :
that was the feeling he left in me ; nor did it alter afterwards,
when I saw a great deal more of him,—without sensible increase
or diminution of the little love he at first inspired in me. Poor
Henry, he shot fiery arrows about, too ; but they told nowhere.
I was never tempted to become more intimate with him ;
though he now and then seemed willing enough. *Ex nihilo
nihil fit.* He, without unkindness of intention, did my poor
Irving a great deal of ill ; me never any, such my better luck.
His last act was, (about eight or nine years ago), to ask us both [1]
out to Albury on a mistaken day (when he himself was not there)!
Happily my Darling had, at the eleventh hour, decided not to
go ; so that the ugly confusion fell all on me :—and in few
months more, Henry was himself dead ; and no mistake
possible again. Albury, the ancient Earl of Arundel's, the

1 Mr. and Mrs. Carlyle.

recent Prophet-Conference's etc., I had seen for the first, and most likely for the last time. . . .[1]

My business lay with the Bookseller or Publishing world ; my chief intercourse was with the lighter Literary Figures ; in part, too, with the Political, many of whom I transiently saw at Jeffrey's (who was then Lord Advocate) and all of whom I might hear of through him : not in either kind was my appetite very keen, nor did it increase by what it fed on,—rather a " feast of shells," as perhaps I then defined it : people of biggish names, but of substance mainly spilt and wanting. All men were full of the *Reform Bill*, nothing else talked of, written of ; the air loaded with *it* alone ;—which occasioned great obstruction in the publishing of my *Sartor*, I was told. On that latter point I could say much ; but will forbear. Few men ever more surprised me than did the great Albemarle-Street Murray, who had published for Byron and all the great ones for many years, and to whom Jeffrey sent me recommended. Stupider man than the great Murray, in look, in speech, in conduct in regard to this poor *Sartor* question, I imagined I had seldom or never seen ! Afterwards it became apparent to me that partly he was sinking into heaviness of old age ; and partly (still more important) that, in regard to this particular *Sartor* question, his position was an impossible one, position of a poor old man endeavouring to answer " Yes *and* No ! " I had striven and pushed, for some weeks, with him and others, on those impossible principles, till at length discovering,—I, with brevity, demanded back my poor *Manuscript* from Murray ; received it with some apologetic palaver (enclosing an opinion from his *Taster*, which was subsequently printed in one edition), and much hope, etc. etc. ; locked *it* away into fixity of silence for the present (my *Murray* into ditto for ever) ;—and decided to send for the Dear One I had left behind me, and let her too see London which I knew she would like, before we went farther. Ah me, this sunny *Riviera*, which we sometimes vaguely thought of, she does not see along with me : and my thoughts of her here are too sad for words. I will write no more to-day. Oh my Darling, my lost Darling, may the Great God be good to thee. Silence, though ;—and " Hope " if I can !—

My Jeannie came about the end of September. Brother John, by industry of hers and mine (*hers* chiefly), acting on an oppor-

---

[1] A few lines referring to Mr. Thomas Carlyle, *Advocate*, printed in the first edition, are omitted here, as there are good grounds for believing that Carlyle had been misinformed as to this namesake of his.

tunity of Lord Advocate Jeffrey's, had got an appointment for
Italy [1] (" Travelling Physician," by which he has since made
abundance of money, and of work may be said to have translated Dante's *Inferno*, were there nothing more !).—We shifted
from an uncomfortable Lodging (at Irving's youngest Brother
George's, an incipient Surgeon, amiable, and clever superficially,
who soon after died) into a clean quiet and modestly comfortable one, in Ampton Street (same St. Pancras region) ; and
there, ourselves two, Brother John being *off* to Italy, set up for
the winter, under tolerable omens. My Darling was, as ever,
the guardian spirit of the establishment, and made all things
bright and smooth. The Daughter of the house, a fine young
Cockney specimen, fell quite in love with her ; served like a
fairy ; was, next year long after we were gone, for coming to us
at Craigenputtock to be " maid of all work " (an impossible
suggestion !)—and did, in effect, keep up an adoring kind of
intercourse till the fatal day of April last ; never changing at all
in *her* poor tribute of love. A fine outpouring of her grief and
admiring gratitude, written after that event, (letter to me,
signed " Eliza Snowden,"—*Miles* was her maiden name.
" Snowden," once a clerk with her uncle, is, now himself, for
long years back, a prosperous Upholsterer ; and the Sylph-like
Eliza, grown fat enough of shape, is the mother of six or seven
prosperous children to him), was *not* thrown into the fire, half-
read or unread, but is still lying in a drawer at Chelsea, or perhaps adjoined to some of the things I was writing there, as a
genuine human utterance, not without some sad value to me.
My poor little Woman had often indifferent health ; which
seemed rather to worsen than improve while we continued ; but
her spirit was indefatigable, ever cheery, full of grace, ingenuity,
dexterity ; and she much enjoyed London, and the considerable
miscellany of people that came about us.   Charles Buller,
John Mill, several professed " admirers " of mine (among whom
was, and for aught I know still is, the mocking Hayward !) ;
Jeffrey almost daily as an admirer of *hers ;* not to mention Mrs.
Montagu and Co., certain Holcrofts (Badams married to one of
them, a certain Kenny married to the mother of them,—at
whose house, I once saw Godwin, if that were anything), Allan
Cunningham from time to time, and fluctuating Foreigners etc.,

---

[1] Dr. J. A. Carlyle held this appointment for a number of years. His
amiable and kindly disposition made him a favourite with his patient, the
Countess of Clare, with whom he remained on intimate terms of friendship
as long as she lived.

etc.,—we had company rather in superabundance than otherwise ; and a pair of the clearest eyes in the whole world were there to take note of them all, a judgment to compare and contrast them (as I afterwards found she had been doing, the dear soul) with what was already all her own. Ah me, ah me !

Soon after New-Year's Day, a great sorrow came, unexpected news of my Father's death. He had been in bed, as ill, only a few hours, when the last hour proved to be there, unexpectedly to all, except perhaps to himself ; for, ever since my Sister Margaret's death he had been fast failing, though none of us took notice enough, such had been his perfection of health, almost all along through the seventy-three years he lived. I sat plunged into the depths of natural grief ; the pale kingdoms of eternity laid bare to me, and all that was sad and grand, and dark as death, filling my thoughts exclusively, day after day. How beautiful *She* was to me ; how kind and tender ! Till after the Funeral, my Father's noble old face, one of the finest and strongest I have ever seen, was continually before my eyes :—in these and the following days and nights I hastily wrote down some memorials of him ; [1] which I have never since seen, but which still exist somewhere, though indeed they were not worth preserving, still less *are*, after *I* have done with them. " Posterity," that is what I never thought of appealing to ; what possible use can there be in appealing *there*,—in *appealing* anywhere, except by absolute silence to the High Court of Eternity, which *can* do no error ? Poor sickly Transiencies that we are ; coveting we know not what !—In the February ensuing I wrote *Johnson* (the *Bozzy* part was published in *Fraser* for April); a week or two before, we had made acquaintance, by Hunt's own goodness, with Leigh Hunt, and were much struck with him ;—early in April, we got back to Annandale and Craigenputtock (sadly present to my soul, most sadly yet most beautifully, all that, even now !)—

In the course of the winter, sad things had occurred in Irving's history. His enthusiastic studies and preachings were passing into the practically " miraculous ; " and to me the most doleful of all phenomena, the " Gift of Tongues " had fairly broken out among the crazed weakliest of his wholly rather dim and weakly flock. I was never at all in his church, during this visit, being grieved at once and angered at the course he had got into : but once or twice, poor Eliza Miles came running home from some evening sermon there was, all in a tremor of tears over these

[1] See Paper, " James Carlyle," *supra.*

same "Tongues," and a riot from the *dissenting* majority
opposing them : "All a tumult yonder, oh me !"   This did not
happen above twice or so ; Irving (never himself a "Tongue"
performer) having taken some order with the thing, and I think
discouraged and nearly suppressed it as *unfit* during Church
service.   It was greatly talked of ; by certain persons with an
enquiry, "Do you believe in it ?"   "Believe in it ?   As much
as I do in the High Priest of Otaheite !" answered Lockhart
once, to Fraser, the inquiring Bookseller, in my hearing.   Sorrow
and disgust were naturally my own feeling : "How are the
mighty fallen ; my once high Irving come to this, by paltry
popularities, and Cockney admirations, puddling such a head !"
We ourselves saw less and less of Irving ; but one night, in one
of our walks, we did make a call ; and actually heard what they
called the Tongues. It was in a neighbouring room, larger part
of the drawing room belike.   Mrs. Irving had retired thither
with the devotees ; Irving for our sake had staid, and was
pacing about the floor, dandling his youngest child, and talking
to us of this and that, probably about the Tongues withal,—
when there burst forth a shrieky hysterical "Lall-lall-lall !"
(little or nothing else but *l*'s and *a*'s continued for several minutes) ; to which Irving, with singular calmness, said only,
"There, hear you ; there are the Tongues !" and we two,
except by our looks which probably were eloquent, answered
him nothing ; but soon came away, full of distress, provocation
and a kind of shame.   "Why wasn't there a bucket of cold
water to fling on that *lall-lalling* hysterical mad-woman ?"
thought we, or said, to one another :   "Oh Heavens, that it
should come to this !"— —I do not remember any call we made
there afterwards ; of course there was a Farewell call ; but that
too I recollect only obliquely. . . . Seldom was seen a more
tragical scene to us, than this of Irving's London life was now
becoming !

One other time we did see Irving : at our Lodging, where he
had called to take leave of us, a day or two before our quitting
London.   I know not whether the interview had been pre-
concerted between my Darling and me for the sake of our common Friend ; but it was abundantly serious, and affecting to us
all ; and none of the Three, I believe, ever forgot it again.
Preconcerting or not, I had privately determined that I must
tell Irving plainly what I thought of his present course and posture ; and I now did so, breaking in by the first opportunity,
and leading the Dialogue wholly into that channel, till with all

the delicacy but also with all the fidelity possible to me, I put him fully in possession of what my real opinion was. *She*, my noble Jeannie, said hardly anything ; but her looks and here and there a word testified how deep her interest was, how complete her assent. I stated plainly to him that he must permit me a few words for relief of my conscience, before leaving him for we knew not what length of time, on a course which I could not but regard as full of danger to him. That the " *13th of the Corinthians*," to which he always appealed, was surely too narrow a basis for so high a tower as he was building on it ;—a high lean tower, or quasi-*mast*, piece added to piece, till it soared far above all human science and experience, and flatly contradicted all that, —founded solely on a little text of *writing* in an ancient Book ! No sound judgment, on such warranty, could venture on such an enterprise. Authentic " writings " of the Most High, were they found in old Books only ? They were in the stars and on the rocks, and in the brain and heart of every mortal,—*not* dubious there, to any person, as this " *13th of the Corinthians* " very greatly was. That it did not beseem him, Edward Irving, to be hanging on the rearward of mankind, struggling still to chain them to old notions not now well tenable ; but to be foremost in the van, leading on by the light of the eternal stars, across this hideous delirious wilderness where we all were, towards Promised Lands that lay ahead. Bethink you, my Friend, is not that *your* plainly commanded duty ; more plain than any 13th of the Corinthians can be. I bid you pause and consider ; that verily is my solemn advice to you !—I added that, as he knew well, it was in the name of old friendship I was saying all this. That I did not expect he would at once, or soon, renounce his fixed views, connections and methods, for any words of mine : but perhaps at some future time of crisis and questioning dubiety in his own mind, he might remember these words of a well-affected soul, and they might then be of help to him.

During all this, which perhaps lasted about twenty minutes, Irving sat opposite me, within a few feet (my Wife to his right hand and to my left, silent and sad-looking) in the middle of the floor ; Irving with head downcast, face indicating great pain, but without the slightest word or sound from him, till I had altogether ended. He then began with the mildest low tone, and face full of kindness and composed distress, " Dear friend," —and endeavoured to make his apology and defence ; which did not last long, or do anything to convince me ; but was in a style of modesty and friendly magnanimity, which no mortal could surpass, and which remains to me, at this moment, dear and memorable and worthy of all honour. Which done, he went silently his way, no doubt with kindest farewells to us ; and I remember nothing more. Possibly we had already made farewell call in Judd-Street, the day before, and found *him* not there ?—

This was, in a manner, the last visit I ever made to Irving ; the last time either of *us* ever freely saw him, or spoke with him at any length. We had to go our way ; he his,—and his soon proved to be precipitous, full of chasms and plunges, which rapidly led him to the close. Our journey homeward—I have spoken of it elsewhere, and of the dear reminiscences it leaves, ever sad, but also ever blessed to me now. We were far away from Irving, in our solitary moors ; staid still there above two years (one of our winters in Edinburgh) ; and heard of Irving and his catastrophes only from the distance. He had to come to Annan and be expelled from the Scottish Kirk.[1] That scene I remember reading in some Newspaper, with lively conception and emotion. A poor aggregate of Reverend *Sticks* in black gown, sitting in Presbytery, to pass formal condemnation on a Man and a Cause which might have been tried in Patmos, under Presidency of St. John, without the right truth of it being got at ! I knew the " Moderator " (one Roddick, since gone mad) for one of the stupidest and barrenest of living mortals ; also the little phantasm of a creature (Sloan his name ; who went niddy-noddying with his head, and was infinitely conceited and phantasmal), by whom Irving was rebuked with the " Remember where you are, Sir ! " and got answer, " I have not forgotten where I am : it is the Church where I was baptized ; where I was consecrated to preach Christ ; where the bones of my dear ones lie buried ! "—Condemnation, under any circumstances, had to follow ; " *le droit de me damner te reste toujours !* " as poor Danton said, in a far other case.[2]

The feeling of the population was strong and general for Irving ; Reverends Sloan and Roddick were not without their apprehensions of some tumult perhaps,—had not the people been so reverent of the place they were in. Irving sent us no word of himself ; made no appeal to any friend or foe ; unless his preaching to the people, up and down, for some days, partly perhaps in the way of defence, though mostly on general gospel subjects, could be taken as such. He was followed by great

---

[1] Irving was deposed at Annan on the 13th of March 1833.
[2] See *French Revolution* (Library edition), iii. 320.

crowds who eagerly heard him. My Brother Jamie, who had
been at several of those open-air preachings, in different parts
of the Annan neighbourhood, and who much admired and pitied
the great Irving, gave me the last notice I ever had of that
tragic matter, " Irving's vocal *appellatio ad populum*, when
Presbytery had condemned him." This time the assemblage
was at Ecclefechan, probably the final one of all, and the last
time he ever preached to Annandale men. The assemblage was
large and earnest, gathered in the Middlebie road, a little way
off the main Street and Highway. The Preacher stood on some
table or chair, which was fixed against the trunk of a huge,
high, strong and many-branched " Plane-tree " (well known to
me and to every one that passes that way) ; the weather was of
proper [March] quality, grim, fierce, with windy snow-showers
flying ; Irving had a woollen comforter about his neck ; skirts
of comforter, hair, cloak, tossing in the storms ; eloquent voice
well audible under the groaning of the boughs and piping of the
winds. Jamie was on business in the village ; and had paused
awhile, much moved by what he saw and heard. It was our
last of Irving in his native Annandale. Mrs. Oliphant, I think,
relates that, on getting back to London, he was put under a kind
of arrest by certain Angels or Authorities of his New " Irvingite " Church (just established in Newman Street, Oxford Street),
for disobeying regulations (perhaps in regard to those volunteer
Preachings in Annandale) ; and sat with great patience, in some
penitential place among them ; dumb for about a week, till he
had expiated that sin. Irving was now become wholly tragical
to us ; and the least painful we could expect in regard to him
was, what mainly happened, that we heard no news from that
side at all. His health, we vaguely understood, was becoming
uncertain ; news naturally worse than none,—had we much
believed it, which, knowing his old Herculean strength, I suppose
we didn't.

In 1834 came our own removal to London ;—concerning
which are heavy fields of memory, laborious, beautiful, sad and
sacred (my darling Lost One !)—were this the place for them ;
which it isn't. Our winter in Edinburgh ; our haggles and
distresses (badness of servants mainly), our bits of diligences,
strenuous and sometimes happy ;—in fine the clear resolution
that we ought to go. I had been in correspondence with
London (chiefly with John Mill, Leigh Hunt, Mrs. Austin, etc.)
ever since our presence there : " Let us burn our ships,"
said my noble One, " and get on march ! "—I went as pre-

cursor, early in May; ignorantly thinking this was, as in Scotland, the general and sole term for getting Houses in London; and that *after* "May 26th" there would be none but leavings! We were not very *practically* advised, I should think, though there were counsellors many. However I roved lustily about seeking Houses for the next three weeks, while my Darling was still busier at home, getting all things packed, and put under way: what endless toil for her; undertaken with what courage, skill and cheery heroism! By the time of her arrival I had been far and wide round London seeking Houses; had found out that the Western Suburb was, in important respects, the fittest; and had seen nothing I thought so eligible there as a certain *one* of three cheap Houses, which one she, on survey, agreed to be the best,—and which is, in fact, No. 5 Great Cheyne Row, where the rest of our life was to be passed together. Why do I write all this? it is too sad to me to think of it; brokendown and solitary as I am, and the lamp of my life, which " covered everything with gold" as it were, gone out, gone out!—

It was on one of those expeditions, a week or more after my arrival, expedition to take survey of the proposed No. 5, in company with Mrs. Austin, whom I had taken up in Bayswater where she lived, and with whom, attended also by Mrs. Jameson, not known to me before, but found by accident on a call there,— we were proceeding towards Chelsea in the middle of a bright May day, when I noticed, well down in Kensington-Gardens, a dark male figure sitting between two white female ones under a tree; male figure, which abruptly rose and stalked towards me; whom, seeing it was Irving, I hastily disengaged myself, and stept out to meet. It was indeed Irving; but how changed in the two years and two months since I had last seen him! In look he was almost friendlier than ever; but he had suddenly become an old man. His head, which I had left raven-black, was grown grey, on the temples almost snow-white; the face was hollow, wrinkly, collapsed; the figure, still perfectly erect, seemed to have lost all its elasticity and strength. We walked some space slowly together, my heart smitten with various emotions; my speech, however, striving to be cheery and hopeful. He was very kind and loving; it seemed to be a kind of tender grief and regret that my Jeannie and I were taking so important a step, and he not called at all to assist, rendered unable to assist. Certainly in all England was no heart, and in all Scotland only two or three, that wished us half as well. He admitted his weak health, but treated it as temporary, it seemed of small account to him. Friends and doctors had advised him to Bayswater for better air; had got him a lodging there, a stout horse to ride; summer, they expected, would soon set him up again. His tone was not despondent; but it was low, pensive, full of silent sorrow. Once, perhaps twice, I got a small bit of Annandale laugh from him, strangely genuine, though so lamed and overclouded; this was to me the most affecting thing of all, and still is when I recall it. He gave me his address in Bayswater; his hours as near as might be; and I engaged to try and find him there,—I, him, which seemed the likelier method, in our widely diverse elements, both of them so full of bustle, interruption and uncertainty. And so adieu, my friend, adieu! Neither of us had spoken with the women of the other; and each was gone his several road again,—mine not specially remembered farther.

It seems to me I never found Irving in his Bayswater lodging; I distinctly recollect seeing him, one dusty evening about eight, at the door there, mount his horse, a stout firm bay animal, of the kind called Cob; and set out towards Newman-Street, whither he rode perhaps twice or thrice a day for Church-services there were; but this, and his friendly regret at being obliged to go, is all I can recall of interview farther. Neither at the Bayswater Lodging, nor at his own House in Newman-Street when he returned thither, could I for many weeks to come ever find him " at home." In Chelsea, we poor Pair of Immigrants had, of course, much of our own to do,—and right courageously we marched together, my own brave Darling (what a store of humble but high and sacred memories to me!) victoriously carrying the flag. But at length it struck me there was something questionable in these perpetual " not-at-home's " of Irving; and that perhaps his poor jealous anxious and much-bewildered wife had her hand in the phenomenon. As proved to be the fact according. I applied to William Hamilton (excellent City Scotsman, married, not over well I doubt, to a Sister of Mrs. Irving's) with a brief statement of the case; and had immediate remedy: an appointment to dinner Newman-Street on a given day; which I failed not to observe. None but Irving and his wife besides myself were there; the dinner (from a good joint of roast-beef, in a dim but quiet comfortable kind of room) was among the pleasantest of dinners to me; Madam herself wearing nothing but smiles; and soon leaving us together to a fair hour or two of free talk. I think the main topic must have been my own outlooks and affairs, my project of writing on the *French Revolution*, which Irving warmly approved of (either then or some other time) : of his Church matters we now never spoke. I went away gratified ; and, for my own share, glad,—had not the outlooks on his side been so dubious and ominous. He was evidently growing weaker, not stronger ; wearing himself down, as to me seemed too clear, by spiritual agitations, which would kill him, unless checked and ended. Could he but be got to Switzerland, to Italy, I thought ; to some pleasant country, of which the language was unknown to him, where he would be *forced to silence*, the one salutary medicine for him, in body and in soul ! I often thought of this : but he had now no Brother, no Father on whom I could practically urge it, as I would with my whole strength have done, feeling that his life now lay on it : I had to hear of his growing weaker and weaker ; while there was nothing whatever that I could do.

With himself I do not recollect that there was anything more of interview, since that dinner in Newman-Street ; or that I saw him again in the world,—except once only, to be soon noticed. Latish in the Autumn some of the Kirkcaldy Martins had come ; I remember speaking to his Father-in-law, at Hamilton's in Cheapside one evening, and very earnestly on the topic that interested us both : but in Martin too there was nothing of help. " Grows weaker and weaker," said he ; " and no Doctor can find the least disease in him. So weak now, he cannot lift his little baby to his neck ! " In my desperate anxiety at this time, I remember writing a Letter on my Switzerland or Italy scheme to Henry Drummond, whom I yet knew nothing more of, but considered to be probably a man of sense and practical insight ; Letter stating briefly my sad and clear belief that, unless carried into some element of *perfect silence*, poor Irving would soon die ;—Letter which lay some days on the mantelpiece at Chelsea, under some misgivings about sending it ; and was then thrown into the fire. We heard, before long, that it was decided he should journey slowly into Wales, paying visits ; perhaps into Scotland : which seemed the next best to what I would have proposed ; and was of some hope to us. And late one afternoon, soon after, we had a short farewell visit from him ; his first visit to Cheyne Row, and his last,—the last we Two ever saw of him in this world. It was towards sunset,— had there been any sun, that damp dim October [1] day ;—he came ambling gently on his bay horse ; sat some fifteen or

1 It must have been before October, for Irving, as already noted, had left London in the beginning of September.

twenty minutes, and went away while it was still daylight. It was in the ground-floor room where I still write (thanks to *her* last service to me, shifting me thither again, the darling ever-helpful One !)—whether She was sitting with me on his entrance I don't recollect ; but I well do his fine chivalrous demeanour to *her ;* and how he complimented her (as he well might) on the pretty little room she had made for her husband and self, and running his eye over her dainty bits of arrangements, ornamenta-tions, all so frugal, simple, full of grace, propriety and ingenuity as they ever were, said smiling, " You are like an Eve, and make a little Paradise wherever you are ! " His manner was sincere, affectionate, yet with a great suppressed sadness in it, and as if with a feeling that he must not linger. It was perhaps on this occasion that he expressed to me his satisfaction at my having taken to " writing History " (*French Revolution* now begun, I suppose) ; study of History, he seemed to intimate, was the study of things real, practical, and actual, and would bring me closer upon all reality whatsoever. With a fine simplicity of lovingness, he bade us farewell. I followed him to the door ; held his bridle (doubtless) while he mounted, no groom being ever with him on such occasions ; stood on the steps as he quietly walked or ambled up Cheyne Row, quietly turned the corner (at Wright's door, or the Rector's back *garden*-door) into Cook's Grounds,[1]—and had vanished from my eyes for evermore. In this world neither of us ever saw him again. He was off north-ward in a day or two ; died at Glasgow in December following, —age only forty-three gone ; and, except weakness, no disease traceable.

Mrs. Oliphant's Narrative is nowhere so true and touching to me as in that last portion, where it is drawn almost wholly from his own *Letters* to his Wife. All there is true to the life, and recognisable to me as perfect *portraiture ;* what I cannot quite say of any other portion of the Book. All Mrs. Oliphant's delineation shows excellent diligence, loyalty, desire to be faith-ful, and indeed is full of beautiful sympathy and ingenuity ; but nowhere else are the features of Irving or of his Environment and Life recognisably hit, and the pretty Picture, to one who knows, looks throughout more or less romantic, *pictorial,* and " *not like,*"—till we arrive here at the grand close of all ; which to me was of almost *Apocalyptic* impressiveness, when I first read it, some years ago. What a falling of the curtain ; upon what a Drama ! Rustic Annandale begins it, with its homely honesties,

[1] Street at the top of Cheyne Row, Chelsea.

rough vernacularities, safe, innocently kind, ruggedly mother-
like, cheery, wholesome, like its airy hills and clear-rushing
streams ; prurient corrupted London is the middle part, with
its volcanic stupidities and bottomless confusions ;—and the
end is terrible, mysterious, godlike and awful ; what Patmos
could be more so ? It is as if the vials of Heaven's wrath were
pouring down upon a man ; yet not wrath alone, for his heart
is filled with trust in Heaven's goodness withal. It must be
said, Irving nobly expiates whatever errors he has fallen into ;
like an Antique Evangelist he walks his stony course, the fixed
thought of his heart, at all times, " Though He slay me, yet
will I trust in Him ; " and these final deluges of sorrow are but
washing the faithful soul of him clean.

He sent from Glasgow a curious *Letter* to his *Gift-of-Tongues*
Congregation ; full of questionings, dubieties upon the *Tongues*
and such points ; full of wanderings in deep waters, with one
light fixed on high, " Humble ourselves before God, and He will
show us ! "—Letter indicating a sincerity as of very death ;
which these New Church people (Henry Drummond and Co.)
first printed for useful private circulation, and then afterwards
zealously suppressed and destroyed, till almost everybody but
myself had forgotten the existence of it. Luckily, about two
years ago, I still raked out a copy if it for " Rev. Gavin Carlile "
(Nephew of Irving, now editing Irving's *Select Works*, or some
such title) ; by whom I am glad to know it has been printed
and made permanent, as a Document honourable and due to
such a memory. Less *mendacious* soul of a man than my noble
Irving's there could not well be.

It was but a little while before this that he had said to
Drummond, what was mentioned here long since, " I ought to
have seen more of T. Carlyle, and heard him more clearly, than
I have done." And there is one other thing, which dates several
years before, which I always esteem highly honourable to
Irving's memory ; and which I will note here, as my last item,
since it was forgotten at its right date. Right date is that of
German Romance, 1826,[1] *early ;* the report is from my Brother
John, to whom Irving spoke on the subject, which with me he
always rather avoided. Irving did not much know Goethe ; had
generally a dislike to him, as to a kind of Heathen *un*godly
person and idle *Singer*, who had considerably seduced *me* from
the right path, as one sin. He read *Wilhelm Meister's Travels*

---

[1] *German Romance : Specimens of its chief Authors, etc.*, was finished in
1826, but not published until the following year (4 vols. Edinburgh, 1827).

nevertheless ; and he said to John one day : "Very curious, in this German *Poet*, here are some pages about Christ and the Christian Religion, which, as I study and re-study them, have more sense about that matter than I have found in all the Theologians I ever read ! " Was not this a noble thing for such a man to feel and say ? I have a hundred times recommended that Passage in *Wilhelm Meister*, to inquiring and devout souls ; but, I think, never elsewhere met with one who so thoroughly recognised it. One of my last *Letters*, flung into the fire, just before leaving London the other day, was from an Oxford self-styled " religious inquirer," who asks me, if in those pages of *Meister*, there is not a wonderfully distinct foreshadow of Comte and *Positivism ?* Phœbus Apollo god of the Sun ; *foreshadowing* the miserablest phantasmal *algebraic ghost* I have yet met with among the ranks of the living !— —

I have now ended, and am sorry to end, what I had to say of Irving. It is like bidding him farewell, for a second and the last time. He waits in the Eternities; *Another*, his brightest Scholar, has left me and gone thither. God be about us all. Amen, amen.

[Finished at Mentone, 2d January 1867,—looking towards the eastward Hills, bathed in sunshine, under a brisk west-wind ; two P.M.]

———

The following extracts from Carlyle's *Journal* refer to this Paper on Edward Irving :

" *26th September* 1866.—. . . Writing, languidly, something which I call ' Reminiscences of Edward Irving ' ;—which turns out hitherto to be more about myself than him. Perhaps not easy to help its being so, especially thus far ? Continue it, at any rate ; though good for little."

" *3d December*.—. . . Have been writing (under such per-petual interruptions) ' Reminiscences of Edward Irving ' (turn out to be rather, of myself *and* Edward Irving !)—many pages ; not yet finished ; hardly once in the three days can I get to it of late.—Ought probably to be *burnt* when done (and possibly enough shall) ; but in the meanwhile, the writing of it *clears* my own insight into those past days ; has *branches* and sections still dearer to me than Irving ;—and calms and soothes me as I go on."

LORD JEFFREY

(OF FRANCIS JEFFREY, HON. LORD JEFFREY,[1] THE LAWYER AND REVIEWER)

MENTONE, 3*d January* 1867.

FEW sights have been more impressive to me than the sudden one I had of the " Outer House," in Parliament Square, Edinburgh, on the evening of 9th November 1809, some hours after my arrival in that City, for the first time. We had walked some twenty miles that day, the third day of our journey from Ecclefechan ; my companion one " Tom Smail," who had already been to College last year, and was thought to be a safe guide and guardian to me : he was some years older than myself ; had been at School along with me, though never in my class ; —a very innocent conceited, insignificant, but strict-minded orthodox creature, for whom, knowing him to be of no scholarship or strength of judgment, I privately had very small respect, though civilly following him about in things he knew better than I. As in the streets of Edinburgh, for example, on my first evening there ! On our journey thither he had been wearisome, far from entertaining ; mostly silent, having indeed nothing to say, he stalked on generally some steps ahead ; languidly whistling through his teeth some similitude of a wretched Irish tune, which I knew too well as that of a still more wretched doggrel song called " The Belfast Shoemaker,"—most melancholy to poor me, given up to my bits of reflections in the silence of the moors and hills.

How strangely vivid, how remote and wonderful, tinged with the hues of far-off love and sadness, is that Journey to me now, after fifty-seven years of time ! My Mother and Father walking with me, in the dark frosty November morning, through the village, to set us on our way ; my dear, ever-loving Mother and her tremulous affection ; my etc. etc.—But we must get to

---

1 Francis Jeffrey " took his seat on the Bench on the 7th of June 1834. The Scotch Judges are called *Lords ;* a title to which long usage has associated feelings of reverence in the minds of the people, who could not now be soon made to respect *Mr. Justice.*"—Cockburn's *Life of Lord Jeffrey* (2 vols., Edinburgh, 1852), i. p. 365.

Edinburgh, over Moffat, over Eric-stane (Burnswark visible
there for the last time, and my poor little Sister Margaret
" bursting into tears " when she heard of this in my first letter
home) : I hid my sorrow and my weariness, but had abundance
of it, chequering the mysterious hopes and forecastings of what
Edinburgh and the Student element would be. Tom and I had
entered Edinburgh, after twenty miles of walking, between two
and three P.M. ; got a clean-looking, most cheap lodging (" Simon
Square " the poor locality) ; had got ourselves brushed, some
morsel of dinner doubtless ; and Palinurus Tom sallied out into
the streets with me, to show the novice mind a little of Edinburgh before sundown. The novice mind was not excessively
astonished all at once ; but kept its eyes well open, and said
nothing. What streets we went through, I don't the least
recollect ; but have some faint image of St. Giles's High-Kirk,
and of the Luckenbooths there, with their strange little ins and
outs, and eager old women in miniature shops of combs, shoe-
laces and trifles ; still fainter image, if any whatever, of the sublime Horse-Statue in Parliament Square hard by ;—directly
after which Smail, audaciously (so I thought) pushed open a door
(free to all the world), and dragged me in with him to a scene
which I have never forgotten.

An immense Hall, dimly lighted from the top of the walls,
and perhaps with candles burning in it here and there ; all in
strange *chiaroscuro*, and filled with what I thought (exaggera
tively) a thousand or two of human creatures ; all astir in a
boundless buzz of talk, and simmering about in every direction,
some solitary, some in groups. By degrees I noticed that some
were in wig and black gown, some not, but in common clothes,
all well-dressed ; that here and there on the sides of the Hall,
were little thrones with enclosures, and steps leading up ; red-
velvet figures sitting in said thrones, and the black-gowned
eagerly speaking to them,—Advocates pleading to Judges, as
I easily understood. How they could be heard in such a grinding din was somewhat a mystery. Higher up on the walls,
stuck there like swallows in their nests, sat other humbler figures
these I found were the sources of certain wildly plangent lamentable kinds of sounds or echoes which from time to time pierced
the universal noise of feet and voices, and rose unintelligibly
above it, as if in the bitterness of incurable woe ;—Cries of the
Court, I gradually came to understand. And this was Themis
in her Outer House ; such a scene of chaotic din and hurlyburly
as I had never figured before. It seems to me there were four

times or ten times as many people in that Outer House as there now usually are ; and doubtless there is something of fact in this, such have been the curtailments and abatements of Law Practice in the Head Courts since then, and transference of it to the County jurisdictions. Last time I was in that Outer House (some six or seven years ago, in broad daylight), it seemed like a place fallen asleep, fallen almost dead.

Notable figures, now all vanished utterly, were doubtless wandering about as part of that continual hurlyburly, when I first set foot in it, fifty-seven years ago. Great Law Lords This and That, great Advocates *alors célèbres* (as Thiers has it) : Cranstoun, Cockburn,[1] Jeffrey, Walter Scott, John Clerk ; to me at that time they were not even names ; but I have since occasionally thought of that night and place where probably they were living substances, some of them in a kind of relation to me afterwards. Time with his *tenses*, what a miraculous Entity is he always. The only figure I distinctly recollect, and got printed on my brain that night, was John Clerk ; there veritably hitching about, whose grim strong countenance with its black far-projecting brows and look of great sagacity fixed him in my memory. Possibly enough poor Smail named others to me ; Jeffrey perhaps, if we saw him ; though he was not yet quite at the top of his celebrity,—top was some three or four years afterwards, and went on without much drooping for almost twenty years more. But the truth is, except Clerk's, I carried no figure away with me ; nor do I in the least recollect how we made our exit into the streets again, or what we did next : " Outer House," vivid now to a strange degree, is bordered by darkness on both hands. I recal it for Jeffrey's sake ; though we see it is but potentially his ; and I mean not to speak much of his Law Procedures in what follows.

Poor Smail too I may dismiss, as thoroughly insignificant, conceitedly harmless ; he continued in some comradeship with me (or with James Johnstone and me) for perhaps two seasons more ; but gained no regard from me, nor had any effect on me good or bad ;—became, with success, an insignificant flowery Burgher Minister (somewhere in Galloway), and has died only within few years. Poor Jamie Johnstone, also my senior by several years, was far dearer, a man of real merit, with whom

---

[1] Lord Cockburn became Jeffrey's biographer. Of him, of Jeffrey, of Cranstoun and of Clerk, Lockhart gives an entertaining account in *Peter's Letters to his Kinsfolk* (3 vols. Edinburgh, 1819), ii. 43–73. The book contains portraits of Jeffrey and of Clerk.

about my 17th—21st years I had much genial companionship :
but of him also I must not speak. The good, the honest,
not the strong *enough*, much-suffering soul,—he died as Schoolmaster of Haddington, in a time memorable to me.[1] *Ay
de mi !*

It was about 1811 when I began to be familiar with the figure of
Jeffrey, as I saw him in the Courts ; it was in 1812 or 1813 that
he became universally famous, especially in Dumfriesshire, by
his saving from the gallows one " Nell Kennedy," a country
lass who had shocked all Scotland, and especially that region
of it, by a wholesale murder, done on her next Neighbour and
all his Household in mass, in the most cold-blooded and atrocious
manner conceivable to the oldest artist in such horrors. Nell
went down to Ecclefechan one afternoon, purchased a quantity
of arsenic ; walked back with it towards Burnswark Leas, her
Father's Farm ; stopped at Burnswark Farm, which was " old
Tom Stoddart's," a couple of furlongs short of her own home ;
and there sat gossiping till she pretended it was too late, and
that she would now sleep here with the maid. Slept, accordingly,
old Tom giving no welcome, only stingy permission ; rose with
the family next morning ; volunteered to make the porridge
for breakfast ; made it, could herself take none of it, went
home instead, " having headache ; "—and in an hour or so
after, poor old Tom, his Wife, maid, and every living creature
in the house (except a dog who had vomited, and *not* except
the cats who couldn't) was dead or lay dying. Horror was
universal in those solitary quiet regions ;—on the third day,
my Father, finding no lawyer take the least notice, sent a
messenger express to Dumfries ; whereupon the due " pre-
cognitions," due *et-ceteras*, due arrestment of Helen Kennedy
with strict questioning and strict locking-up, as the essential
element. I was in Edinburgh that summer of 1812 ; but heard
enough of the matter there ; in the Border regions, where it
was the universal topic, perhaps not one human creature
doubted but Nell was the criminal, and would get her doom.
Assize-time came, Jeffrey there ; and Jeffrey, by such a play of
advocacy as was never seen before, bewildered the poor jury
into temporary deliquium, or loss of wits (so that the poor
foreman, *Scotticè* " chancellor," on whose casting-vote it turned,
said at last, with the sweat bursting from his brow, " Mercy,
then, mercy ! "), and brought Nell clear off,—home that night,

[1] Died towards the end of 1837. For Carlyle's Letters to Johnstone,
see *Early Letters of Thomas Carlyle* (Macmillan and Co., 1886).

riding gently out of Dumfries in men's clothes to escape the rage
of the mob. The jury-chancellor, they say, on awakening next
morning, smote his now dry brow, with a gesture of despair,
and exclaimed, " Was I mad ? " I have heard from persons
who were at the trial that Jeffrey's art in examining of witnesses
was extreme, that he made them seem to say almost what he
would, and blocked them up from saying what they evidently
wished to say ; his other great resource was urging the " want
of motive " on Nell's part,—no means of fancying how a blousy
rustic lass should go into such a thing ; thing *must* have happened
otherwise ! And indeed, the stagnant stupid soul of Nell,
awake only to its own appetites, and torpid as dead bacon to
all else in this universe, had needed uncommonly little motive :
a blackguard young farmer of the neighbourhood, it was understood, had answered her, in a trying circumstance, " No, oh no,
I cannot marry you : Tom Stoddart has a Bill against me of
£50 ; I have no money, how can I marry ? " " Stoddart ;
£50 ? " thought Nell to herself ; and without difficulty decided
on removing that small obstacle !—

Jeffrey's Advocate-fame from this achievement was, at last,
almost greater than he wished,—as indeed it might well be.
Nell was, next year, indicted again for murdering a child she had
borne (supposed to be the blackguard young farmer's) ; she
escaped this time too, by want of evidence and by good advocacy
(not Jeffrey's, but the very best that could be hired by three
old miser uncles, bringing out for her their long-hoarded stock
with a generosity nigh miraculous) ; Nell, free again, proceeded
next to rob the treasure-chest of these three miraculous uncles,
one night, and leave them with their house on fire, and singular
reflections on so delectable a niece ; after which, for several
years, she continued wandering in the Border byways, smuggling,
stealing, etc. ; only intermittently heard of, but steadily mounting in evil fame, till she had become the *facile princeps* of Border
Devils, and was considered a completely *uncanny* and quasi-
infernal object : was found twice over in Cumberland ships,
endeavouring to get to America, sailors universally refusing to
lift anchor till she were turned out ;—did, at length, most
probably smuggle herself, through Liverpool or some other
place, to America ; at least vanished out of Annandale, and was
no more talked of there. I have seen her Father mowing at
Scotsbrig as a common day-labourer, in subsequent years ; a
snuffling, unpleasant, deceitful-looking body ; very ill thought
of while still a farmer and before his Nell took to murdering.

Nell's three miraculous uncles were maternal, and come of a very honest kin.

The merit of saving such an item of the world's population could not seem to Jeffrey very great; and it was said, his brethren quizzed him upon it, and made him rather uncomfortable. Long afterwards, at Craigenputtock, my Jeannie and I brought him on the topic, which he evidently did not like too well, but was willing to talk of for our sake and perhaps his own. He still affected to think it uncertain whether Nell was really guilty: such an intrepidity, calmness, and steadfast immovability had she exhibited; persisting in mere unshaken " No," under the severest trials by him;—but there was no persuading us that he had the least real doubt, and not some real regret rather. Advocate morality was clearly on his side; it is a strange trade, I have often thought, that of advocate: your intellect, your highest heavenly gift, hung up in the shop-window, like a loaded pistol for sale; will either blow out a pestilent scoundrel's brains, or the scoundrel's salutary sheriff's (in a sense), as you please to choose for your guinea! Jeffrey rose into higher and higher professional repute from this time; and to the last was very celebrated as what his satirists might have called a " Felon's Friend." All this, however, was swallowed among quite nobler kinds of renown, both as Advocate and as Man of Letters and Member of Society; everybody recognising his honourable ingenuity, sagacity, and opulent brilliancy of mind; and nobody ascribing his Felon help to anything but a pitying disposition, and readiness to exercise what faculty one has.

I seem to remember that I dimly rather felt there was something trivial, doubtful, and not quite of the highest type, in our Edinburgh admiration for our great Lights and Law Sages, and for Jeffrey among the rest; but I honestly admired him in a loose way, as my neighbours were doing; was always glad to notice him when I strolled into the Courts; and eagerly enough stept up to hear, if I found him pleading. A delicate, attractive, dainty little figure, as he merely walked about, much more if he were speaking: uncommonly bright black eyes, instinct with vivacity, intelligence and kindly fire; roundish brow, delicate oval face full of rapid expression; figure light, nimble, pretty, though so small, perhaps hardly five feet four in height: he had his gown, almost never any wig, wore his black hair rather closely cropt,—I have seen the back part of it jerk suddenly out in some of the rapid expressions of his face, and knew, even if behind him, that his brow was then puckered, and his eyes looking archly, half-contemptuously out, in conformity to some conclusive little cut his tongue was giving. His voice, clear, harmonious and sonorous, had something of metallic in it, something almost plangent ; never rose into alt, into any dissonance or shrillness, nor carried much the character of humour,— though a fine feeling of the ludicrous always dwelt in him,— as you would notice best, when he got into Scotch dialect, and gave you, with admirable truth of mimicry, old Edinburgh incidents and experiences of his. Very great upon old " Judge Braxie," [1] " Peter Peebles," and the like :—for the rest, his laugh was small, and by no means Homeric ; he never laughed loud (couldn't do it, I should think), and indeed oftener sniggered slightly than laughed in any way.

For above a dozen or fourteen years I had been outwardly familiar with the figure of Jeffrey, before we came to any closer acquaintance, or indeed had the least prospect of any. His sphere lay far away above mine ; to him in his shining elevation, my existence down among the shadows was unknown. In May 1814 I heard him once pleading in the General Assembly, on some poor Cause there ; [2] a notable, but not the notablest thing to me, while I sat looking diligently, though mostly as dramatic spectator, into the procedures of that venerable Church Court, for the first time, which proved also the last. Queer old figures there,—Hill of St. Andrews, Johnston of Crossmichael, Dr. Inglis with the voice jumbling in perpetual unforeseen alternation between deep bass and shrill treble (ridiculous to hear, though shrewd cunning sense lay in it), Dr. Chalmers once, etc. etc.,—all vanished now ! Jeffrey's pleading, the first I had heard of him, seemed to me abundantly clever, full of liveliness, free-flowing ingenuity ; my admiration went frankly with that of others, but I think was hardly of very deep character.

This would be the year I went to Annan, as Teacher of Mathematics,—not a gracious destiny, nor by any means a joyful ; indeed a hateful, sorrowful and *imprisoning* one, could I at all have helped it, which I could not. My second year there, at Rev. Mr. Glen's (" reading Newton's *Principia* till three A.M.," and voraciously many other Books) was greatly more endurable, nay in parts was genial and spirited, though the paltry trade and ditto environment for most part were always odious to me.

---

[1] Lord Braxfield ; in *Peter's Letters to his Kinsfolk*, vols. ii. iii., there is a description of this coarse, vigorous and grotesque old lawyer.

[2] Jeffrey's age at this time was 41. He was born 23d October 1773.

In late Autumn 1816, I went to Kirkcaldy, in like capacity, though in circumstances (what with Edward Irving's company, what with, etc. etc.) which were far superior : there in 1818 I had come to the grim conclusion that Schoolmastering must end, whatsoever pleased to follow ; that " it were better to perish," as I exaggeratively said to myself, " than continue Schoolmastering." I made for Edinburgh,[1] as did Irving too ; intending, I, darkly towards potential " Literature," if I durst have said or thought so ; but hope hardly dwelt in me on that or on any side ; only fierce resolution in abundance to do my best and utmost in all honest ways, and to suffer as silently and stoically as might be, if it proved (as too likely !) that I could do *nothing*. This kind of humour, what I sometimes called of " *desperate* hope," has largely attended me all my life. In short, as has been enough indicated elsewhere, I was advancing towards huge instalments of bodily and spiritual wretchedness in this my Edinburgh Purgatory ; and had to clean and purify myself in penal fire of various kinds for several years coming,— the first and much the worst two or three of which were to be enacted in this once loved City. Horrible to think of, in part, even yet ! The bodily part of them was a kind of base agony (arising mainly in the *want* of any extant or discoverable *fence* between my coarser fellow-creatures and my more sensitive self), and might and could easily (had the Age been pious or thoughtful) have been spared a poor creature like me :—those hideous disturbances to sleep etc., a very little real care and goodness might prevent all that ; and I look back upon it still with a kind of angry protest, and would have my successors saved from it. But perhaps one needs suffering, more than at first seems ; and the spiritual agonies would not have been enough ? These latter seem wholly blessed, in retrospect ; and were infinitely worth suffering,—with whatever addition *was* needful ! God be thanked always.

It was still some eight or ten years before any personal contact occurred between Jeffrey and me ; nor did I ever tell him what a bitter passage, known to only one party, there had been between us. It was probably in 1819–1820 (the coldest winter I ever knew) that I had taken a most private resolution, and executed it in spite of physical and other misery, to try Jeffrey with an actual Contribution to the *Edinburgh Review*. The idea seemed great, and might be tried, though nearly

[1] Carlyle left Kirkcaldy for Edinburgh, 20th November 1818.

desperate. I had got hold somewhere (for even Books were all
but inaccessible to me) of a foolish enough, but new French
Book, a mechanical *Theory of Gravitation*, elaborately worked
out by a late foolish M. Pictet (I think that was the name) in
Geneva ; this I carefully read, judged of, and elaborately dictated
a candid account and condemnation of, or modestly firm
contradiction of (my amanuensis a certain feeble, but inquiring
quasi-disciple of mine, called George Dalgliesh of Annan, from
whom I kept my ulterior purpose quite secret) : well do I yet
remember those dreary evenings in Bristo Street ; oh, what
ghastly passages, and dismal successive spasms of attempt, at
" Literary Enterprise "—*Hevelii Selenographia*,[1] with poor
Horrox's *Venus in sole visa*, intended for some ghastly *Life* of
the said Horrox,—this for one other instance ! I read all
Saussure's four quartos of *Travels in Switzerland*[2] too (and still
remember much of it), I know not with what object ; I was
banished, solitary, as if to the bottom of a cave, and blindly
had to try many impossible roads out ! My *review of Pictet* all
fairly written out, in George Dalgliesh's good clerk hand, I
penned some brief polite Note to the great Editor ; and walked
off with the small Parcel, one night,[3] to his address in George
Street ;—I very well remember leaving it with his valet there,
and disappearing in the night with various thoughts and doubts !
My hopes had never risen high, or in fact risen at all ; but for
a fortnight or so, they did not quite die out,—and then it was in
absolute *zero*, no answer, no return of MS., absolutely no notice
taken ; which was a form of catastrophe more complete than
even I had anticipated ! There rose in my head a pungent
little Note, which might be written to the great man, with
neatly cutting considerations offered him from the small unknown ditto ; but I wisely judged it was still more dignified to
let the matter lie as it was, and take what I had got for my own
benefit only. Nor did I ever mention it to almost anybody ;
least of all to Jeffrey, in subsequent changed times, when at any
rate it was fallen extinct. It was my second, not quite my first
attempt in that fashion ; above two years before, from Kirkcaldy, I had forwarded to some Magazine Editor in Edinburgh

<hr>

[1] Johannes Hevelius (born at Dantzig 1611, died 1688), one of the most
eminent astronomers of his time. His *Selenographia*, Description of the
Moon, was published at Dantzig 1647. In 1662 he added to his *Mercurius
in sole visus*, Horrox's Dissertation on the Transit of Venus, which Horrox
was the first to observe, in 1639. Horrox died, only 22 years old, in 1641.
[2] Saussure, *Voyages dans les Alpes* (4 vols., 4to, *à Genève*, 1779 to 1796).
[3] 24th January 1820.

what perhaps was a likelier little Article (of descriptive Tourist
kind, after a real Tour by Yarrow Country into Annandale),
which also vanished without sign ; not much to my regret, that
first one ; nor indeed very much the second either (a dull affair
altogether, I could not but admit) ;—and no third adventure of
the kind lay ahead for me.   It must be owned my first entrances
into glorious " Literature " were abundantly stinted and pitiful ;
but a man does enter if, even with a small gift, he persist : and
perhaps it is no disadvantage if the door be several times
slammed in his face, as a preliminary.

In spring 1827, I suppose it must have been, a Letter came to
me at Comley Bank from Procter (" Barry Cornwall," my
quondam London acquaintance) offering, with some " congratulations " etc., to introduce me formally to Jeffrey, whom he
certified to be a " very fine fellow," with much kindness in him,
among his other known qualities.   Comley Bank, except for
one Darling Soul, whose heavenly nobleness then as ever afterwards shone on me, and *should* have made the darkest place
bright (ah me, ah me, I only know now how noble She was !),
was a gloomy intricate abode to me ; and, in retrospect, has
little or nothing of pleasant but *Her*.   This of Jeffrey, however,
had a practical character, of some promise ; and I remember
striding off with Procter's introduction, one evening, towards
George Street and Jeffrey (perhaps by appointment of hour and
place by himself), in rather good spirits.   " I shall see the
famous man then," thought I ;   " and if he can do nothing for
me, why *not !* "   I got ready admission into Jeffrey's " study,"
or rather " office," for it had mostly that air ;   a roomy not
over-neat apartment on the ground floor, with a big baize-
covered table, loaded with book rows and paper bundles ;   on
one or perhaps two of the walls were book-shelves, likewise well
filled, but with books in tattery ill-bound or unbound condition,
—" bad new Literature, these will be," thought I ;   " the table
ones are probably on Law ! "   Fire, pair of candles were cheerfully burning, in the light of which sat my famous little gentleman ;   laid aside his work, cheerfully invited me to sit, and began
talking in a perfectly human manner.   Our dialogue was altogether human and successful ;   lasted for perhaps twenty
minutes (for I could not consume a great man's time), turned
upon the usual topics, what I was doing, what I had published,—
German Romance Translations, my last thing ;   to which I
remember he said kindly, " We must give you a lift ! "   an offer
which, in some complimentary way, I managed, to his satis-

faction, to decline. My feeling with him was that of unembarrassment ; a reasonable, veracious little man, I could perceive, with whom any truth one felt good to utter would have a fair chance. Whether much was said of German Literature, whether anything at all on my writing of it for him, I don't recollect : but certainly I took my leave in a gratified successful kind of mood ; and both those topics, the latter in practical form, did soon abundantly spring up between us ; with formal return-call by him (which gave a new speed to intimacy), agreement for a little Paper on *Jean Paul*, and whatever could follow out of an acquaintanceship well begun. The poor Paper on *Jean Paul*, a sturdy Piece, not without humour and substance of my own, appeared in (I suppose) the very next Edinburgh Review ;[1] and made what they call a sensation among the Edinburgh buckrams ; which was greatly heightened, next Number, by the more elaborate and grave article on *German Literature*[2] generally, which set many tongues wagging, and some few brains considering, *What* this strange monster could be that was come to disturb their quiescence, and the established order of Nature ! Some Newspapers or Newspaper took to denouncing " the Mystic School,"—which my bright little Woman declared to consist of me alone, or of her and me ; and, for a long while after, merrily used to designate us by that title ; " Mystic School " signifying " *us*," in the pretty *coterie*-speech, which she was always so ready to adopt, and which lent such a charm to her talk and writing. She was beautifully gay and hopeful under these improved phenomena,—the darling soul ! *Foreign Review, Foreign Quarterly*, etc., followed, to which I was eagerly invited ; Articles for Jeffrey (about parts of which I had always to dispute with him) appeared also, from time to time : in a word, I was now in a sort, fairly launched upon Literature ; and had even, to sections of the public, become a " Mystic School ; "—not quite prematurely, being now of the age of thirty-two, and having had my bits of experiences, and gotten really something which I wished much to say,—and have ever since been saying, the best way I could.

After Jeffrey's call at Comley Bank, the intimacy rapidly increased. He was much taken with my little Jeannie, as he well might be ; one of the brightest and cleverest creatures in the whole world ; full of innocent rustic simplicity and veracity,

---

1 *Edinburgh Review*, No. 91, June 1827.
2 *State of German Literature;* for this, and the Article on *Jean Paul*, see Carlyle's *Miscellanies*, vol. i.

yet with the gracefullest discernment, calmly natural deportment ; instinct with beauty and intelligence to the finger-ends !
He became, in a sort, her would-be openly declared friend and
quasi-lover ; as was his way in such cases. He had much the
habit of flirting about with women, especially pretty women,
much more the both pretty and clever ; all in a weakish, mostly
dramatic, and wholly theoretic way (his age now fifty gone) ;
would daintily kiss their hands in bidding good morning, offer
his due *homage*, as he phrased it ; trip about half like a lap-dog,
half like a human adorer, with speeches pretty and witty,
always of trifling import. I have known some women (not the
prettiest) take offence at it, and awkwardly draw themselves
up,—but without in the least putting him out. The most took
it quietly, kindly ; and found an entertainment to themselves in
cleverly answering it, as he did in pertly offering it ;—pertly,
yet with something of real reverence, and always in a dextrous
light way. Considerable jealousy attended the reigning queen
of his circle, among the now non-reigning; who soon detected her
position, and gave her the triumph of their sonetimes half-
visible spleen. An airy environment of this kind was, wherever
possible, a coveted charm in Jeffrey's way of life.[1] I can fancy
he had seldom made such a surprising and agreeable acquaintance as this new one at Comley Bank ! My little Woman
perfectly understood all that sort of thing, the methods and the
rules of it ; and could lead her clever little gentleman a very
pretty minuet, as far as she saw good. They discovered mutual
old cousinships by the maternal side, soon had common topics
enough ; I believe he really entertained a sincere regard and
affection for her, in the heart of his theoretic dangling, which
latter continued unabated for several years to come,—with not
a little quizzing and light interest on her part, and without
shadow of offence on mine, or on anybody's ; nay I had my
amusements in it too, so naïve, humorous and pretty were her
bits of narratives about it, all her procedures in it so dainty,
delicate and sure. The noble little Soul, suspicion of her nobleness would have been mad in me ;—and could I grudge her the
little bit of entertainment she might be able to extract from

[1] " What I miss most in London are the four or five houses into which
you can go at all hours, and the seven or eight women with whom you are
quite familiar, and with whom you can go and sit and talk at your ease,
dressed or undressed, morning or evening, whenever you have any leisure,
or indisposition to be busy. Here I have only visiting acquaintances, at
least among that sex, and that does not suit or satisfy me."—Jeffrey to
his Father-in-law, 13th April 1822 (*Cockburn,* ii. 201).

this poor harmless sport, in a life so grim as she cheerfully had with me? My Jeannie, oh my bonny little Jeannie, how did I ever deserve so queen-like a heart from thee? Ah me!—

Jeffrey's acquaintanceship seemed, and was for the time, an immense acquisition to me; and everybody regarded it as my highest good fortune,—though in the end it did not practically amount to much. Meantime it was very pleasant; and made us feel as if no longer cut off and isolated, but fairly admitted, or like to be admitted, and taken in tow, by the world and its actualities. Jeffrey had begun to feel some form of bad health at this time (some remains of disease in the *trachea*, caught on circuit somewhere, " successfully defending a murderess " it was said !)—he rode almost daily, in intervals of Court business; a slow amble, easy to accompany on foot; and I had much walking with him, and many a pleasant sprightly dialogue,— cheerful to my fancy (as speech with an important man), but less instructive than I might have hoped. To my regret, he would not talk of his experiences in the world, which I considered would have been so instructive to me, nor of things concrete and current; but was theoretic generally; and seemed bent on, first of all, converting me from what he called my " German Mysticism,"—back merely, as I could perceive, into dead Edinburgh Whiggism, Scepticism, and Materialism; what I felt to be a forever impossible enterprise. We had long discussions, and argumentative parryings and thrustings; which I have known continue, night after night, till two or three in the morning (when I was his guest at Craigcrook,[1] as once or twice happened in coming years); there we went on in brisk logical exercise, with all the rest of the house asleep; and parted usually in good humour, though after a game which was hardly worth the candle. I found him infinitely witty, ingenious, sharp of fence; but not in any sense deep; and used without difficulty to hold my own with him. A pleasant enough exercise, but at last not a very profitable one.

He was ready to have tried anything in practical help of me; and did, on hint given, try two things: vacant " Professorship of Moral Philosophy " at St. Andrews; ditto of something similar (perhaps it was " English Literature ") in the new Gower- Street University at London; but both (thank Heaven) came

---

1 Craigcrook, as already noted, is about three miles to the north-west of Edinburgh, on the eastern slope of Corstorphine Hill. Jeffrey's summers, from 1815 till his death in 1850, were spent there.

summarily to nothing. Nor were his Review Articles any longer such an important employment to me ; nor had they ever been my least troublesome undertakings,—plenty of small discrepancy about details as we went along ; though no serious disagreement ever, and his treatment throughout was liberal and handsome. Indeed he had much patience with me, I must say ; for there was throughout a singular freedom in my way of talk with him ; and, though far from wishing or intending to be disrespectful, I doubt there was at times an unembarrassment and frankness of hitting and repelling, which did not quite beseem our respective ages and positions. He never testified the least offence ; but, possibly enough, remembered it afterwards, being a thin-skinned, sensitive man, with all his pretended pococurantism, and real knowledge of what is called " the world." I remember pleasant strolls out to Craigcrook (one of the prettiest places in the world), where, on a Sunday especially, I might hope, what was itself a rarity with me, to find a companionable human acquaintance, not to say one of such quality as this. He would wander about the woods with me, looking on the Frith, and Fife Hills, on the Pentlands and Edinburgh Castle and City,—nowhere was there such a view ;—perhaps he would walk most of the way back with me ; quietly sparkling and chatting ; probably quizzing me in a kind way, if his Wife were with us, as sometimes happened. If I met him in the streets, in the Parliament House or accidentally anywhere, there ensued, unless he were engaged, a cheerful bit of talk and promenading. He frequently rode round by Comley Bank in returning home ; and there I would see him, or hear something pleasant of him. He never rode but at a walk, and his little horse was steady as machinery : he on horseback, I on foot, was a frequent form of our dialogues. I suppose we must have dined sometimes at Craigcrook, or Moray Place, in this incipient period ; but don't recollect.

The incipient period was probably among the best ; though for a long while afterwards there was no falling off in intimacy and good will. But sunrise is often enough lovelier than noon : much in this first stage was not yet fulfilment, and was enhanced by the colours of hope ; there was the new feeling, too, of what a precious conquest and acquisition had fallen to us, which all the world might envy : certainly in every sense the adventure was a flattering and cheering one, and did both of us good. I forget how long it had lasted, before our resolution to remove to Craigenputtock came to be fulfilled :—it seems to me, some six

or eight months ?   The flitting to Craigenputtock took place in
May 1828 ; we staid a week in Moray Place (Jeffrey's fine new
house there) after our furniture was all on the road, and we were
waiting till it should arrive, and render a new home possible
amid the moors and mountains.   Jeffrey promised to follow us
thither, with Wife and Daughter, for three days in vacation
time ensuing, to see what kind of a thing we were making of it.
Which, of course, was great news.   Doubtless he, like most of
my Edinburgh acquaintances, had been strongly dissuasive of
the step we were taking : but his or other people's arguments
availed nothing, and I have forgotten them ; the step had been
well meditated, saw itself to be founded on irrefragable considerations, of health, *finance*, etc., etc., unknown to bystanders ;
and could not be forborne or altered.   " I will come and see you
at any rate ! " said Jeffrey ; and dismissed us with various
expressions of interest, and no doubt with something of real
regret.

Of our History at Craigenputtock there might a great deal be
written which might amuse the curious : for it was in fact a very
singular scene and arena for such a pair as my Darling and me,
with such a Life ahead ; and bears some analogy to the settlement of Robinson Crusoe in his desert Isle, surrounded mostly
by the wild populations, not wholly helpful or even harmless ;
and requiring, for its equipment into habitability and convenience, infinite contrivance, patient adjustment, and natural
ingenuity in the head of Robinson himself.   It is a History I
by no means intend to write,—with such or with any object.
To me there is a *sacredness* of interest in it ; consistent only with
silence.   It was the field of endless nobleness, and beautiful
talent and virtue, in Her who is now gone ; also of good industry,
and many loving and blessed thoughts in myself, while living
there by her side.   Poverty and mean Obstruction had given
origin to it, and continued to preside over it ; but were transformed, by human valour of various sorts, into a kind of victory
and royalty : something of high and great dwelt in it, though
nothing could be smaller and lower than very many of the
details.   How blessed might poor mortals be, in the straitest
circumstances, *if* only their wisdom, and fidelity to Heaven and
to one another, were *adequately* great !   It looks to me now like
a kind of humble russet-coated *epic*, that seven [1] years' settlement at Craigenputtock ; very poor in this world's goods, but
not without an intrinsic dignity greater and more important

[1] Six years ; May 1828 till May 1834.

than then appeared. Thanks very mainly to Her, and her faculties and magnanimities ; without whom it had not been possible ! I incline to think it the poor-*best* place that could have been selected for the ripening into fixity and composure, of anything useful which there may have been in me, against the years that were coming. And it is certain that for living in, and thinking in, I have never since found in the world a place so favourable. And we were driven and pushed into it, as if by Necessity, and its beneficent though ugly little shocks and pushes, shock after shock gradually compelling us thither ! ' For a Divinity doth shape our ends, rough-hew them how *we* will : ' often in my life, have I been brought to think of this, as probably every considering person is ; and, looking before and after, have felt, though reluctant enough to believe in the importance or significance of so infinitesimally small an atom as oneself, that the Doctrine of a Special Providence is in some sort natural to man. All piety points that way, all logic points the other ;—one has, in one's darkness and limitation, a trembling faith, and can at least say with the *Voices*, " *Wir heissen euch hoffen*,"—if it *be* the will of the Highest.

The Jeffreys failed not to appear at Craigenputtock ; their big Carriage climbed our rugged Hill-roads, landed the Three Guests (young Charlotte, " Sharlie," with Pa and Ma) and the clever old Valet-maid that waited on them ; stood three days under its glazed sheeting in our little back-court,—nothing like a house yet ready for it, and indeed all the outhouses and appurtenances still in a much unfinished state ; and only the main House quite ready and habitable. The visit was pleasant and successful ; but I recollect few or no particulars. Jeffrey and I rode one day (or perhaps this was on another visit ?), round by the flank of Dunscore Craig, the Shilling-land and Craigenvey ; and took a view of Loch-Orr and the black moorlands round us, with the granite mountains of Galloway overhanging in the distance ; not a beautiful landscape, but it answered as well as another. Our party, the head of it especially, was chatty and cheery ; but I remember nothing so well as the consummate art with which my Dear One played the domestic field-marshal, and spread out our exiguous resources, without fuss or bustle, to cover everything [with a] coat of hospitality and even elegance and abundance ; I have been in houses ten times, nay a hundred times, as rich, where things went not so well. Though never bred to this, but brought up in opulent plenty by a mother that could bear no partnership in house-keeping, she, finding it

become necessary, loyally applied herself to it, and soon surpassed in it all the women I have ever seen. My noble one, how
beautiful has our poverty made thee to me ! She was so true
and frank, withal ; nothing of the skulking Balderstone in her :
one day at dinner, I remember, Jeffrey admired the fritters or
bits of pancake he was eating ; and she let him know, not without
some vestige of shock to him, that she had made them. " What ;
you ! Twirl up the frying-pan, and catch them in the air ? "
Even so, my high friend ; and you may turn it over in your
mind !—On the fourth or third day, the Jeffreys went ; and
" carried off our little temporary paradise," as I sorrowfully
expressed it to them, while shutting their Coach door in our back
yard,—to which bit of pathos Jeffrey answered by a friendly
little sniff of quasi-mockery, or laughter through the nose ; and
rolled prosperously away.

They paid at least one other visit ; probably not just next
year, but the one following. We met them, by appointment, at
Dumfries (I think, in the intervening year) ; and passed a night
with them in the King's Arms Inn there, which I well enough
recollect : huge ill-kept " Head-Inn ; " bed opulent in *bugs ;*
waiter, a monstrous baggy unwieldy old figure, hebetated,
dreary, as if parboiled ; upon whom Jeffrey quizzed his Daughter
at breakfast, " Comes all of eating eggs, Sharlie ; poor man as
good as owned it to me ! "—After breakfast, he went across with
my Wife to visit a certain Mrs. Richardson, Authoress of some
Novels ; really a superior kind of woman and much a lady ; who
had been an old flame of his, perhaps twenty-five or thirty years
before. " These old loves don't do ! " said Mrs. Jeffrey, with
easy sarcasm, who was left behind with me. And accordingly
there had been some embarrassment, I afterwards found, but on
both sides a gratifying of some good though melancholy feelings.

This Mrs. Jeffrey was the American Miss Wilkes ; whose
marriage with Jeffrey, or at least his voyage across to marry her,
had made considerable noise in its time.[1] She was mother of

1 Miss Wilkes (daughter of Mr. Charles Wilkes, banker in New York,
who was nephew, not brother, of the famous John) had, in 1810, paid a
visit to some friends in Edinburgh, where Jeffrey became acquainted with
her. They were married in New York in 1813, and returned to Scotland
early in 1814. The " War of 1812 " was then being carried on between
England and America. Before leaving the United States, Jeffrey had to
apply for a cartel for his return home, when he was drawn into conversation
with the Secretary of State, Mr. Monroe, as to the war, its provocations,
principles and probable results. Afterwards, the same day, he dined with
the President, Mr. Madison, when the same topics were discussed for nearly
two hours (see *Cockburn*, i. 227–229). Jeffrey's reports of these conversations could not fail to produce some effect in England at the time.

this "Sharlie" (who is now the widow Mrs. Empson . . .);
Jeffrey had no other child; his first wife, a Hunter of St.
Andrews, had died very soon.[1] This second, the American Miss
Wilkes, was from Pennsylvania, actual Brother's-Daughter of our
Demagogue "Wilkes,"—she was Sister of the "Commodore
Wilkes," who ' boarded the *Trent* ' some years ago; and almost
involved us in war with Yankeeland, during that beautiful
Nigger Agony or "Civil War" of theirs! She was a roundish-
featured, not pretty but comely, sincere and hearty kind of
woman, with a great deal of clear natural insight, often sarcastically turned; to which a certain nervous tic or jerk of the head
gave new emphasis or singularity; for her talk went roving
about in a loose random way, and hit down, like a flail, unexpectedly on this and that, with the jerk for accompaniment, in
a really genial fashion. She and I were mutual favourites; she
liked my sincerity, as I hers. . . .

The "Old-Love" business finished, our friends soon rolled
away; and left us to go home at leisure,—in our good old Gig
(value £11), which I always look back upon with a kind of
veneration, so sound and excellent was it, though so unfashionable; the conquest of good Alick, my ever-shifty Brother;
which carried us many a pleasant mile till Craigenputtock ended.
Probably the Jeffreys were bound for Cumberland on this
occasion, to see Brougham, of whom, as I remember, Mrs. Jeffrey
spoke to me with candour, not with enthusiasm, during that
short "Old-Love" absence. Next year[2] (it must have been)
they all came again to Craigenputtock; and with more success
than ever.

One of the nights, there, on this occasion, encouraged possibly
by the presence of poor James Anderson, an ingenuous simple
youngish man, and our nearest *gentleman* neighbour,—Jeffrey,
in the Drawing-room, was cleverer, brighter and more amusing
than I ever saw him elsewhere. We had got to talk of public
speaking; of which Jeffrey had plenty to say, and found Anderson and all of us ready enough to hear. Before long he fell into
mimicking of public Speakers,—men unknown, perhaps imaginary generic specimens;—and did it with such a felicity, flowing
readiness, ingenuity and perfection of imitation as I never saw
equalled, and had not given him credit for before. Our cosy
little Drawing-room, bright-shining, hidden in the lonely wildernesses, how beautiful it looked to us; become suddenly, as it

1 In 1805, in the fourth year of her married life.
2 September 1830.

were, a Temple of the Muses! The little man strutted about, full of electric fire, with attitudes, with gesticulations, still more with winged words, oftener *broken*-winged, amid our admiring laughter; gave us the windy-grandiloquent specimen, the ponderous-stupid, the airy-ditto, various specimens, as the talk, chiefly his own, spontaneously suggested them, of which there was a little preparatory interstice between each two; and the mimicry was so complete, you would have said, not his mind only, but his very body became the specimen's, his face filled with the expression represented, and his little figure seeming to grow gigantic if the personage required it: at length he gave us the abstruse-costive specimen, which had a meaning and no utterance for it, but went about clambering, stumbling as on a path of loose boulders; and ended in total downbreak, amid peals of the heartiest laughter from us all. This of the aerial little sprite, standing there in fatal collapse, with the brightest of eyes sternly gazing into utter nothingness and dumbness was one of the most tickling and genially ludicrous things I ever saw; and it prettily winded up our little drama.[1] I often thought of it afterwards; and of what a part mimicry plays among human gifts. In its lowest phase, no talent can be lower (for even the Papuans and monkeys have it); but in its highest, where it gives you *domicile* in the spiritual world of a Shakspeare or a Goethe, there are only some few that are higher. No clever man, I suppose, is originally without it. Dickens's essential faculty, I often say, is that of a first-rate Play-actor; had he been born twenty or forty years sooner, we should most probably have had a second and greater Mathews, Incledon, or the like, and no *writing* Dickens.

It was probably next morning after this (one of these mornings it certainly was) that we received, i.e. Jeffrey did (I think through my Brother John, then vaguely trying for "Medical Practice" in London, and present on the scene referred to), a sternly brief Letter from poor Hazlitt; to the effect, and almost in the words, "Dear Sir, I am dying: can you send me £10, and so consummate your many kindnesses to me? W. Hazlitt."

[1] " It may appear an odd thing to say, but it is true, that the listener's pleasure was enhanced by the personal littleness of the speaker. A large man could scarcely have thrown off Jeffrey's conversational flowers without exposing himself to ridicule. But the liveliness of the deep thoughts, and the flow of the bright expressions, that animated his talk, seemed so natural and appropriate to the figure that uttered them, that they were heard with something of the delight with which the slenderness of the trembling throat, and the quivering of the wings, make us enjoy the strength and clearness of the notes of a little bird."—*Cockburn*, i. 364.

This was for Jeffrey ; my Brother's Letter to me, enclosing this, would of course elucidate the situation. Jeffrey with true sympathy, at once wrote a cheque for £50 ;[1] and poor Hazlitt died, in peace from duns at least. He seemed to have no *old* friends about him ; to be left, in his poor Lodging, to the humanity of medical people, and transient recent acquaintances ; and to be dying in a grim stoical humour, like a worn-out soldier in hospital. The new Doctor people reckoned that a certain Dr. Darling, the first called in, had fatally mistreated him. Hazlitt had just finished his toilsome, unrewarded (not quite worthless) *Life of Napoleon,*[2] which at least recorded his own loyal admiration and quasi-adoration of that questionable Person : after which he felt excessively worn and low ; and was, by unlucky Dr. Darling, recommended, not to Port wine, brown soup, and the like generous regimen, but to a course of purgatives and blue pills, which irrecoverably wasted his last remnants of strength, and brought him to his end in this sad way. Poor Hazlitt, he was never admirable to me ; but I had my estimation of him, my pity for him ;—a man recognisably of fine natural talents and aspirations, but of no sound culture whatever, and flung into the roaring cauldron of stupid prurient anarchic London, there to try if he could find some culture for himself !

This was Jeffrey's last visit to Craigenputtock ; I forget when it was (probably next Autumn late) that we made our fortnight's visit to Craigcrook and him. That was a shining sort of affair ; but did not, in effect, accomplish much for any of us. Perhaps for one thing, we staid too long ; Jeffrey was beginning to be seriously incommoded in health,—had bad sleep, cared not how late he sat ; and we had now more than ever a series of sharp fencing-bouts, night after night ; which could decide nothing for either of us, except our radical incompatibility in respect of World-Theory, and the incurable divergence of our opinions on the most important matters. " You are so dreadfully in earnest ! " said he to me, once or oftener. Besides, I own now, I was deficient in reverence to him ; and had not then, nor, alas, have ever acquired in my solitary and mostly silent existence, the art

[1] Carlyle has mentioned this before. The sum requested was £100, and Jeffrey's £50 never reached Hazlitt. In a letter, dated 18th September 1830, to his brother John, in London, Carlyle says : " He [Jeffrey] has got a letter from Hazlitt, strangely requesting £100 from him, and determines to consult you on the subject, and in the meantime to send £50 through your hands." Dr. Carlyle's reply to this letter, dated 25th October 1830, says that Jeffrey's kind gift did not arrive until after Hazlitt's death, which occurred on the 18th September 1830.
[2] Hazlitt's *Life of Napoleon* (4 vols. London, 1827).

of gently saying strong things, or of insinuating my dissent, instead of uttering it right out, at the risk of offence or otherwise. At bottom, I did not find his the highest kind of insight, in regard to any province whatever. In Literature he had a respectable range of reading, but discovered little serious study ; and had no views which I could adopt in preference. On all subjects, I had to refuse him the title of deep ; and secretly to acquiesce in much that the new Opposition Party (Wilson, Lockhart, etc., who had broken out so outrageously in *Blackwood* for the last ten years) were alleging against the old excessive Edinburgh Hero-worship. An unpleasant fact, which probably was not quite hidden to so keen a pair of eyes. One thing struck me, in sad elucidation of his forensic glories : I found that essentially he was always as if speaking to a jury ; that the thing of which he could not convince fifteen clear-headed men, was to him a nothing,—good only to be flung over the lists, and left lying without notice farther.[1] This seemed to me a very sad result of Law ! For " the Highest cannot be spoken of in words," as Goethe truly says,—as, in fact, all truly deep men say or know. I urged this on his consideration now and then ; but without the least acceptance. These " stormy sittings," as Mrs. Jeffrey laughingly called them, did not improve our relation to one another. But these were the last we had, of that nature. In other respects Edinburgh had been barren : effulgences of " Edinburgh Society," big dinners, parties, we in due measure had ; but nothing there was very interesting either to *Her* or to me, and all of it passed away as an obliging pageant merely. Well do I remember our return to Craigenputtock, after nightfall amid the clammy yellow leaves, and desolate rains, with the clink of Alick's *stithy* alone audible of human ; and have marked it elsewhere.

A great deal of correspondence there still was, and all along had been. Many Jeffrey Letters to me, and many to Her ; which were all cheerfully answered : I know not what has become of all these papers ;[2] by me they never were destroyed,— though indeed neither Hers nor mine were ever of much import-

---

[1] " The authority of our own opinion," Jeffrey says in 1790, " though perhaps the least dangerous of any, still participates in those inconveniences which all species of authority create, and while a man's powers are unimpaired, it were a lucky thing if he could every day forget the sentiments of the former, that they might receive the correction or confirmation of a second judgment."—*Cockburn*, i. 25.

[2] These were given to Lord Jeffrey's daughter, Mrs. Empson, after the publication of the Reminiscence in 1881.

ance except for the passing moment. I ought to add that Jeffrey about this time, (next summer, I should think) generously offered to confer on me an annuity of £100 ;—which annual sum, had it fallen on me from the clouds, would have been of very high convenience at that time ; but which I could not, for a moment, have dreamt of accepting as gift or subventionary help from any fellow-mortal. It was at once, in my handsomest, gratefullest, but brief and conclusive way [declined] from Jeffrey : " Republican Equality the silently fixed law of human society at present ; each man to live on his own resources, and have an *Equality* of economies with every other man ; dangerous, and not possible except through cowardice or folly, to depart from said clear rule, —till perhaps a better era rise on us again ! " Jeffrey returned to the charge, twice over, in handsome enough sort ; but my new answer was, in briefest words, a repetition of the former, and the second time I answered nothing at all, but stood by other topics ; upon which the matter dropped altogether. It was not mere pride of mine that frustrated this generous resolution ; but sober calculation as well, and correct weighing of the results probable in so dangerous a copartnery as that proposed. In no condition well conceivable to me could such a proposal have been accepted ; and though I could not doubt but Jeffrey had intended an act of real generosity, for which I was and am grateful, perhaps there was something in the manner of it that savoured of consciousness, and of screwing one's self up to the point ; less of godlike pity for a fine fellow and his struggles, than of human determination to do a fine action of one's own ;—which might add to the promptitude of my refusal. He had abundance of money ; but he was not of that opulence which could render such an " annuity," in case I should accept it, totally insensible to him : I therefore *endeavoured* all the more to be thankful ; and if the heart would not quite do (as was perhaps the case), forced the intellect to take part, which it does at this day. Jeffrey's beneficence was undoubted ; and his gifts to poor people in distress were a known feature of his way of life. I once, some months after this, borrowed £100 from him (my pitiful bits of " Periodical-Literature " incomings having gone awry, as they were too liable to do), but was able, I still remember with what satisfaction, to repay punctually within a few weeks :—and this was all of pecuniary chivalry *we* two ever had between us.

Probably he was rather cooling in his feelings towards me, if they ever had been very warm : so obstinate and rugged had he found me, " so dreadfully in earnest " ! And now the time of

the Reform Bill was coming on ; Jeffrey and all high Whigs
getting summoned into an Official career ;—and a scene opening,
which (in effect), instead of irradiating with new glory and
value, completely clouded the remaining years of Jeffrey's life.
His health had for some years been getting weaker,—and proved
now unequal to his new honours: that was the fatal circumstance,
which rendered all the others irredeemable.   He was not what
you could call ambitious, rather the reverse of that ; though
he relished public honours, especially if they could be inter-
preted to signify public love : I remember his great pleasure
in having been elected Dean of Faculty,[1] perhaps a year or so
before anything of this Reform agitation ; and my surprise
at the real delight he showed in this proof of general regard
from his fellow Advocates.   But now, ambitious or not, he found
the career flung open, all barriers thrown down, and was forced
to enter, all the world at his back crushing him in.

He was, naturally, appointed Lord Advocate[2] (political
president of Scotland), had to get shoved into Parliament,—
some vacancy created for him by the great Whigs, " Malton in
Yorkshire " the place : and was whirled away to London and
Public Life ; age now about fifty-six, and health bad.   I
remember, in his correspondence, considerable misgivings, and
gloomy forecastings, about all this, which, in my inexperience,
and the general exultation then prevalent, I had treated with
far less regard than they merited.   He found them too true ;
and, what I as bystander could not quite see till long after, that
his worst expectations were realised.   The exciting agitated
scene, abroad and at home ; the unwholesome hours, bad air,

1 Elected Dean of the Faculty of Advocates, 2d July 1829.—*Cockburn,*
i. 283.
2 In December 1830.—" There is no situation native to Scotland of
greater trust or dignity than that of Lord-Advocate. . . . In so far as each
is the legal adviser of the crown in their respective countries, the Lord-
Advocate is in Scotland something like the Attorney-General in England.
But, practically, their positions are very different. The total official
emoluments of the Lord-Advocate are, on an average, not above £3000
a-year ; in addition to which, his only other reward, or hope of reward,
consists in the chance of judicial promotion. His direct patronage is
exceedingly slender, and for the patron, patronage is more of a torture
than of a reward. For these considerations he has to obtain a seat, or
seats, in Parliament ; which, between December 1830 and May 1832, cost
Jeffrey about £10,000. Then he has to go to London, and to return so often,
or to remain so long, that his practice is greatly injured and generally
extinguished . . . if an eminent lawyer, without parliamentary ambition,
and with no taste for sweltering in London, but making a respectable
income, and living at home in peace, wishes to be sleepless all night, and
hot all day, and not half so useful as he might be, let him become Lord-
Advocate."—*Cockburn,* i. 307, 309.

noisy hubbub of St. Stephen's, and at home the incessant press
of crowds, and of business mostly new to him,—rendered his life
completely miserable; and gradually broke down his health
altogether. He had some momentary glows of exultation,—
and dashed off triumphant bits of *Letters* to my Wife, which I
remember we both of us thought somewhat juvenile and idyllic
(especially one written in the House of Commons Library, just
after his ' Great Speech,' [1] and " with the cheers of that House
still ringing in my ears "), and which neither of us pitied withal
to the due degree; for there was in the heart of all of them,—
even of that ' great speech ' one,—a deep misery traceable; a
feeling how blessed the old peace and rest would be, and that
peace and rest were now fled far away ! We laughed considerably
at this huge hurlyburly, comparable in certain features to a huge
Sorcerers' Sabbath prosperously dancing itself out in the distance;
and little knew how lucky we were, instead of unlucky (as perhaps was sometimes one's idea in perverse moments) to have no
concern with it except as spectators in the shilling gallery or the
two-shilling !—

About the middle of August [1831], as elsewhere marked, I
set off for London, with *Sartor Resartus* in my Pocket. I found
Jeffrey much preoccupied and bothered, but willing to assist
me with Bookseller Murray and the like, and studious to be
cheerful. He lived in Jermyn Street, Wife and Daughter with
him; in lodgings at £11 a week, in melancholy contrast to the
beautiful tenements and perfect equipments they had left in the
North: on the Ground-floor, in a room of fair size, was a kind of
Secretary, a blear-eyed, tacit Scotch figure, standing or sitting
at a desk with many papers; this room seemed also to be ante-
room, or waiting-room, into which I was once or twice shown if
important company were upstairs. The Secretary never spoke;
hardly even answered when spoken to, except by an ambiguous
smile or sardonic grin. He seemed a shrewd enough fellow, and
to stick faithfully by his own trade. Upstairs on the first-
floor were the apartments of the family; Lord Advocate's bedroom, the back portion of the sitting-room, shut off from it
merely by a folding door. If I called in the morning, in quest
perhaps of Letters [2] (though I don't recollect much troubling *him*
in that way), I would find the family still at breakfast, ten A.M.
or later; and have seen poor Jeffrey emerge in flowered dressing-

---

[1] Speech on the Reform Bill, delivered March 1831.
[2] Letters for Carlyle addressed to Jeffrey's care,—Letters to Members
of Parliament being conveyed free of cost in those days.

gown, with a most boiled and suffering expression of face ; like one who had slept miserably, and now awoke mainly to paltry misery and bother,—poor Official man ! " I am made a mere Post-Office of ! " I heard him once grumble, after tearing open several Packets, not one of which was internally for himself.

Later in the day you were apt to find certain Scotch people dangling about, on business or otherwise,—Rutherfurd the advocate [1] a frequent figure, I never asked or guessed on what errand ; he, florid fat and joyous, his old Chieftain very lean and dreary. On the whole, I saw little of the latter in those first weeks ; and might have recognised more than I did, how to me he strove always to be cheerful and obliging, though himself so heavy-laden and internally wretched. One day he did my Brother John, for my sake (or perhaps for *Hers* still more) an easy service, which proved very important. A Dr. Baron of Gloucester had called one day, and incidentally noticed that " the Lady Clare " (a great, though most unfortunate, and at length professedly valetudinary Lady) " wanted a Travelling Physician, being bound forthwith to Rome." Jeffrey, the same day, on my calling, asked " Wouldn't it suit your Brother ? " and in a day or two the thing was completely settled ; and John, to his and our great satisfaction (I still remember him on the Coach-box in Regent's Circus), under way into his new Roman locality, and what proved his new career. My Darling had arrived before this last step of the process ; and was much obliged by what her little " Duke " had done. Duke was the name we called him by ;—for a foolish reason, connected with one of Macaulay's swaggering Articles in the *Edinburgh Review*, and an insolent response to it in *Blackwood :* " horse-whipped by a Duke," Macaulay had said of his victim, in the Article ;— " Duke, quotha," answered Blackwood ; " such a set of *Dukes !* " —and hinted that " Duke Macaulay " and " the Duke of Craigcrook " were extremely unheraldic dignitaries both of them !

By my Jeannie, too, had come, for John and me, the last Note we ever had from our Father : it was full of the profoundest *sorrow* (now that I recal it), " drawing nigh to the gates of Death ; "—which none of us regarded as other than common dispiritment, and the weak chagrin of old age. Ah me, how blind, how indifferent are all of us to sorrows that lie remote from us, and in a sphere not ours ! In vain did our brave old

[1] Afterwards The Right Hon. Andrew Rutherfurd, Jeffrey's successor as Lord-Advocate.

Father, sinking in the black gulfs of eternity, seek even to convince us that he was sinking. Alone, left alone, with only a tremulous and fitful, though eternal star of hope, *he* had to front that adventure for himself,—with an awestruck imagination of it, such as few or none of men now know. More valiant soul I have never seen ; nor one to whom Death was more unspeakably " the *King of Terrors*." Death, and the *Judgment-Bar* of the Almighty following it, may well be terrible to the bravest ; Death, with *nothing* of that kind following it,—one readily enough finds cases where that is insignificant to very mean and silly creatures. Within three months my Father was suddenly gone. I might have noticed something of what the old Scotch people used to call *fey* in his last parting with me (though I did not then so read it, nor do superstitiously now, but only *understand* it and the superstition) : it is visible in Friedrich Wilhelm's ultimatum too. But nothing of all that belongs to this place !— My Jeannie had brought us *silhouettes* of all the faces she had found at Scotsbrig ; one of them, and I find they are all still at Chelsea, is the only outward shadow of my Father's face now left me :—thanks to her for this also, the dear and ever helpful One !—

After her arrival, and our settlement in the Miles's lodgings (" 4 Ampton Street, Gray's Inn Lane ; " a place I will go to see if I return !), Jeffrey's appearances were more frequent and satisfactory : very often in the afternoon he came to call, for her sake mainly I believe, though mostly I was there too ;—I perceive now, his little visits to that unfashionable place were probably the golden item of his bad and troublous day ; poor Official man begirt with empty botherations ! I heard gradually that he was not reckoned " successful " in Public Life ; that as Lord Advocate, the Scotch with their multifarious businesses found him irritable, impatient (which I don't wonder at) ; that his " great Speech " with " the cheers of that House," etc. etc., had been a Parliamentary failure rather, unadapted to the place,[1] —and, what was itself very mortifying, that the Reporters had complained of his " Scotch accent " to excuse themselves for various omissions they had made ! His accent was indeed

---

[1] " It is certainly general, and too much above the common grapple of parliamentary contention ; but out of the whole speeches that were delivered throughout the two years that the question was discussed, no better argument in favour of the principle and necessity of the measure, on its general grounds, is extractable. Still, as a debating speech, it fell below the expectations both of his friends and of himself."— *Cockburn*, i. 314.

singular, but it was by no means Scotch : at his first going to
Oxford (where he did not stay long),[1] he had peremptorily
crushed down his Scotch (which he privately had in store, in
excellent condition, to the very end of his life, producible with
highly ludicrous effect on occasion), and adopted instead of a
strange swift, sharp-sounding, fitful modulation, part of it
pungent, quasi-latrant, other parts of it cooing, bantery, lovingly
quizzical ; which no charm of his fine ringing voice (*metallic*
tenor, of sweet tone), and of his vivacious rapid looks and pretty
little attitudes and gestures, could altogether reconcile you to ;
but in which he persisted through good report and bad.   Old
Braxie (Macqueen, ' Lord *Braxfield*,' a sad old cynic, on whom
Jeffrey used to set me laughing often enough) was commonly
reported to have said, on hearing Jeffrey again after that Oxford
sojourn, " The laddie has clean tint his Scotch, and found nae
English ! "—which was an exaggerative reading of the fact, his
vowels and syllables being elaborately English (or English and
more, e.g. " heppy," " My Lud," etc. etc.), while the *tune* he
sang them to was all his own.

There was not much of interest in what the Lord Advocate
brought to us in Ampton Street ; but there was something
friendly and home-like in his manners there ; and a kind of
interest and sympathy in the extra-official fact of his seeking
temporary shelter in that obscure retreat.   How he found his
way thither I know not (perhaps in a cab, if quite lost in his
azimuths) ; but I have more than once led him back through
Lincoln's Inn Fields, launched him safe in Long-Acre, with
nothing but Leicester Square and Piccadilly ahead ; and he
never once could find his way home.   Wandered about, and
would discover at last that he had got into Lincoln's Inn Fields
again !   He used to tell us sometimes of Ministerial things ;
not often, nor ever to the kindling of any admiration in either of
us ; how Lord Althorp would bluffly say etc. etc. (some very
dull piece of bluff candour) ; more sparingly, what the aspects
and likelihoods were : in which my too Radical humour but little
sympathised.   He was often unwell ; hidden for a week at
Wimbledon Park (Lord Althorp's, and then a beautiful secluded
place) for quiet and rural air.   We seldom called at Jermyn
Street ;—but did once, in a damp clammy evening, which I still
fondly recollect, ah me ! . . .

We were at first rather surprised that Jeffrey did not introduce
me to some of his grand literary figures, or try in some way to be

[1] Nine months.

of help to one for whom he evidently had a value : the explanation, I think, partly was, That I myself expressed no trace of aspiration that way ; that his grand literary or other figures were clearly by no means so adorable to the rustic, hopelessly *Germanised* soul, as an introducer of me might have wished ;— and chiefly that in fact Jeffrey did not consort with literary or other grand people, but only with ——s and bores in this bad time ; that it was practically the very worst of times for him, and that he was himself so heartily miserable as to think me and his other fellow-creatures happy in comparison, and to have no care left to bestow on us. I never doubted his real wish to help me, should an opportunity offer ; and while it did not, we had no want of him, but plenty of Society, of resources, outlooks, and interests otherwise. Truly one might have pitied him, in this his influx of unexpected Dignities,—as I hope I, in silence, loyally, sometimes did. So beautiful and radiant a little soul ; plunged on the sudden into such a Mother of (*Gilt*) Dead Dogs ! But it is often so : and many an envied man fares like that mythic Irishman who had resolved on treating himself to a sedan-chair, and on whom the mischievous chairmen, giving one another the wink, *left the bottom open*, and ran away with him, to the sorrow of his poor shins. " And that's your sedan-chair ! " said the Irish gentleman, paying his shilling, and satisfied to finish the experiment.

In March or the end of February I set to writing *Johnson ;* and, having found a *steady* table (what *fettling* [1] in that poor room, and how kind and beautiful *She* was to me !), I wrote it, by her side for most part ; pushing my way through the mud elements, with a certain glow of victory now and then. This finished, this and other little objects and arrangements (Jeffrey much in abeyance, to judge by my memory now so blank), we made our adieus (Irving, Badams, Mill, Leigh Hunt, who was a *new* acquaintance, but an interesting), and, by Birmingham, Liverpool, Scotsbrig, with incidents all fresh in mind to me just now, arrived safely home, well pleased with our London sojourn, and feeling our poor life to a certain degree made richer by it. Ah me, so strange, so sad, the days that are no more !

Jeffrey's correspondence continued, brisk as ever ; but it was now chiefly to Her address ; and I regarded it little ; feeling, as she too did, that it greatly wanted practicality, and amounted mainly to a flourish of fine words, and the pleasant expenditure now and then of an idle hour, in intervals of worry. My time,

[1] Adapting and arranging.

with little *Goethe* papers and excerptings (*Das Mährchen* etc.),
printing of *Sartor* piecemeal in *Fraser*, and London correspondings, went more prosperously than heretofore ;—had there been
good servants procurable, as there were *not*, one might almost
have called it a happy time, this at Craigenputtock, and it might
have lasted longer.   But permanent, we both silently felt it
could not be,—nor even very lasting, as matters stood.   I think
it must have been the latter part of next year (1833) when
Jeffrey's correspondence with me sputtered out into something
of sudden life again,—and something so unlucky that it proved
to be, essentially, death instead !   The case was this :   We
heard copiously, in the Newspapers, that the Edinburgh people,
in a meritorious scientific spirit, were about remodelling their
old Astronomical Observatory ;   and at length that they had
brought it to the proper pitch of real equipment, and that
nothing now was wanting but a fit Observer to make it scientifi-
cally useful and notable.   I had hardly ever looked through a
telescope, but I had good strength in Mathematics, in Astronomy,
and did not doubt but I could soon be at home in such an enterprise, if I fairly entered on it.   My old enthusiasms, I felt too, were
not dead, though so long asleep.   We were eagerly desirous of
some humblest anchorage, in the finance way, among our fellow-
creatures ;—my heart's desire, for many years past and coming,
was always, To find *any* honest employment by which one might
regularly gain one's daily bread !   Often, long after this (while
hopelessly writing the *French Revolution*, for example, hopelessly of *money* or other success from it) I thought my case so
tragically hard :   " *Could* learn to do honestly so many things,
nearly all the things I have ever seen done, from the making
of shoes, up to the engineering of canals, architecture of mansions as palatial as you liked, and perhaps to still higher things
of the physical or spiritual kind ;   *would*, moreover, toil so
loyally to do my task right, not wrong ;—and am forbidden to
try any of them ;   see the practical world closed against me as
with brazen doors ;   and must stand here, and perish idle ! "

   In a word, I had got into considerable spirits about that
Astronomical employment ;   fancied myself in the silent midnight interrogating the eternal Stars etc., with something of real
geniality,—in addition to financial considerations ;—and, after
a few days, in the light friendly tone, with modesty and brevity,
applied to my Lord Advocate for his countenance as the first or
preliminary step of procedure.   Or perhaps it was virtually in
his own appointment ?   Or perhaps again (for I quite forget),

I wrote, rather as inquiring what he would think of me in reference to it ? The poor bit of Letter still seems to me unexcep-
tionable ; and the answer was prompt and surprising ! Almost
or quite by return of post, I got, not a flat refusal only, but an
angry, vehement, almost shrill-sounding and scolding one,—as
if it had been a crime and an insolence in the like of me to think
of such a thing. Thing was intended, as I soon found, for his old
Jermyn Street secretary (my taciturn friend, with the blear eyes),
and it was indeed a plain inconvenience that the like of me
should apply for it, but not a crime or an insolence by any means.
" The like of me ? " thought I ; and my provocation quickly
subsided into contempt. For I had, in Edinburgh, a kind of
Mathematical reputation withal, and could have expected votes
far stronger than Jeffrey's on that subject. But I perceived the
thing to be settled ; believed withal that the poor Secretary,
though blear-eyed when I last saw him, would do well enough
(as in effect I understood he did) ; that his master might have
reasons of his own for wishing a provisionary settlement to the
poor man ;—and that in short I was an outsider, and had nothing
to say to all that. By the first post, I accordingly answered, in
the old light style ; thanking briefly for at least the swift dis-
patch ; affirming the maxim, *bis dat qui cito dat* even in case of
refusal ; and good-humouredly enough leaving the matter to
rest on its own basis. Jeffrey returned to it, evidently somewhat in repentant mood (for his tone had really been splenetic,
sputtery and improper, poor worried man) ; but I took no
notice : and only marked, for my own private behoof, what
exiguous resource of practical help for me lay in that quarter,
and how, there as elsewhere, the economically useful would
always override the sentimental and ornamental. I had internally no kind of anger against my would-be generous friend ;—
had not he, after all, a kind of gratuitous regard for me ; perhaps as much as I for him ? Nor was there a diminution of
respect ; perhaps only a clearer view how little respect there had
been ! My own poor task was abundantly serious, my posture
in it solitary ; and I felt that silence would be fittest. Then and
subsequently I exchanged one or two little Notes of business
with Jeffrey ; but this, of late autumn 1833, was the last of our
sentimental passages ; and may be said to have closed what of
Correspondence we had in the friendly or effusive strain. For
several years more, he continued corresponding with my Wife ;
and had, I think, to the end a kind of lurking regard to us,
willing to show itself. But our own struggle with the world

was now become stern and grim ; not fitly to be interrupted by these theoretic flourishes of epistolary trumpeting ;—and (towards the finale of *French Revolution*, if I recollect) my Dearest also gave him up, and nearly altogether ceased corresponding.

What a finger of Providence, once more, was this of the Edinburgh Observatory ; to which, had Jeffrey assented, I should certainly have gone rejoicing ! These things really strike one's heart. The good Lord Advocate, who really was pitiable, and miserably ill off, in his eminent position, showed visible embarrassment at sight of me (in 1834), come to settle in London, without furtherance asked or given ; and indeed, on other occasions, seemed to recollect the Astronomical catastrophe, in a way which touched me, and was of generous origin or indication. He was quitting his Lord Advocateship, and returning home to old courses and habits ; a solidly wise resolution. He always assiduously called on us, in his subsequent visits to London ; and we had our kind thoughts, our pleasant reminiscences, and loyal pities of the once brilliant man and friend : but he was now practically become little or nothing to us; and had withdrawn, as it were, to the sphere of the Past. I have chanced to meet him in a London party ; found him curiously exotic. I used punctually to call, if passing through Edinburgh ; some recollection I have of an evening, perhaps a night, at Craigcrook ; pleasantly hospitable, with Empson (Son-in-law) there, and talk about Dickens, etc. Jeffrey was now a Judge, and giving great satisfaction in that Office, " seldom a better Judge," said everybody ; his health was weak, and age advancing, but he had escaped his old London miseries, like a sailor from shipwreck, and might now be accounted a lucky man again. The last time I saw him was on my return from Glen Truim in Invernessshire, and my Ashburton visit there (in 1849) : he was then, at least for the time, withdrawn from Judging, and was reported very weak in health ; his Wife and he, sauntering together for a little exercise on the shore at Newhaven, had stumbled over some cable and both of them fallen and hurt themselves,—his Wife so ill that I did not see her at all. Jeffrey I did see, after some delay, and we talked and strolled slowly some hours together ; but there was no longer stay possible, such the evident distress and embarrassment Craigcrook was in : I had got breakfast, on very kind terms, from Mrs. Empson with Husband and three or four children . . . ; Jeffrey himself, on coming down was very kind to me, but sadly weak ; much worn away in body, and in mind more thin and sensitive than ever. He talked a good deal, distantly alluding once to our *changed* courses, in a friendly (not a very dextrous way) ; was throughout friendly, good, but tremulous, thin, almost affecting, in contrast with old times. Grown *Lunar* now, not Solar any more ! He took me, baggage and all, in his carriage to the railway station, Mrs. Empson escorting ; and there said Farewell,— for the last time, as it proved. Going to the Grange, some three or four months after this, I accidentally learned from some Newspaper or miscellaneous fellow-passenger, as the news of the morning, That Lord Jeffrey at Edinburgh was dead.[1] Dull and heavy, somewhere in the Basingstoke localities, the tidings fell on me,—awakening frozen memories not a few. He had died, I afterwards heard, with great constancy and firmness ; lifted his finger, as if in cheerful encouragement, amid the lamenting loved ones, and silently passed away. After that autumn morning at Craigcrook, I have never seen one of those friendly souls, not even the place itself again. A few months afterwards Mrs. Jeffrey followed her Husband ; in a year or two at Haileybury (some East India College where he had an office or presidency), Empson died,[2]—'correcting proof sheets of the *Edinburgh Review*,' as appears, 'while waiting daily for death ;' a most quiet editorial procedure, which I have often thought of ! Craigcrook was sold ; Mrs. Empson with her children vanished mournfully into the dumb distance ; and all was over there, and a life-scene, once so bright for us and others, had ended, and was gone like a dream.

Jeffrey was perhaps at the height of his reputation about 1816 ; his *Edinburgh Review* a kind of Delphic Oracle, and Voice of the Inspired, for great majorities of what is called the " Intelligent Public " ; and himself regarded universally as a man of consummate penetration, and the *facile princeps* in the department he had chosen to cultivate and practise. In the half-century that has followed, what a change in all this : the fine gold become dim to such a degree ; and the Trismegistus hardly now regarded as a *Megas* by any one, or by the generality remembered at all ! He may be said to have begun the rash reckless style of criticising everything in Heaven and Earth by appeal to *Molière's Maid ; "* Do *you* like it ? *Don't* you like it ? " —a style which in hands more and more inferior to that sound-

---

[1] Jeffrey died at Craigcrook, 26th January 1850 ; Mrs. Jeffrey died at Haileybury, 18th May following.

[2] Professor William Empson died at Haileybury, 10th December 1852, aged 62.

hearted old lady and him, has since grown gradually to such immeasurable lengths among us ;—and he himself is one of the first that suffers by it. If praise and blame are to be perfected, not in the mouth of Molière's Maid only, but in that of mischievous precocious babes and sucklings, you will arrive at singular judgments by degrees !—Jeffrey was by no means the Supreme in Criticism or in anything else ; but it is certain there has no Critic appeared among us since who was worth naming beside him ;—and his influence, for good and for evil, in Literature and otherwise, has been very great. " Democracy," the gradual uprise, and rule in all things, of roaring, million-headed, unreflecting, darkly suffering, darkly sinning " Demos," come to call its old superiors to account, at *its* maddest of tribunals : nothing in my time has so forwarded all this as Jeffrey and his once famous *Edinburgh Review.*

He was not deep enough, pious or reverent enough, to have been great in Literature ; but he was a man intrinsically of veracity ; said nothing without meaning it in some considerable degree ; had the quickest perceptions, excellent practical discernment of what lay before him ; was in earnest, too, though not " dreadfully in earnest ; "—in short was well fitted to set forth that *Edinburgh Review* (at the dull opening of our now so tumultuous Century),—and become *Coryphæus* of his generation in the waste, wide-spreading and incalculable course appointed *it* among the Centuries !—I used to find in him a finer talent than any he has evidenced in writing : this was chiefly when he got to speak Scotch, and gave me anecdotes of old Scotch *Braxfields,* and vernacular (often enough, but not always, *cynical*) curiosities of that type. Which he did with a greatness of *gusto* quite peculiar to the topic ; with a fine and deep sense of humour, of real comic mirth, much beyond what was noticeable in him otherwise ; not to speak of the perfection of the mimicry, which itself was something. I used to think to myself, " Here is a man whom they have kneaded into the shape of an *Edinburgh Reviewer,* and clothed the soul of in Whig formulas, and blue-and-yellow ; but he might have been a beautiful Goldoni, too, or something better in that kind, and have given us beautiful *Comedies,* and aerial pictures, true and poetic, of Human Life in a far other way ! "—There was something of Voltaire in him ; something even in bodily features : those bright-beaming, swift and piercing hazel-eyes, with their accompaniment of rapid keen expressions in the other lineaments of face, resembled one's notion of Voltaire ; and in the voice too there was a fine, half-plangent, kind of metallic ringing tone, which used to remind me of what I fancied Voltaire's voice might have been : " *voix sombre et majestueuse*," Duvernet calls it. The culture, and respective natal scenes, of the two men had been very different ; nor was their *magnitude* of faculty anything like the same,—had their respective *kinds* of it been much more identical than they were. You could not define Jeffrey to be more than a potential Voltaire ; say " *Scotch* Voltaire " ; with about as much reason (which was not very much) as they used in Edinburgh to call old Playfair the " Scotch D'Alembert." Our Voltaire too, whatever else might be said of him, was at least worth a large multiple of our D'Alembert ! A beautiful little man, the former of these, and a bright island to me, and to mine, in the sea of things ; of whom it is now again mournful and painful to take farewell.

[*Finished* at Mentone, this Saturday, 19 January 1867 ; day bright as June (while all from London to Avignon seems to be choked under snow and frost), other conditions, especially the *internal*, not good, but baddish or bad !]

The following extracts from Carlyle's *Journal* show under what conditions the Reminiscences of Irving and of Jeffrey were written :

" Mentone, on the Riviera, *20th January* 1867.—. . . I have finished the *Edward Irving* ' Reminiscences ' ; and, yesterday, a short Paper on Jeffrey ditto ;—both of them now lie labelled in bottom drawer of the big *Looking-glass* Press of my bedroom. It was *her* connexion with them that chiefly impelled me ; both are superficially, ill and poorly done, especially the *latter :* but there is something of value for oneself in reawakening the Sleep of the Past, and bringing old years carefully to survey again by our new eyes ; a certain solemn tenderness, too, in these two cases, dwells in it for me ;—and, in fine, doing anything not wicked is better than doing nothing. I must carefully endeavour to find out some new work for myself ;—but as yet am quite at a loss. Unless the forepart of my day is passed in *writing*, I feel too discontented with it, as if it had been *idle* altogether. What *shall* I take to ? Perhaps better, with this *head* and *liver* to go into the open air, and consider !

" *21st January*.—. . . This morning I feel dreadfully in want of some *Task* again ; and cannot find one. . . . Some minutes past noon ; Day rapidly *going* whether it have a 'task' or none !

   " 28*th January*.—Whole week spent in writing letters, mostly bad, factitious, hitting wide, and all *involuntary*, which indeed is perhaps the *father* of all their ill qualities ! . . . Task being undiscoverable, am about beginning (Paper laid *out*, all ready) a Quasi-Task, *Reminiscences of Sundry Notable or Noted Persons.*"

REMINISCENCES OF SUNDRY

[Begun at Mentone (Alpes Maritimes), Monday, 28th January 1867.]

MANY Literary, and one or two Political or otherwise Public Persons, more or less superior to the common run of men [I have met with in my life] ; but perhaps none of them really great, or worth more than a transient remembrance, loud as the talk about them once may have been ; and certainly none of them, what is more to the purpose here, ever vitally interesting or consummately admirable to myself : so that if I do, for want of something else to occupy me better, mark down something of what I recollect concerning some of them, who seemed the greatest, or stood the nearest to me, it surely ought to be with extreme brevity ! With rapid succinctness (if I can) ; at all events, with austere candour, and avoidance of anything which I can suspect to be untrue. Perhaps nobody but myself will ever read this,— but that is not infallibly certain :—and even in regard to myself, the one possible profit of such a thing is, That it be not false or incorrect in any point, but correspond to the fact in all.

[SOUTHEY]

When it was that I first got acquainted with Southey's Books, I do not now recollect ; except that it must have been several years after he had been familiar to me as a Name, and many years after the Public had been familiar with him as a Poet and politically and otherwise Didactic Writer. His Laureateship provoked a great deal of vulgar jesting ; about the " butt of sack," etc. : for the Newspaper public, by far the greater number of them Radically given, had him considerably in abhorrence, and called him not only Tory, but " Renegade," who had traitorously deserted, and gone over to the bad cause. It was at Kirkcaldy that we all read a " slashing article " (by Brougham I should now guess,—were it of the least moment) on Southey's *Letter to W. Smith, M.P.* of Norwich, a small Socinian personage, conscious of meaning grandly and well, who had been denouncing him as " renegade " (probably contrasting the once *Wat Tyler* with the now *Laureateship*) in the House of Commons ; a second back-stroke, which, in the irritating circumstances of the *Wat* itself (republished by some sharking Bookseller) had driven Southey to his fighting gear, or polemical pen. The Pamphlet itself we did not see, except in Review quotations, which were naturally the shrillest and weakest discoverable,— with citations from *Wat Tyler* to accompany :—but the slash Reviewer understood his trade ; and I can remember how we all cackled and triumphed over Southey along with him, as over a slashed and well slain foe to us and to mankind : for we were all Radicals in heart, Irving and I as much as any of the others ; and were not very wise, nor had looked into the *per contra* side. I retract now on many points ; on that of " Barabbas " in particular, which example Southey cited, as characteristic of Democracy, greatly to my dissent, till I had much better, and for many years, considered the subject !

That bout of Pamphleteering had brought Southey much nearer me ; but had sensibly diminished my esteem of him, and would naturally slacken my desire for further acquaintance. It must have been a year or two later when his *Thalaba, Curse of Kehama, Joan of Arc*, etc. came into my hands, or some one of them came, which invoked new effort for the others : I recollect the much kindlier and more respectful feeling these awoke in me, which has continued ever since. I much recognised the piety, the gentle deep affection, the reverence for God and man, which reigned in these Pieces ; full of soft pity, like the wailings of a mother, and yet with a clang of chivalrous valour finely audible too. One could not help loving such a man ;—and yet I rather felt too as if he were a shrillish thin kind of man, the feminine element perhaps considerably predominating and limiting. However, I always afterwards looked out for his Books, new or old, as for a thing of value : and, in particular, read his Articles in the *Quarterly*, which were the most accessible productions. In spite of my Radicalism, I found very much in these Toryisms, which was greatly according to my heart ; things rare and worthy, at once pious and true, which were always welcome to me, though I strove to base them on a better ground than his,—his being no eternal or time-defying one, as I could see ; and time in fact, in my own case, having already *done* its work there. In this manner our innocently pleasant relation, as writer and written-for, had gone on, without serious shock, though, after *Kehama*, not with much growth in quality or quantity, for perhaps ten years.

It was probably in 1836 or 7,[1] the second or third year after our removal to London, that Henry Taylor, author of *Artevelde* and various similar things, with whom I had made acquaintance, and whose early regard, constant esteem, and readiness to be helpful and friendly, should be among my *memorabilia* of those years, invited me to come to him one evening, and have a little speech with Southey, whom he judged me to be curious about, and to like, perhaps more than I did. Taylor himself, a solid, sound-headed, faithful, but not a well-read or wide-minded man, though of marked veracity, in all senses of that deep-reaching word, and with a fine readiness to apprehend new truth, and stand by it, was in personal intimacy with the " Lake " Sages and Poets, especially with Southey, and considered that, in Wordsworth and the rest of them, was embodied all of pious wisdom that our Age had, and could not doubt but the sight of Southey would be welcome to me. I readily consented to come ; none but we three present, Southey to be Taylor's guest at dinner, I to join them after ;—which was done. Taylor, still little turned of thirty, lived miscellaneously about, in bachelor's lodgings, or sometimes for a month or two during " the season " [in the house of his relative, Miss Fenwick] where he could receive guests. In the former I never saw him, nor to the latter did I go but when invited. It was in a quiet ground-floor, of the latter character as I conjectured, somewhere near Downing Street, and looking into St. James's Park, that I found Taylor and Southey, with their wine before them, which they hardly seemed to be minding ; very quiet this seemed to be, quiet their discourse too ; to all which, not sorry at the omen, I quietly joined myself. Southey was a man well up in the fifties ;[2] hair gray, not yet hoary, well setting off his fine clear-brown complexion ; head and face both smallish, as indeed the figure was *while seated ;* features finely cut ; eyes, brow, mouth, good in their kind ; expressive all, and even vehemently so, but betokening rather keenness than depth either of intellect or character ; a serious, human, honest, but sharp almost fierce-looking thin man, with very much of the *militant* in his aspect,—in the eyes especially was legible a mixture of sorrow and of anger, or of angry contempt, as if his indignant fight with the world had not yet ended in victory, but also never should

1 It was in 1835.
2 Southey (born 1774) was sixty-one in 1835.

in defeat. A man you were willing to hear speak. We got to
talk of Parliament, Public Speaking and the like (perhaps some
electioneering then afoot ?)—on my mentioning the Candidate
at Bristol, with his " I say ditto to Mr. Burke ! " Southey
eagerly added, " Hah, I myself heard that " (had been a boy
listening when that was said) ! His contempt for the existing
set of Parliaments was great and fixed ; especially for what
produced it, the present electoral temper ;—though in the future
too, except through Parliaments and elections, he seemed to see
no hope. He took to repeating in a low, sorrowfully mocking
tone, certain verses (I supposed of his own), emphatically in
that vein, which seemed to me bitter and exaggerative, not
without ingenuity, but exhibiting no trace of genius. Partly
in response, or rather as sole articulate response, I asked who had
made those verses ? Southey answered carelessly, " Praed
they say, Praed, I suppose." My notion was, he was merely
putting me off, and that the verses were his own, though he
disliked confessing to them. A year or two ago, looking into
some *review* of a Reprint of Praed's *Works*, I came upon the
verses again, among other excerpts of a similar genus ; and
found that they verily were Praed's : my wonder now was that
Southey had charged his memory with the like of them. This
Praed was a young M.P. who had gained distinction at Oxford
or Cambridge ; as he now spoke and wrote without scruple
against the late illustrious *Reform Bill*, and sovereign Reform
Doctrine in general, great things were expected of him by his
Party, now sitting cowed into silence ; and his name was very
current in the Newspapers for a few months ; till suddenly
(soon after this of Southey), the poor young man died,[1] and sank
at once into oblivion,—tragical, though not unmerited, nor
extraordinary, as I judged from the contents of that late *Reprint*,
and Biographical Sketch, by some pious and regretful old
friend of his. That Southey had some of Praed's verses by heart
(verses about Hon. Mr. This moving, say, to abolish Death and
the Devil ; Hon. Mr. B., to change, for improvement's sake, the
Obliquity of the Ecliptic, etc. etc) is perhaps a kind of honour
to poor Praed,—whose inexorable fate, cutting short his " career
of ambition " in that manner, is perhaps as sad and tragical to
me as to another.— —After Southey's bit of recitation I think
the party must have soon broken up ; I recollect nothing more
of it, except my astonishment, when Southey at last completely

1 W. M. Praed, born 1802, died 1839. His *Works* were published in
1864.

rose from his chair to shake hands : he had only half-risen and nodded on my coming in ; and all along I had counted him a lean little man ; but now he shot suddenly aloft into a lean tall one ; all legs ; in shape and stature like a pair of tongs,—which peculiarity my surprise doubtless exaggerated to me, but only made it the more notable and entertaining. Nothing had happened throughout that was other than moderately pleasant ; and I returned home (I conclude) well enough content with my evening. Southey's *sensitiveness* I had noticed on this first occasion as one of his characteristic qualities ; but was nothing like aware of the extent of it till our next meeting.

This was a few evenings afterwards ; Taylor giving some dinner, or party, party in honour of his guest ;—if dinner I was not at that, but must have undertaken for the evening sequel, as less incommodious to me, less unwholesome more especially. I remember entering, in the same house, but upstairs this time, a pleasant little drawing-room, in which, in well-lighted, serene enough condition, sat Southey in full dress, silently reclining ; and as yet no other company. We saluted suitably, touched ditto on the vague initiatory points ; and were still there, when by way of coming closer, I asked mildly, with no appearance of special interest, but with more than I really felt, " Do you know De Quincey ? " (the *Opium-eater*, whom I knew to have lived in Cumberland as his neighbour). " Yes, sir," answered Southey, with extraordinary animation ; " and if you have opportunity, I'll thank you to tell him he is one of the greatest scoundrels living ! " I laughed lightly ; said, I had myself little acquaintance with the man ; and could not wish to recommend myself by that message. Southey's face as I looked at it, was become of slate-colour, the eyes glancing, the attitude rigid ; the figure altogether a picture of Rhadamanthine rage,—that is, rage conscious to itself of being *just*. He doubtless felt I would expect some explanation from him : " I have told Hartley Coleridge," said he, " that he ought to take a strong cudgel, proceed straight to Edinburgh, and give De Quincey, publicly on the streets there, a sound beating ! "—As a calumniator, cowardly spy, traitor, base betrayer of the hospitable social hearth, for one thing ! It appeared De Quincey was then, and for some time past, writing in [*Tait's*] *Magazine* something of Autobiographic nature, a series of Papers on the *Lake* period of his life,—merely for sake of the highly needful trifle of money, poor soul, and with no wish to be untrue (I could believe) or to hurt anybody, though not without his own bits of splenetic convictions also ;—to which latter, in regard of Coleridge in particular, he had given more rein than was agreeable to parties concerned.   I believe I had myself read the Paper on Coleridge ; one Paper on him I certainly had ; and had been the reverse of tempted by it to look after the others ; finding in this, *e.g.*, that " Coleridge had the greatest intellect perhaps ever given to man," but that he wanted, or as good as wanted, common honesty in applying it ; which seemed to me a miserable contradiction in terms, and threw light, if not on Coleridge, yet on De Quincey's faculty of judging him or others.   In this Paper there were probably withal some domestic details or allusions ; to which, as familiar to rumour, I had paid little heed : but certainly, of general reverence for Coleridge and his gifts and deeds, I had traced, not deficiency in this Paper but glaring exaggeration, coupled with De Quincean drawbacks, which latter had alone struck Southey with such poignancy.   Or perhaps there had been other more criminal Papers which Southey knew of, and not I ?   In few minutes he let the topic drop, I helping what I could ; [1] and seemed to feel as if he had done a little wrong ; and was bound to show himself more than usually amiable and social, especially with me, for the rest of the evening, which he did in effect ;—though I quite forget the details ; only that I had a good deal of talk with him, in the circle of the others ; and had again more than once to notice the singular readiness of the *blushes,*—amiable *red* blush, beautiful like a young girl's, when you touched genially the pleasant theme ;

[1] There is a slight mistake here as to the occasion of this conversation with Southey.   Carlyle writes : " Went last night (in bad wet weather) to Taylor's to meet Southey ; who received me kindly.   A lean gray-white-headed man, of dusky complexion ; unexpectedly tall when he rises, and still *leaner* then.   The shallowest chin ; prominent snubbed-Roman nose ; small care-lined brow, huge brush of white-gray hair, on high crown, and projecting on all sides ; the most *vehement* pair of faint-hazel eyes I have ever seen.   Our talk was of Dutch Poets (Vondel etc., whom he had read), of Orators, Colonies, Schools, Swift, Sterne, Berkeley, Burke : all in the touch-and-go way.   A well-read, honest, limited (strait-laced even), kindly-hearted, most irritable man.   We parted kindly ; with no great purpose on either side, I imagine, to meet again.   De Quincey was mentioned in answer to a question of mine : ' Yes I do know him,' answered Southey, ' and know him to be a great rascal : and, if you have opportunity, I will thank you to tell him so : ' his brown-dun face was overspread suddenly almost with black.   I ' trusted ' in return that ' Some other than I might be the bearer of that comfortable message, as I had no intercourse with De Quincey, and had not seen him for seven years.'   The fault was some stuff poor De Quincey had been writing in *Tait's Magazine* about Coleridge.   I got the thing at last wound up with a hearty laugh.—Southey believes in the Church of England : this is notable ; notabler (and honourable) that he has made such belief serve him so well."—Carlyle's *Journal,* 26th February 1835.

and serpent-like flash of *blue* or black blush (this far, very far the *rarer* kind, though it did recur, too), when you struck upon the opposite. All details of the evening, except that primary one, are clean gone; but the effect was interesting, pleasantly stimulating and surprising. I said to myself, " How has this man contrived, with such a nervous-system, to keep alive for near sixty years? Now blushing, under his gray hairs, rosy like a maiden of fifteen; now *slaty* almost, like a rattle-snake, or fiery serpent? How has he not been torn to pieces long since, under such furious pulling this way and that? He must have somewhere a great deal of methodic virtue in him; I suppose, too, his heart is thoroughly honest, which helps considerably! " I didn't fancy myself to have made personally the least impression on Southey; but, on those terms, I accepted him for a loyal kind of man; and was content and thankful to know of his existing in the world, near me or still far from me, as the Fates should have determined.

For perhaps two years I saw no more of him; heard only, from Taylor in particular, that he was overwhelmed in misery, and imprudently refusing to yield, or screen himself in any particular, —imprudently, thought Taylor and his other friends. For not only had he been, for several continuous years, toiling and fagging at a *Collective Edition* of his Works, which cost him a great deal of incessant labour; but, far worse, his poor Wife had sunk into insanity, and moreover he would not, such his feeling on the tragic matter, be persuaded to send her to an asylum, or trust her out of his own sight and keeping! Figure such a scene; and what the most sensitive of mankind must have felt under it. This, then, is the garland and crown of " victory " provided for an old man, when he arrives, spent with his fifty years of climbing and of running, and has what you call *won* the race?— —

It was after I had finished the *French Revolution*, and perhaps after my Annandale journey to recover from this adventure, that I heard of Southey's being in Town again. His *Collective Edition* was complete, his poor Wife was dead and at rest:[1] his work was done, in fact (had he known it) all his work in the world was done;—and he had determined on a few weeks of wandering, and trying to repose and recreate himself, among old friends and scenes. I saw him twice or thrice on this occasion; it was our second and last piece of intercourse, and much the more interesting,—to me at least, and for a reason that will

[1] Mrs. Southey died 1837.

appear. My wild excitation of nerves, after finishing that grim Book on *French Revolution*, was something strange. The desperate nature of our circumstances and outlooks while writing it ; the thorough possession it had taken of me, dwelling in me day and night, keeping me in constant fellowship with such a " flamy cut-throat scene of things," infernal and celestial both in one, with no fixed prospect but that of writing *it*, though I should die,—had held me in a fever-blaze for three years long ; and now the blaze had ceased, problem *taliter qualiter* was actually done ; and my humour and way of thought about all things was of an altogether ghastly, dim-smouldering, and as if preternatural sort. I well remember that ten-minutes' survey I had of Annan and its vicinity, the forenoon after my landing there : Brother Alick must have met me at the Steamboat Harbour, I suppose ; at any rate we were walking towards Scotsbrig together, and at Mount-Annan [1] Gate, bottom of Landheads Hamlet, he had left me for a moment till he called somewhere ; I stood leaning against a stone or milestone, face towards Annan, of which with the two miles of variegated cheerful green slope that intervened, and then of the Solway Frith far and wide, from Gretna to St. Bees Head, and beyond it, of the grand and lovely Cumberland mountains, with Helvellyn and even with Ingleborough in the rearward, there was magnificent view well known to me. Stone itself was well known to me : this had been my road to Annan School from my tenth year onward ; right sharp was my knowledge of every item in this scene, thousandfold my memories connected with it, and mournful and painful, rather than joyful, too many of them ! And now here it was again ; and here was I again. Words cannot utter the wild and ghastly expressiveness of that scene to me ; it seemed as if Hades itself and the gloomy Realms of Death and Eternity were looking out on me through those poor old familiar objects ; as if no miracle could be more miraculous than this same bit of Space and bit of Time spread out before me. I felt withal how wretchedly unwell I must be ; and was glad, no doubt when Alick returned, and we took the road again. What precedes and what follows this clear bit of memory, are alike gone : but for seven or more weeks after, I rode often down and up this same road, silent, solitary, weird of mood, to bathe in the Solway ; and not even my dear old Mother's love and cheery helpfulness (for she was then still strong for her age) could raise

---

[1] The house of General Dirom ; Carlyle had been tutor to his sons there in 1814.

my spirits out of utter grimness, and fixed contemptuous disbelief in the future.   Hope of having succeeded, of ever succeeding, I had not the faintest,—was not even at the pains to wish it ; said only in a dim mute way, " Very well, then ; be it just *so*, then ! "   A foolish young neighbour, not an ill-disposed, sent me a Number of the *Athenæum* (Literary Journal of the day) in which I was placidly, with some elaboration, set down as blockhead and strenuous *failure :* the last words were, " Readers, have we made out our case ? "   I read it without pain, or pain the least to signify ; laid it aside for a day or two ; then one morning, in some strait about our breakfast tea-kettle, slipt the peccant Number under that, and had my cup of excellent hot tea from it.   The foolish neighbour, who was " filing the *Athenæum* " (more power to him !), found a *lacuna* in his set at this point ; might know better another time, it was hoped ! Thackeray's laudation, in the *Times*, I also recollect the arrival of (how pathetic now *Her* mirth over it to me !)—but neither did Thackeray inspire me with any emotion, still less with any ray of exultation : " One other poor judge voting," I said to myself ; " but what is he, or such as he ? The fate of that thing is *fixed !* I *have* written it ; that is all my result."   Nothing now strikes me as affecting in all this, but *Her* noble attempt to cheer me on my return home to her, still sick and sad ; and how she poured out on me her melodious joy, and all her bits of confirmatory anecdotes and narratives ; " Oh, it has had a great success, Dear ! "—and not even she could irradiate my darkness, beautifully as she tried for a long time, as I sat at her feet again by our own parlour-fire.   " Ah, you are an unbelieving creature ! " said she at last, starting up, probably to give me some tea. There was, and is, in all this something heavenly ;—the rest is all of it smoke, and has gone up the chimney, inferior in benefit and quality to what my pipe yielded me.   I was rich once, had I known it, very rich ; and now I am become poor to the end.

Such being my posture and humour at that time, fancy my surprise at finding Southey full of sympathy, assent, and recognition of the amplest kind, for my poor new Book !   We talked largely on the huge Event itself, which he had dwelt with openly or privately ever since his youth, and tended to interpret exactly as I,—the suicidal explosion of an old wicked world, too wicked, false and impious for living longer ;—and seemed gratified, and as if grateful, that a strong voice had at last expressed that meaning.   My poor *French Revolution* evidently appeared to him a Good Deed, a salutary bit of " scriptural " exposition for the public and for mankind ; and this, I could perceive, was the soul of a great many minor approbations and admirations of detail, which he was too polite to speak of.   As Southey was the only man of eminence that had ever taken such a view of me, and especially of this my first considerable Book, it seems strange that I should have felt so little real triumph in it as I did.   For all other eminent men, in regard to all my Books and Writings hitherto, and most of all in regard to this latest, had stood pointedly silent ; dubitative, disapprobatory, many of them shaking their heads.   Thus, when poor *Sartor* got passed through *Fraser*, and was done up from the *Fraser* types as a separate thing, perhaps about fifty copies being struck off,—I sent six copies to six Edinburgh Literary Friends ; from not one of whom did I get the smallest whisper even of receipt ;—a thing disappointing more or less to human nature, and which has silently and insensibly led me, Never since to send any copy of a book to Edinburgh, or indeed to Scotland at all, except to my own kindred there, and in one or two specific *un*literary cases more.   The *Plebs* of Literature might be divided in their verdicts about me (though, by count of heads, I always suspect the " *Guilties* " clean had it) ; but the Conscript Fathers declined to vote at all.   And yet here was a Conscript Father voting in a very pregnant manner ; and it seems I felt but little joy even in that !   Truly I can say for myself, Southey's approbation, though very privately I doubtless had my pride in it, did not the least tend to swell me ;—though on the other hand, I must own to very great gloom of mind, sullen some part of it, which is possibly a worse fault than what it saved me from.   I remember now how polite and delicate his praises of me were ; never given direct or in over-measure, but always obliquely, in the way of hint or inference left for me ; and how kind, sincere and courteous, his manner throughout was.   Our mutual considerations about French Revolution, about its incidents, catastrophes, or about its characters, Danton, Camille, etc., and contrasts and comparisons of them with their (probable) English congeners of the day,—yielded pleasant and copious material for dialogue when we met. Literature was hardly touched upon ; our discourse came almost always upon moral and social topics.   Southey's look, I remarked, was strangely careworn, anxious, though he seemed to like talking, and both talked and listened well ; his eyes especially were as if full of gloomy bewilderment and incurable sorrow. He had got to be about sixty-three ; had buried all his suffering loved ones, wound up forty years of incessant, vehement labour, much of it more or less uncongenial to him; and in fact, though he knew it not, had finished his work in the world; and might well be looking back on it with a kind of ghastly astonishment rather than with triumph or joy!——

I forget how often we met; it was not very often; it was always at H. Taylor's, or through Taylor.[1] One day, for the first and last time, he made us a visit at Chelsea; a certain old Lady-cousin of Taylor's [whose guest Taylor sometimes was] for a month or two in the Town Season, a Miss Fenwick, of provincial accent and type, but very wise, discreet and well-bred,— had come driving down with him. Their arrival, and loud-thundering knock at the door, is very memorable to me;—the moment being unusually critical in our poor household! My little Jeannie was in hands with the *marmalade* that day:— none ever made such marmalade for me, pure as liquid amber, in taste and in look almost *poetically* delicate, and it was the only one of her pretty and industrious confitures that I individually cared for; which made her doubly diligent and punctual about it. (Ah me, ah me!)—The kitchen fire, I suppose, had not been brisk enough, free enough; so she had had the large brass pan and contents brought up to the brisker parlour-fire; and was there victoriously boiling it,—when it boiled over, in huge blaze, set the chimney on fire;—and I (from my writing upstairs, I suppose) had been suddenly summoned to the rescue. What a moment, what an outlook! The kindling of the chimney-soot was itself a grave matter, involving fine of £10, if the fire-engines had to come. My first and immediate step was to parry this; by at once letting down the grate-valve, and cutting quite off the supply of oxygen or atmosphere; which of course was effectual, though at the expense of a little smoke in the room meanwhile. The brass pan, and remaining contents (not much wasted or injured) she had herself snatched off and set on the hearth; I was pulling down the back-window, which would have completed the temporary settlement,—when, hardly three yards from us, broke out the thundering door-knocker; and before the brass pan could be got away, Miss Fenwick and Southey were let in. Southey I don't think my Darling had yet seen; but her own fine modest composure, and

---

1 " Saw Southey, once here, another time at Miss Fenwick's; very kind to me; and fond of talking, especially about French Revolution, book and thing. The excitablest man I ever saw. Very strange that I should be a *toleratus*, a *laudatus* with him."—Carlyle's *Journal*, 13th April 1838.

presence of mind, never in any other greatest *presence*, forsook her. I remember how daintily she made the salutations, brief quizzical bit of explanation, got the wreck to vanish ; and sat down as member of our little party. Southey and I were on the sofa together ; she nearer Miss Fenwick, for a little of feminine " *aside* " now and then : the colloquy did not last long ;—I recollect no point of it, except that Southey and I got to speaking about Shelley (whom perhaps I remembered to have lived in the Lake Country for some time, and had started on Shelley as a practicable topic) : Southey did not rise into admiration of Shelley either for talent or conduct ; spoke of him and his Life, without bitterness, but with contemptuous sorrow, and evident aversion mingled with his pity.   To me also poor Shelley always was, and is, a kind of ghastly object ; colourless, pallid, tuneless, without health or warmth of vigour ; the sound of him shrieky, frosty, as if a *ghost* were trying to " sing " to us ; the temperament of him, spasmodic, hysterical, instead of strong or robust ; with fine affections and aspirations, gone all such a road :—a man infinitely too *weak* for that solitary scaling of the Alps which he undertook in spite of all the world.   At some point of the dialogue I said to Southey, " A haggard existence that of his."   I remember Southey's pause, and the tone and air with which he answered, " It *is* a haggard existence ! " His look, at this moment, was unusually gloomy and heavy-laden, full of confused distress ;—as if in retrospect of his own existence, and the haggard battle it too had been !—

He was now about sixty-[four] ; his work all done, but his heart as if broken : a certain Miss Bowles, given to scribbling, with its affectations, its sentimentalities, and perhaps twenty years younger than he,[1] had (as I afterwards understood) heroically *volunteered* to marry him, " for the purpose of con-soling," etc., etc. ; to which he heroically had assented ; and was now on the road towards Bristol, or the western region where Miss Bowles lived, for completing that poor hope of his and hers. A second wedlock ; in what contrast almost dismal, almost horrible, with a former there had been !   Far away that former one ; but it had been illuminated by the hopes and radiances of very Heaven ; this second one was to be celebrated under sepulchral lamps, and as if in the forecourt of the charnel-house ! Southey's deep misery of aspect I should have better understood, had this been known to me ; but it was known to Taylor alone, who kept it locked from everybody.

[1] Miss Bowles was *twelve* years younger than Southey.

The last time I saw Southey was on an evening at Taylor's, nobody there but myself ; I think he meant to leave Town next morning, and had wished to say farewell to me first.   We sat on the sofa together ; our talk was long and earnest ; topic ultimately the usual one, steady approach of democracy, with revolution (probably *explosive*), and a *finis* incomputable to man,—steady decay of all morality, political, social, individual, this once noble England getting more and more ignoble and untrue in every fibre of it, till the *gold* (see Goethe's *Composite King*) would *all* be eaten out, and noble England would have to collapse in shapeless ruin, whether *forever* or not none of us could know.   Our perfect consent on these matters gave an animation to the Dialogue, which I remember as copious and pleasant. Southey's last word was in answer to some tirade of mine about universal Mammon-worship, gradual accelerating decay of mutual humanity, of piety and fidelity to God or man, in all our relations and performances,—the whole illustrated by examples, I suppose ;—to which he answered, not with levity, yet with a cheerful tone in his seriousness, " It will not, and it cannot come to good ! "   This he spoke standing ; I had risen, checking my tirade, intimating that, alas, I must go.   He invited me to Cumberland, to " see the Lakes again " ; and added, " Let us know beforehand ; that the rites of hospitality—"   I had already shaken hands, and now answered from beyond the door of the apartment, " Ah, yes ; thanks, thanks ! " little thinking that it was my last farewell of Southey.

He went to the Western Country ; got wedded,[1] went back to Keswick ; and I heard once or so some shallow jest about his promptitude in wedding : but before long, the news came, first in whispers, then public and undeniable, that his mind was going or gone, memory quite, and the rest hopelessly following it.   The new Mrs. Southey had not succeeded in " consoling and comforting " him ; but far the reverse.   We understood afterwards that the grown-up Daughters and their Stepmother " had agreed ill," that perhaps neither they nor she were very wise, nor the arrangement itself very wise or well-contrived.   *Better* perhaps that poor Southey was veiled from it ; shrouded away in curtains of his own, and deaf to all discords henceforth !   We heard of him from Miss Fenwick now and then (I think for a year or two more) till the end came : he was usually altogether placid and quiet, without memory, more and more without thought.   One day they had tried him

[1] 4th June 1839.

with some fine bit of his own Poetry : he woke into beautiful consciousness, eyes and features shining with their old brightness (and perhaps a few words of rational speech coming) ; but it lasted only some minutes, till all lapsed into the old blank again. By degrees all intellect had melted away from him ; and quietly unconsciously he died.[1] There was little noise in the public on this occurrence ; nor could his private friends do other than, in silence, mournfully yet almost gratefully acquiesce. There came out by and by *two* Lives of him ; one by his widow, one by his son (such the family discrepancies, happily *inaudible* where they would have cut sharpest) ; neither of these books did I look into.

Southey I used to construe to myself as a man of slight build, but of sound and elegant ; with considerable genius in him, considerable faculty of *speed* and rhythmic insight, and with a morality that shone distinguished among his contemporaries. I reckoned him (with those *blue* blushes and those red) to be the perhaps excitablest of all men ; and that a deep mute monition of Conscience had spoken to him, " You are capable of running mad, if you don't take care. Acquire *habitudes ;* stick firm as adamant to them at all times, and work, continually work ! " This, for thirty or forty years, he had punctually and impetu- ously done ;—no man so *habitual*, we were told ; gave up his Poetry, at a given hour, on stroke of the clock, and took to Prose, etc. etc. ; and, as to diligence and velocity, employed his very walking hours, walked with a Book in his hand ;—and by these methods of his, had got through perhaps a greater amount of work, counting quantity and quality, than any other man whatever in those years of his ;—till all suddenly ended. I likened him to one of those huge sandstone grinding-cylinders which I had seen at Manchester, turning with inconceivable velocity (in the condemned room of the Iron Factory, where " the men die of lung disease at forty," but are *permitted to smoke* in their damp cellar, and think that a rich recompense !) —with inconceivable velocity turn those huge grinding-stones, screaming harshly victorious, harshly glad ; and shooting out, each of them, its big sheet of fire (*yellow*, star-light, etc. accord- ing as it is *brass* or other kind of metal that you grind and polish there)—beautiful sheets of fire, pouring out each as if from the paper-*cap* of its low-stooping fated grinder, when you look from rearward :—for many years these stones grind so, at such a rate ; till at last (in some cases) comes a moment when the

[1] 21st March 1843.

stone's cohesion is quite worn-out, overcome by the stupendous velocity long-continued ; and, while grinding its fastest, it flies off altogether, and settles some yards from you, a grinding-stone no longer, but a cartload of quiet sand.—[Finished at Mentone, 8th February 1867.]

[WORDSWORTH [1]]

OF Wordsworth I have little to write that could ever be of use to myself or others. I did not see him much, or till latish in my course see him at all ; nor did we deeply admire one another at any time ! Of me in my first times he had little knowledge ; and any feeling he had towards me, I suspect, was largely blended with abhorrence and perhaps a kind of fear. His works I knew ; but never considerably reverenced,—could not, on attempting it. A man recognisably of strong intellectual powers, strong character ; given to meditation, and much contemptuous of the *un*meditative world and its noisy nothing-nesses ; had a fine limpid style of writing and delineating, in his small way ; a fine limpid vein of melody too in him (as of an honest rustic *fiddle*, good, and well handled, but *wanting* two or more of the *strings*, and not capable of much !)—in fact, a rather dull, hard-tempered, unproductive and almost wearisome kind of man ; not adorable, by any means, as a great Poetic Genius, much less as the Trismegistus of such ; whom only a select few could even read, instead of mis-reading, which was the opinion his worshippers confidently entertained of him ! Privately I had a real respect for him withal, founded on his early Bio-graphy, which Wilson of Edinburgh had painted to me as of antique greatness signifying : " Poverty and Peasanthood, then ; be it so. But we consecrate ourselves to the Muses, all the same, and will proceed on those terms, Heaven aiding ! " This, and what of faculty I did recognise in the man, gave me a clear esteem of him, as of one remarkable and fairly beyond common ;—not to disturb which, I avoided speaking of him to

[1] Carlyle, when beginning this Paper, writes in his *Journal*, under date 3d March 1867 : " Fallen into a sad abeyance ; caught a baddish cold etc. ; incapable of anything which even I can call ' work ' for two weeks past,—cannot even touch upon the poor babble about Wordsworth (till to-day with effort) :—am, in brief, *below*, not equal to, the paltry complexities of my situation ; and for most part miserable, dismal, oftenest sad *as the grave*. *Pure* sadness of that kind, when it comes *pure*, is in fact my tolerablest mood ; all bitterness and discontent then taken away !—Shakspeare has been my common reading ; far the best for me I can fall upon here."

his worshippers ; or, if the topic turned up, would listen with an acquiescing air.   But to my private self his divine reflections and unfathomabilities seemed stinted, scanty ; palish and uncertain ;—perhaps in part a feeble *reflex* (derived at second hand through Coleridge) of the immense German fund of such ?—and I reckoned his Poetic Storehouse to be far from an opulent or well furnished apartment !

It was perhaps about 1840 that I first had any decisive meeting with Wordsworth, or made any really personal acquaintance with him.[1] In parties at Taylor's I may have seen him before ; but we had no speech together, nor did we specially notice one another :—one such time I do remember (probably *before*, as it was in my earlier days of Sterling acquaintanceship, when Sterling used to argue much with me), Wordsworth sat silent, almost next to me, while Sterling took to asserting the claims of Kotzebue as a Dramatist (" recommended even by Goethe," as he likewise urged) ; whom I with pleasure did my endeavour to explode from that mad notion,—and thought (as I still recollect), " This will perhaps please Wordsworth, too ; " who, however, gave not the least sign of that or any other feeling. I had various dialogues with him in that same room ; but these, I judge, were all or mostly of after date.

On a summer morning (let us call it 1840, then) I was apprised by Taylor that Wordsworth had come to Town ; and would meet a small party of us at a certain Tavern in St. James's Street, at breakfast,—to which I was invited for the given day and hour. We had a pretty little room ; quiet, though looking street-ward (Tavern's *name* is quite lost to me) ; the morning sun was pleasantly tinting the opposite houses, a balmy, calm and bright morning ; Wordsworth, I think, arrived just along with me ; we had still five minutes of sauntering and miscellaneous talking before the whole were assembled.   I do not positively remember any of them, except that James Spedding was there ; and that the others, not above five or six in whole, were polite intelligent quiet persons, and, except Taylor and Wordsworth, not of any special distinction in the world.   Breakfast was pleasant, fairly beyond the common of such things ; Wordsworth seemed in good tone, and, much to Taylor's satisfaction, talked a great deal.   About " poetic " Correspondents of his own (i.e. correspondents for the sake of *his* Poetry,—especially, one such who had sent him, from Canton, an excellent *Chest of Tea*, corre-

---

[1] Carlyle notes in his *Journal*, under date 1st June 1836, that he has " seen Wordsworth again."

spondent grinningly applauded by us all) ; then about ruralities
and miscellanies, "Countess of Pembroke" (antique She-
Clifford, glory of those Northern parts, who was not new to
any of us, but was set forth by Wordsworth with gusto and brief
emphasis, "You lily-livered" etc.) now the only memorable
item under that head : these were the first topics. Then finally
about *Literature*, literary laws, practices, observances,—at
considerable length, and turning wholly on the mechanical part,
including even a good deal of shallow enough *etymology*, from
me and others, which was well received : on all this Wordsworth
enlarged with evident satisfaction, and was joyfully reverent
of the "wells of English undefiled,"—though stone *dumb* as
to the deeper rules, and wells of Eternal Truth and Harmony
you were to try and set forth by said undefiled wells of *English*
or what other Speech you had ! To me a little disappointing,
but not much ;—though it would have given me pleasure, had
the robust veteran man emerged a little out of vocables into
things, now and then, as he never once chanced to do. For the
rest, he talked well in his way ; with veracity, easy brevity
and force ; as a wise tradesman would of his tools and workshop,
—and as no unwise one could. His voice was good, frank and
sonorous, though practically clear, distinct and forcible, rather
than melodious ; the tone of him business-like, sedately con-
fident, no discourtesy, yet no anxiety about being courteous ;
a fine wholesome rusticity, fresh as his mountain breezes, sat
well on the stalwart veteran, and on all he said and did. You
would have said he was a usually taciturn man ; glad to unlock
himself, to audience sympathetic and intelligent, when such
offered itself. His face bore marks of much, not always peaceful,
meditation ; the look of it not bland or benevolent, so much as
close, impregnable and hard : a man *multa tacere loquive paratus*,
in a world where he had experienced no lack of contradictions
as he strode along ! The eyes were not very brilliant, but they
had a quiet clearness ; there was enough of brow, and well
shaped ; rather too much of cheek (" horse-face," I have heard
satirists say), face of squarish shape and decidedly longish,
as I think the head itself was (*its* "length" going *horizontal*) :
he was large-boned, lean, but still firm-knit, tall and strong-
looking when he stood : a right good old steel-gray figure, with
a fine rustic simplicity and dignity about him, and a veracious
strength looking through him which might have suited one of
those old steel-gray *Markgrafs* (Graf = *Grau*, "Steel-gray")
whom Henry the Fowler set up to ward the "marches," and do

battle with the intrusive Heathen, in a stalwart and judicious manner.

On this and other occasional visits of his, I saw Wordsworth a number of times, at dinners, in evening parties ; and we grew a little more familiar, but without much increase of real intimacy or affection springing up between us. He was willing to talk with me in a corner, in noisy extensive circles ; having weak eyes, and little loving the general babble current in such places. One evening, probably about this time, I got him upon the subject of great poets, who I thought might be admirable equally to us both ; but was rather mistaken, as I gradually found. Pope's partial failure I was prepared for ; less for the narrowish limits visible in Milton and others. I tried him with Burns, of whom he had sung tender recognition ; but Burns also turned out to be a limited inferior creature, any genius he had a theme for one's pathos rather ; even Shakspeare himself had his blind sides, his limitations :—gradually it became apparent to me that of transcendent and unlimited there was, to this Critic, probably but one specimen known, Wordsworth himself ! He by no means said so, or hinted so, in words ; but on the whole it was all I gathered from him in this considerable *tête-à-tête* of ours ; and it was not an agreeable conquest. New notion as to Poetry or Poet I had not in the smallest degree got ; but my insight into the depths of Wordsworth's pride in himself had considerably augmented ;—and it did not increase my love of him ; though I did [not] in the least hate it either, so quiet was it, so fixed, *un*appealing, like a dim old lichened crag on the wayside, the private meaning of which, in contrast with any public meaning it had, you recognised with a kind of not wholly melancholy *grin.*—

Another and better corner dialogue I afterwards had with him, possibly also about this time ; which raised him intellectually some real degrees higher in my estimation than any of his deliverances written or oral had ever done ; and which I may reckon as the best of all his discoursings or dialogues with me. He had withdrawn to a corner, out of the light and of the general babble, as usual with him ; I joined him there, and knowing how little fruitful was the Literary topic between us, set him on giving me account of the notable practicalities he had seen in life, especially of the notable men. He went into all this with a certain alacrity ; and was willing to speak, wherever able on the terms. He had been in France in the earlier or secondary stage of the Revolution ; had witnessed the struggle of *Girondins* and *Mountain,* in particular the execution of Gorsas, " the first *Deputy* sent to the Scaffold ; " and testified strongly to the ominous feeling which that event produced in everybody, and of which he himself still seemed to retain something : " Where will it *end,* when you have set an example in *this* kind ? " I knew well about Gorsas ; but had found, in my readings, no trace of the public emotion his death excited ; and perceived now that Wordsworth might be taken as a true supplement to my Book, on this small point. He did not otherwise add to or alter my ideas on the Revolution : nor did we dwell long there ; but hastened over to England and to the noteworthy, or at least noted men of that and the subsequent time. " Noted " and named, I ought perhaps to say, rather than " noteworthy " ; for in general I forget what men they were ; and now remember only the excellent sagacity, distinctness and credibility of Wordsworth's little Biographic Portraitures of them. Never, or never but once, had I seen a stronger intellect, a more luminous and veracious power of insight, directed upon such a survey of fellow-men and their contemporary journey through the world. A great deal of Wordsworth lay in the mode and tone of drawing ; but you perceived it to be faithful, accurate, and altogether life-like, though Wordsworthian. One of the best remembered Sketches (almost the only one now remembered at all) was that of Wilberforce, the famous Nigger-Philanthropist, Drawing-room Christian, and busy man and Politician. In all which capacities Wordsworth's esteem of him seemed to be privately as small as my own private one, and was amusing to gather. No hard word of him did he speak or hint ; told, in brief firm business terms, How he was born at or near the place called *Wilberforce* in Yorkshire (" force " signifying torrent or angry brook, I suppose, as in Cumberland ?), where, probably, his fore-fathers may have been possessors, though he was poorish ; how he did this and that, of insignificant (to Wordsworth, insignific-ant) nature ;—" and then," added Wordsworth, " he took into the *Oil* trade " (I suppose the Hull whaling) ; which lively phrase, and the incomparable historical tone it was given in : " *the* Oil Trade," as a thing perfectly natural, and proper for such a man,—is almost the only point in the delineation which is now vividly present to me. I remember only the rustic Picture, sketched as with a burnt stick on the board of a pair of bellows, seemed to me completely good ; and that the general effect was, one *saw* the great Wilberforce and his existence, visible in all their main lineaments,—but only as through the *reversed* telescope, and reduced to the size of a mouse and its nest, or little more ! This was, in most or in all cases, the result brought out ; oneself and telescope of natural (or perhaps preternatural) size ; but the object, so great to vulgar eyes, *reduced* amazingly, with all its lineaments recognisable. I found a very superior talent in these Wordsworth delineations. They might have reminded me, though I know not whether they did at the time, of a larger series like them, which I had from my Father during two wet days which confined us to the house, the last time we met at Scotsbrig ! These were of select Annandale Figures whom I had seen in my Boyhood ; and of whom, now that they were all vanished, I was glad to have, for the first time, some real knowledge as facts, the outer *simulacra* in all their equipments, being still so pathetically vivid to me. My Father's, in rugged simple force, picturesque ingenuity, veracity and brevity, were, I do judge, superior to even Wordsworth's, as bits of human Portraiture ; *without* flavour of contempt, too, but given out with judicial indifference ;—and intermixed here and there with flashes of the *Poetical* and soberly Pathetic (e.g. the death of Bell of Dunnaby, and *why* the two joiners were seen sawing wood in a pour of rain), which the Wordsworth Sketches, mainly of distant and indifferent persons, altogether wanted. Oh my brave, dear, and ever-honoured Peasant Father, where among the Grandees, Sages, and recognised Poets of the world, did I listen to such sterling speech as yours,—golden product of a heart and brain all sterling and royal ! That is a literal *fact ;*—and it has often filled me with strange reflections, in the whirlpools of this mad world !

During the last seven or ten years of his life, Wordsworth felt himself to be a recognised lion, in certain considerable London Circles ; and was in the habit of coming up to Town with his Wife for a month or two every season, to enjoy his quiet triumph and collect his bits of tribute *tales quales*. The places where I met him oftenest, were Marshall's (the great Leeds linen-manufacturer, an excellent and very opulent man), Spring-Rice's (i.e. Lord Monteagle's, who and whose house was strangely intermarried with this Marshall's), and the *first* Lord Stanley's of Alderley (who then, perhaps, was still Sir Thomas Stanley). Wordsworth took his bit of lionism very quietly, with a smile sardonic rather than triumphant ; and certainly got no harm by it, if he got or expected little good. His Wife, a small, withered, puckered, winking lady, who never spoke, seemed to be more in earnest about the affair ;—and was visibly and sometimes ridiculously assiduous to secure her proper place of precedence at Table.[1] One evening at Lord Monteagle's—Ah, *who* was it that then made me laugh as we went home together: ah me !— —Wordsworth generally spoke a little with me on those occasions ; sometimes, perhaps, we sat by one another ; but there came from him nothing considerable, and happily at least nothing with an effort. " If you think me dull, be it just so ! " this seemed to a most respectable extent to be his inspiring humour. Hardly above once (perhaps at the Stanleys') do I faintly recollect something of the contrary on his part for a little while ; which was not pleasant or successful while it lasted. The light was always afflictive to his eyes ; he carried in his pocket something like a skeleton brass candlestick ; in which, setting it on the dinner-table, between him and the most afflictive or nearest of the chief lights, he touched a little spring, and there flirted out, at the top of his brass implement, a small vertical green circle, which prettily enough threw his eyes into shade, and screened him from that sorrow. In proof of his equanimity as lion I remember, in connection with this green shade, one little glimpse ; which shall be given presently as finis. But first let me say that all these Wordsworth phenomena appear to have been indifferent to [me], and have melted to steamy oblivion, in a singular degree. Of his talk to others in my hearing I remember simply nothing, not even a word or gesture. To myself it seemed once or twice as if he bore suspicions, thinking I was *not* a real worshipper, which threw him into something of embarrassment, till I hastened to get them laid, by frank discourse on some suitable thing (in the Stanley Drawing-room, I remember, he hit a stool, and kicked it over in striding forward to shake hands) ;—nor, when we did talk, was there on his side or on mine the least utterance worth noting. The tone of his voice when I did get him afloat, on some Cumberland or other matter germane to him, had a braced rustic vivacity, willingness, and solid precision, which alone rings in my ear when all else is gone. Of some Druid Circle, for example, he prolonged his response to me with the addition, " And there is another, some miles off ; which the country people call *Long* MEG *and her* DAUGHTERS ; " as to the now ownership of which, " It " etc. ; " *and then* it came into the

---

[1] According to Sir Henry Taylor, Mrs. Wordsworth was " rather tall," and was in all respects so unlike this description that he says " I cannot but think there was simply a mistake of one person for another."—*Nineteenth Century* for June 1881.

hands of a Mr. Crackenthorpe ; "—the *sound* of these two phrases is still lively and present with me ; meaning or sound of absolutely nothing more. Still more memorable is an ocular glimpse I had in one of these Wordsworthian lion-dinners, very symbolic to me of his general deportment there, and far clearer than the little feature of opposite sort, ambiguously given above (recollection of that viz. of unsuccessful *exertion* at a Stanley Dinner being dubious and all but extinct, while this is still vivid to me as of yesternight). Dinner was large, luminous, sumptuous ; I sat a long way from Wordsworth ; dessert I think had come in ; and certainly there reigned in all quarters a cackle as of Babel (only politer perhaps),—which far up, in Wordsworth's quarter (who was leftward on my side of the table), seemed to have taken a sententious, rather louder, logical and quasi-scientific turn,—heartily unimportant to gods and men, so far as I could judge of it and of the other babble reigning. I looked upwards, leftwards, the coast luckily being for a moment clear : there, far off, beautifully screened in the shadow of his vertical green circle, which was on the farther side of him, sat Wordsworth, silent, in rock-like indifference, slowly but steadily gnawing some portion of what I judged to be raisins, with his eye and attention placidly fixed on these and these alone. The sight of whom, and of his rock-like indifference to the babble, quasi-scientific and other, with attention turned on the small practical alone, was comfortable and amusing to me, who felt like him but could not eat raisins. This little glimpse I could still paint, so clear and bright is it, and this shall be symbolical of all.

In a few years, I forget in how many or when, these Wordsworth Appearances in London ceased ; we heard, not of ill-health perhaps, but of increasing love of rest ; at length of the long Sleep's coming ; and never saw Wordsworth more.[1] One felt his death as the extinction of a public light, but not otherwise. The public itself found not much to say of him ; and staggered on to meaner but more pressing objects.— —Why should I continue these melancholy jottings in which I have no interest ; in which the one Figure that could interest me is almost wanting ! I will cease. [Finished, after many miserable interruptions, catarrhal and other, at Mentone, 8th March 1867.]

On the same day Carlyle writes in his *Journal* :
" Finished the rag on Wordsworth to the last tatter ; won't

[1] Wordsworth died 23d April 1850.

begin another : *Cui bono*, it is wearisome and naught even to myself. . . . I live mostly alone ; with vanished Shadows of the Past,—many of them rise for a moment, inexpressibly tender ; One is never long absent from me. Gone, gone, but very dear, very beautiful and dear ! ETERNITY, which cannot be far off, is my one strong city. I look into it fixedly now and then ; all terrors about it seem to me superfluous ; all knowledge about it, any the least glimmer of certain knowledge, impossible to living mortal. The universe is full of love, and also of inexorable sternness and severity : and it remains for ever true that ' GOD reigns.' Patience, silence, hope ! "

[" CHRISTOPHER NORTH "]

[The following article on Professor John Wilson was written by Carlyle in the spring of 1868 when he was over seventy-two years old and in the second year of his widowerhood, in a lonesome, sombre mood, with thoughts habitually dwelling with sad and fond remembrance on bygone days. The Paper seems to have been mislaid and forgotten when the articles which constitute the *Reminiscences* were entrusted to its first Editor. But on its merits it well deserves to be included because it gives the reader a most vivid, graphic and lifelike representation of the man Wilson and his surroundings, at the same time affords some very interesting autobiographical glimpses into the Carlyle of those early years. The text as here printed conforms accurately with Carlyle's manuscript. A few explanatory footnotes have been added.]

WITH Professor Wilson, the famous John Wilson, *alias* Christopher North of Ambrose's Tavern, Edinburgh, and *Blackwood's Magazine*, I never had much acquaintance, never at bottom a superlative esteem for him, though I recognised with admiration his great and singular gifts, liked him really well, and in the then state of my affairs, notions and outlooks, could have well desired more talk and intercourse with him than I ever had. Being mournfully idle (not for want of things I *might* do, were nervous-system, nay were *soul* in better order—shame on me !) —and having been recalled to far gone days in Edinburgh by the scraps I had to write on Sir William Hamilton,—let me now, fast, and with fidelity, not *overlooked* by anybody requesting or prohibiting, fling down what traits I can recall of Wilson.

In my student days the chosen Promenade of Edinburgh was Princes Street ; from the East end of it, to and fro, westward as far as Frederick Street, or farther if you wished to be less jostled, and have the pavement more to yourself : there, on a bright afternoon, in its highest bloom probably about 4–5 P.M., all that was brightest in Edinburgh seemed to have stept out to enjoy, in the fresh pure air, the finest city-prospect in the world and the sight of one another, and was gaily streaming this way and that. From Castle Street or even the extreme west there was a visible increase of bright population, which thickened regularly eastward, and in the sections near the Register Office or extreme east, had become fairly a lively crowd, dense as it could

366

find stepping-ground,—never needed to be denser, or to become a crush, so many side-streets offering you free issue all along, and the possibility of returning by a circuit, instead of abruptly on your steps. The crowd was lively enough, brilliant, many-coloured, many-voiced, clever-looking (beautiful and graceful young womankind a conspicuous element) : crowd altogether elegant, polite, and at its ease tho' on parade ; something as if of unconsciously rhythmic in the movements of it, as if of harmonious in the sound of its cheerful voices, bass and treble, fringed with the light laughters ; a quite pretty kind of natural concert and rhythmus of march ; into which, if at leisure, and carefully enough dressed (as some of us seldom were) you might introduce yourself, and flow for a turn or two with the general flood. It was finely convenient to a stranger in Edinburgh, intent to employ his eyes in instructive recreation ; and see, or hope to see, so much of what was brightest and most distinguished in the place, on those easy terms. As for me, I never could afford to promenade or linger there ; and only a few times, happened to float leisurely thro', on my way elsewhither. Which perhaps makes it look all the brighter now in far-off memory, being so *rare* as, in one sense, it surely is to me ! Nothing of the same kind now remains in Edinburgh ; already in 1832, you in vain sought and inquired Where the general promenade, then, was ? The general promenade was, and continues, nowhere—as so many infinitely nobler things already do !

It must have been on an April Saturday of 1814, probably enough the last time I ever found myself in this fine Princes-Street tide of human life, that an elder comrade and I, passing thro' for some larger stretch of walking, had sight, I for the first time, of a Figure that has rendered it ever since memorable to me. My comrade was by no means an intimate, but he was six or seven years my elder, a polished ingenious enough kind of man, who knew, at least by outside, the lions and the rumours and topics of society, as I by no means did ; and with whom, meeting him by accident, I had willingly consented to join company, on this occasion, and who accordingly proved really entertaining to me. His name was Campbell ; from Galloway somewhere ; went before long to be Minister of Peebles, I think ; and perhaps this was the first and the last walk we ever had together. Our course lay along Princes Street from the west, the promenade all in its beauty, in its sunny gaiety ; well worth looking at, and growing ever denser as we proceeded ; fairly a kind of press in the last division eastward. Not far from the very finis, or

Register Office itself, Campbell nudged me, and in an under-tone, murmured, glancing to a figure near meeting us, " *Isle of Palms* : Wilson ! " I looked duly ; and sure enough, tho' Poem and Poet were as yet only a rumour to me, here was something one could not at once forget. A very tall strong-built and impetuous looking young man, age perhaps about 28, with a profusion of blond hair, with large flashing countenance of the statuesque sort, flashing pair of blue eyes, which were fixed as if on something far off, was impetuously striding along, regarding nobody to right or left, but gently yet rapidly cleaving the press, and with large strides stepping along, as if too late for some appointment far ahead. His clothing was rough (I think some loose, whitish jacket of kersey-stuff), hat of broadish brim, on the big massive head, flanked with such overplus of strong unclipt flaxen hair, seemed to have known many showers in its time ; but what struck one most was the glance of those big blue eyes, stern yet loving, pointing so authentically to something far away. We followed this figure, at least I did, so far as looking over one's shoulder would do : saw it, or the head of it eminent above the general level victoriously speeding on its course, for some considerable distance farther. Whether the general promenade took any notice of this big transit thro' it I do not remember, rather think not ; but from that day, " John Wilson (*Isle of Palms*) " was an additional item in the little Private Gallery of Portraits my memory had taken in.

It was about a dozen years more, before I knew anything personally of Wilson, or almost even had seen the face of him again. His *Isle of Palms* I had read, and recognised the flush of fine sensibilities, efflorescences and talents there ; but found all in too unripe a state, and of little use to me in that stage of their and my development. Next in order, and what I remember better, in the *Edinburgh Review* there by and by came out a Paper *on Byron* by him ; eloquently descanting with abundance of sympathy, and in a great poetic style, on the abysses of Human Life, on *Rousseau's Confessions* and the Byronic character ;—in a somewhat too grandiloquent and as it were *plethoric* strain, thought I. *Trials of Margaret Lindsay*, which was very popular years afterwards in good Scotch houses, I had also read ; again with considerable love and approval, but without change in the above exceptional clauses. " A human character of fine and noble elements," thought I ; but not at one with itself : an exuberant enough, leafy and tropical kind of tree rather exhaling itself in balmy odours than producing fruit.

"CHRISTOPHER NORTH" 369

In the meanwhile, too, perhaps about midway between *Margaret Lindsay* and the *Isle of Palms*, the far bigger and still more questionable efflorescences in *Blackwood's Magazine* had taken place, and were provoking endless loud criticism from all the world ; to me also questionable, but disclosive of singular new qualities in the man ; wild explosions quasi-volcanic of multifarious half-fused conglomerate,—masses of rugged grotesque human sense ; of scorching satire, torrents of wild human fun, not without touches almost of human blackguardism, striving to combine themselves with something of heroic pride, and with notably much of religious piety,—these phenomena were certainly wonderful if not admirable ; and Wilson had become a conspicuous public man, whom in many points I valued as one of the most gifted, and whom at any rate both for his singular gifts, and even for the singular deficiencies conjoined, one could not but be willing to know, should opportunity ever come.

Which with me it had little chance to do quite in a hurry ! I lived much out of Edinburgh, in those years ; and was almost solitary when in it, a prey to my own sad thoughts and problems, far away from those of Wilson. His very *Toryism*,—for I perceived that, like myself, he was among the *born Radicals* of his generation, considerably dissatisfied me ; still more his forced wedlock of Presbyterian Piety with so much of Bluster and Whisky-Punch : "a character not at one with itself," thought I ; —no indeed, but always at *two* with itself, I might have continued to say. Edinburgh was very noisy upon him now ; against rather than for. It was generally understood his Finance-affairs, not to speak of others, were gone extremely to wreck ; handsome fortune of his own, and ditto of his Wife, quite wasted by extravagance, if not of ostentatious expenditure, yet of irregularity and total want of management.[1] Wild stories ran, Of his having once laid a bet to live three months in Ireland as a common beggar, and of his having done it ; of his being once detected serving in some big Hôtel as waiter ; etc. etc. ;—stories which, tho' probably mythical merely, or altogether fabulous and false, I have heard long after, in distant places, repeated by quiet people as facts. Whig-Radical Edinburgh, that is, some nineteen-twentieths of the population then, figured Wilson to

[1] Soon after writing this Carlyle discovered that he had been misinformed in regard to Professor Wilson's finances. For, in his Journal, under date September 1, 1868, he says : "I ought to correct the notion I had that Wilson '*wasted* his 30,000*l*.'—it was 50,000*l*., and an Uncle (one of his Trustees) 'wasted it for him.' Correct that on opportunity."

itself, as a man of fine gifts and possibilities, who had recklessly
squandered them all, and was now fallen into disgust with his
position, and Stoically waiting, grandly inert (except for these
Blackwood explosions), what would become of it and him ;—
" will spend a whole day with his eldest Boy, flinging old shoes
up and down the staircase " (in the way of bandy ; poor Boy
at the top, it is to be presumed !), said rumouring Edinburgh in
those years.

I have myself heard the story ; and remember well enough
that Tory hoisting process—hoisting of Wilson by main force
into the Professorship of " Moral Philosophy," just fallen vacant
by the death of the immaculate Dr. Brown (a really pure, high
if rather shrill and wire-drawing kind of man) ; and how hugely
ill it was taken by the vast majority of talking and newspapering
mankind,—in which feeling, I my silent self, though not without real love for the erring Wilson, shared more or less.   A
pretty Professor " of *Morals* ! " snorted all manner of indignant
Editors and speculative men ;—and indeed it was a rather high
procedure, this of the Tories in respect of Wilson and their Party:
but it turned out better than was expected. " Moral *Philosophy*,"
or " Philosophy " of any kind, Wilson, I suppose, never taught,
or much tried to teach : but he was a most eloquent, fervid, over-
powering kind of man, alive to all high interests and noble objects,
especially of the literary or spiritual sort, and prompt to foster
any germ of talent or aspiration he might notice in that kind,
among his pupils : and he did kindle several of them, to my after
knowledge, into a certain generous, tho' *fuliginous* as well as
flamy, fire and development of intellectual faculty,—preferable,
surely, to the logical frost which would otherwise have been
their Academic portion, had Wilson *not* been there.   So that, I
suppose, he proved really more serviceable, and not less, than
the best of his competitor Candidates could have been in that
office.

Thrice or so, I have strayed in, as an accidental auditor, and
heard him lecture.   Nothing could be more in contrast to the
high-soaring, purely metaphysical (and to me unintelligible, and
uninteresting, and at last almost *ghastly*) Dr. Brown, who had
been my own Professor in the same place.   Nothing of ghastly at
least in this Wilson, nothing of shrill, or metaphysically cob-
webish.   He stood erect like a tower ; cloudy energy, determination, and even sincerity (or the visible wish to be sincere) looking
out from every feature of him ; giving you, among his chaos of
papers there, assurance of a man.   One of the times, and one,

only, he had got some rather strictly scientific or metaphysical point to handle, or to tide over in some plausible way. His internal embarrassment and yet determined outer onrush in this troublesome matter, I still remember well ; and how with wild strokes he plunged about, like a whale among tubs, hither, thither, churning the ocean into foam, for a length of time, and at last in some good way got floated over into more genial waters. All the other times I found him dealing with human life in the concrete ; and this in a style, and with a stormful opulence of faculty, great and peculiar. Glowing pictures, dashed off in rapid powerful strokes, often of a fine poetic and emphatic quality, this, I could see, was his favourite mode of illustrating and teaching : snatches of human portraiture,—savage men careering free and far in their silent deserts, under a silent law of Nature ; spelling out the rudimentals of this universe,—how strange these dim Primordia of Humanity, as yet inarticulate, mostly mute : or again the civilized man, the civilized criminal, in the heart of an Earth and a Heaven become articulate, fancy him at last resolved on the atrocity of murder, finger on the pistol-trigger, trigger not yet drawn tho' fully intended to be, and what an awful never-alterable infinitude of difference to him when once it *is* drawn ; etc. etc. : there seemed to be much of the like of this ; and you easily observed the Professor found his strength to lie that way. He read with energy, almost with impetuosity, in a strong not unmelodious voice, his kindling eyes flashing as if minatory, in certain high passages, and his brow knitting itself ;—always approximately sincere, and very wishful to be wholly so. I could well conceive his effect on raw young minds, of the better sort, and what enthusiasms and grandiloquences (good but not the best) he might kindle among several of them, and gradually get imitated and reproduced over the world. As indeed has been discernible enough, especially in Scotland, in the years that have followed.

It must have been in the end of 1826 that I first had any personal acquaintance with Wilson ; familiar as his name and wild lucubrations now were to me and everybody, I as yet knew nothing farther of him but his figure and his voice. One Gordon, from Kirkcudbright, a visitor at our little Domicile of Comley Bank, and an estimable old acquaintance of mine, often spoke with us about Wilson, and took a certain shine of new dignity from his known familiarity with the famous man and his circle. I suppose it was by him that I was somewhere incidentally on the streets (I quite forget when or where) brought to the enviable honour of a mouthful of speech with the great Professor, and the privilege of speaking two or three words again with him, if it suited both parties, when we chanced to meet. Wilson was of perfectly accessible and affable character, had not the least stiffness, ceremonial reservation, or pride of place ; and was altogether easy to speak with, if he did not dislike you, and you could be yourself easy.   Our little Dialogues on such occasions never amounted to much,—tho' these conditions were tolerably the fact between us ;—nor could I ever be said to attain any intimacy or free familiarity with the big volcano of a man, much less anything of love or friendship, had that latter been my wish, as the former certainly more or less were.   An esteem etc. he evidently had of me far beyond what was requisite for this object, very far beyond what was demanded or expected by me : nevertheless I could perceive we made as good as no progress, but stood as if looking at one another with a walled iron-grating between us, having only the *eyes* free on both sides.   Eyes looking kindly enough it must be owned.   Uniformly I found Wilson amiable, opulent in faculty of talking ; curious touches, little freaks of gay humour, I got now and then ; always a rough basis of truth, of clear and sharp discernment noticeable in them ; but there it had to rest ; we never got to any solid or at all deeper stratum.   I suppose he felt aways, or indeed already knew from the first, that this young fellow did not go into the *Noctes Ambrosianæ* element of things, except as an occasional spectator, merely, as an admirer *cum grano* under drawbacks and exceptions.

I once heard him say, as we walked together (I cannot say *where* having met), speaking about " Testimonials " on behalf of poor commonplace young men in want of a situation, and eagerly trying for every chance of one, what an embarrassment and ever-recurring bother they were to the like of him ;—of which, as his careless custom sometimes was, he gave me a living example (happily unknown to me then or since) : " You cannot write, ' I hereby certify that Mr. — is an Ass ! ' "—with a toss or a snort of ludicrous pathos and disdain, which I still recollect.   To people of any merit, and even of little or none, I believe he was extremely ready to write whatever best certificate he could—the big good-natured careless man.[1]   His conversation, never so

1 When Carlyle was a candidate for the Chair of Moral Philosophy in the University of St. Andrews (January 1828) Professor Wilson sent him a testimonial in the form of a letter, a copy of which (in Mrs. Carlyle's hand) I have found among his papers.   In this he writes : " From my acquaintance with your various writings and with yourself, I have formed

casual, in such brief meetings, had generally something piquant
in it unlike that of other men ; a spicing of wild satire,
caricature, or off-hand quiz, wild not cruel, almost always an
ingredient traceable. And he loved to *dramatise* any fact or
doctrine to you by an example that might come to hand. It was
always evident to me there lay sound sense and discernment in
what he said ; and I always rather liked to fall in with him, even
for a minute or two, and could have liked much more, would he
have consented to be really serious and sincere with me, now and
then, which he never quite was. On serious speculative points
he glided almost immediately into the sentimental ; on practical
or personal points, into the realm of quiz.

As this was all I could get of my Wilson I had to be content
with it, and quietly despair of more. Even so he was better
to me than nobody or than a common dull acquaintance claiming speech. A fine fresh stalwart human brother, something
massive, not in the figure and gait of him only, but in the form
of his address, in the very sound of his voice. He spoke low
rather than otherwise, with a melodious potency and breadth of
tone, accent essentially Scotch, or even Glasgow-Scotch, tho'
with a certain refining tincture of Old-Oxford, too, as if *chemi-
cally* joined there ; voice spreading itself out as if in trustful
exposition of the current something or nothing, in neighbour-
like cordiality, and the determination to be gracious and agreeable,—often a curious overdone self-conscious and self-mocking
style of politeness observable, which tickled you into the due
posture, and was abundantly piquant and peculiar. In fact
Wilson was full of genuine sensibility to human fun ; had a great
deal of real humour in him ; and no man, or hardly any man, was
less of a hypocrite. But laughter, virtual, or actual, was his
panoply and general cloak-of-darkness ; of virtual he had, as
it were, no end ; and the very tones of his voice testified of it :

a very high estimate of your moral and intellectual character ; nor do I
know a man better qualified than you are for the chair to which you now
aspire. On such an occasion there can be no indelicacy in declaring my
belief that you are a man of distinguished abilities, and of great erudition,
—of abilities and erudition that could be brought to bear, with uncommon
effect, on metaphysical and moral science. You have all your life been a
student of human nature—both of books and men,—and your views of
human nature are, in my opinion, true and comprehensive. I have no
doubt that you would, if elected to this chair, discharge its duties conscientiously, ably, and eloquently, and prove an admirable teacher. You
have therefore my warmest wishes for your success ; and little as may be
the influence of my expressed opinion of your qualifications, it is gratifying
to me to assure you of the high esteem and regard in which you are held by
" Your very sincere friend, JOHN WILSON."

actual he could abundantly awaken in others, tho' himself, to my recollection, never laughed at all.

The very tones of his voice, I said :—once, for example, Dr. Brewster and I, strolling up from Heriot Row towards Queen Street and Frederick Street, in the fine open sunshine and spacious quietude there, discoursing, if I recollect, on some project of a *Literary Gazette*, which Brewster, a man ever fertile in projects, was often endeavouring to render plausible to me, were joined by Wilson ; who, curiously enough, announced to me that a certain " young Mr. Bell," whom I had never heard of, tho' Brewster had, was meditating Literary enterprises, and thought an " Edinburgh Literary Gazette " might do considerable things, if I would embark along with him. " I ? But he doesn't know me at all," objected I. Wilson explained in his satirically polished way : " Has heard ; has read ; your *German* faculty, etc."—" Dear me, is that a son of old James Bell ? " interposed Brewster, with more of surprise than enthusiasm. " The same," answered Wilson ; " and is quite bent on going into Literature and doing exploits in that line." " And ready to co-operate with any man," said I. " With *any* man ! " answered Wilson, in such a tone of broad recognition as completely pictured the truth of the phenomenon, and set Brewster and me into a peal of laughter. I never saw this " young Mr. Bell," nor specifically heard of him again ; but I think he is the same Mr. Bell who afterwards in London, " edited the Poets," etc. etc., and in a leanish not uncreditable way laboured in the vineyard here, till his death not long since. There hung always about the name of him to me a kind of tone ; partly *elegiac*, and yet not rightly so,—run athwart by that " any man ! " of Wilson's. These intonations of his, and the multitudinous small play of feature and gesture that accompanied them, like the many-twinkling motion of sunshine or moonshine on the deep sea, still dwell strangely with me, and no doubt were expressive of the man.

For a long time Gordon had been meditating for me a Supper or Night with Wilson, and deeply pondering how it could be brought about. After various failures the night at length was got fixed, and came. At Gordon's rooms, a party of Four ; Wilson *versus* Gordon himself, and a harmless unimportant Lawyer person (whom I never saw again, name, I think Roy) opposite to whom, with Wilson on my right hand, I remember sitting. It was probably soon after nine when we assembled ; dusk of a fine summer day ;—must have been of the year 1827.

Wilson, semi-visible, till lights and supper came, sat interesting us, and flowingly in talk, about a call he had just been making on Lockhart who had arrived on visit to his old friends that afternoon from London : I remember also, his *Life of Burns* (which Wilson spoke of by and by) was just come out ; and that Lockhart had said to him, in regard to London and his element there, " Oh, don't ask me ; don't bid me speak a word of that,—I have run away to forget all that delirious stuff, for a week or two, among you ! " Bedlam or little better, Lockhart seemed to have thought, and Wilson to think. To all which we grinned or hummed assent with the recognition due from us.

Supper was announced straightway, on these good terms ; supper and lights awakened new vivacity, especially the long sequel of whiskey-punch did ; and there arose such a flood or blaze of talk, Wilson the tongue of it, by nine-tenths or more, we the ear mainly, as I never witnessed or listened to before. The night might well be reckoned amusing ; and truly so it was,— tho' one felt it was not very *fine* amusement, but only very new and very *strange*. Far more of wisdom, grace, and even of real ingenuity, cleverness and sprightly entertainment I have had in a night, from some gifted man ; but never from any man such a boundless, quietly volcanic pouring of himself out in spiritual lava,—all a kind of " lava,"—which glowed luminous in the night, and never, for a moment, was mere ashes and soot, tho' perhaps at no moment quite free of those ingredients. For he went along without study or distrust, extempore in all senses ; and gave you, with careless abundance, whatever lay in him on the topic going. Nor was he in the least one of those *soliloquy* talkers (Coleridge, Humboldt, etc., so unendurable, were they eloquent as seraphs), who *pump* their talk into you as if you were a bucket : on the contrary he rather seemed to wait for your inquiry, for your suggestion of a subject ; and never failed to pause at once, when his quick glance told him you nearly had enough. He was ready to talk of anything, even of any person, —and would launch out into blazy high-coloured delineations of distinguished men ; *dramatising* his ideas, often enough (mimicking the great man's words and ways, in dialogues and incidents, which you felt were imaginary and poetised for the nonce) ; giving you a singularly vivid likeness in caricature. Caricature essentially good-natured almost always, with brushfuls of flattering varnish exuberantly laid on,—tho' you felt, nearly always too, that there lurked something of satirical *per-contra* at the bottom, and a clear view of the seamy side withal. Wordsworth,

Coleridge, and the minor Lakers, he gave us at great length, in this serio-comic or comico-serious, vein ; of De Quincey (who, I think, was then, or had lately been, his guest for a good while) he had much to say, in farce-tragedy style, wildly coruscating and caricaturing ; Brougham, too, Dugald Stewart, at last even Jeffrey, and his own Edinburgh rivals, all done with swift broad strokes, not insincere, and with abundance of flattering varnish and formal *kowtow*ing :—I find our talk, thro' those five hours, was principally of Distinguished Persons whom Wilson knew ; Wilson nothing loth of that unsafe theme, the intrinsically guileless, childlike man. There rose, by intervals, plenty of other speculative neutral topics ; but this had proved to be the fruitfullest, and we always gravitated back to it. I think it was for most part I that started the game ; and probably it was for me mainly that he shaped his volcanic discoursings, —tho' by no means formally for me, all the rest sharing and co-operating throughout, Gordon by some *hotch* of smothered laughter now and then (uncommonly genial of its kind), and Roy by his constant air of intelligence and interested attention. And so the volcano went, five hours of it; and the spiritual lava, never failing or flagging. Till the actual sun came beaming through the window-shutters, and everybody had to think of moving.

Spiritual lava I called it, but indeed it was *spirituous* as well, or fully more ! Wilson drank a great deal of whisky-punch ; steadily, not in haste, but without rest, and as a business, all night ; solid part of supper, to him especially, was nothing ; the essence of it *drink*, by way of keeping *talk* on flame. This too was essentially our case (what we ate, or whether we ate anything, I totally forget) ; but our aim was, to hear Wilson talk, and we cheerfully (for there was no pressing, or speech about drink) conformed to his law. Gordon and Roy, perhaps, did a little to follow suit afar off ; I went upon sipping warm-water, reinforced at long intervals by a spoonful of port-wine negus. Wilson, I think, must have had in all about fourteen tumblers, —considerably above a bottle of " pure *aquavitae*," diluted with sugar and hot water.[1] He also incidentally consumed quantities

---

[1] In the Memoir of her father, Mrs. Gordon gives equally striking testimony to the Professor's extraordinary feats in whisky-drinking : One day, after a long walk in the country, he called at a farm-house, the mistress of which came in " with a bottleful and can of milk with a tumbler. Instead of a tumbler, he requested a bowl and poured the half of the whisky in, along with half of the milk. He drank the mixture at a draught, and while his kind hostess was looking on with amazement, he poured the remainder of the whisky and milk into the bowl and drank that also."—*Memoir of John Wilson*, p. 137.

of snuff,—a box of hendy-fort laid duly beside him for accompaniment ; tho' usually, I think, he did not wear a snuff-box at all.
By degrees his upper lip (a scornful kind of lip, and *short* for a
man of genius) got considerably browned or yellowed by the
snuff, which gave him a still more off-hand, defiant kind of air.
For the rest, the stout whisky-punch, 14 tumblers of it,
seemed to produce no effect on him whatever ; no more than if
you had poured them into an iron pump, which only kept
volcanically talking all the same.   Towards morning you could
perhaps notice that his complexion seemed as if getting half-
perceptibly something of a grey-blue tinge intermingled ; that
the snuffy lip had a still more off-hand defiant look ;—and, on
the whole, that internally the temper was getting visibly a shade
fiercer.   Once, I remarked, and once only among the whole of
us, poor Roy got a slight brief pat : in some interval, Roy, not a
little delighted with his position and entertainment, was ventur-
ing to illustrate something by a bit of eulogy on really good business talents ;   Wilson with a dangerous smile, broke in : " Do
you know, Mr. Roy, there's nothing I so much detest as an
excellent man of business ! "—which completely finished that.
I remarked too that in speaking of distinguished persons (Dugald
Stewart and the like sublimities), tho' his formal flattery and
kowtowing of them was more exuberant than ever, there was
now first clearly discernible across it a substratum of authentic
per-contra ;   and it seemed to me as if here were a lion, wild
monarch of the woods, licking all manner of pretended favourites,
but with every stroke of the tongue bringing away *blood*.   In
fine, things having got to this pass, and the ruddy sun-rays shining visibly in on us, we all rose to go,—loth, all of us, in a sort,
—and went our ways.   Wilson's way and mine were the same,
for half my distance ;   and he listened or talked humanely to me,
till in Glo'ster Place, perhaps to the relief of both, we could
shake ourselves loose.   At Comley Bank I was surprised, and
at first almost shocked, to find a pure white Spirit, lovely and
loving, " sitting up for me,"—quietly reading and waiting, hour
after hour, till I should come.   Ah me, ah me !—In this way
had ended my Night with Wilson, the only one I ever had with
him, or again attempted to have.

For another year we continued to fall in with one another
transiently up and down, and to have a little off-hand discourse ;
offence there never was on either side, always the contrary indeed :
but our intimacy grew no farther, merely continued grown at
the small height it had reached, and to me privately declared

itself incapable of much growing.   Once, perhaps twice, on some
trifling occasion I have been in his house for half an hour ; once
only do I recollect his having been in ours.   One of my little
errands to him was concerning a *letter* and certain medals of
Goethe's, which I was to deliver to Sir Walter Scott : Sir Walter
(to my then great sorrow) had gone out of Town ; I too was
just going.   He said at parting, " Yes, I will come and see you,
Craigenputtock and you, for certain I will : but you must write
specially to ask me ! " I wrote ; but knew beforehand, there
would nothing come, not even an answer.   Forty years afterwards my poor bit of *Letter*, Wilson now gone, came back to me
in a Newspaper,—some Biographer of his had found it and
thought it printable.[1]

Once or so in those years, Wilson gave me a kind word in
Blackwood, never an unkind one at that epoch (or almost at all,
that I ever heard of) : good, good ;—but I perceived there was
not, in my case, much of discernment in either kind of words
from him, rather little even of sincerity ; and my gratitude was
silent, and not very great.   In fact I dimly perceived that my
big volcano of a man was much of a child withal, innocent
spoiled child ; and I consented well enough to love him as I
could from the distance, and enjoy his coruscations and explosions, with such admiration, or such questionable wonder, as a
willing but unconcerned spectator might have.   Those wild
Noctes Anbrosianae of his were uniformly a great entertainment
to me ; admirable flashes of broad strong insight, genially
triumphant sarcasm, humour and satire ; beautiful bits of poetic
delineation, wild tones of piety and melody : but all imbedded
in such an element of drunken semi-frenzy,—sad to me to think
they were *lost*, jewels thrown into a sea of conflagration, inextric-
ably inextricable, there !   I always felt there was in Wilson,
more approximately than in anybody I had (or yet have) ever
seen, the *making* of a great man ; very nearly all the grandest
qualities and opulencies that go to that result ;—but not quite
all[2] ; and that, in fine, the great man never could be *made*.
Which did prove, more sadly than I then expected, the result
of his blazing course.

[1] Carlyle's letter to Wilson is dated December 19, 1829, and may be
read in Mrs. Gordon's *Memoir of John Wilson*.
[2] Wilson himself seems to have been conscious of the lack of one of these
grandest qualities—perhaps the grandest of all—for he wrote to his friend
Mr. Harden, in the year 1809 ; " I do not, I hope, want either ballast or
cargo or sail, but I do want an anchor most confoundedly, and without it,
I shall keep beating about the great sea of life to very little purpose."—
Mrs. Gordon's *Memoir of John Wilson*, p. 109.

That night in Gordon's, I believe, was pretty much the sample of six nights out of every seven of Wilson's for the next twelve or fifteen years. Six nights out of seven (not that he cared very much about Sunday, but that the Edinburgh Public fancied it did), Wilson was likeliest to be dining abroad, with some sympathising jolly company (far jollier, at least far louder than we could pretend to have been), whom his conversation was keeping in a roar. Who his principal hosts or companions, or indeed who any of them were, I never knew : it was not understood he was fastidious or at all select in choice ; but he did dislike, and even " detest " any naturally base fellow, and would much shun to sit with that kind ; *item* equally or more, with the kind that were unfriendly to him, irrecognisant, unjust or stingy to his real merits, pretensions and intentions (which he did not swagger with at all, but was conscious of),—this would be a still unsafer kind to plant beside him. He liked, we need not doubt, kindly intelligent faces, jovial laughers, perfect freedom, and plenty of whisky-punch ; and Edinburgh had circles enough of this type, enough and to spare, of whom Wilson could be the charm. He drank largely I doubt not, but was never heard of as being drunk :—" fourteen tumblers poured as if into an iron pump ! " He was in his best years (40 to 50) ; had health like an athlete ; and certainly in the matter of dining or otherwise he took no charge of it, had no care about it. I remember meeting him one wintry day, the streets all in snow slush ; he was splashing along regardless in very thin shoes, talking to some insignificant friend hooked upon him, his look vivid, rapid but not comfortable : I remonstrated upon the thin shoes, which were evidently quite soaked : " Hm, yes," said he ; " but one hasn't time "—and drawing his finger across mid thigh, added briskly, " Up to here, I have no consciousness of having legs or feet ! " I could only shake my head (thinking of yesternight's probable punch), and step on.

The *Noctes Ambrosianae* themselves, I suppose, were imaginary dinners out, and done in intervals of the real,—probably the chief " rest " from the real. Plenty of punch seemed to be evident in them, and an imaginary circle beaming with approval, and inextinguishable Hahas. This was a mad enough element for one's pursuit of welfare, for one's health either of body or of spirit ! But Wilson had got into it, and couldn't get out again.[1] Intrinsically he meant nothing ill ; intrinsically he

[1] It is pleasing to find that Wilson did escape, for a while, at least, in his later years, from the thraldom of drink ; but, alas, not before much harm

was a lovable guileless kind of man,—kind of wasted giant.
Malice was not in him ; though one often heard him accused of
bitter and inveterate malice ; of long-continued hatreds and
unjust persecutions of innocent men, and even unfortunate as
well,—" Leigh Hunt and the Cockney School," for instance.
This cannot be defended ; but it was not altogether malice, or
malice as of a grown man,—it was malice as of a child rather ;
spoiled child, disobedient, sensitive, impatient, whose jealousies,
affections, whims, you must not cross, under penalties, but
whose worst rages are transitory and of no depth. Wilson,
suddenly one month (in *Blackwood*), whirled round on Hunt,
I believe, and assured him he had loved him all this while, and
would never abuse him more ! It was not in the big man
to hate anybody ; and he saw privately, well enough, what
excellent, loveable, or pretty qualities might lie withal in anybody he was wroth with. Hunt had been his scolding-stock for
many years ; but only as representative and scapegoat of that
" Cockney School," whose sins were, in effect, considerable not
to Wilson alone of mankind. He was not a deliberate man, a
judicial or coherent, far far the contrary ! He hung together
only like the whirlwind, like the smoke-cloud, by law of gravitation and impact. His whole existence yawned in inconsistencies,
which he had lost hope of reconciling. A born Radical, as
intense as you could meet with, yet knowing high chivalrous
things, and obliged to bid vulgar Radicalism, which knew them
not, his fierce *Apage* ; a nobly pious kind of soul, full of tender
and quasi-sacred recollections in that kind, to whom vulgar
free-thinking was an unbearable nuisance, and yet with no
Religion he could give the least account of : seldom had a man
more overwhelming inconsistencies to deal with. He looked at
them with steady front, mournful, gloomy often, but steady ;
did not " deal " with them at all,—only refused to have any fear
of them. " A very wild existence and Life-scene," you might
say ; tropically verdant and luxuriant so much of it, yet riven
into thunder-peaks, split asunder by abysses and impassable

had been wrought on his health of mind and body. An intimate friend of
Carlyle and Wilson, Dr. Samuel Brown (cousin of the more widely known
John Brown, of *Rab and his Friends*, etc.) wrote to Carlyle, in March 1844 :
" By the way the Professor [Wilson] is recovering his youth, and a beautiful second youth it is. For three years he has drunk only Hermitage, by
which I mean not the wine of that name but cold water ; and as he was
never an Epicure, and never used tobacco or opium, he has become very
fresh and funny. But his humour is so mellow as only to beautify the
simple piety of his heart. He talks much of sorrow and death now, but
in a vein of pleasant contemplation. You are a great favourite with him."

chasms ; " unity " forever impossible there :—" well ; *fill* the abysses with whisky-punch, let deluges of that maintain a kind of unity and level ! "

After Spring 1828,[1] we saw no more of Wilson, heard little of him, and from himself nothing. His *Noctes* or *Blackwood* we did not see. From 1834 and our removal to London, he had as it were altogether vanished and gone out of memory. He said something bad about the *French Revolution*, a little word, which somebody, or some chance, brought me sight of. " Malice as of a child ! " said I ; which indeed it was,—and had something *flattering*, when I reflected. Once after that he wrote a stiff embarrassed kind of Note, recommending some Edinburgh lad of his acquaintance ; to whom I duly attended here, immediately assuring Wilson that I would. Not very long after, we read in the Newspapers that an apoplectic stroke had come upon him ; then that he had retired into the Country, to his children and quietude ; and in a year or two more that he had gone on the Long Journey, and all his wild eloquence was fallen silent forever.[2] Adieu to him, a kind and sad adieu. (26 March 1868).

[SIR WILLIAM HAMILTON]

I HAVE in my memory nothing that is worth recording about Sir William Hamilton ; pleasant as all my recollections of him are, they cover but a small space, and that not in the conspicuous or famous portion of his life ; and can have nothing new to those that had the honour of any acquaintance with him. Here, nevertheless, they are, *tales quales*.

Well onward in my student-life at Edinburgh—I think it may have been in 1819 or 1820—I used to pass, most mornings, on my way college-ward, by the east side of St Andrew Square, and a certain alley or short cut thereabouts called *Gabriel's Road*, which led out to the very end of Princes Street, directly opposite the North Bridge—close by the place which afterwards became famous as *Ambrose's Tavern*. Both Gabriel and Ambrose, I find, are now abolished, and the locality not recognisable ; but doubtless many remember it for one reason or another, as I do for the following.

1 When the Carlyles removed from Edinburgh to Craigenputtock.
2 Wilson died on the 3rd of April 1854 ; and soon after hearing of his death Carlyle wrote in his *Journal* (April 29) a couple of pages on lines similar, so far as they go, to this article, but somewhat less appreciative and kindly. These have been published in a wretchedly distorted form in *Carlyle's Life in London*.

Somewhere in Gabriel's Road, there looked out on me, from the Princes Street or St David Street side,[1] a back window on the ground-floor of a handsome enough house ; window which had no curtains ; and visible on the sill of it were a quantity of books lying about, gilt quartos and conspicuous volumes, several of them ;—evidently the sitting room and working room of a studious man, whose lot, in this safe seclusion, I viewed with a certain loyal respect. "Has a fine silent neighbourhood," thought I ; " a fine north light, and wishes to save it all." Inhabitant within I never noticed by any other symptom ; but from my comrades soon learned whose house and place of study this was.

The name of Sir William Hamilton I had before heard ; but this was the first time he appeared definitely before my memory or imagination ; in which his place was permanent thenceforth. A man of good birth, I was told, though of small fortune, who had deep faculties and an insatiable appetite for wise knowledge ; was titularly an advocate here, but had no practice, nor sought any ; had gathered his modest means thriftily together, and sat down here, with his mother and sister (cousin, I believe, it really was), and his ample store of books ; frankly renouncing all lower ambitions, and indeed all ambitions together, except what I well recognised to be the highest and one real ambition in this dark ambiguous world. A man honourable to me, a man lovingly enviable ; to whom, in silence, I heartily bade good speed. It was also an interesting circumstance, which did not fail of mention, that his ancestor, Hamilton of Preston, was leader of the Cameronians at Bothwell Brig, and had stood by the Covenant and Cause of Scotland in that old time and form. " This baronetcy, if carried forward on those principles, may well enough be poor," thought I ; " and beautifully well may it issue in such a Hamilton as this one aims to be, still piously bearing aloft, on the new terms, *his* God's-Banner intrepidly against the World and the Devil ! "

It was years after this, perhaps four or five, before I had the honour of any personal acquaintance with Sir William ; his figure on the street had become familiar, but I forget, too, when this was first pointed out to me ; and cannot recollect even when I first came to speech with him, which must have been by accident and his own voluntary favour, on some slight occasion, probably at *The Advocates' Library*, which was my principal or almost sole literary resource (lasting thanks to *it*, alone of

---

[1] There is an inaccuracy here respecting the locality of the house.   At this period Sir William was living in Howe Street.

Scottish institutions !) in those obstructed, neglectful, and grimly-forbidding years. Perhaps it was in 1824 or 1825. I recollect right well the bright affable manners of Sir William, radiant with frank kindliness, honest humanity, and intelligence ready to help ; and how completely prepossessing they were. A fine firm figure of middle height ; one of the finest cheerfully-serious human faces, of square, solid, and yet rather *aquiline* type ; a little marked with smallpox—marked, not deformed, but rather the reverse [1] (like a rock rough-hewn, not spoiled by polishing) ; and a pair of the beautifullest kindly-beaming hazel eyes, well open, and every now and then with a lambency of smiling fire in them, which I always remember as if with trust and gratitude. Our conversation did not amount to much, in those times ; mainly about German books, philosophies and persons, it is like ; and my usual place of abode was in the country then. Letter to him, or from, I do not recollect there was ever any ; though there might well enough have been, had either of us been prone that way.

In the end of 1826 I came to live in Edinburgh under circumstances new and ever memorable to me : from then till the spring of 1828—and, still more, once again in 1832-33, when I had brought my little household to Edinburgh for the winter—must have been the chief times of personal intercourse between us. I recollect hearing much more of him, in 1826 and onward, than formerly : to what depths he had gone in study and philosophy ; of his simple, independent, meditative habits, ruggedly athletic modes of exercise, fondness for his big dog, &c. &c. : everybody seemed to speak of him with favour, those of his immediate acquaintance uniformly with affectionate respect.

I did not witness, much less share in, any of his swimming or other athletic prowesses. I have once or twice been on long walks with him in the Edinburgh environs, oftenest with some other companion, or perhaps even two, whom he had found vigorous and worthy : pleasant walks and abundantly enlivened with speech from Sir William. He was willing to talk of any humanly-interesting subject ; and threw out sound observations upon any topic started : if left to his own choice, he circled and gravitated, naturally, into subjects that were his own, and were habitually occupying him ;—of which, I can still remember animal magnetism and the German revival of it, not yet known of in England, was one that frequently turned up. Mesmer and

---

[1] This impression is not correct. Sir William's face had no marks of smallpox.

his " four Academicians," he assured us, had *not* been the finale
of that matter ; that it was a matter tending into realities far
deeper and more intricate than had been supposed ;—of which,
for the rest, he did not seem to augur much good, but rather folly
and mischief.   Craniology, too, he had been examining ; but
freely allowed us to reckon that an extremely ignorant story.
On German bibliography and authors, especially of the learned
kind—Erasmus, Ruhnken, Ulrich von Hutten—he could descant
copiously, and liked to be inquired of.   On Kant, Reid, and the
metaphysicians, German and other, though there was such
abundance to have said, he did not often speak ; but politely
abstained rather, when not expressly called on.

He was finely social and human, in these walks or interviews.
Honesty, frankness, friendly veracity, courageous trust in
humanity and in you, were charmingly visible.   His talk was
forcible, copious, discursive, careless rather than otherwise ; and,
on abstruse topics, I observed, was apt to become embroiled and
revelly, much less perspicuous and elucidative than with a little
deliberation he could have made it.   " The fact is," he would
often say : and then plunging into new circuitous depths and
distinctions, again on a new grand, " The fact is," and still again,
—till what the essential " fact " might be was not a little obscure
to you.   He evidently had not been engaged in *speaking* these
things, but only in thinking them, for his own behoof, not yours.
By lucid questioning you could get lucidity from him on any
topic.   Nowhere did he give you the least notion of his not
understanding the thing himself ; but it lay like an unwinnowed
threshing-floor, the corn-grains, the natural chaff, and somewhat
even of the straw, still unseparated there.   This sometimes would
befall, not only when the meaning itself was delicate or abstruse,
but also if several were listening, and he doubted whether they
could understand.   On solid realistic points he was abundantly
luminous ; promptitude, solid sense, free-flowing intelligibility
always the characteristics.   The tones of his voice were themselves attractive, physiognomic of the man : a strong, carelessly-
melodious, tenor voice, the sound of it betokening seriousness
and cheerfulness ; occasionally something of slightly remonstra-
tive was in the undertones, indicating, well in the background,
possibilities of virtuous wrath and fire ; seldom anything of
laughter, of levity never anything : thoroughly a serious,
cheerful, sincere, and kindly voice, with looks corresponding.   In
dialogue, face to face, with one he trusted, his speech, both voice
and words, was still more engaging ; lucid, free, persuasive, with a

bell-like harmony, and from time to time, in the bright eyes, a beaming smile, which was the crown and seal of all to you.

In the winter 1832-33, Captain Hamilton, Sir William's brother, was likewise resident in Edinburgh ; a pleasant, very courteous, and intelligently-talking man, enduring, in a cheery military humour, his old Peninsular hurts, and printing his Peninsular and other books. At his house I have been of literary parties,—of one, at least, which I still remember in an indistinct but agreeable way. Of a similar party at Sir William's I have a still brighter recollection, and of his fine nobly simple ways there ; especially of one little radiancy (his look and his smile the now memorable part of it) privately addressed to myself on the mode of supping I had selected ; supper of one excellent and excellently-boiled potato, of fair size, with salt for seasoning,— at an epoch when excellent potatoes yet were. This evening was altogether pleasant, the talk lively and amusing : the Captain, I remember, quizzed me, and obliquely his brother, in a gay good-natured tone on Goethe's " Last Will " : the other Edinburgh figures I have entirely forgotten, except a Mr * * *,[1] newspaper editor, author of some book on the *Highlands*, whom I otherwise knew by sight and rumour (called at that time " Captain Cloud " from his occasionally fabulous turn), and who died not long after.

I think, though he stood so high in my esteem as a man of intellect and knowledge, I had yet read nothing by Sir William, nor indeed did I ever read anything considerable of what has sent his name over the world;—having years before, for good reasons of my own, renounced all metaphysical study or inquiry, and ceased altogether (as a master phrases it) to " think *about thinking*." One evening I recollect listening to a paper *on Phrenology*, read by him in the Royal Society ; in deliberate examination and refutation of that self-styled science. The meeting was very much larger than usual ; and sat in the deepest silence and attention, and, as it gradually appeared, approval and assent. My own private assent, I know, was complete ; I only wished the subject had been more important or more dubious to me. The argument, grounded on cerebral anatomy (osteology), philosophy, and human sense, I remember, went on in the true style of *vires acquirit* ; and the crowning finish of it was this : " Here are two skulls " (or rather, here *were*, for the experiment was but reported to us), " two noteworthy skulls ; let us carefully make trial and comparison of them. One is the skull of a Malay robber and cut-throat, who ended by murdering

[1] Not identified.

his mistress and getting hanged ; skull sent me by so-and-so "
(some principal official at Penang) ; " the other is George
Buchanan's skull, preserved in the University here.   One is
presumably a very bad specimen of a nation reckoned morally
and intellectually bad ; the other a very good, of a nation which
surely reckons itself good.   One is probably among the best of
mankind, the other among the worst.   Let us take our callipers,
and measure them bump after bump.   Bump of benevolence is
so-and-so, bump of ideality,—and in result, adding all, and
balancing all, your callipers declare the Malay to transcend in
goodness the Buchanan, by such and such a cipher of inches.   A
better man, in intellect and heart, that Malay, if there be truth in
arithmetic and these callipers of yours ! "   Which latter
implement, it seemed to me, was finally closed and done for.   I
said to Sir William next time we met, " Were I in your place I
would decline to say another word on that subject.   Malay cut-
throat *versus* Buchanan ; explain me that ; till then I say
nothing."

In April 1833 we left Edinburgh ; next year went to London ;
and I think Sir William and I never met again.   For the next
thirty and odd years I rarely came to Edinburgh, and then only
in transit, and usually at a season when all my friends (of whom
he surely was among the chief there) were out of town.   From
time to time there passed little mementos between us ; sometimes accidental, unintentional, and of a mute nature, which to
me were very precious, from a fellow-soldier whom I took to be
on the same side with me, and always well assured of my regard
as I was of his.   In Fife once or twice I heard with regret that his
health was failing ; once that he *had been* lately within reach of
where I now was, but had left and was gone.   We were to meet
in this world no more.

CHELSEA, 19*th February* 1868.

BIOGRAPHIES OF PRINCIPAL CHARACTERS RECALLED IN THE 'REMINISCENCES'.

I. JAMES CARLYLE, the author's father (1758–1832), was born in Annandale into a very poor family. After enduring hardships as a child and young man, he settled in Ecclefechan as a stonemason. He entered business with his brothers, and among other undertakings he constructed the famous 'arched house' in which Thomas Carlyle was born. Like his brothers, James Carlyle was noted for inflexible piety, sharp temper and an astonishing gift of words. After Thomas had grown up and left for university, the family left Ecclefechan and James Carlyle became a farmer. He had mixed success in this, and often the family knew poverty, but never actual want. He married twice. His first wife died soon after the birth of their son John, who later emigrated to Canada. James Carlyle then married Margaret Aitken, and Thomas Carlyle was their eldest child. Outwardly unremarkable, James Carlyle was remembered widely not only as the father of Thomas Carlyle, but for his gifts of speech. He wrote only with difficulty, but in his character can be seen many of the distinguishing features of his son's style, in both written and spoken words.

II. JANE WELSH CARLYLE (1801-1866) was born in Haddington, near Edinburgh, to a well-to-do doctor's household. Her father, also a remarkably strong character, was working to establish himself in what seemed a successful career when he was struck down by cholera and died in 1819. Jane Welsh and her mother remained in Haddington for many years, and it was there that Carlyle first met them in 1821. Although outwardly comfortable and elegant, they had in fact very little money, and their two sharp characters led to frequent quarrels. Jane had shown precocious talent, and although her formal schooling finished early she continued to educate herself to the best of her ability. Thomas Carlyle, then a gauche but intense freelance in Edinburgh literary circles, offered her books, advice, insight into German literature and thought. Their intimacy deepened into love, and in 1826 they married. After happy years in Edinburgh, and years of mixed fortune in Craigenputtoch, they settled in London in 1834. Jane was a brilliant talker, a witty friend, an entertaining hostess, and her value to Carlyle was incalculable. She captivated such men as Dickens, who came to Chelsea to visit not only Carlyle, the brilliant talker and 'prophet', but his charming and witty wife.

Beneath this surface there ran strong currents that led to clashes of personality and to disagreement. Both were difficult to live with, both had sensitive nerves and were easily disturbed. Stories of domestic earthquakes are part of the folklore of nineteenth-century studies. Jane was easily offended, jealous and had a wicked tongue, so many people found her intolerable. Like her husband, she was a genius of many sides.

Her health declined steadily in the 1850s, and in the 1860s she was a semi-invalid. She stayed in London in 1866 when Thomas Carlyle came to be installed as Lord Rector of Edinburgh University. She received the news of his success with tremendous relief, then a few days later died, suddenly, apparently of a stroke. Literary London was dismayed, Carlyle was thunderstruck, and the *Reminiscences* owe their existence to this catastrophe.

III. EDWARD IRVING (1792–1834) was born in Annan, and educated in a pattern which closely resembled Carlyle's own early years. He left Edinburgh University in 1809, just as Carlyle was beginning his student years, and taught first in Haddington (where he met, and taught, Jane Welsh) and then in Kirkcaldy, where in 1816 he befriended Thomas Carlyle. Irving left Kirkcaldy in 1818 to prepare himself for his career in the ministry of the Church of Scotland, and in 1819 was appointed to an excellent post in Glasgow. In 1821 he introduced Thomas Carlyle to Jane Welsh; many have speculated as to whether he would not himself have liked to marry his vivacious and pretty pupil, but he was engaged to the minister's daughter of Kirkcaldy, and this engagement he honoured. In 1822 he began his famous ministry at Cross Street Chapel, Hatton Garden, London, and for several years was enormously successful as orator and minister to the Scottish congregation in the city. His fame dimmed as he became more and more interested in the works of those who believed that divine messages could be delivered on earth by those possessed of 'gifts of tongues'; members of the congregations (probably under the influence of hysteria) were encouraged to interrupt the services with unintelligible but terrifying 'tongues' which served to dishearten most members, and actually to terrify some. Irving tolerated, then encouraged, what he took to be a manifestation of divine will. This, coupled with heretical beliefs he possessed about the divinity of Christ the Man, led to his suspension from his London charge in 1832, and from the ministry of the Church of Scotland in 1833. Many followed him, even after these reversals, but he died a broken man in 1834.

All his life he was a loyal and true friend to Carlyle, and gave him practical help whenever he could. He was a man of commanding presence and immense oratorical gifts, and in his heyday he single-handedly caused what amounted to a religious revolution in many Church circles. For further information see A. L. Drummond's biography (1937).

IV. FRANCIS JEFFREY (1773–1850) was the most prominent member of Edinburgh literary society at the time Carlyle was living in or near the city. After an extensive education in Edinburgh, Glasgow and Oxford Jeffrey was trained for a legal career, in which he succeeded brilliantly. Admitted to the Scottish bar in 1794, he rose to be (1829) Dean of the Faculty of Advocates, (1830) Lord Advocate and eventually (1834) a judge, Lord Jeffrey. In addition to this he had a brief but brilliant parliamentary career, helping to push through the business of the first Reformed Parliament in the early 1830s as Lord Advocate.

Such was the energy of Francis Jeffrey that this was only half his life's work. In 1802, with a talented circle of friends, including Brougham, Sydney Smith and Horner, Jeffrey founded *The Edinburgh Review*, and edited it till 1829. The *Review*, a Whig periodical which surveyed the literary, cultural and social scene, infuriated many but captivated all of literary Britain. Jeffrey's word as critic was law for thousands, and his reviews could influence a book's career profoundly. Such was his effect that Tory circles hastened to found *Blackwood's*, the rival magazine.

A small, energetic, precise, witty, immensely sociable man, Jeffrey was popular throughout Edinburgh. When he befriended Carlyle, he showed him unstinted kindness, and ignored many of Carlyle's gaucher replies to well-meant offers of help. He was obviously attracted to Mrs Carlyle, but his kindness to her husband was sincere and unbounded.

The best life of Jeffrey is still Cockburn's (1852), but there is interesting critical material in J. Clive's *Scotch Reviewers* (1957) and J. Greig's *Francis Jeffrey of the 'Edinburgh Review'* (1948).

V. ROBERT SOUTHEY (1774–1843), poet, historian and essayist, was born in Bristol and educated at Oxford. Although educated in the law, he found literature more absorbing, and owed much to his meeting in 1794 with Coleridge. Coleridge was a close friend, and an enormous personal inspiration to Southey. Southey was a complex personality, and had warm friends as well as bitter enemies. His friends included Scott and Wordsworth; his enemies Byron and Jeffrey. His poems and historical works, much read at the time, have fallen out of favour more recently, but Southey was a widely-travelled and well-informed member of literary circles, and an important figure in the story of the English romantic poets.

VI. WILLIAM WORDSWORTH (1770–1850), one of the greatest English poets, was born in Cockermouth in a modest home which rapidly became a straitened one following the death of both his parents. In 1787 the poet was nevertheless sent to Cambridge, where he benefited greatly from his companions, from the stimulus of new ideas and from the enlargement of his ideas. He travelled widely in Europe in his early years, made friends and was for a time caught up in the spirit of the French Revolution. Most important of the friends he made was Coleridge, whom he met in 1795 or 1796. The *Lyrical Ballads* of 1798, which came from their friendship and discussions on poetical topics, are one of the milestones in the development of English poety. Although their practice and their theories differed widely, they could work well together, and stimulated each other's output.

In 1805 Wordsworth completed the *Prelude*, still the best introduction to his work. The poem was never published in Wordsworth's lifetime, but carefully and endlessly revised and polished. Wordsworth retired more and more from public life, and settled in the Lake District among the influences of Nature, in his poetry a moving and living force. His devoted sister Dorothy accompanied him often on his walks, and helped him to order his thoughts towards the production of his poems. He was a meticulous craftsman as well as a profound thinker about man and his relation with the universe, but above all he had a rare gift for expressing his conclusions on these topics—very difficult to talk about—in great poetry which compels the attention of modern readers. Although he and Carlyle stood at opposite poles in their attitudes to many affairs, they both represent a profoundly important influence on the thought of their times.

VII. 'CHRISTOPHER NORTH', John Wilson (1785–1854), had a very similar early career to that of Jeffrey. After leaving Oxford he tried unsuccessfully to make a career in law, but soon found his taste to lie in literature. He was already by this time (1815) a mildly successful poet, but he first rose to wide public notice when in 1817 he took over the nearmoribund *Blackwood's Magazine*, and with Lockhart's help transformed it into an outrageous, challenging, libellous, brilliant, savage Tory review, in direct opposition to the *Edinburgh*. His own contributions included reviews, essays, and from 1822 onwards the brilliant fictitious *Noctes Ambrosianae*, fantasy conversations over the punchbowl between Wilson and his friends (notably James Hogg) on the affairs of the day, witty, penetrating, always entertaining. In 1820 Wilson was elected to the Chair of Moral Philosophy at Edinburgh, largely through party influence, and to the exclusion of the very worthy William Hamilton. As professor Wilson was not original, but enormously inspiring, and he managed to combine the duties of his post with the running of *Blackwood's*. Physically he was an enormous man, a powerful athlete of striking appearance. His original and penetrating writing in criticism animated much of Edinburgh's literary thought in the 1830s and 1840s, when the impetus of the age of Scott was waning. His poems are little remembered, his sentimental short stories wisely forgotten. He is remembered for his critical powers, and his stimulating effect on Edinburgh. Carlyle's brief glimpse of him tallies with this judgment.

VIII. WILLIAM HAMILTON, along with Wilson, was a prominent figure in the declining years of Edinburgh's importance in the nineteenth century. Born in 1788, he was educated at Glasgow and Oxford, and was a philosopher of extraordinary talent. Rebuffed by the electors who refused him Wilson's chair in 1820, he employed himself in a variety of minor jobs until he was elected to the Chair of Logic in Edinburgh in 1836. There he showed himself a lecturer of talent, and a philosopher of some genius. His students found him weighty where Wilson was flashy, although he lacked Wilson's ability to convey enthusiasm and dedication. Hamilton's works helped to explain the philosophers of the preceding generation in Scotland, and to keep Edinburgh abreast of the changes in philosophical thought which were current in the 1830s and 1840s. Carlyle seems to have had a sincere and quite unqualified enthusiasm for Hamilton as a man and scholar, and this testifies to Hamilton's personal impact. The best memoir of him is Veitch's of 1869; it included a requested contribution from Carlyle, which is reprinted here as the last of the *Reminiscences*.

INDEX